STONEWALL JACKSON

VOL. I.

"STONEWALL" JACKSON

STONEWALL JACKSON

AND THE

AMERICAN CIVIL WAR

BY

LIEUT.-COL. G. F. R. HENDERSON, C.B.

AUTHOR OF 'THE BATTLE OF SPICHEREN, A TACTICAL STUDY'
AND 'THE CAMPAIGN OF FREDERICKSBURG'

WITH AN INTRODUCTION BY FIELD-MARSHAL
THE RIGHT HON. VISCOUNT WOLSELEY, K.P., G.C.B., G.C.M.G. &c.

TWO VOLUMES IN ONE—VOL. I

WITH PORTRAITS, MAPS, AND PLANS

Konecky & Konecky
156 Fifth Avenue
New York, NY 10010

Copyright © by William S. Konecky Associates, Inc.

ISBN 0-914427-77-6

Printed in the United States of America

INTRODUCTION

BEFORE the great Republic of the West had completed a century of independent national existence, its political fabric was subjected to the strain of a terrible internecine war. That the true cause of conflict was the antagonism between the spirit of Federalism and the theory of 'States' Rights' is very clearly explained in the following pages, and the author exactly expresses the feeling with which most Englishmen regard the question of Secession, when he implies that had he been a New Englander he would have fought to the death to preserve the Union, while had he been born in Virginia he would have done as much in defence of a right the South believed inalienable. The war thus brought about dragged on its weary length from the spring of 1861 to the same season of 1865. During its progress reputations were made that will live for ever in American history, and many remarkable men came to the front. Among these not the least prominent was 'Stonewall Jackson,' who to the renown of a great soldier and unselfish patriot added the brighter fame of a Christian hero; and to those who would know what manner of man this Stonewall Jackson was, and why he was so universally revered, so beloved, so trusted by his men, I can cordially recommend Colonel Henderson's delightful volumes. From their perusal I have derived real pleasure and sound instruction. They have taught me much; they have made me think still more; and I hope they may do the same for many others in the British Army. They are worth the closest study, for few

military writers have possessed Colonel Henderson's grasp
of tactical and strategical principles, or his knowledge of
the methods which have controlled their application by the
most famous soldiers, from Hannibal to Von Moltke.
Gifted with a rare power of describing not only great
military events but the localities where they occurred, he
places clearly before his readers, in logical sequence, the
circumstances which brought them about. He has
accomplished, too, the difficult task of combining with a
brilliant and critical history of a great war the life-story
of a great commander, of a most singular and remarkable
man. The figure, the character, the idiosyncrasies of the
famous Virginian, as well as the lofty motives which
influenced him throughout, are most sympathetically
pourtrayed.

There have been few more fitted by natural instincts,
by education, by study, and by self-discipline to become
leaders of men than Stonewall Jackson. From the day he
joined that admirable school at West Point he may be said
to have trained himself mentally, morally, and physically,
for the position to which he aspired, and which it would
seem he always believed he would reach. Shy as a lad,
reserved as a man, speaking little but thinking much, he
led his own life, devouring the experiences of great men, as
recorded in military history, in order that when his time
came he should be capable of handling his troops as they
did. A man of very simple tastes and habits, but of strong
religious principles, drawn directly from the Bible ; a child
in purity; a child in faith; the Almighty always in his
thoughts, his stay in trouble, his guide in every difficulty,
Jackson's individuality was more striking and more complete than that of all others who played leading parts
in the great tragedy of Secession. The most reckless
and irreligious of the Confederate soldiers were silent in
his presence, and stood awestruck and abashed before this
great God-fearing man ; and even in the far-off Northern
States the hatred of the formidable 'rebel' was tempered
by an irrepressible admiration of his piety, his sincerity,
and his resolution. The passions then naturally excited

have now calmed down, and are remembered no more by a reunited and chivalrous nation. With that innate love of virtue and real worth which has always distinguished the American people, there has long been growing up, even among those who were the fiercest foes of the South, a feeling of love and reverence for the memory of this great and true-hearted man of war, who fell in what he firmly believed to be a sacred cause. The fame of Stonewall Jackson is no longer the exclusive property of Virginia and the South; it has become the birthright of every man privileged to call himself an American.

Colonel Henderson has made a special study of the Secession War, and it would be difficult, in my opinion, to find a man better qualified in every respect for the task he has undertaken. I may express the hope that he will soon give us the history of the war from the death of Stonewall Jackson to the fall of Richmond. Extending as it did over a period of four years, and marked by achievements which are a lasting honour to the Anglo-Saxon name, the struggle of the South for independence is from every point of view one of the most important events in the second half of the century, and it should not be left half told. Until the battle where Stonewall Jackson fell, the tide of success was flowing, and had borne the flag of the new Confederacy within sight of the gates of Washington. Colonel Henderson deals only with what I think may be called the period of Southern victories, for the tide began to ebb when Jackson fell; and those who read his volumes will, I am convinced, look forward eagerly to his story of the years which followed, when Grant, with the skill of a practised strategist, threw a net round the Confederate capital, drawing it gradually together until he imprisoned its starving garrison, and compelled Lee, the ablest commander of his day, to surrender at discretion.

But the application of strategical and tactical principles, and the example of noble lives, are not the only or even the most valuable lessons of great wars. There are lessons which concern nations rather than individuals; and there are two to be learnt from the Secession War which are of peculiar value to both England and the United States, whose armies are comparatively small and raised by voluntary enlistment. The first is the necessity of maintaining at all times (for it is impossible to predict what to-morrow may have in store for us) a well-organised standing army in the highest state of efficiency, and composed of thoroughly-trained and full-grown men. This army to be large enough for our military requirements, and adapted to the character, the habits, and the traditions of the people. It is not necessary that the whole force should be actually serving during peace : one half of it, provided it is periodically drilled and exercised, can be formed into a Reserve ; the essential thing is that it should be as perfect a weapon as can be forged.

The second lesson is that to hand over to civilians the administration and organisation of the army, whether in peace or in war, or to allow them to interfere in the selection of officers for command or promotion, is most injurious to efficiency ; while, during war, to allow them, no matter how high their political capacity, to dictate to commanders in the field any line of conduct, after the army has once received its commission, is simply to ensure disaster.

The first of these lessons is brought home to us by the opening events of this unreasonably protracted war. As I have elsewhere said, most military students will admit that had the United States been able, early in 1861, to put into the field, in addition to their volunteers, one Army Corps of regular troops, the war would have ended in a few months. An enormous expenditure of life and money, as well as a serious dislocation and loss of trade, would have been thus avoided. Never have the evil consequences which follow upon the absence of an adequate and well-organised army been more forcibly exemplified.

But, alas ! when this lesson is preached in a country governed alternately by rival political parties, and when there is no immediate prospect of national danger, it falls on deaf ears. The demands made by the soldiers to put the army on a thoroughly efficient footing are persistently ignored, for the necessary means are almost invariably required for some other object, more popular at the moment and in a parliamentary—or party—sense more useful. The most scathing comment on such a system of administration is furnished in the story told by Colonel Henderson. The fearful trials to which the United States were subjected expose the folly and self-deception of which even well-meaning party leaders are too often capable. Ministers bluster about fighting and yet refuse to spend enough money on the army to make it fit for use ; and on both sides of the Atlantic the lessons taught by the Peninsula, the Crimea, and the Secession War are but seldom remembered.

The pleasing notion that, whenever war comes, money can obtain for the nation all that it requires is still, it would seem, an article of at least lip-faith with the politicians of the English-speaking race throughout the world. Gold will certainly buy a nation powder, pills, and provisions ; but no amount of wealth, even when supported by a patriotic willingness to enlist, can buy discipline, training, and skilful leading. Without these there can be no such thing as an efficient army, and success in the field against serious opposition is merely the idle dream of those who know not war.

If any nation could improvise an army at short notice it would be the United States, for its men, all round, are more hardy, more self-reliant, and quicker to learn than those of older communities. But, notwithstanding this advantage, both in 1861 and 1898 the United States failed to create the thoroughly efficient armies so suddenly required, and in both instances the unnecessary sufferings of the private soldier were the price paid for the weakness and folly of the politicians. In 1861 the Governors of the several Northern States were ordered to call for volunteers to enlist for ninety days, the men electing their own officers. It was generally believed throughout the North that all Southern resistance would collapse before the great armies that would thus be raised. But the troops sent out to crush the rebellion, when they first came under fire, were soldiers only in outward garb, and at Bull Run, face to face with shot and shell, they soon lapsed into the condition of a terrified rabble, and ran away from another rabble almost equally demoralised; and this, not because they were cowards, for they were of the same breed as the young regular soldiers who retreated from the same field in such excellent order, but because they neither understood what discipline was nor the necessity for it, and because the staff and regimental officers, with few exceptions, were untrained and inexperienced.

Mr. Davis, having prevented the Southern army from following up the victory at Bull Run, gave the Northern States some breathing time. Mr. Lincoln was thus able to raise a new army of over 200,000 men for the projected advance on Richmond.

The new army was liberally supplied with guns, pontoons, balloons, hospitals, and wagons; but, with the exception of a few officers spared from the regular army, it was without trained soldiers to lead it, or staff officers to move and to administer its Divisions. It must be admitted, I think, that General McClellan did all that a man could do in the way of training this huge mass. But when the day came for it to move forward, it was still unfit for an offensive campaign against a regular army. To the practised eye of an able and experienced soldier who accompanied McClellan, the Federal host was an army only in name. He likened it to a giant lying prone upon the earth, in appearance a Hercules, but wanting the bone, the muscle, and the nervous organisation necessary to set the great frame in motion. Even when the army was landed in the Peninsula, although the process of training and organisation had been going on for over six months, it was still a most unwieldy force. Fortunately for the Union, the Confederate army, except as regards the superior leaders and the cavalry, was hardly more efficient.

The United States, fully realising their need of a larger regular army, are now on the point of increasing their existing force to treble its present strength. Their troops, like our own, are raised by voluntary enlistment for a short period of service with the colours.

England has always very great difficulty in filling the ranks even with undeveloped youths. The United States obtain as many full-grown men as they require, because they have the wisdom to pay their men well, on a scale corresponding to the market rate of wages. Here they are fortunate ; but men are not everything, and I will still draw the moral that a nation is more than blind when it deliberately elects to entrust its defence to an army that is not as perfect as training and discipline can make it, that is not led by practised officers, staff and regimental, and that is not provided with a powerful and efficient artillery. Overwhelming disaster is in store for such nation if it be attacked by a large regular army; and when it falls there will be none to pity. To hang the ministers who led them astray, and who believed they knew better than any soldier how the army should be administered, will be but poor consolation to an angry and deluded people.

Let me now dwell briefly upon the second of the two great national lessons taught by the Secession War. I shall say nothing here upon civilian meddling with army organisation and with the selection of officers for command, but I wish particularly to point out the result of interference on the part of a legislative assembly or minister with the plans and dispositions of the generals commanding in the field. Take first the notorious instance of Mr. Lincoln's interference with McClellan in the spring of 1862. McClellan, who was selected to command the army which was to capture Richmond and end the war, was a soldier of known ability, and, in my opinion, if he had not been interfered with by the Cabinet in Washington, he would probably have succeeded. It is true, as Colonel Henderson has said, that he made a mistake in not playing up to Lincoln's susceptibilities with regard to the safety of the Federal capital. But Lincoln made a far greater mistake in suddenly reducing McClellan's army by 40,000 men, and by removing Banks from his jurisdiction, when the plan of campaign had been approved by the Cabinet, and it was already too late to change it. It is possible, considering the political situation, that the garrison of Washington was too small, and it was certainly inefficient; but the best way of protecting Washington was to give McClellan the means of advancing rapidly upon Richmond. Such an advance would have made a Confederate counterstroke against the Northern capital, or even a demonstration, impossible. But to take away from McClellan 40,000 men, the very force with which he intended to turn the Yorktown lines and drive the enemy back on Richmond, and at the same time to isolate Banks in the Shenandoah Valley, was simply playing into the enemy's hands. What Lincoln did not see was that to divide the Federal army into three portions, working on three separate lines, was to run a far greater risk than would be incurred by leaving Washington weakly garrisoned. I cannot bring myself to believe that he in the least realised all that was involved in changing a plan of operations so vast as McClellan's.

Again, look at the folly of which Mr. Benjamin, the Confederate Secretary of War, was guilty at the same period. The reader should carefully study the chapter in which Colonel Henderson describes Stonewall Jackson's resignation of his command when his arrangements in the field were altered, without his cognisance, by the Secretary of War.

I should like to emphasize his words: 'That the soldier,' he says, 'is but the servant of the statesman, as war is but an instrument of diplomacy, no educated soldier will deny. Politics must always exercise a supreme influence on strategy; yet it cannot be gainsaid that interference with the commander in the field is fraught with the gravest danger.' [1]

The absolute truth of this remark is proved, not only by many instances in his own volumes, but by the history of war in all ages, and the principle for which Jackson contended when he sent in his resignation would seem too well founded to be open to the slightest question. Yet there are those who, oblivious of the fact that neglect of this principle has been always responsible for protracted wars, for useless slaughter, and costly failures, still insist on the omniscience

[1] Vol. i. p. 206.

of statesmen ; who regard the protest of the soldier as the mere outcome of injured vanity, and believe that politics must suffer unless the politician controls strategy as well as the finances. Colonel Henderson's pages supply an instructive commentary on these ideas. In the first three years of the Secession War, when Mr. Lincoln and Mr. Stanton practically controlled the movements of the Federal forces, the Confederates were generally successful. Further, the most glorious epoch of the Confederacy was the critical period of 1862, when Lee was allowed to exercise the full authority of Commander-in-Chief; and lastly, the Northern prospects did not begin to brighten until Mr. Lincoln, in March 1864, with that unselfish intelligence which distinguished him, abdicated his military functions in favour of General Grant. And yet while Lee and Grant had a free hand over the military resources of their respective nations the political situation suffered no harm whatever, no extravagant demands were made upon the exchequer, and the Government derived fresh strength from the successes of the armies.

The truth is that a certain class of civilians cannot rid themselves of the suspicion that soldiers are consumed by an inordinate and bloodthirsty ambition. They cannot understand that a man brought up from his youth to render loyal obedience is less likely than most others to run counter to constituted authority. They will not see that a soldier's pride in his own army and in the manhood of his own race tends to make him a devoted patriot. They do not realise that a commander's familiarity with war, whether gained by study or experience, must, unless his ability be limited, enable him to accommodate his strategy to political exigencies. Nor will they admit that he can possess a due sense of economy, although none knows better than an educated soldier the part played in war by a sound and thrifty administration of the national resources.

The soldier, on the other hand, knows that his art is most difficult, that to apply strategical principles correctly experience, study, knowledge of men, and an intimate acquaintance with questions of supply, transport, and the movement of masses, are absolutely necessary. He is aware that what may seem matters of small moment to the civilian—such as the position of a brigade, the strength of a garrison, the command of a detachment—may affect the whole course of a campaign; and consequently, even if he had not the historical examples of Aulic Councils and other such assemblies to warn him, he would rebel against the meddling of amateurs. Let it not be forgotten that an enormous responsibility rests on the shoulders of a commander in the field : the honour of the army committed to his charge, the lives of the brave men under him, perhaps the existence of his country ; and that failure, even if he can plead that he only obeyed the orders of his Government, or that he was supplied with inadequate means, will be laid at his door. McDowell received no mercy after Bull Run, although he had protested against attacking the Confederates ; and it was long before the reputation of Sir John Moore was cleared in the eyes of the English people.

Such, to my mind, are the most important lessons to be drawn from this history of the first period of the Secession War. But it is not alone to draw attention to the teaching on these points that I have acceded, as an old friend, to Colonel Henderson's request that I should write an Introduction to his second edition. In these days of sensational literature and superficial study there is a prejudice against the story that fills more than one volume. But the reader who opens these pages is so carried away by the intense interest of the subject, clothed as it is in forcible and yet graceful language, that he closes them with regret ; and I am only too glad to ask others to share the very great pleasure I have myself enjoyed in reading them. I know of no book which will add more largely to the soldier's knowledge of strategy and the art of war; and the ordinary reader will find in this Life of Stonewall Jackson, true and accurate as it is, all the charm and fascination of a great historical romance.

CONTENTS

OF

THE FIRST VOLUME

ILLUSTRATIONS IN VOL. I

PORTRAITS

MAPS

STONEWALL JACKSON

CHAPTER I

WEST POINT [1]

In the first quarter of the century, on the hills which stand above the Ohio River, but in different States of the Union, were born two children, destined, to all appearance, to lives of narrow interests and thankless toil. They were the sons of poor parents, without influence or expectations; their native villages, deep in the solitudes of the West, and remote from the promise and possibilities of great cities, offered no road to fortune. In the days before the railway, escape from the wilderness, except for those with long purses, was very difficult; and for those who remained, if their means were small, the farm and the store were the only occupations. But a farmer without capital was little better than a hired hand; trade was confined to the petty dealings of a country market; and although thrift and energy, even under such depressing conditions, might eventually win a competence, the most ardent ambition could hardly hope for more. Never was an obscure existence more irretrievably marked out than for these children of the Ohio; and yet, before either had grown grey, the names of Abraham Lincoln, President of the United States, and of Stonewall Jackson, Lieutenant-General in the Confederate Army, were household words in both America and Europe. Descendants of the pioneers, those hardy borderers, half soldiers and half

farmers, who held and reclaimed, through long years of
Indian warfare, the valleys and prairies of the West,
they inherited the best attributes of a frank and valiant
race.   Simple yet wise, strong yet gentle, they were gifted
with all the qualities which make leaders of men.
Actuated by the highest principles, they both ennobled the
cause for which they fought ; and while the opposition of
such kindred natures adds to the dramatic interest of the
Civil War, the career of the great soldier, although a
theme perhaps less generally attractive, may be followed
as profitably as that of the great statesman.   Providence
dealt with them very differently.   The one was struck down
by a mortal wound before his task was well begun ; his life,
to all human seeming, was given in vain, and his name will
ever be associated with the mournful memories of a lost
cause and a vanished army.   The other, ere he fell beneath
the assassin's stroke, had seen the abundant fruits of his
mighty labours ; his sun set in a cloudless sky.   And yet
the resemblance between them is very close.   Both dared

> For that sweet mother-land which gave them birth
> Nobly to do, nobly to die.   Their names,
> Graven on memorial columns, are a song
> Heard in the future ; . . .   more than wall
> And rampart, their examples reach a hand
> Far thro' all years, and everywhere they meet
> And kindle generous purpose, and the strength
> To mould it into action pure as theirs.

Jackson, in one respect, was more fortunate than
Lincoln.   Although born to poverty, he came of a Virginia
family which was neither unknown nor undistinguished ;
and, as showing the influences which went to form his
character, its history and traditions may be briefly related.

It is an article of popular belief that the State of
Virginia, the Old Dominion of the British Crown, owes
her fame to the blood of the English Cavaliers.   The
idea, however, has small foundation in fact.   Not a few
of her great names are derived from a less romantic
source, and the Confederate general, like many of his
neighbours in the western portion of the State, traced his

origin to the Lowlands of Scotland. An ingenious author of the last century, himself born on Tweed-side, declares that those Scotch families whose patronymics end in 'son,' although numerous and respectable, and descended, as the distinctive syllable denotes, from the Vikings, have seldom been pre-eminent either in peace or war. And certainly, as regards the Jacksons of bygone centuries, the assertion seems justified. The name is almost unknown to Border history. In neither lay nor legend has it been preserved; and even in the 'black lists' of the wardens, where the more enterprising of the community were continually proclaimed as thieves and malefactors, it is seldom honoured with notice. The omission might be held as evidence that the family was of peculiar honesty, but, in reality, it is only a proof that it was insignificant. It is not improbable that the Jacksons were one of the landless clans, whose only heritages were their rude 'peel' towers, and who, with no acknowledged chief of their own race, followed, as much for protection as for plunder, the banner of some more powerful house. In course of time, when the Marches grew peaceful and morals improved, when cattle-lifting, no longer profitable, ceased to be an honourable occupation, such humbler marauders drifted away into the wide world, leaving no trace behind, save the grey ruins of their grim fortalices, and the incidental mention of some probably disreputable scion in a chapman's ballad. Neither mark nor memory of the Jacksons remains in Scotland. We only know that some members of the clan, impelled probably by religious persecution, made their way to Ulster, where a strong colony of Lowlanders had already been established.

Under a milder sky and a less drastic government the expatriated Scots lost nothing of their individuality. Masterful and independent from the beginning, masterful and independent they remained, inflexible of purpose, impatient of injustice, and staunch to their ideals. Something, perhaps, they owed to contact with the Celt. Wherever the Ulster folk have made their home, the breath of the wholesome North has followed them, preserving untainted their hereditary virtues. Shrewd, practical, and thrifty, prosperity has consistently rewarded them; and yet, in common with the Irishmen of English stock, they have found in the trade of arms the most congenial outlet for their energies. An abiding love of peace can hardly be enumerated amongst their more prominent characteristics; and it is a remarkable fact, which, unless there is some mysterious property in the air, can only be explained by the intermixture of races, that Ireland 'within the Pale' has been peculiarly prolific of military genius. As England has bred admirals, so the sister isle has bred soldiers. The tenacious courage of the Anglo-Saxon, blended with the spirit of that people which above all others delights in war, has proved on both sides of the Atlantic a most powerful combination of martial qualities. The same mixed strain which gave England Wolfe and Wellington, the Napiers and the Lawrences, has given America some of her greatest captains; and not the least famous of her Presidents is that General Jackson who won the battle of New Orleans in 1814. So, early in the century the name became known beyond the seas; but whether the same blood ran in the veins of the Confederate general and of the soldier President is a matter of some doubt. The former, in almost every single respect, save his warm heart, was the exact converse of the typical Irishman; the latter had a hot temper and a ready wit. Both, however, were undeniably fond of fighting, and a letter still preserved attests that their ancestors had lived in the same parish of Londonderry.[1]

John Jackson, the great-grandfather of our hero, landed in America in 1748, and it was not long before he set
1748.   his face towards the wilderness. The emigrants from Ulster appear as a rule to have moved westward. The States along the coast were already colonised, and, despite its fertility, the country was little to their taste. But beyond the border, in the broad Appalachian valley which runs from the St. Lawrence to Alabama, on the

[1] This letter is in the possession of Thomas Jackson Arnold, Esq., of Beverly, West Va., nephew of General 'Stonewall' Jackson.

banks of the great rivers, the Susquehanna, the Ohio, the Cumberland, and the Tennessee, they found a land after their own heart, a soil with whose properties they were familiar, the sweet grasses and soft contours of their native hills. Here, too, there was ample room for their communities, for the West was as yet but sparsely tenanted. No inconsiderable number, penetrating far into the interior, settled eventually about the headwaters of the Potomac and the James. This highland region was the debateable ground of the United States. So late as 1756 the State of Virginia extended no further than the crests of the Blue Ridge. Two hundred miles westward forts flying French colours dominated the valley of the Ohio, and the wild and inhospitable tract, a very labyrinth of mountains, which lay between, was held by the fierce tribes of the 'Six Nations' and the Leni-Lenape. Two years later the French had been driven back to Canada; but it was not till near the close of the century that the savage was finally dispossessed of his spacious hunting grounds.

It was on these green uplands, where fight and foray were as frequent as once on the Scottish border, that John Jackson and his wife, a fellow passenger to America, by name Elizabeth Cummins, first pitched their camp, and here is still the home of their descendants.

In the little town of Clarksburg, now the county-seat of Harrison, but then no more than a village in the Virginia Jan. 21, backwoods, Thomas Jonathan Jackson was born 1824. on January 21, 1824. His father was a lawyer, clever and popular, who had inherited a comfortable patrimony. The New World had been generous to the Jacksons. The emigrant of 1748 left a valuable estate, and his many sons were uniformly prosperous. Nor was their affluence the reward of energy and thrift alone, for the lands reclaimed by axe and plough were held by a charter of sword and musket. The redskin fought hard for his ancestral domains. The stockaded forts, which stood as a citadel of refuge in every settlement, were often the scene of fierce attack and weary leaguer, and the nursing mothers of the frontier families were no strangers to war and bloodshed. The last great battle with the Indians east of the Ohio was fought in 1774, but the military experience of the pioneers was not confined to the warfare of the border. John Jackson and his sons bore arms in the War of Independence, and the trained riflemen of West Virginia were welcome recruits in the colonial ranks. With the exception of the Highlanders of the '45, who had been deported in droves to the plantations, no race had less cause to remain loyal to the Crown than the men of Ulster blood. Even after the siege of Londonderry they had been proscribed and persecuted ; and in the War of Independence the fiercest enemies of King George were the descendants of the same Scotch-Irish who had held the north of Ireland for King William.

In Washington's campaigns more than one of the Jacksons won rank and reputation ; and when peace was established they married into influential families. Nor was the next generation less successful. Judges, senators, and soldiers upheld the honour of the name, and proved the worth of the ancestral stock. They were marked, it is said, by strong and characteristic features, by a warm feeling of clanship, a capacity for hard work, and a decided love of roving. Some became hunters, others explorers, and the race is now scattered from Virginia to Oregon. A passion for litigation was a general failing, and none of them could resist the fascination of machinery. Every Jackson owned a mill or factory of some sort—many of them more than one—and their ventures were not always profitable. Jackson's father, among others, found it easier to make money than to keep it. Generous and incautious, he became deeply involved by becoming security for others ; high play increased his embarrassments ; and when he died in 1827 every vestige of his property was swept away. His young widow, left with three small children, two sons and a daughter, became dependent on the assistance of her kinsfolk for a livelihood, and on the charity of the Freemasons for a roof. When Thomas, her second son, was six years old, she married a Captain Woodson ; but her second matrimonial venture was not more fortunate than her first. Her husband's means were small, and necessity soon compelled her to commit her two boys to the care of their father's relatives. Within a year the children stood round her dying bed, and at a very early age our little Virginian found himself a penniless orphan. But, as he never regretted his poverty, so he never forgot his mother. To the latest hour of his life he loved to recall her memory, and years after she had passed away her influence still remained. Her beauty, her counsels, their last parting, and her happy death, for she was a woman of deep religious feeling, made a profound impression on him. To his childhood's fancy she was the embodiment of every grace; and so strong had been the sympathy between them, that even in the midst of his campaigns she was seldom absent from his thoughts. After her death the children found a home with their father's half-brother, who had inherited the family estates, and was one of the largest slave-owners in the district. Their surroundings, however, could hardly be called luxurious. Life on the Ohio was very different from life on the coast. The western counties of Virginia were still practically on the frontier of the United States. The axe had thinned the interminable woods; mills were busy on each mountain stream, and the sunny valleys were rich in fruit and corn. But as yet there was little traffic. Steam had not yet come to open up the wilderness. The population was small and widely scattered; and the country was cut off as much by nature as by distance from the older civilisation of the East. The parallel ranges of the Alleghanies, with their pathless forests and great cañons, were a formidable barrier to all intercourse. The West was a world in itself. The only outlets eastward were the valleys of the Potomac and the James, the one leading to Washington, the other to Richmond; and so seldom were they used that the yeomen of the Ohio uplands were almost as much opposed, both in character and in mode of life, to the planters beyond the Blue Ridge, as the Covenanters of Bothwell Brig to the gentlemen of Dundee's Life Guards.

Although the sturdy independence and simple habits of

1831.

the borderers were not affected by contact with wealthier communities, isolation was not in every way a blessing. Served by throngs of slaves, the great landowners of East Virginia found leisure to cultivate the arts which make life more pleasant. The rambling houses on the banks of the James, the Rappahannock, and the Potomac, built on the model of English manors, had their libraries and picture-galleries. A classical academy was the boast of every town, and a university training was considered as essential to the son of a planter as to the heir of an English squire. A true aristocracy, in habit and in lineage, the gentlemen of Virginia long swayed the councils of the nation, and among them were many who were intimate with the best representatives of European culture. Beyond the Alleghanies there were no facilities for education; and even had opportunities offered few would have had the leisure to enjoy them. Labour was scarce, either slave or hired. The owners of farms and mills were their own managers and overseers, and young men had to serve a practical apprenticeship to lumbering and agriculture. To this rule, despite his uncle's wealth, Jackson was no exception. He had to fight his own battle, to rub shoulders with all sorts and conditions of men, and to hold his own as best he could.

It was a hard school, then, in which he grew to manhood. But for that very reason it was a good school for the future soldier. For a man who has to push his own way in the world, more especially if he has to carve it with his sword, a boyhood passed amidst surroundings which boast of no luxury and demand much endurance, is the best probation. Von Moltke has recorded that the comfortless routine of the Military Academy at Copenhagen inured him to privation, and Jackson learned the great lesson of self-reliance in the rough life of his uncle's homestead.

The story of his early years is soon told. As a blue-eyed child, with long fair hair, he was curiously thoughtful and exceedingly affectionate. His temper was generous and cheerful. His truthfulness was proverbial, and his little sister found in him the kindest of playmates and the sturdiest of protectors. He was distinguished, too, for his politeness, although good manners were by no means rare in the rustic West. The manly courtesy of the true American is no exotic product; nor is the universal deference to woman peculiar to any single class. The farmer of the backwoods might be ignorant of the conventionalities, but the simplicity and unselfishness which are the root of all good breeding could be learned in West Virginia as readily as in Richmond.

Once, tempted by his brother, the boy left his adopted home, and the two children, for the elder was no more than twelve, wandered down the Ohio to the Mississippi, and spent the summer on a lonely and malarious island, cutting wood for passing steamers. No one opposed their going, and it seems to have been considered quite natural in that independent community that the veriest urchins should be allowed to seek their fortunes for themselves. Returning, ragged and fever-stricken, the little adventurers submitted once more to the routine of the farm and to the intermittent studies of a country school. After his failure as a man of business, our small hero showed no further inclination to seek his fortunes far afield. He was fond of his home. His uncle, attracted by his steadiness and good sense, treated him more as a companion than a child; and in everything connected with the farm, as well as in the sports of the country side, the boy took the keenest interest. Delicate by nature, with a tendency to consumption inherited from his mother, his physique and constitution benefited by a life of constant exercise and wholesome toil. At school he was a leader in every game, and his proficiency in the saddle proved him a true Virginian. Fox-hunting and horse-racing were popular amusements, and his uncle not only kept a stable of well-bred horses, but had a four-mile race-course on his own grounds. As a light-weight jockey the future general was a useful member of the household, and it was the opinion of the neighbourhood that 'if a horse had any winning qualities whatever in him, young Jackson never failed to bring them out.'

In the management of the estate he learned early to put

his shoulder to the wheel. Transporting timber from the forest to the saw-mill was one of his most frequent tasks, and tradition records that if a tree were to be moved from ground of unusual difficulty, or if there were one more gigantic than the rest, the party of labourers was put under his control, and the work was sure to be effected.

One who knew him well has described his character. 'He was a youth of exemplary habits, of indomitable will and undoubted courage. He was not what is nowadays termed brilliant, but he was one of those untiring, matter-of-fact persons who would never give up an undertaking until he accomplished his object. He learned slowly, but what he got into his head he never forgot. He was not quick to decide, except when excited. and then, when he made up his mind to do a thing, he did it on short notice and in quick time. Once, while on his way to school, an over-grown rustic behaved rudely to one of the school-girls. Jackson fired up, and told him he must apologise at once or he would thrash him. The big fellow, supposing that he was more than a match for him, refused, whereupon Jackson pitched into him, and gave him a severe pounding.'

His surroundings, then, although neither refined nor elevating, were not unwholesome ; but of the moral influences to which he was subjected, so much cannot be said. The stock of piety that the original settlers had brought with them had long since vanished. Irregularity of life was the general rule ; religion was simply a matter to which men gave no thought, and young Jackson drifted with the tide. Yet there was something that preserved him from contamination. His uncle, kindest of guardians, was as unscrupulous as he was violent. His associates were by no means the most respectable of the neighbourhood, and the morals of the sporting fraternity of a frontier settlement are not likely to have been edifying. That his nephew, as he himself declares, was an ardent frequenter of races, 'house-raisings,'[1] and country dances is hardly surprising, and it is assuredly no ground whatever for reproach. But it is strange that, amid much laxity, he should have retained his integrity,

[1] Anglicè, 'house-warmings.'

that his regard for truth should have remained untarnished, and that he should have consistently held aloof from all that was mean and vile. His mother was no mere memory to that affectionate nature.

His good qualities, however, would scarcely of themselves have done more than raise him to a respectable rank amongst the farmers of West Virginia. A spur was wanting to urge him beyond the limits of so contracted an existence, and that spur was supplied by an honourable ambition. Penniless and dependent as he was, he still remembered that his ancestors had been distinguished beyond the confines of their native county, and this legitimate pride in his own people, a far-off reflection, perhaps, of the traditional Scottish attitude towards name and pedigree, exercised a marked influence on his whole career. 'To prove himself worthy of his forefathers was the purpose of his early manhood. It gives us a key to many of the singularities of his character; to his hunger for self-improvement; to his punctilious observance, from a boy, of the essentials of gentlemanly bearing, and to the uniform assertion of his self-respect.'[1]

It was his openly expressed wish for larger advantages than those offered by a country school that brought about his opportunity. In 1841, at the age of seventeen, he became a constable of the county. A sort of minor sheriff, he had to execute the decrees of the justices, to serve their warrants, to collect small debts, and to summon witnesses. It was a curious office for a boy, but a year or two before he had been seized with some obscure form of dyspepsia, and the idea that a life on horseback, which his duties necessitated, might restore his health, had induced his relatives to obtain the post for him. Jackson himself seems to have been influenced by the hope that his salary would help towards his education, and by the wish to become independent of his uncle's bounty. His new duties were uncongenial, but, despite his youth, he faced his responsibilities with a determination which men of maturer years might well have envied. In everything

1841.

[1] Dabney, vol. i. p. 29.

he was scrupulously exact. His accounts were accurately
kept ; he was punctuality itself, and his patience was inexhaustible. For two years he submitted cheerfully to the
drudgery of his position, re-establishing his health, but
without advancing a single step towards the goal of his
ambition. But before he was nineteen his hopes were
unexpectedly realised. The Military Academy at West
Point not only provided, at the expense of the nation,
a sound and liberal education, but offered an opening to
an honourable career. Nominations to cadetships were
made by the Secretary of War, on the recommendation of
1842.   members of Congress, and in 1842 a vacancy
occurred which was to be filled by a youth from
the Congressional District in which Clarksburg was included. Jackson, informed of the chance by a friendly
blacksmith, eagerly embraced it, and left no stone unturned
to attain his object. Every possible influence that could be
brought to bear on the member for the district was immediately enlisted. To those who objected that his education
was too imperfect to enable him even to enter the Academy,
he replied that he had the necessary application, that
he hoped he had the capacity, and that he was at least
determined to try. His earnestness and courage won upon
all. His application was strongly backed by those who
had learned to value his integrity and exactness, and
Mr. Hays, the member for the district, wrote that he would
do all in his power to secure the appointment. No sooner
had the letter been read than Jackson determined to go at
once to Washington, in order that he might be ready to
proceed to West Point without a moment's delay. Packing
a few clothes into a pair of saddlebags, he mounted his
horse, and accompanied by a servant, who was to bring the
animal home, rode off to catch the coach at Clarksburg.
It had already passed, but galloping on, he overtook it at
the next stage, and on his arrival at Washington, Mr.
Hays at once introduced him to the Secretary of War. On
presenting him, he explained the disadvantages of his education, but begged indulgence for him on account of his pluck
and determination. The Secretary plied him with questions,

but Jackson was not to be diverted from his purpose ; and so good was the impression which he made that he then and there received his warrant, accompanied by some excellent advice. 'Sir,' said the Secretary, 'you have a good name. Go to West Point, and the first man who insults you, knock him down, and have it charged to my account !'

Mr. Hays proposed that the new-fledged cadet should stay with him for a few days in order to see the sights of Washington. But as the Academy was already in session, Jackson, with a strong appreciation of the value of time, begged to decline. He was content to ascend to the roof of the Capitol, then still building, and look once on the magnificent panorama of which it is the centre.

At his feet lay the city, with its busy streets and imposing edifices. To the south ran the Potomac, bearing on its ample tide the snowy sails of many merchantmen, and spanned by a bridge more than a mile in length. Over against the Capitol, looking down on that wide-watered shore, stood the white porch of Arlington, once the property of Washington, and now the home of a young officer of the United States army, Robert Edward Lee. Beyond Arlington lay Virginia, Jackson's native State, stretching back in leafy hills and verdant pastures, and far and low upon the western horizon his own mountains loomed faintly through the summer haze. It was a strange freak of fortune that placed him at the very outset of his career within sight of the theatre of his most famous victories. It was a still stranger caprice that was to make the name of the simple country youth, ill-educated and penniless, as terrible in Washington as the name of the Black Douglas was once in Durham and Carlisle.

It was in July 1842 that one of America's greatest soldiers first answered to his name on the parade-ground
1842.   at West Point. Shy and silent, clad in Virginia homespun, with the whole of his personal effects carried in a pair of weatherstained saddlebags, the impression that he made on his future comrades, as the Secretary of War appears to have anticipated, was by no means favourable. The West Point cadets were then, as now, remarkable

for their upright carriage, the neatness of their appointments, and their soldierly bearing towards their officers and
towards each other.   The grey coatee, decorated with
bright buttons and broad gold lace, the shako with tall
plumes, the spotless white trousers, set off the trim young
figures to the best advantage ; and the full-dress parade of
the cadet battalion, marked by discipline and precision in
every movement, is still one of the most attractive of
military spectacles.

These natty young gentlemen were not slow to detect
the superficial deficiencies of the newcomer.   A system of
practical joking, carried to extremes, had long been a
feature of West Point life.   Jackson, with the rusticity of
the backwoods apparent at every turn, promised the
highest sport.   And here it may be written, once for all,
that however nearly in point of character the intended
victim reached the heroic standard, his outward graces were
few.   His features were well cut, his forehead high, his
mouth small and firm, and his complexion fresh.   Yet the
ensemble was not striking, nor was it redeemed by grave
eyes and a heavy jaw, a strong but angular frame, a certain
awkwardness of movement, and large hands and feet.   His
would-be tormentors, however, soon found they had mistaken
their man.   The homespun jacket covered a natural shrewd-
ness which had been sharpened by responsibility.   The
readiness of resource which had characterised the whilom
constable was more than a match for their most ingenious
schemes; and baffled by a temper which they were powerless
to disturb, their attempts at persecution, apparently more
productive of amusement to their victim than to themselves, were soon abandoned.

Rough as was the life of the Virginia border, it had
done something to fit this unpromising recruit for the give
and take of his new existence.   Culture might be lacking
in the distant West, but the air men breathed was at least
the blessed breath of independence.   Each was what he
made himself.   A man's standing depended on his success
in life, and success was within the reach of all.   There,
like his neighbours, Jackson had learned to take his

own part ; like them he acknowledged no superiority
save that of actual merit, and believing that the richest
prize might be won by energy and perseverance, without
diffidence or misgiving he faced his future. He knew
nothing of the life of the great nation of which he was so
insignificant an atom, of the duties of the army, of the
manners of its officers. He knew only that even as regards
education he had an uphill task before him. He was
indeed on the threshold of a new world, with his own way
to make, and apparently no single advantage in his favour.
But he came of a fighting race ; he had his own inflexible
resolution to support him, and his determination expressed
itself in his very bearing. Four cadets, three of whom were
afterwards Confederate generals,[1] were standing together
when he first entered the gates of the Academy. ' There
was about him,' says one of them, ' so sturdy an expression
of purpose that I remarked, "That fellow looks as if he
had come to stay." '

Jackson's educational deficiencies were more difficult of
conquest than the goodwill of his comrades. His want of
previous training placed him at a great disadvantage. He
commenced his career amongst ' the Immortals ' (the last
section of the class), and it was only by the most strenuous
efforts that he maintained his place. His struggles at the
blackboard were often painful to witness. In the struggle to
solve a problem he invariably covered both his face and uniform with chalk, and he perspired so freely, even in the
coldest weather, that the cadets, with boyish exaggeration,
declared that whenever ' the General,' as he had at once been
dubbed in honour of his namesake, the victor of New Orleans,
got a difficult proposition he was certain to flood the class-
room. It was all he could do to pass his first examination.[2]

' We were studying,' writes a classmate, ' algebra and
analytical geometry that winter, and Jackson was very low
in his class. Just before the signal "lights out" he would
pile up his grate with anthracite coal, and lying prone
before it on the floor, would work away at his lessons by

---

[1] A. P. Hill, G. E. Pickett, and D. H. Maury.
[2] Communicated by General John Gibbon, U.S.A.

the glare of the fire, which scorched his very brain, till a
late hour of the night. This evident determination to
succeed not only aided his own efforts directly, but impressed his instructors in his favour. If he could not
master the portion of the text-book assigned for the
day, he would not pass it over, but continued to work at
it till he understood it. Thus it often happened that when
he was called out to repeat his task, he had to reply that
he had not yet reached the lesson of the day, but was
employed upon the previous one. There was then no alternative but to mark him as unprepared, a proceeding which
did not in the least affect his resolution.'

Despite all drawbacks, his four years at the Academy
were years of steady progress. 'The Immortals' were soon
left far behind. At the end of the first twelve months he
stood fifty-first in a class of seventy-two, but when he entered
the first class, and commenced the study of logic, that
bugbear to the majority, he shot from near the foot of the
class to the top. In the final examination he came out
seventeenth, notwithstanding that the less successful years
were taken into account, and it was a frequent remark
amongst his brother cadets that if the course had been a
year longer he would have come out first. His own
satisfaction was complete. Not only was his perseverance
rewarded by a place sufficiently high to give him a commission in the artillery, but his cravings for knowledge
had been fully gratified. West Point was much more than
a military school. It was a university, and a university
under the very strictest discipline, where the science of the
soldier formed only a portion of the course. Subjects
which are now considered essential to a military education
were not taught at all. The art of war gave place to
ethics and engineering ; and mathematics and chemistry
were considered of far more importance than topography
and fortification. Yet with French, history, and drawing,
it will be admitted that the course was sufficiently comprehensive. No cadet was permitted to graduate unless he
had reached a high standard of proficiency. Failures were
numerous. In the four years the classes grew gradually

smaller, and the survival of the fittest was a principle of administration which was rigidly observed.

The fact, then, that a man had passed the final examination at West Point was a sufficient certificate that he had received a thorough education, that his mental faculties had been strengthened by four years of hard work, and that he was well equipped to take his place amongst his fellow men. And it was more than this. Four years of the strictest discipline, for the cadets were allowed only one vacation during their whole course, were sufficient to break in even the most careless and the most slovenly to neatness, obedience, and punctuality. Such habits are not easily unlearned, and the West Point certificate was thus a guarantee of qualities that are everywhere useful. It did not necessarily follow that because a cadet won a commission he remained a soldier. Many went to civil life, and the Academy was an excellent school for men who intended to find a career as surveyors or engineers. The great railway system of the United States was then in its infancy; its development offered endless possibilities, and the work of extending civilisation in a vast and rapidly improving country had perhaps more attraction for the ambitious than the career of arms. The training and discipline of West Point were not, then, concentrated in one profession, but were disseminated throughout the States; and it was with this purpose that the institution of the Academy had been approved by Congress.

In the wars with England the militia of the different States had furnished the means both of resistance and aggression, but their grave shortcomings, owing principally to the lack of competent officers, had been painfully conspicuous. After 1814, the principle that the militia was the first line of defence was still adhered to, and the standing army was merely maintained as a school for generals and a frontier guard. It was expected, however, that in case of war the West Point graduates would supply the national forces with a large number of officers who, despite their civil avocations, would at least be familiar with drill and discipline. This fact is to be borne in mind

in view of the Civil War.   The demands of the enormous
armies then put into the field were utterly unprecedented,
and the supply of West Pointers was altogether inadequate
to meet them ; but the influence of the Military Academy
was conspicuous throughout.   Not a few of the most able
generals were little more than boys ; and yet, as a rule,
they were far superior to those who came from the militia
or volunteers.   Four years of strict routine, of constant
drill, and implicit subordination, at the most impressionable
period of life, proved a far better training for command than
the desultory and intermittent service of a citizen army.

During his stay at West Point Jackson's development
was not all in one direction.   He gained in health and
strength.   When he joined he had not yet attained his
full height, which fell short of six feet by two inches.   The
constant drilling developed his frame.   He grew rapidly,
and soon acquired the erect bearing of the soldier ; but
notwithstanding the incessant practice in riding, fencing
and marching, his anatomical peculiarities still asserted
themselves.   It was with great difficulty that he mastered
the elementary process of keeping step, and despite his
youthful proficiency as a jockey, the regulation seat of the
dragoon, to be acquired on the back of a rough cavalry
trooper, was an accomplishment which he never mastered.
If it be added that his shyness never thawed, that he was
habitually silent, it is hardly surprising to find that he had
few intimates at the Academy.   Caring nothing for the
opinion of others, and tolerant of association rather than
seeking it, his self-contained nature asked neither sympathy
nor affection.   His studious habits never left him.   His
only recreation was a rapid walk in the intervals of the
classes.   His whole thoughts and his whole energy were
centred on doing his duty, and passing into the army
with all the credit he could possibly attain.   Although he
was thoroughly happy at West Point, life to him, even at
that early age, was a serious business, and most seriously
he set about it.

Still, unsociable and irresponsive as he was, there were
those in whose company he found pleasure, cadets who had

studied subjects not included in the West Point course, and from whom there was something to be learned. It was an unwritten law of the Academy that those of the senior year should not make companions of their juniors. But Jackson paid no heed to the traditionary code of etiquette. His acquaintances were chosen regardless of standing, as often from the class below him as his own; and in yet another fashion his strength of character was displayed. Towards those who were guilty of dishonourable conduct he was merciless almost to vindictiveness. He had his own code of right and wrong, and from one who infringed it he would accept neither apology nor excuse. His musket, which was always scrupulously clean, was one day replaced by another in most slovenly order. He called the attention of his captain to his loss, and described the private mark by which it was to be identified. That evening, at the inspection of arms, it was found in the hands of another cadet, who, when taxed with his offence, endeavoured to shield himself by falsehood. Jackson's anger was unbounded, and for the moment his habitual shyness completely disappeared. He declared that such a creature should not continue a member of the Academy, and demanded that he should be tried by court-martial and expelled. It was only by means of the most persevering remonstrances on the part of his comrades and his officers that he could be induced to waive his right of pressing the charge. His regard for duty, too, was no less marked than his respect for truth. During one half-year his room-mate was orderly-sergeant of his company, and this good-natured if perfunctory young gentleman often told Jackson that he need not attend the *réveille* roll-call, at which every cadet was supposed to answer to his name. Not once, however, did he avail himself of the privilege.[1]

At the same time he was not altogether so uncompromising as at first sight he appeared. At West Point, as in after years, those who saw him interested or excited noticed that his smile was singularly sweet, and the cadets knew that it revealed a warm heart within. Whenever, from sickness or misfortune, a comrade stood in need of

[1] Communicated by Colonel P. T. Turnley.

sympathy, Jackson was the first to offer it, and he would devote himself to his help with a tenderness so womanly that it sometimes excited ridicule. Sensitive he was not, for of vanity he had not the slightest taint; but of tact and sensibility he possessed more than his share. If he was careless of what others thought of him, he thought much of them. Though no one made more light of pain on his own account, no one could have more carefully avoided giving pain to others, except when duty demanded it; and one of his classmates [1] testifies that he went through the trying ordeal of four years. at West Point without ever having a hard word or bad feeling from cadet or professor.

Nor did his comrades fail to remember that when he was unjustly blamed he chose to bear the imputation silently rather than expose those who were really at fault. And so, even in that lighthearted battalion, his sterling worth compelled respect. All honoured his efforts and wished him God-speed. 'While there were many,' says Colonel Turnley, ' who seemed to surpass him in intellect, in geniality, and in good-fellowship, there was no one of our class who more absolutely possessed the respect and confidence of all; and in the end " Old Jack," as he was always called, with his desperate earnestness, his unflinching straightforwardness, and his high sense of honour, came to be regarded by his comrades with something very like affection.'

One peculiarity cannot be passed by.

When at study he always sat bolt upright at his table with his book open before him, and when he was not using pencil and paper to solve a problem, he would often keep his eyes fixed on the wall or ceiling in the most profound abstraction. 'No one I have ever known,' says a cadet who shared his barrack-room, ' could so perfectly withdraw his mind from surrounding objects or influences, and so thoroughly involve his whole being in the subject under consideration. His lessons were uppermost in his mind, and to thoroughly understand them was always his deter-

[1] Colonel Turnley.

mined effort. To make the author's knowledge his own was ever the point at which he aimed. This intense application of mind was naturally strengthened by constant exercise, and month by month, and year by year, his faculties of perception developed rapidly, until he grasped with unerring quickness the inceptive points of all ethical and mathematical problems.'

This power of abstraction and of application is well worth noting, for not only was it remarkable in a boy, but, as we shall see hereafter, it had much to do with the making of the soldier.

At West Point Jackson was troubled with the return of the obscure complaint which had already threatened him, and he there began that rigid observance of the laws of health which afterwards developed to almost an eccentricity. His peculiar attitude when studying was due to the fear that if he bent over his work the compression of his internal organs might increase their tendency to disease.

And not only did he lay down rules for his physical regimen. A book of maxims which he drew up at West Point has been preserved, and we learn that his scrupulous exactness, his punctilious courtesy, and his choice of companions were the outcome of much deliberation.

Nothing in this curious volume occurs to show that his thoughts had yet been turned to religion. It is as free from all reference to the teachings of Christianity as the maxims of Marcus Aurelius.

Every line there written shows that at this period of Jackson's life devotion to duty was his guiding rule; and, notwithstanding his remarkable freedom from egotism, the traces of an engrossing ambition and of absolute self-dependence are everywhere apparent. Many of the sentiments he would have repudiated in after-life as inconsistent with humility; but there can be no question that it was a strong and fearless hand that penned on a conspicuous page the sentence: 'You can be what you resolve to be.'

Jackson was already a man in years when he passed his final examination, and here the record of his boyhood

may fitly close.   He had made no particular mark at the
Academy. His memory, in the minds of his comrades, was
       1846.   associated with his gravity, his silence, his kind
              heart, and his awkward movements.   No one sus-
pected him of nobler qualities than dogged perseverance and
a strict regard for truth.   The officers and sergeants of the
cadet battalion were supplied by the cadets themselves;
but Jackson was never promoted.   In the mimic warfare
of the playground at Brienne Napoleon was master of the
revels.   His capacity for command had already been
detected; but neither comrade nor teacher saw beneath
the unpromising exterior of the West Point student a trace
of aught save what was commonplace.

And yet there is much in the boyhood of Stonewall
Jackson that resembles the boyhood of Napoleon, of all
great soldiers the most original.   Both were affectionate.
Napoleon lived on bread and water that he might educate
his brothers; Jackson saved his cadet's pay to give his sister
a silk dress.   Both were indefatigable students, impressed
with the conviction that the world was to be conquered by
force of intellect.   Jackson, burning his lessons into his
brain, is but the counterpart of the young officer who lodged
with a professor of mathematics that he might attend his
classes, and who would wait to explain the lectures to those
who had not clearly understood them.   Both were provin-
cial, neither was prepossessing.   If the West Point cadets
laughed at Jackson's large hands and feet, was not Napoleon,
with his thin legs thrust into enormous boots, saluted by his
friend's children, on his first appearance in uniform, with
the nickname of *Le Chat Botté*?   It is hard to say which
was the more laughable : the spare and bony figure of the
cadet, sitting bolt upright like a graven image in a tight
uniform, with his eyes glued to the ceiling of his barrack-
room, or the young man, with gaunt features, round
shoulders, and uncombed hair, who wandered alone about
the streets of Paris in 1795.

They had the same love of method and of order.   The
accounts of the Virginian constable were not more scrupulously kept than the ledgers of Napoleon's household, nor

could they show a greater regard for economy than the tailor's bill, still extant, on which the future Emperor gained a reduction of four *sous*. But it was not on such trivial lines alone that they run parallel. An inflexibility of purpose, an absolute disregard of popular opinion, and an unswerving belief in their own capacity, were predominant in both. They could say 'No.' Neither sought sympathy, and both felt that they were masters of their own fate. 'You can be whatever you resolve to be' may be well placed alongside the speech of the brigadier of five-and-twenty : 'Have patience. I will command in Paris presently. What should I do there now?'

But here the parallel ends. In Jackson, even as a cadet, self was subordinate to duty. Pride was foreign to his nature. He was incapable of pretence, and his simplicity was inspired by that disdain of all meanness which had been his characteristic from a child. His brain was disturbed by no wild visions ; no intemperate ambition confused his sense of right and wrong. 'The essence of his mind,' as has been said of another of like mould, 'was clearness, healthy purity, incompatibility with fraud in any of its forms.' It was his instinct to be true and straightforward as it was Napoleon's to be false and subtle. And if, as a youth, he showed no trace of marked intellectual power ; if his instructors saw no sign of masterful resolution and a genius for command, it was because at West Point, as elsewhere, his great qualities lay dormant, awaiting the emergency that should call them forth.

CHAPTER II

MEXICO [1]

On June 30, 1846, Jackson received the brevet rank of second lieutenant of artillery. He was fortunate from the very outset of his military career. The officers of the United States army, thanks to the thorough education and Spartan discipline of West Point, were fine soldiers ; but their scope was limited. On the western frontier, far beyond the confines of civilisation, stood a long line of forts, often hundreds of miles apart, garrisoned by a few troops of cavalry or companies of infantry. It is true that there was little chance of soldierly capacity rusting in these solitary posts. From the borders of Canada to the banks of the Rio Grande swarmed thousands of savage warriors, ever watchful for an opportunity to pay back with bloody interest the aggression of the whites. Murder, robbery, and massacre followed each other in rapid succession, and the troops were allowed few intervals of rest. But the warfare was inglorious—a mere series of petty incidents, the punishment of a raid, or the crushing of an isolated revolt. The scanty butcher's bills of the so-called battles made small appeal to the popular imagination, and the deeds of the soldiers in the western wilderness, gallant as they might be, aroused less interest in the States than the conflicts of the police with the New York mob. But although pursuits which carried the adversaries half across the continent, forays which were of longer duration than a European war, and fights against overwhelming odds, where no quarter was asked or given, kept the American officers constantly employed, their

1846.

training was hardly sufficient for the needs of a great campaign. In the running fights against Apache or Blackfoot the rules of strategy and tactics were of small account. The soldier was constrained to acknowledge 'the brave' and the trapper as his teachers; and Moltke himself, with all his lore, would have been utterly baffled by the cunning of the Indian. Before the war of 1845–6 the strength of the regular army was not more than 8,500 men; and the whole of this force, with the exception of a few batteries, was scattered in small detachments along the frontier. The troops were never brought together in considerable bodies; and although they were well drilled and under the strictest discipline, neither the commanders nor the staff had the least experience of handling men in masses. Many of the infantry officers had never drilled with a whole battalion since they left West Point. A brigade of cavalry—that is, two or three regiments working together as a single unit—had never been assembled; and scarcely a single general had ever commanded a force composed of the three arms, either on service or on parade. 'During my twenty years of service on the frontier,' said one of the most famous of the Confederate leaders,[1] 'I learned all about commanding fifty United States dragoons and forgot everything else.'

Nevertheless, this life of enterprise and hard work, the constant struggle against nature, for the illimitable space of the inhospitable wilderness was a more formidable antagonist than the stealthy savage, benefited the American soldier in more ways than one. He grew accustomed to danger and privation. He learned to use his wits; to adapt his means to his end; to depend on his intelligence rather than on rule. Above all, even the most junior had experience of independent command before the enemy. A ready assumption of responsibility and a prompt initiative distinguished the regular officers from the very outset of the Civil War; and these characteristics had been acquired on the western prairies.

But the warfare of the frontier had none of the glamour

[1] General R. S. Ewell.

of the warfare which is waged with equal arms against an
equal enemy, of the conflict of nation against nation. To
bring the foe to bay was a matter of the utmost difficulty.
A fight at close quarters was of rare occurrence, and
the most successful campaign ended in the destruction of
a cluster of dirty wigwams, or the surrender of a handful
of starving savages. In such unsatisfactory service Jackson
was not called upon to take a part. It is doubtful if he
ever crossed the Mississippi. His first experience of campaigning was to be on a field where gleams of glory were
not wanting. The ink on his commission was scarcely dry
when the artillery subaltern was ordered to join his regiment, the First Artillery, in Mexico. The war with the
Southern Republic had blazed out on the Texan border in
1845, and the American Government had now decided to
carry it into the heart of the hostile territory. With the
cause of quarrel we have no concern. General Grant has
condemned the war as ' one of the most unjust ever waged
by a stronger against a weaker nation.' [1] Be this as it may,
it is doubtful whether any of Grant's brother officers
troubled themselves at all with the equity of invasion. It
was enough for them that the expedition meant a struggle
with a numerous enemy, armed and organised on the European model, and with much experience of war; that it
promised a campaign in a country which was the very region
of romance, possessing a lovely climate, historic cities, and
magnificent scenery. The genius of Prescott had just
disentombed from dusty archives the marvellous story of
the Spanish conquest, and the imagination of many a youthful soldier had been already kindled by his glowing pages.
To follow the path of Cortez, to traverse the golden realms of
Montezuma, to look upon the lakes and palaces of Mexico,
the most ancient city of America, to encamp among the
temples of a vanished race, and to hear, while the fireflies
flitted through the perfumed night, the music of the black-
eyed maidens of New Spain—was ever more fascinating
prospect offered to a subaltern of two-and-twenty?
The companies of the First Artillery which had been

[1] Grant's *Memoirs*, vol. i. p. 53.

detailed for foreign service were first transferred to Point Isabel, at the mouth of the Rio Grande. Several engagements had already taken place. Palo Alto, Resaca de la Palma, and Monterey were brilliant American victories, won by hard fighting over superior numbers; and a vast extent of territory had been overrun. But the Mexicans were still unconquered. The provinces they had lost were but the fringe of the national domains; the heart of the Republic had not yet felt the pressure of war, and more than six hundred miles of difficult country intervened between the invaders and the capital. The American proposals for peace had been summarily rejected. A new President, General Santa Anna, had been raised to power, and under his vigorous administration the war threatened to assume a phase sufficiently embarrassing to the United States.

Jackson had been attached to a heavy battery, and his first duty was to transport guns and mortars to the forts which protected Point Isabel. The prospect of immediate employment before the enemy was small. Operations had come to a standstill. It was already apparent that a direct advance upon the capital, through the northern provinces, was an enterprise which would demand an army much larger than the Government was disposed to furnish. It seemed as if the First Artillery had come too late. Jackson was fearful that the war might come to an end before his regiment should be sent to the front. The shy cadet had a decided taste for fighting. 'I envy you men,' he said to a comrade more fortunate than himself,[1] 'who have been in battle. How I should like to be in *one* battle!' His longing for action was soon gratified. Mexico had no navy and a long sea-board. The fleet of the United States was strong, their maritime resources ample, and to land an army on a shorter route to the distant capital was no difficult undertaking.

General Winfield Scott, who had been sent out as commander-in-chief, was permitted, early in 1847, to organise a combined naval and military expedition for the reduction of Vera Cruz, the principal port of the Republic,

[1] Lieutenant D. H. Hill, afterwards his brother-in-law.

whence a good road leads to Mexico. The line of advance
would be thus reduced to two hundred and sixty
miles ; and the natural obstacles, though numerous
enough, were far less serious than the deserts which barred
invasion from the north.   For this enterprise most of the
regular regiments were withdrawn from the Rio Grande ;
and General Taylor, the hero of Palo Alto and Monterey, was
left with a small army, composed principally of volunteers,
to hold the conquered provinces.   Scott's troops assembled
in the first instance at Tampico.   The transports, eighty
in number, having embarked their freight, were directed to
rendezvous in the roadstead of Lobos, one hundred and
twenty miles north of Vera Cruz ; and when the whole
had assembled, the fleet set sail for Los Sacrificios,
the island where Cortez had landed in 1520, three miles
south of the city.   The army of invasion, in which the
First Regiment of Artillery was included, consisted of
13,000 men.   On the morning of March 9 the
sun shone propitiously on the expedition.   The
surf-boats, each holding from seventy to eighty men,
were quickly arrayed in line.   Then, dashing forward
simultaneously, with the strains of martial music sweeping over the smooth waters of the bay, they neared the
shore.   The landing was covered by seven armed vessels,
and as the boats touched the beach the foremost men
leaped into the water and ran up the sandy shore.   In one
hour General Worth's division, numbering 4,500 men, was
disembarked ; and by the same precise arrangements the
whole army was landed in six hours without accident or
confusion.   To the astonishment of the Americans the
enemy offered no resistance, and the troops bivouacked in
line of battle on the beach.

Little more than a mile north, across a waste of sand-
hills, rose the white walls of Vera Cruz.   The city was held
by 4,000 men, and its armament was formidable.   The
troops, however, but partially organised, were incapable of
operations in the open field.   The garrison had not been
reinforced.   Santa Anna, on learning that the American
army on the Rio Grande had been reduced, had acted with

1847.

March 9.

commendable promptitude. Collecting all the troops that were available he had marched northwards, expecting, doubtless, to overwhelm Taylor and still to be in time to prevent Scott from seizing a good harbour. But distance was against him, and his precautions were inadequate. Even if he defeated Taylor, he would have to march more than a thousand miles to encounter Scott, and Vera Cruz was ill provided for a siege. It was difficult, it is true, for the Mexican general to anticipate the point at which the Americans would disembark. An army that moves by sea possesses the advantage that its movements are completely veiled. But Vera Cruz was decidedly the most probable objective of the invaders, and, had it been made secure, the venture of the Americans would have been rendered hazardous. As it was, with Santa Anna's army far away, the reduction of the fortress presented little difficulty. An immediate assault would in all likelihood have proved successful. Scott, however, decided on a regular siege. His army was small, and a march on the capital was in prospect. The Government grudged both men and money, and an assault would have cost more lives than could well be spared. On March 18 the trenches were completed. Four days later, sufficient heavy ordnance having been landed, the bombardment was begun. On the March 27. 27th the town surrendered; the garrison laid down their arms, and 400 cannon, many of large calibre, fell into the hands of the Americans.

The fall of Vera Cruz was brought about by the heavy artillery, aided by the sailors, and the First Regiment was continuously engaged. The Mexican fire, notwithstanding their array of guns, was comparatively harmless. The garrison attempted no sortie; and only 64 of the investing force were killed or wounded. Nevertheless, Jackson's behaviour under fire attracted notice, and a few months later he was promoted to first lieutenant ' for gallant and meritorious conduct at the siege of Vera Cruz.' [1]

[1] He had been promoted second lieutenant on March 3. *Records of the First Regiment of Artillery.*

Scott had now secured an admirable line of operations; but the projected march upon the city of Mexico was a far more arduous undertaking than the capture of the port. The ancient capital of Montezuma stands high above the sea. The famous valley which surrounds it is embosomed in the heart of a vast plateau, and the roads which lead to this lofty region wind by steep gradients over successive ranges of rugged and precipitous mountains. Between Vera Cruz and the upland lies a level plain, sixty miles broad, and covered with tropical forest. Had it been possible to follow up the initial victory by a rapid advance, Cerro Gordo, the first, and the most difficult, of the mountain passes, might have been occupied without a blow. Santa Anna, defeated by Taylor at Buena Vista, but returning hot foot to block Scott's path, was still distant, and Cerro Gordo was undefended. But the progress of the Americans was arrested by the difficulties inherent in all maritime expeditions.

An army landing on a hostile coast has to endure a certain period of inactivity. Under ordinary circumstances, as at Vera Cruz, the process of disembarking men is rapidly accomplished. The field-guns follow with but little delay, and a certain proportion of cavalry becomes early available. But the disembarkation of the impedimenta—the stores, waggons, hospitals, ammunition, and transport animals— even where ample facilities exist, demands far more time than the disembarkation of the fighting force. In the present case, as all the animals had to be requisitioned in the country, it was not till the middle of April that supplies and transport sufficient to warrant further movement had been accumulated; and meanwhile General Santa Anna, halting in the mountains, had occupied the pass of Cerro Gordo with 13,000 men and 42 pieces of artillery. The Mexican position was exceedingly strong. The right rested on a deep ravine, with precipitous cliffs; the left, on the hill of Cerro Gordo, covered with batteries, and towering to the height of several hundred feet above the surrounding ridges; while the front, strongly intrenched, and commanding the road which wound zigzag fashion up the steep ascent, followed the crest of a lofty ridge.

The Americans reached the foot of the pass without difficulty. The enemy had made no attempt to check their passage through the forest. Confident in the inaccessibility of his mountain crags, in his numerous guns and massive breastworks, Santa Anna reserved his strength for battle on ground of his own selection.

Several days were consumed in reconnaissance. The engineers, to whom this duty was generally assigned in the American army, pushed their explorations to either flank. At length the quick eye of a young officer, Captain Robert Lee, already noted for his services at Vera Cruz, discovered a line of approach, hidden from the enemy, by which the position might be turned. In three days a rough road was constructed by which guns could be brought to bear on the hill of Cerro Gordo, and infantry marched round to strike the Mexicans in rear. The attack, delivered at daylight on April 18, was brilliantly successful. The enemy was completely surprised. Cerro Gordo was stormed with the

April 18. bayonet, and Santa Anna's right, assaulted from a direction whence he confessed that he had not believed a goat could approach his lines, was rolled back in confusion on his centre. 1,200 Mexicans were killed and wounded, and 3,000 captured, together with the whole of their artillery.[1] The next day the pursuit was pushed with uncompromising resolution. Amidst pathless mountains, 6,000 feet above the sea, where every spur formed a strong position, the defeated army was permitted neither halt nor respite. The American dragoons, undeterred by numbers, pressed forward along the road, making hundreds of prisoners, and spreading panic in the broken ranks. The infantry followed, sturdily breasting the long ascent; a second intrenched position, barring the La Hoya pass,

May 15. was abandoned on their approach; the strong castle of Perote, with an armament of 60 guns and mortars, opened its gates without firing a shot,

---

[1] The Americans had about 8,500 men upon the field, and their loss was 431, including two generals. *Memoirs of Lieut.-General Scott.*

and on May 15 the great city of Puebla, surrounded by
glens of astonishing fertility, and only eighty miles from
Mexico, was occupied without resistance.

At Cerro Gordo the First Artillery were employed as
infantry.   Their colours were amongst the first to be
planted on the enemy's breastworks.   But in none of the
reports does Jackson's name occur.[1]   The battle, however,
brought him good luck.   Captain Magruder, an officer of his
own regiment, who was to win distinction on wider fields,
had captured a Mexican field battery, which Scott presented
to him as a reward for his gallantry.   Indian wars had
done but little towards teaching American soldiers the true
use of artillery.   Against a rapidly moving enemy, who
systematically forebore exposing himself in mass, and in a
country where no roads existed, only the fire-arm was
effective.   But already, at Palo Alto and Resaca, against
the serried lines and thronging cavalry of the Mexicans,
light field-guns had done extraordinary execution.   The
heavy artillery, hitherto the more favoured service, saw
itself eclipsed.   The First Regiment, however, had already
been prominent on the fighting line.   It had won reputation
with the bayonet at Cerro Gordo, and before Mexico was
reached there were other battles to be fought, and other
positions to be stormed.   A youth with a predilection for
hard knocks might have been content with the chances
offered to the foot-soldier.   But Jackson's partiality for his
own arm was as marked as was Napoleon's, and the decisive
effect of a well-placed battery appealed to his instincts with
greater force than the wild rush of a charge of infantry.
Skilful manœuvring was more to his taste than the mere
bludgeon work of fighting at close quarters.

Two subalterns were required for the new battery.
The position meant much hard work, and possibly much
discomfort.   Magruder was restless and hot-tempered, and
the young officers of artillery showed no eagerness to go
through the campaign as his subordinates.   Not so Jackson.   He foresaw that service with a light battery, under

---

[1] According to the Regimental Records his company (K) was not engaged
in the battle, but only in the pursuit.

a bold and energetic leader, was likely to present peculiar opportunities; and with his thorough devotion to duty, his habits of industry, and his strong sense of self-reliance, he had little fear of disappointing the expectations of the most exacting superior. 'I wanted to see active service,' he said in after years, 'to be near the enemy in the fight; and when I heard that John Magruder had got his battery I bent all my energies to be with him, for I knew if any fighting was to be done, Magruder would be "on hand."' His soldierly ambition won its due reward. The favours of fortune fall to the men who woo more often than to those who wait. The barrack-room proverb which declares that ill-luck follows the volunteer must assuredly have germinated in a commonplace brain. It is characteristic of men who have cut their way to fame that they have never allowed the opportunity to escape them. The successful man pushes to the front and seeks his chance; those of a temper less ardent wait till duty calls and the call may never come. Once before, when, despite his manifold disadvantages, he secured his nomination to West Point, Jackson had shown how readily he recognised an opening; now, when his comrades held back, he eagerly stepped forward, to prove anew the truth of the vigorous adage, 'Providence helps those who help themselves.'

The American army was delayed long at Puebla. Several regiments of volunteers, who had engaged only for a short term of service, demanded their discharge, and reinforcements were slow in arriving. It was not until the first week in August that Scott was able to move upon the capital. The army now numbered 14,000 men. Several hundred were sick in hospital, and 600 convalescents, together with 600 effectives, were left to garrison Puebla. The field force was organised in four divisions: the first, under Major-General Worth; the second, under Major-General Twiggs; the third, to which Magruder's battery was attached, under Major-General Pillow; the fourth (volunteers and marines), under Major-General Pierce. Four field batteries, a small brigade of dragoons, and a still

Aug. 7.

smaller siege train [1] made up a total of 11,500 officers and
men.   During the three months that his enemy was idle
at Puebla, Santa Anna had reorganised his army;   and
30,000 Mexicans, including a formidable body of cavalry,
fine horsemen and well trained,[2] and a large number of
heavy batteries, were now ready to oppose the advance of
the invaders.

On August 10 the American army crossed the Rio Frio
Mountains, 10,000 feet above the sea; the highest point
between the Atlantic and the Pacific, and as the troops
descended the western slopes the valley of Mexico first broke
upon their view.   There, beneath the shadow of her mighty
mountains, capped with eternal snows, stood

> The Imperial city, her far circling walls,
> Her garden groves, and stately palaces.

There lay the broad plain of Tenochtitlan, with all its
wealth of light and colour, the verdure of the forest, the
warmer hues of the great corn-fields, ripening to the harvest,
and the sheen and sparkle of the distant lakes.   There it
lay, as it burst upon the awe-struck vision of Cortez and
his companions, 'bathed in the golden sunshine, stretched
out as it were in slumber, in the arms of the giant hills.'

On every hand were the signs of a teeming population.
White villages and substantial haciendas glistened in the
woodlands; roads broad and well-travelled crossed the level;
and in the clear atmosphere of those lofty altitudes the vast
size of the city was plainly visible.   The whole army of Mexico
formed the garrison;   hills crowned with batteries commanded the approaches, while a network of canals on either
flank and a broad area of deep water enhanced the difficulties of manœuvre.   The line of communication, far too
long to be maintained by the small force at Scott's
disposal, had already been abandoned.   The army depended
for subsistence on what it could purchase in the country;
the sick and wounded were carried with the troops, and

---

[1] Two 24-pounders, two 8-inch howitzers, and two light pieces.   Ripley's
History of the Mexican War.

[2] It is said, however, that their horses were little more than ponies, and
far too light for a charge.   Semmes' *Campaign of General Scott*.

there was no further reserve of ammunition than that which was packed in the regimental waggons. Cortez and his four hundred when they essayed the same enterprise were not more completely isolated, for, while the Spaniard had staunch allies in the hereditary foes of the Aztecs, Scott's nearest supports were at Puebla, eighty miles from Mexico, and these numbered only 1,200 effective soldiers. The most adventurous of leaders might well have hesitated ere he plunged into the great valley, swarming with enemies, and defended by all the resources of a civilised State. But there was no misgiving in the ranks of the Americans. With that wholesome contempt for a foreign foe which has wrought more good than evil for the Anglo-Saxon race, the army moved forward without a halt. 'Recovering,' says Scott, ' from the trance into which the magnificent spectacle had thrown them, probably not a man in the column failed to say to his neighbour or himself, "That splendid city shall soon be ours ! " '

The fortifications which protected Mexico on the east were found to be impregnable. The high ridge of El Peñon, manned by nearly the whole of Santa Anna's army, blocked the passage between the lakes, and deep morasses added to the difficulties of approach. To the south, how- ever, on the far side of Lake Chalco, lay a more level tract, but accessible only by roads which the Mexicans deemed impracticable. Despite the difficulties of the route, the manœuvre of Cerro Gordo was repeated on a grander scale. After a toilsome march of seven-and-twenty miles from Ayotla,

August 16–18. over the spurs of the sierras, the troops reached the great road which leads to the capital from the south.

Across this road was more than one line of forti- fications, to which the Mexican army had been hurriedly transferred. The hacienda of San Antonio, six miles from the city, strengthened by field-works and defended by heavy guns, commanded the highway. To the east was a morass, and beyond the morass were the blue waters of Lake Chalco ; while to the west the Pedregal, a barren tract of volcanic scoriæ, over whose sharp rocks and deep fissures neither horse nor vehicle could move, flanked the American

line of march. The morass was absolutely impassable. **The**
gloomy solitude of the Pedregal, extending to the mountains,
five miles distant, seemed equally forbidding; but the
engineer officers came once more to the rescue. A road
across the Pedregal, little better than a mule track, was
discovered by Captain Lee. Under cover of a strong
escort it was rapidly improved, and Pillow's and
Aug. 19.   Worth's divisions, accompanied by Magruder's
battery, were directed to cross the waste of rocks. Beyond
the Pedregal was a good road, approaching the city from
the south-west; and by this road the post of San Antonio
might be assailed in rear.

Overlooking the road, however, as well as the issues
from the Pedregal, was a high ridge, backed by the
mountains, and held by 6,000 Mexicans. Opposite this
ridge the Americans came out on cultivated ground, but all
further progress was completely checked. Shortly after
midday the leading brigade, with Magruder's battery 'on
hand,' reached the summit of a hill within a thousand yards
of the enemy's breastworks. Magruder came at once into
action, and the infantry attempted to push forward. But
the Mexican artillery was far superior, both in number of
pieces and weight of metal, and the ground was eminently
unfavourable for attack. Two-and-twenty heavy cannon
swept the front; the right of the position was secured by a
deep ravine; masses of infantry were observed in rear of
the intrenchments, and several regiments of lancers were
in close support. For three hours the battle raged fiercely.
On the right the Americans pushed forward, crossing with
extreme difficulty an outlying angle of the Pedregal, covered
with dense scrub, and occupied the village of Contreras. But
elsewhere they made no impression. They were without
cavalry, and Magruder's guns were far too few and feeble
to keep down the fire of the hostile batteries. 'The
infantry,' says Scott, 'could not advance in column without
being mowed down by grape and canister, nor advance in
line without being ridden down by the enemy's numerous
horsemen.' Nor were the Mexicans content on this occasion
to remain passively in their works. Both infantry and

cavalry attempted to drive the assailants back upon the Pedregal; and, although these counterstrokes were successfully repulsed, when darkness fell the situation of the troops was by no means favourable. Heavy columns of Mexicans were approaching from the city; the remainder of the American army was opposite San Antonio, five miles distant, on the far side of the Pedregal, and no support could be expected. To add to their discomfort, it rained heavily; the thunder crashed in the mountains, and torrents of water choked the streams. The men stood in the darkness drenched and dispirited, and an attack made by a Mexican battalion induced General Pillow to withdraw Magruder's battery from the ridge. The senior subaltern had been killed. 15 gunners and as many horses had fallen. The slopes were covered with huge boulders, and it was only by dint of the most strenuous exertions that the guns were brought down in safety to the lower ground.

A council of war was then held in Contreras Church, and, contrary to the traditionary conduct of such conventions, a most desperate expedient was adopted. The Mexican reinforcements, 12,000 strong, had halted on the main road, their advanced-guard within a few hundred yards of the village. Leaving two regiments to hold this imposing force in check, it was determined to make a night march and turn the rear of the intrenchments on the ridge. The Commander-in-Chief was beyond the Pedregal, opposite San Antonio, and it was necessary that he should be informed of the projected movement.

'I have always understood,' says an officer present in this quarter of the field, 'that what was devised and determined on was suggested by Captain Lee; at all events the council was closed by his saying that he desired to return to General Scott with the decision, and that, as it was late, the decision must be given as soon as possible, since General Scott wished him to return in time to give directions for co-operation. During the council, and for hours after, the rain fell in torrents, whilst the darkness was so intense that one could move only by groping.'

The Pedregal was infested by straggling bands of

Mexicans; and yet, over those five miles of desolation, with no guide but the wind, or an occasional flash of lightning, Lee, unaccompanied by a single orderly, made his way to Scott's headquarters. This perilous adventure was characterised by the Commander-in-Chief as 'the greatest feat of physical and moral courage performed by any individual during the entire campaign.'

The night march, although it entailed the passage of a deep ravine, and was so slow that one company in two hours made no more than four hundred yards, was completely successful. The Mexicans, trusting to the strength of their position, and to the presence of the reinforcements, had neglected to guard their left. The lesson of Cerro Gordo had been forgotten. The storming parties, guided by the engineers, Lee, Beauregard, and Gustavus Smith, established themselves, under cover of the darkness, within five hundred paces of the intrenchments, and as the day broke the works were carried at the first rush. Seventeen minutes after the signal had been given, the garrison, attacked in front and rear simultaneously,

Aug. 20. was completely dispersed. 800 Mexicans were captured, and nearly as many killed.[1] The reinforcements, unable to intervene, and probably demoralised by this unlooked-for defeat, fell back to the village of Churubusco, and San Antonio was evacuated. The pursuit was hotly pressed. Churubusco was heavily bombarded. For two hours the American batteries played upon the church and hacienda, both strongly fortified, and after a counterstroke had been beaten back a vigorous onslaught, made by the whole line of battle, compelled the enemy to give way. A brilliant charge of General Shields' brigade dispersed their last reserves, and the whole of the hostile army fled in confusion to the city. The American cavalry followed at speed, using their sabres freely on the panic-stricken masses, and one squadron, not hearing the recall, dashed up to the very gates of the city. Scott's losses amounted to 1,053, including 76 officers. The Mexican casualties

[1] 4,500 Americans (rank and file) were engaged, and the losses did not exceed 50. Scott's *Memoirs*.

were 3,000 prisoners, and 3,250 killed and wounded. 37 field-guns were abandoned, and, a still more valuable capture, a large supply of ammunition fell into the hands of the victors.

Magruder's battery, it appears, was retained in reserve throughout the battle of Churubusco, and Jackson's share in the victory was confined to the engagement of the previous day. But his small charge of three guns had been handled with skill and daring. Magruder was more than satisfied. ' In a few moments,' ran his official report, ' Lieutenant Jackson, commanding the second section of the battery, who had opened fire upon the enemy's works from a position on the right, hearing our fire still further in front, advanced in handsome style, and kept up the fire with equal briskness and effect. His conduct was equally conspicuous during the whole day, and I cannot too highly commend him to the Major-General's favourable consideration.'

The extreme vigour with which the Americans had prosecuted their operations now came to an untimely pause. After his double victory at Contreras and Churubusco, General Scott proposed an armistice. The whole of the Mexican army had been encountered. It had been decisively defeated. Its losses, in men and *matériel*, had been very heavy. The troops were utterly demoralised. The people were filled with consternation, and a rapid advance would probably have been followed by an immediate peace. But Scott was unwilling to drive his foes to desperation, and he appears to have believed that if they were spared all further humiliation they would accede without further resistance to his demands.

The Mexicans, however, were only playing for time. During the negotiations, in direct defiance of the terms of the armistice, Santa Anna strengthened his fortifications, rallied his scattered army, and prepared once more to confront the invader. Scott's ultimatum was rejected, and on September 5 hostilities were renewed. Three
Sept. 8.   days later the position of Molino del Rey, garrisoned by the choicest of the Mexican troops, was

stormed at dawn. But the enemy had benefited by his
respite. The fighting was desperate. 800 Americans were
killed and wounded before the intrenchments and strong
buildings were finally carried ; and although the Mexicans
again lost 3,000 men, including two generals, their spirit of
resistance was not yet wholly crushed.

Driven from their outworks, they had fallen back on a
still more formidable line. Behind the Molino del Rey
rose the hill of Chapultepec, crowned by the great castle
which had been the palace of Montezuma and of the
Spanish viceroys, now the military college of the Republic
and the strongest of her fortresses. Three miles from the
city walls, the stronghold completely barred the line of
advance on the San Cosme Gate. Heavy guns mounted on
the lofty bastions which encircled the citadel, commanded
every road, and the outflanking movements which had
hitherto set at nought the walls and parapets of the Mexicans
were here impracticable. Still, careful reconnaissance had
shown that, with all its difficulties, this was the most favourable approach for the invading army. The gates of Belen
and San Antonio were beset by obstacles even more impracticable. The ground over which the troops would advance to
storm the fortress was far firmer than elsewhere, there was
ample space for the American batteries, and if the hill
were taken, the Mexicans, retreating along two narrow
causeways, with deep marshes on either hand, might easily
be deprived of all opportunity of rallying.

On the night of the 11th four batteries of heavy guns
were established within easy range. On the 12th they
opened fire ; and the next morning the American
Sept. 13. army, covered by the fire of the artillery, advanced
to the assault. In the victory of Molino del Rey, Magruder's
battery had taken little part. Jackson, posted with his
section on the extreme flank of the line, had dispersed a
column of cavalry which threatened a charge ; but, with this
brief interlude of action, he had been merely a spectator.
At Chapultepec he was more fortunate. Pillow's division,
to which the battery was attached, attacked the Mexicans
in front, while Worth's division assailed them from the

north. The 14th Infantry, connecting the two attacks, moved along a road which skirts the base of the hill, and Magruder was ordered to detach a section of his battery in support. Jackson was selected for the duty, and as he approached the enemy's position dangers multiplied at every step. The ground alongside was so marshy that the guns were unable to leave the road. A Mexican field-piece, covered by a breastwork, raked the causeway from end to end, while from the heights of Chapultepec cannon of large calibre poured down a destructive fire. The infantry suffered terribly. It was impossible to advance along the narrow track; and when the guns were ordered up the situation was in no way bettered. Nearly every horse was killed or wounded. A deep ditch, cut across the road, hindered effective action, and the only position where reply to the enemy's fire was possible lay beyond this obstacle. Despite the losses of his command Jackson managed to lift one gun across by hand. But his men became demoralised. They left their posts. The example of their lieutenant, walking up and down on the shot-swept road and exclaiming calmly, 'There is no danger: see! I am not hit,' failed to inspire them with confidence. Many had already fallen. The infantry, with the exception of a small escort, which held its ground with difficulty, had disappeared; and General Worth, observing Jackson's perilous situation, sent him orders to retire. He replied it was more dangerous to withdraw than to stand fast, and if they would give him fifty veterans he would rather attempt the capture of the breastwork. At this juncture Magruder, losing his horse as he galloped forward, reached the road.

The ditch was crowded with soldiers; many wounded; many already dead; many whose hearts had failed them. Beyond, on the narrow causeway, the one gun which Jackson had brought across the ditch was still in action.

Deserted by his gunners, and abandoned by the escort which had been ordered to support him, the young subaltern still held his ground. With the sole assistance of a sergeant, of stauncher mettle than the rest, he was loading and firing his solitary field-piece, rejoicing, as became the son of a warrior race, in the hot breath of battle, and still more in the isolation of his perilous position. To stand alone, in the forefront of the fight, defying the terrors from which others shrank, was the situation which of all others he most coveted; and under the walls of Chapultepec, answering shot for shot, and plying sponge and handspike with desperate energy, the fierce instincts of the soldier were fully gratified. Nor was Magruder the man to proffer prudent counsels. A second gun was hoisted across the ditch; the men rallied; the Mexican artillery was gradually overpowered, and the breastwork stormed. The crisis of the struggle was already past. Pillow's troops had driven the enemy from their intrenchments at the base of the hill, and beneath the shadows of the majestic cypresses, which still bear the name of the Grove of Monte-zuma, and up the rugged slopes which tower above them, pressed the assaulting columns. A redoubt which stood midway up the height was carried. The Mexicans fell back from shelter to shelter; but amid smoke and flame the scaling ladders were borne across the castle ditch, and reared against the lofty walls were soon covered with streams of men. The leaders, hurled from the battlements on to the crowd below, failed to make good their footing, but there were others to take their places. The supports came thronging up; the enemy, assailed in front and flank, drew back disheartened, and after a short struggle the American colours, displayed upon the keep, announced to the citizens of Mexico that Chapultepec had been captured. Yet the victory was not complete. The greater part of the garrison had fled from their intrenchments before the castle had been stormed; and infantry, cavalry, and artillery, in wild confusion, were crowding in panic on the causeways. But their numbers were formidable, and the city, should the army be rallied, was capable of a protracted defence. Not a moment was to be lost if the battle was to be decisive of the war. The disorder on Chapultepec was hardly less than that which existed in the ranks of the defeated

Mexicans. Many of the stormers had dispersed in search of plunder, and regiments and brigades had become hopelessly intermingled in the assault of the rocky hill. Still the pursuit was prompt. Towards the San Cosme Gate several of the younger officers, a lieutenant by name Ulysses Grant amongst the foremost, followed the enemy with such men as they could collect, and Jackson's guns were soon abreast of the fighting line. His teams had been destroyed by the fire of the Mexican batteries. Those of his waggons, posted further to the rear, had partially escaped. To disengage the dead animals from the limbers and to replace them by others would have wasted many minutes, and he had eagerly suggested to Magruder that the guns should be attached to the waggon-limbers instead of to their own. Permission was given, and in a few moments his section was thundering past the cliffs of Chapultepec. Coming into action within close range of the flying Mexicans, every shot told on their demoralised masses; but before the San Cosme Gate the enemy made a last effort to avert defeat. Fresh troops were brought up to man the outworks; the houses and gardens which lined the road were filled with skirmishers; from the high parapets of the flat house-tops a hail of bullets struck the head of the pursuing column; and again and again the American infantry, without cover and with little space for movement, recoiled from the attack.

The situation of the invading army, despite the brilliant victory of Chapultepec, was not yet free from peril. The greater part of the Mexican forces was still intact. The city contained 180,000 inhabitants, and General Scott's battalions had dwindled to the strength of a small division. In the various battles before the capital nearly 3,000 officers and men had fallen, and the soldiers who encompassed the walls of the great metropolis were spent with fighting.[1] One spark of the stubborn courage which bore Cortez and his paladins through the hosts of Montezuma might have made of that stately city a second Saragossa. It was eminently defensible. The churches, the convents,

[1] 862 officers and men fell at Chapultepec. Scott's *Memoirs*.

the public buildings, constructed with that solidity which is peculiarly Spanish, formed each of them a fortress. The broad streets, crossing each other at right angles, rendered concentration at any threatened point an easy matter, and beyond the walls were broad ditches and a deep canal.

Nor was the strength of the city the greatest of Scott's difficulties. Vera Cruz, his base of operations, was two hundred and sixty miles distant; Puebla, his nearest supply-depôt, eighty miles. He had abandoned his communications. His army was dependent for food on a hostile population. In moving round Lake Chalco, and attacking the city from the south, he had burned his boats. A siege or an investment were alike impossible. A short march would place the enemy's army across his line of retreat, and nothing would have been easier for the Mexicans than to block the road where it passes between the sierras and the lake. Guerillas were already hovering in the hills; one single repulse before the gates of the capital would have raised the country in rear; and hemmed in by superior numbers, and harassed by a cavalry which was at least equal to the task of cutting off supplies, the handful of Americans must have cut their way through to Puebla or have succumbed to starvation.

Such considerations had doubtless been at the root of the temporising policy which had been pursued after Churubusco. But the uselessness of half-measures had then been proved. The conviction had become general that a desperate enterprise could only be pushed to a successful issue by desperate tactics, and every available battalion was hurried forward to the assault. Before the San Cosme Gate the pioneers were ordered up, and within the suburb pick and crowbar forced a passage from house to house. The guns, moving slowly forward, battered the crumbling masonry at closest range. The Mexicans were driven back from breastwork to breastwork; and a mountain howitzer, which Lieutenant Grant had posted on the tower of a neighbouring church, played with terrible effect, at a range of two or three hundred yards, on the defenders of the Gate.

By eight o'clock in the evening the suburb had been cleared, and the Americans were firmly established within the walls. To the south-east, before the Belen Gate, another column had been equally successful. During the night Santa Anna withdrew his troops, and when day dawned the white flag was seen flying from the citadel. After a sharp fight with 2,000 convicts whom the fugitive President had released, the invaders occupied the city, and the war was virtually at an end. From Cerro Gordo to Chapultepec the power of discipline had triumphed. An army of 30,000 men, fighting in their own country, and supported by a numerous artillery, had been defeated by an invading force of one-third the strength. Yet the Mexicans had shown no lack of courage. 'At Chapultepec and Molino del Rey, as on many other occasions,' says Grant, 'they stood up as well as any troops ever did.'[1] But their officers were inexperienced; the men were ill-instructed; and against an army of regular soldiers, well led and obedient, their untutored valour, notwithstanding their superior numbers, had proved of no avail. They had early become demoralised. Their strongest positions had been rendered useless by the able manœuvres of their adversaries. Everywhere they had been out-generalled. They had never been permitted to fight on the ground which they had prepared, and in almost every single engagement they had been surprised. Nor had the Government escaped the infection which had turned the hearts of the troops to water. The energy of the pursuit after the fall of Chapultepec had wrought its full effect, and on September 14 the city of Mexico was surrendered, without further parley, to a force which, all told, amounted to less than 7,000 men.[2]

Sept. 14.

With such portion of his force as had not disbanded Santa Anna undertook the siege of Puebla; and the guerillas, largely reinforced from the army, waged a desultory warfare in the mountains. But these despairing

[1] Grant's *Memoirs*, vol. i. p. 169.
[2] The total loss in the battles before the capital was 2,703, including 383 officers. Scott's *Memoirs*.

efforts were without effect upon the occupation of the
capital. The Puebla garrison beat back every attack; and
the bands of irregular horsemen were easily dispersed.
During these operations Magruder's battery remained with
headquarters near the capital, and so far as Jackson was
concerned all opportunities for distinction were past. The
peace negotiations were protracted from September to the following February, and in their camps
beyond the walls the American soldiers were fain
to content themselves with their ordinary duties.

Feb.
1848.

It cannot be said that Jackson had failed to take
advantage of the opportunities which fortune had thrown
in his way. As eagerly as he had snatched at the chance
of employment in the field artillery he had welcomed the
tactical emergency which had given him sole command of
his section at Chapultepec. It was a small charge; but he
had utilised it to the utmost, and it had filled the cup of
his ambition to the brim. Ambitious he certainly was.
' He confessed,' says Dabney, ' to an intimate friend that
the order of General Pillow, separating his section on the
day of Chapultepec from his captain, had excited his abiding
gratitude; so much so that while the regular officers were
rather inclined to depreciate the general as an unprofessional
soldier, he loved him because he gave him an opportunity
to win distinction.' His friends asked him, long after the
war, if he felt no trepidation when so many were falling
round him. He replied: ' No; the only anxiety of which
I was conscious during the engagements was a fear lest I
should not meet danger enough to make my conduct
conspicuous.'

His share of glory was more than ample. Contreras
gave him the brevet rank of captain. For his conduct at
Chapultepec he was mentioned in the Commander-in-
Chief's dispatches, and publicly complimented on his
courage. Shortly after the capture of the city, General
Scott held a levée, and amongst others presented to him
was Lieutenant Jackson. When he heard the name, the
general drew himself up to his full height, and, placing his
hands behind him, said with affected sternness, ' I don't

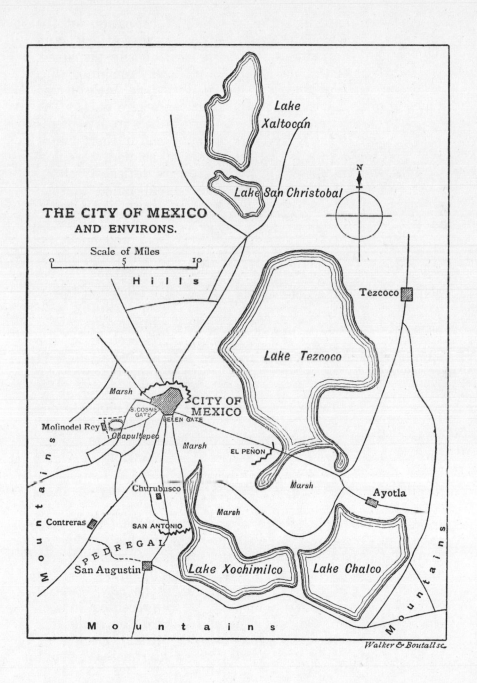

Lake Xaltocán

Lake San Christobal

THE CITY OF MEXICO
AND ENVIRONS.

Scale of Miles
0   5   10

H i l l s

N

Tezcoco

Lake Tezcoco

Marsh

S.COSME GATE
City OF MEXICO
BELEN GATE

Molinodel Rey
Chapultepec

Marsh

EL PEÑON

Marsh

M o u n t a i n s

Churubusco

Marsh

Ayotla

Contreras

SAN ANTONIO

P E D R E G A L

San Augustin

Lake Xochimilco

Lake Chalco

M o u n t a i n s

M o u n t a i n s

Walker & Boutall sc.

know that I shall shake hands with Mr. Jackson.' Jackson, blushing like a girl, was overwhelmed with confusion. General Scott, seeing that he had called the attention of every one in the room, said, ' If you can forgive yourself for the way in which you slaughtered those poor Mexicans with your guns, I am not sure that I can,' and then held out his hand. ' No greater compliment,' says General Gibbon, ' could have been paid a young officer, and Jackson apparently did not know he had done anything remarkable till his general told him so.' [1] Magruder could find no praise high enough for his industry, his capacity, and his gallantry, and within eighteen months of his first joining his regiment he was breveted major. Such promotion was phenomenal even in the Mexican war, and none of his West Point comrades made so great a stride in rank. His future in his profession was assured. He had acquired something more than the spurs of a field officer in his seven months of service. A subaltern, it has been said, learns but little of the higher art of war in the course of a campaign. His daily work so engrosses his attention that he has little leisure to reflect on the lessons in strategy and tactics which unfold themselves before him. Without maps, and without that information of the enemy's numbers and dispositions which alone renders the manœuvres intelligible, it is difficult, even where the inclination exists, to discuss or criticise the problems, tactical and strategical, with which the general has to deal. But siege and battle, long marches and rough roads, gave the young American officers an insight into the practical difficulties of war. It is something to have seen how human nature shows itself under fire ; how easily panics may be generated ; how positions that seem impregnable may be rendered weak ; to have witnessed the effect of surprise, and to have realised the strength of a vigorous attack. It is something, too, if a man learns his own worth in situations of doubt and danger ; and if he finds, as did Jackson, that battle sharpens his faculties, and makes his self-control more perfect, his judgment

[1] Letter to the author.

clearer and more prompt, the gain in self-confidence is of
the utmost value.

Moreover, whether a young soldier learns much or
little from his first campaign depends on his intellectual
powers and his previous training. Jackson's brain, as
his steady progress at West Point proves, was of a capacity
beyond the average. He was naturally reflective. If, at
the Military Academy, he had heard little of war; if,
during his service in Mexico, his knowledge was insufficient
to enable him to compare General Scott's operations with
those of the great captains, he had at least been trained to
think. It is difficult to suppose that his experience was cast
away. He was no thoughtless subaltern, but already an
earnest soldier; and in after times, when he came to study
for himself the campaigns of Washington and Napoleon, we
may be certain that the teaching he found there was made
doubly impressive when read by the light of what he had
seen himself. Nor is it mere conjecture to assert that in
his first campaign his experience was of peculiar value to
a future general of the Southern Confederacy. Some of
the regiments who fought under Scott and Taylor were
volunteers, civilians, like their successors in the great Civil
War, in all but name, enlisted for the war only, or even for a
shorter term, and serving under their own officers. Several
of these regiments had fought well; others had behaved
indifferently; and the problem of how discipline was to be
maintained in battle amongst these unprofessional soldiers
obtruded itself as unpleasantly in Mexico as it had in
the wars with England. Amongst the regular officers,
accustomed to the absolute subordination of the army, the
question provoked perplexity and discussion.

So small was the military establishment of the States
that in case of any future war, the army, as in Mexico, would
be largely composed of volunteers; and, despite the high
intelligence and warlike enthusiasm of the citizen battalions,
it was evident that they were far less reliable than the
regulars. Even General Grant, partial as he was to the
volunteers, admitted the superiority conferred by drill,
discipline, and highly trained officers. 'A better army,' he

wrote, 'man for man, probably never faced an enemy than the one commanded by General Taylor in the earlier engagements of the Mexican war.'[1] These troops were all regulars, and they were those who carried Scott in triumph from the shores of the Gulf to the palace of Santa Anna. The volunteers had proved themselves exceedingly liable to panic. Their superior intelligence had not enabled them to master the instincts of human nature, and, although they had behaved well in camp and on the march, in battle their discipline had fallen to pieces.[2] It could hardly be otherwise. Men without ingrained habits of obedience, who have not been trained to subordinate their will to another's, cannot be expected to render implicit obedience in moments of danger and excitement; nor can they be expected, under such circumstances, to follow officers in whom they can have but little confidence. The ideal of battle is a combined effort, directed by a trained leader. Unless troops are thoroughly well disciplined such effort is impossible; the leaders are ignored, and the spasmodic action of the individual is substituted for the concentrated pressure of the mass. The cavalry which dissolves into a mob before it strikes the enemy but seldom attains success; and infantry out of hand is hardly more effective. In the Mexican campaign the volunteers, although on many occasions they behaved with admirable courage, continually broke loose from control under the fire of the enemy. As individuals they fought well; as organised bodies, capable of manœuvring under fire and of combined effort, they proved to be comparatively worthless.

So Jackson, observant as he was, gained on Mexican battle-fields some knowledge of the shortcomings inherent in half-trained troops. And this was not all. The expedition had demanded the services of nearly every officer in the army of the United States, and in the toils of the march, in the close companionship of the camp, in the excitement of battle, the shrewder spirits probed the characters of their comrades to the quick. In the history of the Civil War

[1] Grant's *Memoirs*, vol. i. p. 168.
[2] Ripley's *History of the Mexican War*, vol. ii. p. 73, &c.

there are few things more remarkable than the use which was made of the knowledge thus acquired. The clue to many an enterprise, daring even to foolhardiness, is to be found in this. A leader so intimately acquainted with the character of his opponent as to be able to predict with certainty what he will do under any given circumstances may set aside with impunity every established rule of war. 'All the older officers, who became conspicuous in the rebellion,' says Grant, 'I had also served with and known in Mexico. The acquaintance thus formed was of immense service to me in the War of the Rebellion—I mean what I learned of the characters of those to whom I was afterwards opposed. I do not pretend to say that all my movements, or even many of them, were made with special reference to the characteristics of the commander against whom they were directed. But my appreciation of my enemies was certainly affected by this knowledge.' [1]

Many of the generals with whom Jackson became intimately connected, either as friends or enemies, are named in Scott's dispatches. Magruder, Hooker, McDowell, and Ambrose Hill belonged to his own regiment. McClellan, Beauregard, and Gustavus Smith served on the same staff as Lee. Joseph E. Johnston, twice severely wounded, was everywhere conspicuous for dashing gallantry. Shields commanded a brigade with marked ability. Pope was a staff officer. Lieutenant D. H. Hill received two brevets. Lieutenant Longstreet, struck down whilst carrying the colours at Chapultepec, was bracketed for conspicuous conduct with Lieutenant Pickett. Lieutenant Edward Johnson is mentioned as having specially distinguished himself in the same battle. Captain Huger, together with Lieutenants Porter and Reno, did good service with the artillery, and Lieutenant Ewell had two horses killed under him at Churubusco.

So having proved his mettle and 'drunk delight of battle with his peers,' Jackson spent nine pleasant months in the conquered city. The peace negotiations were protracted. The United States coveted the auriferous provinces

[1] Grant's *Memoirs*, vol. i. p. 192.

of California and New Mexico, a tract as large as a European kingdom, and far more wealthy. Loth to lose their birthright, yet powerless to resist, the Mexicans could only haggle for a price. The States were not disposed to be ungenerous, but the transfer of so vast a territory could not be accomplished in a moment, and the victorious army remained in occupation of the capital.

Beneath the shadow of the Stars and Stripes conqueror and conquered lived in harmony. Mexico was tired of war. Since the downfall of Spanish rule revolution had followed revolution with startling rapidity. The beneficent despotism of the great viceroys had been succeeded by the cruel exactions of petty tyrants, and for many a long year the country had been ravaged by their armies. The capital itself had enjoyed but a few brief intervals of peace, and now, although the bayonets of an alien race were the pledge of their repose, the citizens revelled in the unaccustomed luxury. Nor were they ungrateful to those who brought them a respite from alarms and anarchy. Under the mild administration of the American generals the streets resumed their wonted aspect. The great markets teemed with busy crowds. Across the long causeways rolled the creaking waggons, laden with the produce of far-distant haciendas. Trade was restored, and even the most patriotic merchants were not proof against the influence of the American dollar. Between the soldiers and the people was much friendly intercourse. Even the religious orders did not disdain to offer their hospitality to the heretics. The uniforms of the victorious army were to be seen at every festive gathering, and the graceful Mexicañas were by no means insensible to the admiration of the stalwart Northerners. Those blue-eyed and fair-haired invaders were not so very terrible after all ; and the beauties of the capital, accustomed to be wooed in liquid accents and flowery phrases, listened without reluctance to harsher tones and less polished compliments. Travellers of many races have borne willing witness to the charms and virtues of the women of Mexico. 'True daughters of Spain,' it has been said, ' they unite the grace of Castile to the vivacity of Andalusia ; and more sterling qualities are by no means wanting. Gentle and refined, unaffectedly pleasing in manners and conversation, they evince a warmth of heart which wins for them the respect and esteem of all strangers.' To the homes made bright by the presence of these fair specimens of womanhood Scott's officers were always welcome ; and Jackson, for the first time in his life, found himself within the sphere of feminine attractions. The effect on the stripling soldier, who, stark fighter as he was, had seen no more of life than was to be found in a country village or within the precincts of West Point, may be easily imagined. Who the magnet was he never confessed; but that he went near losing his heart to some charming señorita of *sangre azul* he more than once acknowledged, and he took much trouble to appear to advantage in her eyes. The deficiencies in his education which prevented his full enjoyment of social pleasures were soon made up. He not only learned to dance, an accomplishment which must have taxed his perseverance to the utmost, but he spent some months in learning Spanish; and it is significant that to the end of his life he retained a copious vocabulary of those tender diminutives which fall so gracefully from Spanish lips.

But during his stay in Mexico other and more lasting influences were at work. Despite the delights of her delicious climate, where the roses bloom the whole year round, the charms of her romantic scenery, and the fascinations of her laughter-loving daughters, Jackson's serious nature soon asserted itself. The constant round of light amusements and simple duties grew distasteful. The impress of his mother's teachings and example was there to guide him, and his native reverence for all that was good and true received an unexpected impulse. There were not wanting in the American army men who had a higher ideal of duty than mere devotion to the business of their profession. The officer commanding the First Artillery, Colonel Frank Taylor, possessed that earnest faith which is not content with solitude. 'This good man,' says Dabney, 'was accustomed to labour as a father for the religious welfare of his young officers, and during the summer campaign his instructions and prayers had produced so much effect as to awake an abiding anxiety and spirit of inquiry in Jackson's mind.' The latter had little prejudice in favour of any particular sect or church. There was no State Establishment in the United States. His youth had been passed in a household where Christianity was practically unknown, and with characteristic independence he determined to discover for himself the rule that he should follow. His researches took a course which his Presbyterian ancestors would assuredly have condemned. But Jackson's mind was singularly open, and he was the last man in the world to yield to prejudice. Soon after peace was declared, he had made the acquaintance of a number of priests belonging to one of the great religious orders of the Catholic Church. They had invited him to take up his quarters with them, and when he determined to examine for himself into the doctrine of the ancient faith, he applied through them for an introduction to the Archbishop of Mexico. Several interviews took place between the aged ecclesiastic and the young soldier. Jackson departed unsatisfied. He acknowledged that the prelate was a sincere and devout Christian, and he was impressed as much with his kindness as his learning. But he left Mexico without any settled convictions on the subject which now absorbed his thoughts.

On June 12, peace having been signed at the end of May, the last of the American troops marched out of the conquered capital. Jackson's battery was sent to June 12. Fort Hamilton, on Long Island, seven miles below New York, and there, with his honours thick upon him, he settled down to the quiet life of a small garrison. He had gone out to Mexico a second lieutenant; he had come back a field-officer. He had won a name in the army, and his native State had enrolled him amongst her heroes. He had gone out an unformed youth; he had come back a man and a proved leader of men. He had been known merely as an indefatigable student and a somewhat unsociable companion. He had come back with a reputation for daring courage, not only the courage which glories in swift action and the excitement of the charge, but courage

of an enduring quality. And in that distant country he
had won more than fame. He had already learned something of the vanity of temporal success. He had gone out
with a vague notion of ruling his life in accordance with
moral precepts and philosophic maxims; but he was to
be guided henceforward by loftier principles than even
devotion to duty and regard for honour, and from the
path he had marked out for himself in Mexico he never
deviated.

STONEWALL JACKSON, ÆT. 24.

(*From a Daguerreotype.*)

CHAPTER III

LEXINGTON. 1851—1861

OF Jackson's life at Fort Hamilton there is little to tell. His friend and mentor, Colonel Taylor, was in command. The chaplain, once an officer of dragoons, was a man of persuasive eloquence and earnest zeal ; and surrounded by influences which had now become congenial, the young major of artillery pursued the religious studies he had begun in Mexico. There was some doubt whether he had been baptised as a child. He was anxious that no uncertainty should exist as to his adhesion to Christianity, but he was unwilling that the sacrament should bind him to any particular sect. On the understanding that no surrender of judgment would be involved, he was baptised and received his first communion in the Episcopal Church.

1848.

1849.

Two years passed without incident, and then Jackson was transferred to Florida. In his new quarters his stay was brief. In March 1851 he was appointed Professor of Artillery Tactics and Natural Philosophy at the Virginia Military Institute. His success, for such he deemed it, was due to his own merit. One of his Mexican comrades, Major D. H. Hill, afterwards his brother-in-law, was a professor in a neighbouring institution, Washington College, and had been consulted by the Superintendent of the Institute as to the filling of the vacant chair.

1851.

Hill remembered what had been said of Jackson at West Point : 'If the course had been one year longer he would have graduated at the head of his class.' This voluntary testimonial of his brother cadets had not passed unheeded. It had weight, as the best evidence of his thoroughness and application, with the Board of Visitors, and Jackson was unanimously elected.

The Military Institute, founded twelve years previously on the model of West Point, was attended by several hundred youths from Virginia and other Southern States. At Lexington, in the county of Rockbridge, a hundred miles west of Richmond, stand the castellated buildings and the wide parade ground which formed the nursery of so many Confederate soldiers. To the east rise the lofty masses of the Blue Ridge. To the north successive ranges of rolling hills, green with copse and woodland, fall gently to the lower levels; and stretching far away at their feet, watered by that lovely river which the Indians in melodious syllables called Shenandoah, 'bright daughter of the Stars,' the great Valley of Virginia,

> Deep-meadowed, happy, fair with orchard lawns
> And bowery hollows,

lies embosomed within its mountain walls. Of all its pleasant market towns, Lexington is not the least attractive; and in this pastoral region, where the great forests stand round about the corn-fields, and the breezes blow untainted from the uplands, had been built the College which Washington, greatest of Virginians and greatest of American soldiers, had endowed. Under the shadow of its towers the State had found an appropriate site for her military school.

The cadets of the Institute, although they wore a uniform, were taught by officers of the regular army, were disciplined as soldiers, and spent some months of their course in camp, were not destined for a military career. All aspirants for commissions in the United States army had to pass through West Point; and the training of the State colleges—for Virginia was not solitary in the possession of such an institution—however much it may have benefited both the minds and bodies of the rising generation, was of immediate value only to those who became officers of the State militia. Still in all essential respects the Military Institute was little behind West Point. The discipline was as strict, the drill but little less precise. The cadets had their own officers and their own sergeants, and the whole establishment was administered on a military footing. No pains were spared either by the State or the faculty to maintain the peculiar character of the school; and the little battalion, although the members were hardly likely to see service, was as carefully trained as if each private in the ranks might one day become a general officer. It was fortunate indeed for Virginia, when she submitted her destinies to the arbitrament of war, that some amongst her statesmen had been firm to the conviction that to defend one's country is a task not a whit less honourable than to serve her in the ways of peace. She was unable to avert defeat. But she more than redeemed her honour; and the efficiency of her troops was in no small degree due to the training so many of her officers had received at the Military Institute.

Still, notwithstanding its practical use to the State, the offer of a chair at Lexington would probably have attracted but few of Jackson's contemporaries. But while campaigning was entirely to his taste, life in barracks was the reverse. In those unenlightened days to be known as an able and zealous soldier was no passport to preferment. So long as an officer escaped censure his promotion was sure; he might reach without further effort the highest prizes the service offered, and the chances of the dull and indolent were quite as good as those of the capable and energetic. The one had no need for, the other no incentive to, self-improvement, and it was very generally neglected. Unless war intervened—and nothing seemed more improbable than another campaign—even a Napoleon would have had to submit to the inevitable. Jackson caught eagerly at the opportunity of freeing himself from an unprofitable groove.

'He believed,' he said, 'that a man who had turned, with a good military reputation, to pursuits of a semi-civilian character, and had vigorously prosecuted his mental improvement, would have more chance of success

in war than those who had remained in the treadmill of
the garrison.'

It was with a view, then, of fitting himself for command
that Jackson broke away from the restraints of regimental
life ; not because those restraints were burdensome or distasteful in themselves, but because he felt that whilst making
the machine they might destroy the man. Those responsible for the efficiency of the United States army had not
yet learned that the mind must be trained as well as
the body, that drill is not the beginning and the end of
the soldier's education, that unless an officer is trusted
with responsibility in peace he is but too apt to lose all
power of initiative in war. That Jackson's ideas were
sound may be inferred from the fact that many of the
most distinguished generals in the Civil War were
men whose previous career had been analogous to his
own.[1]

His duties at Lexington were peculiar. As Professor
of Artillery he was responsible for little more than the
drill of the cadets and their instruction in the theory of
gunnery. The tactics of artillery, as the word is understood in Europe, he was not called upon to impart.
Optics, mechanics, and astronomy were his special subjects, and he seems strangely out of place in expounding
their dry formulas.

In the well-stocked library of the Institute he found
every opportunity of increasing his professional knowledge.
He was an untiring reader, and he read to learn. The
wars of Napoleon were his constant study. He was an
enthusiastic admirer of his genius ; the swiftness, the
daring, and the energy of his movements appealed to his
every instinct. Unfortunately, both for the Institute and
his popularity, it was not his business to lecture on military
history. We can well imagine him, as a teacher of the
art of war, describing to the impressionable youths around

---

[1] Amongst these may be mentioned Grant, Sherman, and McClellan.
Lee himself, as an engineer, had but small acquaintance with regimental life.
The men who saved India for England in the Great Mutiny were of the
same type.

him the dramatic incidents of some famous campaign, following step by step the skilful strategy that brought about such victories as Austerlitz and Jena. The advantage would then have been with his pupils; in the work assigned to him it was the teacher that benefited. He was by no means successful as an instructor of the higher mathematics. Although the theories of light and motion were doubtless a branch of learning which the cadets particularly detested, his methods of teaching made it even more repellent. A thorough master of his subject, he lacked altogether the power of aiding others to master it. No flashes of humour relieved the tedium of his long and closely-reasoned demonstrations. He never descended to the level of his pupils' understanding, nor did he appreciate their difficulties. Facts presented themselves to his intellect in few lights. As one of his chief characteristics as a commander was the clearness with which he perceived the end to be aimed at and the shortest way of reaching it, so, in his explanations to his stumbling class, he could only repeat the process by which he himself had solved the problem at issue. We may well believe that his self-reliant nature, trained to intense application, overlooked the fact that others, weaker and less gifted, could not surmount unaided the obstacles which only aroused his own masterful instincts. Nevertheless, his conscientious industry was not entirely thrown away. To the brighter intellects in his class he communicated accurate scholarship; and although the majority lagged far behind, the thoroughness of his mental drill was most useful, to himself perhaps even more than to the cadets.

The death of his first wife, daughter of the Rev. Dr. Junkin, President of Washington College, after they had been married but fourteen months; the solution of his religious difficulties, and his reception into the Presbyterian Church; a five months' tour in Europe, through Scotland, England, Germany, Switzerland, and Italy; his marriage to Miss Morrison, daughter of a North Carolina clergyman: such were the chief landmarks of his life at Lexington. Ten years,

1854.

1857.

with their burden of joy and sorrow, passed away, of intense interest to the individual, but to the world a story dull and commonplace. Jackson was by no means a man of mark in Rockbridge county. Although his early shyness had somewhat worn off, he was still as reserved as he had been at West Point. His confidence was rarely given outside his own home. Intimates he had few, either at the Institute or elsewhere. Still he was not in the least unsociable, and there were many houses where he was always welcome. The academic atmosphere of Lexington did not preclude a certain amount of gaiety. The presence of Washington College and the Military Institute drew together a large number of families during the summer, and fair visitors thronged the leafy avenues of the little town. During these pleasant months the officers and cadets, as became their cloth, were always well to the fore. Recreation was the order of the day, and a round of entertainments enlivened the 'Commencements.' Major Jackson attended these gatherings with unfailing regularity, but soon after his arrival he drew the line at dancing, and musical parties became the limit of his dissipation. He was anything but a convivial companion. He never smoked, he was a strict teetotaller, and he never touched a card. His diet, for reasons of health, was of a most sparing kind; nothing could tempt him to partake of food between his regular hours, and for many years he abstained from both tea and coffee. In those peaceful times, moreover, there was nothing either commanding or captivating about the Professor of Artillery. His little romance in Mexico had given him no taste for trivial pleasures; and his somewhat formal manner was not redeemed by any special charm of feature. The brow and jaw were undoubtedly powerful; but the eyes were gentle, and the voice so mild and soft as to belie altogether the set determination of the thin straight lips. Yet, at the same time, if Jackson was not formed for general society, he was none the less capable of making himself exceedingly agreeable in a restricted and congenial circle. Young and old, when once they had gained his confidence, came under the spell of his noble nature; and if his friends were few they were very firm.

Why Jackson should have preferred the Presbyterian denomination to all others we are nowhere told. But whatever his reasons may have been, he was a most zealous and hardworking member of his church. He was not content with perfunctory attendances at the services. He became a deacon, and a large portion of his leisure time was devoted to the work which thus devolved on him. His duties were to collect alms and to distribute to the destitute, and nothing was permitted to interfere with their exact performance. He was exceedingly charitable himself—one tenth of his income was laid aside for the church, and he gave freely to all causes of benevolence and public enterprise. At the church meetings, whether for business or prayer, he was a regular attendant, and between himself and his pastor existed the most confidential relations. Nor did he consider that this was all that was demanded of him. In Lexington, as in other Southern towns, there were many poor negroes, and the condition of these ignorant and helpless creatures, especially of the children, excited his compassion. Out of his own means he established a Sunday school, in which he and his wife were the principal teachers. His friends were asked to send their slaves, and the experiment was successful. The benches were always crowded, and the rows of black, bright-eyed faces were a source of as much pride to him as the martial appearance of the cadet battalion.

Jackson's religion entered into every action of his life. No duty, however trivial, was begun without asking a blessing, or ended without returning thanks. 'He had long cultivated,' he said, ' the habit of connecting the most trivial and customary acts of life with a silent prayer.' He took the Bible as his guide, and it is possible that his literal interpretation of its precepts caused many to regard him as a fanatic. His observance of the Sabbath was hardly in accordance with ordinary usage. He never read a letter on that day, nor posted one; he believed that the Government in carrying the mails were violating a divine

law, and he considered the suppression of such traffic one
of the most important duties of the legislature.   Such
opinions were uncommon, even amongst the Presbyterians,
and his rigid respect for truth served to strengthen the
impression that he was morbidly scrupulous.   If he un-
intentionally made a misstatement—even about some
trifling matter—as soon as he discovered his mistake he
would lose no time and spare no trouble in hastening to
correct it.   'Why, in the name of reason,' he was asked,
'do you walk a mile in the rain for a perfectly unimportant
thing?'   'Simply because I have discovered that it was a
misstatement, and I could not sleep comfortably unless I
put it right.'

He had occasion to censure a cadet who had given,
as Jackson believed, the wrong solution of a problem.
On thinking the matter over at home he found that the
pupil was right and the teacher wrong.   It was late at
night and in the depth of winter, but he immediately
started off to the Institute, some distance from his quarters,
and sent for the cadet.   The delinquent, answering with
much trepidation the untimely summons, found himself to
his astonishment the recipient of a frank apology.   Jackson's
scruples carried him even further.   Persons who interlarded
their conversation with the unmeaning phrase 'you know'
were often astonished by the blunt interruption that he did
not know; and when he was entreated at parties or receptions
to break through his dietary rules, and for courtesy's sake
to seem to accept some delicacy, he would always refuse
with the reply that he had 'no genius for seeming.'
But if he carried his conscientiousness to extremes, if
he laid down stringent rules for his own governance, he
neither set himself up for a model nor did he attempt to
force his convictions upon others.   He was always
tolerant; he knew his own faults, and his own temptations, and if he could say nothing good of a man he
would not speak of him at all.   But he was by no means
disposed to overlook conduct of which he disapproved, and
undue leniency was a weakness to which he never yielded.
If he once lost confidence or discovered deception on the

part of one he trusted, he withdrew himself as far as possible from any further dealings with him; and whether with the cadets, or with his brother-officers, if an offence had been committed of which he was called upon to take notice, he was absolutely inflexible. Punishment or report inevitably followed. No excuses, no personal feelings, no appeals to the suffering which might be brought upon the innocent, were permitted to interfere with the execution of his duty.

Such were the chief characteristics of the great Confederate as he appeared to the little world of Lexington. The tall figure, clad in the blue uniform of the United States army, always scrupulously neat, striding to and from the Institute, or standing in the centre of the parade-ground, while the cadet battalion wheeled and deployed at his command, was familiar to the whole community. But Jackson's heart was not worn on his sleeve. Shy and silent as he was, the knowledge that even his closest acquaintances had of him was hardly more than superficial. A man who was always chary of expressing his opinions, unless they were asked for, who declined argument, and used as few words as possible, attracted but little notice. A few recognised his clear good sense; the majority considered that if he said little it was because he had nothing worth saying. Because he went his own way and lived by his own rules he was considered eccentric; because he was sometimes absent-minded, and apt to become absorbed in his own thoughts, he was set down as unpractical; his literal accuracy of statement was construed as the mark of a narrow intellect, and his exceeding modesty served to keep him in the background.

At the Institute, despite his reputation for courage, he was no favourite even with the cadets. He was hardly in sympathy with them. His temper was always equable. Whatever he may have felt he never betrayed irritation, and in the lecture-room or elsewhere he was kindness itself; but his own life had been filled from boyhood with earnest purpose and high ambition. Hard work was more to his taste than amusement. Time, to his mind, was far too valuable to be wasted, and he made few allowances for the thoughtlessness and indolence of irresponsible youth. As a relief possibly to the educational treadmill, his class delighted in listening to the story of Contreras and Chapultepec ; but there was nothing about Jackson which corresponded with a boy's idea of a hero. His aggressive punctuality, his strict observance of military etiquette, his precise interpretation of orders, seemed to have as little in common with the fierce excitement of battle as the uninteresting occupations of the Presbyterian deacon, who kept a Sunday school for negroes, had with the reckless gaiety of the traditional *sabreur*.

'And yet,' says one who knew him, 'they imbibed the principles he taught. Slowly and certainly were they trained in the direction which the teacher wished. Jackson justly believed that the chief value of the Institute consisted in the habits of system and obedience which it impressed on the ductile characters of the cadets, and regarded any relaxation of the rules as tending to destroy its usefulness. His conscientiousness seemed absurd to the young gentlemen who had no idea of the importance of military orders or of the implicit obedience which a good soldier deems it his duty to pay to them. But which was right—the laughing young cadet or the grave major of artillery ? Let the thousands who in the bitter and arduous struggle of the Civil War were taught by stern experience the necessity of strict compliance with all orders, to the very letter, answer the question.' [1]

'As exact as the multiplication table, and as full of things military as an arsenal,' was the verdict passed on Jackson by one of his townsmen, and it appears to have been the opinion of the community at large.

Jackson, indeed, was as inarticulate as Cromwell. Like the great Protector he 'lived silent,' and like him he was often misunderstood. Stories which have been repeated by writer after writer attribute to him the most grotesque eccentricities of manner, and exhibit his lofty piety as the harsh intolerance of a fanatic. He has been

[1] Cooke, p. 28.

represented as the narrowest of Calvinists; and so general was the belief in his stern and merciless nature that a great poet did not scruple to link his name with a deed which, had it actually occurred, would have been one of almost unexampled cruelty. Such calumnies as Whittier's 'Barbara Fritchie' may possibly have found their source in the impression made upon some of Jackson's acquaintances at Lexington, who, out of all sympathy with his high ideal of life and duty, regarded him as morose and morbid; and when in after years the fierce and relentless pursuit of the Confederate general piled the dead high upon the battle-field, this conception of his character was readily accepted. As he rose to fame, men listened greedily to those who could speak of him from personal knowledge; the anecdotes which they related were quickly distorted; the slightest peculiarities of walk, speech, or gesture were greatly exaggerated; and even Virginians seemed to vie with one another in representing the humble and kind-hearted soldier as the most bigoted of Christians and the most pitiless of men.

But just as the majority of ridiculous stories which cluster round his name rest on the very flimsiest foundation, so the popular conception of his character during his life at Lexington was absolutely erroneous. It was only within the portals of his home that his real nature disclosed itself. The simple and pathetic pages in which his widow has recorded the story of their married life unfold an almost ideal picture of domestic happiness, unchequered by the faintest glimpse of austerity or gloom. That quiet home was the abode of much content; the sunshine of sweet temper flooded every nook and corner; and although the pervading atmosphere was essentially religious, mirth and laughter were familiar guests.

'Those who knew General Jackson only as they saw him in public would have found it hard to believe that there could be such a transformation as he exhibited in his domestic life. He luxuriated in the freedom and liberty of his home, and his buoyancy and joyousness often ran into a playfulness and abandon that would have been

F 2

incredible to those who saw him only when he put on his
official dignity.'[1]   It was seldom, indeed, except under his
own roof, or in the company of his intimates, that his
reserve was broken through; in society he was always on
his guard, fearful lest any chance word might be misconstrued or give offence.   It is no wonder, then, that Lexington misjudged him.   Nor were those who knew him only
when he was absorbed in the cares of command before the
enemy likely to see far below the surface.   The dominant
trait in Jackson's character was his intense earnestness,
and when work was doing, every faculty of his nature was
engrossed in the accomplishment of the task on hand.   But
precise, methodical, and matter-of-fact as he appeared, his
was no commonplace and prosaic nature.   He had 'the
delicacy and the tenderness which are the rarest and most
beautiful ornament of the strong.'[2]   Beneath his habitual
gravity a vivid imagination, restrained indeed by strong
sense and indulging in no vain visions, was ever at work;
and a lofty enthusiasm, which seldom betrayed itself in
words, inspired his whole being.   He was essentially
chivalrous.   His deference to woman, even in a land where
such deference was still the fashion, was remarkable, and
his sympathy with the oppressed was as deep as his loyalty
to Virginia.   He was an ardent lover of nature.   The
autumnal glories of the forest, the songs of the birds, the
splendours of the sunset, were sources of unfailing pleasure.
More than all, the strength of his imagination carried him
further than the confines of the material world, and he saw
with unclouded vision the radiant heights that lie beyond.

Jackson, then, was something more than a man of
virile temperament; he was gifted with other qualities than
energy, determination, and common sense.   He was not
witty.   He had no talent for repartee, and the most
industrious collector of anecdotes will find few good things
attributed to him.   But he possessed a kindly humour
which found vent in playful expressions of endearment, or
in practical jokes of the most innocent description; and
if these outbursts of high spirits were confined to the

[1] *Memoirs of Stonewall Jackson*, p. 108.   [2] Marion Crawford.

precincts of his own home, they proved at least that neither by temperament nor principle was he inclined to look upon the darker side. His eye for a ludicrous situation was very quick, and a joke which told against himself always caused him the most intense amusement. It is impossible to read the letters which Mrs. Jackson has published and to entertain the belief that his temper was ever in the least degree morose. To use her own words, 'they are the overflow of a heart full of tenderness;' it is true that they seldom omit some reference to that higher life which both husband and wife were striving hand in hand to lead, but they are instinct from first to last with the serene happiness of a contented mind.

Even more marked than his habitual cheerfulness was his almost feminine sympathy with the poor and feeble. His servants, as was the universal rule in Virginia, were his slaves; but his relations with his black dependents were of almost a paternal character, and his kindness was repaid by that childlike devotion peculiar to the negro race. More than one of these servants—so great was his reputation for kindness—had begged him to buy them from their former owners. Their interests were his special care; in sickness they received all the attention and comfort that the house afforded; to his favourite virtues, politeness and punctuality, they were trained by their master himself, and their moral education was a task he cheerfully undertook. 'There was one little servant in the family,' says Mrs. Jackson, 'whom my husband took under his sheltering roof at the solicitations of an aged lady; to whom the child became a care after having been left an orphan. She was not bright, but he persevered in drilling her into memorising a child's catechism, and it was a most amusing picture to see her standing before him with fixed attention, as if she were straining every nerve, and reciting her answers with the drop of a curtsey at each word. She had not been taught to do this, but it was such an effort for her to learn that she assumed the motion involuntarily.'

Jackson's home was childless. A little daughter, born at Lexington, lived only for a few weeks, and her place remained unfilled. His sorrow, although he submitted uncomplainingly, was very bitter, for his love for children was very great. 'A gentleman,' says Mrs. Jackson, 'who spent the night with us was accompanied by his daughter, but four years of age. It was the first time the child had been separated from her mother, and my husband suggested that she should be committed to my care during the night, but she clung to her father. After our guests had both sunk in slumber, the father was aroused by some one leaning over his little girl and drawing the covering more closely round her. It was only his thoughtful host, who felt anxious lest his little guest should miss her mother's guardian care under his roof, and could not go to sleep himself until he was satisfied that all was well with the child.'

These incidents are little more than trivial. The attributes they reveal seem of small import. They are not such as go towards building up a successful career either in war or politics. And yet to arrive at a true conception of Jackson's character it is necessary that such incidents should be recorded. That character will not appear the less admirable because its strength and energy were tempered by softer virtues; and when we remember the great soldier teaching a negro child, or ministering to the comfort of a sick slave, it becomes easy to understand the feelings with which his veterans regarded him. The quiet home at Lexington reveals more of the real man than the camps and conflicts of the Civil War, and no picture of Stonewall Jackson would be complete without some reference to his domestic life.

'His life at home,' says his wife, 'was perfectly regular and systematic. He arose about six o'clock, and first knelt in secret prayer; then he took a cold bath, which was never omitted even in the coldest days of winter. This was followed by a brisk walk, in rain or shine.

'Seven o'clock was the hour for family prayers, which he required all his servants to attend promptly and regularly. He never waited for anyone, not even his wife. Breakfast followed prayers, after which he left immediately for the Institute, his classes opening at eight o'clock and continuing to eleven. Upon his return home at eleven o'clock he devoted himself to study until one. The first book he took up daily was his Bible, which he read with a commentary, and the many pencil marks upon it showed with what care he bent over its pages. From his Bible lesson he turned to his text-books. During those hours of study he would permit no interruption, and stood all the time in front of a high desk. After dinner he gave himself up for half an hour or more to leisure and conversation, and this was one of the brightest periods in his home life. He then went into his garden, or out to his farm to superintend his servants, and frequently joined them in manual labour. He would often drive me to the farm, and find a shady spot for me under the trees, while he attended to the work of the field. When this was not the case, he always returned in time to take me, if the weather permitted, for an evening walk or drive. In summer we often took our drives by moonlight, and in the beautiful Valley of Virginia the queen of night seemed to shine with more brightness than elsewhere. When at home he would indulge himself in a season of rest and recreation after supper, thinking it was injurious to health to go to work immediately. As it was a rule with him never to use his eyes by artificial light, he formed the habit of studying mentally for an hour or so without a book. After going over his lessons in the morning, he thus reviewed them at night, and in order to abstract his thoughts from surrounding objects—a habit which he had cultivated to a remarkable degree—he would, if alone with his wife, ask that he might not be disturbed by any conversation; he would then take his seat with his face to the wall, and remain in perfect abstraction until he finished his mental task. He was very fond of being read to, and much of our time in the evening was passed in my ministering to him in this way. He had a library, which, though small, was select, composed chiefly of scientific, historical, and religious books, with some of a lighter character, and some in Spanish and French. Nearly all of them were full of his pencil marks, made with a view to future reference.' Next to the Bible, history, both ancient

and modern, was his favourite study.   Plutarch, Josephus,
Rollin, Robertson, Hallam, Macaulay, and Bancroft were
his constant companions.   Shakespeare held an honoured
place upon his shelves; and when a novel fell into his
hands he became so absorbed in the story that he eventually avoided such literature as a waste of time.   'I am
anxious,' he wrote to a relative, ' to devote myself to study
until I shall become master of my profession.'

The Jacksons were far from affluent.   The professor
had nothing but his salary, and his wife, one of a large
family, brought no increase to their income.   But the
traditional hospitality of Virginia was a virtue by no means
neglected.   He was generous but unostentatious in his
mode of living, and nothing gave him more pleasure than
to bid his friends welcome to his own home.

His outdoor recreations were healthful but not exciting.
The hills round Lexington teemed with game, the rivers
with fish, and shooting and fishing were the favourite
amusements of his colleagues.   But Jackson found no
pleasure in rod or gun; and although fond of riding and
a good horseman, he never appears to have joined in any
of those equestrian sports to which the Virginians were
much addicted.   He neither followed the hunt nor tilted at
the ring.   His exercise was taken after more utilitarian
fashion, in the garden or the farm.

It need hardly be said that such a lover of order and
method was strictly economical, and the wise administration
of the farm and household permitted an annual expenditure
on travel.   Many of the most beautiful localities and famous
cities of the east and north were visited in these excursions.
Sometimes he wandered with his wife in search of health;
more often the object of their journey was to see with their
own eyes the splendid scenery of their native land.   The
associations which were ever connected in Jackson's mind
with his tour through Europe show how intensely he
appreciated the marvels both of nature and of art.

'I would advise you,' he wrote to a friend, 'never to
name my European trip to me unless you are blest with a
superabundance of patience, as its very mention is calculated

to bring up with it an almost inexhaustible assemblage of grand and beautiful associations. Passing over the works of the Creator, which are far the most impressive, it is difficult to conceive of the influences which even the works of His creatures exercise over the mind of one who lingers amidst their master productions. Well do I remember the influence of sculpture upon me during my short stay in Florence, and how there I began to realise the sentiment of the Florentine : " Take from me my liberty, take what you will, but leave me my statuary, leave me these entrancing productions of art." And similar to this is the influence of painting.'

But delightful as were these holiday expeditions, the day of Jackson's return to Lexington and his duties never came too soon. In the quiet routine of his home life, in his work at the Institute, in the supervision of his farm and garden, in his evenings with his books, and in the services of his church, he was more than contented. Whatever remained of soldierly ambition had long been eradicated. Man of action as he essentially was, he evinced no longing for a wider sphere of intellectual activity or for a more active existence. Under his own roof-tree he found all that he desired. 'There,' says his wife, ' all that was best in his nature shone forth ; ' and that temper was surely of the sweetest which could utter no sterner rebuke than ' Ah ! that is not the way to be happy ! '

Nor was it merely his own gentleness of disposition and the many graces of his charming helpmate that secured so large a degree of peace and happiness. Jackson's religion played even a greater part. It was not of the kind which is more concerned with the terrors of hell than the glories of paradise. The world to him was no place of woe and lamentation, its beauties vanity, and its affections a snare. As he gazed with delight on the gorgeous tints of the autumnal forests, and the lovely landscapes of his mountain home, so he enjoyed to the utmost the life and love which had fallen to his lot, and thanked God for that capacity for happiness with which his nature was so largely gifted. Yet it cannot be said that he practised no self-denial. His life, in many respects, was one of constant self-discipline, and when his time came to sacrifice himself, he submitted without a murmur.   But in his creed fear had no place.   His faith was great.   It was not, however, a mere belief in God's omnipotence and God's justice, but a deep and abiding confidence in His infinite compassion and infinite love; and it created in him an almost startling consciousness of the nearness and reality of the invisible world.   In a letter to his wife it is revealed in all its strength:

'You must not be discouraged at the slowness of recovery.   Look up to Him who giveth liberally for faith to be resigned to His divine will, and trust Him for that measure of health which will most glorify Him, and advance to the greatest extent your own real happiness.   We are sometimes suffered to be in a state of perplexity that our faith may be tried and grow stronger.   See if you cannot spend a short time after dark in looking out of your window into space, and meditating upon heaven, with all its joys unspeakable and full of glory. . . . "All things work together for good" to God's children.   Try to look up and be cheerful, and not desponding.   Trust our kind Heavenly Father, and by the eye of faith see that all things are right and for your best interests.   The clouds come, pass over us, and are followed by bright sunshine; so in God's moral dealings with us, He permits to have trouble awhile. But let us, even in the most trying dispensations of His Providence, be cheered by the brightness which is a little ahead.'

It would serve no useful purpose to discuss Jackson's views on controversial questions.   It may be well, however, to correct a common error.   It has been asserted that he was a fatalist, and therefore careless of a future over which he believed he had no control.   Not a word, however, either in his letters or in his recorded conversations warrants the assumption.   It is true that his favourite maxim was 'Duty is ours, consequences are God's,' and that knowing 'all things work together for good,' he looked forward to the future without misgiving or apprehension.

But none the less he believed implicitly that the destiny of men and of nations is in their own hands.   His faith was as sane as it was humble, without a touch of that presumptuous fanaticism which stains the memory of Cromwell, to whom he has been so often compared. He never imagined, even at the height of his renown, when victory on victory crowned his banners, that he was 'the scourge of God,' the chosen instrument of His vengeance. He prayed without ceasing, under fire as in the camp; but he never mistook his own impulse for a revelation of the divine will. He prayed for help to do his duty, and he prayed for success. He knew that

> 'More things are wrought by prayer
> Than this world dreams of;'

but he knew, also, that prayer is not always answered in the way which man would have it. He went into battle with supreme confidence, not, as has been alleged, that the Lord had delivered the enemy into his hands, but that whatever happened would be the best that could happen. And he was as free from cant as from self-deception. It may be said of Jackson, as has been said so eloquently of the men whom, in some respects, he closely resembled, that 'his Bible was literally food to his understanding and a guide to his conduct. He saw the visible finger of God in every incident of life. . . . That which in our day devout men and women feel in their earnest moments of prayer, the devout Puritan felt, as a second nature, in his rising up and in his lying down; in the market-place and in the home; in society and in business; in Parliament, in Council, and on the field of battle. And feeling this, the Puritan had no shame in uttering the very words of the Bible wherein he had learned so to feel; nay, he would have burned with shame had he faltered in using the words. It is very hard for us now to grasp what this implies. . . . But there was a generation in which this phraseology was the natural speech of men.'[1] Of this generation, although later in time, was Stonewall Jackson. To him such language as he used in his letters to his wife, in conversation with his intimates, and not rarely in his official

---

[1] *Oliver Cromwell*, by Frederic Harrison, p. 29.

correspondence, was 'the literal assertion of truths which he felt to the roots of his being,' which absorbed his thoughts, which coloured every action of his life, and which, from the abundance of his heart, rose most naturally to his lips.

There is no need for further allusion to his domestic or religious life. If in general society Jackson was wanting in geniality ; if he was so little a man of the world that his example lost much of the influence which, had he stood less aloof from others, it must have exercised, it was the fruit of his early training, his natural reserve, and his extreme humility. It is impossible, however, that so pure a life should have been altogether without reflex upon others. If the cadets profited but indirectly, the slaves had cause to bless his practical Christianity ; the poor and the widow knew him as a friend, and his neighbours looked up to him as the soul of sincerity, the enemy of all that was false and vile. And for himself—what share had those years of quiet study, of self-communing, and of self-discipline, in shaping the triumphs of the Confederate arms ? The story of his military career is the reply.

Men of action have before now deplored the incessant press of business which leaves them no leisure to think out the problems which may confront them in the future. Experience is of little value without reflection, and leisure has its advantages. 'One can comprehend,' says Dabney, referring to Jackson's peculiar form of mental exercise, 'how valuable was the training which his mind received for his work as a soldier. Command over his attention was formed into a habit which no tempest of confusion could disturb. His power of abstraction became unrivalled. His imagination was trained and invigorated until it became capable of grouping the most extensive and complex considerations. The power of his mind was drilled like the strength of an athlete, and his self-concentration became unsurpassed.'

Such training was undoubtedly the very best foundation for the intellectual side of a general's business. War presents a constant succession of problems to be solved by

mental processes. For some experience and resource supply
a ready solution. Others, involving the movements of large
bodies, considerations of time and space, and the thousand
and one circumstances, such as food, weather, roads, topography, and *moral*, which a general must always bear in
mind, are composed of so many factors, that only a brain
accustomed to hard thinking can deal with them successfully.
Of this nature are the problems of strategy—those which
confront a general in command of an army or of a detached
portion of an army, and which are worked out on the map.
The problems of the battle-field are of a different order. The
natural characteristics which, when fortified by experience,
carry men through any dangerous enterprise, win the
majority of victories. But men may win battles and be very
poor generals. They may be born leaders of men, and yet absolutely unfitted for independent command. Their courage,
coolness, and common sense may accomplish the enemy's
overthrow on the field, but with strategical considerations
their intellects may be absolutely incapable of grappling. In
the great wars of the early part of the century Ney and
Blucher were probably the best fighting generals of France
and Prussia. But neither could be trusted to conduct a
campaign. Blucher, pre-eminent on the battle-field, knew
nothing of the grand combinations which prepare and complete success. If he was the strong right hand of the Prussian army, his chief of the staff was the brain. 'Gneisenau,'
said the old Marshal, 'makes the pills which I administer.'
'Ney's best qualities,' says Jomini, who served long on his
staff, ' his heroic valour, his quick *coup d'œil*, and his energy,
diminished in the same proportion that the extent of his
command increased his responsibility. Admirable on the
field of battle, he displayed less assurance, not only in
council, but whenever he was not actually face to face
with the enemy.' It is not of such material as Ney and
Blucher, mistrustful of their own ability, that great captains are made. Marked intellectual capacity is the chief
characteristic of the most famous soldiers. Alexander,
Hannibal, Cæsar, Marlborough, Washington, Frederick,
Napoleon, Wellington, and Nelson were each and all of

them something more than mere fighting men. Few of their age rivalled them in strength of intellect. It was this, combined with the best qualities of Ney and Blucher, that made them masters of strategy, and lifted them high above those who were tacticians and nothing more; and it was strength of intellect that Jackson cultivated at Lexington.

So, in that quiet home amidst the Virginian mountains, the years sped by, peaceful and uneventful, varied only by the holiday excursions of successive summers. By day, the lecture at the Institute, the drill of the cadet battery, the work of the church, the pleasant toil of the farm and garden. When night fell, and the curtains were drawn across the windows that looked upon the quiet street, there in that home where order reigned supreme, where, as the master wished, 'each door turned softly on a golden hinge,' came those hours of thought and analysis which were to fit him for great deeds.

The even tenor of this calm existence was broken, however, by an incident which intensified the bitter feeling which already divided the Northern and Southern sections of the United States. During the month of January, 1859, Jackson had marched with the cadet battalion to Harper's Ferry, where, on the northern frontier of Virginia, the fanatic, John Brown, had attempted to raise an insurrection amongst the negroes, and had been hung after trial in presence of the troops. By the South Brown was regarded as a madman and a murderer; by many in the North he was glorified as a martyr; and so acute was the tension that early in 1860, during a short absence from Lexington, Jackson wrote in a letter to his wife, 'What do you think about the state of the country? Viewing things at Washington from human appearances, I think we have great reason for alarm.' A great crisis was indeed at hand. But if to her who was ever beside him, while the storm clouds were rising dark and terrible over the fair skies of the prosperous Republic, the Christian soldier seemed the man best fitted to lead the people, it was not so outside. None doubted his sincerity or questioned his resolution, but few had penetrated his reserve. As the playful tenderness he displayed at home was never suspected, so the consuming earnestness, the absolute fearlessness, whether of danger or of responsibility, the utter disregard of man, and the unquestioning faith in the Almighty, which made up the individuality which men called Stonewall Jackson, remained hidden from all but one.

To his wife his inward graces idealised his outward seeming; but others, noting his peculiarities, and deceived by his modesty, saw little that was remarkable and much that was singular in the staid professor. Few detected, beneath that quiet demeanour and absent manner, the existence of energy incarnate and an iron will; and still fewer beheld, in the plain figure of the Presbyterian deacon, the potential leader of great armies, inspiring the devotion of his soldiers, and riding in the forefront of victorious battle.

CHAPTER IV

SECESSION. 1860-61

JACKSON spent ten years at Lexington, and he was just five-and-thirty when he left it. For ten years he had seen no

1861. more of military service than the drills of the cadet battalion. He had lost all touch with the army. His name had been forgotten, except by his comrades of the Mexican campaign, and he had hardly seen a regular soldier since he resigned his commission. But, even from a military point of view, those ten years had not been wasted. His mind had a wider grasp, and his brain was more active. Striving to fit himself for such duties as might devolve on him, should he be summoned to the field, like all great men and all practical men he had gone to the best masters. In the campaigns of Napoleon he had found instruction in the highest branch of his profession, and had made his own the methods of war which the greatest of modern soldiers both preached and practised. Strengthened, too, by constant exercise was his control over his physical wants, over his temper and his temptations. Maturer years and the search for wisdom had steadied his restless daring; and his devotion to duty, always remarkable, had become a second nature. His health, under careful and self-imposed treatment, had much improved, and the year 1861 found him in the prime of physical and mental vigour. Already it had become apparent that his life at Lexington was soon to end. The Damascus blade was not to rust upon the shelf. During the winter of 1860-61 the probability of a conflict between the free and slave-holding States, that is, between North and South, had become almost a certainty. South Carolina, Mississippi, Alabama, Florida, Georgia,

Louisiana, and Texas, had formally seceded from the Union; and establishing a Provisional Government, with Jefferson Davis as President, at Montgomery in Alabama, had proclaimed a new Republic, under the title of the Confederate States of America. In order to explain Jackson's attitude at this momentous crisis, it will be necessary to discuss the action of Virginia, and to investigate the motives which led her to take the side she did.

Forces which it was impossible to curb, and which but few detected, were at the root of the secession movement. The ostensible cause was the future status of the negro.

Slavery was recognised in fifteen States of the Union. In the North it had long been abolished, but this made no difference to its existence in the South. The States which composed the Union were semi-independent communities, with their own legislatures, their own magistracies, their own militia, and the power of the purse. How far their sovereign rights extended was a matter of contention; but, under the terms of the Constitution, slavery was a domestic institution, which each individual State was at liberty to retain or discard at will, and over which the Federal Government had no control whatever. Congress would have been no more justified in declaring that the slaves in Virginia were free men than in demanding that Russian conspirators should be tried by jury. Nor was the philanthropy of the Northern people, generally speaking, of an enthusiastic nature. The majority regarded slavery as a necessary evil; and, if they deplored the reproach to the Republic, they made little parade of their sentiments. A large number of Southerners believed it to be the happiest condition for the African race; but the best men, especially in the border States, of which Virginia was the principal, would have welcomed emancipation. But neither Northerner nor Southerner saw a practicable method of giving freedom to the negro. Such a measure, if carried out in its entirety, meant ruin to the South. Cotton and tobacco, the principal and most lucrative crops, required an immense number of hands, and in those hands—

his negro slaves—the capital of the planter was locked up. Emancipation would have swept the whole of this capital away. Compensation, the remedy applied by England to Jamaica and South Africa, was hardly to be thought of. Instead of twenty millions sterling, it would have cost four hundred millions. It was doubtful, too, if compensation would have staved off the ruin of the planters. The labour of the free negro, naturally indolent and improvident, was well known to be most inefficient as compared with that of the slave. For some years, to say the least, after emancipation it would have been impossible to work the plantations except at a heavy loss. Moreover, abolition, in the judgment of all who knew him, meant ruin to the negro. Under the system of the plantations, honesty and morality were being gradually instilled into the coloured race. But these virtues had as yet made little progress ; the Christianity of the slaves was but skin-deep ; and if all restraint were removed, if the old ties were broken, and the influence of the planter and his family should cease to operate, it was only too probable that the four millions of Africans would relapse into the barbaric vices of their original condition. The hideous massacres which had followed emancipation in San Domingo had not yet been forgotten. It is little wonder, then, that the majority shrank before a problem involving such tremendous consequences.

A party, however, conspicuous both in New England and the West, had taken abolition for its watchword. Small in numbers, but vehement in denunciation, its voice was heard throughout the Union. Zeal for universal liberty rose superior to the Constitution. That instrument was repudiated as an iniquitous document. The sovereign rights of the individual States were indignantly denied. Slavery was denounced as the sum of all villainies, the slave-holder as the worst of tyrants ; and no concealment was made of the intention, should political power be secured, of compelling the South to set the negroes free. In the autumn of 1860 came the Presidential election. Hitherto, of the two great political parties, the Democrats had long ruled the councils of the nation, and nearly the whole South was Democratic. The South, as regards population, was numerically inferior to the North ; but the Democratic party had more than held its own at the ballot-boxes, for the reason that it had many adherents in the North. So long as the Southern and Northern Democrats held together, they far outnumbered the Republicans. In 1860, however, the two sections of the Democratic party split asunder. The Republicans, favoured by the schism, carried their own candidate, and Abraham Lincoln became President. South Carolina at once seceded and the Confederacy was soon afterwards established.

It is not at first sight apparent why a change of government should have caused so sudden a disruption of the Union. The Republican party, however, embraced sections of various shades of thought. One of these, rising every day to greater prominence, was that which advocated immediate abolition ; and to this section, designated by the South as 'Black Republicans,' the new President was believed to belong. It is possible that, on his advent to office, the political leaders of the South, despite the safeguards of the Constitution, saw in the near future the unconditional emancipation of the slaves ; and not only this, but that the emancipated slaves would receive the right of suffrage, and be placed on a footing of complete equality with their former masters.[1] As in many districts the whites were far outnumbered by the negroes, this was tantamount to transferring all local government into the hands of the latter, and surrendering the planters to the mercies of their former bondsmen.

It is hardly necessary to say that an act of such gross injustice was never contemplated, except by hysterical abolitionists and those who truckled for their votes. It was certainly not contemplated by Mr. Lincoln ; and it was hardly likely that a President who had been elected by a minority of the people would dare, even if he were so inclined, to assume unconstitutional powers. The Democratic party, taking both sections together, was still the stronger ;

[1] Grant's *Memoirs*, vol. i., p. 214.

and the Northern Democrats, temporarily severed as they
were from their Southern brethren, would most assuredly
have united with them in resisting any unconstitutional
action on the part of the Republicans.

If, then, it might be asked, slavery ran no risk of unconditional abolition, why should the Southern political leaders
have acted with such extraordinary precipitation? Why,
in a country in which, to all appearances, the two sections
had been cordially united, should the advent to power of
one political party have been the signal for so much dis-
quietude on the part of the other? Had the presidential
seat been suddenly usurped by an abolitionist tyrant of the
type of Robespierre the South could hardly have exhibited
greater apprehension. Few Americans denied that a permanent Union, such as had been designed by the founders of
the Republic, was the best guarantee of prosperity and peace.
And yet because a certain number of misguided if well-
meaning men clamoured for emancipation, the South chose
to bring down in ruin the splendid fabric which their forefathers had constructed. In thus refusing to trust the good
sense and fair dealing of the Republicans, it would seem, at a
superficial glance, that the course adopted by the members
of the new Confederacy, whether legitimate or not, could
not possibly be justified.[1]

Unfortunately, something more than mere political
rancour was at work. The areas of slave and of free
labour were divided by an artificial frontier. 'Mason and

---

[1] I have been somewhat severely taken to task for attaching the epi-
thets 'misguided,' 'unpractical,' 'fanatical,' to the abolitionists. I see no
reason, however, to modify my language. It is too often the case that men
of the loftiest ideals seek to attain them by the most objectionable means,
and the maxim 'Fiat justitia ruat cœlum' cannot be literally applied to
great affairs. The conversion of the Mahomedan world to Christianity
would be a nobler work than even the emancipation of the negro, but the
missionary who began with reviling the faithful, and then proceeded to
threaten them with fire and the sword unless they changed their creed,
would justly be called a fanatic. Yet the abolitionists did worse than this,
for they incited the negroes to insurrection. Nor do I think that the question is affected by the fact that many of the abolitionists were upright,
earnest, and devout. A good man is not necessarily a wise man, and I
remember that Samuel Johnson and John Wesley supported King George
against the American colonists.

Dixon's line,' originally fixed as the boundary between
Pennsylvania on the north and Virginia and Maryland on
the south, cut the territory of the United States into two
distinct sections ; and, little by little, these two sections,
geographically as well as politically severed, had resolved
themselves into what might almost be termed two distinct
nations.

Many circumstances tended to increase the cleavage.
The South was purely agricultural; the most prosperous
part of the North was purely industrial. In the South,
the great planters formed a landed aristocracy ; the claims
of birth were ungrudgingly admitted; class barriers were, to
a certain extent, a recognised part of the social system, and
the sons of the old houses were accepted as the natural
leaders of the people. In the North, on the contrary, the only
aristocracy was that of wealth ; and even wealth, apart
from merit, had no hold on the respect of the community.
The distinctions of caste were slight in the extreme. The
descendants of the Puritans, of those English country gentlemen who had preferred to ride with Cromwell rather
than with Rupert, to pray with Baxter rather than with
Laud, made no parade of their ancestry; and among the
extreme Republicans existed an innate but decided aversion to the recognition of social grades. Moreover, diver-
gent interests demanded different fiscal treatment. The
cotton and tobacco of the South, monopolising the markets
of the world, asked for free trade. The manufacturers of
New England, struggling against foreign competition, were
strong protectionists, and they were powerful enough to
enforce their will in the shape of an oppressive tariff.
Thus the planters of Virginia paid high prices in order
that mills might flourish in Connecticut; and the
sovereign States of the South, to their own detriment,
were compelled to contribute to the abundance of the
wealthier North. The interests of labour were not less
conflicting. The competition between free and forced
labour, side by side on the same continent, was bound
in itself, sooner or later, to breed dissension ; and if it
had not yet reached an acute stage, it had at least

created a certain degree of bitter feeling. But more than all—and the fact must be borne in mind if the character of the Civil War is to be fully appreciated—the natural ties which should have linked together the States on either side of Mason and Dixon's line had weakened to a mere mechanical bond. The intercourse between North and South, social or commercial, was hardly more than that which exists between two foreign nations. The two sections knew but little of each other, and that little was not the good points but the bad.

For more than fifty years after the election of the first President, while as yet the crust of European tradition overlaid the young shoots of democracy, the supremacy, social and political, of the great landowners of the South had been practically undisputed. But when the young Republic began to take its place amongst the nations, men found that the wealth and talents which led it forward belonged as much to the busy cities of New England as to the plantations of Virginia and the Carolinas; and with the growing sentiment in favour of universal equality began the revolt against the dominion of a caste. Those who had carved out their own fortunes by sheer hard work and ability questioned the superiority of men whose positions were no guarantee of personal capacity, and whose wealth was not of their own making. Those who had borne the heat and burden of the day deemed themselves the equals and more than equals of those who had loitered in the shade; and, esteeming men for their own worth and not for that of some forgotten ancestor, they had come to despise those who toiled not neither did they spin. Tenaciously the Southerners clung to the supremacy they had inherited from a bygone age. The contempt of the Northerner was repaid in kind. In the political arena the struggle was fierce and keen. Mutual hatred, fanned by unscrupulous agitators, increased in bitterness; and, hindering reconciliation, rose the fatal barrier of slavery.

It is true that, prior to 1860, the abolitionists were not numerous in the North; and it is equally true that by many of the best men in the South the institution which had been bequeathed to them was thoroughly detested. Looking back over the years which have elapsed since the slaves were freed, the errors of the two factions are sufficiently manifest. If, on the one hand, the abolitionist, denouncing sternly, in season and out of season, the existence of slavery on the free soil of America, was unjust and worse to the slave-owner, who, to say the least, was in no way responsible for the inhuman and short-sighted policy of a former generation; on the other hand the high-principled Southerner, although in his heart deploring the condition of the negro, and sometimes imitating the example of Washington, whose dying bequest gave freedom to his slaves, made no attempt to find a remedy.[1]

The latter had the better excuse. He knew, were emancipation granted, that years must elapse before the negro could be trained to the responsibilities of freedom, and that those years would impoverish the South. It appears to have been forgotten by the abolitionists that all races upon earth have required a protracted probation to fit them for the rights of citizenship and the duties of free men. Here was a people, hardly emerged from the grossest barbarism, and possibly, from the very beginning,

[1] On the publication of the first edition my views on the action of the abolitionists were traversed by critics whose opinions demand consideration. They implied that in condemning the unwisdom and violence of the anti-slavery party, I had not taken into account the aggressive tendencies of the Southern politicians from 1850 onwards, that I had ignored the attempts to extend slavery to the Territories, and that I had overlooked the effect of the Fugitive Slave Law. A close study of abolitionist literature, however, had made it very clear to me that the advocates of emancipation, although actuated by the highest motives, never at any time approached the question in a conciliatory spirit; and that long before 1850 their fierce cries for vengeance had roused the very bitterest feelings in the South. In fact they had already made war inevitable. Draper, the Northern historian, admits that so early as 1844 ' the contest between the abolitionists on one side and the slave-holders on the other hand had become *a mortal duel.*' It may be argued, perhaps, that the abolitionists saw that the slave-power would never yield except to armed force, and that they therefore showed good judgment in provoking the South into secession and civil war. But forcing the hand of the Almighty is something more than a questionable doctrine.

of inferior natural endowment, on whom they proposed to confer the same rights without any probation whatsoever. A glance at the world around them should have induced reflection. The experience of other countries was not encouraging. Hayti, where the blacks had long been masters of the soil, was still a pandemonium ; and in Jamaica and South Africa the precipitate action of zealous but unpractical philanthropists had wrought incalculable mischief. Even Lincoln himself, redemption by purchase being impracticable, saw no other way out of the difficulty than the wholesale deportation of the negroes to West Africa.

In time, perhaps, under the influence of such men as Lincoln and Lee, the nation might have found a solution of the problem, and North and South have combined to rid their common country of the curse of human servitude. But between fanaticism on the one side and helplessness on the other there was no common ground. The fierce invectives of the reformers forbade all hope of temperate discussion, and their unreasoning denunciations only provoked resentment. And this resentment became the more bitter because in demanding emancipation, either by fair means or forcible, and in expressing their intention of making it a national question, the abolitionists were directly striking at a right which the people of the South held sacred.

It had never been questioned, hitherto, that the several States of the Union, so far at least as concerned their domestic institutions, were each and all of them, under the Constitution, absolutely self-governing. But the threats which the ' Black Republicans ' held out were tantamount to a proposal to set the Constitution aside. It was their charter of liberty, therefore, and not only their material prosperity, which the States that first seceded believed to be endangered by Lincoln's election. Ignorant of the temper of the great mass of the Northern people, as loyal in reality to the Constitution as themselves, they were only too ready to be convinced that the denunciations of the abolitionists were the first presage of the storm that was presently to overwhelm them, to reduce their States to provinces, to wrest from them the freedom they had inherited, and to make them hewers of wood and drawers of water to the detested plutocrats of New England.

But the gravamen of the indictment against the Southern people is not that they seceded, but that they seceded in order to preserve and to perpetuate slavery; or, to put it more forcibly, that the liberty to enslave others was the right which most they valued. This charge, put forward by the abolitionists in order to cloak their own revolt against the Constitution, is true as regards a certain section, but as regards the South as a nation it is quite untenable, for three-fourths of the population derived rather injury than benefit from the presence in their midst of four million serfs.[1] 'Had slavery continued, the system of labour,' says General Grant, 'would soon have impoverished the soil and left the country poor. The non-slave-holder must have left the country, and the small slave-holder have sold out to his more fortunate neighbour.'[2] The slaves neither bought nor sold. Their wants were supplied almost entirely by their own labour; and the local markets of the South would have drawn far larger profit from a few thousand white labourers than they did from the multitude of negroes. It is true that a party in the South, more numerous perhaps among the political leaders than among the people at large, was averse to emancipation under any form or shape. There were men who looked upon their bondsmen as mere beasts of burden, more valuable but hardly more human than the cattle in their fields, and who would not only have perpetuated but have extended slavery. There were others who conscientiously believed that the negro was unfit for freedom, that he was incapable of self-improvement, and that he was far happier and more contented as a slave. Among these were ministers of the Gospel, in no small number, who, appealing to the Old Testament, preached boldly that the institution was of divine origin, that the coloured race

---

[1] Of 8,300,000 whites in the fifteen slave-holding States, only 346,000 were slave-holders, and of these 69,000 owned only one negro.

[2] *Battles and Leaders*, vol. iii., p. 689.

had been created for servitude, and that to advocate emancipation was to impugn the wisdom of the Almighty.

But there were still others, including many of those who were not slave-owners, who, while they acquiesced in the existence of an institution for which they were not personally accountable, looked forward to its ultimate extinction by the voluntary action of the States concerned. It was impossible as yet to touch the question openly, for the invectives and injustice of the abolitionists had so wrought upon the Southern people, that such action would have been deemed a base surrender to the dictation of the enemy; but they trusted to time, to the spread of education, and to a feeling in favour of emancipation which was gradually pervading the whole country.[1]

The opinions of this party, with which, it may be said, the bulk of the Northern people was in close sympathy,[2] are perhaps best expressed in a letter written by Colonel Robert Lee, the head of one of the oldest families in Virginia, a large landed proprietor and slave-holder, and the same officer who had won such well-deserved renown in Mexico. ‘In this enlightened age,’ wrote the future general-in-chief of the Confederate army, ‘there are few, I believe, but will acknowledge that slavery as an institution is a moral and political evil. It is useless to expatiate on its disadvantages. I think it a greater evil to the white than to the coloured race, and while my feelings are strongly interested in the latter, my sympathies are more deeply engaged for the former. The blacks are immeasurably better off here than in Africa—morally, socially, and physically. The painful discipline they are undergoing is necessary for their instruction as a race, and, I hope, will prepare them for better things. How long their subjection may be necessary is known and ordered by a merciful Providence. Their emancipation will sooner result from the mild and

---

[1] There is no doubt that a feeling of aversion to slavery was fast spreading among a numerous and powerful class in the South. In Maryland, Kentucky, and Missouri the number of slaves was decreasing, and in Delaware the institution had almost disappeared.

[2] Grant's *Memoirs*, p. 214.

melting influence of Christianity than from the storms and contests of fiery controversy. This influence, though slow, is sure. The doctrines and miracles of our Saviour have required nearly two thousand years to convert but a small part of the human race, and even among Christian nations what gross errors still exist! While we see the course of the final abolition of slavery is still onward, and we give it the aid of our prayers and all justifiable means in our power, we must leave the progress as well as the result in His hands, who sees the end and who chooses to work by slow things, and with whom a thousand years are but as a single day. The abolitionist must know this, and must see that he has neither the right nor the power of operating except by moral means and suasion; if he means well to the slave, he must not create angry feelings in the master. Although he may not approve of the mode by which it pleases Providence to accomplish its purposes, the result will nevertheless be the same; and the reason he gives for interference in what he has no concern holds good for every kind of interference with our neighbours when we disapprove of their conduct.'

With this view of the question Jackson was in perfect agreement. 'I am very confident,' says his wife, 'that he would never have fought for the sole object of perpetuating slavery. . . . He found the institution a responsible and troublesome one, and I have heard him say that he would prefer to see the negroes free, but he believed that the Bible taught that slavery was sanctioned by the Creator Himself, who maketh all men to differ, and instituted laws for the bond and free. He therefore accepted slavery, as it existed in the South, not as a thing desirable in itself, but as allowed by Providence for ends which it was not his business to determine.'

It may perhaps be maintained that to have had no dealings with 'the accursed thing,' and to have publicly advocated some process of gradual emancipation, would have been the nobler course. But, setting aside the teaching of the Churches, and the bitter temper of the time, it should be remembered that slavery, although its hardships were admitted, presented itself in no repulsive aspect to the people of the Confederate States. They regarded it with feelings very different from those of the abolitionists, whose acquaintance with the condition they reprobated was small in the extreme. The lot of the slaves, the Southerners were well aware, was far preferable to that of the poor and the destitute of great cities, of the victims of the sweater and the inmates of the fever dens. The helpless negro had more hands to succour him in Virginia than the starving white man in New England. The children of the plantation enjoyed a far brighter exist- ence than the children of the slums. The worn and feeble were maintained by their masters, and the black labourer, looking forward to an old age of ease and comfort among his own people, was more fortunate than many a Northern artisan. Moreover, the brutalities ascribed to the slave- owners as a class were of rare occurrence. The people of the South were neither less humane nor less moral than the people of the North or of Europe, and it is absolutely inconceivable that men of high character and women of gentle nature should have looked with leniency on cruelty, or have failed to visit the offender with some- thing more than reprobation. Had the calumnies [1] which were scattered broadcast by the abolitionists possessed more than a vestige of truth, men like Lee and Jackson would never have remained silent. In the minds of the Northern people slavery was associated with atrocious cruelty and continual suffering. In the eyes of the Southerners, on the other hand, it was associated with great kindness and the most affectionate relations between the planters and their bondsmen. And if the Southerners were blind, it is most difficult to explain the remarkable fact that throughout the war, although thousands of plan- tations and farms, together with thousands of women and children, all of whose male relatives were in the Con- federate armies, were left entirely to the care of the negroes, both life and property were perfectly secure.

Such, then, was the attitude of the South towards

[1] *Uncle Tom's Cabin* to wit.

slavery. The institution had many advocates, uncompromising and aggressive, but taking the people as a whole it was rather tolerated than approved; and, even if no evidence to the contrary were forthcoming, we should find it hard to believe that a civilised community would have plunged into revolution in order to maintain it. There can be no question but that secession was revolution; and revolutions, as has been well said, are not made for the sake of 'greased cartridges.' To bring about such unanimity of purpose as took possession of the whole South, such passionate loyalty to the new Confederacy, such intense determination to resist coercion to the bitter end, needed some motive of unusual potency, and the perpetuation of slavery was not a sufficient motive. The great bulk of the population neither owned slaves nor was connected with those who did; many favoured emancipation; and the working men, a rapidly increasing class, were distinctly antagonistic to slave-labour. Moreover, the Southerners were not only warmly attached to the Union, which they had done so much to establish, but their pride in their common country, in its strength, its prestige, and its prosperity, was very great. Why, then, should they break away? History supplies us with a pertinent example.

Previous to 1765 the honour of England was dear to the people of the American colonies. King George had no more devoted subjects; his enemies no fiercer foes. And yet it required very little to reverse the scroll. The right claimed by the Crown to tax the colonists hardly menaced their material prosperity. A few shillings more or less would neither have added to the burdens nor have diminished the comforts of a well-to-do and thrifty people, and there was some justice in the demand that they should contribute to the defence of the British Empire. But the demand, as formulated by the Government, involved a principle which they were unwilling to admit, and in defence of their birthright as free citizens they flew to arms. So, in defence of the principle of States' Rights the Southern people resolved upon secession with all its consequences.

It might be said, however, that South Carolina and her

sister States seceded under the threat of a mere faction; that there was nothing in the attitude of the Federal Government to justify the apprehension that the Constitution would be set aside; and that their action, therefore, was neither more nor less than rank rebellion. But, whether their rights had been infringed or not, a large majority of the Southern people believed that secession, at any moment and for any cause, was perfectly legitimate. The several States of the Union, according to their political creed, were each and all of them sovereign and independent nations. The Constitution, they held, was nothing more than a treaty which they had entered into for their own convenience, and which, in the exercise of their sovereign powers, individually or collectively, they might abrogate when they pleased. This interpretation was not admitted in the North, either by Republicans or Democrats; yet there was nothing in the letter of the Constitution which denied it, and as regards the spirit of that covenant North and South held opposite opinions. But both were perfectly sincere, and in leaving the Union, therefore, and in creating for themselves a new government, the people of the seceding States considered that they were absolutely within their right.[1]

It must be admitted, at the same time, that the action of the States which first seceded was marked by a petulant haste; and it is only too probable that the people of these States suffered themselves to be too easily persuaded that the North meant mischief. It is impossible to determine how far the professional politician was responsible for the Civil War. But when we recall the fact that secession followed close on the overthrow of a faction which had long monopolised the spoils of office, and that this faction found compensation in the establishment of a new government, it is not easy to resist the suspicion that the secession movement was neither more nor less than a conspiracy, hatched by a clever and unscrupulous cabal.

It would be unwise, however, to brand the whole, or even the majority, of the Southern leaders as selfish and un-

---

[1] For an admirable statement of the Southern doctrine, see Ropes' *History of the Civil War*, vol. i., chap. i.

principled. Unless he has real grievances on which to work, or unless those who listen to him are supremely ignorant, the mere agitator is powerless ; and it is most assuredly incredible that seven millions of Anglo-Saxons, and Anglo-Saxons of the purest strain—English, Lowland Scottish, and North Irish—should have been beguiled by silver tongues of a few ambitious or hare-brained demagogues. The latter undoubtedly had a share in bringing matters to a crisis. But the South was ripe for revolution long before the presidential election. The forces which were at work needed no artificial impulse to propel them forward. It was instinctively recognised that the nation had outgrown the Constitution ; and it was to this, and not to the attacks upon slavery, that secession was really due. The North had come to regard the American people as one nation, and the will of the majority as paramount.[1] The South, on the other hand, holding, as it had always held, that each State was a nation in itself, denied *in toto* that the will of the majority, except in certain specified cases, had any power whatever ; and where political creeds were in such direct antagonism no compromise was possible. Moreover, as the action of the abolitionists very plainly showed, there was a growing tendency in the North to disregard altogether the rights of the minority. Secession, in fact, was a protest against mob rule. The weaker community, hopeless of maintaining its most cherished principles within the Union, was ready to seize the first pretext for leaving it ; and the strength of the popular sentiment may be measured by the willingness of every class, gentle and simple, rich and poor, to risk all and to suffer all, in order to free themselves from bonds which must soon have become unbearable. It is always difficult to analyse the motives of those by whom revolution is provoked ; but if a whole people acquiesce, it is a certain proof

---

[1] ' The Government had been Federal under the Articles of Confederation (1781), but the [Northern] people quickly recognised that that relation was changing under the Constitution (1789). They began to discern that the power they thought they had delegated was in fact surrendered, and that henceforth no single State could meet the general Government as sovereign and equal.' —Draper's *History of the American Civil War*, vol. i., p. 286.

of the existence of universal apprehension and deep-rooted discontent. The spirit of self-sacrifice which animated the Confederate South has been characteristic of every revolution which has been the expression of a nation's wrongs, but it has never yet accompanied mere factious insurrection.

When, in process of time, the history of Secession comes to be viewed with the same freedom from prejudice as the history of the seventeenth and eighteenth centuries, it will be clear that the fourth great Revolution of the English-speaking race differs in no essential characteristic from those which preceded it. It was not simply because the five members were illegally impeached in 1642, the seven bishops illegally tried in 1688, men shot at Lexington in 1775, or slavery threatened in 1861, that the people rose. These were the occasions, not the causes of revolt. In each case a great principle was at stake: in 1642 the liberty of the subject; in 1688 the integrity of the Protestant faith; in 1775 taxation only with consent of the taxed; in 1861 the sovereignty of the individual States.[1]

The accuracy of this statement, as already suggested, has been consistently denied. That the only principle involved in Secession was the establishment of slavery on a firmer basis, and that the cry of States' Rights was raised only by way of securing sympathy, is a very general opinion. But before it can be accepted, it is necessary to make several admissions; first, that the Southerners were absolutely callous to the evils produced by the institution they had determined to make permanent; second, that they had persuaded themselves, in face of the tendencies of civilisation, that it was possible to make it permanent; and third, that they conscientiously held their progress and

[1] It has been remarked that States' Rights, as a political principle, cannot be placed on the same plane as those with which it is here grouped. History, however, proves conclusively that, although it may be less vital to the common weal, the right of self-government is just as deeply cherished. A people that has once enjoyed independence can seldom be brought to admit that a Union with others deprives it of the prerogatives of sovereignty, and it would seem that the treatment of this instinct of nationality is one of the most delicate and important tasks of statesmanship.

prosperity to be dependent on its continued existence. Are we to believe that the standard of morals and intelligence was so low as these admissions would indicate ? Are we to believe that if they had been approached in a charitable spirit, that if the Republican party, disclaiming all right of interference, had offered to aid them in substituting, by some means which would have provided for the control of the negro and, at the same time, have prevented an entire collapse of the social fabric, a system more consonant with humanity, the Southerners would have still preferred to leave the Union, and by creating a great slave-power earn the execration of the Christian world ?

Unless the South be credited with an unusual measure of depravity and of short-sightedness, the reply can hardly be in the affirmative. And if it be otherwise, there remains but one explanation of the conduct of the seceding States viz. the dread that if they remained in the Union they would not be fairly treated.

It is futile to argue that the people were dragooned into secession by the slave-holders. What power had the slave-holders over the great mass of the population, over the professional classes, over the small farmer, the mechanic, the tradesman, the labourer ? Yet it is constantly asserted by Northern writers, although the statement is virtually an admission that only the few were prepared to fight for slavery, that the Federal sentiment was so strong among the Southerners that terrorism must have had a large share in turning them into Separatists. The answer, putting aside the very patent fact that the Southerner was not easily coerced, is very plain. Undoubtedly, throughout the South there was much affection for the Union ; but so in the first Revolution there was much loyalty to the Crown, and yet it has never been asserted that the people of Virginia or of New England were forced into sedition against their will. The truth is that there were many Southerners who, in the vain hope of compromise, would have postponed the rupture ; but when the right of secession was questioned, and the right of coercion was proclaimed, all differences of opinion were swept away, and the people, thenceforward, were of one heart and mind. The action of Virginia is a striking illustration.

The great border State, the most important of those south of Mason and Dixon's line, was not a member of the Confederacy when the Provisional Government was established at Montgomery. Nor did the secession movement secure any strong measure of approval. In fact, the people of Virginia, owing to their closer proximity to, and to their more intimate knowledge of, the North, were by no means inclined to make of the 'Black Republican' President the bugbear he appeared to the States which bordered on the Gulf of Mexico. Whilst acknowledging that the South had grievances, they saw no reason to believe that redress might not be obtained by constitutional means. At the same time, although they questioned the expediency, they held no half-hearted opinion as to the right, of secession, and in their particular case the right seems undeniable. When the Constitution of the United States was ratified, Virginia, by the mouth of its Legislature, had solemnly declared 'that the powers granted [to the Federal Government] under the Constitution, being truly derived from the people of the United States, may be resumed by them whenever the same shall be perverted to their injury and oppression.' And this declaration had been more than once reaffirmed. As already stated, this view of the political status of the Virginia citizen was not endorsed by the North. Nevertheless, it was not definitely rejected. The majority of the Northern people held the Federal Government paramount, but, at the same time, they held that it had no power either to punish or coerce the individual States. This had been the attitude of the founders of the Republic, and it is perfectly clear that their interpretation of the Constitution was this : although the several States were morally bound to maintain the compact into which they had voluntarily entered, the obligation, if any one State chose to repudiate it, could not be legally enforced. Their ideal was a Union based upon fraternal affection ; and in the halcyon days of Washington's first presidency, when the long and victorious struggle against a common enemy was still fresh in men's minds, and the sun of liberty shone in an unclouded sky, a vision so Utopian perhaps seemed capable of realisation. At all events, the promise of a new era of unbroken peace and prosperity was not to be sullied by cold precautions against civil dissensions and conflicting interests. The new order, under which every man was his own sovereign, would surely strengthen the links of kindly sympathy, and by those links alone it was believed that the Union would be held together. Such was the dream of the unselfish patriots who ruled the destinies of the infant Republic. Such were the ideas that so far influenced their deliberations that, with all their wisdom, they left a legacy to their posterity which deluged the land in blood.

Mr. Lincoln's predecessor in the presidential chair had publicly proclaimed that coercion was both illegal and inexpedient; and for the three months which intervened between the secession of South Carolina and the inauguration of the Republican President, the Government made not the slightest attempt to interfere with the peaceable establishment of the new Confederacy. Not a single soldier reinforced the garrisons of the military posts in the South. Not a single regiment was recalled from the western frontiers; and the seceded States, without a word of protest, were permitted to take possession, with few exceptions, of the forts, arsenals, navy yards and custom houses which stood on their own territory. It seemed that the Federal Government was only waiting until an amicable arrangement might be arrived at as to the terms of separation.

If, in addition to the words in which she had assented to the Constitution, further justification were needed for the belief of Virginia in the right of secession, it was assuredly to be found in the apparent want of unanimity on so grave a question even in the Republican party, and in the acquiescent attitude of the Federal Government.

The people of Virginia, however, saw in the election of a Republican President no immediate danger of the Constitution being 'perverted to their injury and oppression.' The North, generally speaking, regarded the action of the secessionists with that strange and good-humoured

tolerance with which the American citizen too often regards
internal politics.   The common-sense of the nation asserted
itself in all its strength.   A Union which could only be
maintained by force was a strange and obnoxious idea to the
majority.   Amid the storm of abuse and insult in which
the two extreme parties indulged, the abolitionists on the
one side, the politicians on the other, Lincoln,

'The still strong man in a blatant land,'

stood calm and steadfast, promising justice to the South,
and eager for reconciliation.   And Lincoln represented the
real temper of the Northern people.

So, in the earlier months of 1861, there was no sign
whatever that the Old Dominion might be compelled to
use the alternative her original representatives had reserved.
The question of slavery was no longer to the fore.   While
reprobating the action of the Confederates, the President,
in his inaugural address (March 4, 1861), had declared that
the Government had no right to interfere with the domestic
institutions of the individual States ; and throughout
Virginia the feeling was strong in favour of the Union.
Earnest endeavours were made to effect a compromise,
under which the seceded communities might renew the
Federal compact.   The Legislature called a Convention of
the People to deliberate on the part that the State should
play, and the other States were invited to join in a Peace
Conference at Washington.

It need hardly be said that during the period of negotia-
tion excitement rose to the highest pitch.   The political
situation was the sole theme of discussion.   In Lexington
as elsewhere the one absorbing topic ousted all others, and
in Lexington as elsewhere there was much difference of
opinion.   But the general sentiment was strongly Unionist,
and in the election of members of the Convention an
overwhelming majority had pronounced against secession.
Between the two parties, however, there were sharp conflicts.
A flagstaff flying the national ensign had been erected
in Main Street, Lexington.   The cadets fired on the flag,

and substituting the State colours placed a guard over them. Next morning a report reached the Institute that the local company of volunteers had driven off the guard, and were about to restore the Stars and Stripes. It was a holiday, and there were no officers present. The drums beat to arms. The boys rushed down to their parade-ground, buckling on their belts, and carrying their rifles. Ammunition was distributed, and the whole battalion, under the cadet officers, marched out of the Institute gates, determined to lower the emblem of Northern tyranny and drive away the volunteers. A collision would certainly have ensued had not the attacking column been met by the Commandant.

In every discussion on the action of the State Jackson had spoken strongly on the side of the majority. In terse phrase he had summed up his view of the situation. He was no advocate of secession. He deprecated the hasty action of South Carolina. 'It is better,' he said, 'for the South to fight for her rights in the Union than out of it.' But much as they loved the Union, the people of Virginia revered still more the principles inculcated by their fore-fathers, the right of secession and the illegality of coercion. And when the proposals of the Peace Conference came to nothing, when all hope of compromise died away, and the Federal Government showed no sign of recognising the Provisional Government, it became evident even to the staunchest Unionist that civil war could no longer be postponed. From the very first no shadow of a doubt had existed in Jackson's mind as to the side he should espouse, or the course he should pursue. 'If I know myself,' he wrote, 'all I am and all I have is at the service of my country.'

According to his political creed his country was his native State, and such was the creed of the whole South. In conforming to the Ordinance of Secession enacted by the legislatures of their own States, the people, according to their reading of the Constitution, acted as loyal and patriotic citizens; to resist that ordinance was treason and rebellion; and in taking up arms 'they were not, in their own opinion, rebels at all; they were defending their States—that is, the nations to which they conceived themselves to belong, from invasion and conquest.'[1]

When, after the incident described above, the cadets marched back to barracks, it was already so certain that the Stars and Stripes would soon be torn down from every flagstaff in Virginia that their breach of discipline was easily condoned. They were addressed by the Commandant, and amid growing excitement officer after officer, hardly concealing his sympathy with their action, gave vent to his opinions on the approaching crisis. Jackson was silent. At length, perhaps in anticipation of some amusement, for he was known to be a stumbling speaker, the cadets called on him by name. In answer to the summons he stood before them, not, as was his wont in public assemblies, with ill-dissembled shyness and awkward gesture, but with body erect and eyes sparkling. 'Soldiers,' he said, 'when they make speeches should say but few words, and speak them to the point, and I admire, young gentlemen, the spirit you have shown in rushing to the defence of your comrades; but I must commend you particularly for the readiness with which you listened to the counsel and obeyed the commands of your superior officer. The time may come,' he continued, and the deep tones, vibrating with unsuspected resolution, held his audience spellbound, 'when your State will need your services; and if that time does come, then draw your swords and throw away the scabbards.'

The crisis was not long postponed. Fort Sumter, in Charleston Harbour, the port of South Carolina, was held by a Federal garrison. The State had demanded its surrender, but no reply had been vouchsafed by Lincoln. On April 8 a message was conveyed to the Governor of the State that an attempt would be made to supply the troops with provisions. This message was telegraphed to Montgomery, still the capital of the Confederacy, and the Government ordered the reduction of the fort. On the morning of April 12 the Southern batteries opened fire, and the next day, when the flames were already scorching the doors

---

[1] *History of the Civil War*, Ropes, chap. i., p. 3.

of the magazine, the standard of the Union was hauled down.

Two days later Lincoln spoke with no uncertain voice. 75,000 militia were called out to suppress the 'rebellion.' The North gave the President loyal support. The insult to the flag set the blood of the nation, of Democrat and Republican, aflame. The time for reconciliation was passed. The Confederates had committed an unpardonable crime. They had forfeited all title to consideration ; and even in the minds of those Northerners who had shared their political creed the memory of their grievances was obliterated.

So far Virginia had given no overt sign of sympathy with the revolution. But she was now called upon to furnish her quota of regiments for the Federal army. To have acceded to the demand would have been to abjure the most cherished principles of her political existence. As the Federal Government, according to her political faith, had no jurisdiction whatever within the boundaries of States which had chosen to secede, it had not the slightest right to maintain a garrison in Fort Sumter. The action of the Confederacy in enforcing the withdrawal of the troops was not generally approved of, but it was held to be perfectly legitimate ; and Mr. Lincoln's appeal to arms, for the purpose of suppressing what, in the opinion of Virginia, was a strictly constitutional movement, was instantly and fiercely challenged.

Neutrality was impossible. She was bound to furnish her tale of troops, and thus belie her principles ; or to secede at once, and reject with a clean conscience the President's mandate. On April 17 she chose the latter, deliberately and with her eyes open, knowing that war would be the result, and knowing the vast resources of the North. She was followed by Arkansas, Tennessee, and North Carolina.[1]

The world has long since done justice to the motives of Cromwell and of Washington, and signs are not wanting

[1] Kentucky and Missouri attempted to remain neutral. Maryland was held in check by the Federal Government, and Delaware sided with the North. The first three, however, supplied large contingents to the Confederate armies.

that before many years have passed it will do justice to the
motives of the Southern people. They were true to their
interpretation of the Constitution ; and if the morality of
secession may be questioned, if South Carolina acted with
undue haste and without sufficient provocation, if certain
of the Southern politicians desired emancipation for themselves that they might continue to enslave others, it can
hardly be denied that the action of Virginia was not only
fully justified, but beyond suspicion. The wildest threats
of the ' Black Republicans,' their loudly expressed determination, in defiance of the Constitution, to abolish slavery,
if necessary by the bullet and the sabre, shook in no
degree whatever her loyalty to the Union. Her best
endeavours were exerted to maintain the peace between
the hostile sections ; and not till her liberties were
menaced did she repudiate a compact which had become
intolerable. It was to preserve the freedom which her
forefathers had bequeathed her, and which she desired
to hand down unsullied to future generations, that she
acquiesced in the revolution.

The North, in resolving to maintain the Union by force
of arms, was upheld by the belief that she was acting in
accordance with the Constitution. The South, in asserting
her independence and resisting coercion, found moral
support in the same conviction, and the patriotism of
those who fought for the Union was neither purer nor more
ardent than the patriotism of those who fought for States'
Rights. Long ago, a parliament of that nation to which
Jackson and so many of his compatriots owed their origin
made petition to the Pope that he should require the
English king ' to respect the independence of Scotland, and
to mind his own affairs. So long as a hundred of us are
left alive,' said the signatories, ' we will never in any degree
be subjected to the English. It is not for glory, or for
riches, or for honour that we fight, but for liberty alone,
which no good man loses but with his life.' More than five
hundred years later, for the same noble cause and in the
same uncompromising spirit, the people of Virginia made
appeal to the God of battles.

CHAPTER V

HARPER'S FERRY

IMMEDIATELY it became apparent that the North was bent
upon re-conquest Jackson offered his sword to his native
State. He was determined to take his share in
defending her rights and liberties, even if it were
only as a private soldier. Devotion to Virginia was his sole
motive. He shrank from the horrors of civil strife. The
thought that the land he loved so well was to be deluged
with the blood of her own children, that the happy hearths
of America were to be desecrated by the hideous image of
war, stifled the promptings of professional ambition. 'If
the general Government,' he said, 'should persist in the
measures now threatened, there must be war. It is painful
enough to discover with what unconcern they speak of war,
and threaten it. They do not know its horrors. I have
seen enough of it to make me look upon it as the sum of
all evils.'

The methods he resorted to in order that the conflict
might be averted were characteristic. He proposed to the
minister of his church that all Christian people should be
called upon to unite in prayer; and in his own devotions,
says his wife, he asked with importunity that, if it were
God's will, the whole land might be at peace.

His work, after the Ordinance of Secession had been
passed, was constant and absorbing. The Governor of
Virginia had informed the Superintendent of the Institute
that he should need the services of the more advanced
classes as drill-masters, and that they must be prepared to
leave for Richmond, under the command of Major Jackson,
at a moment's notice.

1861.

The Lexington Presbytery was holding its spring meeting in the church which Jackson attended, and some of the
members were entertained at his house; but he found no
time to attend a single service—every hour was devoted to
the duty he had in hand.

On the Saturday of that eventful week he expressed
the hope that he would not be called upon to leave till
Monday; and, bidding his wife dismiss from her thoughts
everything pertaining to the war and his departure, they
spent that evening as they had been accustomed, reading
aloud from religious magazines, and studying together the
lesson which was to be taught on the morrow in the
Sunday-school.

But at dawn the next morning came a telegram, directing
Major Jackson to bring the cadets to Richmond immediately. He repaired at once to the Institute; and at one
o'clock, after divine service, at his request, had been held
at the head of the command, the cadet battalion marched
to Staunton, on the Virginia Central Railway, and there
took train.

Camp Lee, the rendezvous of the Virginia army, presented a peculiar if animated scene. With few exceptions,
every man capable of serving in the field belonged either to
the militia or the volunteers. Some of the companies had
a smattering of drill, but the majority were absolutely un-
taught, and the whole were without the slightest conception
of what was meant by discipline. And it was difficult to
teach them. The non-commissioned officers and men of
the United States army were either Irish or Germans, without State ties, and they had consequently no inducement
to join the South. With the officers it was different. They
were citizens first, and soldiers afterwards; and as citizens,
their allegiance, so far as those of Southern birth were concerned, was due to their native States. Out of the twelve
hundred graduates of West Point who, at the beginning
of 1861, were still fit for service, a fourth were Southerners,
and these, almost without exception, at once took service
with the Confederacy. But the regular officers were almost
all required for the higher commands, for technical duties,

and the staff; thus very few were left to instruct the volunteers. The intelligence of the men was high, for every profession and every class was represented in the ranks, and many of the wealthiest planters preferred, so earnest was their patriotism, to serve as privates; but as yet they were merely the elements of a fine army, and nothing more. Their equipment left as much to be desired as their training. Arms were far scarcer than men. The limited supply of rifles in the State arsenals was soon exhausted. Flintlock muskets, converted to percussion action, were then supplied; but no inconsiderable numbers of fowling-pieces and shot-guns were to be seen amongst the infantry, while the cavalry, in default of sabres, carried rude lances fabricated by country blacksmiths. Some of the troops wore uniform, the blue of the militia or the grey of the cadet; but many of the companies drilled and manœuvred in plain clothes; and it was not till three months later, on the eve of the first great battle, that the whole of the infantry had received their bayonets and cartridge boxes.

An assemblage so motley could hardly be called an army; and the daring of the Government, who, with this *levée en masse* as their only bulwark against invasion, had defied a great power, seems at first sight strongly allied to folly. But there was little cause for apprehension. The Federal authorities were as yet powerless to enforce the policy of invasion on which the President had resolved. The great bulk of the Northern troops were just as far from being soldiers as the Virginians, and the regular army was too small to be feared.

The people of the United States had long cherished the Utopian dream that war was impossible upon their favoured soil. The militia was considered an archæological absurdity. The regular troops, admirable as was their work upon the frontier, were far from being a source of national pride. The uniform was held to be a badge of servitude. The drunken loafer, bartering his vote for a dollar or a dram, looked down with the contempt of a sovereign citizen upon men who submitted to the indignity of discipline; and, in denouncing the expense of a standing army, unscrupulous politicians found a sure path to popular favour. So, when secession became something more than a mere threat, the armed forces of the commonwealth had been reduced almost to extinction; and when the flag was fired upon, the nation found itself powerless to resent the insult. The military establishment mustered no more than 16,000 officers and men. There was no reserve, no transport, no organisation for war, and the troops were scattered in distant garrisons. The navy consisted of six screw-frigates, only one of which was in commission, of five steam sloops, some twenty sailing ships, and a few gun-boats. The majority of the vessels, although well armed, were out of date. 9,000 officers and men were the extent of the *personnel*, and several useful craft, together with more than 1,200 guns, were laid up in Norfolk dockyard, on the coast of Virginia, within a hundred miles of Richmond.[1]

The cause of the Confederacy, although her white population of seven million souls was smaller by two-thirds than that of the North, was thus far from hopeless. The North undoubtedly possessed immense resources. But an efficient army, even when the supply of men and arms be unlimited, cannot be created in a few weeks, or even in a few months, least of all an army of invasion. Undisciplined troops, if the enemy be ill-handled, may possibly stand their ground on the defensive, as did Jackson's riflemen at New Orleans, or the colonials at Bunker's Hill. But fighting behind earthworks is a very different matter to making long marches, and executing complicated manœuvres under heavy fire. Without a trained staff and an efficient administration, an army is incapable of movement. Even with a well-organised commissariat it is a most difficult business to keep a marching column supplied with food and forage; and the problem of transport, unless a railway or

[1] Strength of the Federal Navy at different periods:—

March 4, 1861	.	.	.	.	42 ships in commission.
December 1, 1861	.	.	.	.	264 ,, ,,
December 1, 1862	.	.	.	.	427 ,, ,,
December 1, 1863	.	.	.	.	588 ,, ,,
December 1, 1864	.	.	.	.	671 ,, ,,

a river be available, taxes the ability of the most experienced leader. A march of eighty or one hundred miles into an enemy's country sounds a simple feat, but unless every detail has been most carefully thought out, it will not improbably be more disastrous than a lost battle. A march of two or three hundred miles is a great military operation; a march of six hundred an enterprise of which there are few examples. To handle an army in battle is much less difficult than to bring it on to the field in good condition; and the student of the Civil War may note with profit how exceedingly chary were the generals, during the first campaigns, of leaving their magazines. It was not till their auxiliary services had gained experience that they dared to manœuvre freely; and the reason lay not only in deficiencies of organisation, but in the nature of the country. Even for a stationary force, standing on the defensive, unless immediately backed by a large town or a railway, the difficulties of bringing up supplies were enormous. For an invading army, increasing day by day the distance from its base, they became almost insuperable. In 1861, the population of the United States, spread over a territory as large as Europe, was less than that of England, and a great part of that territory was practically unexplored. Even at the present day their seventy millions are but a handful in comparison with the size of their dominions, and their extraordinary material progress is not much more than a scratch on the surface of the continent. In Europe Nature has long since receded before the works of man. In America the struggle between them has but just begun; and except upon the Atlantic seaboard man is almost lost to sight in the vast spaces he has yet to conquer. In many of the oldest States of the Union the cities seem set in clearings of the primeval forest. The wild woodland encroaches on the suburbs, and within easy reach of the very capital are districts where the Indian hunter might still roam undisturbed. The traveller lands in a metropolis as large as Paris; before a few hours have passed he may find himself in a wilderness as solitary as the Transvaal; and although within the boundaries of the townships he sees little that differs from the England of the nineteenth century—beyond them there is much that resembles the England of the Restoration. Except over a comparatively small area an army operating in the United States would meet with the same obstacles as did the soldiers of Cromwell and Turenne. Roads are few and indifferent; towns few and far between; food and forage are not easily obtainable, for the country is but partially cultivated; great rivers, bridged at rare intervals, issue from the barren solitudes of rugged plateaus; in many low-lying regions a single storm is sufficient to convert the undrained alluvial into a fetid swamp, and tracts as large as an English county are covered with pathless forest. Steam and the telegraph, penetrating even the most lonely jungles, afford, it is true, such facilities for moving and feeding large bodies of men that the difficulties presented by untamed Nature have undoubtedly been much reduced. Nevertheless the whole country, even to-day, would be essentially different from any European theatre of war, save the steppes of Russia; and in 1861 railways were few, and the population comparatively insignificant.

The impediments, then, in the way of military operations were such as no soldier of experience would willingly encounter with an improvised army. It was no petty republic that the North had undertaken to coerce. The frontiers of the Confederacy were far apart. The coast washed by the Gulf of Mexico is eight hundred miles south of Harper's Ferry on the Potomac; the Rio Grande, the river boundary of Texas, is seventeen hundred miles west of Charleston on the Atlantic. And over this vast expanse ran but six continuous lines of railway:—

From the Potomac.

1. [Washington,] Richmond, Lynchburg, Chattanooga, Memphis, New Orleans.
2. [Washington,] Richmond, Weldon, Greensboro, Columbia, Atlanta, New Orleans.
   (These connected Richmond with the Mississippi.)

From the Ohio.

3. Cairo, Memphis, New Orleans.
4. Cairo, Corinth, Mobile.

5. Louisville, Nashville, Dalton, Atlanta, Mobile.
    (These connected the Ohio with the Gulf of Mexico.)
6. Richmond, Wilmington, Charleston, Savannah.
    (This connected Richmond with the ports on the Atlantic.)

Although in the Potomac and the Ohio the Federals possessed two excellent bases of invasion, on which it was easy to accumulate both men and supplies, the task before them, even had the regular army been large and well equipped, would have been sufficiently formidable. The city of Atlanta, which may be considered as the heart of the Confederacy, was sixty days' march from the Potomac, the same distance as Vienna from the English Channel, or Moscow from the Niemen. New Orleans, the commercial metropolis, was thirty-six days' march from the Ohio, the same distance as Berlin from the Moselle. Thus space was all in favour of the South ; even should the enemy overrun her borders, her principal cities, few in number, were far removed from the hostile bases, and the important railway junctions were perfectly secure from sudden attack. And space, especially when means of communication are scanty, and the country affords few supplies, is the greatest of all obstacles. The hostile territory must be subjugated piecemeal, state by state, province by province, as was Asia by Alexander ; and after each victory a new base of supply must be provisioned and secured, no matter at what cost of time, before a further advance can be attempted. Had Napoleon in the campaign against Russia remained for the winter at Smolensko, and firmly established himself in Poland, Moscow might have been captured and held during the ensuing summer. But the occupation of Moscow would not have ended the war. Russia in many respects was not unlike the Confederacy. She had given no hostages to fortune in the shape of rich commercial towns ; she possessed no historic fortresses ; and so offered but few objectives to an invader. If defeated or retreating, her armies could always find refuge in distant fastnesses. The climate was severe ; the internal trade inconsiderable ; to bring the burden of war home to the

mass of the population was difficult, and to hold the
country by force impracticable.   Such were the difficulties
which the genius of Napoleon was powerless to overcome,
and Napoleon invaded Russia with half a million of seasoned
soldiers.

And yet with an army of 75,000 volunteers, and
without the least preparation, the Federal Government
was about to attempt an enterprise of even greater magnitude.   The Northern States were not bent merely on
invasion, but on re-conquest ; not merely on defeating the
hostile armies, on occupying their capital, and exacting
contributions, but on forcing a proud people to surrender
their most cherished principles, to give up their own
government, and to submit themselves, for good and all, to
what was practically a foreign yoke.   And this was not all.
It has been well said by a soldier of Napoleon, writing of
the war in Spain, that neither the government nor the
army are the real bulwarks against foreign aggression, but
the national character.   The downfall of Austria and of
Prussia was practically decided by the first great battle.
The nations yielded without further struggle.   Strangers
to freedom, crushed by military absolutism, the prostration
of each and all to an irresponsible despot had paralysed
individual energy.   Spain, on the other hand, without an
army and without a ruler, but deriving new strength from
each successive defeat, first taught Napoleon that he was not
invincible.   And the same spirit of liberty which inspired
the people of the Peninsula inspired, to an even higher
degree, the people of the Confederate States.

The Northern States, moreover, were about to make a
new departure in war.   The manhood of a country has often
been called upon to defend its borders ; but never before
had it been proposed to invade a vast territory with a
civilian army, composed, it is true, of the best blood in the
Republic, but without the least tincture of military experience. Nor did the senior officers, professionals though they
were, appear more fitted for the enterprise than the men
they led.   The command of a company or squadron against
the redskins was hardly an adequate probation for the

THE UNITED STATES
1861.

English Miles

0 50 100 150 200 250 300

Walker & Boutall sc.

command of an army,[1] or even a brigade, of raw troops against a well-armed foe. Had the volunteers been associated with an equal number of trained and disciplined soldiers, as had been the case in Mexico,[2] they would have derived both confidence from their presence, and stability from their example ; had there been even an experienced staff, capable of dealing with large forces, and an efficient commissariat, capable of rapid expansion, they might have crushed all organised opposition. But only 3,000 regulars could be drawn from the Western borders ; the staff was as feeble as the commissariat ; and so, from a purely military point of view, the conquest of the South appeared impossible. Her self-sustaining power was far greater than has been usually imagined. On the broad prairies of Texas, Arkansas, and Louisiana ranged innumerable herds. The area under cultivation was almost equal to that north of the Potomac and the Ohio. The pastoral districts—the beautiful Valley of Virginia, the great plains of Georgia, the fertile bottoms of Alabama, were inexhaustible granaries. The amount of live stock—horses, mules, oxen, and sheep—was actually larger than in the North ; and if the acreage under wheat was less extensive, the deficiency was more than balanced by the great harvests of rice and maize.[3] Men of high ability, but profoundly ignorant of the conditions which govern military operations, prophesied that the South would be brought back to the Union within ninety days ; General Winfield Scott, on the other hand, Commander-in-Chief of the Federal armies, declared that its conquest might be achieved ' in two or three years, by a young and able general—a Wolfe, a Desaix, a Hoche—with 300,000 disciplined men kept up to that number.'

Nevertheless, despite the extent of her territory and her scanty means of communication, the South was peculiarly vulnerable. Few factories or foundries had been established

[1] Even after the Peninsular War had enlarged the experience of the British army, Sir Charles Napier declared that he knew but one general who could handle 100,000 men, and that was the Duke of Wellington.

[2] Grant's *Memoirs*, vol. i., p. 168.

[3] Cf. U.S. Census Returns, 1860.

within her frontiers.   She manufactured nothing ; and not only for all luxuries, but for almost every necessary of life, she was dependent upon others.   Her cotton and tobacco brought leather and cloth in exchange from England. Metals, machinery, rails, rolling stock, salt, and even medicines came, for the most part, from the North.   The weapons which she put into her soldiers' hands during the first year of the war, her cannon, powder, and ammunition, were of foreign make.   More than all, her mercantile marine was very small.   Her foreign trade was in the hands of Northern merchants.   She had ship-yards, for Norfolk and Pensacola, both national establishments, were within her boundaries ; but her seafaring population was inconsiderable, and shipbuilding was almost an unknown industry.   Strong on land, she was powerless at sea, and yet it was on the sea that her prosperity depended.   Cotton, the principal staple of her wealth, demanded free access to the European markets.   But without a navy, and without the means of constructing one, or of manning the vessels that she might easily have purchased, she was unable to keep open her communications across the Atlantic.

Nor was it on the ocean alone that the South was at a disadvantage.   The Mississippi, the main artery of her commerce, which brought the harvests of the plantations to New Orleans, and which divided her territory into two distinct portions, was navigable throughout ; while other great rivers and many estuaries, leading into the heart of her dominions, formed the easiest of highways for the advance of an invading army.   Very early had her fatal weakness been detected.   Immediately Fort Sumter fell, Lincoln had taken measures to isolate the seceding States, to close every channel by which they could receive either succour or supplies, and if need be to starve them into submission.   The maritime resources of the Union were so large that the navy was rapidly expanded. Numbers of trained seamen, recruited from the merchant service and the fisheries, were at once available.

The Northern shipbuilders had long been famous ; and both men and vessels, if the necessity should arise, might be procured in Europe. Judicious indeed was the policy which, at the very outset of the war, brought the tremendous pressure of the sea-power to bear against the South ; and, had her statesmen possessed the knowledge of what that pressure meant, they must have realised that Abraham Lincoln was no ordinary foe. In forcing the Confederates to become the aggressors, and to fire on the national ensign, he had created a united North ; in establishing a blockade of their coasts he brought into play a force, which, like the mills of God, ' grinds slowly, but grinds exceeding small.'

But for the present the Federal navy was far too small to watch three thousand miles of littoral indented by spacious harbours and secluded bays, protected in many cases by natural breakwaters, and communicating by numerous channels with the open sea. Moreover, it was still an even chance whether cotton became a source of weakness to the Confederacy or a source of strength. If the markets of Europe were closed to her by the hostile battle-ships, the credit of the young Republic would undoubtedly be seriously impaired ; but the majority of the Southern politicians believed that the great powers beyond the Atlantic would never allow the North to enforce her restrictive policy. England and France, a large portion of whose population depended for their livelihood on the harvests of the South, were especially interested ; and England and France, both great maritime States, were not likely to brook interference with their trade. Nor had the Southern people a high opinion of Northern patriotism. They could hardly conceive that the maintenance of the Union, which they themselves considered so light a bond, had been exalted elsewhere to the height of a sacred principle. Least of all did they believe that the great Democratic party, which embraced so large a proportion of the Northern people, and which, for so many years, had been in close sympathy with themselves, would support the President in his coercive measures.

History, moreover, not always an infallible guide, supplied many plausible arguments to those who sought to forecast the immediate future. In the War of Independence, not only had the impracticable nature of the country, especially of the South, baffled the armies of Great Britain, but the European powers, actuated by old grudges and commercial jealousy, had come to the aid of the insurgents. On a theatre of war where trained and well-organised forces had failed, it was hardly to be expected that raw levies would succeed ; and if England, opposed in 1782 by the fleets of France, Spain, and Holland, had been compelled to let the colonies go, it was hardly likely that the North, confronted by the naval strength of England and France, would long maintain the struggle with the South. Trusting then to foreign intervention, to the dissensions of their opponents, and to their own hardihood and unanimity, the Southerners faced the future with few misgivings.

At Richmond, finding himself without occupation, Major Jackson volunteered to assist in the drilling of the new levies. The duty to which he was first assigned was distasteful. He was an indifferent draughtsman, and a post in the topographical department was one for which he was hardly fitted. The appointment, fortunately, was not confirmed. Some of his friends in the Confederate Congress proposed that he should be sent to command at Harper's Ferry, an important outpost on the northern frontier of Virginia. There was some opposition, not personal to Jackson and of little moment, but it called forth a remark that shows the estimation in which he was held by men who knew him.

'Who is this Major Jackson ?' it was asked.

'He is one,' was the reply, ' who, if you order him to hold a post, will never leave it alive to be occupied by the enemy.'

Harper's Ferry, the spot where the first collision might confidently be expected, was a charge after Jackson's own heart.

'Last Saturday,' he writes to his wife, ' the Governor handed me my commission as Colonel of Virginia
April 26. Volunteers, the post I prefer above all others, and has given me an independent command. Little one, you must not expect to hear from me very often, as I expect to have more work than I ever had in the same

length of time before; but don't be concerned about your husband, for our kind Heavenly Father will give every needful aid.'

The garrison at Harper's Ferry consisted of a large number of independent companies of infantry, a few light companies, as they were called, of cavalry, and fifteen smooth-bore cannon of small calibre. This force numbered 4,500 officers and men, of whom all but 400 were Virginians. Jackson's appearance was not hailed with acclamation. The officers of the State militia had hitherto exercised the functions of command over the ill-knit concourse of enthusiastic patriots. The militia, however, was hardly more than a force on paper, and the camps swarmed with generals and field-officers who were merely civilians in gaudy uniform. By order of the State Legislature these gentlemen were now deprived of their fine feathers. Every militia officer above the rank of captain was deposed; and the Governor of Virginia was authorised to fill the vacancies. This measure was by no means popular. Both by officers and men it was denounced as an outrage on freemen and volunteers; and the companies met in convention for the purpose of passing denunciatory resolutions.

Their new commander was a sorry substitute for the brilliant figures he had superseded. The militia generals had surrounded themselves with a numerous staff, and on fine afternoons, it was said, the official display in Harper's Ferry would have done no discredit to the Champs-Elysées. Jackson had but two assistants, who, like himself, still wore the plain blue uniform of the Military Institute. To eyes accustomed to the splendid trappings and prancing steeds of his predecessors there seemed an almost painful want of pomp and circumstance about the colonel of volunteers. There was not a particle of gold lace about him. He rode a horse as quiet as himself. His seat in the saddle was ungraceful. His well-worn cadet cap was always tilted over his eyes; he was sparing of speech; his voice was very quiet, and he seldom smiled. He made no orations, he held no reviews, and his orders were remarkable for their brevity. Even with his officers he had little intercourse. He confided his plans to no one, and not a single item of information, useful or otherwise, escaped his lips.

Some members of the Maryland Legislature, a body whom it was important to conciliate, visited Harper's Ferry during his tenure of command. They were received with the utmost politeness, and in return plied the general with many questions. His answers were unsatisfactory, and at length one more bold than the rest asked him frankly how many men he had at his disposal. 'Sir,' was the reply, 'I should be glad if President Lincoln thought I had fifty thousand.' Nor was this reticence observed only towards those whose discretion he mistrusted. He was silent on principle. In the campaign of 1814, the distribution of the French troops at a most critical moment was made known to the allies by the capture of a courier carrying a letter from Napoleon to the Empress. There was little chance of a letter to Mrs. Jackson, who was now in North Carolina, falling into the hands of the Federals; but even in so small a matter Jackson was consistent.

'You say,' he wrote, 'that your husband never writes you any news. I suppose you mean military news, for I have written you a great deal about your *sposo* and how much he loves you. What do you want with military news? Don't you know that it is unmilitary and unlike an officer to write news respecting one's post? You couldn't wish your husband to do an unofficer-like thing, could you?'

And then, the claims of duty being thus clearly defined, he proceeds to describe the roses which climbed round the window of his temporary quarters, adding, with that lover-like devotion which every letter betrays, 'but my sweet little sunny face is what I want to see most of all.'

Careful as he was to keep the enemy in the dark, he was exceedingly particular when he visited his distant posts on the Potomac that his presence should be unobserved. Had it become known to the Federal generals that the commander at Harper's Ferry had reconnoitred a certain point of passage, a clue might have been given to his designs. The Confederate officers, therefore, in charge of these posts, were told that Colonel Jackson did not wish them to recognise him. He rode out accompanied by a single staff officer, and the men were seldom aware that the brigadier had been through their camps.

Never was a commander who fell so far short of the popular idea of a dashing leader. This quiet gentleman, who came and went unnoticed, who had nothing to say, and was so anxious to avoid observation, was a type of soldier unfamiliar to the volunteers. He was duty personified and nothing more.

But at the same time the troops instinctively felt that this absence of ostentation meant hard work. They began to realise the magnitude of the obligations they had assumed. Soldiering was evidently something more than a series of brilliant spectacles and social gatherings. Here was a man in earnest, who looked upon war as a serious business, who was completely oblivious to what people said or thought; and his example was not without effect. The conventions came to nothing; and when the companies were organised in battalions, and some of the deposed officers were reappointed to command, the men went willingly to work. Their previous knowledge, even of drill, was of the scantiest. Officers and men had to begin as recruits, and Jackson was not the man to cut short essential prelimi-naries. Seven hours' drill daily was a heavy tax upon enthusiasm; but it was severely enforced, and the garrison of the frontier post soon learned the elements of manœuvre. Discipline was a lesson more difficult than drill. The military code, in all its rigour, could not be at once applied to a body of high-spirited and inexperienced civilians. Undue severity might have produced the very worst results. The observance, therefore, of those regulations which were not in themselves essential to efficiency or health was not insisted on. Lapses in military etiquette were suffered to pass un-noticed; no attempt was made to draw a hard and fast line between officers and men; and many things which in a regular army would be considered grossly irregular were tacitly permitted. Jackson was well aware that volunteers of the type he commanded needed most delicate and

tactful handling.   The chief use of minute regulations
and exacting routine is the creation of the instinct of
obedience.   Time was wanting to instil such instinct into
the Confederate troops ; and the intelligence and patriotism
of the men, largely of high class and good position, who
filled the ranks, might be relied upon to prevent serious
misconduct. Had they been burdened with the constant ac-
knowledgment of superior authority which becomes a second
nature to the regular soldier, disgust and discontent might
have taken the place of high spirit and good-will.   But
at the same time wilful misbehaviour was severely checked.
Neglect of duty and insubordination were crimes which
Jackson never forgave, and deliberate disobedience was in
his eyes as unmanly an offence as cowardice.   He knew
when to be firm as well as when to relax, and it was not
only in the administration of discipline that he showed
his tact.   He was the most patient of instructors.   So
long as those under him were trying to do their best,
no one could have been kinder or more forbearing ; and he
constantly urged his officers to come to his tent when they
required explanation as to the details of their duty.

Besides discipline and instruction, Jackson had the
entire administration of his command upon his hands.
Ammunition was exceedingly scarce, and he had to provide
for the manufacture of ball-cartridges.   Transport there was
none, but the great waggons of the Valley farmers supplied
the deficiency.   The equipment of the artillery left much to
be desired, and ammunition carts (or caissons) were constructed by fixing roughly made chests on the running gear
of waggons.   The supply and medical services were non-
existent, and everything had to be organised *de novo*.   Thus
the officer in command at Harper's Ferry had his hands
full ; and in addition to his administrative labours there
was the enemy to be watched, information to be obtained,
and measures of defence to be considered.   A glance at
the map will show the responsibilities of Jackson's position.

The Virginia of the Confederacy was cut in two by the
Blue Ridge, a chain of mountains three hundred and thirty
miles in length, which, rising in North Carolina, passes

under different names through Maryland, Pennsylvania, New York, and Vermont, and sinks to the level on the Canadian frontier.

The Blue Ridge varies in height from 2,000 to 6,000 feet. Densely wooded, it is traversed in Virginia only by the 'Gaps,' through which ran three railways and several roads. These Gaps were of great strategic importance, for if they were once secured, a Northern army, moving up the Valley of the Shenandoah, would find a covered line of approach towards the Virginia and Tennessee railway, which connected Richmond with the Mississippi. Nor was this the only advantage it would gain. From Lexington at its head, to Harper's Ferry, where it strikes the Potomac, throughout its whole length of one hundred and forty miles, the Valley was rich in agricultural produce. Its average width, for it is bounded on the west by the eastern ranges of the Alleghanies, is not more than four-and-twenty miles ; but there are few districts of the earth's surface, of equal extent, more favoured by Nature or more highly cultivated. It was the granary of Virginia ; and not Richmond only, but the frontier garrisons, depended largely for subsistence on the farms of the Shenandoah.

Moreover, if the Valley were occupied by the Federals, North-western Virginia would be cut off from the Confederacy ; and Jackson's native mountains, inhabited by a brave and hardy race, would be lost as a recruiting ground.

In order, then, to secure the loyalty of the mountaineers, to supply the armies, and to protect the railways, the retention of the Valley was of the utmost importance to the Confederacy. The key of the communication with the North-west was Winchester, the chief town of the lower Valley, twenty-six miles, in an air-line, south-west of Harper's Ferry. From Winchester two highways lead westward, by Romney and Moorefield ; four lead east and south-east, crossing the Blue Ridge by Snicker's, Ashby's, Manassas, and Chester's Gaps ; and the first object of the Confederate force at Harper's Ferry was to cover this nucleus of roads.

During the month of May the garrison of the frontier

post was undisturbed by the enemy.   Lincoln's first call
had been for 75,000 volunteers.   On May 3 he asked for an
additional 40,000 ; these when trained, with 18,000 seamen
and a detachment of regulars, would place at his disposal
150,000 men.   The greater part of this force had assembled
at Washington ; but a contingent of 10,000 or 12,000 men
under General Patterson, a regular officer of many years'
service, was collecting in Pennsylvania, and an outpost
of 3,000 men was established at Chambersburg, forty-five
miles north of Harper's Ferry.

These troops, however, though formidable in numbers,
were as ill-prepared for war as the Confederates, and no
immediate movement was to be anticipated.   Not only
had the Federal authorities to equip and organise their
levies, but the position of Washington was the cause of
much embarrassment.   The District of Columbia—the sixty
square miles set apart for the seat of the Federal Government—lies on the Potomac, fifty miles south-east of
Harper's Ferry, wedged in between Virginia on the one
side and Maryland on the other.

The loyalty of Maryland to the Union was more than
doubtful.   As a slave-holding State, her sympathies were
strongly Southern ; and it was only her geographical situation, north of the Potomac, and with no strong frontier to protect her from invasion, which had held her back from joining
the Confederacy.   As only a single line of railway connected
Washington with the North, passing through Baltimore,
the chief city of Maryland, a very hot-bed of secession
sentiment, the attitude of the State was a matter of the
utmost anxiety to the Federal Government.   An attempt
to send troops through Baltimore to Washington had
provoked a popular commotion and some bloodshed.   Stern
measures had been necessary to keep the railway open.
Baltimore was placed under martial law, and strongly
garrisoned.   But despite these precautions, for some weeks
the feeling in Maryland was so hostile to the Union that
it was not considered safe for the Northern troops to cross
her territory except in large numbers ; and the concentration

at Washington of a force sufficient to defend it was thus attended with much difficulty.

A single railroad, too, the Baltimore and Ohio, connected Washington with the West. Crossing the Potomac at Harper's Ferry, and following the course of the river, it ran for one hundred and twenty miles within the confines of Virginia. Thus the district commanded by Jackson embraced an artery of supply and communication which was of great importance to the enemy. The natural course would have been to destroy the line at once ; but the susceptibilities of both Maryland and West Virginia had to be considered. The stoppage of all traffic on their main trade route would have done much to alienate the people from the South, and there was still hope that Maryland might throw in her lot with her seceded sisters.

The line was therefore left intact, and the company was permitted to maintain the regular service of trains, including the mails. For this privilege, however, Jackson exacted toll. The Confederate railways were deficient in rolling stock, and he determined to effect a large transfer from the Baltimore and Ohio. From Point of Rocks, twelve miles east of Harper's Ferry, to Martinsburg, fifteen miles west, the line was double. 'The coal traffic along it,' says General Imboden, 'was immense, for the Washington Government was accumulating supplies of coal on the seaboard. These coal trains passed Harper's Ferry at all hours of the day and night, and thus furnished Jackson with a pretext for arranging a brilliant capture. A detachment was posted at Point of Rocks, and the 5th Virginia Infantry at Martinsburg. He then complained to the President of the Baltimore and Ohio that the night trains, eastward bound, disturbed the repose of his camp, and requested a change of schedule that would pass all east-bound trains by Harper's Ferry between eleven and one o'clock in the daytime. The request was complied with, and thereafter for several days was heard the constant roar of passing trains for an hour before and an hour after noon. But since the "empties" were sent up the road at night, Jackson again complained that the nuisance was as great as ever, and, as the road had two tracks, said he must insist that the west-bound trains should pass during the same hour as those going east.   Again he was obliged, and we then had, for two hours every day, the liveliest railroad in America.

'One night, as soon as the schedule was working at its best, Jackson instructed the officer commanding at Point of Rocks to take a force of men across to the Maryland side of the river the next day at eleven o'clock, and letting all west-bound trains pass till twelve o'clock, to permit none to go east.   He ordered the reverse to be done at Martinsburg.

'Thus he caught all the trains that were going east or west between these points, and ran them up to Winchester, thirty-two miles on the branch line, whence they were removed by horse power to the railway at Strasburg, eighteen miles further south.'[1]

This capture was Jackson's only exploit whilst in command at Harper's Ferry.   On May 24 he was relieved by May 24. General Joseph E. Johnston, one of the senior officers of the Confederate army.   The transfer of authority was not, however, at once effected.   Johnston reached Harper's Ferry in advance of his letter of appointment.   Jackson had not been instructed that he was to hand over his command, and, strictly conforming to the regulations, he respectfully declined to vacate his post. Fortunately a communication soon came from General Lee, commanding the Virginia troops, in which he referred to Johnston as in command at Harper's Ferry. Jackson at once recognised this letter as official evidence that he was superseded, and from that time forth rendered his superior the most faithful and zealous support. He seems at first to have expected that he would be sent to North-west Virginia, and his one ambition at this time was to be selected as the instrument of saving his native mountains to the South. But the Confederate Government had other views.   At the beginning of June a more compact organisation was given to the regiments at Harper's Ferry, and Jackson was

[1] *Battles and Leaders*, vol. i.

assigned to the command of the First Brigade of the Army of the Shenandoah.[1]

Recruited in the Valley of the Shenandoah and the western mountains, the brigade consisted of the following regiments :—

The 2nd Virginia, Colonel Allen.
The 4th Virginia, Colonel Preston.
The 5th Virginia, Colonel Harper.
The 27th Virginia, Lieutenant-Colonel Echols.
The 33rd Virginia, Colonel Cummings.

A battery of artillery, raised in Rockbridge County, was attached to the brigade. Commanded by the Rev. Dr. Pendleton, the rector of Lexington, an old West Point graduate, who was afterwards distinguished as Lee's chief of artillery, and recruited largely from theological colleges, it soon became peculiarly efficient.[2]

No better material for soldiers ever existed than the men of the Valley. Most of them were of Scotch-Irish descent, but from the more northern counties came many of English blood, and from those in the centre of Swiss and German. But whatever their origin, they were thoroughly well qualified for their new trade. All classes mingled in the ranks, and all ages ; the heirs of the oldest families, and the humblest of the sons of toil; boys whom it was impossible to keep at school, and men whose white beards hung below their cross-belts ; youths who had been reared in luxury, and rough hunters from their lonely cabins. They were a mountain people, nurtured in a wholesome climate, bred to manly sports, and hardened by the free life of the field and forest. To social distinctions they gave little heed. They were united for a common purpose; they had taken arms to defend Virginia and to maintain her rights; and their patriotism was

---

[1] The Virginia troops were merged in the army of the Confederate States on June 8, 1861. The total strength was 40,000 men and 115 guns. O. R., vol. ii., p. 928.

[2] When the battery arrived at Harper's Ferry, it was quartered in a church, already occupied by a company called the 'Grayson Dare-devils,' who, wishing to show their hospitality, assigned the pulpit to Captain Pendleton as an appropriate lodging. The four guns were at once christened Matthew, Mark, Luke, and John.

proved by the sacrifice of all personal consideration and individual interest. Nor is the purity of their motives to be questioned. They had implicit faith in the righteousness of their cause. Slave-owners were few in the Valley, and the farms were tilled mainly by free labour. The abolition of negro servitude would have affected but little the population west of the Blue Ridge. But, nevertheless, west of the Blue Ridge the doctrine of State Rights was as firmly rooted as in the Carolinas, the idea that a State could be coerced into remaining within the Union as fiercely repudiated; and the men of the Valley faced the gathering hosts of the North in the same spirit that they would have faced the hosts of a foreign foe.

In the first weeks of June the military situation became more threatening. The Union armies were taking shape. The levies of volunteers seemed sufficiently trained to render reconquest practicable, and the great wave of invasion had already mounted the horizon. A force of 25,000 men, based on the Ohio, threatened North-west Virginia. There had been collisions on the Atlantic sea-board, where the Federals held Fortress Monroe, a strong citadel within eighty miles of Richmond, and Richmond had become the capital of the Confederacy. There had been fighting in Missouri, and the partisans of the South in that State had already been badly worsted. The vast power of the North was making itself felt on land, and on the sea had asserted an ascendency which it never lost. The blue waters of the Gulf of Mexico were patrolled by a fleet with which the Confederates had no means of coping. From the sea-wall of Charleston, the great Atlantic port of the South, the masts of the blockading squadron were visible in the offing; and beyond the mouths of the Mississippi, closing the approaches to New Orleans, the long black hulls steamed slowly to and fro.

But it was about Manassas Junction—thirty miles south-west of Washington and barring the road to Richmond—that all interest centred during the first campaign. Here was posted the main army of the Confederacy, 20,000 volunteers under General Beauregard.

the Manassas Gap Railway forming an easy means of communication with the Army of the Shenandoah.

Johnston's force had been gradually increased to 10,000 officers and men. But the general was by no means convinced of the desirability of holding Harper's Ferry. The place itself was insignificant. It had contained an arsenal, but this had been burnt by the Federals when they evacuated the post; and it was absolutely untenable against attack. To the east runs the Shenandoah; and immediately above the river stands a spur of the Blue Ridge, the Loudoun Heights, completely commanding the little town. Beyond the Potomac is a crest of equal altitude, covered with forest trees and under-growth, and bearing the name of the Maryland Heights.

Jackson, without waiting for instructions, had taken on himself to hold and fortify the Maryland Heights. 'I am of opinion,' he had written to General Lee, 'that this place should be defended with the spirit which actuated the defenders of Thermopylæ, and if left to myself such is my determination. The fall of this place would, I fear, result in the loss of the north-western part of the State, and who can estimate the moral power thus gained to the enemy and lost to ourselves?'[1]

Lee, also, was averse to evacuation. Such a measure, he said, would be depressing to the cause of the South, and would leave Maryland isolated. The post, it was true, could be easily turned. By crossing the Potomac, at Williamsport and Shepherdstown, twenty and ten miles north-west respectively, the Federals would threaten the communications of the garrison with Winchester; in case they were attacked, the Confederates would have to fight with their backs to the Shenandoah, broad, deep, and unbridged; and the ground westward of Harper's Ferry was ill adapted for defence. Attack, in Lee's opinion, would have been best met by a resolute offensive.[2] Johnston, however, believed his troops unfitted for active manœuvres, and he was permitted to choose his own course. The incident is of small import-

[1] O. R., vol. ii., p. 814.
[2] Ibid., pp. 881, 889, 897, 898, 901, 923.

ance, but it serves to show an identity of opinion between Lee and Jackson, and a regard for the moral aspect of the situation which was to make itself manifest, with extraordinary results, at a later period. On June 14, Johnston

June 14. destroyed the railway bridge over the Potomac, removed the machinery that had been rescued from the arsenal, burned the public buildings, and the next day retired on Winchester. His immediate opponent, General Patterson, had crossed the Pennsylvania border, and, moving through Maryland, had occupied Williamsport with 14,000 men. A detachment of Confederate militia had been driven from Romney, thirty-five miles north-west of Winchester, and the general forward movement of the enemy had become pronounced.

On June 20 Jackson's brigade was ordered to destroy the workshops of the Baltimore and Ohio Railway at Martinsburg, together with the whole of the rolling

June 20. stock that might there be found, and to support the cavalry. The first of these tasks, although Martinsburg is no more than ten miles distant from Williamsport, was easily accomplished. Four locomotives were sent back to Winchester, drawn by teams of horses; and several more, together with many waggons, were given to the flames. The second task demanded no unusual exertions. The Federals, as yet, manifested no intention of marching upon Winchester, nor was the Confederate cavalry in need of immediate assistance. The force numbered 300 sabres. The men were untrained; but they were first-rate horsemen, they knew every inch of the country, and they were exceedingly well commanded. Lieutenant-Colonel J. E. B. Stuart, who had been a captain of dragoons in the United States army, had already given token of those remarkable qualities which were afterwards to make him famous. Of an old Virginia family, he was the very type of the Cavalier, fearless and untiring, ' boisterous as March, yet fresh as May.'

'Educated at West Point, and trained in Indian fighting in the prairies, he brought to the great struggle upon which he had now entered a thorough knowledge of

arms, a bold and fertile conception, and a constitution of
body which enabled him to bear up against fatigues which
would have prostrated the strength of other men. Those
who saw him at this time are eloquent in their description
of the energy and the habits of the man. They tell how
he remained almost constantly in the saddle; how he
never failed to instruct personally every squad which went
out on picket; how he was everywhere present, at all
hours of the day and night, along the line which he
guarded; and how, by infusing into the raw cavalry his
own activity and watchfulness, he was enabled, in spite of
the small force which he commanded, to observe the whole
part of the Potomac from Point of Rocks to beyond
Williamsport. His animal spirits were unconquerable, his
gaiety and humour unfailing; he had a ready jest for all,
and made the forests ring with his songs as he marched at
the head of his column. So great was his activity that
General Johnston compared him to that species of hornet
called "a yellow jacket," and said that "he was no sooner
brushed off than he lit back again." When the general
was subsequently transferred to the West he wrote to
Stuart: "How can I eat, sleep, or rest in peace without
you upon the outpost?"[1]

No officer in the Confederacy was more trusted by his
superiors or more popular with the men; and Jackson was
no more proof than others against the attractions of his
sunny and noble nature. As a soldier, Stuart was a colleague after his own heart; and, as a man, he was hardly
less congenial. The dashing horseman of eight-and-twenty,
who rivalled Murat in his fondness for gay colours, and to
all appearance looked upon war as a delightful frolic, held
a rule of life as strict as that of his Presbyterian comrade;
and outwardly a sharp contrast, inwardly they were in the
closest sympathy. Stuart's fame as a leader was to be won
in larger fields than those west of the Blue Ridge, and,
although sprung from the same Scotch-Irish stock, he was
in no way connected with the Valley soldiers. But from the
very outbreak of the war he was intimately associated with

[1] Cooke, p. 47.

K 2

Jackson and his men. Fortune seemed to take a curious delight in bringing them together; they were together in their first skirmish, and in their last great victory; and now, on the banks of the Potomac, watching the hostile masses that were assembling on the further shore, they first learned to know each other's worth.

On July 2 Patterson crossed the river. The movement was at once reported by Stuart, and Jackson, with the 5th Virginia and a battery, advanced to meet the enemy. His instructions from Johnston were to ascertain the strength of the hostile force, and then to retire under cover of the cavalry. Four regiments of his brigade were therefore left in camp; the baggage was sent back, and when the 5th Virginia had marched out a short distance, three of the four guns were halted. Near Falling Waters, a country church some five miles south of the Potomac, Patterson's advanced-guard was discovered on the road. The country on either hand, like the greater part of the Valley, was open, undulating, and highly cultivated, view and movement being obstructed only by rail fences and patches of high timber.

The Virginians were partially concealed by a strip of woodland, and when the Federal skirmishers, deployed on either side of the highway, moved forward to the attack, they were received by a heavy and unexpected fire. As the enemy fell back, a portion of the Confederate line was thrown forward, occupying a house and barn; and despite the fire of two guns which the Federals had brought up, the men, with the impetuous rashness of young troops, dashed out to the attack. But Jackson intervened. The enemy, who had two brigades of infantry well closed up, was deploying a heavy force; his skirmishers were again advancing, and the 5th Virginia, in danger of being outflanked, was ordered to retire to its first position. The movement was misconstrued by the Federals, and down the high road, in solid column, came the pursuing cavalry. A well-aimed shot from the single field-piece sufficed to check their progress; a confused mass of horsemen went flying to the rear; and the Confederate gunners turned their attention to the hostile battery. Stuart, at the same time, performed a notable feat. He had moved with fifty troopers to attack the enemy's right flank, and in reconnoitring through the woods had become detached for the moment from his command. As he rode along a winding lane he saw resting in a field a company of Federal infantry. He still wore the uniform of the United States army; the enemy suspected nothing, taking him for one of their own cavalry, and he determined to effect their capture. Riding up to the fence he bade one of the men remove the bars. This was done with respectful alacrity, and he then galloped among them, shouting 'Throw down your arms, or you are all dead men!' The stentorian order was at once obeyed: the raw troops not only dropped their rifles but fell upon their faces, and the Confederate troopers, coming to their leader's aid, marched the whole company as prisoners to the rear.

So firm was the attitude of Jackson's command that General Patterson was thoroughly imposed upon. Slowly and cautiously he pushed out right and left, and it was not till near noon that the Confederates were finally ordered to retreat. Beyond desultory skirmishing there was no further fighting. The 5th Virginia fell back on the main body; Stuart came in with his string of captives, and leaving the cavalry to watch the enemy, the First Brigade went into camp some two miles south of Martinsburg. Patterson reported to his Government that he had been opposed by 3,500 men, exactly ten times Jackson's actual number.[1] The losses on either side were inconsiderable, a few men killed and 10 or 15 wounded; and if the Confederates carried off 50 prisoners, the Federals had the satisfaction of burning some tents which Jackson had been unable to remove. The engagement, however, had the best effect on the *moral* of the Southern troops, and they were not so ignorant as to overlook the skill and coolness with which they had been manœuvred. It is possible that their commander appeared in an unexpected light, and that they had watched his behaviour with some amount of curiosity. They certainly discovered that a dis-

[1] O. R., vol. ii., p. 157.

taste for show and frippery is no indication of an unwarlike spirit. In the midst of the action, while he was writing a dispatch, a cannon ball had torn a tree above his head to splinters. Not a muscle moved, and he wrote on as if he were seated in his own tent.

The day after Falling Waters, on Johnston's recommendation, Jackson received from General Lee his com-
July 3.   mission as brigadier-general in the Confederate army. 'My promotion,' he wrote to his wife, 'was beyond what I had anticipated, as I only expected it to be in the Volunteer forces of the State. One of my greatest desires for advancement is the gratification it will give my darling, and (the opportunity) of serving my country more efficiently. I have had all that I ought to desire in the line of promotion. I should be very ungrateful if I were not contented, and exceedingly thankful to our kind Heavenly Father.'

Of Patterson's further movements it is unnecessary to speak at length. The Federal army crawled on to Martinsburg. Halting seven miles south-west Jackson was reinforced by Johnston's whole command ; and here, for four days, the Confederates, drawn up in line of battle, awaited attack. But the Federals stood fast in Martinsburg ; and on the fourth day Johnston withdrew to Winchester. The Virginia soldiers were bitterly dissatisfied. At first even Jackson chafed. He was eager for further action. His experiences at Falling Waters had given him no exalted notion of the enemy's prowess, and he was ready to engage them single-handed. 'I want my brigade,' he said, 'to feel that it can itself whip Patterson's whole army, and I believe we can do it.' But Johnston's self-control was admirable. He was ready to receive attack, believing that, in his selected position, he could repulse superior numbers. But he was deaf to all who clamoured for an offensive movement, to the murmurs of the men, and to the remonstrances of the officers. The stone houses of Martinsburg and its walled inclosures were proof against assault, and promised at most a bloody victory. His stock of ammunition was scanty in the extreme ; the infantry had but fourteen cartridges apiece ; and although his patience was construed by his troops as a want of enterprise, he had in truth displayed great daring in offering battle south of Martinsburg.

The Federal army at Washington, commanded by General McDowell, amounted to 50,000 men ; a portion of this force was already south of the Potomac, and Beauregard's 20,000 Confederates, at Manassas Junction, were seriously threatened. In West Virginia the enemy had advanced, moving, fortunately, in the direction of Staunton, at the southern end of the Valley, and not on Winchester. On July 11, this force of 20,000 men defeated a Confederate detachment at Rich Mountain, not far from

July 11. Jackson's birthplace ; and although it was still in the heart of the Alleghanies, a few marches, which there were practically no troops to oppose, would give it the control of the Upper Valley.

Thus menaced by three columns of invasion, numbering together over 80,000 men, the chances of the Confederates, who mustered no more than 32,000 all told, looked small indeed. But the three Federal columns were widely separated, and it was possible, by means of the Manassas Gap Railway, for Johnston and Beauregard to unite with greater rapidity than their opponents.

President Davis, acting on the advice of General Lee, had therefore determined to concentrate the whole available force at Manassas Junction, and to meet at that point the column advancing from Washington.[1] The difficulty was for the Army of the Shenandoah to give Patterson the slip. This could easily have been done while that officer stood fast at Martinsburg ; but, in Lee's opinion, if the enemy found that the whole force of the Confederacy was concentrating at Manassas Junction, the Washington column would remain within its intrenchments round the capital, and the Confederates 'would be put to the great disadvantage of achieving nothing, and leaving the other points (Winchester and Staunton) exposed.' The concen-

[1] O. R., vol. ii., p. 515.

tration, therefore, was to be postponed until the Washington column advanced.[1]

But by that time Patterson might be close to Winchester or threatening the Manassas Railway. Johnston had thus a most delicate task before him; and in view of the superior numbers which the Federals could bring against Manassas, it was essential that not a man should be wasted in minor enterprises. The defeat of Patterson, even had it been practicable, would not have prevented the Washington column from advancing; and every Confederate rifleman who fell in the Valley would be one the less at Manassas.

On July 15 Patterson left Martinsburg and moved in the direction of Winchester. On the 16th he remained halted at Bunker's Hill, nine miles north; and on the 17th, instead of continuing his advance, moved to his left and occupied Charlestown. His indecision was manifest. He, too, had no easy part to play. His instructions were to hold Johnston in the Valley, while McDowell advanced against Beauregard. But his instructions were either too definite or not definite enough, and he himself was overcautious. He believed, and so did General Scott, that Johnston might be retained at Winchester by demonstrations—that is, by making a show of strength and by feigned attacks. For more vigorous action Patterson was not in the least inclined; and we can hardly wonder if he hesitated to trust his ill-trained regiments to the confusion and chances of an attack. Even in that day of raw soldiers and inexperienced leaders his troops had an unenviable reputation. They had enlisted for three months, and their term of service was nearly up. Their commander had no influence with them; and, turning a deaf ear to his appeals, they stubbornly refused to remain with the colours even for a few days over their term of service. They were possibly disgusted with the treatment they had received from the Government. The men had received no pay. Many were without shoes, and others, according to their general, were ' without pants!' 'They cannot march,' he adds, 'and, un-

July 15

---

[1] O. R., vol. ii., p. 507.

less a paymaster goes with them, they will be indecently clad and have just cause of complaint.'[1]

Nevertheless, the Federal authorities made a grievous mistake when they allowed Patterson and his *sans-culottes* to move to Charlestown. McDowell marched against Beauregard on the afternoon of the 16th, and Patterson should have been instructed to attack Johnston at any cost. Even had the latter been successful, he could hardly have reinforced the main army in time to meet McDowell.

At 1 A.M. on the morning of the 18th Johnston received a telegram from the President to the effect that McDowell was advancing on Manassas. Stuart was immediately directed to keep Patterson amused; and leaving July 18. their sick, 1,700 in number, to the care of Winchester, the troops were ordered to strike tents and prepare to march. No man knew the object of the movement, and when the regiments passed through Winchester, marching southward, with their backs to the enemy, the step was lagging and the men dispirited. A few miles out, as they turned eastward, the brigades were halted and an order was read to them. 'Our gallant army under General Beauregard is now attacked by overwhelming numbers. The Commanding General hopes that his troops will step out like men, and make a forced march to save the country.' The effect of this stirring appeal was instantaneous. 'The soldiers,' says Jackson, 'rent the air with shouts of joy, and all was eagerness and animation.' The march was resumed, and as mile after mile was passed, although there was much useless delay and the pace was slow, the faint outlines of the Blue Ridge, rising high above the Valley, changed imperceptibly to a mighty wall of rock and forest. As the night came down a long reach of the Shenandoah crossed the road. The ford was waist-deep, but the tall Virginians, plunging without hesitation into the strong current, gained the opposite shore with little loss of time. The guns and waggons followed in long succession through the darkling waters, and still the heavy tramp of the toiling column passed eastward through the quiet fields.

[1] O. R., vol. ii., pp. 169, 170.

The Blue Ridge was crossed at Ashby's Gap; and at two o'clock in the morning, near the little village of Paris, the First Brigade was halted on the further slope.   They had marched over twenty miles, and so great was their exhaustion that the men sank prostrate on the ground beside their muskets.[1]   They were already sleeping, when an officer reminded Jackson that there were no pickets round the bivouac.   'Let the poor fellows sleep,' was the reply; 'I will guard the camp myself.'   And so, through the watches of the summer night, the general himself stood sentry over his unconscious troops.[2]

[1] 'The discouragements of that day's march,' says Johnston, 'to one accustomed to the steady gait of regular soldiers, is indescribable.   The views of military obedience and command then taken both by officers and men confined their duties and obligations almost exclusively to the drill-ground and guards.   In camps and marches they were scarcely known.   Consequently, frequent and unreasonable delays caused so slow a rate of marching as to make me despair of joining General Beauregard in time to aid him.'—Johnston's *Narrative*.

[2] Letter to Mrs. Jackson, *Memoirs*, p. 176.

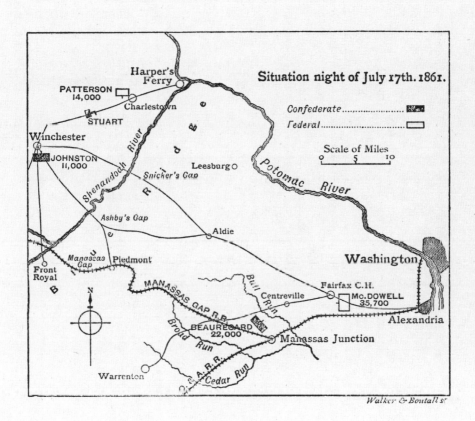

Situation night of July 17th. 1861.

Confederate......................
Federal.............................

Scale of Miles
0   5   10

Harper's Ferry
PATTERSON 14,000
Charlestown
STUART
Winchester
JOHNSTON 11,000
Shenandoah River
Snicker's Gap
Leesburg
Ashby's Gap
Aldie
Potomac River
Manassas Gap
Piedmont
Front Royal
MANASSAS GAP R.R.
Bull Run
Centreville
Fairfax C.H.
Washington
Mc.DOWELL 35,700
Alexandria
BEAUREGARD 22,000
Manassas Junction
Broad Run
O. & A. R.R.
Cedar Run
Warrenton

N

Walker & Boutall sc.

CHAPTER VI

THE FIRST BATTLE OF MANASSAS OR BULL RUN

AT the first streak of dawn, Jackson aroused his men and resumed the march. Before the column gained the plain, Stuart's cavalry clattered past, leaving July 19. Patterson at Charlestown, in ignorance of his adversary's escape, and congratulating himself on the success of his cautious strategy. At Piedmont, a station at the foot of the Blue Ridge, trains were waiting for the conveyance of the troops; and at four o'clock in the afternoon Jackson and his brigade had reached Manassas Junction. The cavalry, artillery, and waggons moved by road; and the remainder of Johnston's infantry was expected to follow the First Brigade without delay. But in war, unless there has been ample time for preparation, railways are not always an expeditious means of travel. The line was single; so short notice had been given that it was impossible to collect enough rolling-stock; the officials were inexperienced; there was much mismanagement; and on the morning of Sunday, July 21, only three brigades of the Army of the Shenandoah—Jackson's, Bee's, and Bartow's—together with the cavalry and artillery, had joined Beauregard. Kirby Smith's brigade, about 1,900 strong, was still upon the railway.

The delay might easily have been disastrous. Happily, the Federal movements were even more tardy. Had the invading army been well organised, Beauregard would probably have been defeated before Johnston could have reached him. McDowell had advanced from Washington on the afternoon of the 16th with 35,000 men. On the morning of the 18th, the greater part of his force was concentrated at Centreville, twenty-two miles from Washington, and five and a half north-east of Manassas Junction. Beauregard's outposts had already fallen back to the banks of Bull Run, a stream made difficult by wooded and precipitous banks, from two to three miles south, and of much the same width as the Thames at Oxford.

It would have been possible to have attacked on the morning of the 19th, but the Federal commander was confronted by many obstacles. He knew little of the country. Although it was almost within sight of the capital, the maps were indifferent. Guides who could describe roads and positions from a military point of view were not forthcoming. All information had to be procured by personal reconnaissance, and few of his officers had been trained to such work. Moreover, the army was most unwieldy. 35,000 men, together with ten batteries, and the requisite train of waggons, was a force far larger than any American officer had yet set eyes upon ; and the movement of such a mass demanded precise arrangement on the part of the staff, and on the part of the troops most careful attention to order and punctuality ; but of these both staff and troops were incapable. The invading force might have done well in a defensive position, which it would have had time to occupy, and where the supply of food and forage, carried on from stationary magazines, would have been comparatively easy; but directly it was put in motion, inexperience and indiscipline stood like giants in the path. The Federal troops were utterly unfitted for offensive movement, and both Scott and McDowell had protested against an immediate advance. The regiments had only been organised in brigades a week previously. They had never been exercised in mass. Deployment for battle had not yet been practised, and to deploy 10,000 or 20,000 men for attack is a difficult operation, even with well-drilled troops and an experienced staff. Nor were the supply arrangements yet completed. The full complement of waggons had not arrived, and the drivers on the spot were as ignorant as they were insubordinate. The troops had received no instruction in musketry, and many of the regiments went into action without having once fired their rifles. But the protests of the generals were of no effect. The Federal Cabinet decided that in face of the public impatience it was impossible to postpone the movement. 'On to Richmond' was the universal cry. The halls of Congress resounded with the fervid eloquence of the politicians. The press teemed with bombastic articles, in which the Northern troops were favourably compared with the regular armies of Europe, and the need of discipline and training for the fearless and intelligent representatives of the sovereign people was scornfully repudiated. Ignorance of war and contempt for the lessons of history were to cost the nation dear.

The march from Washington was a brilliant spectacle. The roads south of the Potomac were covered with masses of men, well armed and well clothed, amply furnished with artillery, and led by regular officers. To the sound of martial music they had defiled before the President. They were accompanied by scores of carriages. Senators, members of Congress, and even ladies swelled the long procession. A crowd of reporters rode beside the columns; and the return of a victorious army could hardly have been hailed with more enthusiasm than the departure of these untrained and unblooded volunteers. Yet, pitiful masquerade as the march must have appeared to a soldier's eye, the majority of those who broke camp that summer morning were brave men and good Americans. To restore the Union, to avenge the insult to their country's flag, they had come forward with no other compulsion than the love of their mother-land. If their self-confidence was supreme and even arrogant, it was the self-confidence of a strong and a fearless people, and their patriotism was of the loftiest kind. It would have been easy for the North, with her enormous wealth, to have organised a vast army of mercenaries wherewith to crush the South. But no! her sons were not willing that their country's honour should be committed to meaner hands.

As they advanced into Virginia, the men, animated by their surroundings, stepped briskly forward, and the country-side was gay with fantastic uniforms and gorgeous standards. But the heat was oppressive, and the roads lay deep in dust. Knapsack, rifle, and blankets became a grievous burden. The excitement died away, and un-broken to the monotonous exertion of the march the three-months' recruits lost all semblance of subordination. The compact array of the columns was gradually lost, and a tail of laggards, rapidly increasing, brought up the rear. Regiment mingled with regiment. By each roadside brook the men fell out in numbers. Every blackberry bush was surrounded by a knot of stragglers; and, heedless of the orders of those officers who still attempted to keep them in the ranks, scores of so-called soldiers sought the cool shade of the surrounding woods.[1] When darkness fell the army was but six miles from its morning bivouacs; and it was not till late the next day that the stragglers rejoined their regiments.

McDowell had intended to attack at once. 'But I could not,' he says, 'get the troops forward earlier than we did. I wished them to go to Centreville the second day, but when I went to urge them forward, I was told that it was impossible for the men to march further. They had only come from Vienna, about six miles, and it was not more than six and a half miles further to Centreville, in all a march of twelve and a half miles; but the men were foot-weary —not so much, I was told, by the distance marched, as by the time they had been on foot, caused by the obstructions in the road, and the slow pace we had to move to avoid ambuscades. The men were, moreover, unaccustomed to marching, and not used to carrying even the load of " light marching order." . . . The trains, hurriedly gotten together, with horses, waggons, drivers, and waggon-masters all new and unused to each other, moved with difficulty and disorder, and were the cause of a day's delay in get-ting the provisions forward.'[2]

On the morning of the 18th, in order to attract the enemy's attention from his right, a brigade was sent south,

[1] *Sherman's Memoirs*, vol. i., p. 181.
[2] O. R., vol. ii., p. 324. McDowell's Report.

in the direction of Bull Run.   The Confederate outposts fell
back over Blackburn's Ford.   The woods about the stream
concealed the defenders' forces, and the Federals pushed
on, bringing artillery into action.   Two Confederate guns,
after firing a few shots, were withdrawn under cover, and
the attacking troops reached the ford.   Suddenly, from the
high timber on the further bank, volleys of musketry blazed
out in their very faces, and then came proof that some at least
of the Federal regiments were no more to be relied upon in
action than on the march.   A portion of the force, despite
the strong position of the enemy and the heavy fire,
showed a bold front, but at least one regiment turned and
fled, and was only rallied far in rear.   The whole affair was
a mistake on the part of the commander.   His troops had
been heedlessly pushed forward, and General Longstreet,
commanding the opposing brigade, by carefully concealing his infantry, had drawn him into an ambuscade.
The results of the action were not without importance.
The Federals fell back with a loss of 83 officers and men,
and the Confederates were much elated at their easy
success.   Among some of the Northerners, on the other
hand, the sudden check to the advance, and the bold bearing
of the enemy, turned confidence and enthusiasm into
irrational despondency.   A regiment and a battery, which
had enlisted for three months and whose time was up,
demanded their discharge, and notwithstanding the appeals
of the Secretary of War, ' moved to the rear to the sound
of the enemy's cannon.' [1]

McDowell's plans were affected by the behaviour of
his troops.   He was still ignorant, so skilfully had the
march from the Valley been carried out, that Johnston
had escaped Patterson.   He was well aware, however, that
such movement was within the bounds of possibility, yet he
found himself compelled to postpone attack until the 21st.
The 19th and 20th were spent in reconnaissance, and in
bringing up supplies; and the lack of organisation made
the issue of rations a long process.   But it was the general's

[1] O. R., vol. ii., p. 324.   McDowell's Report.

want of confidence in his soldiers that was the main cause
of delay.

The Confederates were strongly posted.   The bridges
and fords across Bull Run, with the exception of Sudley
Ford, a long way up stream to the Federal right, were obstructed with felled trees, and covered by rude intrenchments.   Even with regular troops a direct attack on a
single point of passage would have been difficult.
McDowell's first idea was to pass across the front of the
defences, and turn the right at Wolf Run Shoals, five miles
south-east of Union Mills.   The country, however, on this
flank was found to be unfit for the operations of large
masses, and it was consequently determined to turn the
Confederate left by way of Sudley Springs.

The Federal army consisted of five divisions of infantry,
forty-three guns, and seven troops of regular cavalry. Nine
batteries and eight companies of infantry were supplied by
the United States army, and there was a small battalion of
marines.   The strength of the force told off for the attack
amounted to 30,000 all told.[1]

The Confederates, along the banks of Bull Run, disposed of 26,000 infantry, 2,500 cavalry, and 55 guns.
Johnston, who had arrived on the 20th, had assumed command ; but, ignorant of the country, he had allowed Beauregard to make the dispositions for the expected battle.
The line occupied was extensive, six miles in length,
stretching from the Stone Bridge, where the Warrenton
highroad crosses Bull Run, on the left, to the ford at

[1] The rifles (muzzle-loaders) used throughout the war by both Federals
and Confederates compare as follows with more modern weapons :—

	Sighted to	Effective range
American	1,000 yards	250 yards
Needle-gun (1866 and 1870) .	660 ,,	250 ,,
Chassepôt (1870) . . .	1,320 ,,	350 ,,
Martini-Henry	2,100 ,,	400 ,,
Magazine	3,200 ,,	600 ,,

By effective range is meant the distance where, under ordinary conditions,
the enemy's losses are sufficient to stop his advance.   The effective range of
Brown Bess was about 60 yards.   The American rifled artillery was effective,
in clear weather, at 2,000 yards, the 12-pounder smooth-bore at 1,600, the
6-pounder at 1,200.

Union Mills on the right. Besides these two points of passage there were no less than six fords, to each of which ran a road from Centreville. The country to the north was undulating and densely wooded, and it would have been possible for the Federals, especially as the Southern cavalry was held back south of the stream, to mass before any one of the fords, unobserved, in superior numbers. Several of the fords, moreover, were weakly guarded, for Beauregard, who had made up his mind to attack, had massed the greater part of his army near the railroad. The Shenandoah troops were in reserve; Bee's and Bartow's brigades between McLean's and Blackburn's fords, Jackson's between Blackburn's and Mitchell's fords, in rear of the right centre.

The position south of Bull Run, originally selected by General Lee,[1] was better adapted for defence than for attack. The stream, with its high banks, ran like the ditch of a fortress along the front; and to the south was the plateau on which stands Manassas Junction. The plateau is intersected by several creeks, running through deep depressions, and dividing the high ground into a series of bold undulations, level on the top, and with gentle slopes. The most important of the creeks is Young's Branch, surrounding on two sides the commanding eminence crowned by the Henry House, and joining Bull Run a short distance below the Stone Bridge. That part of the field which borders on Flat Run, and lies immediately north of Manassas Junction, is generally thickly wooded; but shortly after passing New Market, the Manassas-Sudley road, running north-west, emerges into more open country, and, from the Henry House onward, passes over several parallel ridges, deep in grass and corn, and studded between with groves of oak and pine. Here the large fields, without hedges, and scantily fenced, formed an admirable manœuvre ground; the wide depressions of the creeks, separating the crests of the ridges by a space of fifteen or sixteen hundred yards, gave free play to the artillery; the long easy slopes could be swept by fire, and the groves were no obstruction to the view.

[1] O. R., vol. ii., p. 505.

L 2

The left flank of the Confederate position, facing north, on either side of the Manassas-Sudley road, was thus an ideal battle-field.

Sunday morning, the 21st of July, broke clear and warm. Through a miscarriage of orders, the Confederate offensive movement was delayed; and soon after six o'clock the July 21. Federals opened with musketry and artillery 6.30 A.M. against the small brigade commanded by Colonel Evans, which held the Stone Bridge on the extreme left of the Confederate line. An hour later the Shenandoah brigades, Bee's, Bartow's, and Jackson's, together with Bonham's, were ordered up in support. The attack was 8.30 A.M. feebly pressed, and at 8.30 Evans, observing a heavy cloud of dust rising above the woods to the north of the Warrenton road, became satisfied that the movement to his front was but a feint, and that a column of the enemy was meanwhile marching to turn his flank by way of Sudley Springs, about two miles north-west. Sending back this information to the next brigade, he left four companies to hold the bridge; and with six companies of riflemen, a battalion called the Louisiana Tigers, and two six-pounder howitzers, he moved across Young's Branch, and took post on 9 A.M. the Matthews Hill, a long ridge, which, at the same elevation, faces the Henry Hill.

Evans' soldierly instinct had penetrated the design of the Federal commander, and his ready assumption of responsibility threw a strong force across the path of the turning column, and gave time for his superiors to alter their dispositions and bring up the reserves.

The Federal force opposite the Stone Bridge consisted of a whole division; and its commander, General Tyler, had been instructed to divert attention, by means of a vigorous demonstration, from the march of Hunter's and Heintzleman's divisions to a ford near Sudley Springs. Part of the Fifth Division was retained in reserve at Centreville, and part threatened the fords over Bull Run below the Stone Bridge. The Fourth Division had been left upon the railroad, seven miles in rear of Centreville, in order to guard the communications with Washington.

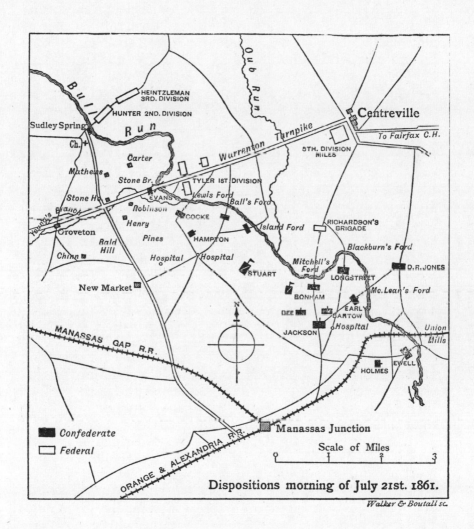

Walker & Boutall sc.

HEINTZLEMAN 3RD. DIVISION

HUNTER 2ND. DIVISION

Sudley Spring
Ch.

Bull

Run

Oub Run

Centreville

To Fairfax C.H.

Carter

Warrenton Turnpike

5TH. DIVISION MILES

Matheus

Stone Br.

TYLER 1ST DIVISION

Stone Ho.

Lewis Ford

Ball's Ford

Young's Branch

EVANS

Robinson

COCKE

Island Ford

RICHARDSON'S BRIGADE

Groveton

Henry

Bald Hill

Pines

HAMPTON

Blackburn's Ford

Chinn

Hospital

Hospital

Mitchell's Ford

LONGSTREET

D.R.JONES

STUART

Mc. Lean's Ford

New Market

BONHAM

DEE

EARLY BARTOW

Hospital

JACKSON

Union Mills

MANASSAS GAP R.R.

N

HOLMES

EWELL

■ *Confederate*

□ *Federal*

Manassas Junction

Scale of Miles

0   1   2   3

ORANGE & ALEXANDRIA R.R.

Dispositions morning of July 21st. 1861.

Already, in forming the line of march, there had been much confusion. The divisions had bivouacked in loose order, without any regard for the morrow's movements, and their concentration previous to the advance was very tedious. The brigades crossed each other's route; the march was slow; and the turning column, blocked by Tyler's division on its way to the Stone Bridge, was delayed for nearly three hours. At last, however, Hunter and Heintzleman crossed Sudley Ford; and after marching a mile in the direction of Manassas Junction, the leading brigade struck Evans' riflemen.

9.30 A.M. The Confederates were concealed by a fringe of woods, and the Federals were twice repulsed. But supports came crowding up, and Evans sent back for reinforcements. The fight had lasted for an hour. It was near eleven o'clock, and the check to the enemy's advance had given time for the Confederates to form a line of battle on the Henry Hill. Bee and Bartow, accompanied by Imboden's battery, were in position; Hampton's Legion, a regiment raised and commanded by an officer who was one of the wealthiest planters in South Carolina, and who became one of the finest soldiers in the Confederacy, was not far behind; and Jackson was coming up.[1]

Again the situation was saved by the prompt initiative of a brigade commander. Bee had been ordered to support the troops at the Stone Bridge. Moving forward towards the Henry Hill, he had been informed by a mounted orderly that the whole Federal army seemed to be moving to the north-west. A signal officer on the plateau who had caught the glint of the brass field-pieces which accompanied the hostile column, still several miles distant, had sent the message. Bee waited for no further instructions. Ordering Bartow to follow, he climbed the Henry Hill. The wide and beautiful landscape lay spread before him; Evans' small command was nearly a mile distant, on the Matthews

---

[1] Hunter and Heintzleman had 13,200 officers and men; Tyler, 12,000. Bee and Bartow had 3,200 officers and men; Hampton, 630; Jackson, 3,000.

Hill; and on the ridges to the far north-west he saw the glitter of many bayonets.

Rapidly placing his battery in position near the Henry House, Bee formed a line of battle on the crest above Young's Branch; but very shortly afterwards, acceding to an appeal for help from Evans, he hurried his troops forward to the Matthews Hill. His new position protected the rear of the companies which held the Stone Bridge; and so long as the bridge was held the two wings of the Federal army were unable to co-operate. But on the Matthews Hill, the enemy's strength, especially in artillery, was overwhelming; and the Confederates were soon compelled to fall back to the Henry Hill. McDowell had already sent word to Tyler to force the Stone Bridge; and Sherman's brigade of this division, passing the stream by a ford, threatened the flank of Bee and Evans as they retreated across Young's Branch.

11 A.M.

The Federals now swarmed over the Matthews Hill; but Imboden's battery, which Bee had again posted on the Henry Hill, and Hampton's Legion, occupying the Robinson House, a wooden tenement on the open spur which projects towards the Stone Bridge, covered the retirement of the discomfited brigades. They were not, however, suffered to fall back unharassed.

A long line of guns, following fast upon their tracks, and crossing the fields at a gallop, came into action on the opposite slope. In vain Imboden's gunners, with their pieces well placed behind a swell of ground, strove to divert their attention from the retreating infantry, now climbing the slopes of the Henry Hill. The Federal batteries, powerful in numbers, in discipline, and in *matériel*, plied their fire fast. The shells fell in quick succession amongst the disordered ranks of the Southern regiments, and not all the efforts of their officers could stay their flight.

The day seemed lost. Strong masses of Northern infantry were moving forward past the Stone House on the Warrenton turnpike. Hampton's Legion was retiring on the right. Imboden's battery, with but three rounds remaining for each piece, galloped back across the Henry Hill, and this commanding height, the key of the battle-ground, was abandoned to the enemy. But help was at hand. Jackson, like Bee and Bartow, had been ordered to the Stone Bridge. Hearing the heavy fire to his left increasing in intensity, he had turned the head of his column towards the most pressing danger, and had sent a messenger to Bee to announce his coming. As he pushed rapidly forward, part of the troops he intended to support swept by in disorder to the rear. Imboden's battery came dashing back, and that officer, meeting Jackson, expressed with a profanity which was evidently displeasing to the general his disgust at being left without support. 'I'll support your battery,' was the brief reply; 'unlimber right here.' At this moment appeared General Bee, approaching at full gallop, and he and Jackson met face to face. The 11.30 A.M. latter was cool and composed; Bee covered with dust and sweat, his sword in his hand, and his horse foaming. 'General,' he said, 'they are beating us back!' 'Then, sir, we will give them the bayonet;' the thin lips closed like a vice, and the First Brigade, pressing up the slope, formed into line on the eastern edge of the Henry Hill.

Jackson's determined bearing inspired Bee with renewed confidence. He turned bridle and galloped back to the ravine where his officers were attempting to reform their broken companies. Riding into the midst of the throng, he pointed with his sword to the Virginia regiments, deployed in well-ordered array on the height above. 'Look!' he shouted, 'there is Jackson standing like a stone wall! Rally behind the Virginians!' The men took up the cry; and the happy augury of the expression, applied at a time when defeat seemed imminent and hearts were failing, was remembered when the danger had passed away.

The position which Jackson had occupied was the strongest that could be found. He had not gone forward to the crest which looks down upon Young's Branch, and commands the slopes by which the Federals were advancing. From that crest extended a wide view, and a wide field of fire; but both flanks would have been exposed. The

Henry House was nothing more than a cottage; neither here nor elsewhere was there shelter for his riflemen, and they would have been exposed to the full force of the Federal artillery without power of reply. But on the eastern edge of the hill, where he had chosen to deploy, ran a belt of young pines, affording excellent cover, which merged into a dense oak wood near the Sudley road.

Along the edge of the pines Jackson placed his regiments, with six guns to support them. Lying in rear of the guns were the 4th and 27th Virginia; on the right was the 5th; on the left the 2nd and 33rd. Both flanks were in the woods, and Stuart, whom Jackson had called upon to secure his left, was watching the ground beyond the road. To the front, for a space of five hundred yards, stretched the level crest of the hill; and the ground beyond the Henry House, dipping to the valley of Young's Branch, where the Federals were now gathering, was wholly unseen. But as the tactics of Wellington so often proved, a position from which the view is limited, well in rear of a crest line, may be exceedingly strong for defence, provided that troops who hold it can use the bayonet. It would be difficult in the extreme for the Federals to pave the way for their attack with artillery. From the guns on the Matthews Hill the Virginia regiments were well sheltered, and the range was long. To do effective work the hostile batteries would have to cross Young's Branch, ascend the Henry Hill, and come into action within five hundred yards of Jackson's line. Even if they were able to hold their ground at so short a range, they could make no accurate practice under the fire of the Confederate marksmen.

In rear of Jackson's line, Bee, Bartow, and Evans were rallying their men, when Johnston and Beauregard, 12 noon. compelled, by the unexpected movement of the Federals, to abandon all idea of attack, appeared upon the Henry Hill. They were accompanied by two batteries of artillery, Pendleton's and Alburtis'. The colours of the broken regiments were ordered to the front, and the men rallied, taking post on Jackson's right. The

moment was critical.   The blue masses of the Federals, the
dust rolling high above them, were already descending the
opposite slopes.   The guns flashed fiercely through the
yellow cloud ; and the Confederate force was but a handful.
Three brigades had been summoned from the fords ; but
the nearest was four miles distant, and many of the troops
upon the plateau were already half-demoralised by retreat.
The generals set themselves to revive the courage of their
soldiers.   Beauregard galloped along the line, cheering the
regiments in every portion of the field, and then, with the
colour-bearers accompanying him, rode forward to the crest.
Johnston was equally conspicuous.   The enemy's shells
were bursting on every side, and the shouts of the Confederates, recognising their leaders as they dashed across
the front, redoubled the uproar.   Meanwhile, before the
centre of his line, with an unconcern which had a marvellous
effect on his untried command, Jackson rode slowly to
and fro.   Except that his face was a little paler, and his
eyes brighter, he looked exactly as his men had seen him
so often on parade ; and as he passed along the crest above
them they heard from time to time the reassuring words,
uttered in a tone which betrayed no trace of excitement,
' Steady, men ! steady ! all's well ! '
    It was at this juncture, while the confusion of taking
up a new position with shattered and ill-drilled troops was
at the highest, that the battle lulled.   The Federal infantry, after defeating Bee and Evans, had to cross the deep
gully and marshy banks of Young's Branch, to climb the
slope of the Henry Hill, and to form for a fresh attack.
Even with trained soldiers a hot fight is so conducive of disorder, that it is difficult to initiate a rapid pursuit, and the
Northern regiments were very slow in resuming their formations.   At the same time, too, the fire of their batteries
became less heavy.   From their position beyond Young's
Branch the rifled guns had been able to ply the Confederate
lines with shell, and their effective practice had rendered
the work of rallying the troops exceedingly difficult.   But
when his infantry advanced, McDowell ordered one half
of his artillery, two fine batteries of regulars, made up

principally of rifled guns, to cross Young's Branch. This
respite was of the utmost value to the Confederates. The
men, encouraged by the gallant bearing of their leaders,
fell in at once upon the colours, and when Hunter's
regiments appeared on the further rim of the plateau
they were received with a fire which for a moment
drove them back. But the regular batteries were close at
hand, and as they came into action the battle became
general on the Henry Hill. The Federals had 16,000
infantry available ; the Confederates no more than 6,500.
But the latter were superior in artillery, 16 pieces confronting 12. The Federal guns, however, were of heavier
calibre ; the gunners were old soldiers, and both friend
and foe testify to the accuracy of their fire, their fine
discipline, and staunch endurance. The infantry, on the
other hand, was not well handled. The attack was purely
frontal. No attempt whatever was made to turn the
Confederate flanks, although the Stone Bridge, except for
the abattis, was now open, and Johnston's line might
easily have been taken in reverse. Nor does it appear that
the cavalry was employed to ascertain where the flanks
rested. Moreover, instead of massing the troops for a determined onslaught, driven home by sheer weight of numbers,
the attack was made by successive brigades, those in rear
waiting till those in front had been defeated ; and, in the
same manner, the brigades attacked by successive regiments. Such tactics were inexcusable. It was certainly
necessary to push the attack home before the Confederate
reinforcements could get up ; and troops who had never
drilled in mass would have taken much time to assume
the orthodox formation of several lines of battle, closely
supporting one another. Yet there was no valid reason,
beyond the inexperience of the generals in dealing with
large bodies, that brigades should have been sent into action
piecemeal, or that the flanks of the defence should have
been neglected. The fighting, nevertheless, was fierce. The
Federal regiments, inspirited by their success on the
Matthews Hill, advanced with confidence, and soon pushed
forward past the Henry House. 'The contest that ensued,'

says General Imboden, ' was terrific. Jackson ordered me
to go from battery to battery and see that the guns were
properly aimed and the fuses cut the right length. This
was the work of but a few minutes. On returning to the left
of the line of guns, I stopped to ask General Jackson's permission to rejoin my battery. The fight was just then hot
enough to make him feel well. His eyes fairly blazed. He
had a way of throwing up his left hand with the open palm
towards the person he was addressing. And, as he told me
to go, he made this gesture. The air was full of flying
missiles, and as he spoke he jerked down his hand, and I
saw that blood was streaming from it. I exclaimed,
"General, you are wounded." "Only a scratch—a mere
scratch," he replied, and binding it hastily with a handkerchief, he galloped away along his line.' [1]

When the battle was at its height, and across that narrow
space, not more than five hundred yards in width, the
cannon thundered, and the long lines of infantry struggled
for the mastery, the two Federal batteries, protected by
two regiments of infantry on their right, advanced
to a more effective position. The movement was
fatal. Stuart, still guarding the Confederate left, was eagerly
awaiting his opportunity, and now, with 150 troopers, filing
through the fences on Bald Hill, he boldly charged the
enemy's right. The regiment thus assailed, a body of
Zouaves, in blue and scarlet, with white turbans, was
ridden down, and almost at the same moment the 33rd
Virginia, posted on Jackson's left, charged forward from
the copse in which they had been hidden. The uniforms
in the two armies at this time were much alike, and from
the direction of their approach it was difficult at first for
the officers in charge of the Federal batteries to make
sure that the advancing troops were not their own. A
moment more and the doubtful regiment proved its identity
by a deadly volley, delivered at a range of seventy yards.
Every gunner was shot down; the teams were almost annihilated, and several officers fell killed or wounded. The
Zouaves, already much shaken by Stuart's well-timed

1.30 P.M.

[1] *Battles and Leaders*, vol. i., p. 236.

charge, fled down the slopes, dragging with them another regiment of infantry.

Three guns alone escaped the marksmen of the 33rd. The remainder stood upon the field, silent and abandoned, surrounded by dying horses, midway between the opposing lines.

This success, however, brought but short relief to the Confederates. The enemy was not yet done with. Fresh regiments passed to the attack. The 33rd was driven back, and the thin line upon the plateau was hard put to it to retain its ground. The Southerners had lost heavily. Bee and Bartow had been killed, and Hampton wounded. Few reinforcements had reached the Henry Hill. Stragglers and skulkers were streaming to the rear. The Federals were thronging forward, and it seemed that the exhausted defenders must inevitably give way before the successive blows of superior numbers. The troops were losing confidence. Yet no thought of defeat crossed Jackson's mind. 'General,' said an officer, riding hastily towards him, 'the day is going against us.' 'If you think so, sir,' was the quiet reply, 'you had better not say anything about it.' And although affairs seemed desperate, in reality the crisis of the battle had already passed. McDowell had but two brigades remaining in reserve, and one of these—of Tyler's division—was still beyond Bull Run. His troops were thoroughly exhausted; they had been marching and fighting since midnight; the day was intensely hot; they had encountered fierce resistance ; their rifled batteries had been silenced, and the Confederate reinforcements were coming up. Two of Bonham's regiments had taken post on Jackson's right, and a heavy force was approaching on the left. Kirby Smith's brigade, of the Army of the Shenandoah, coming up by train, had reached Manassas Junction while the battle was in progress. It was immediately ordered to the field, and had been already instructed by Johnston to turn the enemy's right.

But before the weight of Smith's 1,900 bayonets could be thrown into the scale, the Federals made a vigorous effort to carry the Henry Hill. Those portions of the Confederate line which stood on the open ground gave way before them. Some of the guns, ordered to take up a position from which they could cover the retreat, were limbering up ; and with the exception of the belt of pines, the plateau was abandoned to the hostile infantry, who were beginning to press forward at every point. The Federal engineers were already clearing away the abattis from the Stone Bridge, in order to give passage to Tyler's third brigade and a battery of artillery ; 'and all were certain,' says McDowell, 'that the day was ours.'

Jackson's men were lying beneath the crest of the plateau. Only one of his regiments—the 33rd—had as yet 2.45 P.M. been engaged in the open, and his guns in front still held their own. Riding to the centre of his line, where the 2nd and 4th Virginia were stationed, he gave orders for a counterstroke. 'Reserve your fire till they come within fifty yards, then fire and give them the bayonet ; and when you charge, yell like furies!' Right well did the hot Virginian blood respond. Inactive from the stroke of noon till three o'clock, with the crash and cries of battle in their ears, and the shells ploughing gaps in their recumbent ranks, the men were chafing under the stern discipline which held them back from the conflict they longed to join. The Federals swept on, extending from the right and left, cheering as they came, and following the flying batteries in the ardour of success. Suddenly, a long grey line sprang from the ground in their very faces ; a rolling volley threw them back in confusion ; and then, with their fierce shouts pealing high above the tumult, the 2nd and 4th Virginia, supported by the 5th, charged forward across the hill. At the same moment that the enemy's centre was thus unexpectedly assailed, Kirby Smith's fresh brigade bore down upon the flank,[1] and Beauregard, with ready judgment, dispatched his staff officers to order a general advance. The broken remnants of Bee, Hampton, and Evans advanced upon Jackson's right, and victory, long wavering, crowned the standards of the South. The Federals were driven past

[1] General Kirby Smith being severely wounded, the command of this brigade devolved upon Colonel Elzey.

the guns, now finally abandoned, past the Henry House, and down the slope.   McDowell made one desperate endeavour to stay the rout.   Howard's brigade was rapidly thrown in. But the centre had been completely broken by Jackson's charge ; the right was giving way, and the Confederates, manning the captured guns, turned them on the masses which covered the fields below.

Howard, although his men fought bravely, was easily repulsed; in a few minutes not a single Federal soldier, save the dead and dying, was to be seen upon the plateau.

A final stand was made by McDowell along Young's
3.30 P.M. Branch; and there, at half-past three, a line of battle was once more established, the battalion of regular infantry forming a strong centre.   But another Confederate brigade, under General Early, had now arrived, and again the enemy's right was overthrown, while Beauregard, leaving Jackson, whose brigade had lost all order and many men in its swift advance, to hold the plateau, swept forward towards the Matthews Hill.   The movement was decisive. McDowell's volunteers broke up in the utmost confusion. The Confederate infantry was in no condition to pursue, but the cavalry was let loose, and before long the retreat became a panic.   The regular battalion, composed of young soldiers, but led by experienced officers, alone preserved its discipline, moving steadily in close order through the throng of fugitives, and checking the pursuing troopers by its firm and confident bearing.   The remainder of the army dissolved into a mob. It was not that the men were completely demoralised, but simply that discipline had not become a habit.   They had marched as individuals, going just so far as they pleased, and halting when they pleased ; they had fought as individuals, bravely enough, but with little combination ; and when they found that they were beaten, as individuals they retreated. ' The old soldier,' wrote one of the regular officers a week later, 'feels safe in the ranks, unsafe out of the ranks, and the greater the danger the more pertinaciously he clings to his place.   The volunteer of three months never attains this instinct of discipline.   Under danger, and

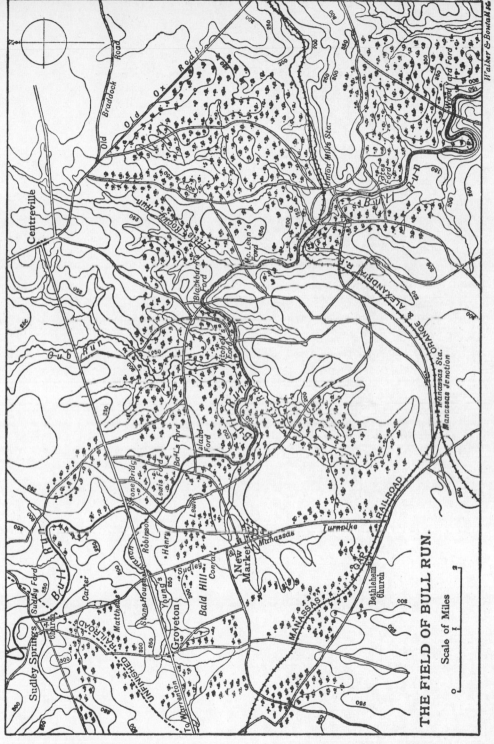

THE FIELD OF BULL RUN.

Scale of Miles

VOL. I.

M

even under mere excitement, he flies away from his ranks, and hopes for safety in dispersion. At four o'clock in the afternoon of the 21st there were more than 12,000 volunteers on the battle-field of Bull Run who had entirely lost their regimental organisation. They could no longer be handled as troops, for the officers and men were not together. Men and officers mingled together promiscuously; and it is worthy of remark that this disorganisation did not result from defeat or fear, for up to four o'clock we had been uniformly successful. The instinct of discipline which keeps every man in his place had not been acquired. We cannot suppose that the enemy had attained a higher degree of discipline than our own, but they acted on the defensive, and were not equally exposed to disorganisation.'[1]

'Cohesion was lost,' says one of McDowell's staff; 'and the men walked quietly off. There was no special excitement except that arising from the frantic efforts of officers to stop men who paid little or no attention to anything that was said; and there was no panic, in the ordinary sense and meaning of the word, until the retiring soldiers, guns, waggons, Congressmen and carriages, were fired upon, on the road east of Bull Run.'[2]

At Centreville the reserve division stood fast; and the fact that these troops were proof against the infection of panic and the exaggerated stories of the fugitives is in itself strong testimony to the native courage of the soldiery.

A lack of competent Staff officers, which, earlier in the day, had prevented an advance on Centreville by the Confederate right, brought Johnston's arrangements for pursuit to naught. The cavalry, weak in numbers, was soon incumbered with squads of prisoners; darkness fell upon the field, and the defeated army streamed over the roads to Washington, followed only by its own fears.

Why the Confederate generals did not follow up their success on the following day is a question round which controversy raged for many a year. Deficiencies in com-

[1] Report of Captain Woodbury, U.S. Engineers, O. R., vol. ii., p. 334.
[2] General J. B. Fry, *Battles and Leaders*, vol. i., p. 191.

M 2

missariat and transport; the disorganisation of the army after the victory; the difficulties of a direct attack upon Washington, defended as it was by a river a mile broad, with but a single bridge, and patrolled by gunboats; the determination of the Government to limit its military operations to a passive defence of Confederate territory, have all been pressed into service as excuses. 'Give me 10,000 fresh troops,' said Jackson, as the surgeon dressed his wound, 'and I would be in Washington to-morrow.' Before twenty-four hours had passed reinforcements had increased the strength of Johnston's army to 40,000. Want of organisation had undoubtedly prevented McDowell from winning a victory on the 19th or 20th, but pursuit is a far less difficult business than attack. There was nothing to interfere with a forward movement. There were supplies along the railway, and if the mechanism for their distribution and the means for their carriage were wanting, the counties adjoining the Potomac were rich and fertile. Herds of bullocks were grazing in the pastures, and the barns of the farmers were loaded with grain. It was not a long supply train that was lacking, nor an experienced staff, nor even well-disciplined battalions; but a general who grasped the full meaning of victory, who understood how a defeated army, more especially of new troops, yields at a touch, and who, above all, saw the necessity of giving the North no leisure to develop her immense resources. For three days Jackson impatiently awaited the order to advance, and his men were held ready with three days' cooked rations in their haversacks. But his superiors gave no sign, and he was reluctantly compelled to abandon all hope of reaping the fruits of victory.

It is true that the Confederates were no more fit for offensive operations than McDowell's troops. 'Our army,' says General Johnston, 'was more disorganised by victory than that of the United States by defeat.' But it is to be remembered that if the Southerners had moved into Maryland, crossing the Potomac by some of the numerous fords near Harper's Ferry, they would have found no organised opposition, save the *débris* of McDowell's army, between them

and the Northern capital.   On July 26, five days after the
battle, the general who was to succeed McDowell arrived in
Washington and rode round the city.   ' I found,' he wrote,
' no preparations whatever for defence, not even to the extent
of putting the troops in military position.   Not a regiment
was properly encamped, not a single avenue of approach
guarded.   All was chaos, and the streets, hotels, and bar-
rooms were filled with drunken officers and men, absent from
their regiments without leave, a perfect pandemonium.
Many had even gone to their homes, their flight from Bull
Run terminating in New York, or even in New Hampshire
and Maine.   There was really nothing to prevent a small
cavalry force from riding into the city.   A determined attack
would doubtless have carried Arlington Heights and placed
the city at the mercy of a battery of rifled guns.   If the
Secessionists attached any value to the possession of
Washington, they committed their greatest error in not
following up the victory of Bull Run.'   On the same date,
the Secretary of War, Mr. Stanton, wrote as follows :
' The capture of Washington seems now to be inevitable ;
during the whole of Monday and Tuesday [July 22 and 23]
it might have been taken without resistance.   The rout,
overthrow, and demoralisation of the whole army were
complete.' [1]

Of his own share in the battle, either at the time or
afterwards, Jackson said but little.   A day or two after the
battle an anxious crowd was gathered round the post-office
at Lexington, awaiting intelligence from the front.   A letter
was handed to the Rev. Dr. White, who, recognising the
handwriting, exclaimed to the eager groups about him,
' Now we shall know all the facts.'   On opening it he found
the following, and no more :

' My dear Pastor,—In my tent last night, after a fatiguing
day's service, I remembered that I had failed to send you my
contribution to our coloured Sunday school.   Enclosed you
will find my check for that object, which please acknowledge
at your earliest convenience, and oblige yours faithfully,
T. J. Jackson.'

[1] *McClellan's Own Story*, pp. 66, 67.

To his wife, however, he was less reserved. 'Yesterday,' he wrote, we 'fought a great battle and gained a great victory, for which all the glory is due to God alone. . . . Whilst great credit is due to other parts of our gallant army, God made my brigade more instrumental than any other in repulsing the main attack. This is for your information only—say nothing about it. Let others speak praise, not myself.'

Again, on August 5: 'And so you think the papers ought to say more about your husband. My brigade is not a brigade of newspaper correspondents. I know that the First Brigade was the first to meet and pass our retreating forces—to push on with no other aid than the smiles of God; to boldly take up its position with the artillery that was under my command—to arrest the victorious foe in his onward progress—to hold him in check until the reinforcements arrived—and finally to charge bayonets, and, thus advancing, to pierce the enemy's centre. I am well satisfied with what it did, and so are my generals, Johnston and Beauregard. It is not to be expected that I should receive the credit that Generals Johnston and Beauregard would, because I was under them; but I am thankful to my ever-kind Heavenly Father that He makes me content to await His own good time and pleasure for commendation—knowing that all things work together for my good. If my brigade can always play so important and useful a part as it did in the last battle, I trust I shall ever be most grateful. As you think the papers do not notice me enough, I send a specimen, which you will see from the upper part of the paper is a " leader." My darling, never distrust our God, Who doeth all things well. In due time He will make manifest all His pleasure, which is all His people should desire. You must not be concerned at seeing other parts of the army lauded, and my brigade not mentioned. Truth is mighty and will prevail. When the official reports are published, if not before, I expect to see justice done to this noble body of patriots.' [1]

These letters reveal a generous pride in the valour of his

---

[1] Both Johnston and Beauregard, in their official reports, did full justice to Jackson and his brigade.

troops, and a very human love of approbation struggles with the curb which his religious principles had placed on his ambition. Like Nelson, he felt perhaps that before long he would have ' a Gazette of his own.' But still, of his own achievements, of his skilful tactics, of his personal behaviour, of his well-timed orders, he spoke no word, and the victory was ascribed to a higher power. ' The charge of the 2nd and 4th Virginia,' he wrote in his modest report, ' through the blessing of God, Who gave us the victory, pierced the centre of the enemy.' [1]

And Jackson's attitude was that of the Southern people. When the news of Bull Run reached Richmond, and through the crowds that thronged the streets passed the tidings of the victory, there was neither wild excitement nor uproarious joy. No bonfires lit the darkness of the night ; no cannon thundered out salutes ; the steeples were silent till the morrow, and then were heard only the solemn tones that called the people to prayer. It was resolved, on the day following the battle, by the Confederate Congress : ' That we recognise the hand of the Most High God, the King of kings and Lord of lords, in the glorious victory with which He has crowned our arms at Manassas, and that the people of these Confederate States are invited, by appropriate services on the ensuing Sabbath, to offer up their united thanksgivings and prayers for this mighty deliverance.'

The spoils of Bull Run were large ; 1,500 prisoners, 25 guns, ten stand of colours, several thousand rifles, a large quantity of ammunition and hospital stores, twenty-six waggons, and several ambulances were left in the victors' hands. The Federal losses were 460 killed and 1,124 wounded ; the Confederate, 387 killed, 1,582 wounded, and 13 missing. The First Brigade suffered more severely than any other in the Southern army. Of 3,000 officers and men, 488 were killed or wounded, nearly a fourth of the total loss.

A few days after the battle Johnston advanced to Centreville, and from the heights above the broad Potomac his cavalry vedettes looked upon the spires of Washington.

[1] O. R., vol. ii., p. 482.

But it was in vain that the Confederate troopers rode to and fro on the river bank and watered their horses within sight of the Capitol. The enemy was not to be beguiled across the protecting stream. But it was not from fear. Although the disaster had been as crushing as unexpected, it was bravely met. The President's demand for another army was cheerfully complied with. Volunteers poured in from every State. The men were no longer asked to serve for three months, but for three years. Washington became transformed into an enormous camp; great earthworks rose on the surrounding heights; and the training of the new levies went steadily forward. There was no cry for immediate action. Men were not wanting who believed that the task of coercion was impossible. Able statesmen and influential journalists advised the President to abandon the attempt. But Lincoln, true to the trust which had been committed to his keeping, never flinched from his resolve that the Union should be restored. He, too, stood like a wall between his defeated legions and the victorious foe. Nor was the nation less determined. The dregs of humiliation had been drained, and though the draught was bitter it was salutary. The President was sustained with no half-hearted loyalty. His political opponents raved and threatened; but under the storm of recrimination the work of reorganising the army went steadily forward, and the people were content that until the generals declared the army fit for action the hour of vengeance should be postponed.

To the South, Bull Run was a Pyrrhic victory. It relieved Virginia of the pressure of the invasion; it proved to the world that the attitude of the Confederacy was something more than the reckless revolt of a small section; but it led the Government to indulge vain hopes of foreign intervention, and it increased the universal contempt for the military qualities of the Northern soldiers. The hasty judgment of the people construed a single victory as proof of their superior capacity for war, and the defeat of McDowell's army was attributed to the cowardice of his volunteers. The opinion was absolutely erroneous. Some of the Federal regiments had misbehaved, it is true ; seized with sudden panic, to which all raw troops are peculiarly susceptible, they had dispersed before the strong counter-stroke of the Confederates. But the majority had displayed a sterling courage. There can be little question that the spirit of the infantry depends greatly on the staunchness of the artillery. A single battery, pushed boldly forward into the front of battle, has often restored the vigour of a waver-ing line. Although the losses it inflicts may not be large, the moral effect of its support is undeniable. So long as the guns hold fast victory seems possible. But when these useful auxiliaries are driven back or captured a general depression becomes inevitable. The retreat of the artillery strikes a chill into the fighting line which is ominous of defeat, and it is a wise regulation that compels the bat-teries, even when their ammunition is exhausted, to stand their ground. The Federal infantry at Bull Run had seen their artillery overwhelmed, the teams destroyed, the gunners shot down, and the enemy's riflemen swarming amongst the abandoned pieces. But so vigorous had been their efforts to restore the battle, that the front of the defence had been with difficulty maintained ; the guns, though they were eventually lost, had been retaken ; and without the assistance of their artillery, but exposed to the fire, at closest range, of more than one battery, the Northern regiments had boldly pushed forward across the Henry Hill. The Con-federates, during the greater part of the battle, were certainly outnumbered ; but at the close they were the stronger, and the piecemeal attacks of the Federals neutralised the superiority which the invading army originally possessed.

McDowell appears to have employed 18,000 troops in the attack ; Johnston and Beauregard about the same number.[1]

A comparison of the relative strength of the two armies, considering that raw troops have a decided advantage on the defensive, detracts, to a certain degree, from the credit of the victory ; and it will hardly be questioned that had

[1] For the strength of divisions and brigades, see the Note at the end of the chapter.

the tactics of the Federals been better the victory would have been theirs. The turning movement by Sudley Springs was a skilful manœuvre, and completely surprised both Johnston and Beauregard. It was undoubtedly risky, but it was far less dangerous than a direct attack on the strong position along Bull Run.

The retention of the Fourth Division between Washington and Centreville would seem to have been a blunder; another 5,000 men on the field of battle should certainly have turned the scale. But more men were hardly wanted. The Federals during the first period of the fight were strong enough to have seized the Henry Hill. Bee, Bartow, Evans, and Hampton had been driven in, and Jackson alone stood fast. A strong and sustained attack, supported by the fire of the regular batteries, must have succeeded.[1] The Federal regiments, however, were practically incapable of movement under fire. The least change of position broke them into fragments; there was much wild firing; it was impossible to manœuvre; and the courage of individuals proved a sorry substitute for order and cohesion. The Confederates owed their victory simply and solely to the fact that their enemies had not yet learned to use their strength.

The summer months went by without further fighting on the Potomac; but the camps at Fairfax and at Centreville saw the army of Manassas thinned by furloughs and by sickness. The Southern youth had come out for battle, and the monotonous routine of the outpost line and the parade-ground was little to their taste. The Government dared not refuse the numberless applications for leave of absence, the more so that in the crowded camps the sultry heat of the Virginia woodlands bred disease of a virulent type. The First Brigade seems to have escaped from all these evils. Its commander found his health improved by his life in the open air. His wound

---

[1] 'Had an attack,' said General Johnston, 'been made in force, with double line of battle, such as any major-general in the United States service would now make, we could not have held [the position] half an hour, for they would have enveloped us on both flanks.'—*Campaigns of the Army of the Potomac*, W. Swinton, p. 58.

had been painful. A finger was broken, but the hand was saved, and some temporary inconvenience alone resulted. As he claimed no furlough for himself, so he permitted no absence from duty among his troops. 'I can't be absent,' he wrote to his wife, ' as my attention is necessary in preparing my troops for hard fighting, should it be required; and as my officers and soldiers are not permitted to visit their wives and families, I ought not to see mine. It might make the troops feel that they are badly treated, and that I consult my own comfort, regardless of theirs.'

In September his wife joined him for a few days at Centreville, and later came Dr. White, at his invitation, to preach to his command. Beyond a few fruitless marches to support the cavalry on the outposts, of active service there was none. But Jackson was not the man to let the time pass uselessly. He had his whole brigade under his hand, a force which wanted but one quality to make it an instrument worthy of the hand that wielded it, and that quality was discipline. Courage and enthusiasm it possessed in abundance; and when both were untrained the Confederate was a more useful soldier than the Northerner. In the South nearly every man was a hunter, accustomed from boyhood to the use of firearms. Game was abundant, and it was free to all. Sport in one form or another was the chief recreation of the people, and their pastoral pursuits left them much leisure for its indulgence. Every great plantation had its pack of hounds, and fox-hunting, an heirloom from the English colonists, still flourished. His stud was the pride of every Southern gentleman, and the love of horse-flesh was inherent in the whole population. No man walked when he could ride, and hundreds of fine horsemen, mounted on steeds of famous lineage, recruited the Confederate squadrons.

But, despite their skill with the rifle, their hunter's craft, and their dashing horsemanship, the first great battle had been hardly won. The city-bred Northerners, unused to arms and uninured to hardship, had fought with extraordinary determination; and the same want of discipline that had driven them in rout to Washington had dissolved the victorious Confederates into a tumultuous mob.[1] If Jackson knew the worth of his volunteers, he was no stranger to their shortcomings. His thoughts might be crystallised in the words of Wellington, words which should never be forgotten by those nations which depend for their defence on the services of their citizen soldiery.

'They want,' said the great Duke, speaking of the Portuguese in 1809, 'the habits and the spirit of soldiers, —the habits of command on one side, and of obedience on the other—mutual confidence between officers and men.'

In order that during the respite now offered he might instil these habits into his brigade, Jackson neither took furlough himself nor granted it to others. His regiments were constantly exercised on the parade-ground. Shoulder to shoulder they advanced and retired, marched and countermarched, massed in column, formed line to front or flank, until they learned to move as a machine, until the limbs obeyed before the order had passed from ear to brain, until obedience became an instinct and cohesion a necessity of their nature. They learned to listen for the word of the officer, to look to him before they moved hand or foot; and, in that subjection of their own individuality to the will of their superior, they acquired that steadiness in battle, that energy on the march, that discipline in quarters which made the First Brigade worthy of the name it had already won. 'Every officer and soldier,' said their commander, 'who is able to do duty ought to be busily engaged in military preparation by hard drilling, in order that, through the blessing of God, we may be victorious in the battles which in His all-wise providence may await us.'

Jackson's tactical ideas, as regards the fire of infantry, expressed at this time, are worth recording. 'I rather think,' he said, 'that fire by file [independent firing] is best on the whole, for it gives the enemy an idea that the

---

[1] Colonel Williams, of the 5th Virginia, writes that the Stonewall Brigade was a notable exception to the general disintegration, and that it was in good condition for immediate service on the morning after the battle.

fire is heavier than if it was by company or battalion
(volley firing). Sometimes, however, one may be best,
sometimes the other, according to circumstances. But my
opinion is that there ought not to be much firing at all.
My idea is that the best mode of fighting is to reserve
your fire till the enemy get—or you get them—to close
quarters. Then deliver one deadly, deliberate fire—and
charge ! '

Although the newspapers did scant justice to the part
played by the brigade in the battle of Bull Run, Bee's
epithet survived, and Jackson became known as ' Stonewall '
throughout the army. To one of his acquaintances the
general revealed the source of his composure under fire.
' Three days after the battle, hearing that Jackson was
suffering from his wound, I rode,' writes Imboden, ' to his
quarters near Centreville. Of course the battle was the only
topic discussed during breakfast. " General," I remarked,
" how is it that you can keep so cool, and appear so utterly
insensible to danger in such a storm of shell and bullets as
rained about you when your hand was hit ? " He instantly
became grave and reverential in his manner, and answered,
in a low tone of great earnestness : " Captain, my religious
belief teaches me to feel as safe in battle as in bed. God
has fixed the time for my death. I do not concern myself
about that, but to be always ready, no matter when it may
overtake me." He added, after a pause, looking me full in
the face : " That is the way all men should live, and then
all would be equally brave." ' [1]

Although the war upon the borders had not yet
touched the cities of the South, the patriotism of Virginia
saw with uneasiness the inroads of the enemy in that portion of the State which lies beyond the Alleghanies, especially
the north-west. The country was overrun with Federal
soldiers, and part of the population of the district had
declared openly for the Union. In that district was
Jackson's birth-place, the home of his childhood, and his
mother's grave. His interest and his affections were
bound by many ties to the country and the people, and in

[1] *Battles and Leaders*, vol. i., pp. 122, 123.

the autumn of 1861 he had not yet come to believe that they were at heart disloyal to their native State. A vigorous effort, he believed, might still restore to the Confederacy a splendid recruiting-ground, and he made no secret of his desire for employment in that region. The strategical advantages of this corner of Virginia were clearly apparent, as will be seen hereafter, to his perception. Along its western border runs the Ohio, a river navigable to its junction with the Mississippi, and giving an easy line of communication into the heart of Kentucky. Through its northern counties passed the Baltimore and Ohio Railroad, the main line of communication between Washington and the West; and alongside the railway ran the Chesapeake and Ohio Canal, a second and most important line of supply. Above all, projecting as it did towards the great lakes of the North, the north-western angle, or Virginia 'Panhandle,' narrowed the passage between East and West to an isthmus not more than a hundred miles in breadth. With this territory in the possession of the Confederates, the Federal dominions would be practically cut in two; and in North-western Virginia, traversed by many ranges of well-nigh pathless mountains, with few towns and still fewer roads, a small army might defy a large one with impunity.

On November 4 Jackson's wish was partially granted. He was assigned to the command of the Shenandoah Valley District, embracing the northern part of the area
Nov. 4. between the Alleghanies and the Blue Ridge. The order was received with gratitude, but dashed by the fact that he had to depart alone. 'Had this communication,' he said to Dr. White, 'not come as an order, I should instantly have declined it, and continued in command of my brave old brigade.'

Whether he or his soldiers felt the parting most it is hard to say. Certain it is that the men had a warm regard for their leader. There was no more about him at Centreville to attract the popular fancy than there had been at Harper's Ferry. When the troops passed in review the eye of the spectator turned at once to the trim carriage of Johnston and of Beauregard, to the glittering uniform of Stuart, to the superb chargers and the martial bearing of young officers fresh from the Indian frontier. The silent professor, absent and unsmiling, who dressed as plainly as he lived, had little in common with those dashing soldiers. The tent where every night the general and his staff gathered together for their evening devotions, where the conversation ran not on the merits of horse and hound, on strategy and tactics, but on the power of faith and the mysteries of the redemption, seemed out of place in an army of high-spirited youths. But, while they smiled at his peculiarities, the Confederate soldiers remembered the fierce counterstroke on the heights above Bull Run. If the Presbyterian general was earnest in prayer, they knew that he was prompt in battle and indefatigable in quarters. He had the respect of all men, and from his own brigade he had something more. Very early in their service, away by the rippling Shenandoah, they had heard the stories of his daring in Mexico. They had experienced his skill and coolness at Falling Waters; they had seen at Bull Run, while the shells burst in never-ending succession among the pines, the quiet figure riding slowly to and fro on the crest above them; they had heard the stern command, 'Wait till they come within fifty yards and then give them the bayonet,' and they had followed him far in that victorious rush into the receding ranks of their astonished foe.

Little wonder that these enthusiastic youths, new to the soldier's trade, should have been captivated by a nature so strong and fearless. The Stonewall Brigade had made Jackson a hero, and he had won more from them than their admiration. His incessant watchfulness for their comfort and well-being; the patient care with which he instructed them; his courtesy to the youngest private; the tact and thoughtfulness he showed in all his relations with them, had won their affection. His very peculiarities endeared him to them. 'Old Jack' or 'Stonewall' were his nicknames in the lines of his own command, and stories went round the camp fire of how he had been seen walking in the woods round Centreville absorbed in prayer, or lifting his left hand with that peculiar gesture which the men believed was an appeal to Heaven, but which, in reality, was made to relieve the pain of his wounded finger. But while they discussed his oddities, not a man in the brigade but acknowledged his ability, and when the time came not a man but regretted his departure.

His farewell to his troops was a striking scene. The forest, already donning its gorgeous autumnal robes, shut in the grassy clearing where the troops were drawn up. There stood the grey columns of the five regiments, with the colours, already tattered, waving in the mild November air. The general rode up, their own general, and not a sound was heard. Motionless and silent they stood, a veritable stone wall, whilst his eye ran along the ranks and scanned the familiar faces. ' I am not here to make a speech,' he said, ' but simply to say farewell. I first met you at Harper's Ferry, at the commencement of the war, and I cannot take leave of you without giving expression to my admiration of your conduct from that day to this, whether on the march, in the bivouac, or on the bloody plains of Manassas, where you gained the well-deserved reputation of having decided the fate of battle.

' Throughout the broad extent of country through which you have marched, by your respect for the rights and property of citizens, you have shown that you are soldiers not only to defend, but able and willing both to defend and protect. You have already won a brilliant reputation throughout the army of the whole Confederacy ; and I trust, in the future, by your deeds in the field, and by the assistance of the same kind Providence who has hitherto favoured our cause, you will win more victories and add lustre to the reputation you now enjoy. You have already gained a proud position in the future history of this our second War of Independence. I shall look with great anxiety to your future movements, and I trust whenever I shall hear of the First Brigade on the field of battle, it will be of still nobler deeds achieved, and higher reputation won ! ' Then there was a pause ; general and soldiers looked upon each other, and the heart of the leader went out to those who had followed him with such devotion. He had spoken his words of formal praise, but both he and they knew the bonds between them were too strong to be thus coldly severed.   For once he gave way to impulse; his eye kindled, and rising in his stirrups and throwing the reins upon his horse's neck, he spoke in tones which betrayed the proud memories that thronged upon him :—

'In the Army of the Shenandoah you were the First Brigade !   In the Army of the Potomac you were the First Brigade !   In the Second Corps of the army you are the First Brigade !   You are the First Brigade in the affections of your general, and I hope by your future deeds and bearing you will be handed down to posterity as the First Brigade in this our second War of Independence.   Farewell !'

For a moment there was silence ; then the pent-up feeling found expression, and cheer upon cheer burst forth from the ranks of the Valley regiments.   Waving his hand in token of farewell, Jackson galloped from the field.

NOTE I

THE TROOPS EMPLOYED ON THE HENRY HILL

FEDERAL.

First Division : TYLER

Brigade   .   .   .   . Keyes
,, ... Sherman   .   .   .   . = 4,500
,, ... Schenck

Second Division : HUNTER

,, ... Porter
,, ... Burnside   .   .   .   . = 6,000

Third Division : HEINTZLEMAN

,, ... Franklin
,, ... Wilcox   .   .   .   . = 7,500
,, ... Howard

Total 18,000, and 30 guns.

CONFEDERATE.

Army of the Shenandoah [JOHNSTON]

Brigade   .   .   .   . Jackson
,, ... Bee
,, ... Bartow   .   .   . = 8,700
,, ... Kirby Smith

Army of the Potomac [BEAUREGARD]

Brigade   .   .   .   . Bonham
,, ... Cocke
,, ... Early
7th Louisiana Regiment .   .   .   . = 9,300
8th   ,,   ,,   .
Hampton's Legion .   .
Cavalry   .   .   .   .

Total 18,000, and 21 guns.

NOTE II

THE COST OF AN INADEQUATE ARMY

Lord Wolseley has been somewhat severely criticised for asserting that in the Civil War, 'from first to last, the co-operation of even one army corps (35,000 men) of regular troops would have given complete victory to whichever side it fought on.' Whatever may be argued as to the latter period of the conflict, it is impossible for anyone who understands the power of organisation, of discipline, of training, and of a proper system of command, to dispute the accuracy of this statement as regards the year 1861, that is, for the first eight months.

It is far too often assumed that the number of able-bodied men is the true criterion of national strength. In the Confederate States, for instance, there were probably 750,000 citizens who were liable for service in the militia, and yet had the United States possessed a single regular army corps, with a trained staff, an efficient commissariat, and a fully-organised system of transport, it is difficult to see how these 750,000 Southerners could have done more than wage a guerilla warfare. The army corps would have absorbed into itself the best of the Northern militia and volunteers; the staff and commissariat would have given them mobility, and 60,000 or 70,000 men, moving on Richmond directly Sumter fell, with the speed and certainty which organisation gives, would have marched from victory to victory. Their 750,000 enemies would never have had time to arm, to assemble, to organise, to create an army, to train a staff, or to arrange for their supplies. Each gathering of volunteers would have been swept away before it had attained consistency, and Virginia, at least, must have been conquered in the first few months.

And matters would have been no different if the army corps had been directed against the Union. In the Northern States there were over 2,000,000 men who were liable for service; and yet the Union States, notwithstanding their superior resources, were just as vulnerable as the Confederacy. Numbers, even if they amount to millions, are useless, and worse than useless, without training and organisation; the more men that are collected on the battle-field, the more crushing and far-reaching their defeat. Nor can the theory be sustained that a small army, invading a rich and populous country, would be ' stung to death' by the numbers of its foes, even if they dared not oppose it in the open field. Of what avail were the stupendous efforts of the French Republic in 1870–71 ? Enormous armies were raised and equipped; the ranks were filled with brave men; the generals were not unskilful; and yet time after time they were defeated by the far inferior forces of their seasoned enemies. Even in America itself, on two occasions, at Sharpsburg in 1862, and at Gettysburg in 1863, it was admitted by the North that the Southerners were ' within a stone's throw of independence.' And yet hundreds of thousands of able-bodied men had not yet joined the Federal armies. Nor can Spain be quoted as an instance of an unconquerable nation. Throughout the war with Napoleon the English armies, not only that under Wellington, but those at Cadiz, Tarifa, and Gibraltar, afforded solid rallying-points for the defeated Spaniards, and by a succession of victories inspired the whole Peninsula with hope and courage.

The patriot with a rifle may be equal, or even superior, man for man, to the professional soldier; but even patriots must be fed, and to win victories they must be able to manœuvre, and to manœuvre they must have leaders. If it could remain stationary, protected by earthworks, and supplied by railways, with which the enemy did not interfere, a host of hastily raised levies, if armed and equipped, might hold its own against even a regular army. But against troops which can manœuvre earthworks are useless, as the history of Sherman's brilliant operations in 1864 conclusively shows. To win battles and to protect their country armies must be capable of counter-manœuvre, and it is when troops are set in motion that the real difficulty of supplying them begins.

If it is nothing else, the War of Secession, with its awful expenditure of blood and treasure, is a most startling object-lesson in National Insurance.

CHAPTER VII

ROMNEY

WHILE the Indian summer still held carnival in the forests of Virginia, Jackson found himself once more on the Shenandoah. Some regiments of militia, the greater part of which were armed with flint-lock muskets, and a few squadrons of irregular cavalry formed his sole command.

1861
November.

The autumn of 1861 was a comparatively quiet season. The North, silent but determined, was preparing to put forth her stupendous strength. Scott had resigned; McDowell had been superseded; but the President had found a general who had caught the confidence of the nation. In the same month that had witnessed McDowell's defeat, a young officer had gained a cheap victory over a small Confederate force in West Virginia, and his grandiloquent dispatches had magnified the achievement in the eyes of the Northern people. He was at once nicknamed the 'Young Napoleon,' and his accession to the chief command of the Federal armies was enthusiastically approved. General McClellan had been educated at West Point, and had graduated first of the class in which Jackson was seventeenth. He had been appointed to the engineers, had served on the staff in the war with Mexico, and as United States Commissioner with the Allied armies in the Crimea. In 1857 he resigned, to become president of a railway company, and when the war broke out he was commissioned by the State of Ohio as Major-General of Volunteers. His reputation at the Military Academy and in the regular army had been high. His ability and industry were unquestioned. His physique was powerful, and he was a fine horseman. His influence over his troops was remarkable, and he was emphatically a gentleman.

It was most fortunate for the Union at this juncture that caution and method were his distinguishing characteristics. The States had placed at Lincoln's disposal sufficient troops to form an army seven times greater than that which had been defeated at Bull Run. McClellan, however, had no thought of committing the new levies to an enterprise for which they were unfitted. He had determined that the army should make no move till it could do so with the certainty of success, and the winter months were to be devoted to training and organisation. Nor was there any cry for immediate action. The experiment of a civilian army had proved a terrible failure. The nation that had been so confident of capturing Richmond, was now anxious for the security of Washington. The war had been in progress for nearly six months, and yet the troops were manifestly unfit for offensive operations. Even the crude strategists of the press had become alive to the importance of drill and discipline. A reconnaissance in force, pushed (contrary to McClellan's orders) across the Potomac, Oct. 21 was repulsed by General Evans at Ball's Bluff with heavy loss; and mismanagement and misconduct were so evident that the defeat did much towards inculcating patience.

So the work went on, quietly but surely, the general supported by the President, and the nation giving men and money without remonstrance. The South, on the other hand, was still apathetic. The people, deluded by their decisive victory, underrated the latent strength of their mighty adversary. They appear to have believed that the earthworks which had transformed Centreville into a formidable fortress, manned by the Army of Northern Virginia, as the force under Johnston was now designated, were sufficient in themselves to end the war. They had not yet learned that there were many roads to Richmond, and that a passive defence is no safeguard against a persevering foe. The Government, expecting much from the intervention of the European Powers, did nothing to press the advantage already gained. In vain the generals urged the President to reinforce the army at Centreville to 60,000 men, and to give it transport and supplies sufficient to permit the passage of the Potomac above Washington.

In vain they pointed out, in answer to the reply that the Government could furnish neither men nor arms, that large bodies of troops were retained at points the occupation of which by the enemy would cause only a local inconvenience. ' Was it not possible,' they asked the President, ' by stripping other points to the last they would bear, and even risking defeat at all other places, to put the Virginian army in condition for a forward movement ? Success,' they said, ' in the neighbourhood of Washington was success everywhere, and it was upon the north-eastern frontier that all the available force of the Confederacy should be concentrated.'

Mr. Davis was immovable. Although Lee, who had been appointed to a command in West Virginia almost immediately after Bull Run, was no longer at hand to advise him, he probably saw the strategical requirements of the situation. That a concentrated attack on a vital point is a better measure of security than dissemination along a frontier, that the counter-stroke is the soul of the defence, and that the true policy of the State which is compelled to take up arms against a superior foe is to allow that foe no breathing-space, are truisms which it would be an insult to his ability to say that he did not realise. But to have surrendered territory to the temporary occupation of the enemy, in order to seek a problematical victory elsewhere, would have probably provoked a storm of discontent. The authority of the new Government was not yet firmly established ; nor was the patriotism of the Southern people so entirely unselfish as to render them willing to endure minor evils in order to achieve a great result. They were willing to fight, but they were unwilling that their own States should be left unprotected. To apply Frederick the Great's maxim [1]

---

[1] 'A defensive war is apt to betray us into too frequent detachments. Those generals who have had but little experience attempt to protect every

requires greater strength of will in the statesman than in
the soldier. The cries and complaints of those who find
themselves abandoned do not penetrate to the camp, but
they may bring down an administration. It is easy to
contrive excuses for the inaction of the President, and it
is no new thing to find the demands of strategy sacrificed
to political expediency. Nor did the army which had
suffered so heavily on the banks of Bull Run evince any
marked desire to be led across the Potomac. Furloughs were
liberally granted. Officers and privates dispersed to look
after their farms and their plantations. The harvests had to
be gathered, the negroes required the master's eye, and
even the counties of Virginia asked that part of the contingents they had furnished might be permitted to return
to agricultural pursuits.

The senior generals of the Virginia army were not
alone in believing that the victory they had won would
be barren of result unless it were at once utilised as a
basis for further action. Jackson, engrossed as he was
with the training of his command, found time to reflect
on the broader aspects of the war. Before he left for the
Shenandoah Valley he sought an interview with General
G. W. Smith, recently appointed to the command of his
division. 'Finding me lying down in my tent,' writes this
officer, 'he expressed regret that I was sick, and said he
had come to confer with me on a subject of great importance, but would not then trouble me with it. I told
him that I wished to hear whatever he desired to say,
and could rest whilst he was talking. He immediately sat
down on the ground, near the head of the cot on which
I was lying, and entered on the subject of his visit.

' " McClellan," he said, " with his army of recruits, will
not attempt to come out against us this autumn. If we
remain inactive they will have greatly the advantage over
us next spring. Their raw recruits will have then become

point, while those who are better acquainted with their profession, having
only the capital object in view, guard against a decisive blow, and acquiesce
in smaller misfortunes to avoid greater.'—Frederick the Great's *Instructions
to his Generals.*

an organised army, vastly superior in numbers to our own. We are ready at the present moment for active operations in the field, while they are not. We ought to invade their country now, and not wait for them to make the necessary preparations to invade ours. If the President would reinforce this army by taking troops from other points not threatened, and let us make an active campaign of invasion before winter sets in, McClellan's raw recruits could not stand against us in the field.

'"Crossing the Upper Potomac, occupying Baltimore, and taking possession of Maryland, we could cut off the communications of Washington, force the Federal Government to abandon the capital, beat McClellan's army if it came out against us in the open country, destroy industrial establishments wherever we found them, break up the lines of interior commercial intercourse, close the coal mines, seize and, if necessary, destroy the manufactories and commerce of Philadelphia, and of other large cities within our reach; take and hold the narrow neck of country between Pittsburg and Lake Erie; subsist mainly on the country we traverse, and making unrelenting war amidst their homes, force the people of the North to understand what it will cost them to hold the South in the Union at the bayonet's point."

'He then requested me to use my influence with Generals Johnston and Beauregard in favour of immediate aggressive operations. I told him that I was sure that an attempt on my part to exert any influence in favour of his proposition would do no good. Not content with my answer he repeated his arguments, dwelling more at length on the advantages of such strategy to ourselves and its disadvantages to the enemy, and again urged me to use my influence to secure its adoption. I gave him the same reply I had already made.

'After a few minutes' thought he abruptly said: "General, you have not expressed any opinion in regard to the views I have laid before you. But I feel assured that you favour them, and I think you ought to do all in your power to have them carried into effect."

'I then said, "I will tell you a secret."

'He replied, "Please do not tell me any secret. I would prefer not to hear it." I answered, "I must tell it to you, and I have no hesitation in doing so, because I am certain that it will not be divulged." I then explained to him that these views had already been laid before the Government, in a conference which had taken place at Fairfax Court House, in the first days of October, between President Davis, Generals Johnston, Beauregard, and myself, and told him the result.

'When I had finished, he rose from the ground, on which he had been seated, shook my hand warmly, and said, "I am sorry, very sorry."

'Without another word he went slowly out to his horse, a few feet in front of my tent, mounted very deliberately, and rode sadly away. A few days afterwards he was ordered to the Valley.' [1]

It was under such depressing circumstances that Jackson quitted the army which, boldly used, might have ensured the existence of the Confederacy. His head-quarters were established at Winchester ; and, in communication with Centreville by road, rail, and telegraph, although sixty miles distant, he was still subordinate to Johnston. The Confederate front extended from Fredericksburg on the Rappahannock to Winchester on the Opequon. Jackson's force, holding the Valley of the Shenandoah and the line of the Potomac westward of Point of Rocks, was the extreme outpost on the left, and was connected with the main body by a detachment at Leesburg, on the other side of the Blue Ridge, under his brother-in-law, General D. H. Hill.

Nov. 5.

At Winchester his wife joined him, and of their first meeting she tells a pretty story :—

'It can readily be imagined with what delight General Jackson's domestic plans for the winter were hailed by me, and without waiting for the promised "aide" to be sent on escort, I joined some friends who were going to Richmond, where I spent a few days to shop, to secure a passport, and

[1] Letter of General G. W. Smith to the author.

to await an escort to Winchester. The latter was soon found in a kind-hearted, absent-minded old clergyman. We travelled by stage coach from Strasburg, and were told, before reaching Winchester, that General Jackson was not there, having gone with his command on an expedition. It was therefore with a feeling of sad disappointment and loneliness that I alighted in front of Taylor's hotel, at midnight, in the early part of dreary cold December, and no husband to meet me with a glad welcome. By the dim lamplight I noticed a small group of soldiers standing in the wide hall, but they remained silent spectators, and my escort led me up the big stairway, doubtless feeling disappointed that he still had me on his hands. Just before reaching the landing I turned to look back, for one figure among the group looked startlingly familiar, but as he had not come forward, I felt that I must be mistaken. However, my backward glance revealed an officer muffled up in a military greatcoat, cap drawn down over his eyes, following us in rapid pursuit, and by the time we were upon the top step a pair of strong arms caught me; the captive's head was thrown back, and she was kissed again and again by her husband before she could recover from the delightful surprise he had given her. The good old minister chuckled gleefully, and was no doubt a sincere sharer in the joy and relief experienced by his charge. When I asked my husband why he did not come forward when I got out of the coach, he said he wanted to assure himself that it was his own wife, as he didn't want to commit the blunder of kissing anybody else's *esposa*! '

The people amongst whom they found themselves were Virginian to the core. In Winchester itself the feeling against the North was exceptionally bitter. The town was no mushroom settlement; its history stretched back to the old colonial days; the grass-grown intrenchments on the surrounding hills had been raised by Washington during the Indian wars, and the traditions of the first struggle for independence were not yet forgotten. No single section of the South was more conservative. Although the citizens had been strong Unionists, nowhere were the principles which their fathers had respected, the sovereignty of the individual State and the right of secession, more strongly held, and nowhere had the hereditary spirit of resistance to coercive legislation blazed up more fiercely. The soldiers of Bull Run, who had driven the invader from the soil of Virginia, were the heroes of the hour, and the leader of the Stonewall Brigade had peculiar claims on the hospitality of the town. It was to the people of the Valley that he owed his command. 'With one voice,' wrote the Secretary of War, 'have they made constant and urgent appeals that to you, in whom they have confidence, their defence should be assigned.'

'The Winchester ladies,' says Mrs. Jackson, 'were amongst the most famous of Virginia housekeepers, and lived in a good deal of old-fashioned elegance and profusion. The old border town had not then changed hands with the conflicting armies, as it was destined to do so many times during the war. Under the rose-coloured light in which I viewed everything that winter, it seemed to me that no people could have been more cultivated, attractive, and noble-hearted. Winchester was rich in happy homes and pleasant people ; and the extreme kindness and appreciation shown to General Jackson by all bound us to them so closely and warmly that ever after that winter he called the place our " war home." '

But amid congenial acquaintances and lovely surroundings, with the tumult of war quiescent, and the domestic happiness so dear to him restored, Jackson allowed no relaxation either to himself or to his men. His first care was to train and organise his new regiments. The ranks were filled with recruits, and to their instruction he devoted himself with unwearied energy. His small force of cavalry, commanded by Colonel Turner Ashby, a gentleman of Virginia, whose name was to become famous in the annals of the Confederacy, he at once despatched to patrol the frontier.

Prompt measures were taken to discipline the troops, and that this last was a task of no little difficulty the following incident suggests. In the middle of November, to Jackson's great delight, the Stonewall Brigade had been sent to him from Manassas, and after its arrival an order was issued which forbade all officers leaving the camp except upon passes from headquarters. A protest was immediately drawn up by the regimental commanders, and laid before the general. They complained that the obnoxious order was 'an unwarranted assumption of authority, disparaged their dignity, and detracted from that respect of the force under their command which was necessary to maintain their authority and enforce obedience.' Jackson's reply well illustrates his own idea of discipline, and of the manner in which it should be upheld. His adjutant-general wrote as follows to the discontented officers :—

'The Major-General Commanding desires me to say that the within combined protest is in violation of army regulations and subversive of military discipline. He claims the right to give his pickets such instructions as in his opinion the interests of the service require.

'Colonels —— and —— on the day that their regiments arrived at their present encampment, either from incompetency to control their commands, or from neglect of duty, so permitted their commands to become disorganised and their officers and men to enter Winchester without permission, as to render several arrests of officers necessary.

'If officers desire to have control over their commands, they must remain habitually with them, industriously attend to their instruction and comfort, and in battle lead them well, and in such a manner as to command their admiration.

'Such officers need not apprehend loss of respect resulting from inserting in a written pass the words "on duty," or "on private business," should they have occasion to pass the pickets.'

Even the Stonewall Brigade had yet much to learn.

At this time Jackson was besieged with numerous applications for service on his staff. The majority of these were from persons without experience, and they were made to the wrong man. 'My desire,' he wrote, 'is to get a staff specially qualified for their specific duties. I know Mr. —— personally, and was favourably impressed by him. But if a person desires office in these times, the best thing for him to do is to pitch into service somewhere, and work with such energy, skill, and success as to impress those round him with the conviction that such are his merits that he must be advanced, or the interests of the service must suffer. . . . My desire is to make merit the basis of my recommendations.'

Social claims had no weight with him whatever. He felt that the interests at stake were too great to be sacrificed to favouritism or friendship, and he had seen enough of war to know the importance of staff work. Nor was he in the unfortunate position of being compelled to accept the nominees of his superiors. The Confederate authorities were wise enough to permit their generals to choose for themselves the instruments on which they would have to rely for the execution of their designs. Wellington, in 1815, had forced on him by the Horse Guards, in the teeth of his indignant remonstrances, incompetent officers whom he did not know and whom he could not trust. Jackson, in a country which knew little of war, was allowed to please himself. He need appoint no one without learning all about him, and his inquiries were searching. Was he intelligent? Was he trustworthy? Was he industrious? Did he get up early? If a man was wanting in any one of these qualifications he would reject him, however highly recommended. That his strict investigations and his insistence on the possession of certain essential characteristics bore good fruit it is impossible to gainsay. The absence of mishaps and errors in his often complicated manœuvres is sufficient proof that he was exceedingly well served by his subordinates. The influence of a good staff is seldom apparent except to the initiated. If a combination succeeds, the general gets all the credit. If it fails, he gets all the blame; and while no agents, however efficient, can compensate by their own efforts for the weakness of a conception that is radically unsound, many a brilliant plan has failed in execution through the inefficiency of the staff. In his selection of such capable men as his assistants must needs have been

Jackson gave proof that he possessed one at least of the attributes of a great leader. He was not only a judge of character, but he could place men in the positions to which they were best suited. His personal predilections were never allowed to interfere. For some months his chief of the staff was a Presbyterian clergyman, while his chief quartermaster was one of the hardest swearers in Virginia. The fact that the former could combine the duties of spiritual adviser with those of his official position made him a congenial comrade; but it was his energy and ability rather than this unusual qualification which attracted Jackson; and although the profanity of the quartermaster offended his susceptibilities, their relations were always cordial. It was to the intelligence of his staff officers, their energy and their loyalty, that he looked; for the business in hand these qualities were more important than their morals.

That a civilian should be found serving as chief of the staff to a general of division, one of the most important posts in the military hierarchy, is a curious comment on the organisation of the Confederate army. The regular officers who had thrown in their lot with the South had, as a rule, been appointed to commands, and the generals of lower rank had to seek their staff officers amongst the volunteers. It may be noticed, however, that Jackson was by no means bigoted in favour of his own cloth. He showed no anxiety to secure their services on his staff. He thought many of them unfitted for duties which brought them in immediate contact with the volunteers. In dealing with such troops, tact and temper are of more importance than where obedience has become mechanical, and the claims of rank are instinctively respected. In all his campaigns, too, Jackson was practically his own chief of the staff. He consulted no one. He never divulged his plans. He gave his orders, and his staff had only to see that these orders were obeyed. His topographical engineer, his medical director, his commissary and his quartermaster, were selected, it is true, by reason of their special qualifications. Captain Hotchkiss, who filled the first position, was a young man of twenty-six, whose abilities as a surveyor were well known in the Valley. Major Harman, his chief quartermaster, was one of the proprietors of a line of stage coaches and a large farmer, and Major Hawks, his commissary, was the owner of a carriage manufactory. But the remainder of his assistants, with the exception of the chief of artillery, owed their appointments rather to their character than to their professional abilities. It is not to be understood, at the same time, that Jackson underrated soldierly acquirements. He left no complaints on record, like so many of his West Point comrades, of the ignorance of the volunteer officers, and of the consequent difficulties which attended every combination. But he was none the less alive to their deficiencies. Early in 1862, when the military system of the Confederacy was about to be reorganised, he urged upon the Government, through the member of Congress for the district where he commanded, that regimental promotion should not be obtained by seniority, unless the applicant were approved by a board of examination; and it was due to his representations that this regulation, to the great benefit of the army, was shortly afterwards adopted. With all his appreciation of natural aptitude for the soldier's trade, so close a student of Napoleon could scarcely be blind to the fact that the most heroic character, unsustained by knowledge, is practically useless. If Napoleon himself, more highly endowed by nature with every military attribute than any other general of the Christian era, thought it essential to teach himself his business by incessant study, how much more is such study necessary for ordinary men?

But no man was less likely than Jackson to place an exaggerated value on theoretical acquirements. No one realised more fully that Napoleon's character won more victories than Napoleon's knowledge. The qualities he demanded in his subordinates were those which were conspicuous in Napoleon. Who was more industrious than the great Corsican? Who displayed an intenser energy? Whose intelligence was brighter? Who understood human nature better, or handled men with more consummate tact?

These were the very attributes which distinguished Jackson himself. They are the key-note to his success, more so than his knowledge of strategy and tactics, of the mechanism of march and battle, and of the principles of the military art. In selecting his staff officers, therefore, he deemed character of more importance than erudition.

The men of the Stonewall Brigade had a saying that Jackson always marched at dawn, except when he started the night before, and it was perhaps this habit, which his enemies found so unreasonable, that led him to lay so much stress on early rising. It is certain that, like Wellington, he preferred 'three o'clock in the morning men.' In a letter to his wife he says :—

'If you will vouch for your brother's being an early riser during the remainder of the war, I will give him an aide-ship. I do not want to make an appointment on my staff except of such as are early risers ; but if you will vouch for him to rise regularly at dawn, I will offer him the position.'

Another characteristic he looked for was reticence ; and it was undeniably of the utmost importance, especially in an army which spoke the same language as the enemy, where desertion was not uncommon, and spies could easily escape detection, that the men who might become cognisant of the plans of the commander should be gifted with dis- cretion. Absolute concealment is generally impracticable in a camp. Maps must be drawn, and reports furnished. Reconnoitring parties must be sent out, roads examined, positions surveyed, and shelter and supplies requisitioned in advance. Thus the movements of staff officers are a clue to the projected movements of the army, and the smallest hint may set a hundred brains to the work of surmise. There will always be many who are just as anxious to discover the general's intentions as he is to conceal them ; and if, by any possibility whatever, the gossip and guesses of the camp may come to the enemy's ears, it is well that curiosity should be baulked. Nor is it undesirable that the privacy of headquarters should be respected. The vanity of a little brief authority has before now tempted subordinate officers to hint at weaknesses on the part of their superiors. Ignorance of war and of the situation has induced them to criticise and to condemn; and idle words, greedily listened to, and quickly exaggerated, may easily destroy the confidence of the soldiery in the abilities of their leader.

By the middle of December Jackson's small army had become fairly effective. Its duties were simple. To watch the enemy, to keep open the communication with Manassas, so as to be ready to join the main army should McClellan advance—such were Johnston's orders. The Upper Potomac was held by the enemy in force. General Banks, a volunteer officer, who was yet to learn more of Stonewall Jackson, was in command. The headquarters of his division, 18,000 strong, were at Frederick City in Maryland; but his charge extended seventy-five miles further west, as far as Cumberland on the Potomac. In addition to Banks, General Kelly with 5,000 men was at Romney, on the South Branch of the Potomac, thirty-five miles north-west of Winchester by a good road. The Federal troops guarding the Chesapeake and Ohio Canal and that portion of the Baltimore and Ohio Railroad which was still intact were necessarily much dispersed, for the Confederate guerillas were active, and dam and aqueduct, tunnel and viaduct, offered tempting objectives to Ashby's cavalry. Still the force which confronted Jackson was far superior to his own; the Potomac was broad and bridgeless, and his orders appeared to impose a defensive attitude. But he was not the man to rest inactive, no matter what the odds against him, or to watch the enemy's growing strength without an endeavour to interfere. Within the limits of his own command he was permitted every latitude; and he was determined to apply the aggressive strategy which he was so firmly convinced should be adopted by the whole army. The Secretary of War, Mr. Benjamin, in detaching him to the Valley, had asked him to ' forward suggestions as to the means of rendering his measures of defence effectual.' [1]

The earliest information he had received on his arrival

---

[1] O. R., vol. v., p. 909.

at Winchester pointed to the conclusion that the enemy was meditating an advance by way of Harper's Ferry. His first suggestion thereupon was, that he should be reinforced by a division under General Loring and a brigade under Colonel Edward Johnson, which were stationed within the Alleghanies on the great highways leading to the Ohio, covering Staunton from the west.[1] His next was to the effect that he should be permitted to organise an expedition for the recapture and occupation of Romney. If he could seize this village, the junction of several roads, more decisive operations would at once become feasible. It has been said that the force of old associations urged Jackson to drive the invader from the soil which held his mother's grave; but, even if we had not the evidence of his interview with General G. W. Smith,[2] a glance at the map would in itself be sufficient to assure us that strategy prevailed with him rather than sentiment.

The plan of campaign which first suggested itself to him was sufficiently comprehensive.

'While the Northern people and the Federal authorities were still a prey to the demoralisation which had followed Bull Run, he proposed to advance with 10,000 troops into North-west Virginia, where he would reclaim the whole country, and summon the inhabitants of Southern sentiment to join his army. His information was extensive and reliable, and he did not doubt his ability to recruit between 15,000 and 20,000 men, enough for his designs. These were bold and simple. While the enemy was under the impression that his only object was to reclaim and occupy North-west Virginia, he would move his whole force rapidly across to the Monongahela, march down upon Pittsburg, destroy the United States arsenal, and then, in conjunction with Johnston's army (which was to cross the Potomac at Leesburg), advance upon Harrisburg, the

---

[1] Loring was at Huntersville, Johnson on Alleghany Mountain, not far from Monterey. General Lee, unable with an inferior force to drive the enemy from West Virginia, had been transferred to South Carolina on November 1.

[2] *Ante*, p. 174.

capital of Pennsylvania. From Harrisburg he proposed that the army should advance upon Philadelphia.'[1]

These suggestions, however, went no further than his friends in the Legislative Assembly. Although, for his conduct at Bull Run, he had now been promoted to major-general, the Lexington professor had as yet no voice in the councils of the young republic. Nevertheless, the President read and approved the less ambitious proposal for an attack on the Federal force at Romney.

Romney, the county seat of Hampshire, lies in a rich district watered by the South Branch of the Potomac. For more than a hundred miles, from source to mouth, the river is bordered by alluvial meadows of extraordinary fertility. Their prodigal harvests, together with the sweetness of the upland pastures, make them the paradise of the grazier; the farms which rest beneath the hills are of manorial proportions, and the valley of the beautiful South Branch is a land of easy wealth and old-fashioned plenty. From Romney an excellent road runs south-east to Winchester, and another south-west by Moorefield and Franklin to Monterey, where it intersects the great road, constructed by one of Napoleon's engineers, that leads from Staunton in the Valley to Parkersburg on the Ohio.

When Jackson advocated the occupation of this important point the whole of West Virginia, between the Alleghanies and the Ohio, was in possession of the Federals. The army of occupation, under General Rosecrans, amounted to 27,000 men and over 40 guns; but the troops were dispersed in detachments from Romney to Gauley Bridge, a distance of near two hundred miles, their communications were exposed, and, owing to the mountains, co-operation was almost impracticable.

5,000 men, based on Grafton, occupied Romney.

18,700, based on Clarksburg, occupied the passes south-east of Beverley.

9,000, based on the Ohio, were stationed on the Great

[1] Cooke, p. 87.

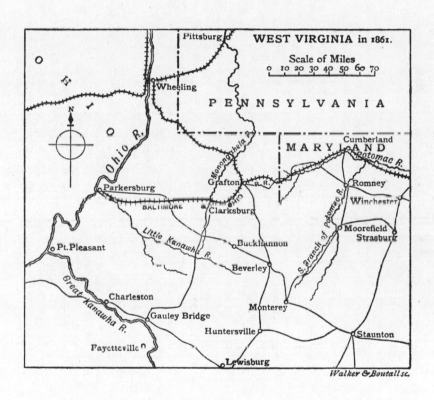

WEST VIRGINIA in 1861.

Scale of Miles

0 10 20 30 40 50 60 70

Walker & Boutall sc.

Kanawha, a river which is navigable for small steamers to within a few miles of Gauley Bridge.

4,000 protected the lines of communication.

Jackson's letter to the Secretary of War was as follows:—

'Deeply impressed with the importance of absolute secrecy respecting military operations, I have made it a point to say but little respecting my proposed movements in the event of sufficient reinforcements arriving, but since conversing with Lieutenant-Colonel Preston [his adjutant-general], upon his return from General Loring, and ascertaining the disposition of the general's forces, I venture to respectfully urge that after concentrating all his troops here, an attempt should be made to capture the Federal forces at Romney. The attack on Romney would probably induce McClellan to believe that General Johnston's army had been so weakened as to justify him in making an advance on Centreville; but should this not induce him to advance, I do not believe anything will, during this winter.

Nov. 20.

'Should General Johnston be attacked, I would be at once prepared to reinforce him with my present force, increased by General Loring's. After repulsing the enemy at Manassas, let the troops that marched on Romney return to the Valley, and move rapidly westward to the waters of the Monongahela and Little Kanawha. I deem it of very great importance that North-western Virginia be occupied by Confederate troops this winter. At present it is to be presumed that the enemy are not expecting an attack there, and the resources of that region, necessary for the subsistence of our troops, are in greater abundance than in almost any other season of the year. Postpone the occupation of that section until spring, and we may expect to find the enemy prepared for us, and the resources to which I have referred greatly exhausted. I know that what I have proposed will be an arduous undertaking and cannot be accomplished without the sacrifice of much personal comfort; but I feel that the troops will be prepared to make the sacrifice when animated by the prospects of important results to our cause, and distinction to themselves. It may be urged against this plan that the enemy will advance [from Beverley and the Great Kanawha] on Staunton or Huntersville. I am well satisfied that such a step would but make their destruction sure. When North-western Virginia is occupied in force, the Kanawha Valley, unless it be the lower part of it, must be evacuated by the Federal forces, or otherwise their safety will be endangered by forcing a column across from the Little Kanawha between them and the Ohio River.

'Admitting that the season is too far advanced, or that from other causes all cannot be accomplished that has been named, yet through the blessing of God, who has thus far wonderfully prospered our cause, much more may be expected from General Loring's troops, according to this programme, than can be expected from them where they are.'[1]

This scheme was endorsed by Johnston. 'I submit,' he wrote, 'that the troops under General Loring might render valuable services by taking the field with General Jackson, instead of going into winter quarters as now proposed.'

In accordance with Jackson's suggestion, Loring was ordered to join him. Edward Johnson, however, was withheld. The Confederate authorities seem to have considered it injudicious to leave unguarded the mountain roads which lead into the Valley from the west. Jackson, with a wider grasp of war, held that concentration at Winchester was a sounder measure of security. 'Should the Federals' (at Beverley), he said, 'take advantage of the withdrawal of Johnson's troops, and cross the mountains, so much the worse for them. While they were marching eastwards, involving themselves amongst interminable obstacles, he [Jackson] would place himself on their communications and close in behind them, making their destruction the more certain the further they advanced towards their imaginary prize.'[2]

While waiting for Loring, Jackson resolved to complete the education of his new battalions in the field. The raw

[1] O. R., vol. v., p. 965.   [2] Dabney, vol. i., p. 298

troops who garrisoned the Northern border were not formidable enemies, and a sudden rush upon some ill-defended post would give to the staff and soldiery that first taste of success which gives heart and backbone to inexpe-

Dec. 6–9.   rienced troops.   The first enterprise, however, was only partially successful.   The destruction of a dam on the Chesapeake and Ohio Canal, one of the main arteries of communication between Washington and the West, by which coal, hay, and forage reached the Union capital, was the result of a few days' hard marching and hard work.   Two companies of the Stonewall Brigade volunteered to go down by night and cut the cribs.   Standing waist deep in the cold water, and under the constant fire of the enemy, they effected a partial breach; but it was repaired by the Federals within two days.   Jackson's loss was one man killed.   While engaged in this expedition news reached him of the decisive repulse by Colonel Edward Johnson of an attack on his position on Alleghany Mountain.   Jackson again asked that this brigade might be sent to his support, but it was again refused, notwithstanding Johnston's endorsement of his request.

Loring reached Winchester on Christmas Day.   Once more the enemy threatened to advance, and information had been received that he had been largely strengthened. Jackson was of opinion that the true policy of the Federals would be to concentrate at Martinsburg, midway between Romney and Frederick, and ' to march on Winchester over a road that presented no very strong positions.' To counteract such a combination, he determined to anticipate their movements, and to attack them before they received additional reinforcements.

On January 1, 1862, 9,000 Confederates marched from Winchester towards the Potomac.   Jackson's first ob-

1862.   jectives were the villages of Bath and Hancock,
Jan. 1.   on the Baltimore and Ohio Railway, held by Federal garrisons.   By dispersing these detachments he would prevent support being sent to Romney; by cutting the telegraph along the railroad he would sever the communication between Banks at Frederick and Rosecrans

in West Virginia, and compel Kelly either to evacuate
Romney or fight him single-handed. To deal with his
enemy in detail, to crush his detachments in succession,
and with superior force, such was the essence of his plan.

The weather when the expedition started was bright
and pleasant, so much so that the troops, with the im-
providence of young soldiers, left their coats and blankets
in the waggons. That very afternoon, however, the
temperature underwent a sudden change.   Under cold grey
skies the column scaled the mountain ridges, and on the
winter wind came a fierce storm of snow and hail.   In order
to conceal the march as far as possible from the enemy's
observations the brigades had marched by country roads,
and delayed by steep gradients and slippery tracks, it was
not till the next morning that the supply waggons came up.
The troops, hurried suddenly from comfortable winter
quarters, suffered much. The bivouac was as cheerless as
the march. Without rations and without covering, the
men lay shivering round the camp fires.   The third day out,
even the commander of the Stonewall Brigade took it upon
himself to halt his wearied men. Jackson became restive.
Riding along the column he found his old regiments
halted by the roadside, and asked the reason for the delay.

'I have halted to let the men cook their rations,'
was General Garnett's reply. 'There is no time for
that.' 'But it is impossible for the men to march
further without them.' '*I* never found anything impossible with this brigade!' and Jackson rode on. His
plans admitted of no delay. He intended to surprise the

Jan. 3. enemy. In this expectation, however, he was
        disappointed. A few miles distant from Bath his
advanced-guard fell in with a Federal reconnaissance, and at
nightfall the Confederates had not yet reached the outskirts
of the town. Once more they had to bivouac in the open,
and rations, tents, and blankets were still behind. When
the day broke over the Shenandoah Mountains the country
was white with snow, and the sleeping soldiers were covered
as with a winding-sheet. After a hasty meal an attempt
was made to surround the village, and to cut off the retreat

of the garrison. The outflanking movements, made in a
blinding storm, failed in combination. The roads were too
bad, the subordinate commanders too inexperienced; the
three hostile regiments escaped across the river in their
boats, and only 16 prisoners were captured. Still, the advantages of their unexpected movement were not altogether
lost to the Confederates. The Federals, ignorant as yet of
the restless energy of the foe who held command at Winchester, had settled themselves cosily in winter quarters.
The intelligence of Jackson's march had come too late
to enable them to remove the stores which had been
collected at Bath, and on the night of January 4 the
Virginians revelled in warmth and luxury. The next morning they moved forward to the river. On the opposite
Jan. 5. bank stood the village of Hancock, and after a
demand to surrender had been refused, Jackson
ordered his batteries to open fire.[1] Shepherdstown, a little
Virginia town south of the Potomac, had been repeatedly
shelled, even when unoccupied by Confederate troops. In
order to intimate that such outrages must cease a few shells
were thrown into Hancock. The next day the bombardment was resumed, but with little apparent effect; and
strong reinforcements having joined the enemy, Jackson
ceased fire and withdrew. A bridge was already in
process of construction two miles above the town, but
to have crossed the river, a wide though shallow stream,
in face of a considerable force, would have been a useless
and a costly operation. The annihilation of the Federal
garrison would have scarcely repaid the Southerners for
the loss of life that must have been incurred. At the
same time, while Jackson's batteries had been at work,
his infantry had done a good deal of mischief. Two
regiments had burned the bridge by which the Baltimore
and Ohio Railway crosses the Great Cacapon River, the canal
dam was breached, and many miles of track and telegraph
were destroyed. The enemy's communications between
Frederick and Romney were thus effectually severed,

[1] The Federal commander was granted two hours in which to remove
the women and children.

and a large amount of captured stores were sent to Winchester. It was with the design of covering these operations that the bombardment had been continued, and the summons to surrender was probably no more than a ruse to attract the attention of the Federal commander from the attack on the Cacapon Bridge. On the morning of the 7th Jackson moved southward to Unger's Store. Here, however, the expedition came to a standstill. The precaution of rough-shoeing the horses before leaving Winchester had been neglected, and it was found necessary to refit the teams and rest the men.

After halting for four days the Confederates, on January 13, renewed their march. The outlook was unpromising. Although cavalry patrols had been despatched in every direction, a detachment of militia, which had acted as flank-guard in the direction of Romney while Jackson was moving to Unger's Store, had been surprised and defeated, with the loss of two guns, at Hanging Rock. The weather, too, grew colder and colder, and the mountain roads were little more than sheets of ice. The sleet beat fiercely down upon the crawling column. The men stumbled and fell on the slippery tracks; many waggons were overturned, and the bloody knees and muzzles of the horses bore painful witness to the severity of the march. The bivouacs were more comfortless than before. The provision train lagged far in rear. Axes there were none; and had not the fence-rails afforded a supply of firewood, the sufferings of the troops would have been intense. As it was, despite the example of their commander, they pushed forward but slowly through the bitter weather. Jackson was everywhere; here, putting his shoulder to the wheel of a gun that the exhausted team could no longer move; there, urging the wearied soldiers, or rebuking the officers for want of energy. Attentive as he was to the health and comfort of his men in quarters, on the line of march he looked only to the success of the Confederate arms. The hardships of the winter operations were to him but a necessary concomitant of his designs, and it mattered but little if the weak and sickly should succumb.

Jan. 13.

Commanders who are over-chary of their soldiers' lives, who forget that their men have voluntarily offered themselves as food for powder, often miss great opportunities. To die doing his duty was to Jackson the most desirable consummation of the soldier's existence, and where duty was concerned or victory in doubt he was as careless of life and suffering as Napoleon himself. The well-being of an individual or even of an army were as nothing compared with the interests of Virginia. And, in the end, his indomitable will triumphed over every obstacle. Romney village came at length in sight, Jan. 10. lonely and deserted amid the mountain snows, for the Federal garrison had vanished, abandoning its camp-equipment and its magazines.

No pursuit was attempted. Jackson had resolved on further operations. It was now in his power to strike at the Federal communications, marching along the Baltimore and Ohio Railway in the direction of Grafton, seventy-five miles west of Romney. In order to leave all safe behind him, he determined, as a first step, to destroy the bridge by which the Baltimore and Ohio Railway crossed the Potomac in the neighbourhood of Cumberland. The Federal forces at Williamstown and Frederick drew the greater part of their supplies from the West; and so serious an interruption in the line of communication would compel them to give up all thought of offensive enterprises in the Valley. But the sufferings that his green soldiers had undergone had sapped their discipline. Loring's division, nearly two-thirds of the command, was so discontented as to be untrustworthy. It was useless with such troops to dream of further movements among the inhospitable hills. Many had deserted during the march from Unger's Store; many had succumbed to the exposure of the bivouacs; and, more than all, the commander had been disloyal to his superior. Although a regular officer of long service, he had permitted himself a license of speech which was absolutely unjustifiable, and throughout the operations had shown his unfitness for his position. Placed under the command of an officer who had been his junior in the Army of the United States, his sense of discipline was

overborne by the slight to his vanity ; and not for the first
time nor the last the resentment of a petty mind ruined an
enterprise which would have profited a nation.   Compelled
to abandon his projected march against the enemy, Jackson
determined to leave a strong garrison in Romney and the
surrounding district, while the remainder of the force withdrew to Winchester.   The two towns were connected by a
good high-road, and by establishing telegraphic communication between them, he believed that despite the Federal
numbers he could maintain his hold on these important
posts.   Many precautions were taken to secure Romney
from surprise.   Three militia regiments, recruited in the
country, and thus not only familiar with every road, but
able to procure ample information, were posted in the
neighbourhood of the town ; and with the militia were
left three companies of cavalry, one of which had already
been employed in this region.

In detailing Loring's division as the garrison of Romney
Jackson seems to have made a grave mistake.   He had
much reason to be dissatisfied with the commander, and
the men were already demoralised.   Troops unfit to march
against the enemy were not the men to be trusted with
the security of an important outpost, within thirty miles of
the Federal camps at Cumberland, far from their supports,
and surrounded by bleak and lonely mountains.   A man
of wider sympathy with human weakness, and with less
rigid ideas of discipline, might possibly have arranged
matters so that the Stonewall Brigade might have remained
at Romney, while Loring and his division were transferred to less exacting duties and more comfortable
quarters.   But Loring's division constituted two-thirds of
Jackson's force, and Romney, more exposed than Winchester, required the stronger garrison.   A general of
Loring's temper and pretensions would scarcely have
submitted to the separation of his brigades, and would
probably have become even more discontented had Garnett,
the leader of the Stonewall Brigade, been left in command
at Romney, while he himself played a subordinate part at
Winchester.   It is only too possible, however, that matters

were past mending. The feeble discipline of Loring's troops had broken down; their enthusiasm had not been proof against the physical suffering of these winter operations.

The Stonewall Brigade, on the other hand, was still staunch. ' I am well assured,' wrote Jackson at this time, ' that had an order been issued for its march, even through the depth of winter and in any direction, it would have sustained its reputation; for although it was not under fire during the expedition at Romney, yet the alacrity with which it responded to the call of duty and overcame obstacles showed that it was still animated by the same spirit that characterised it at Manassas.' But Jackson's old regiments were now tried soldiers, inspirited by the memories of the great victory they had done so much to win, improved by association with Johnston's army, and welded together by a discipline far stricter than that which obtained in commands like Loring's.

On January 24 Jackson returned to Winchester. His strategy had been successful. He had driven the enemy across the Potomac. He had destroyed for a time an important line of supply. He had captured a few prisoners and many stores; and this with a loss of 4 men killed and 28 wounded. The Federal forces along the border were far superior to his own. The dispersion of these forces from Cumberland to Frederick, a distance of eighty miles, had doubtless been much in his favour. But when he marched from Winchester he had reason to believe that 8,000 men were posted at Frederick, 2,000 at Hagerstown, 2,000 at Williamsport, 2,000 at Hancock, and 12,000 at Cumberland and Romney. The actual effective strength of these garrisons may possibly have been smaller than had been reported, but such were the numbers which he had to take into consideration when planning his operations. It would appear from the map that while he was at Romney, 12,000 Federals might have moved out from Williamsport and Harper's Ferry and have cut him off from Winchester. This danger had to be kept in view. But the enemy had made no preparations

Jan. 24.

for crossing the Potomac ; the river was a difficult obstacle ; and Banks was not the man to run risks.[1]

At the same time, while Jackson was in all probability perfectly aware of the difficulties which Banks refused to face, and counted on that commander's hesitation, it must be admitted that his manœuvres had been daring, and that the mere thought of the enemy's superior numbers would have tied down a general of inferior ability to the passive defence of Winchester. Moreover, the results attained were out of all proportion to the trifling loss which had been incurred. An important recruiting-ground had been secured. The development of Union sentiment, which, since the occupation of Romney by the Federals, had been gradually increasing along the Upper Potomac, would be checked by the presence of Southern troops. A base for further operations against the Federal detachments in West Virginia had been established, and a fertile region opened to the operations of the Confederate commissaries. These strategic advantages, however, were by no means appreciated by the people of Virginia. The sufferings of the troops appealed more forcibly to their imagination than the prospective benefit to be derived by the Confederacy. Jackson's secrecy, as absolute as that of the grave, had an ill effect. Unable to comprehend his combinations, even his own officers ascribed his manœuvres to a restless craving for personal distinction ; while civilian wiseacres, with their ears full of the exaggerated stories of Loring's stragglers, saw in the relentless energy with which he had pressed the march on Romney not only the evidence of a callous in-difference to suffering, but the symptoms of a diseased mind. They refused to consider that the general had shared the hardships of the troops, faring as simply and roughly as any private in the ranks. He was charged with partiality to

[1] 'Any attempt,' Banks reported to McClellan, ' to intercept the enemy would have been unsuccessful. . . It would have resulted in almost certain failure to cut him off, and have brought an exhausted force into his presence to fight him in his stronghold at Winchester. In any case, it promised no positive prospect of success, nor did it exclude large chances of disaster.' — O. R., vol. v., p. 694.

the Stonewall Brigade. 'It was said that he kept it in the rear, while other troops were constantly thrust into danger ; and that now, while Loring's command was left in mid-winter in an alpine region, almost within the jaws of a powerful enemy, these favoured regiments were brought back to the comforts and hospitalities of the town; whereas in truth, while the forces in Romney were ordered into huts, the brigade was three miles below Winchester, in tents, and under the most rigid discipline.' [1]

It should not be forgotten, however, that Loring's troops were little more as yet than a levy of armed civilians, ignorant of war ; and this was one reason the more that during those cruel marches the hand that held the reins should have been a light one. A leader more genial and less rigid would have found a means to sustain their courage. Napoleon, with the captivating familiarity he used so well, would have laughed the grumblers out of their ill-humour, and have nerved the fainting by pointing to the glory to be won. Nelson would have struck the chord of patriotism. Skobeleff, taking the very privates into his confidence, would have enlisted their personal interest in the success of the enterprise, and the eccentric speeches of 'Father' Suvoroff would have cheered them like a cordial. There are occasions when both officers and men are the better for a little humouring, and the march to Romney was one. A few words of hearty praise, a stirring appeal to their nobler instincts, a touch of sym-pathy, might have worked wonders. But whatever of per-sonal magnetism existed in Stonewall Jackson found no utterance in words. Whilst his soldiers struggled painfully towards Romney in the teeth of the winter storm, his lips were never opened save for sharp rebuke or peremptory order, and Loring's men had some reason to complain of his fanatical regard for the very letter of the law. On the most inclement of those January nights the captain of a Virginia company, on whose property they happened to have halted, had allowed them to use the fence-rails for the camp fires. Jackson, ever careful of private rights, had

[1] Dabney, vol. i., p. 320.

issued an order that fences should not be burnt, and the generous donor was suspended from duty on the charge of giving away his own property without first asking leave! Well might the soldiers think that their commander regarded them as mere machines.

His own men knew his worth. Bull Run had shown them the measure of his courage and his ability; in a single battle he had won that respect and confidence which go so far towards establishing discipline. But over Loring's men his personal ascendency was not yet established. They had not yet seen him under fire. The fighting in the Romney campaign had been confined to skirmishing. Much spoil had been gathered in, but there were no trophies to show in the shape of guns or colours; no important victory had raised their self-respect. It is not too much to say that the silent soldier who insisted on such constant exertion and such unceasing vigilance was positively hated.

'They were unaccustomed to a military regimen so energetic as his. Personally the most modest of men, officially he was the most exacting of commanders, and his purpose to enforce a thorough performance of duty, and his stern disapprobation of remissness and self-indulgence were veiled by no affectations of politeness. Those who came to serve near his person, if they were not wholly like-minded with himself, usually underwent, at first, a sort of breaking in, accompanied with no little chafing to restless spirits. The expedition to Romney was, to such officers, just such an apprenticeship to Jackson's methods of making war. All this was fully known to him; but while he keenly felt the injustice, he disdained to resent it, or to condescend to any explanation.'[1]

Jackson returned to Winchester with no anticipation that the darkest days of his military life were close at hand. 'Little Sorrel,' the charger he had ridden at Bull Run, leaving the senior members of the staff toiling far in rear, had covered forty miles of mountain roads in one short winter day. 'After going to an hotel and divesting

[1] Dabney, vol. i., p. 321.

himself of the mud which had bespattered him in his
rapid ride, he proceeded to Dr. Graham's.   In order to
give his wife a surprise he had not intimated when he
would return.   As soon as the first glad greetings were
over, before taking his seat, with a face all aglow with
delight, he glanced round the room, and was so impressed
with the cosy and cheerful aspect of the fireside, as we all
sat round it that winter evening, that he exclaimed : " This
is the very essence of comfort." '[1]

He had already put aside the unpleasant memories of
the expedition, and had resigned himself to rest content
with the measure of success that had been attained.
Romney at least was occupied, and operations might be
effectively resumed at a more propitious season.

Six days later, however, Jackson received a peremptory
message from the Secretary of War : ' Our news indicates
that a movement is making to cut off General Loring's
command ; order him back immediately.'[2]

This order had been issued without reference to General
Johnston, Jackson's immediate superior, and so marked a
departure from ordinary procedure could not possibly be
construed except as a severe reflection on Jackson's judgment.   Nor could it have other than a most fatal effect on
the discipline of the Valley troops.   It had been brought
about by most discreditable means.   Loring's officers had
sat in judgment on their commander.   Those who had
been granted leave at the close of the expedition had
repaired to Richmond, and had filled the ears of the
Government and the columns of the newspapers with
complaints.   Those who remained at Romney formulated their grievance in an official remonstrance, which
Loring was indiscreet enough to approve and forward.
A council of subordinate officers had the effrontery to record
their opinion that ' Romney was a place of no strategical importance,' and to suggest that the division might be ' maintained much more comfortably, at much less expense, and
with every military advantage, at almost any other place.'[3]

---

[1] *Memoirs of Stonewall Jackson.*   [2] O. R., vol. v., p. 1053.
[3] *Ibid.*, pp. 1046 8.

Discomfort was the burden of their complaint. They had been serving continuously for eight months. Their present position imposed upon them even greater vigilance and more constant exertion than had hitherto been demanded of them, and their one thought was to escape from a situation which they characterised as 'one of the most disagreeable and unfavourable that could well be imagined.' Only a single pertinent argument was brought forward. The Confederate soldiers had enlisted only for twelve months, and the Government was about to ask them to volunteer for the duration of the war. It was urged by Loring's officers that with the present prospect before them there was much doubt that a single man of the division would re-enlist. 'With some regard for its comfort,' added the general, 'a large portion, if not the whole, may be prevailed upon to do so.'

It does not seem to have occurred to these officers that soldiers in the near vicinity of the enemy, wherever they may be placed, must always be subject to privations, and that at any other point of the Confederate frontier—at Winchester with Jackson, at Leesburg with Hill, or at Centreville with Johnston—their troops would be exposed to the same risks and the same discomforts as at Romney. That the occupation of a dangerous outpost is in itself an honour never entered their minds; and it would have been more honest, instead of reviling the climate and the country, had they frankly declared that they had had enough for the present of active service, and had no mind to make further sacrifices in the cause for which they had taken arms. With the Jan. 31. Secretary's order Jackson at once complied. Loring was recalled to Winchester, but before his command arrived Jackson's resignation had gone in.

His letter, forwarded through Johnston, ran as follows:

'Headquarters, Valley District, Winchester, Va.:
'Jan. 31, 1862.
'Hon. J. P. Benjamin, Secretary of War,

'Sir,—Your order, requiring me to direct General Loring to return with his command to Winchester immediately, has been received and promptly complied with.

'With such interference in my command I cannot expect to be of much service in the field, and, accordingly, respectfully request to be ordered to report for duty to the Superintendent of the Virginia Military Institute at Lexington, as has been done in the case of other professors. Should this application not be granted, I respectfully request that the President will accept my resignation from the army.' [1]

The danger apprehended by the Secretary of War, that Loring's division, if left at Romney, might be cut off, did not exist. General Lander, an able and energetic officer, now in command of the Federal force at Cumberland, had put forward proposals for an active campaign in the Shenandoah Valley; but there was no possibility of such an enterprise being immediately undertaken. The Potomac was still a formidable obstacle; artillery and cavalry were both deficient; the troops were scattered, and their discipline was indifferent. Lander's command, according to his official despatches, was 'more like an armed mob than an army.' [2] Romney, therefore, was in little danger; and Jackson, who had so lately been in contact with the Federal troops, whose cavalry patrolled the banks of the Potomac, and who was in constant receipt of information of the enemy's attitude and condition, was certainly a better judge of what was probable than any official in the Confederate capital. There were doubtless objections to the retention of Romney. An enormous army, in the intrenched camp at Washington, threatened Centreville; and in the event of that army advancing, Jackson would be called upon to reinforce Johnston, just as Johnston had reinforced Beauregard before Bull Run. With the greater part of his force at Romney such an operation would be delayed by at least two days. Even Johnston himself, although careful to leave his subordinate a free hand, suggested that the occupation of Romney, and the consequent dispersion of Jackson's force, might enable the enemy to cut in effectively between the Valley troops and the main army. It is beyond question, however, that Jackson had carefully

[1] O. R., vol. v., p. 1053. [2] Ibid., pp. 702, 703.

studied the situation. There was no danger of his forgetting that his was merely a detached force, or of his overlooking, in the interests of his own projected operations, the more important interests of the main army; and if his judgment of the situation differed from that of his superior, it was because he had been indefatigable in his search for information.

He had agents everywhere.[1] His intelligence was more ample than that supplied by the Confederate spies in Washington itself. No reinforcements could reach the Federals on the Potomac without his knowledge. He was always accurately informed of the strength and movements of their detachments. Nor had he failed to take the precautions which minimise the evils arising from dissemination. He had constructed a line of telegraph from Charlestown, within seven miles of Harper's Ferry, to Winchester, and another line was to have been constructed to Romney. He had established relays of couriers through his district. By this means he could communicate with Hill at Leesburg in three hours, and by another line of posts with Johnston at Centreville.

But his chief reason for believing that Romney might be occupied without risk to a junction between himself and Johnston lay in the impassable condition of the Virginia roads. McClellan's huge army could not drag its guns and waggons through the slough of mud which lay between Washington and Centreville. Banks' command at Frederick was in no condition for a rapid advance either upon Leesburg or on Winchester; and it was evident that little was to be feared from Lander until he had completed the work, on which he was now actively engaged, of repairing the communications which Jackson's raid had temporarily interrupted. With the information we have now before us, it is clear that Jackson's view of the situation was absolutely correct; that for the present Romney might be

---

[1] 'I have taken special pains,' he writes on January 17, 'to obtain information respecting General Banks, but I have not been informed of his having gone east. I will see what can be effected through the Catholic priests at Martinsburg.'—O. R., vol. v., p. 1036.

advantageously retained, and recruiting pushed forward in this section of Virginia. If, when McClellan advanced, the Confederates were to confine themselves to the defensive, the post would undoubtedly have to be abandoned. But if, instead of tamely surrendering the initiative, the Government were to adopt the bolder strategy which Jackson had already advocated, and Johnston's army, moving westward to the Valley, were to utilise the natural line of invasion by way of Harper's Ferry, the occupation of Romney would secure the flank, and give the invading force a fertile district from which to draw supplies.

It was not, however, on the Secretary's misconception of the situation that Jackson's request for relief was based. Nor was it the slur on his judgment that led him to resign. The injury that had been inflicted by Mr. Benjamin's unfortunate letter was not personal to himself. It affected the whole army. It was a direct blow to discipline, and struck at the very heart of military efficiency. Not only would Jackson himself be unable to enforce his authority over troops who had so successfully defied his orders; but the whole edifice of command, throughout the length and breadth of the Confederacy, would, if he tamely submitted to the Secretary's extraordinary action, be shaken to its foundations. Johnston, still smarting under Mr. Davis's rejection of his strategical views, felt this as acutely as did Jackson. 'The discipline of the army,' he wrote to the Secretary of War, 'cannot be maintained under such circumstances. The direct tendency of such orders is to insulate the commanding general from his troops, to diminish his moral as well as his official control, and to harass him with the constant fear that his most matured plans may be marred by orders from his Government which it is impossible for him to anticipate.' [1]

To Jackson he wrote advising the withdrawal of his resignation. 'Under ordinary circumstances a due sense of one's own dignity, as well as care for professional character and official rights, would demand such a course as yours, but the character of this war, the great energy exhibited

[1] O. R., vol. v., pp. 1057, 1058.

by the Government of the United States, the danger in which our very existence as an independent people lies, requires sacrifices from us all who have been educated as soldiers.

'I receive the information of the order of which you have such cause to complain from your letter. Is not that as great an official wrong to me as the order itself to you? Let us dispassionately reason with the Government on this subject of command, and if we fail to influence its practice, then ask to be relieved from positions the authority of which is exercised by the War Department, while the responsibilities are left to us.

'I have taken the liberty to detain your letter to make this appeal to your patriotism, not merely from common feelings of personal regard, but from the official opinion which makes me regard you as necessary to the service of the country in your present position.' [1]

But Johnston, when he wrote, was not aware of the remonstrance of Loring's officers. His protest, in his letter to the Secretary of War, deprecated the action of the department in ignoring the authority of the military chiefs; it had no reference to the graver evil of yielding to the representations of irresponsible subordinates. Considering the circumstances, as he believed them to exist, his advice was doubtless prudent. But it found Jackson in no compromising mood.

'Sacrifices!' he exclaimed; 'have I not made them? What is my life here but a daily sacrifice? Nor shall I ever withhold sacrifices for my country, where they will avail anything. I intend to serve here, anywhere, in any way I can, even if it be as a private soldier. But if this method of making war is to prevail, the country is ruined. My duty to Virginia requires that I shall utter my protest against it in the most energetic form in my power, and that is to resign. The authorities at Richmond must be taught a lesson, or the next victims of their meddling will be Johnston and Lee.'

Fortunately for the Confederacy, the Virginia officers

[1] O. R., vol. v., pp. 1059, 1060.

possessed a staunch supporter in the Governor of the State. Mr. Letcher knew Jackson's worth, and he knew the estimation in which he was already held by the Virginia people. The battle of Manassas had attained the dignity of a great historical event, and those whose share in the victory had been conspicuous were regarded with the same respect as the heroes of the Revolution. In the spring of 1862 Manassas stood alone, the supreme incident of the war ; its fame was not yet overshadowed by mightier conflicts, and it had taken rank in the popular mind with the decisive battles of the world.

Jackson, at the same time that he addressed Johnston, wrote to Letcher. It is possible that he anticipated the course the Governor would adopt. He certainly took care that if a protest were made it should be backed with convincing argument.

' The order from the War Department,' he wrote, ' was given without consulting me, and is abandoning to the enemy what has cost much preparation, expense, and exposure to secure, is in direct conflict with my military plans, implies a want of confidence in my capacity to judge when General Loring's troops should fall back, and is an attempt to control military operations in details from the Secretary's desk at a distance. . . . As a single order like that of the Secretary's may destroy the entire fruits of a campaign, I cannot reasonably expect, if my operations are thus to be interfered with, to be of much service in the field. . . . If I ever acquired, through the blessing of Providence, any influence over troops, this undoing my work by the Secretary may greatly diminish that influence. I regard the recent expedition as a great success. . . . I desire to say nothing against the Secretary of War. I take it for granted that he has done what he believes to be best, but I regard such policy as ruinous.' [1]

This letter had the desired result. Not content with reminding Jackson of the effect his resignation would have on the people of Virginia, and begging him to withdraw it, Governor Letcher took the Secretary of War to task. Mr.

[1] *Memoirs*, pp. 232, 233.

Benjamin, who had probably acted in ignorance rather than
in defiance of the military necessities, at once gave way.
Governor Letcher, assured that it was not the intention of
the Government to interfere with the plans of the general,
withdrew the resignation : Jackson had already yielded to
his representations.

'In this transaction,' says his chief of the staff, ' Jackson gained one of his most important victories for the Confederate States.   Had the system of encouragement to the
insubordination of inferiors, and of interference with the
responsibilities of commanders in the field, which was
initiated in his case, become established, military success
could only have been won by accident.   By his firmness
the evil usage was arrested, and a lesson impressed both
upon the Government and the people of the South.' [1]

That the soldier is but the servant of the statesman, as
war is but an instrument of diplomacy, no educated soldier
will deny.   Politics must always exercise a supreme influence on strategy ; yet it cannot be gainsaid that interference with the commanders in the field is fraught with
the gravest danger.   Mr. Benjamin's action was without
excuse.   In listening to the malcontents he ignored the
claims of discipline.   In cancelling Jackson's orders he
struck a blow at the confidence of the men in their commander.   In directing that Romney should not be held he
decided on a question which was not only purely military,
but of which the man on the spot, actually in touch with
the situation and with the enemy, could alone be judge.[2]
Even Johnston, a most able and experienced soldier,
although he was evidently apprehensive that Jackson's
front was too extended, forbore to do more than warn.
Nor was his interference the crown of Mr. Benjamin's

---

[1] Dabney, vol. i., p. 327.
[2] The inexpediency of evacuating Romney was soon made apparent. The
enemy reoccupied the village, seized Moorefield, and, with the valley of
the South Branch in their possession, threatened the rear of Edward
Johnson's position on the Alleghany Mountain so closely that he was compelled to retreat.   Three fertile counties were thus abandoned to the enemy,
and the Confederate sympathisers in North-west Virginia were proportionately discouraged.

offence. The omniscient lawyer asked no advice ; but believing, as many still believe, that neither special knowledge nor practical acquaintance with the working of the military machine is necessary in order to manœuvre armies, he had acted entirely on his own initiative. It was indeed time that he received a lesson.

Well would it have been for the Confederacy had the President himself been wise enough to apply the warning to its full extent. We have already seen that after the victory of Manassas, in his capacity of Commander-in-Chief, he refused to denude the Southern coasts of their garrisons in order to reinforce Johnston's army and strike a decisive blow in Northern territory. Had he but once recognised that he too was an amateur, that it was impossible for one man to combine effectively in his own person the duties of Head of the Government and of Commander-in-Chief, he would have handed over the management of his huge armies, and the direction of all military movements, to the most capable soldier the Confederacy could produce. Capable soldiers were not wanting ; and had the control of military operations been frankly committed to a trained strategist, and the military resources of the Southern States been placed unreservedly at the disposal of either Lee or Johnston, combined operations would have taken the place of disjointed enterprises, and the full strength of the country have been concentrated at the decisive point. It can hardly, however, be imputed as a fault to Mr. Davis that he did not anticipate a system which achieved such astonishing success in Prussia's campaigns of '66 and '70. It was not through vanity alone that he retained in his own hands the supreme control of military affairs. The Confederate system of government was but an imitation of that which existed in the United States ; and in Washington, as in Richmond, the President was not only Commander-in-Chief in name, but the arbiter on all questions of strategy and organisation ; while, to go still further back, the English Cabinet had exercised the same power since Parliament became supreme. The American people may be forgiven for their failure to recognise the deplorable results of the system they

had inherited from the mother-country. The English
people had been equally blind, and in their case there was
no excuse. The mismanagement of the national resources
in the war with France was condoned by the victories of
Wellington. The vicious conceptions of the Government,
responsible for so many useless enterprises, for waste
of life, of treasure, of opportunity, were lost in the blaze
of triumph in which the struggle ended. Forty years
later it had been forgotten that the Cabinet of 1815 had
done its best to lose the battle of Waterloo; the lessons of
the great war were disregarded, and the Cabinet of 1853-4
was allowed to work its will on the army of the Crimea.

It is a significant fact that, during the War of Secession,
for the three years the control of the armies of the North
remained in the hands of the Cabinet the balance of success
lay with the Confederates. But in March 1864 Grant was
appointed Commander-in-Chief; Lincoln abdicated his
military functions in his favour, and the Secretary of War
had nothing more to do than to comply with his requisitions. Then, for the first time, the enormous armies of the
Union were manœuvred in harmonious combination, and
the superior force was exerted to its full effect. Nor is it
less significant that during the most critical period of the
1862 campaign, the most glorious to the Confederacy, Lee
was Commander-in-Chief of the Southern armies. But
when Lee left Richmond for the Northern border, Davis
once more assumed supreme control, retaining it until it
was too late to stave off ruin.

Yet the Southern soldiers had never to complain of
such constant interference on the part of the Cabinet as
had the Northern; and to Jackson it was due that each
Confederate general, with few exceptions, was henceforward
left unhampered in his own theatre of operations. His
threat of resignation at least effected this, and, although
the President still managed or mismanaged the grand
operations, the Secretary of War was muzzled.

It might be objected that in this instance Jackson
showed little respect for the discipline he so rigidly enforced, and that in the critical situation of the Confederacy

his action was a breach of duty which was almost dis-
loyalty. Without doubt his resignation would have
seriously embarrassed the Government. To some degree at
least the confidence of both the people and the army in the
Administration would have become impaired. But Jackson
was fighting for a principle which was of even more importance than subordination. Foreseeing as he did the
certain results of civilian meddling, submission to the
Secretary's orders would have been no virtue. His presence
with the army would hardly have counterbalanced the
untrammelled exercise of Mr. Benjamin's military sagacity,
and the inevitable decay of discipline. It was not the
course of a weak man, an apathetic man, or a selfish
man. We may imagine Jackson eating his heart out at
Lexington, while the war was raging on the frontier,
and the Stonewall Brigade was fighting manfully under
another leader against the hosts of the invader. The
independence of his country was the most intense of all
his earthly desires ; and to leave the forefront of the fight
before that desire had been achieved would have been more
to him than most. He would have sacrificed far more in
resigning than in remaining ; and there was always the
possibility that a brilliant success and the rapid termination of the war would place Mr. Benjamin apparently in the
right. How would Jackson look then ? What would be the
reputation of the man who had quitted the army, on what
would have been considered a mere point of etiquette, in
the very heat of the campaign ? No ordinary man would
have faced the alternative, and have risked his reputation
in order to teach the rulers of his country a lesson which
might never reach them. It must be remembered, too,
that Jackson had not yet proved himself indispensable.
He had done good work at Manassas, but so had others.
His name was scarcely known beyond the confines of his
own State, and Virginia had several officers of higher reputation. His immediate superiors knew his value, but the
Confederate authorities, as their action proved, placed little
dependence on his judgment, and in all probability set no
special store upon his services. There was undoubtedly

every chance, had not Governor Letcher intervened, that his resignation would have been accepted. His letter then to the Secretary of War was no mere threat, the outcome of injured vanity, but the earnest and deliberate protest of a man who was ready to sacrifice even his own good name to benefit his country.

The negotiations which followed his application to resign occupied some time. He remained at Winchester, and the pleasant home where he and his wife had found such kindly welcome was the scene of much discussion. Governor Letcher was not alone in his endeavours to alter his decision. Many were the letters that poured in. From every class of Virginians, from public men and private, came the same appeal. But until he was convinced that Virginia would suffer by his action, Jackson was deaf to argument. He had not yet realised the measure of confidence which he had won. To those who sought to move him by saying that his country could not spare his services, or by speaking of his hold upon the troops, he replied that they greatly overestimated his capacity for usefulness, and that his place would readily be filled by a better man. That many of his friends were deeply incensed with the Secretary of War was only natural, and his conduct was bitterly denounced. But Jackson not only forbore to criticise, but in his presence all criticism was forbidden. There can be no doubt that he was deeply wounded. He could be angry when he chose, and his anger was none the less fierce because it was habitually controlled. He never forgave Davis for his want of wisdom after Manassas; and indeed, in future campaigns, the President's action was sufficient to exasperate the most patriotic of his generals. But during this time of trouble not a word escaped Jackson which showed those nearest him that his equanimity was disturbed. Anticipating that he would be ordered to the Military Institute, he was even delighted, says his wife, at the prospect of returning home. The reason of his calmness is not far to seek. He had come to the determination that it was his duty to resign, not, we may be certain, without prayer and self-communing, and when Jackson saw what his duty was, all other considerations were soon dismissed. He was content to leave the future in higher hands. It had been so with him when the question of secession was first broached. 'It was soon after the election of 1860,' wrote one of his clerical friends, 'when the country was beginning to heave in the agony of dissolution. We had just risen from morning prayers in his own house, where at that time I was a guest. Filled with gloom, I was lamenting in strong language the condition and prospect of our beloved country. "Why," said he, " should Christians be disturbed about the dissolution of the Union? It can only come by God's permission, and will only be permitted if for His people's good. I cannot see why we should be distressed about such things, whatever be their consequence."'

For the next month the Stonewall Brigade and its commander enjoyed a well-earned rest. The Federals, on Loring's withdrawal, contented themselves with holding Romney and Moorefield, and on Johnston's recommendation Loring and part of his troops were transferred elsewhere. The enemy showed no intention of advancing. The season was against them. The winter was abnormally wet; the Potomac was higher than it had been for twenty years, and the Virginia roads had disappeared in mud. In order to encourage re-enlistment amongst the men, furloughs were liberally granted by the authorities at Richmond, and for a short season the din of arms was unheard on the Shenandoah.

This peaceful time was one of unalloyed happiness to Jackson. The country round Winchester—the gently rolling ridges, surmounted by groves of forest trees, the great North Mountains to the westward, rising sharply from the Valley, the cosy villages and comfortable farms, and, in the clear blue distance to the south, the towering peaks of the Massanuttons—is a picture not easily forgotten. And the little town, quiet and old-fashioned, with its ample gardens and red-brick pavements, is not unworthy of its surroundings. Up a narrow street, shaded by silver maples, stood the manse, not far from the headquarter offices; and here when his daily work was done Jackson found the happiness of a home, brightened by the winning ways and attractive presence of his wife.   With his host he had much in common.   They were members of the same church, and neither yielded to the other in his high standard of morality.   The great bookcases of the manse were well stocked with appropriate literature, and the cultured intellect of Dr. Graham met more than half-way the somewhat abstruse problems with which Jackson's powerful brain delighted to wrestle.

But Jackson and his host, even had they been so inclined, were not permitted to devote their whole leisure to theological discussion.   Children's laughter broke in upon their arguments.   The young staff officers, with the bright eyes of the Winchester ladies as a lure, found a welcome by that hospitable hearth, and the war was not so absorbing a topic as to drive gaiety afield.

The sedate manse was like to lose its character. There were times when the house overflowed with music and with merriment, and sounds at which a Scotch elder would have shuddered were heard far out in the street.   And the fun and frolic were not confined to the more youthful members of the household.   The Stonewall Brigade would hardly have been surprised had they seen their general surrounded by ponderous volumes, gravely investigating the teaching of departed commentators, or joining with quiet fervour in the family devotions.   But had they seen him running down the stairs with an urchin on his shoulders, laughing like a schoolboy, they would have refused to credit the evidence of their senses.

So the months wore on. 'We spent,' says Mrs. Jackson, 'as happy a winter as ever falls to the lot of mortals upon earth.'   But the brigade was not forgotten, nor the enemy.   Every day the Virginia regiments improved in drill and discipline.   The scouts were busy on the border, and not a movement of the Federal forces was unobserved.   A vigilant watch was indeed necessary. The snows had melted and the roads were slowly drying.   The Army of the Potomac, McClellan's great host, numbering over 200,000 men, encamped around Washington, hardly more than a day's march distant from Centreville, threatened to overwhelm the 32,000 Confederates who held the intrenchments at Centreville and Manassas Junction.   General Lander was dead, but Shields, a veteran of the Mexican campaign, had succeeded him, and the force at both Romney and Frederick had been increased.   In the West things were going badly for the new Republic.   The Union troops had overrun Kentucky, Missouri, and the greater part of Tennessee.   A Confederate army had been defeated ; Confederate forts captured ; and 'the amphibious power' of the North had already been effectively exerted. Various towns on the Atlantic seaboard had been occupied. Not one of the European Powers had evinced a decided intention of espousing the Confederate cause, and the blockade still exercised its relentless pressure.

It was not, however, until the end of February that the great host beyond the Potomac showed symptoms of approaching movement.   But it had long been evident that both Winchester and Centreville must soon be abandoned. Johnston was as powerless before McClellan as Jackson before Banks.   Even if by bringing fortification to their aid they could hold their ground against the direct attack of far superior numbers, they could not prevent their intrenchments being turned.   McClellan had at his disposal the naval resources of the North.   It would be no difficult task to transfer his army by the broad reaches of the Potomac and the Chesapeake to some point on the Virginia coast, and to intervene between Centreville and Richmond.   At the same time the army of Western Virginia, which was now under command of General Frémont, might threaten Jackson in rear by moving on Staunton from Beverley and the Great Kanawha, while Banks assailed him in front.[1]

Johnston was already preparing to retreat.   Jackson,

[1] Fortunately for the Confederates this army had been reduced to 18,000 men, and the want of transport, together with the condition of the mountain roads, kept it stationary until the weather improved.

reluctant to abandon a single acre of his beloved Valley to
the enemy, was nevertheless constrained to face the possibilities of such a course. His wife was sent back to her
father's home in the same train that conveyed his sick to
Staunton; baggage and stores were removed to Mount
Jackson, half-way up the Shenandoah Valley, and his little
army, which had now been increased to three brigades, or
4,600 men all told, was ordered to break up its camps.
38,000 Federals had gradually assembled between Frederick
and Romney. Banks, who commanded the whole force,
was preparing to advance, and his outposts were already
established on the south bank of the Potomac.

But when the Confederate column filed through the
streets of Winchester, it moved not south but north.

Such was Jackson's idea of a retreat. To march
towards the enemy, not away from him; to watch his every
movement; to impose upon him with a bold front; to
delay him to the utmost; and to take advantage of every
opportunity that might offer for offensive action.

Shortly before their departure the troops received a
reminder that their leader brooked no trifling with orders.
Intoxicating liquors were forbidden in the Confederate
lines. But the regulation was systematically evaded, and
the friends of the soldiers smuggled in supplies. When
this breach of discipline was discovered, Jackson put a stop
to the traffic by an order which put the punishment on
the right shoulders. 'Every waggon that came into camp
was to be searched, and if any liquor were found it was to
be spilled out, and the waggon horses turned over to the
quartermaster for the public service.' Nevertheless, when
they left Winchester, so Jackson wrote to his wife, the
troops were in excellent spirits, and their somewhat hypo-
chondriacal general had never for years enjoyed more
perfect health—a blessing for which he had more reason
to be thankful than the Federals.

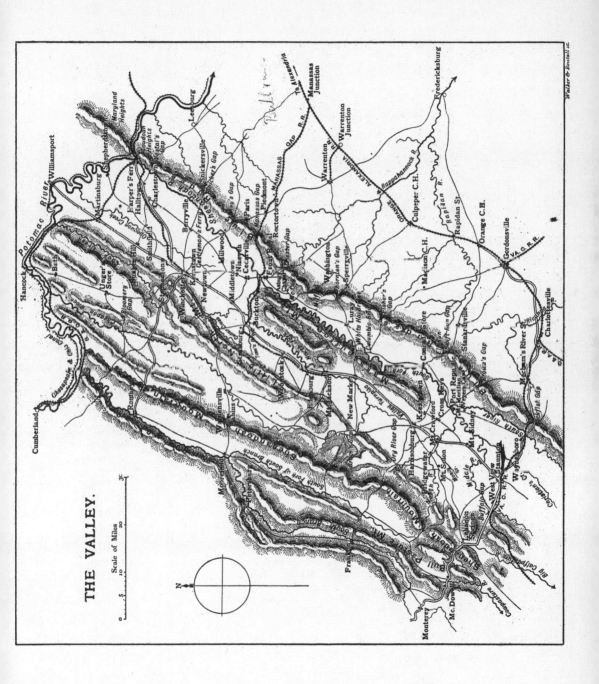

THE VALLEY.

Scale of Miles
0   5   10   20   30

Walker & Boutall sc.

NOTE

The Evils of Civilian Control

It is well worth noticing that the interference of both the Union and Confederate Cabinets was not confined to the movements and location of the troops. The organisation of the armies was very largely the work of the civilian authorities, and the advice of the soldiers was very generally disregarded. The results, it need hardly be said, were deplorable. The Northern wiseacres considered cavalry an encumbrance and a staff a mere ornamental appendage. McClellan, in consequence, was always in difficulties for the want of mounted regiments; and while many regular officers were retained in the command of batteries and companies, the important duties of the staff had sometimes to be assigned to volunteers. The men too, at first, were asked to serve for three months only; that is, they were permitted to take their discharge directly they had learned the rudiments of their work. Again, instead of the ranks of the old regiments being filled up as casualties occurred, the armies, despite McClellan's protests, were recruited by raw regiments, commanded by untrained officers. Mr. Davis, knowing something of war, certainly showed more wisdom. The organisation of the army of Northern Virginia was left, in great measure, to General Lee; so from the very first the Southerners had sufficient cavalry and as good a staff as could be got together. The soldiers, however, were only enlisted at first for twelve months; yet 'Lee,' says Lord Wolseley, 'pleaded in favour of the engagement being for the duration of the war, but he pleaded in vain;' and it was not for many months that the politicians could be induced to cancel the regulation under which the men elected their officers. The President, too, while the markets of Europe were still open, neglected to lay in a store of munitions of war: it was not till May that an order was sent across the seas, and then only for 10,000 muskets! The commissariat department, moreover, was responsible to the President and not to the commander of the armies; this, perhaps, was the worst fault of all. It would seem impossible that such mistakes, in an intelligent community, should be permitted to recur. Yet, in face of the fact that only when the commanders have been given a free hand, as was Marlborough in the Low Countries, or Wellington in the Peninsula, has the English army been thoroughly efficient, the opinion is not uncommon in England that members of Parliament and journalists are far more capable of organising an army than even the most experienced soldier.

Since the above was written the war with Spain has given further proof of how readily even the most intelligent of nations can forget the lessons of the past.

CHAPTER VIII

KERNSTOWN

By the end of February a pontoon bridge had been thrown across the Potomac at Harper's Ferry, and Banks had crossed to the Virginia shore. An army of 38,000 men, including 2,000 cavalry, and accompanied by 80 pieces of artillery, threatened Winchester.

President Lincoln was anxious that the town should be occupied. Banks believed that the opportunity was favourable. 'The roads to Winchester,' he wrote, 'are turnpikes and in tolerable condition. The enemy is weak, demoralised, and depressed.'

But McClellan, who held command of all the Federal forces, had no mind to expose even a detachment to defeat. The main Confederate army at Centreville could, at any moment, dispatch reinforcements by railway to the Valley, reversing the strategic movement which had won Bull Run; while the Army of the Potomac, held fast by the mud, could do nothing to prevent it. Banks was therefore ordered to occupy the line Charlestown-Martinsburg, some two-and-twenty miles from Winchester, to cover the reconstruction of the Baltimore and Ohio Railroad, and to accumulate supplies preparatory to a further advance. The troops, however, did not approve such cautious strategy. 'Their appetite for work,' according to their commander, 'was very sharp.' Banks himself was not less eager. 'If left to our own discretion,' he wrote to McClellan's chief of staff, 'the general desire will be to move early.'

On March 7 General D. H. Hill, acting under instructions, fell back from Leesburg, and two days later Johnston, destroying the railways, abandoned Centreville. The Confederate General-in-Chief had decided to withdraw to near

March 9. Orange Court House, trebling his distance from Washington, and surrendering much territory, but securing, in return, important strategical advantages. Protected by the Rapidan, a stream unfordable in spring, he was well placed to meet a Federal advance, and also, by a rapid march, to anticipate any force which might be transported by water and landed close to Richmond.

Jackson was now left isolated in the Valley. The nearest Confederate infantry were at Culpeper Court House, beyond the Blue Ridge, nearly sixty miles south-east. In his front, within two easy marches, was an army just seven times his strength, at Romney another detachment of several thousand men, and a large force in the Alleghanies. He was in no hurry, however, to abandon Winchester.

Johnston had intended that when the main army fell back towards Richmond his detachments should follow suit. Jackson found a loophole in his instructions which gave him full liberty of action.

'I greatly desire,' he wrote to Johnston on March 8, 'to hold this place [Winchester] so far as may be consistent with your views and plans, and am making arrangements, by constructing works, &c., to make a stand. Though you desired me some time since to fall back in the event of yourself and General Hill's doing so, yet in your letter of the 5th inst. you say, "Delay the enemy as long as you can;" I have felt justified in remaining here for the present.

'And now, General, that Hill has fallen back, can you not send him over here? I greatly need such an officer; one who can be sent off as occasion may offer against an exposed detachment of the enemy for the purpose of capturing it. . . . I believe that if you can spare Hill, and let him move here at once, you will never have occasion to regret it. The very idea of reinforcements coming to Winchester would, I think, be a damper to the enemy, in addition to the fine effect that would be produced on our own troops, already in fine spirits. But if you cannot spare

Hill, can you not send me some other troops? If we cannot be successful in defeating the enemy should he advance, a kind Providence may enable us to inflict a terrible wound and effect a safe retreat in the event of having to fall back. I will keep myself on the alert with respect to communications between us, so as to be able to join you at the earliest possible moment, if such a movement becomes necessary.'[1]

This letter is characteristic. When Jackson asked for reinforcements the cause of the South seemed well-nigh hopeless. Her Western armies were retiring, defeated and demoralised. Several of her Atlantic towns had fallen to the Federal navy, assisted by strong landing parties. The army on which she depended for the defence of Richmond, yielding to the irresistible presence of far superior numbers, was retreating into the interior of Virginia. There was not the faintest sign of help from beyond the sea. The opportunity for a great counterstroke had been suffered to escape. Her forces were too small for aught but defensive action, and it was difficult to conceive that she could hold her own against McClellan's magnificently appointed host. 'Events,' said Davis at this time, 'have cast on our arms and hopes the gloomiest shadows.' But from the Valley, the northern outpost of the Confederate armies, where the danger was most threatening and the means of defence the most inadequate, came not a whisper of apprehension. The troops that held the border were but a handful, but Jackson knew enough of war to be aware that victory does not always side with the big battalions. Neither Johnston nor Davis had yet recognised, as he did, the weak joint in the Federal harness. Why should the appearance of Hill's brigade at Winchester discourage Banks? Johnston had fallen back to the Rapidan, and there was now no fear of the Confederates detaching troops suddenly from Manassas. Why should the bare idea that reinforcements were coming up embarrass the Federals?

The letter itself does not indeed supply a definite answer. Jackson was always most guarded in his correspondence; and, if he could possibly avoid it, he never

[1] O. R., vol. v., p. 1094.

made the slightest allusion to the information on which his plans were based. His staff officers, however, after the campaign was over, were generally enlightened as to the motive of his actions, and we are thus enabled to fill the gap.[1] Jackson demanded reinforcements for the one reason that a blow struck near Winchester would cause alarm in Washington. The communications of the Federal capital with both the North and West passed through or close to Harper's Ferry; and the passage over the Potomac, which Banks was now covering, was thus the most sensitive point in the invader's front. Well aware, as indeed was every statesman and every general in Virginia, of the state of public feeling in the North, Jackson saw with more insight than others the effect that was likely to be produced should the Government, the press, and the people of the Federal States have reason to apprehend that the capital of the Union was in danger.

If the idea of playing on the fears of his opponents by means of the weak detachment under Jackson ever suggested itself to Johnston, he may be forgiven if he dismissed it as chimerical. For 7,600 men[2] to threaten with any useful result a capital which was defended by 250,000 seemed hardly within the bounds of practical strategy. Johnston had nevertheless determined to turn the situation to account. In order to protect the passages of the Upper Potomac, McClellan had been compelled to disseminate his army. Between his main body south of Washington and his right wing under Banks was a gap of fifty miles, and this separation Johnston was determined should be maintained. The President, to whom he had referred Jackson's letter, was unable to spare the reinforcements therein requested, and the defence of the Valley was left to the 4,600 men encamped at Winchester. Jackson was permitted to use his own judgment as to his own position, but something more was required of him than the mere protection of a tract of territory. ' He was to endeavour to employ the invaders in the Valley without exposing himself to the

---

[1] Letter from Major Hotchkiss to the author.
[2] Jackson, 4,600; Hill, 3,000.

danger of defeat, by keeping so near the enemy as to prevent his making any considerable detachment to reinforce McClellan, but not so near that he might be compelled to fight.' [1]

To carry out these instructions Jackson had at his disposal 3,600 infantry, 600 cavalry, and six batteries of 27 guns. Fortunately, they were all Virginians, with the exception of one battalion, the First, which was composed of Irish navvies.

This force, which had now received the title of the Army of the Valley, was organised in three brigades :—

First Brigade (' Stonewall ') : Brigadier-General Garnett	{	2nd Virginia Regiment 4th ,, ,, 5th ,, ,, 27th ,, ,, 33rd ,, ,,
Second Brigade : Col. Burks	{	21st ,, ,, 42nd ,, ,, 48th ,, ,, 1st Regular Battalion (Irish)
Third Brigade : Col. Fulkerson	{	23rd Virginia Regiment 27th ,, ,,

McLaughlin's Battery	.	.	.	. 8 guns
Waters' ,,	.	.	.	. 4 ,,
Carpenter's ,,	.	.	.	. 4 ,,
Marye's ,,	.	.	.	. 4 ,,
Shumaker's ,,	.	.	.	. 4 ,,
Ashby's Regiment of Cavalry				
Chew's Horse-Artillery Battery	.	.	.	3 ,,

The infantry were by this time fairly well armed and equipped, but the field-pieces were mostly smoothbores of small calibre. Of the quality of the troops Bull Run had been sufficient test. Side by side with the sons of the old Virginia houses the hunters and yeomen of the Valley had proved their worth. Their skill as marksmen had stood them in good stead. Men who had been used from boyhood to shoot squirrels in the woodland found the Federal soldier a target difficult to miss. Skirmishing and patrolling came instinctively to those who had stalked the deer and the bear in the mountain forests ; and the simple hardy life of an

[1] Johnston's *Narrative*.

agricultural community was the best probation for the trials of a campaign. The lack of discipline and of competent regimental officers might have placed them at a disadvantage had they been opposed to regulars; but they were already half-broken to the soldier's trade before they joined the ranks. They were no strangers to camp and bivouac, to peril and adventure; their hands could guard their heads. Quick sight and steady nerve, unfailing vigilance and instant resolve, the very qualities which their devotion to field-sports fostered, were those which had so often prevailed in the war of the Revolution over the mechanical tactics of well-disciplined battalions; and on ground with which they were perfectly familiar the men of the Shenandoah were formidable indeed.

They were essentially rough and ready. Their appearance would hardly have captivated a martinet. The eye that lingers lovingly on glittering buttons and spotless belts would have turned away in disdain from Jackson's soldiers. There was nothing bright about them but their rifles. They were as badly dressed, and with as little regard for uniformity, as the defenders of Torres Vedras or the Army of Italy in 1796. Like Wellington and Napoleon, the Confederate generals cared very little what their soldiers wore so long as they did their duty. Least of all can one imagine Stonewall Jackson exercising his mind as to the cut of a tunic or the polish of a buckle. The only standing order in the English army of the Peninsula which referred to dress forbade the wearing of the enemy's uniform. It was the same in the Army of the Valley, although at a later period even this order was of necessity ignored. As their forefathers of the Revolution took post in Washington's ranks clad in hunting shirts and leggings, so the Confederate soldiers preferred the garments spun by their own women to those supplied them by the State. Grey, of all shades, from light blue to butter-nut, was the universal colour. The coatee issued in the early days of the war had already given place to a short-waisted and single-breasted jacket. The blue *képi* held out longer. The soft felt hat which experience soon proved the most serviceable head-dress had not yet become universal.   But the long boots had gone ; and strong brogans, with broad soles and low heels, had been found more comfortable.   Overcoats were soon discarded.   ' The men came to the conclusion that the trouble of carrying them on hot days outweighed their comfort when the cold day arrived.   Besides, they found that life in the open air hardened them to such an extent that changes in temperature were hardly felt.' [1]   Nor did the knapsack long survive.   ' It was found to gall the back and shoulders and weary the man before half the march was accomplished. It did not pay to carry around clean clothes while waiting for the time to use them.' [2]   But the men still clung to their blankets and waterproof sheets, worn in a roll over the left shoulder, and the indispensable haversack carried their whole kit.   Tents—except the enemy's—were rarely seen. The Army of the Valley generally bivouacked in the woods, the men sleeping in pairs, rolled in their blankets and rubber sheets.   The cooking arrangements were primitive.   A few frying-pans and skillets formed the culinary apparatus of a company, with a bucket or two in addition, and the frying-pans were generally carried with their handles stuck in the rifle-barrels !   The tooth-brush was a button-hole ornament, and if, as was sometimes the case, three days' rations were served out at a single issue, the men usually cooked and ate them at once, so as to avoid the labour of carrying them.

Such was Jackson's infantry, a sorry contrast indeed to the soldierly array of the Federals, with their complete appointments and trim blue uniforms.   But ' fine feathers,' though they may have their use, are hardly essential to efficiency in the field ; and whilst it is absolutely true that no soldiers ever marched with less to encumber them than the Confederates, it is no empty boast that ' none ever marched faster or held out longer.'

If the artillery, with a most inferior equipment, was less efficient than the infantry, the cavalry was an invaluable auxiliary.   Ashby was the *beau-idéal* of a captain of light-horse.   His reckless daring, both across-country and under fire, made him the idol of the army.   Nor was

---

[1] *Soldier Life in the Army of Northern Virginia*, chap. ii.   [2] *Ibid.*

his reputation confined to the Confederate ranks. ' I think even our men,' says a Federal officer, ' had a kind of admiration for him, as he sat unmoved upon his horse, and let them pepper away at him as if he enjoyed it.' His one shortcoming was his ignorance of drill and discipline. But in the spring of 1862 these deficiencies were in a fair way of being rectified. He had already learned something of tactics. In command of a few hundred mounted riflemen and a section of horse-artillery he was unsurpassed ; and if his men were apt to get out of hand in battle, his personal activity ensured their strict attention on the outposts. He thought little of riding seventy or eighty miles within the day along his picket line, and it is said that he first recommended himself to Jackson by visiting the Federal camps disguised as a horse doctor. Jackson placed much dependence on his mounted troops. Immediately he arrived in the Valley he established his cavalry outposts far to the front. While the infantry were reposing in their camps near Winchester, the south bank of the Potomac, forty miles northward, was closely and incessantly patrolled. The squadrons never lacked recruits. With the horse-loving Virginians the cavalry was the favourite arm, and the strength of the regiments was only limited by the difficulty of obtaining horses. To the sons of the Valley planters and farmers Ashby's ranks offered a most attractive career. The discipline was easy, and there was no time for drill. But of excitement and adventure there was enough and to spare. Scarcely a day passed without shots being exchanged at one point or another of the picket line. There were the enemy's outposts to be harassed, prisoners to be taken, bridges to be burnt, and convoys to be captured. Many were the opportunities for distinction. Jackson demanded something more from his cavalry than merely guarding the frontier. It was not sufficient for him to receive warning that the enemy was advancing. He wanted information from which he could deduce what he intended doing ; information of the strength of his garrisons, of the dispositions of his camps, of every movement which took place beyond the river. The cavalry had other and more dangerous duties than vedette and escort.　To penetrate the enemy's lines, to approach his camps, and observe his columns—these were the tasks of Ashby's riders, and in these they were unrivalled.　Many of them were no more than boys ; but their qualifications for such a life were undeniable.　A more gallant or high-spirited body of young soldiers never welcomed the 'boot and saddle.'　Their horses were their own, scions of good Virginian stock, with the blood of many a well-known sire—Eclipse, Brighteyes, and Timoleon—in their veins, and they knew how to care for them.　They were acquainted with every country lane and woodland track. They had friends in every village, and their names were known to every farmer.　The night was no hindrance to them, even in the region of the mountain and the forest. The hunter's paths were as familiar to them as the turnpike roads.　They knew the depth and direction of every ford, and could predict the effect of the weather on stream and track.　More admirable material for the service of intelligence could not possibly have been found, and Ashby's audacity in reconnaissance found ready imitators.　A generous rivalry in deeds of daring spread through the command.　Bold enterprises were succeeded by others yet more bold, and, to use the words of a gentleman who, although he was a veteran of four years' service, was but nineteen years of age when Richmond fell, 'We thought no more of riding through the enemy's bivouacs than of riding round our fathers' farms.'　So congenial were the duties of the cavalry, so attractive the life and the associations, that it was no rare thing for a Virginia gentleman to resign a commission in another arm in order to join his friends and kinsmen as a private in Ashby's ranks.　And so before the war had been in progress for many months the fame of the Virginia cavalry rivalled that of their Revolutionary forbears under 'Light-Horse Harry,' the friend of Washington and the father of Lee.

But if the raw material of Jackson's army was all that could be desired, no less so was the material of the force opposed to him.　The regiments of Banks' army corps were recruited as a rule in the Western States ; Ohio,

Indiana, and West Virginia furnished the majority. They too were hunters and farmers, accustomed to firearms, and skilled in woodcraft. No hardier infantry marched beneath the Stars and Stripes; the artillery, armed with a proportion of rifled guns, was more efficient than that of the Confederates; and in cavalry alone were the Federals overmatched. In numbers the latter were far superior to Ashby's squadrons; in everything else they were immeasurably inferior. Throughout the North horsemanship was practically an unknown art. The gentlemen of New England had not inherited the love of their Ironside ancestors for the saddle and the chase. Even in the forests of the West men travelled by waggon and hunted on foot. 'As cavalry,' says one of Banks' brigadiers, 'Ashby's men were greatly superior to ours. In reply to some orders I had given, my cavalry commander replied, "I can't catch them, sir; they leap fences and walls like deer; neither our men nor our horses are so trained." ' [1]

It was easy enough to fill the ranks of the Northern squadrons. Men volunteered freely for what they deemed the more dashing branch of the service, ignorant that its duties were far harder both to learn and to execute than those of the other arms, and expecting, says a Federal officer, that the regiment would be accompanied by an itinerant livery stable! Both horses and men were recruited without the slightest reference to their fitness for cavalry work. No man was rejected, no matter what his size or weight, no matter whether he had ever had anything to do with horseflesh or not, and consequently the proportion of sick horses was enormous. Moreover, while the Southern troopers generally carried a firearm, either rifle or shot-gun, some of the Northern squadrons had only the sabre, and in a wooded country the firearm was master of the situation. During the first two years of the war, therefore, the Federal cavalry, generally speaking, were bad riders and worse horsemasters, unable to move except upon the roads, and as inefficient on reconnaissance as in action. For an invading army, information, ample and accurate, is the first requisite.

[1] *Brook Farm to Cedar Mountain*, General G. H. Gordon, p. 136.

Operating in a country which, almost invariably, must be better known to the defenders, bold scouting alone will secure it from ambush and surprise. Bold scouting was impossible with such mounted troops as Banks possessed, and throughout the Valley campaign the Northern general was simply groping in the dark.

But even had his cavalry been more efficient, it is doubtful whether Banks would have profited. His appointment was political. He was an ardent Abolitionist, but he knew nothing whatever of soldiering. He had begun life as a hand in a cotton factory. By dint of energy and good brains his rise had been rapid; and although, when the war broke out, he was still a young man, he had been Governor of Massachusetts and Speaker of the House of Representatives. What the President expected when he gave him an army corps it is difficult to divine; what might have been expected any soldier could have told him. To gratify an individual, or perhaps to conciliate a political faction, the life of many a private soldier was sacrificed. Lincoln, it is true, was by no means solitary in the unwisdom of his selections for command. His rival in Richmond, it is said, had a fatal *penchant* for his first wife's relations; his political supporters were constantly rewarded by appointments in the field, and the worst disasters that befell the Confederacy were due, in great part, to the blunders of officers promoted for any other reason than efficiency. For Mr. Davis there was little excuse. He had been educated at West Point. He had served in the regular army of the United States, and had been Secretary of War at Washington. Lincoln, on the other hand, knew nothing of war, beyond what he had learned in a border skirmish, and very little of general history. He had not yet got rid of the common Anglo-Saxon idea that a man who has pluck and muscle is already a good soldier, and that the same qualities which serve in a street-brawl are all that is necessary to make a general. Nor were historical precedents wanting for the mistakes of the American statesmen. In both the Peninsula and the Crimea, lives, treasure, and prestige were as recklessly wasted as in Virginia; and staff officers who owed their positions to social influence alone, generals, useless and ignorant, who succeeded to responsible command by virtue of seniority and a long purse, were the standing curse of the English army. At the same time, it may well be questioned whether some of the regular officers would have done better than Banks. He was no fool, and if he had not studied the art of war, there have been barrack-square generals who have showed as much ignorance without one-quarter his ability. Natural common-sense has often a better chance of success than a rusty brain, and a mind narrowed by routine. After serving in twenty campaigns Frederick the Great's mules were still mules. On this very theatre of war, in the forests beyond Romney, an English general had led a detachment of English soldiers to a defeat as crushing as it was disgraceful, and Braddock was a veteran of many wars. Here, too, Patterson, an officer of Volunteers who had seen much service, had allowed Johnston to slip away and join Beauregard on Bull Run. The Northern people, in good truth, had as yet no reason to place implicit confidence in the leading of trained soldiers. They had yet to learn that mere length of service is no test whatever of capacity for command, and that character forti-fied by knowledge is the only charm which attracts success.

Jackson had already some acquaintance with Banks. During the Romney expedition the latter had been posted at Frederick with 16,000 men, and a more enterprising commander would at least have endeavoured to thwart the Confederate movements. Banks, supine in his camps, made neither threat nor demonstration. Throughout the winter, Ashby's troopers had ridden unmolested along the bank of the Potomac. Lander alone had worried the Confederate outposts, driven in their advanced detachments, and drawn supplies from the Virginian farms. Banks had been over-cautious and inactive, and Jackson had not failed to note his characteristics.

Up to March 9 the Federal general, keeping his cavalry in rear, had pushed forward no farther than Charlestown March 9. and Bunker Hill. On that day the news reached McClellan that the Confederates were preparing

to abandon Centreville. He at once determined to push
forward his whole army. Banks was instructed to
move on Winchester, and on the morning of the
12th his leading division occupied the town.

March 12.

Jackson had withdrawn the previous evening. Twice,
on March 7 and again on the 11th, he had offered battle.[1]
His men had remained under arms all day in the hope
that the enemy's advanced-guard might be tempted to
attack. But the activity of Ashby's cavalry, and the boldness with which Jackson maintained his position, impressed
his adversary with the conviction that the Confederate
force was much greater than it really was. It was reported
in the Federal camps that the enemy's strength was from
7,000 to 11,000 men, and that the town was fortified.
Jackson's force did not amount to half that number, and,
according to a Northern officer, ' one could have jumped
over his intrenchments as easily as Remus over the walls
of Rome.'

Jackson abandoned Winchester with extreme reluctance.
Besides being the principal town in that section of the Valley,
it was strategically important to the enemy. Good roads
led in every direction, and communication was easy with
Romney and Cumberland to the north-west, and with
Washington and Manassas to the south-east. Placed at
Winchester, Banks could support, or be supported by, the
troops in West Virginia or the army south of Washington.
A large and fertile district would thus be severed from the
Confederacy, and the line of invasion across the Upper
Potomac completely blocked. Overwhelming as was the
strength of the Union force, exceeding his own by more
than eight to one, great as was the caution of the Federal
leader, it was only an unlucky accident that restrained
Jackson from a resolute endeavour to at least postpone
the capture of the town. He had failed to induce the

[1] Major Harman, of Jackson's staff, writing to his brother on March 6,
says : ' The general told me last night that the Yankees had 17,000 men
at the two points, Charlestown and Bunker Hill.' On March 8 he writes:
' 3,000 effective men is about the number of General Jackson's force. The
sick, those on furlough, and the deserters from the militia, reduce him to
about that number.'—MS.

enemy's advanced guard to attack him in position. To attack himself, in broad daylight, with such vast disproportion of numbers, was out of the question. His resources, however, were not exhausted. After dark on the 12th, when his troops had left the town, he called a council, consisting of General Garnett and the regimental commanders of the Stonewall Brigade, and proposed a night attack on the Federal advance. When the troops had eaten their supper and rested for some hours, they were to march to the neighbourhood of the enemy, some four miles north of Winchester, and make the attack before daylight. The Federal troops were raw and inexperienced. Prestige was on the side of the Confederates, and their *moral* was high. The darkness, the suddenness and energy of the attack, the lack of drill and discipline, would all tend to throw the enemy into confusion; and 'by the vigorous use of the bayonet, and the blessing of divine Providence,' Jackson believed that he would win a signal victory. In the meantime, whilst the council was assembling, he went off, booted and spurred, to make a hasty call on Dr. Graham, whose family he found oppressed with the gloom that overspread the whole town. 'He was so buoyant and hopeful himself that their drooping spirits were revived, and after engaging with them in family worship, he retired, departing with a cheerful "Good evening," merely saying that he intended to dine with them the next day as usual.'

When the council met, however, it was found that someone had blundered. The staff had been at fault. The general had ordered his trains to be parked immediately south of Winchester, but they had been taken by those in charge to Kernstown and Newtown, from three to eight miles distant, and the troops had been marched back to them to get their rations.

Jackson learned for the first time, when he met his officers, that his brigades, instead of being on the outskirts of Winchester, were already five or six miles away. A march of ten miles would thus be needed to bring them into contact with the enemy. This fact and the disapproval of the council caused him to abandon his project.

Before following his troops he once more went back to Dr. Graham's. His cheerful demeanour during his previous visit, although he had been as reticent as ever as to his plans, had produced a false impression, and this he thought it his duty to correct. He explained his plans to his friend, and as he detailed the facts which had induced him to change them, he repeatedly expressed his reluctance to give up Winchester without a blow. 'With slow and desperate earnestness he said, "Let me think—can I not yet carry my plan into execution?" As he uttered these words he grasped the hilt of his sword, and the fierce light that blazed in his eyes revealed to his companion a new man. The next moment he dropped his head and released his sword, with the words, "No, I must not do it; it may cost the lives of too many brave men. I must retreat and wait for a better time."' He had learned a lesson. 'Late in the evening,' says the medical director of the Valley army, 'we withdrew from Winchester. I rode with the general as we left the place, and as we reached a high point overlooking the town we both turned to look at Winchester, now left to the mercy of the Federal soldiers. I think that a man may sometimes yield to overwhelming emotion, and I was utterly overcome by the fact that I was leaving all that I held dear on earth; but my emotion was arrested by one look at Jackson. His face was fairly blazing with the fire of wrath that was burning in him, and I felt awed before him. Presently he cried out, in a tone almost savage, "That is the last council of war I will ever hold!"'

On leaving Winchester Jackson fell back to Strasburg, eighteen miles south. There was no immediate pursuit. Banks, in accordance with his instructions, occupied the

March 18. town, and awaited further orders. These came on the 18th,[1] and Shields' division of 11,000 men with 27 guns was at once pushed on to Strasburg. Jackson had already withdrawn, hoping to draw Banks up the Valley, and was now encamped near Mount Jackson, a strong position twenty-five miles further south, the indefatigable Ashby still skirmishing with the enemy. The unusual

[1] O. R., vol. xii., part i., p. 164.

audacity which prompted the Federal advance was probably due to the fact that the exact strength of the Confederate force had been ascertained in Winchester. At all events, all apprehension of attack had vanished. Jackson's 4,500 men were considered a *quantité négligeable*, a mere corps of observation; and not only was Shields sent forward without support, but a large portion of Banks' corps was ordered to another field. Its *rôle* as an independent force had ceased. Its movements were henceforward to be subordinate to those of the main army, and McClellan designed to bring it into closer connection with his advance on Richmond. How his design was frustrated, how he struggled in vain to correct the original dissemination of his forces, how his right wing was held in a vice by Jackson, and how his initial errors eventually ruined his campaign, is a strategical lesson of the highest import.

From the day McClellan took command the Army of the Potomac had done practically nothing. Throughout the winter troops had poured into Washington at the rate of 40,000 a month. At the end of December there were 148,000 men fit for duty. On March 20 the grand aggregate was 240,000.[1] But during the winter no important enterprise had been undertaken. The colours of the rebels were still flaunting within sight of the forts of Washington, and the mouth of the Potomac was securely closed by Confederate batteries. With a mighty army at their service it is little wonder that the North became restive and reproached their general. It is doubtless true that the first thing needful was organisation. To discipline and consolidate the army so as to make success assured was unquestionably the wiser policy. The impatience of a sovereign people, ignorant of war, is not to be lightly yielded to. At the same time, the desire of a nation cannot be altogether disregarded. A general who obstinately refuses to place himself in accord with the political situation forfeits the confidence of his employers and the cordial support of the Administration. The cry throughout the North was for action. The President took

[1] O. R., vol. xi., part iii., p. 26.

it upon himself to issue a series of orders. The army was
ordered to advance on February 22, a date chosen because
it was Washington's birthday, just as the third and most
disastrous assault on Plevna was delivered on the 'name-
day' of the Czar. McClellan secured delay. His plans
were not yet ripe. The Virginia roads were still impassable.
The season was not yet sufficiently advanced for active
operations, and that his objections were well founded it is
impossible to deny. The prospect of success depended
much upon the weather. Virginia, covered in many places
with dense forests, crossed by many rivers, and with most
indifferent communications, is a most difficult theatre of
war, and the amenities of the Virginian spring are not to
be lightly faced. Napoleon's fifth element, 'mud,' is a
most disturbing factor in military calculations. It is related
that a Federal officer, sent out to reconnoitre a road in a
certain district of Virginia, reported that the road was there,
but that he guessed 'the bottom had fallen out.' Moreover,
McClellan had reason to believe that the Confederate army
at Manassas was more than double its actual strength. His
intelligence department, controlled, not by a trained staff
officer, but by a well-known detective, estimated Johnston's
force at 115,000 men. In reality, including the detachment
on the Shenandoah, it at no time exceeded 50,000. But for
all this there was no reason whatever for absolute inactivity.
The capture of the batteries which barred the entrance to
the Potomac, the defeat of the Confederate detachments
along the river, the occupation of Winchester or of Leesburg, were all feasible operations. By such means the
impatience of the Northern people might have been
assuaged. A few successes, even on a small scale, would
have raised the *moral* of the troops and have trained them
to offensive movements. The general would have retained
the confidence of the Administration, and have secured the
respect of his opponents. Jackson had set him the example.
His winter expeditions had borne fruit. The Federal
generals opposed to him gave him full credit for activity.
'Much dissatisfaction was expressed by the troops,' says
one of Banks' brigadiers, 'that Jackson was permitted to

get away from Winchester without a fight, and but little heed was paid to my assurances that this chieftain would be apt, before the war closed, to give us an entertainment up to the utmost of our aspirations.'[1]

It was not only of McClellan's inactivity that the Government complained. At the end of February he submitted a plan of operations to the President, and with that plan Mr. Lincoln totally disagreed. McClellan, basing his project on the supposition that Johnston had 100,000 men behind formidable intrenchments at Manassas, blocking the road to Richmond, proposed to transfer 150,000 men to the Virginia coast by sea ; and landing either at Urbanna on the Rappahannock, or at Fortress Monroe on the Yorktown peninsula, to intervene between the Confederate army and Richmond, and possibly to capture the Southern capital before Johnston could get back to save it.

The plan at first sight seemed promising. But in Lincoln's eyes it had this great defect : during the time McClellan was moving round by water and disembarking his troops—and this, so few were the transports, would take at least a month—Johnston might make a dash at Washington. The city had been fortified. A cordon of detached forts surrounded it on a circumference of thirty miles. The Potomac formed an additional protection. But a cordon of isolated earthworks does not appeal as an effective barrier to the civilian mind, and above Point of Rocks the great river was easy of passage. Even if Washington were absolutely safe from a *coup de main*, Lincoln had still good reason for apprehension. The Union capital was merely the seat of government. It had no commercial interests. With a population of but 20,000, it was of no more practical importance than Windsor or Versailles. Compared with New York, Pittsburg, or Philadelphia, it was little more than a village. But, in the regard of the Northern people, Washington was the centre of the Union, the keystone of the national existence. The Capitol, the White House, the Treasury, were symbols as sacred to the States as the colours

[1] General G. H. Gordon.

to a regiment.[1] If the nation was set upon the fall of Richmond, it was at least as solicitous for the security of its own
chief city, and an administration that permitted that security
to be endangered would have been compelled to bow to the
popular clamour.   The extraordinary taxation demanded
by the war already pressed heavily on the people.   Stocks
were falling rapidly, and the financial situation was almost
critical.   It is probable, too, that a blow at Washington
would have done more than destroy all confidence in the
Government.   England and France were chafing under the
effects of the blockade.   The marts of Europe were hungry
for cotton.   There was much sympathy beyond seas with
the seceded States ; and, should Washington fall, the South,
in all likelihood, would be recognised as an independent
nation.   Even if the Great Powers were to refuse her active
aid in the shape of fleets and armies, she would at least
have access to the money markets of the world ; and it
was possible that neither England nor France would endure
the closing of her ports.   With the breaking of the blockade,
money, munitions, and perhaps recruits, would be poured
into the Confederacy, and the difficulty of reconquest would
be trebled.   The dread of foreign interference was, therefore,
very real ; and Lincoln, foreseeing the panic that would
shake the nation should a Confederate army cross the
Potomac at Harper's Ferry or Point of Rocks, was quite
justified in insisting on the security of Washington being
placed beyond a doubt.   He knew, as also did Jackson,
that even a mere demonstration against so vital a point
might have the most deplorable effect.   Whatever line of
invasion, he asked, might be adopted, let it be one that
would cover Washington.

Lincoln's remonstrances, however, had no great weight
with McClellan.   The general paid little heed to the political
situation.   His chief argument in favour of the expedition by
sea had been the strength of the fortifications at Manassas.
Johnston's retreat on March 9 removed this obstacle from

[1] For an interesting exposition of the views of the soldiers at Washington,
see evidence of General Hitchcock, U.S.A., acting as Military Adviser to the
President, O. R., vol. xii., part i., p. 221.

his path; but although he immediately marched his whole
army in pursuit, he still remained constant to his favourite
idea. The road to Richmond from Washington involved
a march of one hundred miles, over a difficult country,
with a single railway as the line of supply. The route
from the coast, although little shorter, was certainly
easier. Fortress Monroe had remained in Federal hands.
Landing under the shelter of its guns, he would push forward, aided by the navy, to West Point, the terminus of the
York River Railroad, within thirty miles of Richmond, transporting his supplies by water. Washington, with the garrison he would leave behind, would in his opinion be quite
secure. The Confederates would be compelled to concentrate
for the defence of their capital, and a resolute endeavour
on their part to cross the Potomac was forbidden by every
rule of strategy. Had not Johnston, in his retreat, burnt
the railway bridges? Could there be a surer indication
that he had no intention of returning?

Such was McClellan's reasoning, and, putting politics
aside, it was perfectly sound. Lincoln reluctantly yielded,
and on March 17 the Army of the Potomac, withdrawing
by successive divisions from Centreville to Alexandria,
began its embarkation for the Peninsula, the region, in
McClellan's words, 'of sandy roads and short land transportation.'[1] The vessels assembled at Alexandria could
only carry 10,000 men, thus involving at least fifteen
voyages to and fro. Yet the Commander-in-Chief was full
of confidence. To the little force in the Shenandoah Valley,
flying southward before Shields, he gave no thought. It
would have been nothing short of miraculous had he even
suspected that 4,500 men, under a professor of the higher
mathematics, might bring to naught the operations of his
gigantic host. Jackson was not even to be followed. Of
Banks' three divisions, Shields', Sedgwick's, and Williams',
that of Shields alone was considered sufficient to protect
Harper's Ferry, the Baltimore and Ohio Railway, and the
Chesapeake Canal.[2] Banks, with the remainder of his army,
was to move at once to Manassas, and cover the approaches

[1] O. R., vol. xi., part iii., p. 7.   [2] Ibid., p. 11.

to Washington east of the Blue Ridge. Sedgwick had already been detached to join McClellan; and on March 20 Williams' division began its march towards Manassas, while Shields fell back on Winchester.

On the evening of the 21st Ashby reported to Jackson that the enemy was retreating, and information came to March 21. hand that a long train of waggons, containing the baggage of 12,000 men, had left Winchester for Castleman's Ferry on the Shenandoah. Further reports indicated that Banks' whole force was moving eastward, and Jackson, in accordance with his instructions to hold the enemy in the Valley, at once pushed northward.[1] On the March 22. 22nd, Ashby, with 280 troopers and 3 horse-artillery guns, struck Shields' pickets about a mile south of Winchester. A skirmish ensued, and the presence of infantry, a battery, and some cavalry, was ascertained. Shields, who was wounded during the engagement by a shell, handled his troops ably. His whole division was in the near neighbourhood, but carefully concealed, and Ashby reported to Jackson that only four regiments of infantry, besides the guns and cavalry, remained at Winchester. Information obtained from the townspeople within the Federal lines confirmed the accuracy of his estimate. The enemy's main body, he was told, had already marched, and the troops which had opposed him were under orders to move to Harper's Ferry the next morning.

On receipt of this intelligence Jackson hurried forward from his camp near Woodstock, and that night reached March 23. Strasburg. At dawn on the 23rd four companies were despatched to reinforce Ashby; and under cover of this advanced guard the whole force followed in the direction of Kernstown, a tiny village, near which the Federal outposts were established. At one o'clock the three brigades, wearied by a march of fourteen miles succeeding one of twenty-two on the previous day, arrived

[1] A large portion of the Army of the Potomac, awaiting embarkation, still remained at Centreville. The cavalry had pushed forward towards the Rapidan, and the Confederates, unable to get information, did not suspect that McClellan was moving to the Peninsula until March 25.

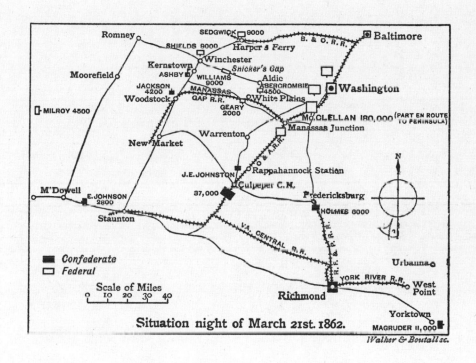

Situation night of March 21st. 1862.

Walker & Boutall sc.

upon the field of action. The ranks, however, were sadly weakened, for many of the men had succumbed to their unusual exertions. Ashby still confronted the enemy; but the Federals had developed a brigade of infantry, supported by two batteries and several squadrons, and the Confederate cavalry were slowly giving ground. On reaching the field Jackson ordered the troops to bivouac. 'Though it was very desirable,' he wrote, 'to prevent the enemy from leaving the Valley, yet I deemed it best not to attack until morning.' An inspection of the ground, however, convinced him that delay was impracticable. 'Ascertaining,' he continued, 'that the Federals had a position from which our forces could be seen, I concluded that it would be dangerous to postpone the attack until next day, as reinforcements might be brought up during the night.'[1] Ashby was directed to detach half his cavalry[2] under Major Funsten in order to cover the left flank; and Jackson, ascertaining that his men were in good spirits at the prospect of meeting the enemy, made his preparations for fighting his first battle.

The position occupied by the Federals was by no means ill-adapted for defence. The country round Winchester, and indeed throughout the Valley of the Shenandoah, resembles in many of its features an English landscape. Low ridges, covered with open woods of oak and pine, overlook green pastures and scattered copses; and the absence of hedgerows and cottages gives a parklike aspect to the broad acres of rich 'blue grass.' But the deep lanes and hollow roads of England find here no counterpart. The tracks are rough and rude, and even the 'pikes,' as the main thoroughfares are generally called, are flush with the fields on either hand. The traffic has not yet worn them to a lower level, and Virginia roadmaking despises such refinements as cuttings or embankments. The highways, even the 'Valley pike' itself, the great road which is inseparably linked with the fame of Stonewall Jackson and

[1] O. R., vol. xii., part i., p. 381. The staff appears to have been at fault. It was certainly of the first importance, whether battle was intended or not, to select a halting-place concealed from the enemy's observation.
[2] 140 sabres.

his brigade, are mere ribbons of metal laid on swell and swale. Fences of the rudest description, zigzags of wooden rails, or walls of loose stone, are the only boundaries, and the land is parcelled out in more generous fashion than in an older and more crowded country. More desirable ground for military operations it would be difficult to find. There are few obstacles to the movement of cavalry and artillery, while the woods and undulations, giving ample cover, afford admirable opportunities for skilful manœuvre. In the spring, however, the condition of the soil would be a drawback. At the date of the battle part of the country round Kernstown was under plough, and the whole was saturated with moisture. Horses sank fetlock-deep in the heavy meadows, and the rough roads, hardly seen for mud, made marching difficult.

The Federal front extended on both sides of the Valley turnpike. To the east was a broad expanse of rolling grassland, stretching away to the horizon; to the west a low knoll, crowned by a few trees, which goes by the name of Pritchard's Hill. Further north was a ridge, covered with brown woods, behind which lies Winchester. This ridge, nowhere more than 100 feet in height, runs somewhat obliquely to the road in a south-westerly direction, and passing within a mile and a half of Pritchard's Hill, sinks into the plain three miles south-west of Kernstown. Some distance beyond this ridge, and separated from it by the narrow valley of the Opequon, rise the towering bluffs of the North Mountain, the western boundary of the Valley, sombre with forest from base to brow.

On leaving Winchester, Williams' division had struck due east, passing through the village of Berryville, and making for Snicker's Gap in the Blue Ridge. The Berryville road had thus become of importance to the garrison of Winchester, for it was from that direction, if they should become necessary, that reinforcements would arrive. General Kimball, commanding in Shields' absence the division which confronted Ashby, had therefore posted the larger portion of his troops eastward of the pike. A strong force of infantry, with waving colours, was plainly visible to the Confederates, and it was seen that the extreme left was protected by several guns. On the right of the road was a line of skirmishers, deployed along the base of Pritchard's Hill, and on the knoll itself stood two batteries. The wooded ridge to westward was as yet unoccupied, except by scouting parties.

Jackson at once determined to turn the enemy's right. An attack upon the Federal left would have to be pushed across the open fields and decided by fair fighting, gun and rifle against gun and rifle, and on that flank the enemy was prepared for battle. Could he seize the wooded ridge on his left, the initiative would be his. His opponent would be compelled to conform to his movements. The advantages of a carefully selected position would be lost. Instead of receiving attack where he stood, the Federal general would have to change front to meet it, to execute movements which he had possibly not foreseen, to fight on ground with which he was unfamiliar; and, instead of carrying out a plan which had been previously thought out, to conceive a new one on the spur of the moment, and to issue immediate orders for a difficult operation. Hesitation and confusion might ensue; and in place of a strongly established line, confidently awaiting the advance, isolated regiments, in all the haste and excitement of rapid move- ment, or hurriedly posted in unfavourable positions, would probably oppose the Confederate onset. Such are the ad- vantages which accrue to the force which delivers an attack where it is not expected; and, to all appearance, Jackson's plan of battle promised to bring them into play to the very fullest extent. The whole force of the enemy, as reported by Ashby, was before him, plainly visible. To seize the wooded ridge, while the cavalry held the Federals fast in front; to pass beyond Pritchard's Hill, and to cut the line of retreat on Winchester, seemed no difficult task. The only danger was the possibility of a counterstroke while the Confederates were executing their turning movement. But the enemy, so far as Jackson's information went, was rapidly withdrawing from the Valley. The force confronting him was no more than a rear-guard; and it was improbable in the extreme that a mere rear-guard would involve itself in a desperate engagement. The moment its line of retreat was threatened it would probably fall back. To provide, however, against all emergencies, Colonel Burks' brigade of three battalions was left for the present in rear of Kernstown, and here, too, remained four of the field batteries. With the remainder of his force, two brigades of infantry and a battery, Jackson moved off to his left. Two companies of the 5th Virginia were recruited from Winchester. Early in the day the general had asked the regiment for a guide familiar with the locality; and, with the soldier showing the way, the 27th Virginia, with two of Carpenter's guns as advanced-guard, struck westward by a waggon track across the meadows, while Ashby pressed the Federals in front of Kernstown. The main body followed in two parallel columns, and the line of march soon brought them within range of the commanding batteries on Pritchard's Hill.[1] At a range of little more than a mile the enemy's gunners poured a heavy fire on the serried ranks, and Carpenter, unlimbering near the Opequon Church, sought to distract their aim.

3.45 P.M.

The Confederate infantry, about 2,000 all told, although moving in mass, and delayed by fences and marshy ground, passed unscathed under the storm of shell, and in twenty minutes the advanced guard had seized the wooded ridge.

Finding a rocky clearing on the crest, about a mile distant from Pritchard's Hill, Jackson sent back for the artillery. Three batteries, escorted by two of Burks' battalions, the 21st Virginia and the Irishmen, pushed across the level as rapidly as the wearied teams could move. Two guns were dismounted by the Federal fire; but, coming into action on the ridge, the remainder engaged the hostile batteries with effect. Meanwhile, breaking their way through the ragged undergrowth of the bare March woods, the infantry, in two lines, was pressing forward along the

---

[1] No hidden line of approach was available. Movement to the south was limited by the course of the Opequon. Fulkerson's brigade, with Carpenter's two guns, marched nearest to the enemy; the Stonewall Brigade was on Fulkerson's left.

ridge. On the right was the 27th Virginia, supported by the 21st; on the left, Fulkerson's two battalions, with the Stonewall Brigade in second line. The 5th Virginia remained at the foot of the ridge near Macauley's cottage, in order to connect with Ashby. Jackson's tactics appeared to be succeeding perfectly. A body of cavalry and infantry, posted behind Pritchard's Hill, was seen to be withdrawing, and the fire of the Federal guns was visibly weakening. Suddenly, in the woods northward of the Confederate batteries, was heard a roar of musketry, and the 27th 4.30 P.M. Virginia came reeling back before the onslaught of superior numbers. But the 21st was hurried to their assistance; the broken ranks rallied from their surprise; and a long line of Federal skirmishers, thronging through the thickets, was twice repulsed by the Southern marksmen.[1]

Fulkerson, further to the left, was more fortunate than the 27th. Before he began his advance along the ridge he had deployed his two battalions under cover, and when the musketry broke out on his right front, they were moving forward over an open field. Half-way across the field ran a stone wall or fence, and beyond the wall were seen the tossing colours and bright bayonets of a line of battle, just emerging from the woods. Then came a race for the wall, and the Confederates won. A heavy fire, at the closest range, blazed out in the face of the charging Federals, and in a few moments the stubble was strewn with dead and wounded. A Pennsylvania regiment, leaving a colour on the field, gave way in panic, and the whole of the enemy's force retreated to the shelter of the woods. An attempt to turn Jackson's left was then easily frustrated; and although the Federals maintained a heavy fire, Fulkerson's men held stubbornly to the wall.

In the centre of the field the Northern riflemen were sheltered by a bank; their numbers continually increased,

---

[1] The Confederate advance was made in the following order:—

23rd Va.	37th Va.		27th Va.	
				21st Va.
	4th Va.	33rd Va.	2nd Va.	
				Irish Battn.

and here the struggle was more severe. The 4th and 33rd Virginia occupied this portion of the line, and they were without support, for the 2nd Virginia and the Irish battalion, the last available reserves upon the ridge, had been already sent forward to reinforce the right.

The right, too, was hardly pressed. The Confederate infantry had everywhere to do with superior numbers, and the artillery, in that wooded ground, could lend but small support. The batteries protected the right flank, but they could take no share in the struggle to the front ; and yet, as the dusk came on, after two long hours of battle, the white colours of the Virginia regiments, fixed fast amongst the rocks, still waved defiant. The long grey line, 'a ragged spray of humanity,' plied the ramrod with still fiercer energy, and pale women on the hills round Winchester listened in terror to the crashing echoes of the leafless woods. But the end could not be long delayed. Ammunition was giving out. Every company which had reached the ridge had joined the fighting line. The ranks were thinning. Many of the bravest officers were down, and the Northern regiments, standing staunchly to their work, had been strongly reinforced.

Ashby for once had been mistaken. It was no rearguard that barred the road to Winchester, but Shields' entire division, numbering at least 9,000 men. A prisoner captured the day before had admitted that the Confederates were under the impression that Winchester had been evacuated, and that Jackson had immediately moved forward. Shields, an able officer, who had commanded a brigade in Mexico, saw his opportunity. He knew something of his opponent, and anticipating that he would be eager to attack, had ordered the greater part of his division to remain concealed. Kimball's brigade and five batteries were sent quietly, under cover of the night, to Pritchard's Hill. Sullivan's brigade was posted in support, hidden from view behind a wood. The cavalry and Tyler's brigade were held in reserve, north of the town, at a distance where they were not likely to be observed by the inhabitants. As soon as the Confederates came in sight, and Kimball deployed across the pike, Tyler was brought through the town and placed in rear of Sullivan, at a point where the road dips down between two parallel ridges. Shields himself, wounded in the skirmish of the preceding day, was not present at the action, although responsible for these dispositions, and the command had devolved on Kimball. That officer, when Jackson's design became apparent, ordered Tyler to occupy the wooded ridge ; and it was his five regiments, over 3,000 strong, which had struck so strongly at the Confederate advance. But although superior in numbers by a third, they were unable to make headway. Kimball, however, rose to the situation before it was too late. Recognising that Ashby's weak attack was nothing more than a demonstration, he hurried nearly the whole of his own brigade, followed by three battalions of Sullivan's, to Tyler's aid, leaving a couple of battalions and the artillery to hold the pike.

'The struggle,' says Shields, 'had been for a short time doubtful,'[1] but this reinforcement of 3,000 bayonets turned the scale. Jackson had ordered the 5th and 42nd Virginia to the ridge, and a messenger was sent back to hurry forward the 48th. But it was too late. Before the 5th could reach the heights the centre of the Confederate line was broken. Garnett, the commander of the Stonewall Brigade, without referring to the general, who was in another part of the field, had given the order to fall back. Fulkerson, whose right was now uncovered, was obliged to conform to the rearward movement, and moving across from Pritchard's Hill, two Federal regiments, despite the fire of the Southern guns, made a vigorous attack on Jackson's right. The whole Confederate line, long since dissolved into a crowd of skirmishers, and with the various regiments much mixed up, fell back, still fighting, through the woods. Across the clearing, through the clouds of smoke, came the Northern masses in pursuit. On the extreme right a hot fire of canister, at a range of two hundred and fifty yards, drove back the troops that had come from Pritchard's Hill; but on the wooded ridge above the artillery was unable to hold its own. The enemy's riflemen swarmed in the thickets,

[1] O. R., vol. xii., part i., p. 341.

and the batteries fell back. As they limbered up one of the six-pounders was overturned. Under a hot fire, delivered at not more than fifty paces distant, the sergeant in charge cut loose the three remaining horses, but the gun was abandoned to the enemy.

Jackson, before the Federal reinforcements had made their presence felt, was watching the progress of the action on the left. Suddenly, to his astonishment and wrath, he saw the lines of his old brigade falter and fall back. Galloping to the spot he imperatively ordered Garnett to hold his ground, and then turned to restore the fight. Seizing a drummer by the shoulder, he dragged him to a rise of ground, in full view of the troops, and bade him in curt, quick tones, to ' Beat the rally ! ' The drum rolled at his order, and with his hand on the frightened boy's shoulder, amidst a storm of balls, he tried to check the flight of his defeated troops. His efforts were useless. His fighting-line was shattered into fragments; and although, according to a Federal officer, ' many of the brave Virginians lingered in rear of their retreating comrades, loading as they slowly retired, and rallying in squads in every ravine and behind every hill— or hiding singly among the trees,'[1] it was impossible to stay the rout. The enemy was pressing forward in heavy force, and their shouts of triumph rang from end to end of the field of battle. No doubt remained as to their overwhelming numbers, and few generals but would have been glad enough to escape without tempting fortune further.

It seemed almost too late to think of even organising a rear-guard. But Jackson, so far from preparing for retreat, had not yet ceased to think of victory. The 5th and 42nd Virginia were coming up, a compact force of 600 bayonets, and a vigorous and sudden counterstroke might yet change the issue of the day. The reinforcements, however, had not yet come in sight, and galloping back to meet them he found that instead of marching resolutely against the enemy, the two regiments had taken post to the rear, on the crest of a wooded swell, in order to cover the retreat. On his way to the front the colonel of the 5th Virginia had

[1] Colonel E. H. C. Cavins, 14th Indiana. *Battles and Leaders*, vol. ii., p. 307.

received an order from Garnett instructing him to occupy a position behind which the fighting-line might recover its formation. Jackson was fain to acquiesce; but the fighting-line was by this time scattered beyond all hope of rallying; the opportunity for the counterstroke had passed away, and the battle was irretrievably lost.

Arrangements were quickly made to enable the broken troops to get away without further molestation. A battery was ordered to take post at the foot of the hill, and Funsten's cavalry was called up from westward of the ridge. The 42nd Virginia came into line on the right of the 5th, and covered by a stone wall and thick timber, these two small regiments, encouraged by the presence of their commander, held stoutly to their ground. The attack was pressed with reckless gallantry. In front of the 5th Virginia the colours of the 5th Ohio changed hands no less than six times, and one of them was pierced by no less than eight-and-forty bullets. The 84th Pennsylvania was twice repulsed and twice rallied, but on the fall of its colonel retreated in confusion. The left of the 14th Indiana broke; but the 13th Indiana now came up, and 'inch by inch,' according to their commanding officer, the Confederates were pushed back. The 5th Virginia was compelled to give way before a flanking fire; but the colonel retired the colours to a short distance, and ordered the regiment to re-form on them. Again the heavy volleys blazed out in the gathering twilight, and the sheaves of death grew thicker every moment on the bare hillside. But still the Federals pressed on, and swinging round both flanks, forced the Confederate rear-guard from the field, while their cavalry, moving up the valley of the Opequon, captured several ambulances and cut off some two or three hundred fugitives.

As the night began to fall the 5th Virginia, retiring steadily towards the pike, filed into a narrow lane, fenced by a stone wall, nearly a mile distant from their last position, and there took post for a final stand. Their left was commanded by the ridge, and on the heights in the rear, coming up from the Opequon valley, appeared a large mass of Northern cavalry. It was a situation sufficiently uncomfortable. If the ground was too difficult for the horse-men to charge over in the gathering darkness, a volley from their carbines could scarcely have failed to clear the wall. 'A single ramrod,' it was said in the Confederate ranks, ' would have spitted the whole battalion.' But not a shot was fired. The pursuit of the Federal infantry had been stayed in the pathless woods, the cavalry was held in check by Funsten's squadrons, and the 5th was permitted to retire unmolested.

The Confederates, with the exception of Ashby, who halted at Bartonsville, a farm upon the pike, a mile and a half from the field of battle, fell back to Newtown, three miles further south, where the trains had been parked. The men were utterly worn out. Three hours of fierce fighting against far superior numbers had brought them to the limit of their endurance. ' In the fence corners, under the trees, and around the waggons they threw themselves down, many too weary to eat, and forgot, in profound slumber, the trials, the dangers, and the disappointments of the day.' [1]

Jackson, when the last sounds of battle had died away, followed his troops. Halting by a camp-fire, he stood and warmed himself for a time, and then, remounting, rode back to Bartonsville. Only one staff officer, his chief commissary, Major Hawks, accompanied him. The rest had dropped away, overcome by exhaustion. ' Turning from the road into an orchard, he fastened up his horse, and asked his companion if he could make a fire, adding, " We shall have to burn fence-rails to-night." The major soon had a roaring fire, and was making a bed of rails, when the general wished to know what he was doing. " Finding a place to sleep," was the reply. " You seem determined to make yourself and those around you comfortable," said Jackson. And knowing the general had fasted all day, he soon obtained some bread and meat from the nearest squad of soldiers, and after they had satisfied their hunger, they slept soundly on the rail-bed in a fence-corner.'

Such was the battle of Kernstown, in which over

[1] *Jackson's Valley Campaign*, Colonel William Allan, C.S.A., p. 54.

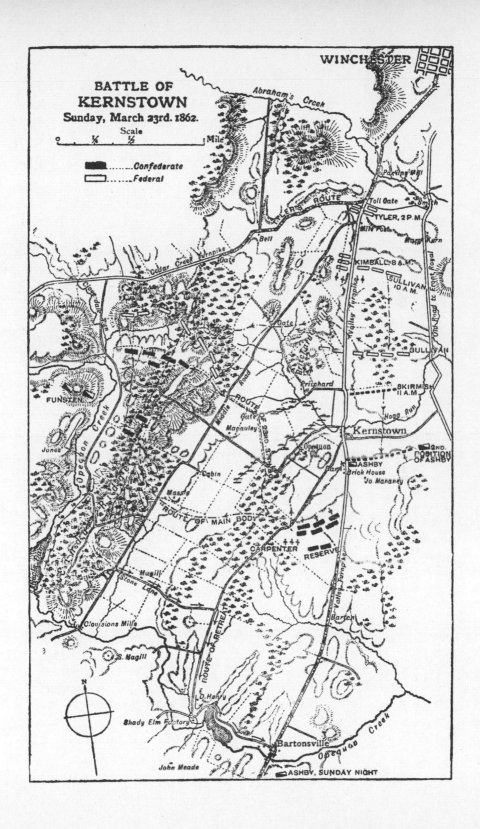

WINCHESTER

BATTLE OF
KERNSTOWN
Sunday, March 23rd. 1862.

Scale

0   ¼   ½   Mile

█████ ....Confederate
▭ ....Federal

Abraham's Creek

Parting Hill

ASHBY ROUTE

Toll Gate   Smith

TYLER, 2 P.M.

Mill Post

Bell

Mary Barn

Cedar Creek Turnpike   Gate

KIMBALL, 8 A.M.

SULLIVAN
10 A.M.

Gate

SULLIVAN

Pritchard

SKIRMISH
11 A.M.

FUNSTEN

Hogg Run

Opequon Creek

Jones

Kernstown

Road

Middle

Gate
Macauley

2ND.
POSITION
OF ASHBY

ROUTE OF 23RD. ST

Opequon Ch.

ASHBY
Brick House
Jo. Mahaney

Cabin

Massie

ROUTE OF MAIN BODY

CARPENTER

RESERVE

Magill

Stone Lane

Valley Turnpike

Barton

Coudons Mills

S. Magill

ROUTE OF RETREAT

N

O. Henry

Shady Elm Factory

Bartonsville

Opequon Creek

John Meade

ASHBY, SUNDAY NIGHT

1,200 men were killed and wounded, the half of them Confederates. Two or three hundred prisoners fell into the hands of the Federals. Nearly one-fourth of Jackson's infantry was *hors de combat*, and he had lost two guns. His troops were undoubtedly depressed. They had anticipated an easy victory; the overwhelming strength of the Federals had surprised them, and their losses had been severe. But no regret disturbed the slumbers of their leader. He had been defeated, it was true; but he looked further than the immediate result of the engagement. 'I feel justified in saying,' he wrote in his short report, 'that, though the battle-field is in the possession of the enemy, yet the most essential fruits of the victory are ours.' As he stood before the camp-fire near Newtown, wrapped in his long cloak, his hands behind his back, and stirring the embers with his foot, one of Ashby's youngest troopers ventured to interrupt his reverie. 'The Yankees don't seem willing to quit Winchester, General!' 'Winchester is a very pleasant place to stay in, sir!' was the quick reply. Nothing daunted, the boy went on: 'It was reported that they were retreating, but I guess they're retreating after us.' With his eyes still fixed on the blazing logs: 'I think I may say I am satisfied, sir!' was Jackson's answer; and with no further notice of the silent circle round the fire, he stood gazing absently into the glowing flames. After a few minutes the tall figure turned away, and without another word strode off into the darkness.

That Jackson divined the full effect of his attack would be to assert too much. That he realised that the battle, though a tactical defeat, was strategically a victory is very evident. He knew something of Banks, he knew more of McClellan, and the bearing of the Valley on the defence of Washington had long been uppermost in his thoughts. He had learned from Napoleon to throw himself into the spirit of his enemy, and it is not improbable that when he stood before the fire near Newtown he had already foreseen, in some degree at least, the events that would follow the news of his attack at Kernstown.

The outcome of the battle was indeed far-reaching. 'Though the battle had been won,' wrote Shields, 'still I could not have believed that Jackson would have hazarded a decisive engagement, so far from the main body, without expecting reinforcements; so, to be prepared for such a contingency, I set to work during the night to bring together all the troops within my reach. I sent an express after Williams' division, requesting the rear brigade, about twenty miles distant, to march all night and join me in the morning. I swept the posts in rear of almost all their guards, hurrying them forward by forced marches, to be with me at daylight.' [1]

General Banks, hearing of the engagement on his way to Washington, halted at Harper's Ferry, and he also ordered Williams' division to return at once to Winchester.

One brigade only, [2] which the order did not reach, continued the march to Manassas. This counter-movement met with McClellan's approval. He now recognised that Jackson's force, commanded as it was, was something more than a mere corps of observation, and that it was essential that it should be crushed. 'Your course was right,' he telegraphed on receiving Banks' report. 'As soon as you are strong enough push Jackson hard and drive him well beyond Strasburg. . . . The very moment the thorough defeat of Jackson will permit it, resume the movement on Manassas, always leaving the whole of Shields' command at or near Strasburg and Winchester until the Manassas Gap Railway is fully repaired. Communicate fully and act vigorously.' [3]

8,000 men (Williams' division) were thus temporarily withdrawn from the force that was to cover Washington from the south. But this was only the first step. Jackson's action had forcibly attracted the attention of the Federal Government to the Upper Potomac. The President was already contemplating the transfer of Blenker's division from McClellan to Frémont; the news of Kernstown decided the

[1] O. R., vol. xii., part i., p. 341.
[2] Abercrombie's, 4,500 men and a battery. The brigade marched to Warrenton, where it remained until it was transferred to McDowell's command.
[3] O. R., vol. xii., part iii., p. 16.

question, and at the end of March these 9,000 men were ordered to West Virginia, halting at Strasburg, in case Banks should then need them, on their way.[1] But even this measure did not altogether allay Mr. Lincoln's apprehensions. McClellan had assured him, on April 1, that 73,000 men would be left for the defence of the capital and its approaches. But in the original arrangement, with which the President had been satisfied, Williams was to have been brought to Manassas, and Shields alone left in the Shenandoah Valley. Under the new distribution the President found that the force at Manassas would be decreased by two brigades; and, at the same time, that while part of the troops McClellan had promised were not forthcoming, a large portion of those actually available were good for nothing. The officer left in command at Washington reported that 'nearly all his force was imperfectly disciplined; that several of the regiments were in a very disorganised condition; that efficient artillery regiments had been removed from the forts, and that he had to relieve them with very new infantry regiments, entirely unacquainted with the duties of that arm.'[2] Lincoln submitted the question to six generals of the regular army, then present in Washington; and these officers replied that, in their opinion, 'the requirement of the President that this city shall be left entirely secure has not been fully complied with.'[3]

On receiving this report, Lincoln ordered the First Army Corps, 37,000 strong, under General McDowell, to remain at Manassas in place of embarking for the Peninsula; and thus McClellan, on the eve of his advance on Richmond, found his original force of 150,000 reduced by 46,000 officers and men. Moreover, not content with detaching McDowell for a time, Lincoln, the next day, assigned that general to an independent command, covering the approaches to Washington; Banks, also, was withdrawn from

[1] Blenker's division was at Hunter's Chapel, south of Washington, when it received the order.
[2] Report of General Wadsworth; O. R., vol. xii., part iii., p. 225.
[3] Letter of Mr. Stanton; O. R., vol. xix., part ii., p. 726.

McClellan's control, and directed to defend the Valley. The original dissemination of the Federal forces was thus gravely accentuated, and the Confederates had now to deal with four distinct armies, McClellan's, McDowell's, Banks', and Frémont's, dependent for co-operation on the orders of two civilians, President Lincoln and his Secretary of War. And this was not all. McDowell had been assigned a most important part in McClellan's plan of invasion. The road from Fortress Monroe was barred by the fortifications of Yorktown. These works could be turned, however, by sending a force up the York River. But the passage of the stream was debarred to the Federal transports by a strong fort at Gloucester Point, on the left bank, and the capture of this work was to be the task of the First Army Corps. No wonder that McClellan, believing that Johnston commanded 100,000 men, declared that in his deliberate judgment the success of the Federal cause was imperilled by the order which detached McDowell from his command. However inadequately the capital might be defended, it was worse than folly to interfere with the general's plans when he was on the eve of executing them. The best way of defending Washington was for McClellan to march rapidly on Richmond, and seize his adversary by the throat. By depriving him of McDowell, Lincoln and his advisers made such a movement difficult, and the grand army of invasion found itself in a most embarrassing situation. Such was the effect of a blow struck at the right place and the right time, though struck by no more than 3,000 bayonets.

The battle of Kernstown was undoubtedly well fought. It is true that Jackson believed that he had no more than four regiments of infantry, a few batteries, and some cavalry before him. But it was a skilful manœuvre, which threw three brigades and three batteries, more than two-thirds of his whole strength, on his opponent's flank. An ordinary general would probably have employed only a small portion of his force in the turning movement. Not so the student of Napoleon. 'In the general's haversack,' says one of Jackson's staff, 'were always three books: the Bible,

Napoleon's Maxims of War, and Webster's Dictionary—for his spelling was uncertain—and these books he constantly consulted.'   Whether the chronicles of the Jewish kings threw any light on the tactical problem involved at Kernstown may be left to the commentators; but there can be no question as to the Maxims.   To hurl overwhelming numbers at the point where the enemy least expects attack is the whole burden of Napoleon's teaching, and there can be no doubt but that the wooded ridge, unoccupied save by a few scouts, was the weakest point of the defence.

The manœuvre certainly surprised the Federals, and it very nearly beat them.   Tyler's brigade was unsupported for nearly an hour and a half.   Had his battalions been less staunch, the tardy reinforcements would have been too late to save the day.   Coming up as they did, not in a mass so strong as to bear all before it by its own inherent weight, but in successive battalions, at wide intervals of time, they would themselves have become involved in a desperate engagement under adverse circumstances. Nor is Kimball to be blamed that he did not throw greater weight on Jackson's turning column at an earlier hour. Like Shields and Banks, he was unable to believe that Jackson was unsupported.   He expected that the flank attack would be followed up by one in superior numbers from the front.   He could hardly credit that an inferior force would deliberately move off to a flank, leaving its line of retreat to be guarded by a few squadrons, weakly supported by infantry; and the audacity of the assailant had the usual effect of deceiving the defender.

Kernstown, moreover, will rank as an example of what determined men can do against superior numbers.   The Confederates on the ridge, throughout the greater part of the fight, hardly exceeded 2,000 muskets.   They were assailed by 3,000, and proved a match for them.   The 3,000 were then reinforced by at least 3,000 more, whilst Jackson could bring up only 600 muskets to support an already broken line.   Nevertheless, these 6,000 Northerners were so roughly handled that there was practically no pursuit.   When the Confederates fell back every one of the

Federal regiments had been engaged, and there were no fresh troops wherewith to follow them. Jackson was perfectly justified in reporting that 'Night and an indisposition of the enemy to press further terminated the battle.' [1]

But the action was attended by features more remarkable than the stubborn resistance of the Virginia regiments. It is seldom that a battle so insignificant as Kernstown has been followed by such extraordinary results. Fortune indeed favoured the Confederates. At the time of the battle a large portion of McClellan's army was at sea, and the attack was delivered at the very moment when it was most dreaded by the Northern Government. Nor was it to the disadvantage of the Southerners that the real head of the Federal army was the President, and that his strategical conceptions were necessarily subservient to the attitude of the Northern people. These were circumstances purely fortuitous, and it might seem, therefore, that Jackson merely blundered into success. But he must be given full credit for recognising that a blow at Banks might be fraught with most important consequences. It was with other ideas than defeating a rear-guard or detaining Banks that he seized the Kernstown ridge. He was not yet aware of McClellan's plan of invasion by sea; but he knew well that any movement that would threaten Washington must prove embarrassing to the Federal Government; that they could not afford to leave the Upper Potomac ill secured; and that the knowledge that an active and enterprising enemy, who had shown himself determined to take instant advantage of every opportunity, was within the Valley, would probably cause them to withdraw troops from McClellan in order to guard the river. A fortnight after the battle, asking for reinforcements, he wrote, 'If Banks is defeated it may greatly retard McClellan's movements.' [2]

Stubborn as had been the fighting of his brigades, Jackson himself was not entirely satisfied with his officers. When Sullivan and Kimball came to Tyler's aid, and a new line of battle threatened to overwhelm the Stone-

[1] O. R., vol. xii., part i., p. 382.
[2] *Ibid.*, part iii., p. 844.

wall regiments, Garnett, on his own responsibility, had given the order to retire. Many of the men, their ammunition exhausted, had fallen to the rear. The exertions of the march had begun to tell. The enemy's attacks had been fiercely pressed, and before the pressure of his fresh brigades the Confederate power of resistance was strained to breaking-point. Garnett had behaved with conspicuous gallantry. The officers of his brigade declared that he was perfectly justified in ordering a retreat. Jackson thought otherwise, and almost immediately after the battle he relieved him of his command, placed him under arrest, and framed charges for his trial by court-martial. He would not accept the excuse that ammunition had given out. At the time the Stonewall Brigade gave back the 5th and 42nd Virginia were at hand. The men had still their bayonets, and he did not consider the means of victory exhausted until the cold steel had been employed. 'He insisted,' says Dabney, 'that a more resolute struggle might have won the field.' [1]

Now, in the first place, it must be conceded that Garnett had not the slightest right to abandon his position without a direct order.[2] In the second, if we turn to the table of losses furnished by the brigade commander, we find that in Garnett's four regiments, numbering 1,100 officers and men, there fell 153. In addition, 148 were reported missing, but, according to the official reports, the majority of these were captured by the Federal cavalry and were unwounded. At most, then, when he gave the order to retreat, Garnett had lost 200, or rather less than 20 per cent.

Such loss was heavy, but by no means excessive. A few months later hardly a brigade in either army would have given way because every fifth man had fallen. A year later and the Stonewall regiments would have considered an action in which they lost 200 men as nothing

[1] Dabney, vol. ii., p. 46.
[2] He was aware, moreover, that supports were coming up, for the order to the 5th Virginia was sent through him. Report of Colonel W. H. Harman, 5th Virginia, O. R., vol. xii., part i., pp. 391, 392.

more than a skirmish.[1]   The truth would seem to be that
the Valley soldiers were not yet 'blooded.' In peace the
individual is everything; material prosperity, self-indulgence, and the preservation of existence are the general
aim.   In war the individual is nothing, and men learn the
lesson of self-sacrifice. But it is only gradually, however
high the enthusiasm which inspires the troops, that the
ideas of peace become effaced, and they must be seasoned
soldiers who will endure, without flinching, the losses of
Waterloo or Gettysburg.   Discipline, which means the
effacement of the individual, does more than break the
soldier to unhesitating obedience; it trains him to die for
duty's sake, and even the Stonewall Brigade, in the spring
of 1862, was not yet thoroughly disciplined.   'The lack of
competent and energetic officers,' writes Jackson's chief of
the staff, 'was at this time the bane of the service.   In
many there was neither an intelligent comprehension of
their duties nor zeal in their performance. Appointed by
the votes of their neighbours and friends, they would
neither exercise that rigidity in governing, nor that detailed
care in providing for the wants of their men, which are
necessary to keep soldiers efficient.   The duties of the
drill and the sentry-post were often negligently performed;
and the most profuse waste of ammunition and other military stores was permitted.   It was seldom that these officers
were guilty of cowardice upon the field of battle, but they
were often in the wrong place, fighting as common soldiers
when they should have been directing others. Above all
was their inefficiency marked in their inability to keep their
men in the ranks. Absenteeism grew under them to a
monstrous evil, and every poltroon and laggard found a
way of escape.   Hence the frequent phenomenon that
regiments, which on the books of the commissary appeared
as consumers of 500 or 1,000 rations, were reported as

---

[1] On March 5, 1811, in the battle fought on the arid ridges of Barossa,
the numbers were almost identical with those engaged at Kernstown.   Out
of 4,000 British soldiers there fell in an hour over 1,200, and of 9,000 French
more than 2,000 were killed or wounded; and yet, although the victors were
twenty-four hours under arms without food, the issue was never doubtful.

carrying into action 250 or 300 bayonets.'[1] It is unlikely that this picture is over-coloured, and it is certainly no reproach to the Virginia soldiers that their discipline was indifferent. There had not yet been time to transform a multitude of raw recruits into the semblance of a regular army. Competent instructors and trained leaders were few in the extreme, and the work had to be left in inexperienced hands. One Stonewall Jackson was insufficient to leaven a division of 5,000 men.

In the second place, Jackson probably remembered that the Stonewall Brigade at Bull Run, dashing out with the bayonet on the advancing Federals, had driven them back on their reserves. It seems hardly probable, had Garnett at Kernstown held his ground a little longer, that the three regiments still intact could have turned the tide of battle. But it is not impossible. The Federals had been roughly handled. Their losses had been heavier than those of the Confederates. A resolute counterstroke has before now changed the face of battle, and among unseasoned soldiers panic spreads with extraordinary effect. So far as can be gathered from the reports, there is no reason to suspect that the vigour of the Federal battalions was as yet relaxed. But no one who was not actually present can presume to judge of the temper of the troops. In every well-contested battle there comes a moment when the combatants on both sides become exhausted, and the general who at that moment finds it in his heart to make one more effort will generally succeed. Such was the experience of Grant, Virginia's stoutest enemy.[2] That moment, perhaps, had come at Kernstown; and Jackson, than whom not Skobeleff himself had clearer vision or cooler brain in the tumult of battle, may have observed it. It cannot be too often repeated that numbers go for little on the battle-field. It is possible that Jackson had in his mind, when he declared that the victory might yet have been won, the decisive counterstroke at Marengo, where 20,000 Austrians, pressing forward in pursuit of a defeated enemy, were utterly overthrown by a

[1] Dabney, vol. ii., pp. 18, 19.
[2] Grant's *Memoirs*.

fresh division of 6,000 men supported by four squadrons.[1]

Tactical unity and *moral* are factors of far more importance in battle than mere numerical strength. Troops that have been hotly engaged, even with success, and whose nerves are wrought up to a high state of tension, are peculiarly susceptible to surprise. If they have lost their order, and the men find themselves under strange officers, with unfamiliar faces beside them, the counterstroke falls with even greater force. It is at such moments that cavalry still finds its opportunity. It is at such moments that a resolute charge, pushed home with drums beating and a loud cheer, may have extraordinary results. On August 6, 1870, on the heights of Wörth, a German *corps d'armée*, emerging, after three hours' fierce fighting, from the great wood on McMahon's flank, bore down upon the last stronghold of the French. The troops were in the utmost confusion. Divisions, brigades, regiments, and companies were mingled in one motley mass. But the enemy was retreating; a heavy force of artillery was close at hand, and the infantry must have numbered at least 10,000 rifles. Suddenly three battalions of Turcos, numbering no more than 1,500 bayonets, charged with wild cries, and without firing, down the grassy slope. The Germans halted, fired a few harmless volleys, and then, turning as one man, bolted to the shelter of the wood, twelve hundred yards in rear.

According to an officer of the 14th Indiana, the Federals at Kernstown were in much the same condition as the Germans at Wörth. 'The Confederates fell back in great disorder, and we advanced in disorder just as great. Over logs, through woods, over hills and fields, the brigades, regiments, and companies advanced, in one promiscuous, mixed, and uncontrollable mass. Officers shouted themselves hoarse in trying to bring order out of confusion, but

[1] The morning after the battle one of the Confederate officers expressed the opinion that even if the counterstroke had been successful, the Federal reserves would have arrested it. Jackson answered, 'No, if I had routed the men on the ridge, they would all have gone off together.'

all their efforts were unavailing along the front line, or rather what ought to have been the front line.' [1]

Garnett's conduct was not the only incident connected with Kernstown that troubled Jackson. March 23 was a Sunday. 'You appear much concerned,' he writes to his wife, 'at my attacking on Sunday. I am greatly concerned too ; but I felt it my duty to do it, in consideration of the ruinous effects that might result from postponing the battle until the morning. So far as I can see, my course was a wise one ; the best that I could do under the circumstances, though very distasteful to my feelings ; and I hope and pray to our Heavenly Father that I may never again be circumstanced as on that day. I believed that, so far as our troops were concerned, necessity and mercy both called for the battle. I do hope that the war will soon be over, and that I shall never again be called upon to take the field. Arms is a profession that, if its principles are adhered to, requires an officer to do what he fears may be wrong, and yet, according to military experience, must be done if success is to be attained. And the fact of its being necessary to success, and being accompanied with success, and that a departure from it is accompanied with disaster, suggests that it must be right. Had I fought the battle on Monday instead of Sunday, I fear our cause would have suffered, whereas, as things turned out, I consider our cause gained much from the engagement.'

We may wonder if his wife detected the unsoundness of the argument. To do wrong—for wrong it was according to her creed—in order that good may ensue is what it comes to. The literal interpretation of the Scriptural rule seems to have led her husband into difficulties ; but the incident may serve to show with what earnestness, in every action of his life, he strove to shape his conduct with what he believed to be his duty.

It has already been observed that Jackson's reticence was remarkable. No general could have been more careful that no inkling of his design should reach the enemy. He had not the slightest hesitation in withholding his plans from

[1] Colonel E. H. C. Cavins, *Battles and Leaders*, vol. ii., p. 307.

even his second in command ; special correspondents were rigorously excluded from his camps ; and even with his most confidential friends his reserve was absolutely impenetrable. During his stay at Winchester, it was his custom directly he rose to repair to headquarters and open his correspondence. When he returned to breakfast at Dr. Graham's there was much anxiety evinced to hear the news from the front. What the enemy was doing across the Potomac, scarce thirty miles away, was naturally of intense interest to the people of the border town. But not the smallest detail of intelligence, however unimportant, escaped his lips. To his wife he was as uncommunicative as to the rest. Neither hint nor suggestion made the least impression, and direct interrogations were put by with a quiet smile. Nor was he too shy to suggest to his superiors that silence was golden. In a report to Johnston, written four days after Kernstown, he administered what can scarcely be considered other than a snub, delicately expressed but unmistakable :—

'It is understood in the Federal army that you have instructed me to keep the forces now in this district and not permit them to cross the Blue Ridge, and that this must be done at every hazard, and that for the purpose of effecting this I made my attack. I have never so much as intimated such a thing to anyone.' [1]

It cannot be said that Jackson's judgment in attacking Shields was at once appreciated in the South. The defeat, at first, was ranked with the disasters in the West. But as soon as the effects upon the enemy were appreciated the tide of popular feeling turned. The gallantry of the Valley regiments was fully recognised, and the thanks of Congress were tendered to Jackson and his troops.

No battle was ever yet fought in exact accordance with the demands of theory, and Kernstown, great in its results, gives openings to the critics. Jackson, it is said, attacked with tired troops, on insufficient information, and contrary to orders. As to the first, it may be said that his decision

[1] O. R., vol. xii., part iii., p. 840.

to give the enemy no time to bring up fresh troops was absolutely justified by events. On hearing of his approach to Kernstown, Banks immediately countermarched a brigade of Williams' division from Castleman's Ferry. A second brigade was recalled from Snicker's Gap on the morning of the 24th, and reached Winchester the same evening, after a march of six-and-twenty miles. Had attack been deferred, Shields would have been strongly reinforced.

As to the second, Jackson had used every means in his power to get accurate intelligence.[1] Ashby had done his best. Although the Federals had 780 cavalry present, and every approach to Winchester was strongly picketed, his scouts had pushed within the Federal lines, and had communicated with the citizens of Winchester. Their reports were confirmed, according to Jackson's despatch, 'from a source which had been remarkable for its reliability,' and for the last two days a retrograde movement towards Snicker's Gap had been reported. The ground, it is true, favoured an ambush. But the strategic situation demanded instant action. McClellan's advanced guard was within fifty miles of Johnston's position on the Rapidan, and a few days' march might bring the main armies into collision. If Jackson was to bring Banks back to the Valley, and himself join Johnston before the expected battle, he had no time to spare. Moreover, the information to hand was quite sufficient to justify him in trusting something to fortune. Even a defeat, if the attack were resolutely pushed, might have the best effect.

The third reproach, that Jackson disobeyed orders, can hardly be sustained. He was in command of a detached force operating at a distance from the main army, and Johnston, with a wise discretion, had given him not orders,

---

[1] The truth is that in war, accurate intelligence, especially when two armies are in close contact, is exceedingly difficult to obtain. At Jena, even after the battle ended, Napoleon believed that the Prussians had put 80,000 men in line instead of 45,000. The night before Eylau, misled by the reports of Murat's cavalry, he was convinced that the Russians were retreating ; and before Ligny he underestimated Blücher's strength by 40,000. The curious misconceptions under which the Germans commenced the battles of Spicheren, Mars-la-Tour, and Gravelotte will also occur to the military reader.

but instructions; that is, the general-in-chief had merely
indicated the purpose for which Jackson's force had been
detached, and left to his judgment the manner in which
that purpose was to be achieved. Johnston had certainly
suggested that he should not expose himself to the danger
of defeat. But when it became clear that he could not
retain the enemy in the Valley unless he closed with him,
to have refrained from attack would have been to disobey
the spirit of his instructions.

Again, when Jackson attacked he had good reason to
believe that he ran no risk of defeat whatever. The force
before him was reported as inferior to his own, and he
might well have argued : ' To confine myself to observation
will be to confess my weakness, and Banks is not likely to
arrest his march to Manassas because of the presence
of an enemy who dare not attack an insignificant rear-
guard.' Demonstrations, such as Johnston had advised,
may undoubtedly serve a temporary purpose, but if protracted the enemy sees through them. On the 22nd, for
instance, it was reported to Banks that the Confederates
were advancing. The rear brigade of Williams' division
was therefore countermarched from Snicker's Gap to
Berryville ; but the other two were suffered to proceed.
Had Jackson remained quiescent in front of Shields, tacitly
admitting his inferiority, the rear brigade would in all
probability have soon been ordered to resume its march;
and Lincoln, with no fear for Washington, would have
allowed Blenker and McDowell to join McClellan.

Johnston, at least, held that his subordinate was
justified. In publishing the thanks of the Confederate
Congress tendered to Jackson and his division, he expressed, at the same time, ' his own sense of their
admirable conduct, by which they fully earned the high
reward bestowed.'

During the evening of the 23rd the medical director of
the Valley army was ordered to collect vehicles, and send
the wounded to the rear before the troops continued their
retreat. Some time after midnight Dr. McGuire, finding
that there were still a large number awaiting removal,

reported the circumstances to the general, adding that he did not know where to get the means of transport, and that unless some expedient were discovered the men must be abandoned. Jackson ordered him to impress carriages in the neighbourhood. 'But,' said the surgeon, 'that requires time ; can you stay till it has been done ?' 'Make yourself easy, sir,' was the reply. 'This army stays here until the last man is removed. Before I leave them to the enemy I will lose many men more.' Fortunately, before daylight the work was finished.

NOTE

The exact losses at Kernstown were as follows :—

CONFEDERATES.

By brigades			Killed	Wounded	Missing	Total
Stonewall Brigade			40	151	152	343
Burks' Brigade			24	114	39	177
Fulkerson's Brigade			15	76	71	162
Cavalry			1	17		18
Artillery				17	1	18
By regiments	Strength					
2nd Va.	320	N.C.O. and men	6	33	51	90
4th	203	„ „	5	23	48	76
5th	450	„ „	9	48	4	61
27th	170	„ „	2	20	35	57
33rd	275	„ „	18	27	14	59
21st	270	officers and men	7	44	9	60
42nd	293	„ ,	11	50	9	70
1st	187	„ „	6	20	21	47
23rd	177	„ „	3	14	32	49
27th	397	N.C.O. and men	12	62	39	113

Total casualties = 718 { 80 k. including 5 officers } 13 p.c. k. and w.
{ 375 w. „ 22 „ } 20 p.c. k., w., and
{ 263 m. „ 10 „ } m.

FEDERALS.

Total casualties = 590 { 118 k. including 6 officers }
{ 450 w. „ 27 „ } 6 p.c.
{ 22 m. }

According to the reports of his regimental commanders, Jackson took into battle (including 48th Va.) 3,087 N.C.O. and men of infantry, 290 cavalry, and 27 guns. 2,742 infantry, 290 cavalry, and 18 guns were engaged, and his total strength, including officers, was probably about 3,500. Shields, in his first report of the battle, put down the strength of his own division as between 7,000 and 8,000 men. Four days later he declared that it did not exceed 7,000, viz. 6,000 infantry, 750 cavalry, and 24 guns. It is probable that only those actually engaged are included in this estimate, for on March 17 he reported the strength of the troops which were present at Kernstown six days later as 8,374 infantry, 608 artillerymen, and 780 cavalry ; total, 9,752.[1]

---

[1] O. R., vol. xii., part iii., p. 4.

CHAPTER IX

M'DOWELL

THE stars were still shining when the Confederates began their retreat from Kernstown. With the exception of seventy,

1862. all the wounded had been brought in, and the army
March 23. followed the ambulances as far as Woodstock.

There was little attempt on the part of the Federals to improve their victory. The hard fighting of the Virginians had left its impress on the generals. Jackson's numbers were estimated at 15,000, and Banks, who arrived in time to take direction of the pursuit, preferred to wait till Williams' two brigades came up before he moved. He encamped that night at Cedar Creek, eight miles from Kernstown.

March 25. The next day he reached Strasburg. The cavalry pushed on to near Woodstock, and there, for the time being, the pursuit terminated. Shields, who remained at Winchester to nurse his wound, sent enthusiastic telegrams announcing that the retreat was a flight, and that the houses along the road were filled with Jackson's dead and dying; yet the truth was that the Confederates were in nowise pressed, and only the hopeless cases had been left behind.[1] Had the 2,000 troopers at Banks' disposal been sent forward at daybreak on the 24th, something might have been done. The squadrons, however, incapable of moving across country, were practically useless in pursuit; and to start even at daybreak was to start too late. If the fruits of victory are to be secured, the work must be put in hand whilst the enemy is still reeling under the shock. A few hours' delay gives him time to recover his equilibrium,

[1] Major Harman wrote on March 26 that 150 wounded had been brought to Woodstock. MS.

to organise a rear-guard, and to gain many miles on his
rearward march.

On the night of the 26th, sixty hours after the battle
ceased, the Federal outposts were established along Tom's
March 26.   Brook, seventeen miles from Kernstown.   On the
           opposite bank were Ashby's cavalry, while Burks'
brigade lay at Woodstock, six miles further south.   The
remainder of the Valley army had reached Mount Jackson.

These positions were occupied until April 1, and for six
whole days Banks, with 19,000 men, was content to observe
a force one-sixth his strength, which had been defeated by
just half the numbers he had now at his disposal.   This
was hardly the 'vigorous action' which McClellan had
demanded.   'As soon as you are strong enough,' he had
telegraphed, 'push Jackson hard, drive him well beyond
Strasburg, pursuing at least as far as Woodstock, if possible,
with cavalry to Mount Jackson.'[1]

In vain he reiterated the message on the 27th: 'Feel
Jackson's rear-guard smartly and push him well.'   Not a
single Federal crossed Tom's Brook.   'The superb scenery
of the Valley,' writes General G. H. Gordon, a comrade of
Jackson's at West Point, and now commanding the 2nd
Massachusetts, one of Banks' best regiments, 'opened
before us—the sparkling waters of the Shenandoah,
winding between the parallel ranges, the groves of cedar
and pine that lined its banks, the rolling surfaces of the
Valley, peacefully resting by the mountain side, and occupied
by rich fields and quiet farms.   A mile beyond I could
see the rebel cavalry.   Sometimes the enemy amused himself by throwing shells at our pickets, when they were a
little too venturesome; but beyond a feeble show of strength
and ugliness, nothing transpired to disturb the dulness of
the camp.'[2]

Banks, far from all support, and with a cavalry unable
to procure information, was by no means free from apprehension.   Johnston had already fallen back into the interior

---

[1] O. R., vol. xii., part iii., p. 16.   The telegrams and letters quoted in
this chapter, unless otherwise stated, are from this volume.

[2] *From Brook Farm to Cedar Mountain*, p. 133.

of Virginia, and the Army of the Potomac, instead of following him, was taking ship at Alexandria.   Information had
reached Strasburg that the Confederates were behind the
Rapidan, with their left at Gordonsville. Now Gordonsville is
sixty-five miles, or four marches, from Mount Jackson, and
there was reason to believe that reinforcements had already
been sent to Jackson from that locality.   On March 25
Banks telegraphed to Mr. Stanton : ' Reported by rebel
Jackson's aide (a prisoner) that they were assured of reinforcements to 30,000, but don't credit it.'   On March 26 :
' The enemy is broken, but will rally. Their purpose is to unite
Jackson's and Longstreet's[1] forces, some 20,000, at New
Market (seven miles south of Mount Jackson) or Washington
(east of Blue Ridge) in order to operate on either side of the
mountains, and will desire to prevent our junction with the
force at Manassas.   At present they will not attack here.
It will relieve me greatly to know how far the enemy
(*i.e.* Johnston) will be pressed in front of Manassas.'   On
the 27th his news was less alarming : ' Enemy is about
four miles below Woodstock. No reinforcement received yet.
Jackson has constant communication with Johnston, who
is east of the mountains, probably at Gordonsville.   His
pickets are very strong and vigilant, none of the country
people being allowed to pass the lines under any circumstances.   The same rule is applied to troops, stragglers
from Winchester not being permitted to enter their lines.
We shall press them further and quickly.'

The pressure, however, was postponed ; and on the 29th
McClellan desired Banks to ascertain the intentions of the
enemy as soon as possible, and if he were in force to drive
him from the Valley of the Shenandoah.   Thus spurred,
Banks at last resolved to cross the Rubicon.   ' Deficiency,'
he replied, ' in ammunition for Shields' artillery detains
us here ; expect it hourly, when we shall push Jackson
sharply.'   It was not, however, till April 2, four days
later, that Mr. Lincoln's *protégé* crossed Tom's Brook.
His advanced-guard, after a brisk skirmish with Ashby,
reached the village of Edenburg, ten miles south, the

---

[1] Commanding a division under Johnston.

same evening. The main body occupied Woodstock, and McClellan telegraphed that he was 'much pleased with the vigorous pursuit !'

It is not impossible that Banks suspected that McClellan's commendations were ironical. In any case, praise had no more effect upon him than a peremptory order or the promise of reinforcements. He was instructed to push forward as far as New Market ; he was told that he would be joined by two regiments of cavalry, and that two brigades of Blenker's division were marching to Strasburg. But Jackson, although Ashby had been driven in, still held obstinately to his position, and from Woodstock and Edenburg Banks refused to move.

On April 4, becoming independent of McClellan,[1] he at once reported to the Secretary of War that he hoped 'immediately to strike Jackson an effective blow.' 'Immediately,' however, in Banks' opinion, was capable of a very liberal interpretation, for it was not till April 17 that he once more broke up his camps. Well might Gordon write that life at Edenburg became monotonous !

It is but fair to mention that during the whole of this time Banks was much troubled about supply and transport. His magazines were at Winchester, connected with Harper's Ferry and Washington by a line of railway which had been rapidly repaired, and on April 12 this line had become unserviceable through the spreading of the road-bed.[2] His waggon train, moreover, had been diverted to Manassas before the fight at Kernstown, and was several days late in reaching Strasburg. The country in which he was operating was rich, and requisitions were made upon the farmers ; but in the absence of the waggons, according to his own report, it was impossible to collect sufficient supplies for a further advance.[3] The weather, too, had been unfavourable. The first days of April were like summer. 'But hardly,' says

---

[1] On this date McClellan ceased to be Commander-in-Chief.

[2] The bridges over the railway between Strasburg and Manassas Gap, which would have made a second line available, had not yet been repaired.

[3] On April 3 Jackson wrote that the country around Banks was 'very much drained of forage.'

Gordon, 'had we begun to feel in harmony with sunny days and blooming peach trees and warm showers, before a chill came over us, bitter as the hatred of the women of Virginia : the ground covered with snow, the air thick with hail, and the mountains hidden in the chilly atmosphere. Our shivering sentinels on the outer lines met at times the gaze of half-frozen horsemen of the enemy, peering through the mist to see what the Yankees had been doing within the last twenty-four hours. It was hard to believe that we were in the "sunny South."'

All this, however, was hardly an excuse for absolute inaction. The Confederate position on the open ridge called Rude's Hill, two and a half miles south of Mount Jackson, was certainly strong. It was defended in front by Mill Creek, swollen by the snows to a turbulent and unfordable river ; and by the North Fork of the Shenandoah. But with all its natural strength Rude's Hill was but weakly held, and Banks knew it. Moreover, it was most unlikely that Jackson would be reinforced, for Johnston's army, with the exception of a detachment under General Ewell, had left Orange Court House for Richmond on April 5. 'The enemy,' Banks wrote to McClellan on April 6, ' is reduced to about 6,000 men (*sic*), much demoralised by defeat, desertion, and the general depression of spirits resting on the Southern army. He is not in a condition to attack, neither to make a strong resistance, and I do not believe he will make a determined stand there. I do not believe Johnston will reinforce him.' If Banks had supplies enough to enable him to remain at Woodstock, there seems to have been no valid reason why he should not have been able to drive away a demoralised enemy, and to hold a position twelve miles further south.

But the Federal commander, despite his brave words, had not yet got rid of his misgivings. Jackson had lured him into a most uncomfortable situation. Between the two branches of the Shenandoah, in the very centre of the Valley, rises a gigantic mass of mountain ridges, parallel throughout their length of fifty miles to the Blue Ridge and the Alleghanies. These are the famous Massanuttons, the glory of the Valley.   The peaks which form their northern faces sink as abruptly to the level near Strasburg as does the single hill which looks down on Harrisonburg.   Dense forests of oak and pine cover ridge and ravine, and 2,500 feet below, on either hand, parted by the mighty barrier, are the dales watered by the Forks of the Shenandoah.   That to the east is the narrower and less open; the Blue Ridge is nowhere more than ten miles distant from the Massanuttons, and the space between them, the Luray or the South Fork Valley, through which a single road leads northward, is clothed by continuous forest.   West of the great mountain, a broad expanse of green pasture and rich arable extends to the foothills of the Alleghanies, dotted with woods and homesteads, and here, in the Valley of the North Fork, is freer air and more space for movement.

The separation of the two valleys is accentuated by the fact that save at one point only the Massanuttons are practically impassable.   From New Market, in the western valley, a good road climbs the heights, and crossing the lofty plateau, sinks sharply down to Luray, the principal village on the South Fork.   Elsewhere precipitous gullies and sheer rock faces forbid all access to the mountain, and a few hunters' paths alone wind tediously through the woods up the steep hillside.   Nor are signal stations to be found on the wide area of unbroken forest which clothes the summit. Except from the peaks at either end, or from one or two points on the New Market-Luray road, the view is intercepted by the sea of foliage and the rolling spurs.

Striking eastward from Luray, two good roads cross the Blue Ridge; one running to Culpeper Court House, through Thornton's Gap; the other through Fisher's Gap to Gordonsville.

It was the Massanuttons that weighed on the mind of Banks.   The Valley of the South Fork gave the Confederates a covered approach against his line of communications.   Issuing from that strait cleft between the mountains Ashby's squadrons might at any time sweep down upon his trains of waggons, his hospitals, and his magazines; and should Jackson be reinforced, Ashby might be supported by infantry and guns, and both Strasburg and Winchester be endangered. It was not within Banks' power to watch the defile. 'His cavalry,' he reported, 'was weak in numbers and spirit, much exhausted with night and day work.' Good cavalry, he declared, would help incalculably, and he admitted that in this arm he was greatly inferior to the enemy.

Nor was he more happy as to the Alleghanies on his right. Frémont was meditating an advance on Lewisburg, Staunton, and the Virginia and Tennessee Railway with 25,000 men.[1] One column was to start from Gauley Bridge, in the Kanawha Valley; the other from the South Branch of the Potomac. Milroy's brigade, from Cheat Mountain, had therefore occupied Monterey, and Schenck's brigade had marched from Romney to Moorefield. But Moorefield was thirty miles west of Woodstock, and between them rose a succession of rugged ridges, within whose deep valleys the Confederate horsemen might find paths by which to reach to Banks' rear.

It was essential, then, that his communications should be strongly guarded, and as he advanced up the Valley his force had diminished at every march. According to his own report he had, on April 6, 16,700 men fit for duty. Of these 4,100 were detached along the road from Woodstock to Harper's Ferry. His effective strength for battle was thus reduced to 12,600, or, including the troops escorting convoys and the garrison of Strasburg, to 14,500 men, with 40 pieces of artillery.[2]

Such were the considerations that influenced the Federal commander. Had he occupied New Market, as McClellan had desired, he would have secured the Luray road, have opened the South Fork Valley to his scouts, and have overcome half the difficulties presented by the Massanuttons. A vigorous advance would have turned the attention of the Confederates from his communications to their own; and to drive Jackson from the Valley was the best method

[1] See *ante*, p. 213.
[2] O.R., vol. xii., part iii., p. 50.

of protecting the trains and the magazines.   But Banks
was not inclined to beard the lion in his den, and on
April 16 Jackson had been unmolested for more than
three weeks.   Ashby's troopers were the only men who
had even seen the enemy.   Daily that indefatigable
soldier had called to arms the Federal outposts. 'Our stay
at Edenburg,' says Gordon, 'was a continuous season
of artillery brawling and picket stalking.   The creek that
separated the outposts was not more than ten yards wide.
About one-fourth of a mile away there was a thick wood, in
which the enemy concealed his batteries until he chose to
stir us up, when he would sneak up behind the cover, open
upon us at an unexpected moment, and retreat rapidly when
we replied.'   It was doubtless by such constant evidence of
his vigilance that Ashby imposed caution on the enemy's
reconnoitring parties.   The fact remains that Jackson's
camps, six miles to the rear, were never once alarmed, nor
could Banks obtain any reliable information.

    This period of repose was spent by Jackson in re-
organising his regiments, in writing letters to his wife, and,
like his old class-mate, Gordon, in admiring the scenery.   It
is not to be supposed that his enforced inaction was altogether
to his taste.   With an enemy within sight of his outposts
his bold and aggressive spirit must have been sorely tried.
But with his inferior numbers prudence cried patience,
and he had reason to be well content with the situation.   He had been instructed to prevent Banks from
detaching troops to reinforce McClellan.   To attain an
object in war the first consideration is to make no mistakes yourself; the next, to take instant advantage of
those made by your opponent.   But compliance with this
rule does not embrace the whole art of generalship.   The
enemy may be too discreet to commit himself to risky
manœuvres.   If the campaigns of the great masters of war
are examined, it will be found that they but seldom
adopted a quiescent attitude, but by one means or another,
by acting on their adversary's *moral*, or by creating false
impressions, they induced him to make a false step, and to
place himself in a position which made it easy for them

to attain their object. The greatest general has been defined as 'he who makes the fewest mistakes;' but 'he who compels his adversary to make the most mistakes' is a definition of equal force; and it may even be questioned whether the general whose imagination is unequal to the stratagems which bring mistakes about is worthy of the name. He may be a trustworthy subordinate, but he can scarcely become a great leader.

Johnston had advised, when, at the beginning of March, the retreat of the Confederates from Winchester was determined on, that Jackson should fall back on Front Royal, and thence, if necessary, up the South Fork of the Shenandoah. His force would thus be in close communication with the main army behind the Rapidan; and it was contrary, in the General-in-Chief's opinion, to all sound discretion to permit the enemy to attain a point, such as Front Royal, which would render it possible for him to place himself between them. Jackson, however, declared his preference for a retreat up the North Fork, in the direction of Staunton. Why should Banks join McClellan at all? McClellan, so Jackson calculated, had already more men with him than he could feed; and he believed, therefore, that Staunton would be Banks' objective, because, by seizing that town, he would threaten Edward Johnson's rear, open the way for Frémont, and then, crossing the Blue Ridge, place himself so near the communications of the main army with Richmond that it would be compelled to fall back to defend them. Nor, in any case, did he agree with Johnston that the occupation of Front Royal would prevent Banks leaving the Valley and marching to Manassas. Twenty miles due east of Winchester is Snicker's Gap, where a good road crosses the Blue Ridge, and eight miles south another turnpike leads over Ashby's Gap. By either of these Banks could reach Manassas just as rapidly as Jackson could join Johnston; and, while 4,500 men could scarcely be expected to detain 20,000, they might very easily be cut off by a portion of the superior force.

If a junction with the main army were absolutely necessary, Jackson was of opinion that the move ought to be made at once, and the Valley abandoned. If, on the other hand, it was desirable to keep Banks and McClellan separated, the best means of doing so was to draw the former up the North Fork ; and at Mount Jackson, covering the New Market-Luray road, the Valley troops would be as near the Rapidan as if they were at Front Royal.[1] The strategical advantages which such a position would offer— the isolation of the troops pursuing him, the chance of striking their communications from the South Fork Valley, and, if reinforcements were granted, of cutting off their retreat by a rapid movement from Luray to Winchester— were always present to Jackson's mind.[2]

An additional argument was that at the time when these alternatives were discussed the road along South Fork was so bad as to make marching difficult ; and it was to this rather than to Jackson's strategical conceptions that Johnston appears to have ultimately yielded.

Be this as it may, the sum of Jackson's operations was satisfactory in the extreme. On March 27 he had written to Johnston, ' I will try and draw the enemy on.' On April 16 Banks was exactly where he wished him, well up the North Fork of the Shenandoah, cut off by the Massanuttons from Manassas, and by the Alleghanies from Frémont. The two detachments which held the Valley, his own force at Mount Jackson, and Edward Johnson's 2,800 on the Shenandoah Mountain, were in close communication, and could at any time, if permitted by the higher authorities, combine against either of the columns which threatened Staunton. 'What I desire,' he said to Mr. Boteler, a friend in the Confederate Congress, ' is to hold the country, as far as practicable, until we are in a condition to advance ; and then, with God's blessing, let us make thorough work of it. But let us start right.'

On April 7 he wrote to his wife as follows :—

'Your sickness gives me great concern ; but so live that it and all your tribulations may be sanctified to you, remembering that our " light afflictions, which are but for a

---

[1] Dabney, vol. ii., pp. 22, 23. O. R., vol. v., p. 1087.
[2] Cf. letters of April 5. O. R., vol. xii., part iii.. pp. 843-4.

moment, work out for us a far more exceeding and eternal weight of glory ! " I trust you and all I have in the hands of a kind Providence, knowing that all things work together for the good of His people. Yesterday was a lovely Sabbath day. Although I had not the privilege of hearing the word of life, yet it felt like a holy Sabbath day, beautiful, serene, and lovely. All it wanted was the church-bell and God's services in the sanctuary to make it complete. Our gallant little army is increasing in numbers, and my prayer is that it may be an army of the living God as well as of its country.'

The troops, notwithstanding their defeat at Kernstown, were in high spirits. The very slackness of the Federal pursuit had made them aware that they had inflicted a heavy blow. They had been thanked by Congress for their valour. The newspapers were full of their praises. Their comrades were returning from hospital and furlough, and recruits were rapidly coming in.[1] The mounted branch attracted the majority, and Ashby's regiment soon numbered more than 2,000 troopers. Their commander, however, knew little of discipline. Besides himself there was but one field-officer for one-and-twenty companies; nor had these companies any regimental organisation. When Jackson attempted to reduce this curiously constituted force to order, his path was once more crossed by the Secretary of War. Mr. Benjamin, dazzled by Ashby's exploits, had given him authority to raise and command a force of independent cavalry. A reference to this authority and a threat of resignation was Ashby's reply to Jackson's orders. 'Knowing Ashby's ascendency over his men, and finding himself thus deprived of legitimate power, the general was constrained to pause, and the cavalry was left unorganised and un-

---

[1] Congress, on April 16, passed a Conscription Act, under which all able-bodied whites, between the ages of eighteen and thirty-five, were compelled to serve. It was not found necessary, however, except in the case of three religious denominations, to enforce the Act in the Valley; and, in dealing with these sectarians, Jackson found a means of reconciling their scruples with their duty to their State. He organised them in companies as teamsters, pledging himself to employ them, so far as practicable, in other ways than fighting. O. R., vol. xii., part iii., p. 835.

disciplined.   One half was rarely available for duty.   The remainder were roaming over the country, imposing upon the generous hospitalities of the citizens, or lurking in their homes.   The exploits of their famous leader were all performed with a few hundreds, or often scores, of men, who followed him from personal devotion rather than force of discipline.' [1]

By April 15 Jackson's force had increased to 6,000 men.[2] McClellan had now landed an army of over 100,000 at Fortress Monroe, on the Yorktown Peninsula, and Johnston had marched thither to oppose him.   The weather had at last cleared; although the mountain pines stood deep in snow the roads were in good order; the rivers were once

April 17.   more fordable; the Manassas Gap Railway had been restored as far as Strasburg, and Banks took heart of grace.   On the 17th his forces were put in motion. One of Ashby's companies was surprised and captured.   A brigade was sent to turn the Confederate left by a ford of the North Fork; and when the Virginians, burning the railway station at Mount Jackson, fell back southwards, the Federal cavalry seized New Market.

For the moment the situation of the Valley army was somewhat critical.   When Johnston marched to the Peninsula he had left a force of 8,000 men, under General Ewell, on the Upper Rappahannock, and with this force Jackson had been instructed to co-operate.   But with the road across the Massanuttons in his possession Banks could move into the Luray Valley, and occupying Swift Run Gap with a detachment, cut the communication between the two Confederate generals.   It was essential, then, that this important pass should be secured, and Jackson's men were

April 18.   called on for a forced march.   On the morning of the 18th they reached Harrisonburg, twenty-

[1] Dabney, vol. ii., p. 49.
[2] On April 5 he had over 4,000 infantry.   O. R., vol. xii., pt. iii., p. 844. The estimate in the text is from Colonel Allan's *Valley Campaign*, p. 64.   On April 9, however, he was so short of arms that 1,000 pikes were ordered from Richmond.   'Under Divine blessing,' he wrote, 'we must rely upon the bayonet when firearms cannot be furnished.'   O. R., vol. xii., part iii., pp. 842, 845.

five miles from Mount Jackson, and halted the same
April 19. evening at Peale's, about six miles east. On the
19th they crossed the Shenandoah at Conrad's
store, and leaving a detachment to hold the bridge, moved
to the foot of Swift Run Gap, and went into camp in Elk
Run Valley. In three days they had marched over fifty
miles. Banks followed with his customary caution, and when,
on the 17th, his cavalry occupied New Market he was congratulated by the Secretary of War on his 'brilliant and successful operations.' On the 19th he led a detachment across
the Massanuttons, and seized the two bridges over the South
Fork at Luray, driving back a squadron which Jackson had
April 22. sent to burn them. On the night of the 22nd
his cavalry reached Harrisonburg, and he reported
that want of supplies alone prevented him from bringing
the Confederates to bay. On the 26th he sent two of his
April 26. five brigades to Harrisonburg, the remainder
halting at New Market, and for the last few days,
according to his own despatches, beef, flour, and forage had
been abundant. Yet it had taken him ten days to march
five-and-thirty miles.

On April 20 General Edward Johnson, menaced in rear
by Banks' advance, in flank by the brigade which Frémont
had placed at Moorefield, and in front by Milroy's brigade,
April 20. which had advanced from Monterey, had fallen
back from the Shenandoah Mountain to West View,
seven miles west of Staunton ; and to all appearance the
Federal prospects were exceedingly favourable.

Harrisonburg is five-and-twenty miles, or two short
marches, north of Staunton. The hamlet of M'Dowell, now
occupied by Milroy, is seven-and-twenty miles north-west.
Proper concert between Banks and Frémont should therefore have ensured the destruction or retreat of Edward
Johnson, and have placed Staunton, as well as the Virginia
Central Railroad, in their hands. But although not a single
picket stood between his outposts and Staunton, Banks
dared not move. By moving to Elk Run Valley Jackson
had barred the way of the Federals more effectively than if
he had intrenched his troops across the Staunton road.

South of Harrisonburg, where the Valley widens to five-and-twenty miles, there was no strong position. And even had such existed, 6,000 men, of which a third were cavalry, could scarcely have hoped to hold it permanently against a far superior force. Moreover, cooped up inside intrenchments, the Army of the Valley would have lost all freedom of action; and Jackson would have been cut off both from Ewell and from Richmond. But, although direct intervention was impracticable, he was none the less resolved that Banks should never set foot in Staunton. The Elk Run Valley was well adapted for his purpose. Spurs of the Blue Ridge, steep, pathless, and densely wooded, covered either flank. The front, protected by the Shenandoah, was very strong. Communication with both Ewell and Richmond was secure, and so long as he held the bridge at Conrad's store he threatened the flank of the Federals should they advance on Staunton. Strategically the position was by no means perfect. The Confederates, to use an expression of General Grant's, applied to a similar situation, were 'in a bottle.' A bold enemy would have seized the bridge, 'corking up' Jackson with a strong detachment, and have marched on Staunton with his main body.

'Had Banks been more enterprising,' says Dabney, 'this objection would have been decisive.' But he was not enterprising, and Jackson knew it.[1] He had had opportunities in plenty of judging his opponent's character. The slow advance on Winchester, the long delay at Woodstock, the cautious approach to New Market, had revealed enough. It was a month since the battle of Kernstown, and yet the Confederate infantry, although for the greater part of the time they had been encamped within a few miles of the enemy's outposts, had not fired a shot.

The tardy progress of the Federals from Woodstock to Harrisonburg had been due rather to the perplexities of

---

[1] 'My own opinion,' he wrote, when this movement was in contemplation, 'is that Banks will not follow me up to the Blue Ridge. My desire is, as far as practicable, to hold the Valley, and I hope that Banks will be deterred from advancing [from New Market] much further toward Staunton by the apprehension of my returning to New Market [by Luray], and thus getting in his rear.'—O. R., vol. xii., part iii., p. 848.

their commander than to the difficulties of supply; and Banks had got clear of the Massanuttons only to meet with fresh embarrassments. Jackson's move to Elk Run Valley was a complete checkmate. His opponent felt that he was dangerously exposed. McClellan had not yet begun his advance on Richmond; and, so long as that city was secure from immediate attack, the Confederates could spare men to reinforce Jackson. The railway ran within easy reach of Swift Run Gap, and the troops need not be long absent from the capital. Ewell, too, with a force of unknown strength, was not far distant. Banks could expect no help from Frémont. Both generals were anxious to work together, and plans had been submitted to Washington which would probably have secured the capture of Staunton and the control of the railway. But the Secretary of War rejected all advice. Frémont was given to understand that under no circumstances was he to count on Banks,[1] and the latter was told to halt at Harrisonburg. 'It is not the desire of the President,' wrote Mr. Stanton on April 26, 'that you should prosecute a further advance towards the south. It is possible that events may make it necessary to transfer the command of General Shields to the department of the Rappahannock [i.e. to the First Army Corps], and you are desired to act accordingly.' To crown all, Blenker's division, which had reached Winchester, instead of being sent to support Banks, forty-five miles distant by the Valley turnpike, was ordered to join Frémont in the Alleghanies by way of Romney, involving a march of one hundred and twenty miles, over bad roads, before it could reinforce his advanced brigade.

Stanton, in writing to Banks, suggested that he should not let his advanced guard get too far ahead of the main body; but he does not appear to have seen that the separation of Banks, Frémont, and Blenker, and the forward position of the two former, which he had determined to maintain, was even more dangerous.[2] His lesson was to come, for

[1] O. R., vol. xii., p. 104.
[2] Jackson had recognised all along the mistake the Federals had made in pushing comparatively small forces up the Valley before McClellan closed in

Jackson, by no means content with arresting Banks' march, was already contemplating that general's destruction.

The situation demanded instant action, and in order that the import of Jackson's movements may be fully realised it is necessary to turn to the main theatre of war. McClellan, on April 5, with the 60,000 men already landed, had moved a few miles up the Peninsula. Near the village of Yorktown, famous for the surrender of Lord Cornwallis and his army in 1782, he found the road blocked by a line of earthworks and numerous guns. Magruder, Jackson's captain in Mexico, was in command; but Johnston was still on the Rapidan, one hundred and thirty miles away, and the Confederates had no more than 15,000 men in position. The flanks, however, were secured by the York and the James rivers, which here expand to wide estuaries, and the works were strong. Yorktown proved almost as fatal to the invaders as to their English predecessors. Before the historic lines their march was suddenly brought up. McClellan, although his army increased in numbers every day, declined the swift process of a storm. Personal reconnaissance convinced him that 'instant assault would have been simple folly,' and he determined to besiege the intrenchments in due form. On April 10 Johnston's army began to arrive at Yorktown, and the lines, hitherto held by a slender garrison, were now manned by 53,000 men.

The Confederate position was by no means impregnable. The river James to the south was held by the 'Merrimac,' an improvised ironclad of novel design, which had already wrought terrible destruction amongst the wooden frigates of the Federals. She was neutralised, however, by her Northern counterpart, the 'Monitor,' and after an indecisive action she had remained inactive for nearly a month. The York was less securely guarded. The channel, nearly a mile wide, was barred only by the fire of two forts; and

on Richmond. On April 5, when Banks was at Woodstock, he wrote: 'Banks is very cautious. As he belongs to McClellan's army, I suppose that McClellan is at the helm, and that he would not, even if Banks so desired, permit him to advance much farther until other parts of his army are farther advanced' (O. R., vol. xii., part iii., p. 843). He did not know that at the date he wrote the President and Mr. Stanton had relieved McClellan at the helm.

that at Gloucester Point, on the north bank, was open to assault from the land side. Had McClellan disembarked a detachment and carried this work, which might easily have been done, the river would have been opened to his gunboats, and Johnston's lines have become untenable. He decided, however, notwithstanding that his army was more than 100,000 strong, that he had no men to spare for such an enterprise.

Magruder's bold stand was of infinite service to the Confederate cause. To both parties time was of the utmost value. The Federals were still over seventy miles from Richmond; and there was always a possibility, if their advance were not rapidly pressed, that Johnston might move on Washington and cause the recall of the army to protect the capital. The Confederates, on the other hand, had been surprised by the landing of McClellan's army. They had been long aware that the flotilla had sailed, but they had not discovered its destination; the detachments which first landed were supposed to be reinforcements for the garrison of the fortress; and when McClellan advanced on Yorktown, Johnston was far to the west of Richmond. The delay had enabled him to reach the lines.[1] But at the time Jackson fell back to Elk Run Valley, April 17–19, fortune seemed inclining to the Federals.

Lincoln had been induced to relax his hold on the army corps which he had held back at Manassas to protect the capital, and McDowell was already moving on Fredericksburg, sixty miles north of Richmond. Here he was to be joined by Shields, bringing his force for the field up to 40,000 men; and the fall of Yorktown was to be the signal for his advance on the Confederate capital. Johnston still held the lines, but he was outnumbered by more than two to one, and the enemy was disembarking heavy ordnance. It was evident that the end could not be long delayed, and

---

[1] The first detachment of Federals embarked at Alexandria on March 16, and the army was thereafter transferred to the Peninsula by successive divisions. On March 25 Johnston was ordered to be ready to move to Richmond. On April 4 he was ordered to move at once. On that date 50,000 Federals had landed.

that in case of retreat every single Confederate soldier, from the Valley and elsewhere, would have to be brought to Richmond for the decisive battle. Jackson was thus bound to his present position, close to the railway, and his orders from Johnston confined him to a strictly defensive attitude. In case Banks advanced eastward he was to combine with Ewell, and receive attack in the passes of the Blue Ridge.

Such cautious strategy, to one so fully alive to the opportunity offered by McClellan's retention before York-town, was by no means acceptable. When his orders reached him, Jackson was already weaving plans for the discomfiture of his immediate adversary, and it may be imagined with what reluctance, although he gave no vent to his chagrin, he accepted the passive *rôle* which had been assigned to him.

No sooner, however, had he reached Elk Run Valley than the telegraph brought most welcome news. In a moment of unwonted wisdom the Confederate President had charged General Lee with the control of all military operations in Virginia, and on April 21 came a letter to Jackson which foreshadowed the downfall of McClellan and the rout of the invaders.

McDowell's advance from Manassas had already become known to the Confederates, and Lee had divined what this movement portended. 'I have no doubt,' he wrote to

April 21.　　Jackson, 'that an attempt will be made to occupy Fredericksburg and use it as a base of operations against Richmond. Our present force there is very small, (2,500 men under General Field), and cannot be reinforced except by weakening other corps. If you can use General Ewell's division in an attack on Banks, it will prove a great relief to the pressure on Fredericksburg.'[1]

This view of the situation was in exact agreement with Jackson's own views. He had already made preparation for combined action with Ewell. For some days they had been in active correspondence. The exact route which Ewell should take to the Blue Ridge had been decided on. The roads had been reconnoitred. Jackson had supplied

[1] O. R., vol. xii., part iii., p. 859.

a map identical with his own, and had furnished an officer to act as guide. A service of couriers had been established across the mountains, and no precaution had been neglected. Ewell was instructed to bring five days' rations. He was warned that there would be no necessity for a forced march; he was to encamp at cross-roads, and he was to rest on Sunday.[1]

Jackson, replying to Lee, stated that he was only waiting a favourable occasion to fall on Banks. 'My object,' he wrote, 'has been to get in his rear at New

April 23.

Market or Harrisonburg, if he gives me an opportunity, and this would be the case should he advance on Staunton with his main body. It appears to me that if I remain quiet a few days more he will probably make a move in some direction, or send a large force towards Harrisonburg, and thus enable me, with the blessing of Providence, to successfully attack his advance. If I am unsuccessful in driving back his entire force he may be induced to move forward from New Market, and attempt to follow me through this Gap, where our forces would have greatly the advantage. . . .

'Under all the circumstances I will direct General Ewell to move to Stanardsville. Should Banks remain in the position of yesterday [cavalry at Harrisonburg; infantry, &c., at New Market] I will try and seek an opportunity of attacking successfully some part of his army, and if circumstances justify press forward. My instructions from General Johnston were to unite with General Ewell near the top of the Blue Ridge, and give battle. The course I propose would be departing from General Johnston's instructions, but I do not believe that Banks will follow me to the Blue Ridge unless I first engage him, and I doubt whether he will then.'

But although authorised to draw Ewell to himself, and to carry out the project on which his heart was set, he still kept in view the general situation. After he had despatched the above letter, a report came in which led him to believe that Ewell was more needed on the Rappahannock than in

[1] O. R., vol. xii., part iii., pp. 849, 854, 857.

the Valley. Lee had already informed him that McDowell's
advanced guard had occupied Falmouth, on the north bank
of the river, opposite Fredericksburg, on April 19, and that
General Field had fallen back.

Jackson, in consequence, permitted Ewell to remain
near Gordonsville, close to the railway; assuring Lee that
'he would make arrangements so as not to be disappointed
should Ewell be ordered to Fredericksburg.'[1]

Nor was this the only instance in which he demonstrated his breadth of view. In planning co-operation with
Ewell, that general had suggested that he should take a
different road to that which had been recommended by
General Johnston, should necessity for a combined movement arise. Jackson protested against the route being
altered. 'General Johnston,' he wrote, 'does not state
why he desires you to go (by this road), but it may be for
the purpose of deceiving the enemy with regard to your
ultimate destination, to be more distant from the enemy
during the movement, and also to be in a more favourable
position for reinforcing some other points should it be
necessary.' The interests of his own force, here as always,
were subordinated to those of the army which was
defending Richmond.

The next information received from General Lee was
that the enemy was collecting in strong force at Fredericksburg. 'For this purpose,' he wrote, 'they must weaken
April 25. other points, and now is the time to concentrate
           on any that may be exposed within our reach.'
He then suggested that, if Banks was too strong in numbers
and position, Jackson and Ewell combined should move
on Warrenton, where a Federal force was reported; or that
Ewell and Field should attack Fredericksburg. 'The blow,'
he added, 'wherever struck, must, to be successful, be
sudden and heavy. The troops must be efficient and light.
I cannot pretend at this distance to direct operations
depending on circumstances unknown to me, and requiring
the exercise of discretion and judgment as to time and

[1] O. R., vol. xii., part iii., pp. 863-4.

execution, but submit these ideas for your consideration.'[1]

On April 26, when Banks moved two brigades to Harrisonburg, Ewell was at once called up to Stanardsville, twelve
miles south-east of Swift Run Gap. No opportunity as
April 26.   yet had offered for attack. 'I have reason to
                   believe,' wrote Jackson to Lee on the 28th, 'that
Banks has 21,000 men within a day's march of me.[2] He
has moved his main body from New Market to Harrisonburg,
leaving probably a brigade at New Market, and between
that town and the Shenandoah (Luray Gap), to guard against
a force getting in his rear. . . . On yesterday week there
were near 7,000 men in the neighbourhood of Winchester,
under Blenker; as yet I have not heard of their having
joined Banks. . . . I propose to attack Banks in front if
you will send me 5,000 more men. . . . Now, as it appears
to me, is the golden opportunity for striking a blow.   Until
I hear from you I will watch an opportunity for striking
some exposed point.'[3]

The next day, April 29, Jackson suggested, if reinforcements could not be spared, that one of three plans should be
April 29.   adopted. 'Either to leave Ewell here (Swift Run
                   Gap) to threaten Banks' rear in the event of his
advancing on Staunton, and move with my command rapidly
on the force in front of General Edward Johnson; or else,
co-operating with Ewell, to attack the enemy's detached
force between New Market and the Shenandoah, and if
successful in this, then to press forward and get in Banks'
rear at New Market, and thus induce him to fall back; the

[1] Jackson himself showed the same wise self-restraint. In his communications with Ewell, after that officer had been placed under his orders,
but before they had joined hands, he suggested certain movements as
advisable, but invariably left the ultimate decision to his subordinate's
judgment.

[2] On April 30 Banks and Shields, who had been reinforced, numbered
20,000 effective officers and men, of whom a portion must have been guarding
the communications. Reports of April 30 and May 31. O.R., vol. xii., part iii.

[3] It is amusing to note how far, at this time, his staff officers were
from understanding their commander. On this very date one of them wrote
in a private letter: 'As sure as you and I live, Jackson is a cracked man, and
the sequel will show it.' A month later he must have been sorry he had
posed as a prophet.

third is to pass down the Shenandoah to Sperryville (east of the Blue Ridge), and thus threaten Winchester *viâ* Front Royal. To get in Banks' rear with my present force would be rather a dangerous undertaking, as I would have to cross the river and immediately cross the Massanutton Mountains, during which the enemy would have the advantage of position. Of the three plans I give the preference to attacking the force west of Staunton [Milroy], for, if successful, I would afterward only have Banks to contend with, and in doing this would be reinforced by General Edward Johnson, and by that time you might be able to give me reinforcements, which, united with the troops under my control, would enable me to defeat Banks. If he should be routed and his command destroyed, nearly all our own forces here could, if necessary, cross the Blue Ridge to Warrenton, Fredericksburg, or any other threatened point.'

Lee's reply was to the effect that no reinforcements could be spared, but that he had carefully considered the three plans of operations proposed, and that the selection was left to Jackson.

The Army of the Valley, when the Commander-in-Chief's letter was received, had already been put in motion. Three roads lead from Conrad's store in the Elk Run Valley to Johnson's position at West View; one through Harrisonburg; the second by Port Republic, Cross Keys, and Mount Sidney; the third, the river road, by Port Republic and Staunton. The first of these was already occupied by the Federals; the second was tortuous, and at places almost within view of the enemy's camps; while the third, though it was nowhere less than ten miles distant, ran obliquely across their front. In fact, to all appearance, Banks with his superior force blocked Jackson's march on Staunton more effectively than did Jackson his.

On the 29th, Ashby, continually watching Banks, made a demonstration in force towards Harrisonburg. On the April 30. 30th he drove the Federal cavalry back upon their camps; and the same afternoon Jackson, leaving Elk Run Valley, which was immediately occupied by Ewell, with 8,000 men, marched up the river to Port

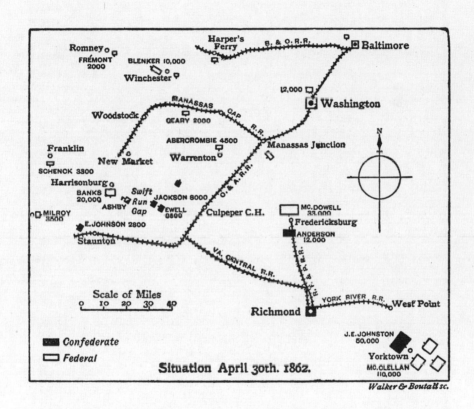

Romney o
FRÉMONT
2000
BLENKER 10,000
Winchester o

Harper's
Ferry
B. & O. R.R.
Baltimore

12,000
Washington

Woodstock o
MANASSAS
GEARY 2000
GAP
R.R.
Manassas Junction

Franklin
o
SCHENCK 3300
ABERCROMBIE 4500
Warrenton
New Market

Harrisonburg o
BANKS
20,000
Swift
JACKSON 8000
Run
ASHBY
Gap
EWELL
8500
MILROY
3500
E. JOHNSON 2800
Staunton

Culpeper C.H.
MC. DOWELL
33,000
o Fredericksburg
ANDERSON
12,000

O. & A. R.R.

V.A. CENTRAL R.R.

N

Scale of Miles
0   10   20   30   40

Richmond
YORK RIVER R.R.
West Point

Confederate
Federal

Situation April 30th. 1862.

J.E. JOHNSTON
50,000
Yorktown
MC. CLELLAN
110,000

Walker & Boutall sc.

Republic. The track, unmetalled and untended, had been turned into a quagmire by the heavy rains of an ungenial spring, and the troops marched only five miles, bivouacking by the roadside. May 1 was a day of continuous rain. The great mountains loomed dimly through the dreary mist. The streams which rushed down the gorges to the Shenandoah had swelled to brawling torrents, and in the hollows of the fields the water stood in sheets. Men and horses floundered through the mud. The guns sunk axle-deep in the treacherous soil; and it was only by the help of large detachments of pioneers that the heavy waggons of the train were able to proceed at all. It was in vain that piles of stones and brushwood were strewn upon the roadway; the quicksands dragged them down as fast as they were placed. The utmost exertions carried the army no more than five miles forward, and the troops bivouacked once more in the dripping woods.

The next day, the third in succession, the struggle with the elements continued. The whole command was called upon to move the guns and waggons. The general and his staff were seen dismounted, urging on the labourers; and Jackson, his uniform bespattered with mud, carried stones and timbers on his own shoulders. But before nightfall the last ambulance had been extricated from the slough, and the men, drenched to the skin, and worn with toil, found a halting-place on firmer ground. But this halting-place was not on the road to Staunton. Before they reached Port Republic, instead of crossing the Shenandoah and passing through the village, the troops had been ordered to change the direction of their march. The spot selected for their bivouac was at the foot of Brown's Gap, not more than twelve miles south-west of the camp in Elk Run Valley.

May 2.

The next morning the clouds broke. The sun, shining with summer warmth, ushered in a glorious May day, and the column, turning its back upon the Valley, took the stony road that led over the Blue Ridge. Upward and eastward the battalions passed, the great forest of oak and pine rising high on either hand, until from the eyry of the

May 3.

mountain-eagles they looked down upon the wide Virginia plains. Far off, away to the south-east, the trails of white smoke from passing trains marked the line of the Central Railroad, and the line of march led directly to the station at Mechum's River. Both officers and men were more than bewildered. Save to his adjutant-general, Jackson had breathed not a whisper of his plan. The soldiers only knew that they were leaving the Valley, and leaving it in the enemy's possession. Winchester, Strasburg, Front Royal, New Market, Harrisonburg, were full of Northern troops. Staunton alone was yet unoccupied. But Staunton was closely threatened; and north of Harrisonburg the blue-coated cavalry were riding far and wide. While the women and old men looked impotently on, village and mill and farm were at the mercy of the invaders. Already the Federal commissaries had laid hands on herds and granaries. It is true that the Northerners waged war like gentlemen; yet for all that the patriotism of the Valley soldiers was sorely tried. They were ready to go to Richmond if the time had come; but it was with heavy hearts that they saw the Blue Ridge rise behind them, and the bivouac on Mechum's River was even more cheerless than the sodden woods near Port Republic. The long lines of cars that awaited them at the station but confirmed their anticipations. They were evidently wanted at the capital, and the need was pressing. Still not a word transpired as to their destination.

The next day was Sunday, and Jackson had intended that the troops should rest. But early in the morning came a message from Edward Johnson. Frémont's advanced guard was pushing forward. 'After hard debate with himself,' says Dabney, who accompanied him, ' and with sore reluctance,' Jackson once more sacrificed his scruples and ordered the command to march. The infantry was to move by rail, the artillery and waggons by road. To their astonishment and delight the troops then heard, for the first time, that their destination was not Richmond but Staunton; and although they were far from understanding the reason for their circuitous march, they began to suspect that it had not been made without good purpose.

May 4.

If the soldiers had been heavy hearted at the prospect of leaving the Valley, the people of Staunton had been plunged in the direst grief. For a long time past they had lived in a pitiable condition of uncertainty. On April 19 the sick and convalescents of the Valley army had been removed to Gordonsville. On the same day Jackson had moved to Elk Run Valley, leaving the road from Harrisonburg completely open; and Edward Johnson evacuated his position on the Shenandoah Mountain. Letters from Jackson's officers, unacquainted with the designs of their commander, had confirmed the apprehension that the Federals were too strong to be resisted. On the Saturday of this anxious week had come the news that the army was crossing the Blue Ridge, and that the Valley had been abandoned to the enemy. Sunday morning was full of rumours and excitement. 10,000 Federals, it was reported, were advancing against Johnson at West View; Banks was moving from Harrisonburg; his cavalry had been seen from the neighbouring hills, and Staunton believed that it was to share the fate of Winchester. Suddenly a train full of soldiers steamed into the station; and as regiment after regiment, clad in their own Confederate grey, swept through the crowded streets, confidence in Stonewall Jackson began once more to revive.

Pickets were immediately posted on all the roads leading to Harrisonburg, and beyond the line of sentries no one, whatever his business might be, was allowed to pass. The following day the remainder of the division arrived, and the junction with Johnson's brigade was virtually effected. May 6 was spent in resting the troops, in making the arrangements for the march, and in getting information. The next morning brought a fresh surprise to both troops and townsfolk. Banks, so the rumour went, was rapidly approaching; and it was confidently expected that the twin hills which stand above the town—christened by some early settler, after two similar heights in far-away Tyrone, Betsy Bell and Mary Gray—would look down upon a bloody battle. But instead of taking post to defend the town, the Valley regiments filed away over the western

May 7.

hills, heading for the Alleghanies ; and Staunton was once more left unprotected. Jackson, although informed by Ashby that Banks, so far from moving forward, was actually retiring on New Market, was still determined to strike first at Milroy, commanding Frémont's advanced guard ; and there can be little question but that his decision was correct. As we have seen, he was under the impression that Banks' strength was 21,000, a force exceeding the united strength of the Confederates by 4,200 men.[1] It was undoubtedly sound strategy to crush the weaker and more exposed of the enemy's detachments first ; and then, having cleared his own rear and prevented all chance of combination between Banks and Frémont, to strike the larger.

There was nothing to be feared from Harrisonburg. Eight days had elapsed since Jackson had marched from Elk Run ; but Banks was still in blissful ignorance of the blow that threatened Frémont's advanced guard.

On April 28 he had telegraphed to Washington that he was 'entirely secure.' Everything was satisfactory. 'The enemy,' he said, 'is in no condition for offensive movements. Our supplies have not been in so good condition nor my command in so good spirits since we left Winchester. General Hatch (commanding cavalry) made a reconnaissance in force yesterday, which resulted in obtaining a complete view of the enemy's position. A negro employed in Jackson's tent came in this morning, and reports preparation for retreat of Jackson to-day. You need have no apprehensions for our safety. I think we are just now in a condition to do all you can desire of us in the Valley—clear the enemy out permanently.'

On the 30th, when Ashby repaid with interest Hatch's reconnaissance in force, he reported : 'All quiet. Some alarm excited by movement of enemy's cavalry. It appears to-day that they were in pursuit of a Union prisoner who escaped to our camp. The day he left Jackson was to be reinforced by Johnson and attack *via* Luray. Another report says Jackson is bound for Richmond. This is the fact, I have no doubt. Jackson is on half-rations, his

[1] Jackson, 6,000 ; Ewell, 8,000 ; E. Johnson, 2,800.

supplies having been cut off by our advance. There is
nothing to be done in this Valley this side of Strasburg.'

The same night, 'after full consultation with all leading officers,' he repeated that his troops were no longer
required in the Valley, and suggested to the Secretary of
War that he should be permitted to cross the Blue Ridge
and clear the whole country north of Gordonsville.
'Enemy's force there is far less than represented in newspapers—not more than 20,000 at the outside. Jackson's
army is reduced, demoralised, on half-rations. They are
all concentrating for Richmond. . . . I am now satisfied
that it is the most safe and effective disposition for our
corps. I pray your favourable consideration. Such order
will electrify our force.' The force was certainly to be
electrified, but the impulse was not to come from Mr.
Secretary Stanton.

Banks, it may have been observed, whenever his
superiors wanted him to move, had invariably the best
of reasons for halting. At one time supplies were most
difficult to arrange for. At another time the enemy was
being reinforced, and his own numbers were small. But
when he was told to halt, he immediately panted to be
let loose. 'The enemy was not half so strong as had been
reported;' 'His men were never in better condition;'
'Supplies were plentiful.' It is not impossible that Mr.
Stanton had by this time discovered, as was said of a certain
Confederate general, a *protégé* of the President, that Banks
had a fine career before him until Lincoln ' undertook to
make of him what the good Lord hadn't, a great general.'
To the daring propositions of the late Governor and
Speaker, the only reply vouchsafed was an order to fall
back on Strasburg, and to transfer Shields' division to
General McDowell at Fredericksburg.

But on May 3, the day Jackson disappeared behind the
Blue Ridge, Banks, to his evident discomfiture, found that
his adversary had not retreated to Richmond after all.
The dashing commander, just now so anxious for one thing
or the other, either to clear the Valley or to sweep the
country north of Gordonsville, disappeared. 'The re-

x 2

duced, demoralised ' enemy assumed alarming proportions. Nothing was said about his half-rations ; and as Ewell had reached Swift Run Gap with a force estimated at 12,000 men, while Jackson, according to the Federal scouts, was still near Port Republic, Banks thought it impossible to divide his force with safety.

Stanton's reply is not on record, but it seems that he permitted Banks to retain Shields until he arrived at Strasburg ; and on May 5 the Federals fell back to New Market, their commander, misled both by his cavalry and his spies, believing that Jackson had marched to Harrisonburg.

On the 7th, the day that Jackson moved west from Staunton, Banks' fears again revived. He was still anxious that Shields should remain with him. 'Our cavalry,' he said, ' from near Harrisonburg report to-night that Jackson occupies that town, and that he has been largely reinforced. Deserters confirm reports of Jackson's movements in this direction.'

Jackson's movements at this juncture are full of interest. Friend and foe were both mystified. Even his own officers might well ask why, in his march to Staunton, he deliberately adopted the terrible road to Port Republic. From Elk Run Valley a metalled road passed over the Blue Ridge to Gordonsville. Staunton by this route was twenty-four miles further than by Port Republic ; but there were no obstacles to rapid marching, and the command would have arrived no later than it actually did. Moreover, in moving to Port Republic, eleven miles only from Harrisonburg, and within sight of the enemy's patrols, it would seem that there was considerable risk. Had Banks attacked the bridge whilst the Confederate artillery was dragging heavily through the mire, the consequences would probably have been unpleasant. Even if he had not carried the bridge, the road which Jackson had chosen ran for several miles over the open plain which lies eastward of the Shenandoah, and from the commanding bluffs on the western bank his column could have been effectively shelled without the power of reply.

In moving to Staunton the Confederate commander had three objects in view :—

1. To strengthen his own force by combining with Edward Johnson.

2. To prevent the Federals combining by keeping Banks stationary and defeating Milroy.

3. To protect Staunton.

The real danger that he had to guard against was that Banks, taking advantage of his absence from the Valley, should move on Staunton. Knowing his adversary as well as he did, he had no reason to apprehend attack during his march to Port Republic. But it was not impossible that when he found out that Jackson had vanished from the Valley, Banks might take heart and join hands with Milroy. It was necessary, therefore, in order to prevent Banks moving, that Jackson's absence from the Valley should be very short; also, in order to prevent Milroy either joining Banks or taking Staunton, that Edward Johnson should be reinforced as rapidly as possible.

These objects would be attained by making use of the road to Port Republic. In the first place, Banks would not dare to move towards Milroy so long as the flank of his line of march was threatened; and in the second place, from Port Republic to Staunton, by Mechum's River, was little more than two days' march. Within forty-eight hours, therefore, using the railway, it would be possible to strengthen Johnson in time to protect Staunton, and to prevent the Federals uniting. It was unlikely that Banks, even if he heard at once that his enemy had vanished, would immediately dash forward; and even if he did he would still have five-and-twenty miles to march before he reached Staunton. Every precaution had been taken, too, that he should not hear of the movement across the Blue Ridge till it was too late to take advantage of it; and, as we have already seen, so late as May 5 he believed that Jackson was at Harrisonburg. Ashby had done his work well.

It might be argued, however, that with an antagonist

so supine as Banks Jackson might have openly marched
to Staunton by the most direct route; in fact, that he need
never have left the Valley at all. But, had he taken the
road across the Valley, he would have advertised his purpose. Milroy would have received long warning of his
approach, and all chance of effecting a surprise would have
been lost.

On April 29, the day on which Jackson began his movement, Richmond was still safe. The Yorktown lines were
intact, held by the 53,000 Confederates under Johnston ; but
it was very evident that they could not be long maintained.

A large siege train had been brought from Washington,
and Johnston had already learned that in a few days one
hundred pieces of the heaviest ordnance would open fire on
his position. His own armament was altogether inadequate
to cope with such ponderous metal. His strength was not
half his adversary's, and he had determined to retreat without waiting to have his works demolished.

But the mighty army in his front was not the only
danger. McDowell, with 35,000 men, had already concentrated near Falmouth. Johnston, in falling back on
Richmond, was in danger of being caught between two fires,
for to oppose McDowell on the Rappahannock Lee had been
unable to assemble more than 12,000 Confederates.

These facts were all known to Jackson. Whether the
march to Mechum's River was intended by him to have any
further effect on the Federals than surprising Milroy,
and clearing the way for an attack on Banks, it is impossible to say. It is indisputable, at the same time, that
his sudden disappearance from the Valley disturbed Mr.
Stanton. The Secretary of War had suspected that
Jackson's occupation of Swift Run Gap meant mischief.
McDowell, who had been instructed to cross the Rappahannock, was ordered in consequence to stand fast at
Falmouth, and was warned that the enemy, amusing
McClellan at Yorktown, might make a sudden dash on
either himself or Banks.

A few days later McDowell reported that Jackson had
passed Gordonsville. The news came from deserters, ' very

intelligent men.' The next day he was informed that Shields was to be transferred to his command, and that he was to bear in mind his instructions as to the defence of Washington. Banks had already been ordered back to Strasburg. Now, a few days previously, Stanton had been talking of co-operation between McClellan and McDowell. Directly he learned that Jackson was east of the Blue Ridge all thought of combination was abandoned; McDowell was held back; Shields was sent to reinforce him; and the possible danger to Washington overrode all other considerations.

The weak point of McClellan's strategy was making itself felt. In advancing on Richmond by way of the Peninsula he had deliberately adopted what are called in strategy 'the exterior lines.' That is, his forces were distributed on the arc of a circle, of which Richmond and the Confederate army were the centre. If, landing on the Peninsula, he had been able to advance at once upon Richmond, the enemy must have concentrated for the defence of his capital, and neither Banks nor Washington would have been disturbed. But the moment his advance was checked, as it was at Yorktown, the enemy could detach at his leisure in any direction that he pleased, and McClellan was absolutely unable to support the threatened point. The strategy of exterior lines demands, for success, a strong and continuous pressure on the enemy's main army, depriving him of the time and the space necessary for counterstroke. If this is impossible, a skilful foe will at once make use of his central position.

Lincoln appears to have had an instinctive apprehension that McClellan might not be able to exert sufficient pressure to hold Johnston fast, and it was for this reason that he had fought so strongly against the Peninsula line of invasion. It was the probability that the Confederates would use their opportunity with which Stanton had now to deal, complicated by the fact that their numbers were believed to be much greater than they really were. Still the problem was not one of insurmountable difficulty. Banks and Frémont united had 40,000 men, McDowell over 30,000. A few marches would have brought these forces into combination.

Banks and Frémont, occupying Staunton, and moving on Gordonsville, would have soon taken up communication with McDowell; an army 70,000 strong, far larger than any force the Confederates could detach against it, would have threatened Richmond from the north and west, and, at the same time, would have covered Washington. This plan, though not without elements of danger, offered some advantages. Nor were soldiers wanting to advise it. Both Rosecrans and Shields had submitted schemes for such a combination. Mr. Stanton, however, preferred to control the chessboard by the light of unaided wisdom; and while McDowell was unnecessarily strengthened, both Banks and Frémont were dangerously weakened.

The only single point where the Secretary showed the slightest sagacity was in apprehending that the Confederates would make use of their opportunity, and overwhelm one of the detachments he had so ingeniously isolated.

On April 29 Johnston proposed to Davis that his army should be withdrawn from the Peninsula, and that the North should be invaded by way of the Valley.[1] Lee, in the name of the President, replied that some such scheme had been for some time under consideration; and the burden of his letters, as we have seen, both to Ewell and Jackson, was that a sudden and heavy blow should be struck at some exposed portion of the invading armies. Mr. Stanton was so far right; but where the blow was to be struck he was absolutely unable to divine.

'It is believed,' he writes to the Assistant Secretary on May 8, ' that a considerable force has been sent toward the Rappahannock and Shenandoah to move on Washington. Jackson is reinforced strongly. Telegraph McDowell, Banks, and Hartsuff (at Warrenton) to keep a sharp look-out. Tell General Hitchcock to see that the force around Washington is in proper condition.'

It was indeed unfortunate for the North that at this juncture the military affairs of the Confederacy should have been placed in the hands of the clearest-sighted soldier in America. It was an unequal match, Lincoln and Stanton

[1] O. R., vol. xi., part iii., p. 477.

against Lee; and the stroke that was to prove the weakness of the Federal strategy was soon to fall. On May 7 Jackson westward marched in the following order: Edward Johnson's regiments led the way, several miles in advance; the Third and Second Brigades followed; the 'Stonewall,' under General Winder, a young West Point officer of exceptional promise, bringing up the rear. 'The corps of cadets of the Virginia Military Institute,' says Dabney, 'was also attached to the expedition; and the spruce equipments and exact drill of the youths, as they stepped out full of enthusiasm to take their first actual look upon the horrid visage of war, under their renowned professor, formed a strong contrast with the war-worn and nonchalant veterans who composed the army.' [1]

Eighteen miles west of Staunton a Federal picket was overrun, and in the pass leading to the Shenandoah Mountain Johnson captured a camp that had just been abandoned. The Federal rear-guard fired a few shells, and the Confederates went into bivouac. Johnson had marched fourteen and Jackson twenty miles.

That night Milroy concentrated his whole brigade of 3,700 men at M'Dowell, a little village at the foot of the Bull Pasture Mountain, and sent back in haste for reinforcements. Frémont's command was much strung out. When Milroy had moved from Cheat Mountain through Monterey, twelve miles west of M'Dowell,[2] the remainder of the army had started up the South Branch Valley to reinforce him. But snowstorms and heavy rains had much delayed the march, and Schenck's brigade had not advanced beyond Franklin, thirty-four miles north of M'Dowell. Frémont himself, with a couple of battalions, was approaching Petersburg, thirty-five miles from Franklin; and Blenker's division, still further to the rear, had not yet quitted Romney.

'On the following morning,' to quote from Jackson's report, 'the march was resumed, General Johnson's brigade still in front. The head of the column was halted near the top of Bull Pasture Mountain, and

May 8.

[1] Dabney, vol. ii., p. 65.   [2] See ante, pp. 185, 269, 275.

General Johnson, accompanied by a party of thirty men and several officers, with a view to a reconnaissance of the enemy's position, ascended Sitlington's Hill, an isolated spur on the left of the turnpike and commanding a full view of the village of M'Dowell. From this point the position, and to some extent the strength, of the enemy could be seen. In the valley in which M'Dowell is situated was observed a considerable force of infantry. To the right, on a height, were two regiments, but too distant for an effective fire to that point. Almost a mile in front was a battery supported by infantry. The enemy, observing a reconnoitring party, sent a small body of skirmishers, which was promptly met by the men with General Johnson and driven back. For the purpose of securing the hill all of General Johnson's regiments were sent to him.'

Jackson had no intention of delivering a direct assault on the Federal position. The ground was altogether unfavourable for attack. The hill on which his advanced guard was now established was more than two miles broad from east to west. But it was no plateau. Rugged and precipitous ridges towered high above the level, and numerous ravines, hidden by thick timber, seamed the surface of the spur. To the front a slope of smooth unbroken greensward dropped sharply down; and five hundred feet below, behind a screen of woods, the Bull Pasture River ran swiftly through its narrow valley. On the river banks were the Federals; and beyond the valley the wooded mountains, a very labyrinth of hills, rose high and higher to the west. To the right was a deep gorge, nearly half a mile across from cliff to cliff, dividing Sitlington's Hill from the heights to northward; and through this dangerous defile ran the turnpike, eventually debouching on a bridge which was raked by the Federal guns. To the left the country presented exactly the same features. Mountain after mountain, ridge after ridge, cleft by shadowy crevasses, and clothed with great tracts of forest, rolled back in tortuous masses to the backbone of the Alleghanies; a narrow pass, leading due westward, marking the route to Monterey and the Ohio River.

Although commanded by Sitlington's Hill, the Federal position was difficult to reach. The river, swollen by rain, protected it in front. The bridge could only be approached by a single road, with inaccessible heights on either hand. The village of M'Dowell was crowded with troops and guns. A low hill five hundred yards beyond the bridge was occupied by infantry and artillery; long lines of tents were ranged on the level valley, and the hum of many voices, excited by the appearance of the enemy, was borne upwards to the heights. Had the Confederate artillery been brought to the brow of Sitlington's Hill, the valley would doubtless soon have become untenable, and the enemy have been compelled to retire through the mountains. It was by no means easy, however, to prevent them from getting away unscathed. But Jackson was not the man to leave the task untried, and to content himself with a mere cannonade. He had reason to hope that Milroy was ignorant of his junction with General Johnson, and that he would suppose he had only the six regiments of the latter with which to deal. The day was far spent, and the Valley brigades, toiling through the mountains, were still some miles behind. He proposed, therefore, while his staff explored the mountains for a track which might lead him the next day to the rear of the Federal position, merely to hold his ground on Sitlington's Hill.

His immediate opponent, however, was a general of more resource and energy than Banks. Milroy was at least able to supply himself with information. On May 7 he had been advised by his scouts and spies that Jackson and Johnson had combined, and that they were advancing to attack him at M'Dowell. At 10 A.M. the next day Schenck's brigade arrived from Franklin, after a march of thirty-four miles in twenty-three hours, and a little later the enemy's scouts were observed on the lofty crest of Sitlington's Hill. The day wore on. The Federal battery, with muzzles elevated and the trails thrust into trenches, threw occasional shells upon the heights, and parties of skirmishers were sent across the river to develop the Confederate strength. Johnson, to whom Jackson had confided the defence of the

position, kept his troops carefully concealed, merely exposing sufficient numbers to repel the Federal patrols. Late
in the afternoon a staff officer reported to Jackson that
he had discovered a rough mountain track, which, passing
through the mountains to the north-west, crossed the Bull-
Pasture River and came out upon the road between
M'Dowell and Franklin. Orders had just been issued to
move a strong detachment of artillery and infantry by this
track during the night, when the Federal infantry, who had
crossed the bridge under shelter of the woods, advanced in
a strong line of battle up the slopes. Their scouts had
observed what they believed to be preparations for establishing a battery on the heights, and Milroy and Schenck, with
a view of gaining time for retreat, had determined on
attack. Johnson had six regiments concealed behind the
crest, in all about 2,800 men. Two regiments of the enemy,
under 1,000 strong, advanced against his front; and
shortly afterwards three regiments, bringing the numbers
of the attack up to 2,500 rifles, assailed his left.

The Ohio and West Virginia Regiments, of which the
Federal force was composed, fought with the vigour which
always characterised the Western troops.[1] The lofty heights
held by the Confederates were but an illusory advantage.
So steep were the slopes in front that the men, for the most
part, had to stand on the crest to deliver their fire, and their
line stood out in bold relief against the evening sky. 'On
the other hand,' says Dabney, 'though the Federal troops
had to scale the steep acclivity of the hill, they reaped the
usual advantage in such cases, resulting from the high firing
of the Confederates.' The 12th Georgia, holding the centre
of Johnson's line, displayed more valour than judgment.
Having been advanced at first in front of the crest, they
could not be persuaded to retire to the reverse of the ridge,
where other regiments found partial protection without

---

[1] Jackson fully recognised the fine fighting qualities of his compatriots
'As Shields' brigade (division),' he wrote on April 5, 'is composed principally
of Western troops, who are familiar with the use of arms, we must calculate
on hard fighting to oust Banks if attacked only in front, and may meet
with obstinate resistance, however the attack may be made.'

sacrificing the efficiency of their fire. Their commander, perceiving their useless exposure, endeavoured again and again to withdraw them; but amidst the roar of the musketry his voice was lifted up in vain, and when by passing along the ranks he persuaded one wing of the regiment to recede, they rushed again to the front while he was gone to expostulate with the other. A tall Georgia youth expressed the spirit of his comrades when he replied the next day to the question why they did not retreat to the shelter of the ridge: 'We did not come all this way to Virginia to run before Yankees.'[1] Nor was the courage of the other troops less ardent. The 44th Virginia was placed in reserve, thirty paces in rear of the centre. 'After the battle became animated,' says the brigadier, 'and my attention was otherwise directed, a large number of the 44th quit their position, and, rushing forward, joined the 58th and engaged in the fight, while the balance of the regiment joined some other brigade.'[2]

The action gradually became so fierce that Jackson sent his Third Brigade to support the advanced guard. These nine regiments now engaged sufficed to hold the enemy in check; the Second Brigade, which moved towards them as darkness fell, was not engaged, and the Stonewall regiments were still in rear. No counterstroke was delivered. Johnson himself was wounded, and had to hand over the command; and after four hours' fighting the Federals fell back in perfect order under cover of the night. Nor was there any endeavour to pursue. The Confederate troops were superior in numbers, but there was much confusion in their ranks; the cavalry could not act on the steep and broken ground, and there were other reasons which rendered a night attack undesirable.

The enemy had been repulsed at every point. The tale of casualties, nevertheless, was by no means small. 498 Confederates, including 54 officers, had fallen. The 12th Georgia paid the penalty for its useless display of valour with the loss of 156 men and 19 officers. The

[1] Dabney, vol. ii., p. 73.
[2] Report of Colonel Scott, 44th Virginia Infantry. O. R., vol. xii., part i., p. 486.

Federals, on the other hand, favoured by the ground, had no more than 256 killed, wounded, and missing. Only three pieces of artillery took part in the engagement. These were Federal guns; but so great was the angle of elevation that but one man on Sitlington's Hill was struck by a piece of shell. Jackson, in order to conceal his actual strength, had declined to order up his artillery. The approach to the position, a narrow steep ravine, wooded, and filled with boulders, forbade the use of horses, and the guns must have been dragged up by hand with great exertion. Moreover, the artillery was destined to form part of the turning column, and had a long night march before it.

'By nine o'clock,' says Dabney, ' the roar of the struggle had passed away, and the green battle-field reposed under the starlight as calmly as when it had been occupied only by its peaceful herds. Detachments of soldiers were silently exploring the ground for their wounded comrades, while the tired troops were slowly filing off to their bivouac. At midnight the last sufferer had been removed and the last picket posted; and then only did Jackson turn to seek a few hours' repose in a neighbouring farmhouse. The valley of M'Dowell lay in equal quiet. The camp-fires of the Federals blazed ostentatiously in long and regular lines, and their troops seemed wrapped in sleep. At one o'clock the general reached his quarters, and threw himself upon a bed. When his mulatto servant, knowing that he had eaten nothing since morning, came in with food, he said, " I want none; nothing but sleep," and in a few minutes he was slumbering like a healthy child.'

It seems, however, that the march of the turning column had already been countermanded. Putting himself in his enemy's place, Jackson had foreseen Milroy's movements. If the one could move by night, so could the other; and when he rode out at dawn, the Federals, as he anticipated, had disappeared. The next day he sent a laconic despatch to Richmond: ' God blessed our arms with victory at M'Dowell yesterday.'

This announcement was doubtless received by the people of Virginia, as Dabney declares, with peculiar delight.

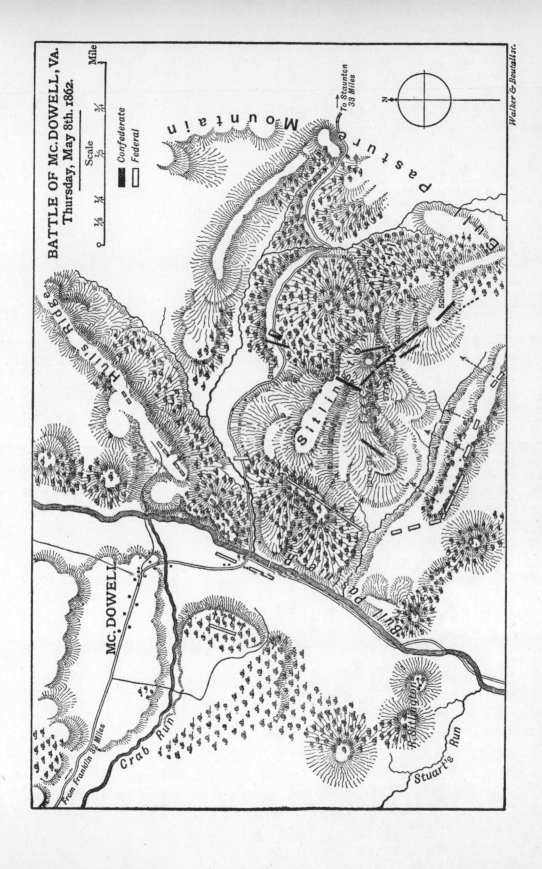

BATTLE OF MC.DOWELL, VA.
Thursday, May 8th. 1862.

Scale

Mile

Confederate
Federal

Walker & Boutall sc.

To Staunton
33 Miles

N

Bull Pasture Mountain

Bull Pasture

Hull's Ridge

Sitlington

Bull Pasture River

MC. DOWELL

From Franklin 32 Miles

Crab Run

R. Sitlington

Stuart's Run

On May 4 Johnston had evacuated Yorktown. On the 5th he had checked the pursuit at Williamsburg, inflicting heavy losses, but had continued his retreat. On the 9th Norfolk was abandoned; and on the 11th the 'Merrimac,' grounding in the James, was destroyed by her commander. 'The victory of M'Dowell was the one gleam of brightness athwart all these clouds.' It must be admitted, however, that the victory was insignificant. The repulse of 2,500 men by 4,000 was not a remarkable feat; and it would even appear that M'Dowell might be ranked with the battles of lost opportunities. A vigorous counterstroke would probably have destroyed the whole of the attacking force. The riflemen of the West, however, were not made of the stuff that yields readily to superior force. The fight for the bridge would have been fierce and bloody. Twilight had fallen before the Confederate reinforcements arrived upon the scene; and under such conditions the losses must have been very heavy. But to lose men was exactly what Jackson wished to avoid. The object of his manœuvres was the destruction not of Frémont's advanced guard, but of Banks' army; and if his numbers were seriously reduced it would be impossible to attain that end. Frémont's brigades, moreover, protected no vital point. A decisive victory at M'Dowell would have produced but little effect at Washington. No great results were to be expected from operations in so distant a section of the strategic theatre; and Jackson aimed at nothing more than driving the enemy so far back as to isolate him from Banks.

The next morning the small force of cavalry crossed the bridge and rode cautiously through the mountain passes.

May 9. The infantry halted for some hours in M'Dowell in order that rations might be issued, but the Federals made three-and-twenty miles, and were already too far ahead to be overtaken. On the 10th and the 11th the Confederates made forced marches, but the enemy set fire to the forests on the mountain-side, and this desperate measure proved eminently successful. 'The sky was overcast with volumes of smoke, which wrapped every distant object in a veil, impenetrable alike to the eyes and telescopes of the officers. Through this sultry canopy the pursuing army felt its way cautiously, cannonaded by the enemy from every advantageous position, while it was protected from ambuscades only by detachments of skirmishers, who scoured the burning woods on either side of the highway. The general, often far in advance of the column in his eagerness to overtake the foe, declared that this was the most adroit expedient to which a retreating army could resort, and that it entailed upon him all the disadvantages of a night attack. By slow approaches, and with constant skirmishing, the Federals were driven back to Franklin village, and the double darkness of the night and the smoke arrested the pursuit.'[1]

On May 12 Jackson resolved to return to the Valley. Frémont, with Blenker's division, was at hand. It was impossible to outflank the enemy's position, and time was precious, 'for he knew not how soon a new emergency at Fredericksburg or at Richmond might occasion the recall of Ewell, and deprive him of the power of striking an effective blow at Banks.'[2] Half the day was granted to the soldiers as a day of rest, to compensate for the Sunday spent in the pursuit, and the following order was issued to the command :—

May 12.

'I congratulate you on your recent victory at M'Dowell. I request you to unite with me in thanksgiving to Almighty God for thus having crowned your arms with success ; and in praying that He will continue to lead you on from victory to victory, until our independence shall be established ; and make us that people whose God is the Lord. The chaplains will hold divine service at 10 A.M. on this day, in their respective regiments.'

Shortly after noon the march to M'Dowell was resumed. On the 15th the army left the mountains and encamped at Lebanon Springs, on the road to Harrisonburg. The 16th was spent in camp, the Confederate President having appointed a day of prayer and

May 15.

[1] Dabney, vol. ii., p. 77.
[2] *Ibid.*, p. 78. On May 9, in anticipation of a movement down the Valley, he had ordered thirty days' forage, besides other supplies, to be accumulated at Staunton. *Harman MS.*

fasting.   On the 17th a halt was made at Mount Solon, and here Jackson was met by Ewell, who had ridden over from Elk Run Valley.   Banks had fallen back to Strasburg, and he was now completely cut off from Frémont.   On the night of the engagement at M'Dowell Captain Hotchkiss had been ordered back to the Valley, and, accompanied by a squadron of Ashby's cavalry, had blocked the passes by which Frémont could cross the mountains and support his colleague.   'Bridges and culverts were destroyed, rocks rolled down, and in one instance trees were felled along the road for nearly a mile.[1]   Jackson's object was thus thoroughly achieved.   All combination between the Federal columns, except by long and devious routes, had now been rendered impracticable; and there was little fear that in any operations down the Valley his own communications would be endangered.   The M'Dowell expedition had neutralised, for the time being, Frémont's 20,000 men; and Banks was now isolated, exposed to the combined attack of Jackson, Ewell, and Edward Johnson.

One incident remains to be mentioned.   During the march to Mount Solon some companies of the 27th Virginia, who had volunteered for twelve months, and whose time had expired, demanded their discharge.   On this being refused, as the Conscription Act was now in force, they threw down their arms, and refused to serve another day. Colonel Grigsby referred to the General for instructions. Jackson's face, when the circumstances were explained, set hard as flint.   'Why,' he said, ' does Colonel Grigsby refer to me to learn how to deal with mutineers? He should shoot them where they stand.'   The rest of the regiment was ordered to parade with loaded muskets; the insubordinate companies were offered the choice of instant death or instant submission.   The men knew their commander, and at once surrendered.   'This,' says Dabney, 'was the last attempt at organised disobedience in the Valley army.'

[1] Frémont's Report, O. R., vol. xii., part i., p. 11.

CHAPTER X

WINCHESTER

THAT week in May when the Army of the Valley marched
back to the Shenandoah was almost the darkest in the
1862.   Confederate annals. The Northern armies, im-
May.   proving daily in discipline and in efficiency,
had attained an ascendency which it seemed impossible to
withstand. In every quarter of the theatre of war success
inclined to the Stars and Stripes. At the end of April New
Orleans, the commercial metropolis of the South, had fallen
to the Federal navy. Earlier in the month a great battle had
been fought at Shiloh, in Tennessee ; one of the most trusted
of the Confederate commanders had been killed ;[1] his troops,
after a gallant struggle, had been repulsed with fearful
losses ; and the upper portion of the Mississippi, from the
source to Memphis, had fallen under the control of the
invader. The wave of conquest, vast and irresistible, swept
up every navigable river of the South ; and if in the West
only the outskirts of her territory were threatened with
destruction, in Virginia the roar of the rising waters was
heard at the very gates of Richmond. McClellan, with
112,000 men, had occupied West Point at the head of the
York River ; and on May 16 his advance reached the White
House, on the Pamunkey, twenty miles from the Confederate
capital. McDowell, with 40,000 men, although still north of
the Rappahannock, was but five short marches distant.[2]

[1] General A. S. Johnston.
[2] Directly McClellan closed in on Richmond, McDowell was ordered, as
soon as Shields should join him, to march from Manassas to his assistance.
Lincoln and Stanton had recovered confidence when Jackson returned to
the Valley from Mechum's Station.

The Federal gunboats were steaming up the James; and Johnston's army, encamped outside the city, was menaced by thrice its numbers.

So black was the situation that military stores had already been removed from the capital, the archives of the Confederacy had been packed, and Mr. Davis had made arrangements for the departure of his family. In spite of the protests of the Virginia people the Government had decided to abandon Richmond. The General Assembly addressed a resolution to the President requiring him to defend the city, if necessary, ' until not a stone was left upon another.' The City Council, enthusiastically supported by the citizens, seconded the appeal. A deputation was sent to Mr. Davis; but while they conferred together, a messenger rode in with the news that the mastheads of the Federal fleet could be seen from the neighbouring hills. Davis dismissed the committee, saying: ' This manifestly concludes the matter.'

The gunboats, however, had still to feel their way up the winding reaches of the James. Their progress was very slow; there was time to obstruct the passage, and batteries were hastily improvised. The people made a mighty effort; and on the commanding heights of Drewry's Bluff, six miles below the city, might be seen senators and merchants, bankers and clergymen, digging parapets and hauling timber, in company with parties of soldiers and gangs of slaves. Heavy guns were mounted. A great boom was constructed across the stream. When the ships approached they were easily driven back, and men once more breathed freely in the streets of Richmond. The example of the ' Unterrified Commonwealth,' as Virginia has been proudly named, inspired the Government, and it was determined, come what might, that Richmond should be held. On the land side it was already fortified. But Lee was unwilling to resign himself to a siege. McClellan had still to cross the Chickahominy, a stream which oozes by many channels through treacherous swamps and an unwholesome jungle; and despite the overwhelming numbers of the invading armies, it was still possible to strike an effective blow.

Few would have seen the opportunity, or, with a great army thundering at the gates of Richmond, have dared to seize it; but it was not McClellan and McDowell whom Lee was fighting, not the enormous hosts which they commanded, nor the vast resources of the North. The power which gave life and motion to the mighty mechanism of the attack lay not within the camps that could be seen from the housetops of Richmond and from the hills round Fredericksburg. Far away to the north, beyond the Potomac, beneath the shadow of the Capitol at Washington, was the mainspring of the invader's strength. The multitudes of armed men that overran Virginia were no more the inanimate pieces of the chess-board. The power which controlled them was the Northern President. It was at Lincoln that Lee was about to strike, at Lincoln and the Northern people, and an effective blow at the point which people and President deemed vital might arrest the progress of their armies as surely as if the Confederates had been reinforced by a hundred thousand men.

On May 16 Lee wrote to Jackson: 'Whatever movement you make against Banks, do it speedily, and if successful drive him back towards the Potomac, and May 16. create the impression, as far as possible, that you design threatening that line.' For this purpose, in addition to Ewell and Johnson's forces, the Army of the Valley was to be reinforced by two brigades, Branch's and Mahone's, of which the former had already reached Gordonsville.

In this letter the idea of playing on the fears of Lincoln for the safety of his capital first sees the light, and it is undoubtedly to be attributed to the brain of Lee. That the same idea had been uppermost in Jackson's mind during the whole course of the campaign is proved not only by the evidence of his chief of the staff, but by his correspondence with headquarters. 'If Banks is defeated,' he had written on April 5, 'it may directly retard McClellan's movements.' It is true that nowhere in his correspondence is the idea of menacing Washington directly mentioned, nor is there the slightest evidence that he suggested it to Lee. But in his letters to his superiors he confines himself strictly to the immediate subject, and on no single occasion does he indulge in speculation on possible results. In the ability of the Commander-in-Chief he had the most implicit confidence. 'Lee,' he said, ' is the only man I know whom I would follow blindfold,' and he was doubtless assured that the embarrassments of the Federal Government were as apparent to Lee as to himself. That the same idea should have suggested itself independently to both is hardly strange. Both looked further than the enemy's camps; both studied the situation in its broadest bearings; both understood the importance of introducing a disturbing element into the enemy's plans; and both were aware that the surest means of winning battles is to upset the mental equilibrium of the opposing leader.

Before he reached Mount Solon Jackson had instructed Ewell to call up Branch's brigade from Gordonsville. He intended to follow Banks with the whole force at his disposal, and in these dispositions Lee had acquiesced. Johnston, however, now at Richmond, had once more resumed charge of the detached forces, and a good deal of confusion ensued. Lee, intent on threatening Washington, was of opinion that Banks should be attacked. Johnston, although at first he favoured such a movement, does not appear to have realised the effect that might be produced by an advance to the Potomac. Information had been received that Banks was constructing intrenchments at Strasburg, and Johnston changed his mind. He thought the attack too hazardous, and Ewell was directed to cross the Blue Ridge and march eastward, while Jackson ' observed ' Banks.

These orders placed Ewell in a dilemma. Under instructions from Lee he was to remain with Jackson. Under instructions from Jackson he was already moving on Luray. Johnston's orders changed his destination. Taking horse in haste he rode across the Valley from Swift Run Gap to Jackson's camp at Mount Solon. Jackson at once telegraphed to Lee: 'I am of opinion that an attempt should be made to defeat Banks, but under instructions from General Johnston I do not feel at liberty to make an attack. Please answer by telegraph at once.' To Ewell he gave orders that he should suspend his movement until a reply was received. 'As you are in the Valley district,' he wrote, 'you constitute part of my command. . . . You will please move so as to encamp between New Market and Mount Jackson on next Wednesday night, unless you receive orders from a superior officer and of a date subsequent to the 16th instant.'

This order was written at Ewell's own suggestion. It was for this he had ridden through the night to Jackson's camp.

Lee's reply was satisfactory. Johnston had already summoned Branch to Richmond, but Ewell was to May 18. remain; and the next morning, May 18, the Confederates moved forward down the Valley. The two days' rest which had been granted to Jackson's troops had fallen at a useful time. They had marches to look back on which had tried their endurance to the utmost. In three days, before and after Kernstown, they had covered fifty-six miles, and had fought a severe engagement. The struggle with the mud on the Port Republic was only surpassed by the hardships of the march to Romney. From Elk Run to Franklin, and from Franklin to Mount Solon, is just two hundred miles, and these they had traversed in eighteen days. But the exertions which had been then demanded from them were trifling in comparison with those which were to come. From Mount Solon to Winchester is eighty miles by the Valley pike; to Harper's Ferry one hundred and ten miles. And Jackson had determined that before many days had passed the Confederate colours should be carried in triumph through the streets of Winchester, and that the gleam of his camp-fires should be reflected in the waters of the Potomac.

Johnston believed that Banks, behind the earthworks at Strasburg, was securely sheltered. Jackson saw that his enemy had made a fatal mistake, and that his earthworks, skilfully and strongly constructed as they were, were no more than a snare and a delusion.

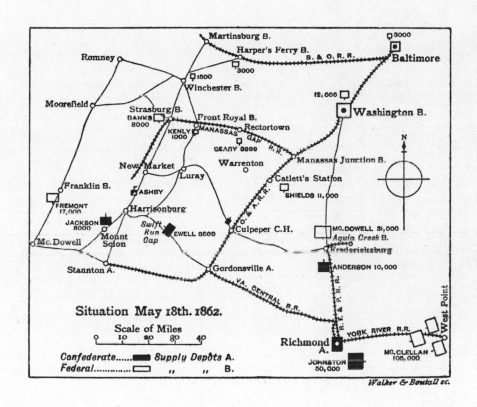

Situation May 18th. 1862.

Scale of Miles

0   10   20   30   40

Confederate...... ■ Supply Depôts A.
Federal............. □   "   "   B.

Walker & Boutall sc.

Ashby had already moved to New Market; and a strong cordon of pickets extended along Pugh's Run near Woodstock, within sight of the Federal outposts, and cutting off all communication between Strasburg and the Upper Valley. Ewell's cavalry regiments, the 2nd and 6th Virginia, held the Luray Valley, with a detachment east of the Blue Ridge. On the 20th Jackson arrived at New Market, thirty miles from Mount Solon. Ewell had meanwhile marched to Luray, and the two wings were now on either side of the Massanuttons. On his way to New Market Jackson had been joined by the Louisiana brigade of Ewell's division. This detachment seems to have been made with the view of inducing Banks to believe, should information filter through Ashby's pickets, that the whole Confederate force was advancing direct on Strasburg.

May 20.

The Army of the Valley numbered nearly 17,000 officers and men.[1] Ewell's effective strength was 7,500; Johnson's 2,500; Jackson's 6,000; and there were eleven batteries.

The troops were now organised in two divisions :—

JACKSON'S DIVISION.

First (Stonewall) Brigade, General Winder: 2nd Virginia, 4th Virginia, 5th Virginia, 27th Virginia, 33rd Virginia.

Second Brigade, Colonel Campbell: 21st Virginia, 42nd Virginia, 48th Virginia, 1st Regulars (Irish).

Third Brigade, Colonel Taliaferro: 10th Virginia, 23rd Virginia, 37th Virginia.

Cavalry, Colonel Ashby: 7th Virginia.

Artillery: 5 batteries (1 horse-artillery), 22 guns.

EWELL'S DIVISION.

Taylor's Brigade: 6th Louisiana, 7th Louisiana, 8th Louisiana, 9th Louisiana, Wheat's Battalion (Louisiana Tigers).

Trimble's Brigade: 21st North Carolina, 21st Georgia, 15th Alabama, 16th Mississippi.

Elzey's Brigade : { 13th Virginia, 31st Virginia, 25th Virginia, 12th Georgia.

(late Johnson's)

Scott's Brigade : { 44th Virginia, 52nd Virginia, 58th Virginia.

---

[1] This estimate is Colonel Allan's. Cf. *The Valley Campaign*, pp. 92–3. Dabney gives 16,000 men.

Maryland Line : 1st Maryland.
Cavalry, General G. H. Steuart : 2nd Virginia, Colonel Munford ;
6th Virginia, Colonel Flournoy.
Artillery : 6 batteries, 26 guns.

For the first time in his career Jackson found himself
in command of a considerable force. The greater part
of the troops were Virginians, and with these he was
personally acquainted. The strange contingents were
Taylor's and Trimble's brigades, and Steuart's cavalry.
These had yet to be broken to his methods of war and
discipline. There was no reason, however, to fear that
they would prove less efficient than his own division.
They had as yet seen little fighting, but they were well
commanded. Ewell was a most able soldier, full of dash
and daring, who had seen much service on the Indian
frontier. He was an admirable subordinate, ready to take
responsibility if orders were not forthcoming, and executing
his instructions to the letter. His character was original.
His modesty was only equalled by his eccentricity.
'Bright, prominent eyes, a bomb-shaped bald head,
and a nose like that of Francis of Valois, gave him a
striking resemblance to a woodcock ; and this was increased by a bird-like habit of putting his head on one side
to utter his quaint speeches. He fancied that he had
some mysterious internal malady, and would eat nothing
but frumenty, a preparation of wheat ; and his plaintive
way of talking of his disease, as if he were someone else,
was droll in the extreme. "What do you suppose President Davis made me a major-general for?" beginning
with a sharp accent, ending with a gentle lisp, was a usual
question to his friends. Superbly mounted, he was the
boldest of horsemen, invariably leaving the roads to take
timber and water ; and with all his oddities, perhaps in
some measure because of them, he was adored by officers
and men.'[1] To Jackson he must have been peculiarly
acceptable ; not indeed as an intimate, for Ewell, at this
period of the war, was by no means regenerate, and
swore like a cowboy : but he knew the value of time, and

---

[1] *Destruction and Reconstruction*, General R. Taylor, pp. 38-9.

rated celerity of movement as high as did Napoleon. His instructions to Branch, when the march against Banks was first projected, might have emanated from Jackson himself: 'You cannot bring tents; tent-flies without poles, or tents cut down to that size, and only as few as are indispensable. No mess-chests, trunks, &c. It is better to leave these things where you are than to throw them away after starting. We can get along without anything but food and ammunition. The road to glory cannot be followed with much baggage.' [1]

Trimble, too, was a good officer, an able tactician and a resolute leader. He had hardly, however, realised as yet that the movements of a brigade must be subordinated to those of the whole army, and he was wont to grumble if his troops were held back, or were not allowed to pursue some local success. Steuart was also a West Pointer, but with much to learn. Taylor and his Louisianians played so important a part in the ensuing operations that they deserve more detailed mention. The command was a mixed one. One of the regiments had been recruited from the roughs of New Orleans. The 7th and 9th were composed of planters and sons of planters, the majority of them men of fortune. 'The 6th,' writes the brigadier, 'were Irishmen, stout, hardy fellows, turbulent in camp and requiring a strong hand, but responding to justice and kindness, and ready to follow their officers to the death. The 8th were from the Attakapas —Acadians, the race of whom Longfellow sings in "Evangeline"—a home-loving, simple people; few spoke English, fewer still had ever moved ten miles from their native cabanas; and the war to them was a liberal education. They had all the light gaiety of the Gaul, and, after the manner of their ancestors, were born cooks. A capital regimental band accompanied them, and whenever weather and ground permitted, even after long marches, they would waltz and polk in couples with as much zest as if their arms encircled the supple waists of the Célestines and Mélazies of their native Téche. The Valley soldiers were largely of the Presbyterian faith, and of a solemn, pious demeanour,

[1] O. R., vol. xii., part iii., p. 890.

and looked askance at the caperings of my Creoles, holding them to be " devices and snares. " '[1]

Taylor himself had been educated at West Point. He was a man of high position, of unquestioned ability, an excellent disciplinarian, and a delightful writer. More than other commanders he had paid great attention to the marching of his men. He had an eye to those practical details which a good regimental officer enforces with so much effect. Boots were properly fitted ; the troops were taught the advantages of cold water, and how to heal abrasions ; halts upon the march were made at frequent intervals, and the men soon held that to fall out on the march was a disgrace. Before a month 'had passed,' he says, 'the brigade had learned how to march, and in the Valley with Jackson covered long distances without leaving a straggler behind.'[2]

Jackson's first meeting with the Louisiana troops has been described by their commander :—

'A mounted officer was despatched to report our approach and select a camp, which proved to be beyond Jackson's forces, then lying in the fields on both sides of the Valley pike. Over 3,000 strong, neat in fresh clothing of grey with white gaiters, bands playing at the head of their regiments—not a straggler, but every man in his place, stepping jauntily as if on parade, though it had marched twenty miles or more—in open column, with the rays of the declining sun flaming on polished bayonets, the brigade moved down the hard smooth pike, and wheeled on to the camping-ground. Jackson's men, by thousands, had gathered on either side of the road to see us pass.

'After attending to necessary camp details, I sought Jackson, whom I had never met. The mounted officer who had been sent on in advance pointed out a figure perched on the topmost rail of a fence overlooking the road and field, and said it was Jackson. Approaching, I saluted and declared my name and rank, then waited for a response. Before this came I had time to see a pair of

---

[1] *Destruction and Reconstruction*, pp. 52-3.
[2] *Ibid.*, p. 37.

cavalry boots covering feet of gigantic size, a mangy cap with visor drawn low, a heavy dark beard and weary eyes, eyes I afterwards saw filled with intense but never brilliant light. A low gentle voice inquired the road and distance marched that day. " Keezleton road, six-and-twenty miles." " You seem to have no stragglers." " Never allow straggling." " You must teach my people; they straggle badly." A bow in reply. Just then my Creoles started their band for a waltz. After a contemplative suck at a lemon, "Thoughtless fellows for serious work " came forth. I expressed a hope that the work would not be less well done because of the gaiety. A return to the lemon gave me the opportunity to retire. Where Jackson got his lemons " No fellow could find out," but he was rarely without one. To have lived twelve miles from that fruit would have disturbed him as much as it did the witty dean.' [1]

The next day, marching in the grey of the morning, the force moved north, the Louisianians in advance. Suddenly, after covering a short distance, the head of the column was turned to the right; and the troops, who had confidently expected that Strasburg would be the scene of their next engagement, found themselves moving eastward and crossing the Massanuttons. The men were utterly at sea as to the intentions of their commander. Taylor's brigade had been encamped near Conrad's Store, only a few miles distant, not many days before, and they had now to solve the problem why they should have made three long marches in order to return to their former position. No word came from Jackson to enlighten them. From time to time a courier would gallop up, report, and return to Luray, but the general, absorbed in thought, rode silently across the mountain, perfectly oblivious of inquiring glances.

May 21.

At New Market the troops had been halted at crossroads, and they had marched by that which they had least expected. The camp at Luray on the 21st presented the same puzzle. One road ran east across the mountains to Warrenton or Culpeper; a second north to Front Royal

[1] *Destruction and Reconstruction*, pp. 54–6.

and Winchester; and the men said that halting them in such a position was an ingenious device of Jackson's to May 22. prevent them fathoming his plans.[1] The next day, the 22nd, the army, with Ewell leading, moved quietly down the Luray Valley, and the advanced guard, Taylor's Louisianians, a six-pounder battery, and the 6th Virginia Cavalry, bivouacked that night within ten miles of Front Royal, held by a strong detachment of Banks' small army.

Since they had left Mount Solon and Elk Run Valley on May 19 the troops in four days had made just sixty miles. Such celerity of movement was unfamiliar to both Banks and Stanton, and on the night of the 22nd neither the Secretary nor the general had the faintest suspicion that the enemy had as yet passed Harrisonburg. There was serenity at Washington. On both sides of the Blue Ridge everything was going well. The attack on Frémont had not been followed up; and McClellan, though calling urgently for reinforcements, was sanguine of success. Mr. Lincoln, reassured by Jackson's retreat from Franklin, had permitted Shields to march to Falmouth; and McDowell, with a portion of his troops, had already crossed the Rappahannock. The President of the Baltimore and Ohio Railroad, an important personage at Washington, appears to have been alone in his apprehension that a storm was gathering in the summer sky. 'The aspect of affairs in the Valley of Virginia,' he wrote to Stanton, 'is becoming very threatening. . . . The enterprise and vigour of Jackson are well known. . . . Under the circumstances will it not be more judicious to order back General Shields to co-operate with General Banks? Such a movement might be accomplished in time to prevent disaster.'[2] The Secretary, however, saw no reason for alarm. His strategical combinations were apparently working without a hitch. Banks at Strasburg was in a strong position; and McDowell was about to lend the aid which would enable McClellan to storm the rebel capital. One of Frémont's columns, under General Cox, a

[1] Compare instructions to Ewell, *ante*, p. 281.
[2] O. R., vol. xii., part iii., p. 201.

most able officer, which was making good progress towards
the Virginia and Tennessee Railroad, had certainly been
compelled to halt when Milroy was driven back to Franklin.
Yet the defeated troops were rapidly reorganising, and
Frémont would soon resume his movement.   Milroy's
defeat was considered no more than an incident of *la petite
guerre*.   Washington seemed so perfectly secure that the
recruiting offices had been closed, and the President and
Secretary, anticipating the immediate fall of Richmond,
left for Fredericksburg the next day.   McDowell was to
march on the 26th, and the departure of his fine army was
to be preceded by a grand review.

Even Banks, though Shields had marched to Fredericksburg, reducing his force by a half, believed that there was
no immediate reason to fear attack.   'I regard it as
certain,' he wrote, 'that Jackson will move north as far as
New Market . . . a position which enables him to co-
operate with General Ewell, who is still at Swift Run Gap.'
Yet he took occasion to remind Mr. Stanton of the 'persistent adherence of Jackson to the defence of the Valley,
and his well-known purpose to expel the Government troops.
This,' he added, 'may be assumed as certain.   There is
probably no one more fixed and determined purpose in the
whole circle of the enemy's plans.'   Banks had certainly
learned something of Jackson by this time, but he did not
yet know all.

So on this night of May 22 the President and his
people were without fear of what the morrow might bring
forth.   The end of the rebellion seemed near at hand.
Washington was full of the anticipated triumph.   The
crowds passed to and fro in the broad avenues, exchanging
congratulations on the success of the Northern arms and
the approaching downfall of the slaveholders.   The theatres
were filled with delighted audiences, who hailed every
scoffing allusion to the 'Southern chivalry' with enthusiasm,
and gaiety and confidence reigned supreme.   Little dreamt
the light-hearted multitude that, in the silent woods of the
Luray Valley, a Confederate army lay asleep beneath the
stars.   Little dreamt Lincoln, or Banks, or Stanton, that

not more than seventy miles from Washington, and less than thirty from Strasburg, the most daring of their enemies, waiting for the dawn to rise above the mountains, was pouring out his soul in prayer,

> Appealing from his native sod
> *In formâ pauperis* to God:
> 'Lay bare Thine arm—stretch forth Thy rod.
> Amen!' That's Stonewall's way.

It is not always joy that cometh in the morning, least of all to generals as ignorant as Banks when they have to do with a skilful foe. It was not altogether Banks' fault that his position was a bad one. Stanton had given him a direct order to take post at Strasburg or its vicinity, and to send two regiments to hold the bridges at Front Royal. But Banks had made no remonstrance. He had either failed to recognise, until it was too late, that the force at Front Royal would be exposed to attack from the Luray Valley, and, if the post fell, that his own communications with both Winchester and Washington would be at once endangered; or he had lost favour with the Secretary. For some time past Mr. Stanton's telegrams had been cold and peremptory. There had been no more effusive praise of 'cautious vigour' and 'interesting manœuvres;' and Banks had gradually fallen from the command of a large army corps to the charge of a single division.

His 10,000 men were thus distributed. At Strasburg were 4,500 infantry, 2,900 cavalry, and 16 guns. At Winchester 850 infantry and 600 cavalry. Two companies of infantry held Buckton station on the Manassas Gap Railway, midway between Strasburg and Front Royal.[1] At Rectortown, east of the Blue Ridge, nineteen miles from Front Royal, was General Geary with 2,000 infantry and cavalry; these troops, however, were independent of Banks.

Front Royal, twelve miles east of Strasburg, was committed to the charge of Colonel Kenly, of the 1st Maryland Regiment in the Federal service, and 1,000 rifles and 2 guns were placed at his disposal. The post itself was

[1] O. R., vol. xii., part i., pp. 523 and 560.

indefensible.   To the west and south-west, about three
miles distant, stand the green peaks of the Massanuttons,
while to the east the lofty spurs of the Blue Ridge look
down into the village streets.   A mile and a half north
the forks of the Shenandoah unite in the broad river that
runs to Harper's Ferry.   The turnpike to Winchester
crosses both forks in succession, at a point where they are
divided by a stretch of meadows a mile in width.   In
addition to these two bridges, a wooden viaduct carried
the railway over the South Fork, whence, passing between
the North Fork and the Massanuttons, it runs south of the
stream to Strasburg.   Kenly had pitched his camp between
the town and the river, covering the bridges, and two
companies were on picket beyond the houses.

In front were the dense forests which fill the Luray
Valley and cover the foothills of the mountains, and the
view of the Federal sentries was very limited.   A strong
patrol of 100 infantry and 30 troopers, which had been
sent out on the 20th, had marched eleven miles south, had
bivouacked in the woods, and had captured a Confederate
straggler.   The officer in command had obtained information, by questioning civilians, that Confederate infantry was
expected, and this was confirmed by his prisoner.   Banks,
however, notwithstanding this report, could not bring
himself to believe that an attack was imminent, and the
cavalry was called back to Strasburg.   For this reason
Kenly had been unable to patrol to any distance on the
22nd, and the security of his camp was practically dependent on the vigilance of his sentries.

On the morning of May 23 there was no token of
the approaching storm.   The day was intensely hot, and
the blue masses of the mountains shimmered in
May 23.   the summer haze.   In the Luray Valley to the south
was no sign of life, save the buzzards sailing lazily above
the slumbrous woods.   Suddenly, and without the least
warning, a long line of skirmishers broke forward from the
forest.   The clear notes of the Confederate bugles, succeeded by the crash of musketry, woke the echoes of
the Blue Ridge, and the Federal pickets were driven in

z 2

confusion through the village. The long roll of the drums beat the startled camp to arms, and Kenly hastily drew up his slender force upon a ridge in rear.

The ground in front of his position was fairly open, and with his two pieces of artillery he was able to check the first rush of the Confederate infantry. The guns which had accompanied their advanced guard were only smooth-bores, and it was some time before a battery capable of making effective reply to the Federal pieces was brought up. As soon as it opened fire the Southern infantry was ordered to attack; and while one regiment, working round through the woods on the enemy's left, endeavoured to outflank his guns, four others, in successive lines, advanced across the plain against his front. The Federals, undismayed by the disparity of numbers, were fighting bravely, and had just been reinforced by a squadron of New York regiment, when word was brought to their commander that a regiment of Southern cavalry had appeared between the rivers to his right rear. He at once gave the order to retire. The movement was carried out in good order, under heavy musketry, and the tents and stores were given to the flames; but an attempt to fire the bridges failed, for the Louisiana infantry, rushing recklessly forward, darted into the flames, and extinguished the burning brands. Sufficient damage was done, however, to render the passage of the North Fork by the Confederates slow and difficult; and Kenly took post on Guard Hill, a commanding ridge beyond the stream. Again there was delay. The smoke of the burning camp, rolling past in dense volumes, formed an impenetrable screen; the river was deep and turbulent, with a strong current; and the Federal guns commanded the single bridge. The cavalry, however, were not long in discovering a practicable ford. The river was soon alive with horsemen; and, forcing their way through the swirling waters, four squadrons of the 6th Virginia, accompanied by Jackson, gained the further bank, and formed up rapidly for pursuit. The enemy had already retired, and the dust of the retreating column was receding fast down the road to Winchester.

Without waiting for reinforcements, and without artillery, Jackson urged the 6th Virginia forward. The country through which the turnpike runs is rolling and well-farmed, and the rail fences on either hand made movement across the fields by no means easy. But the Confederate advance was vigorous. The New York cavalry, pressed at every point, were beginning to waver; and near the little hamlet of Cedarville, some three miles from his last position, Kenly gave orders for his infantry to check the pursuit.

The column had halted. Men were tearing down the fences, and the companies were forming for battle in the fields, when there was a sudden outcry, the rolling thunder of many hoofs, and the sharp rattle of pistol-shots. A dense cloud of dust came whirling down the turnpike, and emerging from the yellow canopy the New York troopers, riding for their lives, dashed through the ranks of the startled infantry, while the Confederate horsemen, extending far to right and left, came surging on their traces.

The leading squadron, keeping to the high road, was formed four abreast, and the deep mass was wedged tightly between the fences. The foremost files were mowed down by a volley at close range, and here, for a moment, the attack was checked. But the Virginians meant riding home. On either flank the supporting squadrons galloped swiftly forward, and up the road and across the fields, while the earth shook beneath their tread, swept their charging lines, the men yelling in their excitement and horses as frenzied as their riders. In vain the Federal officers tried to deploy their companies. Kenly, calling on them to rally round the colours, was cut down with a dreadful wound. The grey troopers fell on them before they could fix bayonets or form a front, and sabre and revolver found an easy mark in the crowded masses of panic-stricken infantry. One of the guns was surrounded, and the gunners were cut to pieces; the other escaped for the moment, but was soon abandoned; and with the appearance of a fresh Confederate squadron on the scene Kenly's whole force dispersed in flight. Through woods and orchards

the chase went on. Escape was impossible. Hundreds
laid down their arms ; and 250 Virginia horsemen, resolutely
handled and charging at exactly the right moment, had the
honour of bringing in as prisoners 600 Federals, including
20 officers and a complete section of artillery. The enemy
lost in addition 32 killed and 122 wounded. The Confederate casualties were 11 killed and 15 wounded, and so
sudden and vigorous was their attack that a Federal colonel
estimated their numbers at 3,000.

Colonel Flournoy, a most daring officer, led the
squadrons to the charge ; but that the opportunity was so
instantly utilised was due to Jackson. ' No sooner,' says
Dabney, ' did he see the enemy than he gave the order to
charge with a voice and air whose peremptory determination was communicated to the whole party. His quick eye
estimated aright the discouragement of the Federals and
their wavering temper. Infusing his own spirit into his
men, he struck the hesitating foe at the decisive moment,
and shattered them.' [1] Yet he took no credit to himself.
He declared afterwards to his staff that he had never, in
all his experience of warfare, seen so gallant and effective a
charge of cavalry, and such commendation, coming from
his guarded lips, was the highest honour that his troopers
could have wished.

While these events were in progress the remainder of
the Confederate cavalry had also been busy. The 7th
Virginia had moved to Buckton. The railway was torn up,
the telegraph line cut, and an urgent message to Banks for
reinforcements was intercepted. The two companies of
Pennsylvania infantry, on picket near the station, occupied a log storehouse and the embankment. Dismounting
his command, Ashby, after a fierce fight, in which two of
his best officers were killed, stormed the building and drove
out the garrison. Two locomotives were standing on the
rails with steam up, and by this means the Federals
attempted to escape. Twice they moved out towards Strasburg, twice they were driven back by the Confederate
carbines, and eventually the two companies surrendered.

[1] Dabney, vol. ii., p. 95.

Jackson's measures had been carefully thought out. Kenly's patrols had failed to discover his advance in the early morning, for at Asbury Chapel, about three and a half miles south of the Federal outpost line, he had turned to the right off the Luray road, and plunging into the woods, had approached Front Royal by a circuitous track, so rough that the enemy had thought it hardly worth while to watch it. The main body of the cavalry left the Luray road at McCoy's Ford, and crossing the South Fork of the Shenandoah, worked through the forest at the foot of the Massanuttons. During the night Ashby had withdrawn the 7th Virginia, with the exception of a few patrols, from in front of Banks, and joining Jackson, by a rough track across the mountains, before daybreak, had been directed to cut the communication between Front Royal and Strasburg. The 6th Virginia had accompanied Jackson, the 2nd, under Colonel Munford, destroyed the railway bridges eastward of Front Royal. Had Kenly retreated on Strasburg he would have found Ashby on his flank. Had reinforcements been despatched from Strasburg they would have had to deal with Ashby before they could reach Kenly. Had the Federals attempted to escape by Manassas Gap they would have found Munford across their path. Meanwhile another party of cavalry had cut the telegraph between Front Royal and Washington ; and a strong detachment, scouring the country east of the Blue Ridge, checked Geary's patrols, and blocked the entrance to the Gap from the direction of Manassas. Within an hour after his pickets were surprised Kenly was completely isolated.[1]

[1] The ingenuous report of a Federal officer engaged at Front Royal is significant of the effect of the sudden attack of the Confederates. He was sick at the time, but managed to escape. 'By considerable coaxing,' he wrote, 'I obtained an entrance to a house near by. I was now completely broken down—so much so that the gentleman prepared a liniment for me, and actually bound up some of my bruises, while the female portion of the household actually screamed for joy at our defeat ! I was helped to bed, and next morning was taken by Mr. Bitzer to Winchester in his carriage. He is a gentleman in all particulars, but his family is the reverse (sic). On reaching Winchester I found things decidedly squally, and concluded to get out. I was carried to Martinsburg, and being offered by the agent of a

A failure in staff duties marred to some extent the Confederate success. 'A vicious usage,' according to Dabney, 'obtained at this time in the Southern armies. This was the custom of temporarily attaching to the staff of a general commanding a division or an army a company of cavalry to do the work of orderlies. By this clumsy contrivance the organisation of the cavalry regiments was broken up, the men detached were deprived of all opportunity for drill, and the general had no evidence whatever of their special fitness for the responsible service confided to them. Nay, the colonel of cavalry required to furnish them was most likely to select the least serviceable company. At the time of the combat of Front Royal the duty of orderlies was performed for General Jackson by a detachment from one of Ashby's undisciplined companies, of whom many were raw youths just recruited and never under fire. As soon as the Federal pickets were driven in, orders were despatched to the rear brigades to avoid the laborious route taken by the advance, and to pursue the direct highway to the town, a level track of three miles, in place of a steep byway of seven or eight. The panic-struck boy by whom the orders were sent was seen no more. When Jackson sent orders to the artillery and rear brigades to hurry the pursuit, instead of being found near at hand, upon the direct road, they were at length overtaken toiling over the hills of the useless circuit, spent with the protracted march. Thus night overtook them by the time they reached the village. This unfortunate incident taught the necessity of a picked company of orderlies, selected for their intelligence and courage, permanently attached to headquarters, and owing no subordination to any other than the general and his staff. Such was the usage that afterwards prevailed in the Confederate armies.' [1]

luggage train to take me to Baltimore, I concluded to accept the offer, and took a sleeping bunk, arriving in Baltimore the next afternoon.' He then proceeded to Philadelphia, and sent for his physician. Several of his officers whom he found in the town he immediately sent back to the colours ; but as he believed that 'the *moral* of his regiment was not as it should be' he remained himself in Philadelphia.

[1] Dabney, vol. ii., pp. 93–94. It may be recalled that Wellington found it necessary to form a corps of the same kind in the Peninsular War ; it is curious that no such organisation exists in regular armies.

General Gordon has described with much minuteness how the news of the disaster was received at Strasburg. The attack had begun at one o'clock, but it was not till four that Banks was made aware that his detachment was in jeopardy. Believing that Jackson was at Harrisonburg, sixty miles distant, he had certainly no cause for immediate apprehension. The Valley towards Woodstock never looked more peaceful than on that sleepy summer afternoon ; the sentries dawdled on their posts, and officers and men alike resigned themselves to its restful influence. Suddenly a mounted orderly dashed violently through the camp, and Strasburg was aroused. By the road to Buckton Banks hastily despatched a regiment and two guns. Then came a lull, and many anxious inquiries: ' What is it ? Is it Stonewall Jackson, or only a cavalry raid ? '

A few hours later reports came in from the field of battle, and Banks telegraphed to Stanton that 5,000 rebels had driven Kenly back on Middletown. ' The force,' he added, ' has been gathering in the mountains, it is said, since Wednesday.'

But still the Federal general showed no undue alarm.

' Nothing was done,' says Gordon, ' towards sending away to Winchester any of the immense quantities of public stores collected at Strasburg ; no movement had been made to place our sick in safety. It did not seem as if Banks interpreted the attack to signify aught of future or further movement by the enemy, or that it betokened any purpose to cut us off from Winchester. I was so fully impressed, however, with Jackson's purpose, that as soon as night set in I sought Banks at his headquarters. I laboured long to impress upon him what I thought a duty, to wit, his immediate retreat upon Winchester, carrying all his sick and all his supplies that he could transport, and destroying the remainder. Notwithstanding all my solicitations and entreaties, he persistently refused to move, ever repeating, ' I must develop the force of the enemy.' [1]

The force that had been sent out on the Buckton road had been soon recalled, without securing further information

[1] *From Brook Farm to Cedar Mountain*, pp. 191, 192.

than that the Confederate pickets were in possession of every road which led west or north from Front Royal.

Again did Gordon, at the request of Banks' chief of the staff, endeavour to persuade the general to abandon Strasburg. ' " It is not a retreat," he urged, " but a true military movement to escape from being cut off; to prevent stores and sick from falling into the hands of the enemy." Moved with an unusual fire, General Banks, who had met all my arguments with the single reply, " I must develop the force of the enemy," rising excitedly from his seat, with much warmth and in loud tones exclaimed, " By God, sir, I will not retreat! We have more to fear, sir, from the opinions of our friends than the bayonets of our enemies! " The thought,' continues the brigadier, ' so long the subject of his meditations was at last out. Banks was afraid of being thought afraid. I rose to take my leave, replying, " This, sir, is not a military reason for occupying a false position." It was eleven o'clock at night when I left him. As I returned through the town I could not perceive that anybody was troubled with anticipation for the morrow. The sutlers were driving sharp bargains with those who had escaped from or those who were not amenable to military discipline. The strolling players were moving crowds to noisy laughter in their canvas booths, through which the lights gleamed and the music sounded with startling shrillness. I thought as I turned towards my camp, how unaware are all of the drama Jackson is pre- paring for us, and what merriment the morning will reveal! '

Fortunately for his own battalions, the brigadier had his camp equipage and baggage packed and sent off then and there to Winchester, and though his men had to spend the night unsheltered under persistent rain, they had reason to bless his foresight a few nights later.

At midnight a report was received from one of the Front Royal fugitives: ' Kenly is killed. First Maryland cut to pieces. Cavalry ditto. The enemy's forces are 15,000 or 20,000 strong, and on the march to Strasburg.'

In forwarding this despatch to Washington Banks

remarked that he thought it much exaggerated.   At 7
A.M. on the 24th he told Stanton that the enemy's force was
from 6,000 to 10,000 ; that it was probably Ewell's division,
and that Jackson was still in his front on the Valley
turnpike.

Three hours later he wrote to Gordon, informing him
that the enemy had fallen back to Front Royal during the
night, that ample reinforcements had been promised from
Washington, and that the division would remain in Strasburg until further orders.

Up to this time he had been convinced that the attack
on Front Royal was merely a raid, and that Jackson would
never dare to insert his whole force between himself and
McDowell.[1]   Suddenly, by what means we are not told, he
was made aware that the Confederates were in overwhelming numbers, and that Jackson was in command.

Scarcely had General Gordon digested the previous
communication when an orderly, galloping furiously to
his side, delivered a pencil note from the chief of staff.
'Orders have just been received for the division to move
at once to Middletown, taking such steps to oppose the
enemy, reported to be on the road between Front Royal and
Middletown, as may seem proper.'   Banks was electrified
at last.   Three weeks previously, in writing to Mr. Stanton,
he had expressed his regret that he was 'not to be included
in active operations during the summer.'   His regret was
wasted.   He was about to take part in operations of which
the activity, on his part at least, was more than
satisfying.

Such blindness as Banks had shown is difficult to
explain.   His latest information, previous to the attack on
Kenly, told him that Jackson's trains were arriving at
Harrisonburg on the 20th, and he should certainly have
inferred that Jackson was in advance of his waggons.
Now from Harrisonburg across the Massanuttons to Front
Royal is fifty-five miles ; so it was well within the bounds
of possibility that the Confederates might reach the

---

[1] Article in *Harper's Weekly* by Colonel Strother, aide-de-camp to General
Banks.

latter village at midday on the 23rd. Moreover, Banks
himself had recognised that Strasburg was an unfavourable position. It is true that it was fortified, but therein
lay the very reason that would induce the enemy to
turn it by Front Royal. Nor did the idea, which seems
to have held possession of his mind throughout the night,
that Ewell alone had been sent to destroy Kenly, and had
afterwards fallen back, show much strategic insight.
Front Royal was the weak point in the Federal position.
It was of all things unlikely that a commander, energetic
and skilful as Jackson was well known to be, would, when
he had once advertised his presence, fail to follow up his
first blow with his whole force and the utmost vigour. It is
only fair to add that the Federal authorities were no wiser
than their general. At two A.M. on the morning of the
24th, although the news of Kenly's disaster had been fully
reported, they still thought that there was time to move
fresh troops to Strasburg from Baltimore and Washington.
It seemed incredible that Jackson could be at Front Royal.
'Arrangements are making,' ran Stanton's telegram to
Banks, 'to send you ample reinforcements. Do not give
up the ship before succour can arrive.'

We may now turn to Jackson.

Up to the present his operations had been perfectly
successful. He had captured over 700 of the enemy, with
a loss of only 40 or 50 to himself. He had seized stores
to the value of three hundred thousand dollars (£60,000),
and a large quantity had been burned by the enemy. He
had turned the intrenched position at Strasburg. He
threatened the Federal line of retreat. Banks was completely at his mercy, and there seemed every prospect of
inflicting on that ill-starred commander a defeat so
decisive as to spread panic in the council chambers of the
Northern capital.

But the problem was not so simple as it seemed. In
the first place, although the positions of the Federals had
been thoroughly examined, both by staff officers and scouts,
the information as to their numbers was somewhat vague.
Banks had actually about 8,000 effectives at Strasburg;

but so far as the Confederates knew it was quite possible that he had from 12,000 to 15,000. There is nothing more difficult in war than to get an accurate estimate of the enemy's numbers, especially when civilians, ignorant of military affairs, are the chief sources of information. The agents on whom Jackson depended for intelligence from within the enemy's lines were not always selected because of their military knowledge. 'On the march to Front Royal,' says General Taylor, 'we reached a wood extending from the mountain to the river, when a mounted officer from the rear called Jackson's attention, who rode back with him. A moment later there rushed out of the wood a young, rather well-looking woman, afterwards widely known as Belle Boyd. Breathless with speed and agitation, some time elapsed before she found her voice. Then, with much volubility, she said we were near Front Royal; that the town was filled with Federals, whose camp was on the west side of the river, where they had guns in position to cover the bridge; that they believed Jackson to be west of the Massanuttons, near Harrisonburg; that General Banks was at Winchester, where he was concentrating his widely scattered forces to meet Jackson's advance, which was expected some days later. All this she told with the precision of a staff officer making a report, and it was true to the letter. Jackson was possessed of this information before he left New Market, and based his movements on it; but it was news to me.'

In the second place, Banks had still the means of escape. He could hardly prevent the Confederates from seizing Winchester, but he might at least save his army from annihilation. Jackson's men were exhausted and the horses jaded. Since the morning of the 19th the whole army had marched over eighty, and Ewell's division over ninety miles. And this average of seventeen miles a day had been maintained on rough and muddy roads, crossed by many unbridged streams, and over a high mountain. The day which had just passed had been especially severe. Ewell, who was in bivouac at Cedarville, five miles north of Front Royal on the Winchester turnpike, had marched more than twenty miles; and Jackson's own division, which had made four - and - twenty, was on foot from five in the morning till nine at night.

Banks' natural line of retreat led through Winchester, and the Confederate advanced guard at Cedarville was two miles nearer that town than were the Federals at Strasburg. But it was still possible that Banks, warned by Kenly's overthrow, might withdraw by night; and even if he deferred retreat until daylight he might, instead of falling back on Winchester, strike boldly for Front Royal and escape by Manassas Gap. Or, lastly, he might remain at Strasburg, at which point he was in communication, although by a long and circuitous road, with Frémont at Franklin.

Jackson had therefore three contingencies to provide against, and during the night which followed the capture of Front Royal he evolved a plan which promised to meet them all. Ashby, at daybreak, was to move with the 7th Virginia cavalry in the direction of Strasburg; and at the same hour a staff officer, with a small escort, supported by Taylor's Louisianians, was to ride towards Middletown, a village five miles north of Strasburg and thirteen from Winchester, and to report frequently. The 2nd and 6th Virginia cavalry, under General Steuart, were to advance to Newtown, also on the Valley turnpike, and eight miles from Winchester; while Ewell, with Trimble's brigade and his artillery, was to move to Nineveh, two miles north of Cedarville, and there halt, awaiting orders. The remainder of the command was to concentrate at Cedarville, preparatory to marching on Middletown; and strong cavalry patrols were to keep close watch on the Strasburg-Front Royal road.[1]

From Cedarville to Middletown is no more than seven miles, and Taylor's brigade is reported to have moved at six A.M., while Ashby had presumably already marched. But notwithstanding the fact that Banks' infantry did not leave Strasburg till ten A.M., and

6 A.M.

[1] Jackson's Report. O. R., vol. xii., part i., p. 703.

that it had five miles to cover before reaching Middletown, when the Confederates reached the turnpike at that village the Federal main body had already passed, and only the rear-guard was encountered.

It seems evident, therefore, that it was not till near noon that Jackson's patrols came in sight of Middletown, and that the Confederate advanced guard had taken at least six hours to cover seven miles. The country, however, between Cedarville and the Valley turnpike was almost a continuous forest; and wood-fighting is very slow fighting. The advance had met with strong resistance. General Gordon had prudently sent the 29th Pennsylvania to Middletown at an early hour, with orders to reconnoitre towards Front Royal, and to cover Middletown until the army had passed through.

Supported by a section of artillery, the regiment had moved eastward till it struck the Confederate scouts some

7 A.M. four miles out on the Cedarville road. After a long skirmish it was withdrawn to Middletown; but the 1st Maine cavalry, and a squadron of the 1st Vermont, about 400 strong, which had been ordered by Banks to proceed in the same direction, made a vigorous demonstration, and then fell back slowly before the advanced guard, showing a bold front, using their carbines freely, and taking advantage of the woods to impose upon the enemy.

These manœuvres succeeded in holding the Confederates in check till after ten o'clock, for the heavy timber concealed the real strength of the Federals, and although

10.15 A.M. Ashby, with the 7th Virginia, had marched to the scene of action, the infantry was not yet up. It is to be remembered that at daybreak the Valley army was by no means concentrated. Jackson had with him at Cedarville only Ewell's division; his own division having halted near Front Royal. This last division, it appears from the reports, did not leave Front Royal until 8 A.M.; a sufficiently early hour, considering the condition of the men and horses, the absence of the trains, and the fact that one of the brigades had bivouacked four miles south of

the village.[1] It was not, then, till between nine and ten that
the column cleared Cedarville, and Middletown was distant
nearly three hours' march, by an exceedingly bad road.

In all probability, if Jackson, at daybreak or soon
afterwards, had marched boldly on Middletown with Ewell's
division, he would have been able to hold Banks on the
Valley turnpike until the rest of his infantry and artillery
arrived. But he had always to bear in mind that the
Federals, finding their retreat on Winchester compromised, might make a dash for Manassas Gap. Now
the road from Strasburg to Manassas Gap was protected throughout its length by the North Fork of the
Shenandoah; and to attack the Federals on the march,
should they take this road, the Confederates would have to
move through Cedarville on Front Royal. This was the
only road by which they could reach the river, and the
bridges at Front Royal were the only available points of
passage. Jackson, it appears, was therefore reluctant
to leave Cedarville, within easy reach of the bridges,
until he received information of his enemy's designs, and
that information, which had to be sought at a distance,
was naturally long in coming.

Criticism, after the event, is easy; but it certainly
seems curious, with his knowledge of Banks, that Jackson
should have believed his opponent capable of so bold a
measure as retreat by way of Manassas Gap. According
to his own report, the feasibility of such a course did
cross Banks' mind; but it might seem that on this
occasion Jackson lost an opportunity through over-caution.
Nevertheless, in desperate situations even the most inert
characters are sometimes capable of desperate resolutions.

Although for the time being Banks was permitted
to extricate his infantry from the toils, the remainder
of his command was less fortunate. The general and his
brigades reached Winchester in safety, but the road between
that town and Strasburg was a scene of dire disaster.

[1] The supply waggons were still eight miles south of Front Royal, in the
Luray Valley.

Steuart, with the 2nd and 6th Virginia, had struck
Newton before noon, and found a convoy of waggons strung
11.30 A.M. out on the Valley turnpike. A few shots threw
everything into confusion. Many of the teamsters
deserted their posts, and fled towards Winchester or
Strasburg. Waggons were upset, several were captured,
and others plundered. But the triumph of the Confederates was short-lived. The Federal infantry had
already reached Middletown; and Banks sent forward a
regiment of cavalry and a brigade of infantry to clear the
way. Steuart was speedily driven back, and the Northerners resumed their march.

At some distance behind the infantry came the Federal
cavalry, about 2,000 strong, accompanied by a battery and
12.15 P.M. a small party of Zouaves; but by the time this
force reached Middletown, Ashby, supported by
the Louisiana brigade, had driven in the regiment hitherto
opposed to him, and, emerging from the forest, with infantry
and guns in close support, was bearing down upon the
village. The batteries opened upon the solid columns of
the Federal horse. The Louisiana regiments, deploying at
the double, dashed forward, and the Northern squadrons,
penned in the narrow streets, found themselves assailed by
a heavy fire. A desperate attempt was made to escape
towards Winchester, and a whirling cloud of dust through
which the sabres gleamed swept northward up the turnpike.
But Ashby's horsemen, galloping across country, headed off
the fugitives; some of the Confederate infantry drew an
abandoned waggon across the road, and others ran forward
to the roadside fences. At such close quarters the effect of
the musketry was terrible. 'In a few moments the turnpike,
which had just before teemed with life, presented a most
appalling spectacle of carnage and destruction. The road
was literally obstructed with the mingled and confused
mass of struggling and dying horses and riders. Amongst
the survivors the wildest confusion ensued, and they
scattered in disorder in various directions, leaving some
200 prisoners in the hands of the Confederates.'[1] Part

[1] Jackson's Report. O. R., vol. xii., part i., p. 704.

dashed back to Strasburg, where the teeming magazines
of the Federal commissaries were already blazing; and
part towards the mountains, flying in small parties
by every country track. The rear regiments, however, still held together. Drawing off westward, in the
hope of gaining the Middle road, and of making his way to
Winchester by a circuitous route, General Hatch, commanding the cavalry brigade, brought his guns into action
on a commanding ridge, about a mile west of the highway,
and still showed a front with his remaining squadrons.
Infantry were with them; more horsemen came thronging
up; their numbers were unknown, and for a moment they
looked threatening. The Confederate batteries trotted
forward, and Taylor's brigade, with the Stonewall and
Campbell's in support, was ordered to attack; whilst Ashby,
accompanied by the Louisiana Tigers and two batteries,
pursued the train of waggons that was flying over the hills
towards Winchester.

The question now to be solved was whether the cavalry
was the advanced or the rear guard of the Federal army.
No message had arrived from Steuart. But the people of
Middletown supplied the information. They reported that
in addition to the convoy a long column of infantry had
passed through the village; and Jackson, directing
his infantry to follow Ashby, sent a message to Ewell
to march on Winchester. Some delay took place before
the three brigades, which had now driven back the Federal
cavalry, could be brought back to the turnpike and re-
3 P.M.   formed; and it was well on in the afternoon
        when, with the Stonewall regiments leading, the
Confederate infantry pushed forward down the pike.

The troops had been on their legs since dawn; some
of them, who had bivouacked south of Front Royal, had
already marched sixteen miles, the Federals had more
than two hours' start, and Winchester was still twelve
miles distant. But the enemy's cavalry had been routed,
and such as remained of the waggons were practically
without a guard. Ashby and Steuart, with three fine
regiments of Virginia cavalry, supported by the horse-

artillery and other batteries, were well to the front, and
'there was every reason to believe,' to use Jackson's own
words, 'that if Banks reached Winchester, it would be
without a train, if not without an army.'

But the irregular organisation of the Valley forces
proved a bar to the fulfilment of Jackson's hopes. On
approaching Newtown he found that the pursuit had been
arrested. Two pieces of artillery were engaging a Federal
battery posted beyond the village, but the Confederate
guns were almost wholly unsupported. Ashby had come
up with the convoy. A few rounds of shell had dispersed
the escort. The teamsters fled, and the supply waggons
and sutlers' carts of the Federal army, filled with luxuries,
proved a temptation which the half-starving Confederates
were unable to resist. 'Nearly the whole of Ashby's
cavalry and a part of the infantry under his command had
turned aside to pillage. Indeed the firing had not ceased,
in the first onset upon the Federal cavalry at Middletown,
before some of Ashby's men might have been seen, with a
quickness more suitable to horse-thieves than to soldiers,
breaking from their ranks, seizing each two or three of the
captured horses and making off across the fields. Nor did
the men pause until they had carried their illegal booty
to their homes, which were, in some instances, at the
distance of one or two days' journey. That such extreme
disorders could occur,' adds Dabney, 'and that they
could be passed over without a bloody punishment, reveals
the curious inefficiency of officers in the Confederate
army.' [1]

---

[1] Dabney, vol. ii., pp. 101-2. 'The difficulty,' says General Taylor,
speaking of the Confederate cavalry, 'of converting raw men into soldiers
is enhanced manifold when they are mounted. Both man and horse require
training, and facilities for rambling, with temptation to do so, are increased.
There was little time, and it may be said less disposition, to establish camps
of instruction. Living on horseback, fearless and dashing, the men of the
South afforded the best possible material for cavalry. They had every
quality but discipline, and resembled Prince Charming, whose manifold
gifts were rendered useless by the malignant fairy. Assuredly our cavalry
rendered much excellent service, especially when dismounted; and such able
officers as Stuart, Hampton, and the younger Lees in the east, Forrest,
Green, and Wheeler in the West, developed much talent for war; but their

Banks, when the pursuit had so suddenly ceased, had determined to save the remnant of his train. Three regiments and a couple of batteries were ordered back from Bartonsville, with Gordon in command; and this rear-guard had not only shown a formidable front, but had actually driven the infantry that still remained with Ashby out of Newtown, and into the woods beyond. General Hatch, who had regained the turnpike with part of his brigade, had now come up; and the addition of six squadrons of cavalry rendered Gordon's force capable of stout resistance. The Federals held a strong position. The Confederates had present but 50 cavalry, 150 infantry, and 5 guns. Nor was there any hope of immediate support, for the remainder of the troops were still several miles in rear, and Steuart's two regiments appear to have rejoined General Ewell on the road for Nineveh.

Shortly before sunset the Confederate artillery was re-inforced. The Stonewall Brigade had also arrived upon the scene; and Gordon, firing such waggons as he could not carry off, as well as the pontoons, fell back on Winchester as the night closed in.

The Confederates had now marched from sixteen to twenty miles, and the men had not eaten since the early morning. But Jackson had determined to press the march till he was within striking distance of the hills which stand round Winchester to the south. It was no time for repose. The Federals had a garrison at Harper's Ferry, a garrison at Romney, detachments along the Baltimore and Ohio Railway; and Washington, within easy distance of Winchester by rail, was full of troops.[1] A few hours' delay, and instead of Banks' solitary division, a large army might bar the way to the Potomac. So, with the remnant of Ashby's cavalry

achievements, however distinguished, fell far below the standard that would have been reached had not the want of discipline impaired their efforts.'— *Destruction and Reconstruction*, pp. 70–71. It is only fair to add, however, that the Confederate troopers had to supply their own horses, receiving no compensation for their loss by disease or capture. This in some measure excuses their anxiety to loot as many chargers as they could lay hands on.

[1] Twenty regiments of infantry and two regiments of cavalry. O. R., vol. xii., part iii., p. 313.

in advance, and the Stonewall Brigade in close support, the column toiled onward through the darkness. But the Federal rear-guard was exceedingly well handled. The 2nd Massachusetts regiment held the post of honour, and, taking advantage of stream and ridge, the gallant New Englanders disputed every mile of road. At Bartonsville, where the Opequon, a broad and marshy creek, crosses the turnpike, they turned stubbornly at bay. A heavy volley, suddenly delivered, drove the Confederate cavalry back in confusion on the infantry supports. The 33rd Virginia was completely broken by the rush of flying horsemen; the guns were overridden; and Jackson and his staff were left alone upon the turnpike. In the pitch darkness it was difficult to ascertain the enemy's numbers, and the flashes of their rifles, dancing along the top of the stone walls, were the only clue to their position. The Confederate column was ordered to deploy, and the Stonewall Brigade, pushing into the fields on either flank, moved slowly forward over the swampy ground. The stream proved an impassable obstacle both below and above the Federal position; but the 27th Virginia, attacking the enemy in front, drove them back and crossed to the further bank.

The pursuit, however, had been much delayed; and the Massachusetts regiment, although ridden into by their own cavalry, fell back in good order, protected by a strong line of skirmishers on either side of the turnpike. The Confederate order of march was now changed. Three companies, who were recruited from the district and knew the ground, were ordered to the front. The 5th Virginia, four or five hundred yards from the skirmish line, were to follow in support. The cavalry and guns were left in rear; and the troops once more took up the line of march.

For more than an hour they tramped slowly forward. The darkness grew more intense, and the chaff and laughter —for the soldiers, elated by success, had hitherto shown no sign of fatigue—died gradually away. Nothing was to be heard but the clang of accoutrements, the long rumble of the guns, and the shuffle of weary feet. Men fell in the ranks, overpowered by sleep or faint with hunger, and the skirmishers, wading through rank fields of wheat and clover, stumbling into ditches, and climbing painfully over high stone walls, made tardy progress. Again and again the enemy's volleys flashed through the darkness; but still there was no halt, for at the head of the regiments, peering eagerly into the darkness, their iron-willed commander still rode forward, as regardless of the sufferings of his men as of the bullets of the Federal rear-guard, with but one thought present to his mind—to bring Banks to battle, and so prevent his escape from Winchester. The student of Napoleon had not forgotten the pregnant phrase: 'Ask me for anything but time!' The indiscipline of Ashby's cavalry had already given Banks a respite; and, undisturbed by his reverses, the Union general had shown himself capable of daring measures. Had the Confederates halted at Newtown or at Bartonsville, the troops would doubtless have been fresher for the next day's work, but the morning might have seen Banks far on his way to the Potomac, or possibly strongly reinforced.

When the Confederate infantry had met and overthrown their enemy it would be time enough to think of food and rest. So long as the men could stand they were to follow on his traces. 'I rode with Jackson,' says General Taylor, 'through the darkness. An officer, riding hard, overtook us, who proved to be the chief quartermaster of the army. He reported the waggon trains far behind, impeded by a bad road in the Luray Valley. "The ammunition waggons?" sternly. "All right, sir. They were in advance, and I doubled teams on them and brought them through." "Ah!" in a tone of relief.

'To give countenance to the quartermaster, if such can be given on a dark night, I remarked jocosely, "Never mind the waggons. There are quantities of stores in Winchester, and the general has invited me to breakfast there to-morrow." Jackson took this seriously, and reached out to touch me on the arm. Without physical wants himself, he forgot that others were differently constituted, and paid little heed to commissariat, but woe to the man who failed to bring up ammunition. In advance his trains were left behind. In retreat he would fight for a wheelbarrow.'[1]

At Kernstown, behind Hogg Run, the Federal rear-guard halted for the last time, but after a short engagement fell back on Winchester. It was now three o'clock, an hour before dawn, and the Massachusetts men became aware that the enemy had halted. Their skirmishers still pressed slowly forward, and an occasional shot flashed out in the darkness. But that noise which once heard on a still night is never forgotten, the solid tramp of a heavy column on a hard road, like the dull roar of a distant cataract, had suddenly died away. As the day broke the Confederate advanced guard, passing Pritchard's Hill and Kernstown battlefield, struck the Federal pickets on Parkin's Hill. In front was a brook which goes by the name of Abraham's Creek; beyond the brook rose the ridge which covers Winchester, and Jackson at last permitted his men to rest. The coveted heights were within easy grasp. The Federal army was still in Winchester, and nothing now remained but to storm the hills, and drive the enemy in panic from the town.

The Confederates, when the order was given to halt, had dropped where they stood, and lay sleeping by the roadside. But their commander permitted himself no repose. For more than an hour, without a cloak to protect him from the chilling dews, listening to every sound that came from the front, he stood like a sentinel over the prostrate ranks. As the dawn rose, in a quiet undertone he gave the word to march. The order was passed down the column, and, in the dim grey light, the men, rising from their short slumbers, stiff, cold, and hungry, advanced to battle.

Jackson had with him on the turnpike, for the most part south of Kernstown, his own division, supported by the brigades of Scott and Elzey and by nine batteries. About a mile eastward on the Front Royal road was Ewell, with Trimble's brigade and ten guns. This detachment had moved on Winchester the preceding evening,

Destruction and Reconstruction, p. 65.

driving in the Federal pickets, and had halted within three miles of the town. During the night Jackson had sent a staff officer with instructions to Ewell. The message, although the bearer had to ride nine-and-twenty miles, by Newton and Nineveh, had reached its destination in good time; and as the Stonewall Brigade moved silently past Pritchard's Hill, Trimble's brigade advanced abreast of it beyond the intervening woods.

On both the Valley turnpike and the Front Royal road the Federals were favoured by the ground, and their position, although the two wings were widely separated, had been skilfully selected. On the turnpike and west of it was Gordon's brigade of four regiments, strengthened by eight guns, and by a strong force of cavalry in reserve. Watching the Front Royal road was Donnelly's brigade, also of four regiments, with eight guns and a few squadrons. The line of defence ran along a broken ridge, lined in many places with stout stone walls, and protected in front by the winding reaches of Abraham's Creek.

Still, strong as was the Federal position, there was little chance of holding it. Banks had been joined during the night by the larger portion of his army, and by the garrison of Winchester, but he was heavily outnumbered. At Front Royal and at Middletown he had lost over 1,500 men; part of his rear-guard had scattered in the mountains, and it was doubtful if he could now muster more than 6,500 effective soldiers. In infantry and artillery the Confederates were more than twice his strength; in cavalry alone were they inferior.

Jackson's plan of action was simple. His advanced guard was to hold Gordon in position; and when Ewell fell on Donnelly, a heavy column would move round Gordon's right.

The Stonewall regiments led the way. The line of heights, west of the turnpike and commanding Abraham's Creek, was 5 A.M. occupied by the Federal outposts, and a general advance of the whole brigade, sweeping across the brook and up the slopes, quickly drove in the pickets.

But the enemy, whether by skill or good fortune, had

occupied with his main line a position admirably adapted
for an inferior force. Four hundred yards beyond the ridge
which the Confederates had seized rose a second swell of
ground; and eight rifled guns, supported by the 2nd Massachusetts, swept the opposite height at effective range.

Jackson immediately ordered up three batteries, posting
them behind the crest; and as the sun rose, drawing up the
mist from the little stream, a fierce duel of artillery began
the battle.

The Confederate gunners, harassed by the enemy's
skirmishers, and overwhelmed with shells, suffered heavily;
one battery was compelled to retire with a loss of
6.30 A.M.   17 men and 9 horses; a second lost all its officers;
and it was not till near seven o'clock that the enemy's eight
guns, with their infantry escort, were finally driven back.

Ewell, meanwhile, had come into action on the right;
but the mist was heavy, and his advanced guard,
received with a heavy fire from behind the stone walls,
was driven back with a loss of 80 officers and men.
Then the fog rose heavily, and for nearly an hour the
engagement on this wing died away. About eight
8 A.M.   o'clock Ewell's batteries again came into action,
and Trimble moved round to take the enemy in flank. But
Jackson, meanwhile, was bringing matters to a crisis on the
left. The Federals still held fast in front; but the
Louisiana, Taliaferro's, and Scott's brigades, retained
hitherto with Elzey in reserve, were now ordered to turn the
enemy's flank. Moving to the left in rear of the Stonewall
Brigade, these eleven regiments, three forming a second
line, faced to the front and climbed the heights.

General Gordon, in anticipation of such a movement,
had already transferred two regiments to his right. The
fire of this force, though delivered at close range, hardly
checked the Confederate onset. Closing the many gaps,
and preserving an alignment that would have been credit-
able on parade, Taylor and Taliaferro moved swiftly forward over rocks and walls. The Federal infantry gave way
in great disorder. The cavalry in support essayed a
charge, but the Confederates, as the squadrons rode boldly

towards them, halted where they stood, and the rolling
volleys of the line of battle drove back the horsemen
with many empty saddles. · Then, as Taylor resumed his
advance, the Stonewall regiments, with Elzey in close
support, rose suddenly from their covert, and the whole
line swept forward across the ridges. The bright sun of
the May morning, dispersing the mists which veiled the
field, shone down upon 10,000 bayonets ; and for the first
time in the Valley 'the rebel yell,' that strange fierce cry
which heralded the Southern charge, rang high above the
storm of battle.

It was impossible, before so strong an onset, for the
Federals to hold their ground. Infantry, artillery, and
cavalry gave way. From east, west, and south the grey
battalions converged on Winchester ; and as the enemy's
columns, covered by the heavy smoke, disappeared into
the streets, Jackson, no longer the imperturbable tactician,
moving his troops like the pieces on a chess-board, but
the very personification of triumphant victory, dashed forward in advance of his old brigade. Riding recklessly
down a rocky slope he raised himself in his stirrups, and
waving his cap in the direction of the retreating foe,
shouted to his officers to 'Press forward to the Potomac ! '
Elzey's, the reserve brigade, was ordered to take up the
pursuit ; and within the town, where the storehouses had
been already fired, the battle was renewed. The Federal
regiments, with the exception of the 2nd Massachusetts, lost
all order in the narrow streets.[1] The roar of battle followed
close ; and with the rattle of musketry, the crash of shells,
and the loud cries of the victors speeding their rapid flight,
the Northern infantry dispersed across the fields. As the
Confederates passed through the town, the people of
Winchester, frantic with triumph after their two months of
captivity, rushed out from every doorway to meet the
troops ; and with weeping and with laughter, with the

[1] Banks' aide-de-camp, Colonel Strother, says, 'For several minutes it
looked like the commencement of a Bull Run panic. The stragglers,' he
adds, 'rapidly increased in numbers, and many threw down their arms.'—
Harper's Weekly. See also Jackson's Report, O. R., vol. xii., part i., p. 706.

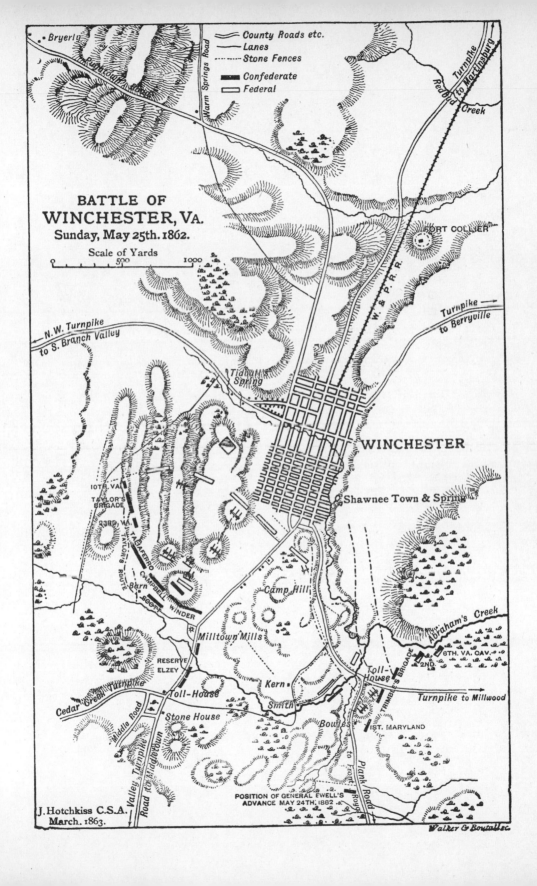

BATTLE OF WINCHESTER, VA.
Sunday, May 25th. 1862.

Scale of Yards

0   500   1000

County Roads etc.
Lanes
Stone Fences
Confederate
Federal

Bryerly

Pughtown Road

Warm Springs Road

Red Bud Creek

Turnpike to Martinsburg

FORT COLLIER

W. & P.R.R.

Turnpike to Berryville

N.W. Turnpike to S. Branch Valley

Tidball's Spring

WINCHESTER

Shawnee Town & Spring

10TH VA.
TAYLOR'S BRIGADE

23RD. VA.
TALIAFERRO

TAYLOR'S ROUTE

CAMPBELL

SCOTT

Barn

WINDER

Camp Hill

Abraham's Creek

6TH. VA. CAV.

Milltown Mills

Toll-House

TRIMBEL'S BRIGADE

2ND.

RESERVE
ELZEY

Toll-House

Kern

Smith

Toll-House

Turnpike to Millwood

Cedar Creek Turnpike

Middle Road

Stone House

Bowles

1ST. MARYLAND

Valley Turnpike

Road to Middletown

Road to Front Royal

Plank Road

POSITION OF GENERAL EWELL'S
ADVANCE MAY 24TH. 1862.

J. Hotchkiss C.S.A.
March. 1863.

Walker & Boutall sc.

blessings of women and the fierce shouts of men, the soldiers of the Valley were urged forward in hot pursuit.

As they emerged from the town, and looked down upon the open pastures through which the Martinsburg turnpike 10 A.M. runs, they saw the country before them covered with crowds of fugitives. Jackson, still in advance, turned round to seek his cavalry. From the head of every street eager columns of infantry were pouring, and, deploying without waiting orders, were pushing hastily across the fields. But not a squadron was in sight. Ashby, with the handful of men that still remained with him, had ridden to Berryville, expecting that the enemy would attempt to escape by Snicker's Gap. Steuart, with the two regiments that had done such service at Front Royal, was with Ewell and Trimble; but although Donnolly's regiments could be seen retiring in good order, they were not followed by a single sabre.

Despatching an aide-de-camp to order Steuart to the front, Jackson called up his batteries. The infantry, too, was hurried forward, in order to prevent the Federals rallying. But after a rapid march of two hours the interval between the Confederates and the enemy was still increasing; and it was evident that without cavalry it was useless to continue the pursuit. Not only was the infantry utterly exhausted, but the horses of the artillery were worn out; and about five miles out of Winchester the troops were ordered to halt and bivouac.[1] The Federals, relieved from the pressure of the hostile fire, gradually reformed their ranks; and Jackson, notwithstanding the extraordinary exertions he had demanded from his troops, his own skilful manœuvres, and the high spirit of his men, saw his opportunity pass away. His impatience was almost uncontrollable. His staff was despatched in all directions to urge forward the remainder of the batteries. 'We must press them to the Potomac!' 'Forward to the Potomac!' Such was the tenor of every order; and at length, as the Federals disappeared in the far distance, he ordered the

---

[1] The greater part of the troops had marched over thirty miles in thirty hours, during which time they had been almost continuously engaged.

artillery teams to be unhitched, and the gunners, thus mounted, to pursue the enemy. But before this strange substitute for cavalry had moved out, the lagging squadrons arrived, and with a few fiery words they were sent at speed down the Valley turnpike. But it was too late. Banks, for the second time, was more fortunate than he deserved.

To the misconduct of Ashby's troopers, and to the pedantic folly of General Steuart, the escape of the Federal army must be attributed.

'Never have I seen an opportunity when it was in the power of cavalry to reap a richer harvest of the fruits of victory. Had the cavalry played its part in this pursuit as well as the four companies under Colonel Flournoy two days before in the pursuit from Front Royal, but a small portion of Banks' army would have made its escape to the Potomac.'

So runs Jackson's official report, and when the disorganised condition of the Federal battalions, as they fled north from Winchester, is recalled, it is difficult to question the opinion therein expressed. The precipitate retreat from Strasburg, accompanied by the loss of waggons and of stores ; the concentrated attack of overwhelming numbers, followed by the disorderly rush through the streets of Winchester, had, for the time being, dissolved the bonds of discipline. It is true that some of the Federal regiments held together ; but many men were missing ; some fell into the hands of the Confederates, others sought safety by devious roads, and there can be little doubt but that those who fled to the Potomac were for the time being utterly demoralised. Had they been resolutely charged before they had reformed their ranks, their rifles would no more have saved them from annihilation than they had saved Kenly's command at Cedarville.

But where was the cavalry ? Ashby's 50 men, all that he had been able to collect, were far away upon the right; out of reach of orders, and in any case too few for effective use. The two regiments under Steuart, 600 or 700 strong, were the force on which Jackson had depended, and Steuart had shown himself in-

capable of command.   He had received Jackson's message
with the reply that he could obey no orders unless they
came through his immediate superior.[1]   Before Ewell
could be found, precious time was wasted, and two hours
elapsed before the cavalry took up the chase.   But the
Federals had now established strong rear-guards.   The
whole of their cavalry, supported by artillery, had been
ordered to cover the retreat; and Steuart, although he
picked up numerous prisoners, and followed as far as
Martinsburg, twenty-two miles north of Winchester, found
no opportunity for attack.

Halting for two and a half hours at Martinsburg, the
Federals continued their retreat at sunset, abandoning the
magazines in the town to their pursuers.   Before midnight
3,000 or 4,000 men had arrived at Williamsport, and by the
ford and ferry, supplemented by a few pontoon boats, the
remnant of Banks' army crossed the broad Potomac.

Although not a single Confederate squadron had followed
him from Martinsburg, the Northern general, elated by his
unexpected escape, spoke of this operation as if it had been
carried out under heavy fire.   'It is seldom,' he reported,
'that a river-crossing of such magnitude is achieved (sic)
with greater success.'   But he added, with more candour,
'there were never more grateful hearts, in the same number
of men, than when at mid-day on the 26th we stood on the
opposite shore;'   and then, with the loss of 2,000 men, a
hundred waggons, the regimental transport of his cavalry,
nearly 800 sick, and a vast quantity of stores, to traverse his
assertion, he stated that his command 'had not suffered an
attack or rout, but had accomplished a premeditated march
of near sixty miles in the face of the enemy, defeating
his plans, and giving him battle wherever he was found!'[2]

---

[1] Jackson's Report.

[2] Some of Banks' officers shared his opinion.   The captain of the
Zouaves d'Afrique, the general's body-guard, who had been cut off at
Strasburg, but rejoined on the Potomac, reported that, 'incredible as it may
appear, my men marched 141 miles in 47 hours, as measured by Captain
Abert,' and concluded by congratulating Banks upon the success of his 'un-
paralleled retreat.'   The Zouaves, at all events, could not complain that
they had been excluded from 'active operations.' Another officer declared that

But the Northern people were not to be deceived.   The truth was but too apparent ; and long before Banks had found leisure to write his report, terror had taken possession of the nation.   While the soldiers of the Valley lay round Winchester, reposing from their fatigues, and regaling themselves on the captured stores, the Governors of thirteen States were calling on their militia to march to the defence of Washington.   Jackson had struck a deadly blow. Lincoln and Stanton were electrified even more effectually than Banks.   They issued an urgent call for more troops. ' There is no doubt,' wrote Stanton to the Governor of Massachusetts, ' that the enemy in great force are marching on Washington.'   In the cities of the North the panic was indescribable.   As the people came out of church the newsboys were crying, ' Defeat of General Banks !   Washington in danger ! '   The newspaper offices were surrounded by anxious crowds.   In the morning edition of the *New York Herald* a leader had appeared which was headed ' Fall of Richmond.'   The same evening it was reported that the whole of the rebel army was marching to the Potomac. Troops were hurried to Harper's Ferry from Baltimore and Washington.   The railways were ordered to place their lines at the disposal of the Government.   McDowell, on the eve of starting to join McClellan, was ordered to lay aside the movement, and to send half his army to the Valley.[1]   Frémont, who was about to join his column from the Great Kanawha, was called upon to support Banks. McClellan was warned, by the President himself, that the enemy was making a general movement northward, and that he must either attack Richmond forthwith or come to the defence of Washington.   A reserve corps of 50,000 men was ordered to be organised at once, and stationed permanently near the capital ; and in one day nearly half a million American citizens offered their services to save the Union.

' we have great reason to be grateful to kind Providence, and applaud the skill and energy of our commanding officers for the miraculous escape of our men from utter annihilation.'   O. R., vol. xii., part i., pp. 573 and 611.

[1] Shields' and Ord's divisions of infantry, and Bayard's brigade of cavalry, numbering all told 21,200 officers and men.

Jackson's success was as complete as it was sudden. The second diversion against Washington was as effective as the first, and the victory at Winchester even more prolific of results than the defeat at Kernstown. Within four-and-twenty hours the storm-cloud which had been gathering about Fredericksburg was dispersed. McDowell's army of 40,000 men and 100 guns was scattered beyond the hope of speedy concentration. McClellan, who had pushed forward his left wing across the Chickahominy, suddenly found himself deprived of the support on which he counted to secure his right ; and Johnston, who had determined to attack his opponent before that support should arrive, was able to postpone operations until the situation should become more favourable.

Immediately after his victory Jackson had sent an officer to Richmond with dispatches explaining his views, and asking for instructions. Lee, in reply, requested him to press the enemy, to threaten an invasion of Maryland, and an assault upon the Federal capital. Early on the 28th, the Stonewall Brigade advanced towards

May 28. Harper's Ferry. At that point, crowded with stores of every description, 7,000 men and 18 guns, under General Saxton, had already been assembled. At Charlestown, Winder's advanced guard struck a reconnoitring detachment, composed of two regiments, a section of artillery, and a cavalry regiment. Within twenty minutes the Federals, already demoralised by the defeat of Banks, were retiring in disorder, abandoning arms, blankets, and haversacks, along the road, and the pursuit was continued until their reserves were descried in strong force on the Bolivar Heights, a low ridge covering Harper's Ferry from the south. The same evening Ewell advanced in support of Winder ; and, on the 29th, the Valley army was concentrated near Halltown, with the exception of the Louisiana brigade, posted near Berryville, the 12th Georgia, with 2 guns, in occupation of Front Royal, and Ashby, on the road to Wardensville, watching Frémont.

During the afternoon the 2nd Virginia Infantry was sent across the Shenandoah, and occupying the Loudoun

Heights, threatened the enemy's position on the ridge below. Saxton, in consequence, withdrew a part of his troops the same night to the left bank of the Potomac; but Jackson, although Harper's Ferry and its magazines might easily have been taken, made no attempt to follow. His scouts, riding far to east and west, had already informed him that McDowell and Frémont were in motion to cut off his retreat. Shields' division, leading McDowell's advance from Fredericksburg, was approaching Manassas Gap; while Frémont, hurrying from Franklin through the passes of the North Mountain, was ten miles east of Moorefield. Lee's instructions had already been carried to the extreme point consistent with safety, and Jackson determined to retreat by the Valley turnpike. Not only was it the one road which was not yet closely threatened, but it was the one road over which the enormous train of captured stores could be rapidly withdrawn.[1] The next morning, therefore, the

May 29. main body of the army marched back to Winchester; Winder, with the Stonewall Brigade and two batteries, remaining before Harper's Ferry to hold Saxton in check. Jackson himself returned to Winchester by the railway, and on the way he was met by untoward news. As the train neared Winchester a staff officer, riding at a gallop across the fields, signalled it to stop, and the general was informed that the 12th Georgia had been driven from Front Royal, burning the stores, but not the bridges, at Front Royal, and that Shields' division was in possession of the village.

The situation had suddenly become more than critical. Front Royal is but twelve miles from Strasburg. Not a single Confederate battalion was within five-and-twenty miles of that town, and Winder was just twice as far away. The next morning might see the Valley turnpike blocked by 10,000 Federals under Shields. Another 10,000, McDowell's Second Division, under General Ord, were already near Front Royal; Frémont, with 15,000, was

---

[1] Jackson, although the harvest was in full swing, had given orders that all waggons in the valley were to be impressed and sent to Winchester and Martinsburg.

pressing forward from the west; and Banks and Saxton, with the same number, were moving south from the Potomac. With resolute management it would seem that 35,000 Federals might have been assembled round Strasburg by midday of the 31st, and that this force might have been increased to 50,000 by the evening of June 1.[1] Desperate indeed appeared the Confederate chances. The waggons which conveyed the spoils of Martinsburg and Charlestown were still at Winchester, and with them were more than 2,000 prisoners. With the utmost expedition it seemed impossible that the Valley army, even if the waggons were abandoned, could reach Strasburg before the evening of the 31st; and the Stonewall Brigade, with fifty miles to march, would be four-and-twenty hours later. Escape, at least by the Valley turnpike, seemed absolutely impossible. Over Pharaoh and his chariots the waters were already closing.

But there is a power in war more potent than mere numbers. The moral difficulties of a situation may render the proudest display of physical force of no avail. Uncertainty and apprehension engender timidity and hesitation, and if the commander is ill at ease the movements of his troops become slow and halting. And when several armies, converging on a single point, are separated by distance or by the enemy, when communication is tedious, and each general is ignorant of his colleagues' movements, uncertainty and apprehension are inevitable. More than ever is this the case when the enemy has a character for swiftness and audacity, and some unfortunate detachment is still reeling under the effects of a crushing and unexpected blow.

Regarding, then, like Napoleon, the difficulties rather than the numbers of his enemies, Jackson held fast to his purpose, and the capture of Front Royal disturbed him little. 'What news?' he asked briefly as the staff officer rode up to the carriage door. 'Colonel Connor has been driven back from Front Royal.' Jackson smiled

[1] For the distribution of the different forces during this period see Note at end of chapter.

grimly, but made no reply. His eyes fixed themselves apparently upon some distant object. Then his preoccupation suddenly disappeared. He read the dispatch which he held in his hand, tore it in pieces, after his accustomed fashion, and, leaning forward, rested his head upon his hands and apparently fell asleep. He soon roused himself, however, and turning to Mr. Boteler, who tells the story, said : ' I am going to send you to Richmond for reinforcements. Banks has halted at Williamsport, and is being reinforced from Pennsylvania. Dix (Saxton) is in my front, and is being reinforced by the Baltimore and Ohio Railway. I have just received a dispatch informing me of the advance of the enemy upon Front Royal, which is captured, and Frémont is now advancing towards Wardensville. Thus, you see, I am nearly surrounded by a very large force.'

' What is your own, General ? ' asked his friend.

' I will tell you, but you must not repeat what I say, except at Richmond. To meet this attack I have only 15,000 effective men.'

' What will you do if they cut you off, General ? '

A moment's hesitation, and then the cool reply : ' I will fall back upon Maryland for reinforcements.'

' Jackson,' says Cooke, ' was in earnest. If his retreat was cut off he intended to advance into Maryland, and doubtless make his way straight to Baltimore and Washington, depending on the Southern sentiment in that portion of the State to bring him reinforcements.' That the Federal Government was apprehensive of some such movement is certain. The wildest rumours were everywhere prevalent. Men throughout the North wore anxious faces, and it is said that one question, ' Where is Jackson ? Has he taken Washington ? ' was on every lip. The best proof, however, that a movement on Washington was actually anticipated by the Federals is the dispatch of the Secretary of War to the Governors of the different States : ' Send forward all the troops that you can, immediately. Banks completely routed. Intelligence from various quarters leaves no doubt that the enemy, in great force, are advancing on Washington.

You will please organise and forward immediately all the
volunteer and militia force in your State.'   Further, on
receiving the news of Banks' defeat, the President had called
King's division of McDowell's army corps to defend the
capital; and his telegram of May 25 to McClellan, already
alluded to, in which that general was warned that he might
have to return to Washington, is significant of what would
have happened had the Confederates entered Maryland.[1]
McClellan's vast army, in all human probability, would
have been hurriedly re-embarked, and Johnston have been
free to follow Jackson.

On the night of the 30th the whole Army of the Valley
was ordered back to Strasburg; and early next morning
May 31.   the prisoners, escorted by the 21st Virginia, and
            followed by the convoy of waggons in double
column, covering seven miles of road, led the way.   Captain
Hotchkiss was sent with orders to Winder to hasten back to
Winchester, and not to halt till he had made some distance
between that place and Strasburg.   'I want you to go to
Charlestown,' were Jackson's instructions to his staff officer,
' and bring up the First Brigade.   I will stay in Winchester
until you get here, if I can, but if I cannot, and the enemy
gets here first, you must conduct it around through the
mountains.'

The march, however, as the general had expected, was
made without molestation, and during the afternoon the
main body reached Strasburg, and camped there for the
night.   The Stonewall Brigade, meanwhile, had passed
through Winchester, halting near Newtown; the 2nd
Virginia Regiment having marched thirty-five miles, and
all the remainder twenty-eight.   Little had been seen of
the enemy.   Frémont had passed Wardensville, and, marching through heavy rain, had halted after nightfall at Cedar
Creek, six miles west of Strasburg.   On the road to Front
Royal, only a few scouts had been encountered by the
Confederate patrols, for Shields, deceived by a demon-

        [1] O. R., vol. xi., part i., p. 31. King's division, when it was found that
Jackson had halted near Winchester, was ordered to Front Royal. The
fourth division, McCall's, was left to defend Fredericksburg.

stration which the Louisiana Brigade had made from Winchester, had let the day pass by without a decisive movement. The difficulties on which Jackson had counted had weighted the feet of his adversaries with lead.[1] Frémont, with two-and-twenty miles to march, had suffered Ashby to delay his progress; and although he had promised Lincoln that he would be in Strasburg at five o'clock that evening, he had halted on the mountains six miles distant. Shields, far ahead of the next division, had done nothing more than push a brigade towards Winchester, and place strong pickets on every road by which the enemy might approach. Neither Federal general could communicate with the other, for the country between them was held by the enemy. Both had been informed of the other's whereabouts, but both were uncertain as to the other's movements; and the dread of encountering, unsupported, the terrible weight of Jackson's onset had sapped their resolution. Both believed the enemy far stronger than he really was. The fugitives from Winchester had spread exaggerated reports of the Confederate numbers, and the prisoners captured at Front Royal had by no means minimised them.[2] Banks, impressed by the long array of bayonets that had crowned the ridge at Winchester, rated them at 20,000 infantry, with cavalry and artillery in addition. Geary, who had retired in hot haste from Rectortown, burning his tents and stores, had learned, he reported, from numerous sources that 10,000 cavalry were passing through Manassas Gap. There were constant rumours that strong reinforcements were coming up from Richmond, and even McDowell believed that the army of invasion consisted of 25,000 to 30,000 men.

---

[1] Up to the time that they arrived within striking distance of Jackson they had acted vigorously, Shields marching eighty miles in five days, and Frémont seventy over a mountain road.

[2] According to the Official Records, 156 men were taken by General Shields. It is said that when Colonel Connor, in command of the 12th Georgia Regiment, reported to Jackson at Winchester, and gave rather a sensational account of his defeat, the General looked up, and asked in his abrupt manner: 'Colonel, how many men had you killed?' 'None, I am glad to say, General.' 'How many wounded?' 'Few or none, sir.' 'Do you call that fighting, sir?' said Jackson, and immediately placed him under arrest, from which he was not released for several months.

Frémont's scouts, as he approached Strasburg, 'represented the Confederate force at 30,000 to 60,000.' Shields, before he crossed the Blue Ridge and found himself in the vicinity of his old opponent, had condemned the panic that had seized his brother generals, and had told McDowell that he would clear the Valley with his own division. But when he reached Front Royal the force that he had scornfully described as insignificant had swelled to 20,000 men. Troops from Richmond, he telegraphed, were marching down the Luray Valley; and he urged that he should be at once supported by two divisions. It cannot be said that Lincoln and Stanton were to blame for the indecision of the generals. They had urged Frémont forward to Strasburg, and Shields to Front Royal. They had informed them, by the telegraph, of each other's situation, and had passed on such intelligence of the enemy's movements as had been acquired at Harper's Ferry; and yet, although the information was sufficiently exact, both Shields and Frémont, just as Jackson anticipated, held back at the decisive moment. The waters had been held back, and the Confederates had passed through them dry-shod. Such is the effect of uncertainty in war; a mighty power in the hands of a general who understands its scope.

On the morning of June 1, Jackson's only remaining anxiety was to bring Winder back, and to expedite the retreat of the convoy. Ewell was therefore ordered to support Ashby, and to hold Frémont in check until the Stonewall Brigade had passed through Strasburg. The task was easily accomplished. At seven in the morning the Confederate pickets were driven in. As they fell back on their supports, the batteries on both sides came rapidly into action, and the Federal infantry pressed forward. But musketry replied to musketry, and finding the road blocked by a line of riflemen, Frémont ordered his troops to occupy a defensive position on Cedar Creek. 'I was entirely ignorant,' he says, 'of what had taken place in the Valley beyond, and it was now evident that Jackson, in superior force, was at or near Strasburg.' His men, also, appear to have caught the spirit of irresolution, for a forward

June 1.

movement on the part of the Confederates drove in Blenker's Germans with the greatest ease. 'Sheep,' says General Taylor, 'would have made as much resistance as we met. Men decamped without firing, or threw down their arms and surrendered. Our whole skirmish line was advancing briskly. I sought Ewell and reported. We had a fine game before us, and the temptation to play it was great; but Jackson's orders were imperative and wise. He had his stores to save, Shields to guard against, Lee's grand strategy to promote. He could not waste time chasing Frémont.' [1]

Winder reached Strasburg about noon. The troops that had been facing Frémont were then withdrawn; and the whole force, now reunited, fell back on Woodstock; Ashby, with the cavalry, holding his old position on Tom's Brook. The retreat was made in full view of the Federal scouts. On the Confederates retiring from before him, Frémont had pushed forward a reconnaissance, and Bayard's cavalry brigade, of McDowell's army, came up in the evening on the other flank. But attack was useless. The Confederate trains were disappearing in the distance, and heavy masses of all arms were moving slowly south. The Federal horsemen were unsupported save by a single battery. McDowell, who had reached Front Royal with part of his Second Division in the morning, had endeavoured to push Shields forward upon Strasburg. But Shields, fearing attack, had dispersed his troops to guard the various roads; and when at last they were assembled, misled by erroneous information, he had directed them on Winchester. Before the mistake was discovered the day had passed away. It was not until the next morning that the Federal columns came into communication, and then Jackson was already south of Woodstock.

On Friday morning, May 29, says Allan, 'Jackson was in front of Harper's Ferry, fifty miles from Strasburg. Frémont was at Fabius, twenty miles from Strasburg; and Shields was not more than twenty miles from Strasburg, for his advance entered Front Royal, which is but twelve miles distant, before mid-day, while McDowell was

---

[1] *Destruction and Reconstruction.* p. 78.

following with two divisions. Yet by Sunday night Jackson had marched between fifty and sixty miles, though encumbered with prisoners and captured stores, had reached Strasburg before either of his adversaries, and had passed safely between their armies, while he held Frémont at bay by a show of force, and blinded and bewildered Shields by the rapidity of his movements.'

From the morning of May 19 to the night of June 1, a period of fourteen days, the Army of the Valley had marched one hundred and seventy miles, had routed a force of 12,500 men, had threatened the North with invasion, had drawn off McDowell from Fredericksburg, had seized the hospitals and supply depôts at Front Royal, Winchester,[1] and Martinsburg, and finally, although surrounded on three sides by 60,000 men, had brought off a huge convoy without losing a single waggon.

This remarkable achievement, moreover, had been comparatively bloodless. The loss of 613 officers and men was a small price to pay for such results.[2]

That Jackson's lucky star was in the ascendant there can be little doubt. But fortune had far less to do with his success than skill and insight; and in two instances—the misconduct of his cavalry, and the surprise of the 12th Georgia—the blind goddess played him false. Not that he trusted to her favours. 'Every movement throughout the whole period,' says one of his staff officers, 'was the result of profound calculation. He knew what his men could do, and to whom he could entrust the execution of important orders.'[3] Nor was his danger of capture, on his retreat from Harper's Ferry, so great as it appeared.

May 31 was the crisis of his operations. On that morning, when the prisoners and the convoy marched out of Winchester, Shields was at Front Royal. But Shields

---

[1] Quartermaster's stores, to the value of 25,000*l*., were captured at Winchester alone, and 9,354 small arms, besides two guns, were carried back to Staunton.

[2] 68 killed; 386 wounded; 3 missing; 156 captured.

[3] Letter from Major Hotchkiss.

was unsupported; Ord's division was fifteen miles in rear, and Bayard's cavalry still further east. Even had he moved boldly on Strasburg he could hardly have seized the town. The ground was in Jackson's favour. The only road available for the Federals was that which runs south of the North Fork and the bridges had been destroyed. At that point, three miles east of Strasburg, a small flank-guard might have blocked the way until the main body of the Confederates had got up. And had Frémont, instead of halting that evening at Cedar Creek, swept Ashby aside and pushed forward to join his colleague, the Valley army might easily have effected its retreat. Winder alone would have been cut off, and Jackson had provided for that emergency.

When the embarrassments under which the Federals laboured are laid bare, the passage of the Confederates between the converging armies loses something of its extraordinary character. Nevertheless, the defeat of the Front Royal garrison and the loss of the bridges was enough to have shaken the strongest nerves. Had Jackson then burnt his convoy, and released his prisoners, few would have blamed him; and the tenacity with which he held to his original purpose, the skill with which he imposed on both Shields and Frémont, are no less admirable than his perception of his opponents' difficulties. Well has it been said : ' What gross ignorance of human nature do those declaimers display who assert that the employing of brute force is the highest qualification of a general ! '

NOTE

Positions of the Troops, May 29 to June 1

Night of May 29

FEDERALS.	CONFEDERATES.
Shields, 10,200, Rectorstown.	Jackson's Division, 7,200, Halltown.
Ord, 9,000, Thoroughfare Gap.	Ewell's Division, 5,000, Halltown
Bayard, 2,000, Catlett's Station.	Ashby, 300, Wardensville road.
Frémont, 15,000, Fabius.	Taylor's Brigade, 3,000, Berryville.
Saxton, 7,000, Harper's Ferry.	12th Georgia Regiment, 450, Front Royal.
Banks, 7,000, Williamsport.	2nd Virginia Regiment, 350, Loudoun Heights.
Geary, 2,000, Middleburg.	

McDowell brackets: Shields, Ord, Bayard.

Night of May 30

FEDERALS.	CONFEDERATES.
Shields, 10,200, Front Royal.	Army of Valley, 13,850, Winchester.
Ord, 9,000, Piedmont.	Stonewall Brigade, 1,600, Halltown.
Bayard, 2,000, Thoroughfare Gap.	2nd Virginia Regiment, 380, Loudoun Heights.
King, 10,000, near Catlett's Station.	Ashby, 300, Wardensville Road.
Saxton, 7,000, Harper's Ferry.	
Banks, 8,600, Williamsport.	
Frémont, 15,000, Wardensville.	
Geary, 2,000, Upperville.	

McDowell brackets: Shields, Ord, Bayard, King.

Night of May 31

FEDERALS.	CONFEDERATES.
Shields, Front Royal.	Army of Valley, Strasburg.
Ord, Manassas Gap.	Stonewall Brigade, Newtown.
King, Catlett's Station.	Ashby, Cedar Creek.
Bayard, Manassas Gap.	
Saxton, Harper's Ferry.	
Banks, Williamsport.	
Frémont, Cedar Creek.	
Geary, Snicker's and Ashby's Gaps.	

McDowell brackets: Shields, Ord, King, Bayard.

Night of June 1.

McDowell
{
Shields, ten miles south of Front Royal.
Ord, Front Royal.
King, Haymarket.
Bayard, Buckton.
}

Saxton, Harper's Ferry.
Banks, Williamsport.
Frémont, Cedar Creek.
Geary, Snicker's and Ashby's Gaps.

Army of Valley, Woodstock
Ashby, Tom's Brook.

TOTAL STRENGTH.

Federal . . . . . 62,000.
Confederate . . . . 16,000.

CHAPTER XI

CROSS KEYS AND PORT REPUBLIC

By the ignorant and the envious success in war is easily explained away. The dead military lion, and, for that matter, even the living, is a fair mark for the heels of a baser animal. The greatest captains have not escaped the critics. The genius of Napoleon has been belittled on the ground that each one of his opponents, except Wellington, was only second-rate. French historians have attributed Wellington's victories to the mutual jealousy of the French marshals; and it has been asserted that Moltke triumphed only because his adversaries blundered. Judged by this rule few reputations would survive. In war, however, it is as impossible to avoid error as it is to avoid loss of life; but it is by no means simple either to detect or to take advantage of mistakes. Before both Napoleon and Wellington an unsound manœuvre was dangerous in the extreme. None were so quick to see the slip, none more prompt to profit by it. Herein, to a very great extent, lay the secret of their success, and herein lies the true measure of military genius. A general is not necessarily incapable because he makes a false move; both Napoleon and Wellington, in the long course of their campaigns, gave many openings to a resolute foe, and both missed opportunities. Under ordinary circumstances mistakes may easily escape notice altogether, or at all events pass unpunished, and the reputation of the leader who commits them will remain untarnished. But if he is pitted against a master of war a single false step may lead to irretrievable ruin; and he will be classed as beneath contempt for a fault which his successful antagonist may have committed with impunity a hundred times over.

So Jackson's escape from Winchester was not due simply to the inefficiency of the Federal generals, or to the ignorance of the Federal President. Lincoln was wrong in dispatching McDowell to Front Royal in order to cut off Jackson. When Shields, in execution of this order, left Fredericksburg, the Confederates were only five miles north of Winchester, and had they at once retreated McDowell must have missed them by many miles. McDowell, hotly protesting, declared, and rightly, that the movement he had been ordered to execute was strategically false. 'It is impossible,' he said, 'that Jackson can have been largely reinforced. He is merely creating a diversion, and the surest way to bring him from the lower Valley is for me to move rapidly on Richmond. In any case, it would be wiser to move on Gordonsville.'[1] His arguments were unavailing. But when Jackson pressed forward to the Potomac, it became possible to intercept him, and the President did all he could to assist his generals. He kept them constantly informed of the movements of the enemy and of each other. He left them a free hand, and with an opponent less able his instructions would have probably brought about complete success. Nor were the generals to blame. They failed to accomplish the task that had been set them, and they made mistakes. But the task was difficult; and, if at the critical moment the hazard of their situation proved too much for their resolution, it was exactly what might have been expected. The initial error of the Federals was in sending two detached forces, under men of no particular strength of character, from opposite points of the compass, to converge upon an enemy who was believed to be superior to either of them. Jackson at once recognised the blunder, and foreseeing the consequences that were certain to ensue, resolved to profit by them. His escape, then, was the reward of his own sagacity.

When once the actual position of the Confederates had been determined, and the dread that reinforcements were coming down the Valley had passed away, the vigour of the Federal pursuit left nothing to be desired. Directly it was found that the Confederates had gone south, on the after-

[1] O. R., vol. xii., part iii., pp. 220, 229 (letter of S. P. Chase).

noon of June 1, Shields was directed on Luray, and
that night his advanced guard was ten miles
beyond Front Royal; on the other side of the
Massanuttons, Frémont, with Bayard's cavalry heading his
advance, moved rapidly on Woodstock.

June 1.

The Federal generals, however, had to do with a foe
who never relaxed his vigilance. Whilst Ashby and Ewell,
on May 31, were engaged with Frémont at Cedar Creek,
Jackson had expected that Shields would advance on Strasburg. But not a single infantry soldier was observed on
the Front Royal road throughout the day. Such inaction
was suspicious, and the probability to which it pointed had
not escaped the penetration of the Confederate leader. His
line of retreat was the familiar route by New Market and
Harrisonburg to Port Republic, and thence to the Gaps of
the Blue Ridge. There he could secure an unassailable
position, within reach of the railway and of Richmond.
But, during the movement, danger threatened from the
valley of the South Fork. Should Shields adopt that line
of advance the White House and Columbia bridges would
give him easy access to New Market; and while Frémont
was pressing the Confederates in rear, their flank might
be assailed by fresh foes from the Luray Gap. And
even if the retiring column should pass New Market in
safety, Shields, holding the bridges at Conrad's Store and
Port Republic, might block the passage to the Blue Ridge.
Jackson, looking at the situation from his enemy's point
of view, came to the conclusion that a movement up the
valley of the South Fork was already in progress, and that
the aim of the Federal commander would be to secure the
bridges. His conjectures hit the mark.

Before leaving Front Royal Shields ordered his
cavalry to march rapidly up the valley of the South
Fork, and seize the bridge at Conrad's Store; the White
House and Columbia bridges he intended to secure himself.
But Jackson was not to be so easily overreached. On the
night of June 2 the Federal cavalry reached
Luray, to find that they had come too late. The
White House and Columbia bridges had both been burned

June 2.

by a detachment of Confederate horse, and Shields was thus cut off from New Market. At dawn on the 4th, after a forced night march, his advanced guard reached Conrad's Store to find that bridge also gone,[1] and he was once more foiled. On his arrival at Luray, the sound of cannon on the other side of the Massanuttons was plainly heard. It seemed probable that Jackson and Frémont were already in collision ; but Shields, who had written a few hours before to Mr. Stanton that with supplies and forage he could 'stampede the enemy to Richmond,' was unable to stir a foot to assist his colleague.

Once again Jackson had turned to account the strategic possibilities of the Massanuttons and the Shenandoah ; and, to increase General Shields' embarrassment, the weather had broken. Heavy and incessant rain-storms submerged the Virginia roads. He was ahead of his supplies ; much hampered by the mud ; and the South Fork of the Shenandoah, cutting him off from Frémont, rolled a volume of rushing water which it was impossible to bridge without long delay.

Meanwhile, west of the great mountain, the tide of war, which had swept with such violence to the Potomac, came surging back. Frémont, by the rapidity of his pursuit, made full amends for his lack of vigour at Cedar Creek. A cloud of horsemen filled the space between the hostile columns. Day after day the quiet farms and sleepy villages on the Valley turnpike heard the thunder of Ashby's guns. Every stream that crossed the road was the scene of a fierce skirmish ; and the ripening corn was trampled under the hoofs of the charging squadrons. On June 2, the first day of the pursuit, between Strasburg and Woodstock the Federals, boldly led by Bayard, gained a distinct advantage. A dashing attack drove in the Confederate rear-guard, swept away the horse artillery, and sent Ashby's and Steuart's regiments, exhausted by hunger and loss of sleep, flying up the Valley. Many prisoners were taken, and the pursuit was

[1] Of the existence of the bridge at Port Republic, held by a party of Confederate cavalry, the Federals do not appear to have been aware.

only checked by a party of infantry stragglers, whom Ashby had succeeded in rallying across the road.

Next day, June 3, the skirmishing was continued; and the Confederates, burning the bridges across the roads, June 4. retreated to Mount Jackson. On the 4th the bridge over the North Fork was given to the flames, Ashby, whose horse was shot under him, remaining to the last; and the deep and turbulent river placed an impassable obstacle between the armies. Under a deluge of rain the Federals attempted to launch their pontoons; but the boats were swept away by the rising flood, and it was not till the next morning that the bridge was made. The Confederates had thus gained twenty-four hours' respite, and contact was not resumed until the June 5. 6th. Jackson, meanwhile, constructing a ferry at Mount Crawford, had sent his sick and wounded to Staunton, thus saving them the long *détour* by Port Republic; and dispatching his stores and prisoners by the more circuitous route, had passed through Harrisonburg to Cross Keys, a clump of buildings on Mill Creek, where, on the night of the 5th, his infantry and artillery, with the exception of a brigade supporting the cavalry, went into bivouac.

On the afternoon of the 6th the Federal cavalry followed Ashby. Some three miles from Harrisonburg is a tract of forest, crowning a long ridge; and within the June 6. timber the Confederate squadrons occupied a strong position. The enemy, 800 strong, pursued without precaution, charged up a gentle hill, and were repulsed by a heavy fire. Then Ashby let loose his mounted men on the broken ranks, and the Federals were driven back to within half a mile of Harrisonburg, losing 4 officers and 30 men.

Smarting under this defeat, Frémont threw forward a still stronger force of cavalry, strengthened by two battalions of infantry. Ashby had already called up a portion of the brigade which supported him, and met the attack in a clearing of the forest. The fight was fierce. The Confederates were roughly handled by the Northern riflemen, and the ranks began to waver. Riding to the front, where the opposing lines were already at close range, Ashby called upon his infantry to charge.

As he gave the order his horse fell heavily to the ground. Leaping to his feet in an instant, again he shouted, 'Charge, men! for God's sake, charge!' The regiments rallied, and inspired by his example swept forward from the wood. But hardly had they left the covert when their leader fell, shot through the heart. He was speedily avenged. The men who followed him, despite the heavy fire, dashed at the enemy in front and flank, and drove them from their ground. The cavalry, meanwhile, had worked round in rear; the horse artillery found an opportunity for action; and under cover of the night the Federals fell back on Harrisonburg.

The losses of the Union troops were heavy; but the Confederate victory was dearly purchased. The death of Ashby was a terrible blow to the Army of the Valley. From the outbreak of the war he had been employed on the Shenandoah, and from Staunton to the Potomac his was the most familiar figure in the Confederate ranks. His daring rides on his famous white charger were already the theme of song and story; and if the tale of his exploits, as told in camp and farm, sometimes bordered on the marvellous, the bare truth, stripped of all exaggeration, was sufficient in itself to make a hero. His reckless courage, his fine horsemanship, his skill in handling his command, and his power of stimulating devotion, were not the only attributes which incited admiration. 'With such qualities,' it is said, 'were united the utmost generosity and unselfishness, and a delicacy of feeling equal to a woman's.' His loss came home with especial force to Jackson. After the unfortunate episode in the pursuit from Middletown, he had rated his cavalry leader in no measured terms for the indiscipline of his command; and for some days their intercourse, usually most cordial, had been simply official. Sensitive in the extreme to any reflection upon himself or his troops, Ashby held aloof; and Jackson, always stern when a breach of duty was concerned, made no overtures for a renewal of friendly intercourse. Fortunately, before the fatal fight near Harrisonburg, they had been fully reconciled; and with no shadow of remorse Jackson was able to offer his tribute to the dead. Entering the room in Port Republic, whither the body had been brought, he remained for a time alone with his old comrade; and in sending an order to his cavalry, added, ' Poor Ashby is dead. He fell gloriously—one of the noblest men and soldiers in the Confederate army.' A more public testimony was to come. In his official report he wrote : ' The close relation General Ashby bore to my command for most of the previous twelve months will justify me in saying that as a partisan officer I never knew his superior. His daring was proverbial, his powers of endurance almost incredible, his character heroic, and his sagacity almost intuitive in divining the purposes and movements of the enemy.'

On the 6th and 7th the Confederate infantry rested on the banks of Mill Creek, near Cross Keys. The cavalry, on either flank of the Massanuttons, watched both Frémont's camps at Harrisonburg and the slow advance of Shields; and on the southern peak of the mountains a party of signallers, under a staff officer, looked down upon the roads which converged on the Confederate position.

June 7 was passed in unwonted quiet. For the first time for fifteen days since the storming of Front Royal the
June 7. boom of the guns was silent. The glory of the summer brooded undisturbed on hill and forest ; and as the escort which followed Ashby to his grave passed down the quiet country roads, the Valley lay still and peaceful in the sunshine. Not a single Federal scout observed the melancholy *cortège*. Frémont's pursuit had been roughly checked. He was uncertain in which direction the main body of the Confederates had retreated ; and it was not till evening that a strong force of infantry, reconnoitring through the woods, struck Jackson's outposts near the hamlet of Cross Keys. Only a few shots were exchanged.

Shields, meanwhile, had concentrated his troops at

c c 2

Columbia Bridge on the 6th, and presuming that Jackson was standing fast on the strong position at Rude's Hill, was preparing to cross the river. Later in the day a patrol, which had managed to communicate with Frémont, informed him that Jackson was retreating, and the instructions he thereupon dispatched to the officer commanding his advanced guard are worthy of record :

'The enemy passed New Market on the 5th; Blenker's division on the 6th in pursuit. The enemy has flung away everything, and their stragglers fill the mountain. They need only a movement on the flank to panic-strike them, and break them into fragments. No man has had such a chance since the war commenced. You are within thirty miles of a broken, retreating enemy, who still hangs together. 10,000 Germans are on his rear, who hang on like bull-dogs. You have only to throw yourself down on Waynesborough before him, and your cavalry will capture them by the thousands, seize his train and abundant supplies.' [1]

In anticipation, therefore, of an easy triumph, and, to use his own words, of 'thundering down on Jackson's rear,' Shields, throwing precaution to the winds, determined to move as rapidly as possible on Port Republic. He had written to Frémont urging a combined attack on ' the demoralised rebels,' and he thought that together they ' would finish Jackson.' His only anxiety was that the enemy might escape, and in his haste he neglected the warning of his Corps commander. McDowell, on dispatching him in pursuit, had directed his attention to the importance of keeping his division well closed up. Jackson's predilection for dealing with exposed detachments had evidently been noted. Shields' force, however, owing to the difficulties of the road, the mud, the quick-sands, and the swollen streams, was already divided into several distinct fractions. His advanced brigade was south of Conrad's Store ; a second was some miles in rear, and two were at Luray, retained at that point in consequence of a report that 8,000 Confederates were crossing the Blue

[1] O. R., vol. xii., part iii., p. 352.

Ridge by Thornton's Gap. To correct this faulty formation before advancing he thought was not worth while. On the night of June 7 he was sure of his prey.

The situation at this juncture was as follows: Shields was stretched out over five-and-twenty miles of road in the valley of the South Fork; Frémont was at Harrisonburg; Ewell's division was near Cross Keys, and the main body of the Valley Army near Port Republic.

During his retreat Jackson had kept his attention fixed on Shields. That ardent Irishman pictured his old enemy flying in confusion, intent only on escape. He would have been much astonished had he learned the truth. From the moment Jackson left Strasburg, during the whole time he was retreating, with the 'bull-dogs' at his heels, he was meditating a counter-stroke, and his victim had already been selected. When Shields rushed boldly up the valley of the South Fork it seemed that an opportunity of avenging Kernstown was about to offer. On June 4, the day that the enemy reached Luray, Ewell was ordered to provide his men with two days' cooked rations and to complete their ammunition 'for active service.' The next day, however, it was found that Shields had halted. Ewell was ordered to stand fast, and Jackson wrote despondently to Lee: 'At present I do not see that I can do much more than rest my command and devote its time to drilling.' On the 6th, however, he learned that Shields' advanced guard had resumed its march; and, like a tiger crouching in the jungle, he prepared to spring upon his prey. But Frémont was close at hand, and Shields and Frémont between them mustered nearly 25,000 men. They were certainly divided by the Shenandoah; but they were fast converging on Port Republic; and in a couple of marches, if not actually within sight of each other's camps, they would come within hearing of each other's guns. Yet, notwithstanding their numbers, Jackson had determined to deal with them in detail.

A few miles from the camp at Port Republic was a hill honeycombed with caverns, known as the Grottoes of the Shenandoah. In the heart of the limestone Nature has built herself a palace of many chambers, vast, silent, and magnificent.   But far beyond the beauty of her mysterious halls was the glorious prospect which lay before the eyes of the Confederate sentries.   Glimmering aisles and dark recesses, where no sunbeam lurks nor summer wind whispers, compared but ill with those fruitful valleys, watered by clear brown rivers, and steeped in the glow of a Virginian June.   To the north stood the Massanuttons, with their forests sleeping in the noon-day ; and to the right of the Massanuttons, displaying, in that transparent atmosphere, every shade of that royal colour from which it takes its name, the Blue Ridge loomed large against the eastern sky.   Summit after summit, each more delicately pencilled than the last, receded to the horizon, and beneath their feet, still, dark, and unbroken as the primeval wilderness, broad leagues of woodland stretched far away over a lonely land.

No battle-field boasts a fairer setting than Port Republic ; but, lover of Nature as he was, the region was attractive to Jackson for reasons of a sterner sort. It was eminently adapted for the purpose he had at heart.

1. The South Fork of the Shenandoah is formed by the junction of two streams, the North and South Rivers ; the village of Port Republic lying on the peninsula between the two.

2. The bridge crosses the North River just above the junction, carrying the Harrisonburg road into Port Republic ; but the South River, which cuts off Port Republic from the Luray Valley, is passable only by two difficult fords.

3. North of the village, on the left bank of the Shenandoah, a line of high bluffs, covered with scattered timber, completely commands the tract of open country which lies between the river and the Blue Ridge, and across this tract ran the road by which Shields was marching.

4. Four miles north-west of Port Republic, near the village of Cross Keys, the road to Harrisonburg crosses Mill Creek, a strong position for defence.

By transferring his army across the Shenandoah, and burning the bridge at Port Republic, Jackson could easily have escaped Frémont, and have met Shields in the Luray Valley with superior force. But the plain where the battle must be fought was commanded by the bluffs on the left bank of the Shenandoah; and should Frémont advance while an engagement was in progress, even though he could not cross the stream, he might assail the Confederates in flank with his numerous batteries. In order, then, to gain time in which to deal with Shields, it was essential that Frémont should be held back, and this could only be done on the left bank. Further, if Frémont could be held back until Shields' force was annihilated, the former would be isolated. If Jackson could hold the bridge at Port Republic, and also prevent Frémont reaching the bluffs, he could recross when he had done with Shields, and fight Frémont without fear of interruption.

To reverse the order, and to annihilate Frémont before falling upon Shields, was out of the question. Whether he advanced against Frémont or whether he stood still to receive his attack, Jackson's rear and communications, threatened by Shields, must be protected by a strong detachment. It would be thus impossible to meet Frémont with superior or even equal numbers, and an army weaker on the battlefield could not make certain of decisive victory.

Jackson had determined to check Frémont at Mill Creek. But the situation was still uncertain. Frémont had halted at Harrisonburg, and it was possible that he might advance no further. So the Confederates were divided, ready to meet either adversary; Ewell remaining at Cross Keys, and the Stonewall division encamping near Port Republic.

On the morning of June 8, however, it was found that Frémont was moving. Ewell's division was already under arms. At 8.30 A.M. his pickets, about two miles to the front, became engaged, and the Confederate regiments moved leisurely into position.

June 8.

The line ran along the crest of a narrow ridge, commanding an open valley, through which Mill Creek, an insignificant brook, ran parallel to the front. The further slopes, open and unobstructed except for scattered trees and a few fences, rose gently to a lower ridge, about a mile distant. The ground held by the Confederates was only partially cleared, and from the Port Republic road in the centre, at a distance of six hundred yards on either flank, were woods of heavy timber, enclosing the valley, and jutting out towards the enemy. The ridge beyond the valley was also thickly wooded; but here, too, there were open spaces on which batteries might be deployed; and the forest in rear, where Ashby had been killed, standing on higher ground, completely concealed the Federal approach. The pickets, however, had given ample warning of the coming attack; and when, at 10 A.M., the hostile artillery appeared on the opposite height, it was received with a heavy fire. 'Eight and a half batteries,' says Frémont, 'were brought into action within thirty minutes.' Against this long array of guns the Confederates massed only five batteries; but these commanded the open ground, and were all in action from the first.

Ewell had with him no more than three brigades. The Louisiana regiments had bivouacked near Port Republic, and were not yet up. The whole strength of the troops which held the ridge was no more than 6,000 infantry, and perhaps 500 cavalry. Frémont had at least 10,000 infantry, twelve batteries, and 2,000 cavalry.

It was then against overwhelming numbers that Ewell was asked to hold his ground, and the remainder of the army was four miles in rear. Jackson himself was still absent from the field. The arrangements for carrying out his ambitious plans had met with an unexpected hitch. In the Luray Valley, from Conrad's Store northwards, the space between the Blue Ridge and the Shenandoah was covered for the most part with dense forest, and through this forest ran the road. Moving beneath the spreading foliage of oak and hickory, Shields' advanced brigade was concealed from the observation of the Confederate cavalry; and the signallers on the mountain, endangered by Frémont's movement, had been withdrawn.

North of Port Republic, between the foot-hills of the

Blue Ridge and the Shenandoah, lies a level tract of arable and meadow, nearly a mile wide, and extending for nearly three miles in a northerly direction. On the plain were the Confederate pickets, furnished by three companies of Ashby's regiment, with their patrols on the roads towards Conrad's Store; and there seemed little chance that Shields would be able to reach the fords over the South River, much less the Port Republic bridge, without long notice being given of his approach. The cavalry, however, as had been already proved, were not entirely to be depended on. Jackson, whose headquarters were within the village, had already mounted his horse to ride forward to Cross Keys, when there was a distant fire, a sudden commotion in the streets, and a breathless messenger from the outposts reported that not only had the squadrons on picket been surprised and scattered, but that the enemy was already fording the South River.

Between the two rivers, south-west of Port Republic, were the Confederate trains, parked in the open fields. Here was Carrington's battery, with a small escort; and now the cavalry had fled there were no other troops, save a single company of the 2nd Virginia, on this side the Shenandoah. The squadron which headed the Federal advanced guard was accompanied by two guns. One piece was sent towards the bridge; the other, unlimbering on the further bank, opened fire on the church, and the horsemen trotted cautiously forward into the village street. Jackson, warned of his danger, had already made for the bridge, and crossing at a gallop escaped capture by the barest margin of time. His chief of artillery, Colonel Crutchfield, was made prisoner, with Dr. McGuire and Captain Willis,[1] and his whole staff was dispersed, save Captain Pendleton, a sterling soldier, though hardly more than a boy in years. And the danger was not over. With the trains was the whole of the reserve ammunition, and it seemed that a crushing disaster was near at hand. The sudden appearance of the enemy caused the greatest consternation amongst the teamsters; several of the waggons went off

[1] All three of these officers escaped from their captors.

by the Staunton road; and, had the Federal cavalry come on, the whole would have been stampeded. But Carrington's battery was called to the front by Captain Moore, commanding the company of infantry in the village. The picket, promptly put into position, opened with a well-aimed volley, and a few rounds checked the enemy's advance; the guns came rapidly and effectively into action, and at this critical moment Jackson intervened with his usual vigour.[1] From the left bank of the North River he saw a gun bearing on the bridge, the village swarming with blue uniforms, and more artillery unlimbering across the river. He had already sent orders for his infantry to fall in, and a six-pounder was hurrying to the front. 'I was surprised,' said the officer to whose battery this piece belonged, 'to see a gun posted on the opposite bank. Although I had met a cavalry man who told me that the enemy were advancing up the river, still I did not think it possible they could have brought any guns into the place in so short a time. It thereupon occurred to me that the piece at the bridge might be one of Carrington's, whose men had new uniforms something like those we saw at the bridge. Upon suggesting this to the general, he reflected a moment, and then riding a few paces to the left and front, he called out, in a tone loud enough to be heard by the enemy, "Bring that gun up here!" but getting no reply, he raised himself in his stirrups, and in a most authoritative and seemingly angry tone he shouted, "Bring that gun up here, I say!" At this they began to move the trail of the gun so as to bring it to bear on us, which, when the general perceived, he turned quickly to the officer in charge of my gun, and said in his sharp, quick way, "Let 'em have it!" The words had scarcely left his lips when Lieutenant Brown, who had his piece charged and aimed, sent a shot right among them, so disconcerting them that theirs in reply went far above us.'[2]

[1] According to General Shields' account his cavalry had reported to him that the bridge at Port Republic had been burned, and he had therefore ordered his advanced guard to take up a defensive position and prevent the Confederates crossing the Shenandoah River. It was the head of this detachment which had dispersed the Confederate squadrons.

[2] Related by Colonel Poague, C.S.A.

The Confederate battalions, some of which had been formed up for inspection, or for the Sunday service, when the alarm was given, had now come up, and the 37th Virginia was ordered to capture the gun, and to clear the village. Without a moment's hesitation the regiment charged with a yell across the bridge, and so sudden was the rush that the Federal artillerymen were surprised. The gun was double-shotted with canister, and the head of the column should have been swept away. But the aim was high and the Confederates escaped. Then, as the limber came forward, the horses, terrified by the heavy fire and the yells of the charging infantry, became unmanageable; and the gunners, abandoning the field-piece, fled through the streets of Port Republic. The 37th rushed forward with a yell. The hostile cavalry, following the gunners, sought safety by the fords; and as the rout dashed through the shallow water, the Confederate batteries, coming into action on the high bluffs west of the Shenandoah, swept the plain below with shot and shell.

The hostile artillery beyond the stream was quickly overpowered; horses were shot down wholesale; a second gun was abandoned on the road; a third, which had only two horses and a driver left, was thrown into a swamp; and a fourth was found on the field without either team or men.

The Federal infantry was not more fortunate. Carroll's brigade of four regiments was close in rear of the artillery when the Confederate batteries opened fire. Catching the contagion from the flying cavalry, it retreated northward in confusion. A second brigade (Tyler's) came up in support; but the bluffs beyond the river were now occupied by Jackson's infantry; a stream of fire swept the plain; and as Shields' advanced guard, followed by the Confederate cavalry, fell back to the woods whence it had emerged, five miles away on the other flank was heard the roar of the cannonade which opened the battle of Cross Keys.

From the hurried flight of the Federals it was evident that Shields' main body was not yet up; so, placing two brigades in position to guard the bridge, Jackson sent the remainder to Ewell, and then rode to the scene of action.

Frémont, under cover of his guns, had made his preparations for attack; but the timidity which he had already displayed when face to face with Jackson had once more taken possession of his faculties. Vigorous in pursuit of a flying enemy, when that enemy turned at bay his courage vanished. The Confederate position was undoubtedly strong, but it was not impregnable. The woods on either flank gave access under cover to the central ridge. The superior weight of his artillery was sufficient to cover an advance across the open; and although he was without maps or guide, the country was not so intersected as to render manœuvring impracticable.

In his official report Frémont lays great stress on the difficulties of the ground; but reading between the lines it is easy to see that it was the military situation which over-burdened him. The vicious strategy of converging columns, where intercommunication is tedious and uncertain, once more exerted its paralysing influence. It was some days since he had heard anything of Shields. That general's dispatch, urging a combined attack, had not yet reached him: whether he had passed Luray or whether he had been already beaten, Frémont was altogether ignorant; and, in his opinion, it was quite possible that the whole of the Confederate army was before him.

A more resolute commander would probably have decided that the shortest way out of the dilemma was a vigorous attack. If Shields was within hearing of the guns—and it was by no means improbable that he was—such a course was the surest means of securing his co-operation; and even if no help came, and the Confederates maintained their position, they might be so crippled as to be unable to pursue. Defeat would not have been an irreparable misfortune. Washington was secure. Banks, Saxton, and McDowell held the approaches; and if Frémont himself were beaten back, the strategic situation could be in no way affected. In fact a defeat, if it had followed an attack so hotly pressed as to paralyse Jackson for the time being, would have been hardly less valuable than a victory.

'Fortune,' it has been well said, 'loves a daring suitor, and he who throws down the gauntlet may always count upon his adversary to help him.' Frémont, however, was more afraid of losing the battle than anxious to win it. 'Taking counsel of his fears,' he would run no risks. But neither could he abstain from action altogether. An enemy was in front of him who for seven days had fled before him, and his own army anticipated an easy triumph.

So, like many another general who has shrunk from the nettle danger, he sought refuge in half-measures, the most damning course of all. Of twenty-four regiments present on the field of battle, five only, of Blenker's Germans, were sent forward to the attack. Their onslaught was directed against the Confederate right; and here, within the woods, Trimble had posted his brigade in a most advantageous position. A flat-topped ridge, covered with great oaks, looked down upon a wide meadow, crossed by a stout fence; and beyond the hollow lay the woods through which the Federals, already in contact with the Confederate outposts, were rapidly advancing. The pickets soon gave way, and crossing the meadow found cover within the thickets, where Trimble's three regiments lay concealed. In hot pursuit came the Federal skirmishers, with the solid lines of their brigade in close support. Steadily moving forward, they climbed the fence and breasted the gentle slope beyond. A few scattered shots, fired by the retreating pickets, were the only indications of the enemy's presence; the groves beyond were dark and silent. The skirmishers had reached the crest of the declivity, and the long wave of bayonets, following close upon their tracks, was within sixty paces of the covert, when the thickets stirred suddenly with sound and movement. The Southern riflemen rose swiftly to their feet. A sheet of fire ran along their line, followed by a crash that resounded through the woods; and the German regiments, after a vigorous effort to hold their ground, fell back in disorder across the clearing. Here, on the further edge, they rallied on their reserves, and the Confederates, who had followed up no further than was sufficient to give impetus to the retreat, were once more withdrawn.

A quarter of an hour passed, and as the enemy showed no inclination to attempt a second advance across the meadow, where the dead and wounded were lying thick, Trimble, sending word to Ewell of his intention, determined to complete his victory. More skilful than his enemies, he sent a regiment against their left, to which a convenient ravine gave easy access, while the troops among the oaks were held back till the flank attack was fully developed. The unexpected movement completely surprised the Federal brigadier. Again his troops were driven in, and the Confederates, now reinforced by six regiments which Ewell had sent up, forced them with heavy losses through the woods, compelled two batteries, after a fierce fight, to limber up, routed a brigade which had been sent by Frémont to support the attack, and pressing slowly but continuously forward, threw the whole of the enemy's left wing, consisting of Blenker's eleven regiments, back to the shelter of his line of guns. Trimble had drawn the 'bulldog's' teeth.

The Confederates had reached the outskirts of the wood. They were a mile in advance of the batteries in the centre; and the Federal position, commanding a tract of open ground, was strong in itself and strongly held. A general counterstroke was outside the scope of Jackson's designs. He had still Shields to deal with. The Federal left wing had been heavily repulsed, but only a portion of Frémont's force had been engaged; to press the attack further would undoubtedly have cost many lives, and even a partial reverse would have interfered with his comprehensive plan.

In other quarters of the battle-field the fighting had been unimportant. The Confederate guns, although heavily outnumbered, held their ground gallantly for more than five hours; and when they eventually retired it was from want of ammunition rather than from loss of *moral*. The waggons which carried their reserve had taken a wrong road, and at the critical moment there were no means of replenishing the supply. But so timid were Frémont's tactics that the blunder passed unpunished. While the battle on the left was raging fiercely he had contented himself elsewhere with tapping feebly at the enemy's lines. In the centre of the field his skirmishers moved against Ewell's batteries, but were routed by a bayonet charge; on the right, Milroy and Schenck, the two generals who had withstood Jackson so stubbornly at M'Dowell, advanced on their own initiative through the woods. They had driven in the Confederate skirmishers, and had induced Ewell to strengthen this portion of his line from his reserve, when they were recalled by Frémont, alarmed by Trimble's vigorous attack, to defend the main position.

The Southerners followed slowly. The day was late, and Ewell, although his troops were eager to crown their victory, was too cool a soldier to yield to their impatience; and, as at Cedar Creek, where also he had driven back the 'Dutch' division, so at Cross Keys he rendered the most loyal support to his commander. Yet he was a dashing fighter, chafing under the restraint of command, and preferring the excitement of the foremost line. 'On two occasions in the Valley,' says General Taylor, 'during the temporary absence of Jackson, he summoned me to his side, and immediately rushed forward amongst the skirmishers, where sharp work was going on. Having refreshed himself, he returned with the hope that "Old Jack would not catch him at it."' [1]

How thoroughly Jackson trusted his subordinate may be inferred from the fact that, although present on the field, he left Ewell to fight his own battle. The only instructions he gave showed that he had fathomed the temper of Frémont's troops. 'Let the Federals,' he said, 'get very close before your infantry fire; they won't stand long.' It was to Ewell's dispositions, his wise use of his reserves, and to Trimble's ready initiative, that Frémont's defeat was due. Beyond sending up a couple of brigades from Port Republic, Jackson gave no orders. His ambition was of too lofty a

[1] *Destruction and Reconstruction*, p. 39.

kind to appropriate the honours which another might fairly claim ; and, when once battle had been joined, interference with the plan on which it was being fought did not commend itself to him as sound generalship. He was not one of those suspicious commanders who believe that no subordinate can act intelligently.   If he demanded the strictest compliance with his instructions, he was always content to leave their execution to the judgment of his generals ; and with supreme confidence in his own capacity, he was still sensible that his juniors in rank might be just as able. His supervision was constant, but his interference rare ; and it was not till some palpable mistake had been committed that he assumed direct control of his divisions or brigades. Nor was any peculiar skill needed to beat back the attack of Frémont.   Nothing proves the Federal leader's want of confidence more clearly than the tale of losses.   The Confederate casualties amounted to 288, of which nearly half occurred in Trimble's counterstroke.   The Federal reports show 684 killed, wounded, and missing, and of these Trimble's riflemen accounted for nearly 500, one regiment, the 8th New York, being almost annihilated ; but such losses, although at one point severe, were altogether insignificant when compared with the total strength ; and it was not the troops who were defeated but the general.[1]

Ewell's division bivouacked within sight of the enemy's watch-fires, and within hearing of his outposts ; and throughout the night the work of removing the wounded, friend and foe alike, went on in the sombre woods.   There was work, too, at Port Republic.   Jackson, while his men slept, was all activity.   His plans were succeeding admirably.   From Frémont, cowering on the defensive before inferior numbers, there was little to be feared.   It was unlikely that after his repulse he would be found more enterprising on the morrow ; a small force would be sufficient to arrest his march until Shields had been crushed ; and then, swinging back across the Shenandoah,

[1] The Confederates at Kernstown lost 20 per cent. ; the Federals at Port Republic 18 per cent.   At Manassas the Stonewall Brigade lost 16 per cent., at Cross Keys Ewell only lost 3 per cent. and Frémont 5 per cent.

the soldiers of the Valley would find ample compensation, in the rout of their most powerful foe, for the enforced rapidity of their retreat from Winchester. But to fight two battles in one day, to disappear completely from Frémont's ken, and to recross the rivers before he had time to seize the bridge, were manœuvres of the utmost delicacy, and needed most careful preparation.

It was Jackson's custom, whenever a subordinate was to be entrusted with an independent mission, to explain the part that he was to play in a personal interview. By such means he made certain, first, that his instructions were thoroughly understood; and, second, that there was no chance of their purport coming to the knowledge of the enemy. Ewell was first summoned to headquarters, and then Patton, whose brigade, together with that of Trimble, was to have the task of checking Frémont the next day. 'I found him at 2 A.M.,' says Patton, 'actively engaged in making his dispositions for battle. He immediately proceeded to give me particular instructions as to the management of the men in covering the rear, saying : " I wish you to throw out all your men, if necessary, as skirmishers, and to make a great show, so as to cause the enemy to think the whole army are behind you. Hold your position as well as you can, then fall back when obliged ; take a new position, hold it in the same way, and I will be back to join you in the morning." '

Colonel Patton reminded him that his brigade was a small one, and that the country between Cross Keys and the Shenandoah offered few advantages for protracting such manœuvres. He desired, therefore, to know for how long he would be expected to hold the enemy in check. Jackson replied, 'By the blessing of Providence, I hope to be back by ten o'clock.' [1]

These interviews were not the only business which occupied the commanding general. He arranged for the feeding of his troops before their march next day,[2] for the

[1] *Southern Historical Society Papers*, vol. ix., p. 372.

[2] Rations appear to have been short, for General Ewell reports that when he marched against Shields the next day many of his men had been without food for four-and-twenty hours.

dispositions of his trains and ammunition waggons; and at the rising of the moon, which occurred about midnight, he was seen on the banks of the South River, superintending the construction of a bridge to carry his infantry dryshod across the stream.

An hour before daybreak he was roused from his short slumbers. Major Imboden, who was in charge of a mule battery,[1] looking for one of the staff, entered by mistake the general's room.

'I opened the door softly, and discovered Jackson lying on his face across the bed, fully dressed, with sword, sash, and boots all on. The low-burnt tallow-candle on the table shed a dim light, yet enough by which to recognise him. I endeavoured to withdraw without waking him. He turned over, sat upon the bed, and called out. "Who is that?"

'He checked my apology with, "That is all right. It's time to be up. I am glad to see you. Were the men all up as you came through camp?"

'"Yes, General, and cooking."

'"That's right; we move at daybreak. Sit down. I want to talk to you."

'I had learned never to ask him questions about his plans, for he would never answer such to anyone. I therefore waited for him to speak first. He referred very feelingly to Ashby's death, and spoke of it as an irreparable loss. When he paused I said, "General, you made a glorious winding-up of your four weeks with yesterday." He replied, "Yes, God blessed our army again yesterday, and I hope with His protection and blessing we shall do still better to-day."'[2] Then followed instructions as to the use of the mule battery in the forests through which lay Shields' line of advance.

Before 5 A.M. the next morning the Stonewall Brigade

---

[1] The mule battery does not appear to have done much more than afford the Confederate soldiers an opportunity of airing their wit. With the air of men anxiously seeking for information they would ask the gunners whether the mule or the gun was intended to go off first? and whether the gun was to fire the mule or the mule the gun?

[2] *Battles and Leaders*, vol. ii., p. 293.

had assembled in Port Republic, and was immediately ordered to advance. On the plain beyond, still dark in the shadow of the mountains, where the cavalry formed the outposts, the fire of the pickets, which had been incessant throughout the night, was increasing in intensity. The Federals were making ready for battle.

Winder had with him four regiments, about 1,200 strong, and two batteries. In rear came Taylor with his Louisianians ; and Jackson, leaving Major Dabney to superintend the passage of the river, rode with the leading brigade. The enemy's pickets were encountered about a mile and a half down the river, beyond a strip of woods, on either side of the Luray road. They were quickly driven in, and the Federal position became revealed. From the foot-hills of the Blue Ridge, clothed to their crests with under-growth and timber, the plain, over a mile in breadth, extended to the Shenandoah. The ground was terraced ; the upper level, immediately beneath the mountain, was densely wooded, and fifty or sixty feet above the open fields round the Lewis House. Here was the hostile front. The Federal force was composed of two brigades of infantry and sixteen guns, not more than 4,000 all told, for Shields, with the remainder of the division, was still far in rear. The right rested on the river ; the left on a ravine of the upper level, through which a shallow stream flowed down from the heights above. On the northern shoulder of this ravine was established a battery of seven guns, sweeping every yard of the ground beneath, and a country road, which led directly to the Shenandoah, running between stiff banks and strongly fenced, was lined with riflemen. Part of the artillery was on the plain, near the Lewis House, with a section near the river ; on the hillside, beyond the seven guns, two regiments were concealed within the forest, and in rear of the battery was a third. The position was strong, and the men who held it were of different calibre from Blenker's Germans, and the leaders of stauncher stuff than Frémont. Six of the seven battalions had fought at Kernstown. Tyler, who on that day had seen the Confederates retreat before him, was in

D D 2

command; and neither general nor soldiers had reason to
dread the name of Stonewall Jackson. In the sturdy
battalions of Ohio and West Virginia the Stonewall
Brigade were face to face with foemen worthy of their
steel; and when Jackson, anxious to get back to Frémont,
ordered Winder to attack, he set him a formidable
task.

It was first necessary to dislodge the hostile guns.
Winder's two batteries were insufficient for the work,
and two of his four regiments were ordered into the
woods on the terrace, in order to outflank the battery
beyond the stream. This detachment, moving with difficulty through the thickets, found a stronger force of
infantry within the forest; the guns opened with grape
at a range of one hundred yards, and the Confederates,
threatened on either flank, fell back in some confusion.

The remainder of Winder's line had meanwhile met with
a decided check. The enemy along the hollow road was
strongly posted. Both guns and skirmishers were hidden
by the embankment; and as the mists of the morning
cleared away, and the sun, rising in splendour above the
mountains, flooded the valley with light, a long line of
hostile infantry, with colours flying and gleaming arms,
was seen advancing steadily into battle. The Federal
commander, observing his opportunity, had, with rare
good judgment, determined on a counterstroke. The
Louisiana brigade was moving up in support of Winder,
but it was still distant. The two regiments which supported the Confederate batteries were suffering from
the heavy artillery fire, and the skirmishers were already
falling back. 'Below,' says General Taylor, 'Ewell was
hurrying his men over the bridge; but it looked as
if we should be doubled up on him ere he could cross
and develop much strength. Jackson was on the road,
a little in advance of his line, where the fire was hottest,
with the reins on his horse's neck. Summoning a
young officer from his staff, he pointed up the mountain. The head of my approaching column was turned
short up the slope, and within the forest came speedily

to a path which came upon the gorge opposite the battery. [1]

But, as Taylor's regiments disappeared within the forest, Winder's brigade was left for the moment isolated, bearing up with difficulty against overwhelming numbers. Ewell's division had found great difficulty in crossing the South River. The bridge, a construction of planks laid on the running gear of waggons, had proved unserviceable. At the deepest part there was a step of two feet between two axle-trees of different height; and the boards of the higher stage, except one, had broken from their fastenings. As the men passed over, several were thrown from their treacherous platform into the rushing stream, until at length they refused to trust themselves except to the centre plank. The column of fours was thus reduced to single file; men, guns, and waggons were huddled in confusion on the river banks; and the officers present neglected to secure the footway, and refused, despite the order of Major Dabney, to force their men through the breast-high ford.

So, while his subordinates were trifling with the time, which, if Frémont was to be defeated as well as Shields, was of such extreme importance, Jackson saw his old brigade assailed by superior numbers in front and flank. The Federals, matching the rifles of the Confederate marksmen with weapons no less deadly, crossed over the road and bore down upon the guns. The 7th Louisiana, the rear regiment of Taylor's column, was hastily called up, and dashed forward in a vain attempt to stem the tide.

A most determined and stubborn conflict now took place, and, as at Kernstown, at the closest range. The Ohio troops repelled every effort to drive them back. Winder's line was thin. Every man was engaged in the

[1] *Destruction and Reconstruction*, p. 90. Jackson's order to the staff officer (Major Hotchkiss) was brief: 'Sweeping with his hand to the eastward, and then towards the Lewis House, where the Federal guns were raking the advance, he said: " Take General Taylor around and take that battery." '

firing line. The flanks were scourged by bursting shells.
The deadly fire from the road held back the front. Men
and officers were falling fast. The stream of wounded
was creeping to the rear ; and after thirty minutes of
fierce fighting, the wavering line of the Confederates,
breaking in disorder, fell back upon the guns. The
artillery, firing a final salvo at a range of two hundred
yards, was ordered to limber up. One gun alone, standing
solitary between the opposing lines, essayed to cover the
retreat ; but the enemy was within a hundred yards, men
and horses were shot down ; despite a shower of grape,
which rent great gaps in the crowded ranks, the long blue
wave swept on, and leaving the captured piece in rear,
advanced in triumph across the fields.

In vain two of Ewell's battalions, hurrying forward to
the sound of battle, were thrown against the flank of the
attack. For an instant the Federal left recoiled, and then,
springing forward with still fiercer energy, dashed back
their new antagonists as they had done the rest. In vain
Jackson, galloping to the front, spurred his horse into the
tumult, and called upon his men to rally. Winder's line,
for the time being at least, had lost all strength and order ;
and although another regiment had now come up, the
enemy's fire was still so heavy that it was impossible to
reform the defeated troops, and two fresh Federal regiments were now advancing to strengthen the attack.
Tyler had ordered his left wing to reinforce the centre ;
and it seemed that the Confederates would be defeated piecemeal. But at this moment the lines of the assailant came
to a sudden halt ; and along the slopes of the Blue Ridge
a heavy crash of musketry, the rapid discharges of the
guns, and the charging yell of the Southern infantry,
told of a renewed attack upon the battery on the mountain
side.

The Louisianians had come up in the very nick of time.
Pursuing his march by the forest path, Taylor had heard
the sounds of battle pass beyond his flank, and the cheers
of the Federals proved that Winder was hard pressed.
Rapidly deploying on his advanced guard, which, led by

Colonel Kelley, of the 8th Louisiana, was already in line, he led his companies across the ravine. Down the broken slopes, covered with great boulders and scattered trees, the men slipped and stumbled, and then, splashing through the stream, swarmed up the face of the bank on which the Federal artillery was in action. Breaking through the undergrowth they threw themselves on the guns. The attention of the enemy had been fixed upon the fight that raged over the plain below, and the thick timber and heavy smoke concealed the approach of Taylor's regiments. The surprise, however, was a failure. The trails were swung round in the new direction, the canister crashed through the laurels, the supporting infantry rushed forward, and the Southerners were driven back. Again, as reinforcements crowded over the ravine, they returned to the charge, and with bayonet and rammer the fight surged to and fro within the battery. For the second time the Federals cleared their front; but some of the Lousiana companies, clambering up the mountain to the right, appeared upon their flank, and once more the stormers, rallying in the hollow, rushed forward with the bayonet. The battery was carried, one gun alone escaping, and the Federal commander saw the key of his position abandoned to the enemy. Not a moment was to be lost. The bank was nearly a mile in rear of his right and centre, and commanded his line of retreat at effective range. Sending his reserves to retake the battery, he directed his attacking line, already pressing heavily on Winder, to fall back at once. But it was even then too late. The rest of Ewell's division had reached the field. One of his brigades had been ordered to sustain the Lousianians; and across the plain a long column of infantry and artillery was hurrying northwards from Port Republic.

The Stonewall Brigade, relieved of the pressure in front, had already rallied; and when Tyler's reserves, with their backs to the river, advanced to retake the battery, Jackson's artillery was once more moving forward. The guns captured by Taylor were turned against the Federals—Ewell, it is said, indulging to the full his passion for hot work, serving as a gunner—and within a short space of time

Tyler was in full retreat, and the Confederate cavalry were thundering on his traces.

It was half-past ten. For nearly five hours the Federals had held their ground, and two of Jackson's best brigades had been severely handled. Even if Trimble and Patton had been successful in holding Frémont back, the Valley soldiers were in no condition for a rapid march and a vigorous attack, and their commander had long since recognised that he must rest content with a single victory.

Before nine o'clock, about the time of Winder's repulse, finding the resistance of the enemy more formidable than he had anticipated, he had recalled his brigades from the opposite bank of the Shenandoah, and had ordered them to burn the bridge. Trimble and Patton abandoned the battle-field of the previous day, and fell back to Port Republic. Hardly a shot was fired during their retreat, and when they took up their march only a single Federal battery had been seen. Frémont's advance was cautious in the extreme. He was actually aware that Shields had two brigades beyond the river, for a scout had reached him, and from the ground about Mill Creek the sound of Tyler's battle could be plainly heard. But he could get no direct information of what was passing. The crest of the Massanuttons, although the sun shone bright on the cliffs below, was shrouded in haze, completely forbidding all observation; and it was not till near noon, after a march of seven miles, which began at dawn and was practically unopposed, that Frémont reached the Shenandoah. There, in the charred and smoking timbers of the bridge, the groups of Federal prisoners on the plain, the Confederates gathering the wounded, and the faint rattle of musketry far down the Luray Valley, he saw the result of his timidity.

Massing his batteries on the western bluffs, and turning his guns in impotent wrath upon the plain, he drove the ambulances and their escort from the field. But the Confederate dead and wounded had already been removed, and the only effect of his spiteful salvoes was that his suffering comrades lay under a drenching rain until he retired to Harrisonburg. By that time many, whom their enemies

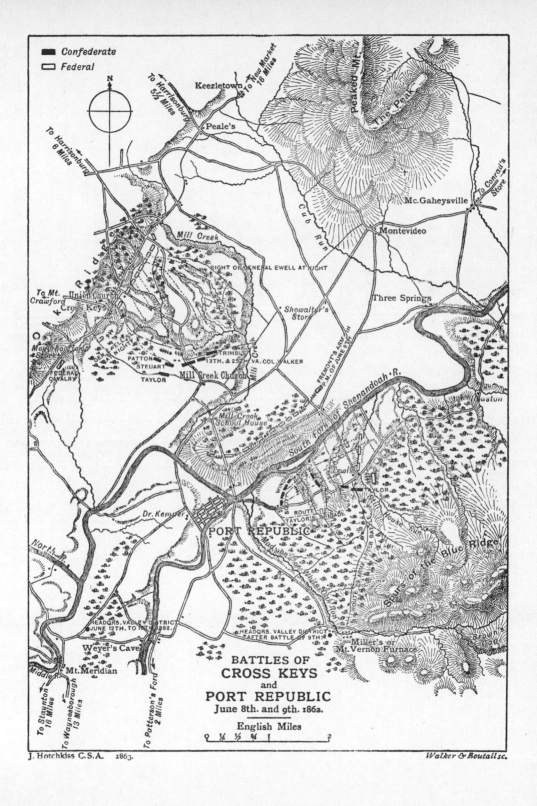

■ *Confederate*
□ *Federal*

To Harrisonburg 5½ Miles
To New Market 16 Miles
Keezletown
Peale's
To Harrisonburg 6 Miles
To Conrad's Store
Mc. Gaheysville
Montevideo
Peaked Mt.
The Peak
Cub Run
Mill Creek
RIGHT OF GENERAL EWELL AT NIGHT
Three Springs
Showalter's Store
To Mt. Crawford
Union Church
Cross Keys
GEN. ELEY'S BRIGADE
PATTON
STEUART
TRIMBLE
13TH. & 25TH VA. COL. WALKER
FREMONT'S ARMY IN P. M. OF JUNE 9TH
Moore's or Ford Store
Federal Cavalry
TAYLOR
Mill Creek Church
Mill Creek School House
South Fork or Shenandoah R.
Ruston
Mill Creek
Dr. Kemper
Lewis
Taylor
ROUTE OF TAYLOR'S BRIGADE
House Run
PORT REPUBLIC
Madison's Run
Spurs of the Blue Ridge
North R.
Brown Gap
HEADQRS. VALLEY DISTRICT JUNE 12TH. TO 16TH. 1862.
HEADQRS. VALLEY DISTRICT AFTER BATTLE OF 9TH.
Weyer's Cave
Miller's or Mt. Vernon Furnace
Middle
Mt. Meridian
To Staunton 16 Miles
To Waynesborough 13 Miles
To Patterson's Ford 2 Miles

BATTLES OF
CROSS KEYS
and
PORT REPUBLIC
June 8th. and 9th. 1862.

English Miles

J. Hotchkiss C.S.A. 1863.

Walker & Boutall sc.

would have rescued, had perished miserably, and 'not a few of the dead, with some perchance of the mangled living, were partially devoured by swine before their burial.' [1]

The pursuit of Tyler was pressed for nine miles down the river. The Ohio regiments, dispersed at first by the Confederate artillery, gathered gradually together, and held the cavalry in check. Near Conrad's Store, where Shields, marching in desperate haste to the sound of the cannonade, had put his two remaining brigades in position across the road, the chase was stayed. The Federal commander admits that he was only just in time. Jackson's horsemen, he says, were enveloping the column; a crowd of fugitives was rushing to the rear, and his own cavalry had dispersed. The Confederate army, of which some of the brigades and nearly the whole artillery had been halted far in rear, was now withdrawn; but, compelled to move by circuitous paths in order to avoid the fire of Frémont's batteries, it was after midnight before the whole had assembled in Brown's Gap. More than one of the regiments had marched over twenty miles and had been heavily engaged.

Port Republic was the battle most costly to the Army of the Valley during the whole campaign. Out of 5,900 Confederates engaged 804 were disabled.[2] The Federal losses were heavier. The killed, wounded, and missing (including 450 captured) amounted to 1,001, or one-fourth of Tyler's strength.

The success which the Confederates had achieved was undoubtedly important. The Valley army, posted in Brown's Gap, was now in direct communication with Richmond. Not only had its pursuers been roughly checked, but

[1] Dabney, vol. ii.
[2] The troops actually engaged were as follows :—

4 Regiments of Winder's Brigade	1,200
The Louisiana Brigade, 5 regiments	2,500
Scott's Brigade, 3 regiments	900
31st Virginia } 40th Virginia }	600
Artillery (5 batteries)	300
Cavalry	400
	5,900

the sudden and unexpected counterstroke, delivered by an enemy whom they believed to be in full flight, had surprised Lincoln and Stanton as effectively as Shields and Frémont. On June 6, the day Jackson halted near Port Republic, McCall's division of McDowell's Army Corps, which had been left at Fredericksburg, had been sent to the Peninsula by water; and two days later McDowell himself, with the remainder of his force, was directed to join McClellan as speedily as possible overland. Frémont, on the same date, was instructed to halt at Harrisonburg, and Shields to march to Fredericksburg. But before Stanton's dispatches reached their destination both Frémont and Shields had been defeated, and the plans of the Northern Cabinet were once more upset.

Instead of moving at once on Fredericksburg, and in spite of McDowell's remonstrances, Shields was detained at Luray, and Ricketts, who had succeeded Ord, at Front Royal; while Frémont, deeming himself too much exposed at Harrisonburg, fell back to Mount Jackson. It was not till June 20 that Ricketts and Shields were permitted to leave the Valley, ten days after the order had been issued for McDowell to move on Richmond. For that space of time, then, his departure was delayed; and there was worse to come. The great strategist at Richmond had not yet done with Lincoln. There was still more profit to be derived from the situation; and from the subsidiary operations in the Valley we may now turn to the main armies.

By Jackson's brilliant manœuvres McDowell had been lured westward at the very moment he was about to join McClellan. The gap between the two Federal armies had been widened from five to fifteen marches, while Jackson at Brown's Gap was no more than nine marches distant from Richmond. McClellan, moreover, had been paralysed by the vigour of Jackson's blows.

On May 16, as already related, he had reached White House on the Pamunkey, twenty miles from the Confederate capital. Ten miles south, and directly across his path, flowed the Chickahominy, a formidable obstacle to the march of a large army.

On the 24th, having already been informed that he was to be reinforced by McDowell, he was told that the movement of the latter for Fredericksburg was postponed until the Valley had been cleared. This change of plan placed him in a most awkward predicament. A portion of his army, in order to lend a hand to McDowell, had already crossed the Chickahominy, a river with but few points of passage, and over which, by reason of the swamps, the construction of military bridges was a difficult and tedious operation. On May 30, two army corps were south of the Chickahominy, covering, in a partially intrenched position, the building of the bridges, while three army corps were still on the further bank.

McClellan's difficulties had not escaped the observation of his watchful adversaries, and on the morning of May 31 the Federal lines were heavily attacked by Johnston. The left of the position on the south side of the Chickahominy was protected by the White Oak Swamp, a broad and almost impassable morass; but the right, thrown back to the river, was unprotected by intrenchments, and thinly manned. The defence of the first line had been assigned to one corps only; the second was five miles in rear. The assailants should have won an easy triumph. But if McClellan had shown but little skill in the distribution of his troops on the defensive, the Confederate arrangements for attack were even more at fault. The country between Richmond and the Chickahominy is level and well wooded. It was intersected by several roads, three of which led directly to the enemy's position. But the roads were bad, and a tremendous rain-storm, which broke on the night of the 30th, transformed the fields into tracts of greasy mud, and rendered the passage of artillery difficult. The natural obstacles, however, were not the chief.

The force detailed for the attack amounted to 40,000 men, or twenty-three brigades. The Federal works were but five miles from Richmond, and the Confederates were ordered to advance at dawn. But it was the first time that an offensive movement on so large a scale had been

attempted; the woods and swamps made supervision difficult, and the staff proved unequal to the task of ensuring
co-operation. The orders for attack were badly framed.
The subordinate generals did not clearly comprehend what
was expected from them. There were misunderstandings
as to the roads to be followed, and as to who was to command
the wings. The columns crossed, and half the day was
wasted in getting into position. It was not till 1 P.M. that the
first gun was fired, and not till 4 P.M. that the commanding
general, stationed with the left wing, was made acquainted
with the progress of his right and centre. When it was at
last delivered, the attack was piecemeal; and although successful in driving the enemy from his intrenchments, it
failed to drive him from the field. The Federals fell back
to a second line of earthworks, and were strongly reinforced from beyond the river. During the battle Johnston
himself was severely wounded, and the command devolved
on General G. W. Smith. Orders were issued that the
attack should be renewed next morning; but for reasons
which have never been satisfactorily explained, only five of
the twenty-three brigades were actively engaged, and the
battle of Seven Pines ended with the unmolested retreat
of the Confederates. Smith fell sick, and General Lee
was ordered by the President to take command of the
army in the field.

McClellan, thanks to the bad work of the Confederate
staff at the battle of Seven Pines, had now succeeded in
securing the passages across the Chickahominy. But for the
present he had given up all idea of an immediate advance.
Two of his army corps had suffered severely, both in men and
in *moral;* the roads were practically impassable for artillery;
the bridges over the Chickahominy had been much injured
by the floods; and it was imperative to re-establish the communications. Such is his own explanation of his inactivity;
but his official correspondence with the Secretary of War
leaves no doubt that his hope of being reinforced by McDowell
was a still more potent reason. During the first three weeks
in June he received repeated assurances from Mr. Stanton
that large bodies of troops were on their way to join him,

and it was for these that he was waiting. This expectant attitude, due to McDowell's non-arrival, entailed on him a serious disadvantage. If he transferred his whole army to the right bank of the Chickahominy, his line of supply, the railway to West Point, would be exposed; and, secondly, when McDowell approached from Fredericksburg, it would be possible for Lee to drive that general back before the Army of the Potomac could give him direct support, or in any case to cut off all communication with him. McClellan was consequently compelled to retain his right wing north of the river; and indeed in so doing he was only obeying his instructions. On May 18 Stanton had telegraphed: 'You are instructed to co-operate so as to establish this communication [with McDowell], by extending your right wing north of Richmond.'

The Federal army, then, whilst awaiting the promised reinforcements, was divided into two parts by a stream which another storm might render impassable. It will thus be seen that Jackson's operations not only deprived McClellan of the immediate aid of 40,000 men and 100 guns, but placed him in a most embarrassing situation. 'The faulty location of the Union army,' says General Porter, commanding the Fifth Federal Army Corps, 'was from the first realised by General McClellan, and became daily an increasing cause of care and anxiety; not the least disturbing element of which was the impossibility of quickly reinforcing his right wing or promptly withdrawing it to the south bank.'[1]

Seeing that the Confederates were no more than 60,000 strong, while the invading army mustered 100,000, it would seem that the knot should have been cut by an immediate attack on the Richmond lines. But McClellan, who had been United States Commissioner in the Crimea, knew something of the strength of earthworks; and moreover, although the comparatively feeble numbers developed by the Confederates at Seven Pines should have enlightened him, he still believed that his enemy's army was far larger than his own. So, notwithstanding his danger, he pre-

[1] *Battles and Leaders*, vol. ii., p. 324.

ferred to postpone his advance till Jackson's defeat should set McDowell free.

Fatal was the mistake which retained McDowell's divisions in the Valley, and sent Shields in pursuit of Jackson. While the Federal army, waiting for reinforcements, lay astride the noisome swamps of the Chickahominy, Lee was preparing a counterstroke on the largest scale.

The first thing to do was to reduce the disparity of numbers; and to effect this troops were to be brought up from the south, Jackson was to come to Richmond, and McDowell was to be kept away. This last was of more importance than the rest, and, at the same time, more difficult of attainment. Jackson was certainly nearer to Richmond than was McDowell; but to defeat McClellan would take some time, and it was essential that Jackson should have a long start, and not arrive upon the battle-field with McDowell on his heels. It was necessary, therefore, that the greater part of the latter's force should be detained on the Shenandoah; and on June 8, while Cross Keys was being fought, Lee wrote to Jackson: ' Should there be nothing requiring your attention in the Valley, so as to prevent you leaving it in a few days, and you can make arrangements to deceive the enemy and impress him with the idea of your presence, please let me know, that you may unite at the decisive moment with the army near Richmond. Make your arrangements accordingly; but should an opportunity occur of striking the enemy a successful blow, do not let it escape you.'

At the same time a detachment of 7,000 infantry was ordered to the Valley. ' Your recent successes,' wrote Lee on the 11th, when the news of Cross Keys and

June 11. Port Republic had been received, ' have been the cause of the liveliest joy in this army as well as in the country. The admiration excited by your skill and boldness has been constantly mingled with solicitude for your situation. The practicability of reinforcing you has been the subject of gravest consideration. It has been determined to do so at the expense of weakening this army. Brigadier-General Lawton with six regiments from Georgia is on his way to you, and Brigadier-General Whiting with eight veteran regiments leaves here to-day. The object is to enable you to crush the forces opposed to you. Leave your enfeebled troops to watch the country and guard the passes covered by your cavalry and artillery, and with your main body, including Ewell's division and Lawton's and Whiting's commands, move rapidly to Ashland by rail or otherwise, as you may find most advantageous, and sweep down between the Chickahominy and the Pamunkey, cutting up the enemy's communications, &c., while this army attacks McClellan in front. He will then, I think, be forced to come out of his intrenchments, where he is strongly posted on the Chickahominy, and apparently preparing to move by gradual approaches on Richmond.' [1]

Before the reinforcements reached the Valley both Frémont and Shields were out of reach. To have followed them down the Valley would have been injudicious. Another victory would have doubtless held McDowell fast, but it would have drawn Jackson too far from Richmond. The Confederate generals, therefore, in order to impose upon their enemies, and to maintain the belief that Washington was threatened, had recourse to stratagem. The departure of Whiting and Lawton for the Valley was ostentatiously announced. Federal prisoners, about to be dismissed upon parole, were allowed to see the trains full of soldiers proceeding westward, to count the regiments, and learn their destination. Thus Lee played his part in the game of deception, and meanwhile Jackson had taken active measures to the same end.

Frémont had retired from Port Republic on the morning of the 10th. On the 11th the Confederate cavalry, now under Colonel Munford, a worthy successor of the indefatigable Ashby, crossed the Shenandoah, and followed the retreating enemy. So active was the pursuit that Frémont evacuated Harrisonburg, abandoning two hundred wounded

[1] O. R., vol. xii., part iii., p. 910.

in the hospitals, besides medical and other stores. 'Significant demonstrations of the enemy,' to use his own words, drove him next day from the strong position at

June 14.   Mount Jackson ; and on June 14 he fell back to Strasburg, Banks, who had advanced to Middletown, being in close support.

On the 12th the Army of the Valley had once more moved westward, and, crossing South River, had encamped in the woods near Mount Meridian. Here for five days, by the sparkling waters of the Shenandoah, the wearied soldiers rested, while their indefatigable leader employed ruse after ruse to delude the enemy. The cavalry, though far from support, was ordered to manœuvre boldly to prevent all information reaching the Federals, and to follow Frémont so long as he retreated.[1] The bearers of flags of truce were impressed with the idea that the Southerners were advancing in great strength. The outpost line was made as close as possible ; no civilians were allowed to pass ; and the troopers, so that they should have nothing to tell if they were captured, were kept in ignorance of the position of their own infantry. The general's real intentions were concealed from everyone except Colonel Munford. The officers of the staff fared worse than the remainder of the army. Not only were they debarred from their commander's confidence, but they became the unconscious instruments whereby false intelligence was spread. 'The engineers were directed to prepare a series of maps of the Valley ; and all who acquired a knowledge of this carefully divulged order told their friends in confidence that Jackson was going at once in pursuit of Frémont. As those friends told their friends without loss of time, it was soon the well-settled conviction of everybody that nothing was further from Jackson's intention than an evacuation of the Valley.'

June 17.   On June 17 arrived a last letter from Lee :—
'From your account of the position of the enemy I think it would be difficult for you to engage him in time to unite with this army in the battle for Richmond. Frémont

[1] 'The only true rule for cavalry is to follow as long as the enemy retreats.' —Jackson to Munford, June 13.

and Shields are apparently retrograding, their troops shaken and disorganised, and some time will be required to set them again in the field. If this is so, the sooner you unite with this army the better. McClellan is being strengthened. . . . There is much sickness in his ranks, but his reinforcements by far exceed his losses. The present, therefore, seems to be favourable for a junction of your army and this. If you agree with me, the sooner you can make arrangements to do so the better. In moving your troops you could let it be understood that it was to pursue the enemy in your front. Dispose those to hold the Valley, so as to deceive the enemy, keeping your cavalry well in their front, and at the proper time suddenly descending upon the Pamunkey. To be efficacious the movement must be secret. Let me know the force you can bring, and be careful to guard from friends and foes your purpose and your intention of personally leaving the Valley. The country is full of spies, and our plans are immediately carried to the enemy.' [1]

The greater part of these instructions Jackson had already carried out on his own initiative. There remained but to give final directions to Colonel Munford, who was to hold the Valley, and to set the army in motion. Munford was instructed to do his best to spread false reports of an advance to the Potomac. Ewell's division was ordered to Charlottesville. The rest of the Valley troops were to follow Ewell; and Whiting and Lawton, who, in order to bewilder Frémont, had been marched from Staunton to Mount Meridian, and then back to Staunton, were to take train to Gordonsville. It was above all things important that the march should be secret. Not only was it essential that Lincoln should not be alarmed into reinforcing McClellan, but it was of even more importance that McClellan should not be alarmed into correcting the faulty distribution of his army. So long as he remained with half his force on one bank of the Chickahominy and half on the other, Lee had a fair chance of concentrating superior numbers against one of the fractions. But if McClellan, warned of Jackson's

---

[1] O. R., vol. xii., part iii., p. 913.

approach, were to mass his whole force on one bank or the other, there would be little hope of success for the Confederates.

The ultimate object of the movement was therefore revealed to no one, and the most rigorous precautions were adopted to conceal it. Jackson s letters from Richmond, in accordance with his own instructions, bore no more explicit address than 'Somewhere.' A long line of cavalry, occupying every road, covered the front, and prevented anyone, soldier or civilian, preceding them toward Richmond. Far out to either flank rode patrols of horsemen, and a strong rear-guard swept before it campfollowers and stragglers. At night, every road which approached the bivouacs was strongly picketed, and the troops were prevented from communicating with the country people. The men were forbidden to ask the names of the villages through which they passed; and it was ordered that to all questions they should make the one answer: 'I don't know.' 'This was just as much license as the men wanted,' says an eye-witness, 'and they forthwith knew nothing of the past, present, or future.' An amusing incident, it is said, grew out of this order. One of General Hood's [1] Texans left the ranks on the march, and was climbing a fence to go to a cherry-tree near at hand, when Jackson rode by and saw him.

'Where are you going?' asked the general.

'I don't know,' replied the soldier.

'To what command do you belong?'

'I don't know.'

'Well, what State are you from?'

'I don't know.'

'What is the meaning of all this?' asked Jackson of another.

'Well,' was the reply, 'Old Stonewall and General Hood gave orders yesterday that we were not to know anything until after the next fight.'

Jackson laughed and rode on.[2]

The men themselves, intelligent as they were, were

[1] Whiting's division.   [2] Cooke, p. 205.

unable to penetrate their general's design. When they reached Charlottesville it was reported in the ranks that the next march would be northwards, to check a movement of Banks across the Blue Ridge. At Gordonsville it was supposed that they would move on Washington.

'I recollect,' says one of the Valley soldiers, 'that the pastor of the Presbyterian church there, with whom Jackson spent the night, told me, as a profound secret, not to be breathed to mortal man, that we would move at daybreak on Culpeper Court House to intercept a column of the enemy coming across the mountains. He said there could be no mistake about this, for he had it from General Jackson himself. We did move at daybreak, but instead of moving on Culpeper Court House we marched in the opposite direction. At Hanover Junction we expected to head towards Fredericksburg to meet McDowell, and the whole movement was so secretly conducted that the troops were uncertain of their destination until the evening of June 26, when they heard A. P. Hill's guns at Mechanicsville, and made the woods vibrate with their shouts of anticipated victory.' [1]

At Gordonsville a rumour, which proved to be false, arrested the march of the army for a whole day. On the 21st the leading division arrived at Frederickshall, fifty miles from Richmond, and there halted for the Sunday. They had already marched fifty miles, and the main body, although the railway had been of much service, was still distant. There was not sufficient rolling stock available to transport all the infantry simultaneously, and, in any case, the cavalry, artillery, and waggons must have proceeded by road. The trains, therefore, moving backwards and forwards along the line, and taking up the rear brigades in succession, forwarded them in a couple of hours a whole day's march. Beyond Frederickshall the line had been destroyed by the enemy's cavalry.

At 1 A.M. on Monday morning, Jackson, accompanied by a single orderly, rode to confer with Lee, near Richmond. He was provided with a pass, which Major Dabney had

[1] Communicated by the Rev. J. W. Jones, D.D.

been instructed to procure from General Whiting, the next
in command, authorising him to impress horses;
           and he had resorted to other expedients to blind
his friends.   The lady of the house which he had made his
headquarters at Frederickshall had sent to ask if the general
would breakfast with her next morning.   He replied that he
would be glad to do so if he were there at breakfast time;
and upon her inquiry as to the time that would be most
convenient, he said: 'Have it at your usual time, and
send for me when it is ready.'   When Mrs. Harris sent for
him, Jim, his coloured servant, replied to the message:
'Sh! you don't 'spec' to find the general here at this hour,
do you?   He left here 'bout midnight, and I 'spec' by this
time he's whippin' Banks in the Valley.'

During the journey his determination to preserve his
incognito was the cause of some embarrassment.   A few
miles from his quarters he was halted by a sentry.   It was
in vain that he represented that he was an officer on duty,
carrying dispatches.   The sentry, one of the Stonewall
Brigade, was inexorable, and quoted Jackson's own
orders.   The utmost that he would concede was that the commander of the picket should be called.   When this officer
came he recognised his general.   Jackson bound them
both to secrecy, and praising the soldier for his obedience,
continued his ride.   Some hours later his horse broke
down.   Proceeding to a plantation near the road, he
told his orderly to request that a couple of horses
might be supplied for an officer on important duty.
It was still dark, and the indignant proprietor, so
unceremoniously disturbed by two unknown soldiers, who
declined to give their names, refused all aid.   After some
parley Jackson and his orderly, finding argument wasted,
proceeded to the stables, selected the two best horses,
shifted the saddles, and left their own chargers as a
temporary exchange.

At three o'clock in the afternoon, after passing rapidly
through Richmond, he reached the headquarters of the
Commander-in-Chief.   It is unfortunate that no record of
the meeting that took place has been preserved.   There

were present, besides Lee and Jackson, the three officers
whose divisions were to be employed in the attack upon
the Federals, Longstreet, A. P. Hill, and D. H. Hill.   The
names of the two former are associated with almost every
Confederate victory won upon the soil of Virginia.   They
were trusted by their great leader, and they were idolised
by their men.   Like others, they made mistakes; the one
was sometimes slow, the other careless; neither gave
the slightest sign that they were capable of independent
command, and both were at times impatient of control.
But, taking them all in all, they were gallant soldiers,
brave to a fault, vigorous in attack, and undaunted by
adverse fortune.   Longstreet, sturdy and sedate, his ' old
war-horse' as Lee affectionately called him, bore on his
broad shoulders the weight of twenty years' service in the
old army.   Hill's slight figure and delicate features, instinct
with life and energy, were a marked contrast to the heavier
frame and rugged lineaments of his older colleague.

   Already they were distinguished.   In the hottest of the
fight they had won the respect that soldiers so readily accord
to valour; yet it is not on these stubborn fighters, not
on their companion, less popular, but hardly less capable,
that the eye of imagination rests.   Were some great
painter, gifted with the sense of historic fitness, to place on
his canvas the council in the Virginia homestead, two
figures only would occupy the foreground: the one weary
with travel, white with the dust of many leagues, and
bearing on his frayed habiliments the traces of rough
bivouacs and mountain roads; the other, tall, straight,
and stately; still, for all his fifty years, remarkable for his
personal beauty, and endowed with all the simple dignity
of a noble character and commanding intellect.   In that
humble chamber, where the only refreshment the Commander-in-Chief could offer was a glass of milk, Lee and
Jackson met for the first time since the war had begun.
Lee's hours of triumph had yet to come.   The South was
aware that he was sage in council; he had yet to prove his
mettle in the field.   But there was at least one Virginia
soldier who knew his worth.   With the prescient sympathy

of a kindred spirit Jackson had divined his daring and his genius, and although he held always to his own opinions, he had no will but that of his great commander. With how absolute a trust his devotion was repaid one of the brightest pages in the history of Virginia tells us; a year crowded with victories bears witness to the strength begotten of their mutual confidence. So long as Lee and Jackson led her armies hope shone on the standards of the South. Great was the constancy of her people; wonderful the fortitude of her soldiers; but on the shoulders of her twin heroes rested the burden of the tremendous struggle.

To his four major-generals Lee explained his plan of attack, and then, retiring to his office, left them to arrange the details. It will be sufficient for the present to state that Jackson's troops were to encamp on the night of the 25th east of Ashland, fifteen miles north of Richmond, between the village and the Virginia Central Railway. The day following the interview, the 24th, he returned to his command, rejoining the column at Beaver Dam Station.

His advanced guard were now within forty miles of Richmond, and, so far from McDowell being on his heels, that June 24. general was still north of Fredericksburg. No reinforcements could reach McClellan for several days; the Confederates were concentrated round Richmond in full strength; and Lee's strategy had been entirely successful. Moreover, with such skill had Jackson's march been made that the Federal generals were absolutely ignorant of his whereabouts. McClellan indeed seems to have had some vague suspicion of his approach; but Lincoln, McDowell, Banks, Frémont, together with the whole of the Northern people and the Northern press, believed that he was still west of Gordonsville. Neither scout, spy, nor patrol was able to penetrate the cordon of Munford's outposts. Beyond his pickets, strongly posted at New Market and Conrad's Store, all was dim and dark. Had Jackson halted, awaiting reinforcements? Was he already in motion, marching swiftly and secretly against some isolated garrison? Was he planning another dash on Washington, this time with a larger army at his back? Would his advance be east or west of the Blue Ridge, across the sources of the Rappahannock, or through the Alleghanies? Had he 15,000 men or 50,000?

Such were the questions which obtruded themselves on the Federal generals, and not one could give a satisfactory reply. That a blow was preparing, and that it would fall where it was least expected, all men knew. 'We have a determined and enterprising enemy to contend with,' wrote one of Lincoln's generals. 'Jackson,' said another, 'marches thirty miles a day.' The successive surprises of the Valley campaign had left their mark; and the correspondence preserved in the Official Records is in itself the highest tribute to Jackson's skill. He had gained something more than the respect of his enemies. He had brought them to fear his name, and from the Potomac to the Rappahannock uncertainty and apprehension reigned supreme. Not a patrol was sent out which did not expect to meet the Confederate columns, pressing swiftly northward; not a general along the whole line, from Romney to Fredericksburg, who did not tremble for his own security.

There was sore trouble on the Shenandoah. The disasters of M'Dowell and Front Royal had taught the Federal officers that when the Valley army was reported to be sixty miles distant, it was probably deploying in the nearest forest; and with the rout of Winchester still fresh in their memories they knew that pursuit would be as vigorous as attack would be sudden. The air was full of rumours, each more alarming than its predecessor, and all of them contradictory. The reports of the cavalry, of spies, of prisoners, of deserters, of escaped negroes, told each a different story.

Jackson, it was at first reported, had been reinforced to the number of 35,000 men.[1] A few days later his army had swelled to 60,000 with 70 guns, and he was rebuilding the bridge at Port Republic in order to follow Frémont.

[1] The telegrams and letters containing the reports quoted on pages 399–400 are to be found in O. R., vol. xi., part iii., and vol. xii., part iii.

On June 13 he was believed to be moving through Charlottesville against one or other of McDowell's divisions. 'He
was either going against Shields at Luray, or King at Catlett's, or Doubleday at Fredericksburg, or going to Richmond.' On the 16th it was absolutely certain that he was
within striking distance of Front Royal. On the 18th he
had gone to Richmond, but Ewell was still in the Valley with
40,000 men. On the 19th Banks had no doubt but that
another immediate movement down the Valley was intended
' with 30,000 or more.' On the 20th Jackson was said to be
moving on Warrenton, east of the Blue Ridge. On the
22nd ' reliable persons' at Harper's Ferry had learned that
he was about to attack Banks at Middletown; and on the
same day Ewell, who was actually near Frederickshall, was
discovered to be moving on Moorefield! On the 25th Frémont had been informed that large reinforcements had
reached Jackson from Tennessee; and Banks was on the
watch for a movement from the west. Frémont heard
that Ewell designed to attack Winchester in rear, and the
threat from so dangerous a quarter made Lincoln anxious.

'We have no definite information,' wrote Stanton
to McClellan, ' as to the numbers or position of Jackson's
force. Within the last two days the evidence is strong
that for some purpose the enemy is circulating rumours of
Jackson's advance in various directions, with a view to
conceal the real point of attack. Neither McDowell nor
Banks nor Frémont appear to have any accurate knowledge of the subject.'

This was on June 25, the day the Valley army halted
at Ashland; but the climax was reached on the 28th. For
forty-eight hours Jackson had been fighting McClellan, yet
Banks, although ' quite confident that he was not within
thirty miles, believed that he was preparing for an attack
on Middletown.' To reach Middletown Jackson would have
had to march one hundred and fifty miles!

Under the influence of these rumours the movements of
the Federal troops were erratic in the extreme.

Frémont, who had originally been ordered to remain at
Harrisonburg, had fallen back on Banks at Middletown,

although ordered to Front Royal, was most reluctant to move so far south. Shields was first ordered to stand fast at Luray, where he would be reinforced by Ricketts, and was then ordered to fall back on Front Royal. Reinforcements were ordered to Romney, to Harper's Ferry, and to Winchester; and McDowell, who kept his head throughout, struggled in vain to reunite his scattered divisions. Divining the true drift of the Confederate strategy, he realised that to protect Washington, and to rescue McClellan, the surest method was for his own army corps to march as rapidly as possible to the Chickahominy. But his pleadings were disregarded. Lincoln and Stanton had not yet discovered that the best defence is generally a vigorous attack. They had learned nothing from the Valley campaign, and they were infected with the fears of Banks and Frémont. Jackson was well on his way to Richmond before Shields and Ricketts were permitted to cross the Blue Ridge; and it was not till the 25th that McDowell's corps was once more concentrated at Fredericksburg. The Confederates had gained a start of five marches, and the Northern Government was still ignorant that they had left the Valley.

McClellan was equally in the dark. Faint rumours had preceded the march of Jackson's army, but he had given them scant credit. On the morning of the 26th, however, he was rudely enlightened. It was but too clear that Jackson, strongly reinforced from Richmond, was bearing down upon his most vulnerable point—his right wing, which, in anticipation of McDowell's advance, remained exposed on the north bank of the Chickahominy.

Nor was this the sum of his troubles. On this same day, when his outposts were falling back before superior numbers, and the Valley regiments were closing round their flank, he received a telegram from Stanton, informing him that the forces commanded by McDowell, Banks, and Frémont were to form one army under Major-General Pope; and that this army was ' to attack and overcome the rebel forces under Jackson and Ewell, and threaten the enemy in the direction of Charlottesville!' All hope of succour passed away, and the ' Young Napoleon ' was left to extricate himself, as best he could, from his many difficulties; difficulties which were due in part to his own political blindness, in part to the ignorance of Lincoln, but, in a far larger degree, to the consummate strategy of Lee and Jackson.

NOTE

The Marches in the Valley Campaign, March 22 to June 25, 1862

		Miles	
March 22.	Mount Jackson—Strasburg	22	
„ 23.	Strasburg—Kernstown—Newtown	18	Battle of Kernstown.
„ 24–26.	Newtown—Mt. Jackson	35	
April 17–19.	Mt. Jackson—Elk Run Valley	50	
„ 30–May 3.	Elk Run Valley—Mechum's River Station	60	
May 7–8.	Staunton—Shenandoah Mt.	32	Battle of M'Dowell.
„ 9–11.	Bull Pasture Mount—Franklin	30	Skirmishes.
„ 12–15.	Franklin—Lebanon Springs	40	
„ 17.	Lebanon Springs—Bridgewater	18	
„ 19–20.	Bridgewater—New Market	24	
„ 21.	New Market—Luray	12	
„ 22.	Luray—Milford	12	
„ 23.	Milford — Front Royal — Cedarville	22	Action at Front Royal.
„ 24.	Cedarville—Abraham's Creek	22	Action at Middletown and Newtown.
„ 25.	Abraham's Creek—Stevenson's	7	Battle of Winchester.
„ 28.	Stevenson's—Charlestown	15	Skirmish.
„ 29.	Charlestown—Halltown	5	Skirmish.
„ 30.	Halltown—Winchester	25	
„ 31.	Winchester—Strasburg	18	
June 1.	Strasburg—Woodstock	12	Skirmish.
„ 2.	Woodstock—Mount Jackson	12	
„ 3.	Mount Jackson—New Market	7	
„ 4–5.	New Market—Port Republic	30	
„ 8.	. . . . . .		Battle of Cross Keys.
„ 9.	Cross Keys—Brown's Gap	16	Battle of Port Republic.
„ 12.	Brown's Gap—Mount Meridian	10	
„ 17–25.	Mount Meridian — Ashland Station (one rest day)	120	
		676	miles in 48 marching days. Average 14 miles per diem.

CHAPTER XII

REVIEW OF THE VALLEY CAMPAIGN

IN March, 1862, more than 200,000 Federals were prepared to invade Virginia. McClellan, before McDowell
was withheld, reckoned on placing 150,000 men at West
Point. Frémont, in West Virginia, commanded 30,000,
including the force in the Kanawha Valley; and Banks
had crossed the Potomac with over 30,000.

Less than 60,000 Confederate soldiers were available to
oppose this enormous host, and the numerical disproportion
was increased by the vast material resources of the North.
The only advantages which the Southerners possessed were
that they were operating in their own country, and that
their cavalry was the more efficient. Their leaders, therefore, could count on receiving more ample and more
accurate information than their adversaries.[1] But, except
in these respects, everything was against them. In mettle
and in discipline the troops were fairly matched. On both
sides the higher commands, with few exceptions, were held
by regular officers, who had received the same training.
On both sides the staff was inexperienced. If the Confederate infantry were better marksmen than the majority
of the Federals, they were not so well armed; and the
Federal artillery, both in *matériel* and in handling, was
the more efficient.

The odds against the South were great; and to those
who believed that Providence sides with the big battalions,

---

[1] 'If I were mindful only of my own glory, I would choose always to
make war in my own country, for there every man is a spy, and the enemy
can make no movement of which I am not informed.'—Frederick the Great's
Instructions to his Generals.

that numbers, armament, discipline, and tactical efficiency, are all that is required to ensure success, the fall of Richmond must have seemed inevitable.

But within three months of the day that McClellan started for the Peninsula the odds had been much reduced. The Confederates had won no startling victories. Except in the Valley, and there only small detachments were concerned, the fighting had been indecisive. The North had no reason to believe that her soldiers, save only the cavalry, were in any way inferior to their adversaries. And yet, on June 26, where were the 'big battalions?' 105,000 men were intrenched within sight of the spires of Richmond; but where were the rest? Where were the 70,000[1] that should have aided McClellan, have encircled the rebel capital on every side, cut the communications, closed the sources of supply, and have overwhelmed the starving garrison? How came it that Frémont and Banks were no further south than they were in March? that the Shenandoah Valley still poured its produce into Richmond? that McDowell had not yet crossed the Rappahannock? What mysterious power had compelled Lincoln to retain a force larger than the whole Confederate army 'to protect the national capital from danger and insult?'

It was not hard fighting. The Valley campaign, from Kernstown to Port Republic, had not cost the Federals more than 7,000 men; and, with the exception of Cross Keys, the battles had been well contested. It was not the difficulties of supply or movement. It was not absence of information; for until Jackson vanished from the sight of both friend and foe on June 17, spies and 'contrabands'[2] (i.e. fugitive slaves) had done good work. Nor was it want of will on the part of the Northern Government. None

---

[1] At the date of the action at Front Royal, May 23, the following was the strength of the detached forces: Banks, 10,000; Frémont, 25,000; McDowell (including Shields, but excluding McCall), 35,000.

[2] The blacks, however, appear to have been as unreliable as regards numbers as McClellan's detectives. 'If a negro were asked how many Confederates he had seen at a certain point, his answer was very likely to be: "I dunno, Massa, but I guess about a million."'—McClellan's Own Story, p. 254.

were more anxious than Lincoln and Stanton to capture
Richmond, to disperse the rebels, and to restore the Union.
They had made stupendous efforts to organise a sufficient
army. To equip that army as no army had ever been
equipped before they had spared neither expense nor
labour ; and it can hardly be denied that they had created
a vast machine, perhaps in part imperfect, but, considering the weakness of the enemy, not ill-adapted for the work
before it.

There was but one thing they had overlooked, and that
was that their host would require intelligent control. So
complete was the mechanism, so simple a matter it
appeared to set the machine in motion, and to keep it in
the right course, that they believed that their untutored
hands, guided by common-sense and sound abilities,
were perfectly capable of guiding it, without mishap, to the
appointed goal. Men who, aware of their ignorance, would
probably have shrunk from assuming charge of a squad
of infantry in action, had no hesitation whatever in
attempting to direct a mighty army, a task which Napoleon
has assured us requires profound study, incessant application, and wide experience.[1]

They were in fact ignorant—and how many statesmen,
and even soldiers, are in like case ?—that strategy, the art of
manœuvring armies, is an art in itself, an art which none
may master by the light of nature, but to which, if he is to
attain success, a man must serve a long apprenticeship.

The rules of strategy are few and simple. They may
be learned in a week. They may be taught by familiar
illustrations or a dozen diagrams. But such knowledge
will no more teach a man to lead an army like Napoleon

[1] ' In consequence of the excessive growth of armies tactics have lost
in weight, and the strategical design, rather than the detail of the movements, has become the decisive factor in the issue of a campaign. The
strategical design depends, as a rule, upon the decision of cabinets, and
upon the resources placed at the disposal of the commander. Consequently,
either the leading statesmen should have correct views of the science of
war, or should make up for their ignorance by giving their entire confidence
to the man to whom the supreme command of the army is entrusted.
Otherwise, the germs of defeat and national ruin may be contained in the
first preparations for war.'—*The Archduke Charles of Austria.*

than a knowledge of grammar will teach him to write like Gibbon. Lincoln, when the army he had so zealously toiled to organise, reeled back in confusion from Virginia, set himself to learn the art of war. He collected, says his biographer, a great library of military books; and, if it were not pathetic, it would be almost ludicrous, to read of the great President, in the midst of his absorbing labours and his ever-growing anxieties, poring night after night, when his capital was asleep, over the pages of Jomini and Clausewitz. And what was the result? In 1864, when Grant was appointed to the command of the Union armies, he said: 'I neither ask nor desire to know anything of your plans. Take the responsibility and act, and call on me for assistance.' He had learned at last that no man is a born strategist.

The mistakes of Lincoln and Stanton are not to be condoned by pointing to McClellan.

McClellan designed the plan for the invasion of Virginia, and the plan failed. But this is not to say that the plan was in itself a bad one. Nine times out of ten it would have succeeded. In many respects it was admirable. It did away with a long line of land communications, passing through a hostile country. It brought the naval power of the Federals into combination with the military. It secured two great waterways, the York and the James, by which the army could be easily supplied, which required no guards, and by which heavy ordnance could be brought up to bombard the fortifications of Richmond. But it had one flaw. It left Washington, in the opinion of the President and of the nation, insecure; and this flaw, which would have escaped the notice of an ordinary enemy, was at once detected by Lee and Jackson. Moreover, had McClellan been left in control of the whole theatre of war, Jackson's manœuvres would probably have failed to produce so decisive an effect. The fight at Kernstown would not have induced McClellan to strike 40,000 men off the strength of the invading army. He had not been deceived when Jackson threatened Harper's Ferry at the end of May. The reinforcements sent from Richmond after Port Republic

had not blinded him, nor did he for a moment believe that
Washington was in actual danger.   There is this, however,
to be said : had McClellan been in sole command, public
opinion, alarmed for Washington, would have possibly
compelled him to do exactly what Lincoln did, and to
retain nearly half the army on the Potomac.

So much for the leading of civilians.   On the other
hand, the failure of the Federals to concentrate more
than 105,000 men at the decisive point, and even to
establish those 105,000 in a favourable position, was
mainly due to the superior strategy of the Confederates.
Those were indeed skilful manoeuvres which prevented
McDowell from marching to the Chickahominy ; and, at
the critical moment, when Lee was on the point of
attacking McClellan, which drew McDowell, Banks, and
Frémont on a wild-goose chase towards Charlottesville.
The weak joint in the enemy's armour, the national anxiety
for Washington, was early recognised.   Kernstown induced
Lincoln, departing from the original scheme of operations,
to form four independent armies, each acting on a different
line.   Two months later, when McClellan was near Richmond, and it was of essential importance that the movements of these armies should be combined, Jackson once
more intervened ; Banks was driven across the Potomac,
and again the Federal concentration was postponed.   Lastly,
the battles of Cross Keys and Port Republic, followed by
the despatch of Whiting and Lawton to the Valley, led the
Northern President to commit his worst mistake.   For the
second time the plan of campaign was changed, and
McClellan was left isolated at the moment he most needed
help.

The brains of two great leaders had done more for
the Confederacy than 200,000 soldiers had done for the
Union.   Without quitting his desk, and leaving the execution of his plans to Jackson, Lee had relieved Richmond
of the pressure of 70,000 Federals, and had lured the
remainder into the position he most wished to find them.
The Confederacy, notwithstanding the enormous disparity of
force, had once more gained the upper hand ; and from this

instance, as from a score of others, it may be deduced that Providence is more inclined to side with the big brains than with the big battalions.

It was not mere natural ability that had triumphed. Lee, in this respect, was assuredly not more highly gifted than Lincoln, or Jackson than McClellan. But, whether by accident or design, Davis had selected for command of the Confederate army, and had retained in the Valley, two past masters in the art of strategy. If it was accident he was singularly favoured by fortune. He might have selected many soldiers of high rank and long service, who would have been as innocent of strategical skill as Lincoln himself. His choice might have fallen on the most dashing leader, the strictest disciplinarian, the best drill, in the Confederate army; and yet the man who united all these qualities might have been altogether ignorant of the higher art of war. Mr. Davis himself had been a soldier. He was a graduate of West Point, and in the Mexican campaign he had commanded a volunteer regiment with much distinction. But as a director of military operations he was a greater marplot than even Stanton. It by no means follows that because a man has lived his life in camp and barrack, has long experience of command, and even long experience of war, that he can apply the rules of strategy before the enemy. In the first place he may lack the character, the inflexible resolution, the broad grasp, the vivid imagination, the power of patient thought, the cool head, and, above all, the moral courage. In the second place, there are few schools where strategy may be learned, and, in any case, a long and laborious course of study is the only means of acquiring the capacity to handle armies and outwit an equal adversary. The light of common-sense alone is insufficient; nor will a few months' reading give more than a smattering of knowledge.

'Read and *re-read*,' said Napoleon, 'the eighty-eight campaigns of Alexander, Hannibal, Cæsar, Gustavus, Turenne, Eugène, and Frederick. Take them as your models, for it is the only means of becoming a great leader, and of mastering the secrets of the art of war. Your intelligence, enlightened by such study, will then reject methods contrary to those adopted by these great men.'

In America, as elsewhere, it had not been recognised before the Civil War, even by the military authorities, that if armies are to be handled with success they must be directed by trained strategists. No *Kriegsakademie* or its equivalent existed in the United States, and the officers whom common-sense induced to follow the advice of Napoleon had to pursue their studies by themselves. To these the campaigns of the great Emperor offered an epitome of all that had gone before; the campaigns of Washington explained how the principles of the art might be best applied to their own country, and Mexico had supplied them with practical experience. Of the West Point graduates there were many who had acquired from these sources a wide knowledge of the art of generalship, and among them were no more earnest students than the three Virginians, Lee, Jackson, and Johnston.

When Jackson accepted an appointment for the Military Institute, it was with the avowed intention of training his intellect for war. In his retirement at Lexington he had kept before his eyes the possibility that he might some day be recalled to the Army. He had already acquired such practical knowledge of his profession as the United States service could afford. He had become familiar with the characteristics of the regular soldier. He knew how to command, to maintain discipline, and the regulations were at his fingers' ends. A few years had been sufficient to teach him all that could be learned from the routine of a regiment, as they had been sufficient to teach Napoleon, Frederick, and Lee. But there remained over and above the intellectual part of war, and with characteristic thoroughness he had set himself to master it. His reward came quickly. The Valley campaign practically saved Richmond. In a few short months the quiet gentleman of Lexington became, in the estimation of both friend and foe, a very thunderbolt of war; and his name, which a year previous had hardly been known beyond the Valley, was already famous.

It is, perhaps, true that Johnston and Lee had a larger share in Jackson's success than has been generally recognised. It was due to Johnston that Jackson was retained in the Valley when McClellan moved to the Peninsula ; and his, too, was the fundamental idea of the campaign, that the Federals in the Valley were to be prevented from reinforcing the army which threatened Richmond. To Lee belongs still further credit. From the moment he assumed command we find the Confederate operations directed on a definite and well-considered plan : a defensive attitude round Richmond, a vigorous offensive in the Valley, leading to the dispersion of the enemy, and a Confederate concentration on the Chickahominy. His operations were very bold. When McClellan, with far superior numbers, was already within twenty miles of Richmond, he had permitted Jackson to retain Ewell's 8,000 in the Valley, and he would have given him the brigades of Branch and Mahone. From Lee, too, came the suggestion that a blow should be struck at Banks, that he should be driven back to the Potomac, and that the North should be threatened with invasion. From him, too, at a moment when McClellan's breastworks could be actually seen from Rich mond, came the 7,000 men under Whiting and Lawton, the news of whose arrival in the Valley had spread such conster- nation amongst the Federals. But it is to be remembered that Jackson viewed the situation in exactly the same light as his superiors. The instructions he received were exactly the instructions he would have given had he been in com- mand at Richmond ; and it may be questioned whether even he would have carried them out with such whole-hearted vigour if he had not thoroughly agreed with every detail.

Lee's strategy was indeed remarkable. He knew McClellan and he knew Lincoln. He knew that the former was over-cautious; he knew that the latter was over-anxious. No sudden assault on the Richmond lines, weak as they were, was to be apprehended, and a threat against Washington was certain to have great results. Hence the audacity which, at a moment apparently most critical, sent 17,000 of the best troops in the Confederacy as

far northward as Harper's Ferry, and, a fortnight later,
weakened the garrison of Richmond by 7,000 infantry.
He was surely a great leader who, in the face of an overwhelming enemy, dared assume so vast a responsibility.
But it is to be remembered that Lee made no suggestion
whatever as to the manner in which his ideas were to be
worked out.   Everything was left to Jackson.   The swift
manœuvres which surprised in succession his various
enemies emanated from himself alone.   It was his brain
that conceived the march by Mechum's Station to M'Dowell,
the march that surprised Frémont and bewildered Banks.
It was his brain that conceived the rapid transfer of the
Valley army from the one side of the Massanuttons to the
other, the march that surprised Kenly and drove Banks
in panic to the Potomac.   It was his brain that
conceived the double victory of Cross Keys and Port
Republic; and if Lee's strategy was brilliant, that displayed
by Jackson on the minor theatre of war was no less
masterly.   The instructions he received at the end of April,
before he moved against Milroy, were simply to the effect
that a successful blow at Banks might have the happiest
results.   But such a blow was not easy.   Banks was strongly
posted and numerically superior to Jackson, while Frémont, in
equal strength, was threatening Staunton.   Taking instant
advantage of the separation of the hostile columns, Jackson
struck at Milroy, and having checked Frémont, returned
to the Valley to find Banks retreating.   At this moment
he received orders from Lee to threaten Washington.
Without an instant's hesitation he marched northward.
By May 23, had the Federals received warning of his
advance, they might have concentrated 30,000 men at
Strasburg and Front Royal; or, while Banks was reinforced, McDowell might have moved on Gordonsville,
cutting Jackson's line of retreat on Richmond.

But Jackson took as little count of numbers as did
Cromwell.   Concealing his march with his usual skill he
dashed with his 16,000 men into the midst of his enemies.
Driving Banks before him, and well aware that Frémont
and McDowell were converging in his rear, he advanced

boldly on Harper's Ferry, routed Saxton's outposts, and remained for two days on the Potomac, with 62,000 Federals within a few days' march. Then, retreating rapidly up the Valley, beneath the southern peaks of the Massanuttons he turned fiercely at bay ; and the pursuing columns, mustering together nearly twice his numbers, were thrust back with heavy loss at the very moment they were combining to crush him.[1] A week later he had vanished, and when he appeared on the Chickahominy, Banks, Frémont, and McDowell were still guarding the roads to Washington, and McClellan was waiting for McDowell. 175,000 men absolutely paralysed by 16,000 ! Only Napoleon's campaign of 1814 affords a parallel to this extraordinary spectacle.[2]

Jackson's task was undoubtedly facilitated by the ignorance of Lincoln and the incapacity of his political generals. But in estimating his achievements, this ignorance and incapacity are only of secondary importance. The historians do not dwell upon the mistakes of Colli, Beaulieu, and Wurmser in 1796, but on the brilliant resolution with which Napoleon took advantage of them ; and the salient features, both of the Valley Campaign and of that of 1796, are the untiring vigilance with which opportunities were looked for, the skill with which they were detected, and the daring rapidity with which they were seized.

History often unconsciously injures the reputation of great soldiers. The more detailed the narrative, the less brilliant seems success, the less excusable defeat. When we are made fully acquainted with the dispositions of both sides, the correct solution of the problem, strategical or tactical, is generally so plain that we may easily be led to believe that it must needs have spontaneously suggested itself to the victorious leader ; and, as a natural corollary, that success is due rather to force of will than to force of intellect ; to vigilance, energy, and audacity, rather than

---

[1] 'An operation which stamps him as a military genius of the highest order.'—Lord Wolseley, *North American Review*, vol. 149, No. 2, p. 166.

[2] 'These brilliant successes appear to me models of their kind, both in conception and execution. They should be closely studied by all officers who wish to learn the art and science of war.'—*Ibid.*

to insight and calculation. It is asserted, for instance, by superficial critics that both Wellington and Napoleon, in the campaign of 1815, committed unpardonable errors. Undoubtedly, at first sight, it is inconceivable that the one should have disregarded the probability of the French invading Belgium by the Charleroi road, or that the other, on the morning of the great battle, should never have suspected that Blücher was close at hand. But the critic's knowledge of the situation is far more ample and accurate than that of either commander. Had either Wellington before Quatre Bras, or Napoleon on the fateful June 18 known what we know now, matters would have turned out very differently. ' If,' said Frederick the Great, ' we had exact information of our enemy's dispositions, we should beat him every time ; ' but exact information is never forthcoming. A general in the field literally walks in darkness, and his success will be in proportion to the facility with which his mental vision can pierce the veil. His manœuvres, to a greater or less degree, must always be based on probabilities, for his most recent reports almost invariably relate to events which, at best, are several hours old ; and, meanwhile, what has the enemy been doing ? This it is the most essential part of his business to discover, and it is a matter of hard thinking and sound judgment. From the indications furnished by his reports, and from the consideration of many circumstances, with some of which he is only imperfectly acquainted, he must divine the intentions of his opponent. It is not pretended that even the widest experience and the finest intellect confer infallibility. But clearness of perception and the power of deduction, together with the strength of purpose which they create, are the fount and origin of great achievements ; and when we find a campaign in which they played a predominant part, we may fairly rate it as a masterpiece of war. It can hardly be disputed that these qualities played such a part on the Shenandoah. For instance ; when Jackson left the Valley to march against Milroy, many things might have happened which would have brought about disaster :—

1. Banks, who was reported to have 21,000 men at Harrisonburg, might have moved on Staunton, joined hands with Milroy, and crushed Edward Johnson.

2. Banks might have attacked Ewell's 8,000 with superior numbers.

3. Frémont, if he got warning of Jackson's purpose, might have reinforced Milroy, occupied a strong position, and requested Banks to threaten or attack the Confederates in rear.

4. Frémont might have withdrawn his advanced brigade, and have reinforced Banks from Moorefield.

5. Banks might have been reinforced by Blenker, of whose whereabouts Jackson was uncertain.

6. Banks might have marched to join McDowell at Fredericksburg.

7. McClellan might have pressed Johnston so closely that a decisive battle could not have been long delayed.

8. McDowell might have marched on Richmond, intervening between the Valley army and the capital.

Such an array of possibilities would have justified a passive attitude on Elk Run. A calculation of the chances, however, showed Jackson that the dangers of action were illusory. 'Never take counsel of your fears,' was a maxim often on his lips. Unlike many others, he first made up his mind what he wanted to do, and then, and not till then, did he consider what his opponents might do to thwart him. To seize the initiative was his chief preoccupation, and in this case it did not seem difficult to do so. He knew that Banks was unenterprising. It was improbable that McDowell would advance until McClellan was near Richmond, and McClellan was very slow. To prevent Frémont getting an inkling of his design in time to cross it was not impossible, and Lincoln's anxiety for Washington might be relied on to keep Banks in the Valley.

It is true that Jackson's force was very small. But the manifestation of military genius is not affected by numbers. The handling of masses is a mechanical art, of which knowledge and experience are the key; but it is the manner in which the grand principles of war are applied which marks the great leader, and these principles may be applied as resolutely and effectively with 10,000 men as with 100,000.

'In meditation,' says Bacon, 'all dangers should be seen; in execution none, unless they are very formidable.' It was on this precept that Jackson acted. Not a single one of his manœuvres but was based on a close and judicial survey of the situation. Every risk was weighed. Nothing was left to chance. 'There was never a commander,' says his chief of the staff, 'whose foresight was more complete. Nothing emerged which had not been considered before in his mind; no possibility was overlooked; he was never surprised.'[1] The character of his opponent, the *moral* of the hostile troops, the nature of the ground, and the manner in which physical features could be turned to account, were all matters of the most careful consideration. He was a constant student of the map, and his topographical engineer was one of the most important officers on his staff. 'It could readily be seen,' writes Major Hotchkiss, 'that in the preparations he made for securing success he had fully in mind what Napoleon had done under similar circumstances; resembling Napoleon especially in this, that he was very particular in securing maps, and in acquiring topographical information. He furnished me with every facility that I desired for securing topographical information and for making maps, allowing me a complete transportation outfit for my exclusive use and sending men into the enemy's country to procure copies of local maps when I expressed a desire to have them. I do not think he had an accurate knowledge of the Valley previous to the war. When I first reported to him for duty, at the beginning of March 1862, he told me that he wanted " a complete map of the entire Shenandoah Valley from Harper's Ferry to Lexington, one showing every point of offence and defence," and to that task I immediately addressed myself. As a rule he did not refer to maps in the field, making his study of them in advance. He undoubtedly had the power of retaining the topo-

[1] Dabney, vol. i., p. 76.

graphy of the country in his imagination. He had spent his youth among the mountains, where there were but few waggon roads but many bridle and foot paths. His early occupation made it necessary for him to become familiar with such intricate ways; and I think this had a very important bearing on his ability to promptly recognise the topographical features of the country, and to recall them whenever it became necessary to make use of them. He was quick in comprehending topographical features. I made it a point, nevertheless, to be always ready to give him a graphic representation of any particular point of the region where operations were going on, making a rapid sketch of the topography in his presence, and using different coloured pencils for greater clearness in the definition of surface features. The carefully prepared map generally had too many points of detail, and did not sufficiently emphasise features apparently insignificant, but from a military standpoint most important. I may add that Jackson not only studied the general maps of the country, but made a particular study of those of any district where he expected to march or fight, constantly using sketch maps made upon the ground to inform him as to portions of the field of operations that did not immediately come under his own observation. I often made rough sketches for him when on the march, or during engagements, in answer to his requests for information.'[1]

It is little wonder that it should have been said by his soldiers that 'he knew every hole and corner of the Valley as if he had made it himself.'

But to give attention to topography was not all that Jackson had learned from Napoleon. 'As a strategist,' says Dabney, 'the first Napoleon was undoubtedly his model. He had studied his campaigns diligently, and he was accustomed to remark with enthusiasm upon the evidences of his genius. "Napoleon," he said, " was the first to show what an army could be made to accomplish. He had shown what was the value of time as an element

[1] Letter to the author.

of strategic combination, and that good troops, if well cared for, could be made to march twenty-five miles daily, and win battles besides." ' And he had learned more than this. 'We must make this campaign,' he said at the beginning of 1863, ' an exceedingly active one. Only thus can a weaker country cope with a stronger ; it must make up in activity what it lacks in strength. A defensive campaign can only be made successful by taking the aggressive at the proper time. Napoleon never waited for his adversary to become fully prepared, but struck him the first blow.'

It would perhaps be difficult, in the writings of Napoleon, to find a passage which embodies his conception of war in terms as definite as these ; but no words could convey it more clearly. It is sometimes forgotten that Napoleon was often outnumbered at the outset of a campaign. It was not only in the campaigns of Italy, of Leipsic, of 1814, and of Waterloo, that the hostile armies were larger than his own. In those of Ulm, Austerlitz, Eckmühl, and Dresden, he was numerically inferior on the whole theatre of war ; but while the French troops were concentrated under a single chief, the armies of the Allies were scattered over a wide area, and unable to support each other. Before they could come together, Napoleon, moving with the utmost rapidity, struck the first blow, and they were defeated in succession. The first principle of war is to concentrate superior force at the decisive point, that is, upon the field of battle. But it is exceedingly seldom that by standing still, and leaving the initiative to the enemy, that this principle can be observed, for a numerically inferior force, if it once permits its enemy to concentrate, can hardly hope for success. True generalship is, therefore, ' to make up in activity for lack of strength ; ' to strike the enemy in detail, and overthrow his columns in succession. And the highest art of all is to compel him to disperse his army, and then to concentrate superior force against each fraction in turn.

It is such strategy as this that 'gains the ends of States and makes men heroes.' Napoleon did not discover **it.** Every single general who deserves to be entitled great has used it. Frederick, threatened by Austria, France, Russia, Saxony, and Sweden, used it in self-defence, and from the Seven Years' War the little kingdom of Prussia emerged as a first-class Power. It was such strategy which won back the Peninsula; not the lines of Torres Vedras, but the bold march northwards to Vittoria.[1] It was on the same lines that Lee and Jackson acted. Lee, in compelling the Federals to keep their columns separated, manœuvred with a skill which has seldom been surpassed; Jackson, falling as it were from the skies into the midst of his astonished foes, struck right and left before they could combine, and defeated in detail every detachment which crossed his path.

It is when regarded in connection with the operations of the main armies that the Valley campaign stands out in its true colours; but, at the same time, even as an isolated incident, it is in the highest degree interesting. It has been compared, and not inaptly, with the Italian campaign of 1796. And it may even be questioned whether, in some respects, it was not more brilliant. The odds against the Confederates were far greater than against the French. Jackson had to deal with a homogeneous enemy, with generals anxious to render each other loyal support, and not with the contingents of different States. His marches were far longer than Napoleon's. The theatre of war was not less difficult. His troops were not veterans, but, in great part, the very rawest of recruits. The enemy's officers and soldiers were not inferior to his own; their leaders were at least equal in capacity to Colli, Beaulieu, and Alvinzi, and the statesmen who directed them were not more purblind than the Aulic Council. Moreover, Jackson was merely the commander of a detached force, which might at any moment be required at Richmond. The risks which Napoleon freely accepted he could not afford. He dared not deliver battle unless he were certain of success,

---

[1] 'In six weeks, Wellington marched with 100,000 men six hundred miles, passed six great rivers, gained one decisive battle, invested two fortresses, and drove 120,000 veteran troops from Spain.'—*The War in the Peninsula*, Napier, vol. v., p. 132.

and his one preoccupation was to lose as few men as possible. But be this as it may, in the secrecy of the Confederate movements, the rapidity of the marches, and the skilful use of topographical features, the Valley campaign bears strong traces of the Napoleonic methods. Seldom has the value of these methods been more forcibly illustrated. Three times was McDowell to have marched to join McClellan: first, at the beginning of April, when he was held back by Kernstown; second, on May 26, when he was held back by Front Royal and Winchester; third, on June 25, when he was held back by Jackson's disappearance after Port Republic. Above all, the campaign reveals a most perfect appreciation of the surest means of dealing with superior numbers. 'In my personal intercourse with Jackson,' writes General Imboden, 'in the early part of the war, he often said that there were two things never to be lost sight of by a military commander. "Always mystify, mislead, and surprise the enemy, if possible; and when you strike and overcome him, never give up the pursuit as long as your men have strength to follow; for an army routed, if hotly pursued, becomes panic-stricken, and can then be destroyed by half their number. The other rule is, never fight against heavy odds, if by any possible manœuvring you can hurl your own force on only a part, and that the weakest part, of your enemy and crush it. Such tactics will win every time, and a small army may thus destroy a large one in detail, and repeated victory will make it invincible."[1] And again: "To move swiftly, strike vigorously, and secure all the fruits of victory, is the secret of successful war."'

These maxims were the outcome of his studies, 'drawn absolutely and merely,' says Lord Wolseley, 'from his knowledge of war, as learned from the great leaders of former days;'[2] and if he made war by rule, as he had regulated his conduct as a cadet, it can hardly be denied that his rules were of the soundest. They are a complete summary of the tactics which wrought such havoc in the

[1] *Battles and Leaders*, vol. ii., p. 297.
[2] *North American Review*, vol. 149, p. 168.

Valley. The order in which they are placed is interesting. 'To mystify, mislead, and surprise,' is the first precept. How thoroughly it was applied! The measures by which his adversaries were to be deceived were as carefully thought out as the maps had been closely studied. The troops moved almost as often by country roads and farm tracks as by the turnpikes. The longer route, even when time was of importance, was often preferred, if it was well concealed, to the shorter. No precaution, however trivial, that might prevent information reaching the enemy was neglected. In order that he might give his final instructions to Colonel Munford before marching to Richmond, he told that officer to meet him at ten o'clock at night in Mount Sidney. 'I will be on my horse,' he wrote, 'at the north end of the town, so you need not inquire after me.'[1] '*Le bon général ordinaire*' would have scoffed at the atmosphere of mystery which enveloped the Confederate camp. The march from Elk Run Valley to Port Republic, with its accompaniments of continuous quagmire and dreary bivouacs, he would have ridiculed as a most useless stratagem. The infinite pains with which Jackson sought to conceal, even from his most trusted staff officers, his movements, his intentions, and his thoughts, a commander less thorough would have pronounced useless. The long night ride to Richmond, on June 22, with its untoward delays and provoking *contretemps*, sounds like an excess of precaution which was absolutely pedantic.[2] But war, according to Napoleon, is made up of accidents. The country was full of spies; the Southern newspapers were sometimes indiscreet; and the simple fact that Jackson had been seen near Richmond would have warned McClellan that his right wing was in jeopardy. Few men would have taken such infinite trouble to hide the departure from the Valley and the march across Virginia to attack McClellan. But soldiers of experience, alive to the full bearing of seem-

---

[1] O. R., vol. xii., part iii., p. 914.
[2] He instructed the orderly that accompanied him, and who knew the roads, to call him 'Colonel.'

ingly petty details, appreciate his skill.[1] According to the dictum of Napoleon, 'there are no such things as trifles in war.'

It was not, however, on such expedients that Jackson principally relied to keep his enemy in the dark. The use he made of his cavalry is perhaps the most brilliant tactical feature of the campaign. Ashby's squadrons were the means whereby the Federals were mystified. Not only was a screen established which perfectly concealed the movements of the Valley army, but constant demonstrations, at far distant points, alarmed and bewildered the Federal commanders. In his employment of cavalry Jackson was in advance of his age. His patrols were kept out two or three marches to front and flank; neither by day nor by night were they permitted to lose touch of the enemy; and thus no movement could take place without their knowledge. Such tactics had not been seen since the days of Napoleon. The Confederate horsemen in the Valley were far better handled than those of France or Austria in 1859, of Prussia or Austria in 1866, of France in 1870, of England, France, or Russia in the Crimea.

In the flank march on Sebastopol the hostile armies passed within a few miles, in an open country, without either of them being aware of the proximity of the other, and the English headquarter staff almost rode into a Russian baggage-train. At Solferino and at Sadowa, armies which were counted by hundreds of thousands encamped almost within sight of each other's watch-fires, without the slightest suspicion that the enemy lay over the next ridge. The practice of Napoleon had been forgotten. The great cloud of horsemen which, riding sometimes a hundred miles to the front, veiled the march of the Grand Army had vanished from memory. The vast importance ascribed by the Emperor to procuring early information of his enemy and hiding his own movements had been overlooked; and it was left to an American soldier to revive his methods.

The application of Jackson's second precept, 'to hurl

---

[1] ' The manner,' says Lord Wolseley, 'in which he thus mystified his enemy regarding this most important movement is a masterpiece.'—*North American Review*, vol. 149, pp. 166, 167.

your own force on the weakest part of the enemy's,' was
made possible by his vigorous application of the first. The
Federals, mystified and misled by demonstrations of the
cavalry, and unable to procure information, never knew at
what point they should concentrate, and support invariably
came too late. Jackson's tactical successes were achieved
over comparatively small forces. Except at Cross Keys, and
there he only intended to check Frémont for the moment,
he never encountered more than 10,000 men on any
single field. No great victory, like Austerlitz or Salamanca,
was won over equal numbers. No Chancellorsville, where
a huge army was overthrown by one scarce half the size, is
reckoned amongst the triumphs of the Valley campaign.
But it is to be remembered that Jackson was always outnumbered, and outnumbered heavily, on the theatre of war ;
and if he defeated his enemies in detail, their overthrow
was not less decisive than if it had been brought about at one
time and at one place. The fact that they were unable
to combine their superior numbers before the blow fell is
in itself the strongest testimony to his ability. 'How
often,' says Napier, 'have we not heard the genius of
Buonaparte slighted, and his victories talked of as destitute
of merit, because, at the point of attack, he was superior
in numbers to his enemies! This very fact, which has been
so often converted into a sort of reproach, constitutes his
greatest and truest praise. He so directed his attack as
at once to divide his enemy, and to fall with the mass of
his own forces upon a point where their division, or the
distribution of their army, left them unable to resist him.
It is not in man to defeat armies by the breath of his mouth ;
nor was Buonaparte commissioned, like Gideon, to con-
found and destroy a host with three hundred men. He knew
that everything depended ultimately upon physical superiority ; and his genius was shown in this, that, though outnumbered on the whole, he was always superior to his
enemies at the decisive point.' [1]

[1] The following table, of which the idea is borrowed from *The Principles
of Strategy*, by Capt. Bigelow, U.S.A., may be found interesting. Under
the heading 'Strategic' appear the numbers available on the theatre

The material results of the Valley campaign were by no means inconsiderable. 3,500 prisoners were either paroled or sent to Richmond. 3,500 Federals were killed or wounded. An immense quantity of stores was captured, and probably as much destroyed. 9 guns were taken and over 10,000 rifles, while the loss of the Confederates was no more than 2,500 killed and wounded, 600 prisoners, and 3 guns. It may be added that the constant surprises, together with the successive conflict with superior numbers, had the worst effect on the *moral* of the Federal soldiers. The troops commanded by Frémont, Shields, Banks, Saxton, and Geary were all infected. Officers resigned and men deserted. On the least alarm there was a decided tendency to 'stampede.' The generals thought only of retreat. Frémont, after Cross Keys, did not think that his men would stand, and many of his men declared that it was 'only murder' to fight without reinforcements.[1]

When to those results is added the strategical effect of the campaign, it can hardly be denied that the success he achieved was out of all proportion to Jackson's strength. Few generals have done so much with means so small. Not only were the Valley troops comparatively few in

of operations; under the heading 'Tactical' the numbers present on the field of battle. See also note at the end of the volume.

	STRATEGIC.	TACTICAL.
M'Dowell.		
Federal . . .	30,000	2,500
Confederate . . .	17,000	6,000
Winchester.		
Federal . . .	60,000	7,500
Confederate . . .	16,000	16,000
Cross Keys.		
Federal . . .	23,000	12,750
Confederate . . .	13,000	8,000
Port Republic.		
Federal . . .	22,000	4,500
Confederate . . .	12,700	6,000

[1] O. R., vol. xii., part iii., p. 402.

numbers, but they were volunteers, and volunteers of a type that was altogether novel. Even in the War of the Revolution many of the regimental officers, and indeed many of the soldiers, were men who had served in the Indian and French wars under the English flag. But there were not more than half a dozen regular officers in the whole Army of the Valley. Except Jackson himself, and his chief of artillery, not one of the staff had more than a year's service. Twelve months previous several of the brigadiers had been civilians. The regimental officers were as green as the men; and although military offences were few, the bonds of discipline were slight. When the march to M'Dowell was begun, which was to end five weeks later at Port Republic, a considerable number of the so-called 'effectives' had only been drilled for a few hours. The cavalry on parade was little better than a mob; on the line of march they kept or left the ranks as the humour took them. It is true that the Federals were hardly more efficient. But Jackson's operations were essentially offensive, and offensive operations, as was shown at Bull Run, are ill-suited to raw troops. Attack cannot be carried to a triumphant issue unless every fraction of the force co-operates with those on either hand; and co-operation is hardly to be expected from inexperienced officers. Moreover, offensive operations, especially when a small force is manœuvring against the fraction of a larger, depend for success on order, rapidity, and endurance; and it is in these qualities, as a rule, that raw troops are particularly deficient. Yet Jackson, like Napoleon at Ulm, might have boasted with truth that he had 'destroyed the enemy merely by marches,' and his men accomplished feats of which the hardiest veterans might well be proud.

From April 29 to June 5, that is, in thirty-eight days, they marched four hundred miles, fought three battles and numerous combats, and were victorious in all. Several of the marches exceeded twenty-five miles a day; and in retreat, from the Potomac to Port Republic, the army made one hundred and four miles between the morning of May 30 and the night of June 5, that is, fifteen miles daily without a rest day intervening. This record, if we take into consideration the infamous roads, is remarkable; and it well may be asked by what means these half-trained troops were enabled to accomplish such a feat?[1]

Jackson's rules for marching have been preserved. 'He never broke down his men by long-continued movement. He rested the whole column very often, but only for a few minutes at a time. He liked to see the men lie flat on the ground to rest, and would say, "A man rests all over when he lies down."'[2] Nor did he often call upon his troops for extraordinary exertions. In the period between his departure from Elk Run Mountain to the battle of Port Republic there were only four series of forced marches.[3] 'The hardships of forced marches,' he said, 'are often more painful than the dangers of battle.' It was only, in short, when he intended a surprise, or when a rapid retreat was imperative, that he sacrificed everything to speed. The troops marched light, carrying only rifles, blankets, haversacks, and ammunition. When long distances were to be covered, those men who still retained their knapsacks were ordered to leave them behind. No heavy trains accompanied the army. The ambulances and ammunition waggons were always present; but the supply waggons were often far in rear. In their haversacks the men carried several days' rations; and when these were consumed they lived either on the farmers, or on the stores they had captured from the enemy.

It is not to be supposed, however, that the ranks

[1] 'Campaigning in France,' says General Sheridan, who was with the Prussian Headquarter Staff in 1870, 'that is, the marching, camping, and subsisting of an army, is an easy matter, very unlike anything we had in the War of the Rebellion. To repeat: the country is rich, beautiful, and densely populated, subsistence abundant, and the roads all macadamised highways; thus the conditions are altogether different from those existing with us. . . . I can but leave to conjecture how the Germans would have got along on bottomless roads—often none at all—through the swamps and quicksands of Northern Virginia.'—*Memoirs*, vol. ii., p. 450.

[2] *Battles and Leaders*, vol. ii., pp. 297, 298.

[3] From April 17 to April 19, when he moved to Elk Run Valley; May 6 to May 8, when he moved against Milroy; May 18 to May 25, when he moved against Banks; and May 29 to June 1, when he passed south between Frémont and Shields.

remained full. 'I had rather,' said Jackson, 'lose one man in marching than five in fighting,' and to this rule he rigorously adhered. He never gave the enemy warning by a deliberate approach along the main roads ; and if there was a chance of effecting a surprise, or if the enemy was already flying, it mattered little how many men fell out. And fall out they did, in large numbers. Between May 17 and the battle of Cross Keys the army was reduced from 16,500 men to 13,000. Not more than 500 had been killed or wounded, so there were no less than 3,000 absentees. Many were footsore and found no place in the ambulances. Many were sick ; others on detachment ; but a large proportion had absented themselves without asking leave. Two days after Winchester, in a letter to Ewell, Jackson writes that 'the evil of straggling has become enormous.'

Such severe exertion as the march against Kenly, the pursuit of Banks, and the retreat from the Potomac, would have told their tale upon the hardiest veterans. When the German armies, suddenly changing direction from west to north, pushed on to Sedan by forced marches, large numbers of the infantry succumbed to pure exhaustion. When the Light Division, in 1813, pressing forward after Sauroren to intercept the French retreat, marched nineteen consecutive hours in very sultry weather, and over forty miles of mountain roads, 'many men fell and died convulsed and frothing at the mouth, while others, whose spirit and strength had never before been quelled, leant on their muskets and muttered in sullen tones that they yielded for the first time.' [1]

But the men that fell out on the march to Sedan and in the passes of the Pyrenees were physically incapable of further effort. They were not stragglers in the true sense of the term ; and in an army broken to discipline straggling on the line of march is practically unknown. The sickly and feeble may fall away, but every sound man may confidently be relied upon to keep his place. The secret of full ranks is good officers and strict discipline ; and the most marked difference between regular troops and those hastily

[1] *The War in the Peninsula*, Napier, vol. v., p. 244.

organised is this—with the former the waste of men will be small, with the latter very great. In all armies, however constituted, there is a large proportion of men whose hearts are not in the business.[1]

When hard marching and heavy fighting are in prospect the inclination of such men is to make themselves scarce, and when discipline is relaxed they will soon find the opportunity. But when their instincts of obedience are strong, when the only home they know is with the colours, when the credit of their regiment is at stake—and even the most worthless have some feeling for their own corps—engrained habit and familiar associations overcome their natural weakness. The troop-horse bereft of his rider at once seeks his comrades, and pushes his way, with empty saddle, into his place in the ranks. And so the soldier by profession, faint-hearted as he may be, marches shoulder to shoulder with his comrades, and acquires a fictitious, but not unuseful, courage from his contact with braver men.

It is true that the want of good boots told heavily on the Confederates. A pair already half-worn, such as many of the men started with, was hardly calculated to last out a march of several hundred miles over rocky tracks, and fresh supplies were seldom forthcoming. There was a dearth both of shoe-leather and shoe-factories in the South; and if Mr. Davis, before the blockade was established, had indented on the shoemakers of Europe, he would have added very largely to the efficiency of his armies. A few cargoes of good boots would have been more useful than a shipload of rifled guns.

Nevertheless, the absentees from the ranks were not all footsore. The vice of straggling was by no means confined to Jackson's command. It was the curse of both armies, Federal and Confederate. The Official Records, as well as the memoirs of participants, teem with references to it. It was an evil which the severest punishments seemed incapable of checking. It was in vain that it was de-

---

[1] General Sheridan is said to have declared that 25 per cent. of the Federal soldiers lacked the military spirit.

nounced in orders, that the men were appealed to, warned, and threatened. Nor were the faint-hearted alone at fault. The day after Jackson's victory at M'Dowell, Johnston, falling back before McClellan, addressed General Lee as follows :—

'Stragglers cover the country, and Richmond is no doubt filled with the absent without leave. . . . The men are full of spirit when near the enemy, but at other times to avoid restraint leave their regiments in crowds.'[1] A letter from a divisional general followed :—

'It is with deep mortification that I report that several thousand soldiers and many individuals with commissions have fled to Richmond under pretext of sickness. They have even thrown away their arms that their flight might not be impeded. Cannot these miserable wretches be arrested and returned to their regiments, where they can have their heads shaved and be drummed out of the service ?'[2]

Jackson, then, had to contend with difficulties which a general in command of regular troops would not have been called on to provide against ; and in other respects also he suffered from the constitution of his army. The one thing lacking in the Valley campaign was a decisive victory over a considerable detachment of the Federal army, the annihilation of one of the converging forces, and large capture of guns and prisoners. A victory as complete as Rivoli would have completed its dramatic interest. But for this Jackson himself was hardly to blame. The misconduct of the Confederate cavalry on May 24 and 25 permitted Banks to escape destruction ; and the delay at the temporary bridge near Port Republic, due, mainly, to the disinclination of the troops to face the ford, and the want of resolute obedience on the part of their commanders, saved Frémont from the same fate. Had Shields' advanced brigades been driven back, as Jackson designed, while the day was still young, the operations of the Valley army would in all probability have been crowned by a brilliant triumph over nearly

[1] O. R., vol. xi., part iii., p. 503.   [2] *Ibid*. p. 506.

equal forces. Frémont, already fearful and irresolute, was hardly the man to withstand the vigour of Jackson's onset; and that onset would assuredly have been made if more careful arrangements had been made to secure the bridge. This was not the only mistake committed by the staff. The needlessly long march of the main body when approaching Front Royal on May 23 might well have been obviated. But for this delay the troops might have pushed on before nightfall to within easy reach of the Valley turnpike, and Banks have been cut off from Winchester.

It is hardly necessary to say that, even with regular troops, the same mistakes might have occurred. They are by no means without parallel, and even those committed by the Federals have their exact counterpart in European warfare. At the beginning of August, 1870, the French army, like Banks' division on May 23, 1862, was in two portions, divided by a range of mountains. The staff was aware that the Germans were in superior strength, but their dispositions were unknown. Like Banks, they neglected to reconnoitre; and when a weak detachment beyond the mountains was suddenly overwhelmed, they still refused to believe that attack was imminent. The crushing defeats of Wörth and Spicheren were the result.

The staff of a regular army is not always infallible. It would be hard to match the extraordinary series of blunders made by the staffs of the three armies—English, French, and Prussian—in the campaign of Waterloo, and yet there was probably no senior officer present in Belgium who had not seen several campaigns. But the art of war has made vast strides since Waterloo, and even since 1870. Under Moltke's system, which has been applied in a greater or less degree to nearly all professional armies, the chance of mistakes has been much reduced. The staff is no longer casually educated and selected haphazard; the peace training of both officers and men is far more thorough; and those essential details on which the most brilliant conceptions, tactical and strategical, depend for success stand much less chance of being overlooked than in 1815. It is by the standard of a modern army, and not of those whose only school in peace was the parade-ground, that the American armies must be judged.

That Jackson's tactical skill, and his quick eye for ground, had much to do with his victories can hardly be questioned. At Kernstown and Port Republic he seized the key of the position without a moment's hesitation. At Winchester, when Ewell was checked upon the right, three strong brigades, suddenly thrown forward on the opposite flank, completely rolled up the Federal line. At Cross Keys the position selected for Ewell proved too formidable for Frémont, despite his superiority in guns. At Port Republic, Taylor's unexpected approach through the tangled forest was at once decisive of the engagement. The cavalry charge at Front Royal was admirably timed ; and the manner in which Ashby was employed throughout the campaign, not only to screen the advance but to check pursuit, was a proof of the highest tactical ability. Nor should the quick insight into the direction of Shields' march on June 1, and the destruction of the bridges by which he could communicate with Frémont, be omitted. It is true that the operations in the Valley were not absolutely faultless. When Jackson was bent on an effective blow his impatience to bring the enemy to bay robbed him more than once of complete success. On the march to M'Dowell Johnson's brigade, the advanced guard, had been permitted to precede the main body by seven miles, and, consequently, when Milroy attacked there was not sufficient force at hand for a decisive counterstroke. Moreover, with an ill-trained staff a careful supervision was most essential, and the waggon-bridge at Port Republic should have been inspected by a trustworthy staff officer before Winder rushed across to fall on Tyler.

Errors of this nature, however instructive they may be to the student of war, are but spots upon the sun ; and in finding in his subordinate such breadth of view and such vigour of execution, Lee was fortunate indeed. Jackson was no less fortunate when Ashby came under his command. That dashing captain of free-lances was undoubtedly a most valuable colleague. It was something to have a cavalry leader who could not only fight and reconnoitre, but who had sagacity enough to divine the enemy's intentions. But the ideas that governed the employment of the cavalry were Jackson's alone. He it was who placed the squadrons across Frémont's road from Wardensville, who ordered the demonstrations against Banks, before both M'Dowell and Front Royal, and those which caused Frémont to retreat after Port Republic. More admirable still was the quickness with which he recognised the use that might be made of mounted riflemen. From the Potomac to Port Republic his horsemen covered his retreat, dismounting behind every stream and along the borders of every wood, checking the pursuers with their fire, compelling them to deploy their infantry, and then retreating rapidly to the next position. Day after day were the Federal advanced guards held in check, their columns delayed, and the generals irritated by their slippery foe. Meanwhile, the Confederate infantry, falling back at their leisure, were relieved of all annoyance. And if the cavalry was suddenly driven in, support was invariably at hand, and a compact brigade of infantry, supported by artillery, sent the pursuing horsemen to the right-about. The retreat of the Valley army was managed with the same skill as its advance, and the rear-guard tactics of the campaign are no less remarkable than those of the attack.

To judge from the Valley campaign, Jackson handled his horsemen with more skill than any other commander, Confederate or Federal. A cavalry that could defend itself on foot as well as charge in the saddle was practically a new arm, of far greater efficiency than cavalry of the old type, and Jackson at once recognised, not only its value; but the manner in which it could be most effectively employed. He was not led away by the specious advantages, so eagerly urged by young and ambitious soldiers, of the so-called raids. Even Lee himself, cool-headed as he was, appears to have been fascinated by the idea of throwing a great body of horsemen across his enemy's communications, spreading terror amongst his supply trains, cutting his telegraphs, and destroying his magazines. In hardly a single instance did such expeditions inflict more than temporary discomfort on the enemy; and the armies were led more than once into false manœuvres, for want of the information which only the cavalry could supply. Lee at Malvern Hill and Gettysburg, Hooker at Chancellorsville, Grant at Spotsylvania, owed defeat, in great measure, to the absence of their mounted troops. In the Valley, on the contrary, success was made possible because the cavalry was kept to its legitimate duty—that is, to procure information, to screen all movements, to take part in battle at the decisive moment, and to carry out the pursuit.

With all his regard for Napoleon's maxims, Jackson was no slave to rule. In war, circumstances vary to such an extent that a manœuvre, which at one time is manifestly unsound, may at another be the most judicious. The so-called rules are never binding; they merely point out the risks which are generally entailed by some particular course of action. There is no principle on which Napoleon lays more stress than that a general should never divide his force, either on the field of battle or the theatre of war. But when he marched to M'Dowell and left Ewell at Swift Run Gap, Jackson deliberately divided his forces and left Banks between them, knowing that the apparent risk, with an opponent like Banks, was no risk at all. At the battle of Winchester, too, there was a gap of a mile between the brigades on the left of the Kernstown road and Ewell on the right; and owing to the intervening hills, one wing was invisible to the other. Here again, like Moltke at Königgrätz, Jackson realised that the principle might be disregarded not only with impunity but with effect. He was not like Lord Galway, 'a man who was in war what Molière's doctors were in medicine, who thought it much more honourable to fail according to rule than to succeed by innovation.'[1]

But the triumphs of the Valley campaign were not due alone to the orders issued by Lee and Jackson. The Confederate troops displayed extraordinary endurance. When

[1] Macaulay.

the stragglers were eliminated their stauncher comrades proved themselves true as steel. In every engagement the regiments fought with stubborn courage. They sometimes failed to break the enemy's line at the first rush; but, except at Kernstown, the Federals never drove them from their position, and Taylor's advance at Winchester, Trimble's counterstroke at Cross Keys, the storming of the battery at Port Republic, and the charge of the cavalry at Cedarville, were the deeds of brave and resolute men.

A retreat is the most exhausting of military movements. It is costly in men, 'more so,' says Napoleon, 'than two battles,' and it shakes the faith of the soldiers in their general and in themselves. Jackson's army retreated for seven days before Frémont, dwindling in numbers at every step, and yet it never fought better than when it turned at bay. From first to last it believed itself superior to its enemies; from first to last it was equal to the tasks which its exacting commander imposed upon it, and its spirit was indomitable throughout. 'One male a week and three foights a day,' according to one of Jackson's Irishmen, was the rule in the campaigns of 1862. The forced marches were not made in luxury. Not seldom only half-rations were issued, and more often none at all. The weather, for many days in succession, was abominable, and the forest bivouacs were comfortless in the extreme. On May 25 twenty per cent. of Trimble's brigade went into action barefoot; and had it not been for the stores captured in Winchester, the march to the Potomac, and the subsequent unmolested retreat to Woodstock, would have been hardly possible.

If the troops were volunteers, weak in discipline and prone to straggling, they none the less bore themselves with conspicuous gallantry. Their native characteristics came prominently to the front. Patient under hardships, vigorous in attack, and stubborn in defence, they showed themselves worthy of their commander. Their enthusiastic patriotism was not without effect on their bearing before the enemy. Every private in the ranks believed that he was fighting in the sacred cause of liberty, and the spirit which nerved the resolution of the Confederate soldier was the same which inspired the resistance of their revolutionary forefathers. His hatred of the Yankee, as he contemptuously styled the Northerner, was even more bitter than the wrath which Washington's soldiers felt towards England; and it was intensified by the fact that his detested foeman had not only dared to invade the South, but had proclaimed his intention, in no uncertain tones, of dealing with the Sovereign States exactly as he pleased.

But it was something more than native courage and enthusiastic patriotism which inspired the barefooted heroes of Winchester. It would be difficult to prove that in other parts of the theatre of war the Confederate troops were inferior to those that held the Valley. Yet they were certainly less successful, and in very many instances they had failed to put forth the same resolute energy as the men who followed Jackson.

But it is hardly possible to discuss the spirit of an army apart from that of its commander. If, in strategy wholly, and in tactics in great part, success emanates from a single brain, the *moral* of the troops is not less dependent on the influence of one man. 'Better an army of stags,' runs the old proverb, 'led by a lion, than an army of lions led by a stag.'

Their leader's character had already made a sensible impression on the Valley soldiers. Jackson was as untheatrical as Wellington. He was hardly to be distinguished, even by his dress, from the private in the ranks. Soon after his arrival at Richmond he called on Mrs. Pendleton, the wife of the reverend captain of the Rockbridge battery. The negro servant left him standing in the hall, thinking that this quiet soldier, clad in a faded and sunburnt uniform, need not be treated with further ceremony.[1] Headquarters in camp were an ordinary bell-tent, or a room in the nearest cottage, and they were often without guard or sentry. In bivouac the general rolled himself in his blankets, and lay down under a tree or in a fence corner. He could sleep

[1] *Memoirs of W. N. Pendleton, D.D., Brigadier-General, C.S.A.*, p. 201.

anywhere, in the saddle, under fire, or in church; and he could compel sleep to come to him when and where he pleased. He cared as little for good quarters as a mountain hunter, and he was as abstemious as a Red Indian on the war-path. He lived as plainly as the men, and often shared their rations. The majority of the cavalry were better mounted, and many of his officers were better dressed. He was not given to addressing his troops, either in mass or as individuals. His praises he reserved for his official reports, and then he was generous. In camp he was as silent as the Sphinx, and he never posed, except in action, as the commander of an army. Off duty he was the gentlest and most unpretentious of men, and the most approachable of generals. He was always scrupulously polite; and the private soldier who asked him a question might be sure of a most courteous reply. But there was no man with whom it was less safe to take liberties; and where duty was concerned he became a different being. The gentle tones grew curt and peremptory, and the absent demeanour gave place to a most purposeful energy. His vigilance was marvellous: his eye was everywhere; he let nothing pass without his personal scrutiny. The unfortunate officer accused of indolence or neglect found the shy and quiet professor transformed into the most implacable of masters. No matter how high the rank of the offender, the crime met with the punishment it deserved. The scouts compared him with Lee. The latter was so genial that it was a pleasure to report to him. Jackson cross-questioned them on every detail, treating them as a lawyer does a hostile witness, and his keen blue eyes seemed to search their very souls.

Nor did the men escape when they misbehaved. Ashby's cavalry were reprimanded in general orders for their indiscipline at Middletown, and again at Port Republic; and if either officer or regiment displeased the general, it was duly mentioned in his published reports.[1]

---

[1] It is worth remark that Jackson's methods of punishment showed his deep knowledge of his soldiers. The sentence on the men who were tempted from their duty, during Banks' retreat, by the plunder on the Winchester road was that they should not be allowed to serve with the advanced guard until

But the troops knew that their grave leader, so uncommunicative in camp, and so unrelenting to misconduct, was constantly occupied with their well-being. They knew that he spared them, when opportunity offered, as he never spared himself. His *camaraderie* was expressed in something more than words. The hospitals constructed in the Valley excited the admiration even of the Federals, and Jackson's wounded were his first care. Whatever it might cost the army, the ambulances must be got safely away, and the sick and disabled soldiers transferred to their own people. But, at the same time, the troops had long since learned that, as administered by Jackson, the military code was a stern reality. They had seen men shot for striking their officers, and they knew that for insubordination or disobedience it was idle to plead excuse. They had thought their general harsh, and even cruel; but as their experience increased they recognised the wisdom of his severity, and when they looked upon that kindly face, grave and determined as it was, they realised how closely his firmness was allied to tenderness. They had learned how highly he esteemed them. Once, in his twelve months of command, he had spoken from his heart. When, on the heights near Centreville, he bade farewell to his old brigade, his pride in their achievements had broken through the barriers of his reserve, and his ringing words had not yet been forgotten. If he was swift to blame, his general orders and official dispatches gave full credit to every gallant action, and each man felt himself a hero because his general so regarded him.

They had learned, too, that Jackson's commendation was worth having. They had seen him in action, the coolest of them all, riding along the line of battle with as much composure as if the hail of bullets was no more than summer rain. They had seen him far in advance of the charging lines, cheering them to the pursuit; and they knew the tremendous vigour of his flank attacks.

But it was not only confidence in the skill of their

further orders. It was considered terribly severe. O. R., vol. xii., part iii. p. 902.

commander that inspired the troops. It was impossible
not to admire the man who, after a sleepless night, a long
march, and hard fighting, would say to his officers, 'We
must push on—we must push on!' as unconcernedly as if
his muscles were of steel and hunger an unknown sensation.
Such fortitude was contagious. The men caught something
of his resolution, of his untiring energy, and his unhesitating audacity. The regiments which drove Banks to the
Potomac were very different from those that crawled to
Romney through the blinding sleet, or that fell back with
the loss of one-sixth their number from the Kernstown
Ridge. It has been related of Jackson that when he had
once made up his mind, 'he seemed to discard all idea of
defeat, and to regard the issue as assured. A man less
open to the conviction that he was beaten could not be
imagined.' To this frame of mind he brought his soldiers.
Jackson's brigade at Bull Run, Jackson's division in the
Valley, Jackson's army corps later in the war, were all
imbued with the characteristics of their leader. The
exertions that he demanded of them seemed beyond the
powers of mortal men, but with Jackson leading them the
troops felt themselves able to accomplish impossibilities.
'I never saw one of Jackson's couriers approach,' said
Ewell, 'without expecting an order to assault the North
Pole!' But had the order been given neither Ewell nor
the Valley troops would have questioned it.

With the senior officers of his little army Jackson's
relations were in some instances less cordial than with
the men. His staff was devoted to him, for they had
learned to know him. At the beginning of the Valley
campaign some of them thought him mad; before it was
over they believed him to be a genius. He lived with his
military family on the most intimate terms, and his
unfailing courtesy, his utter absence of self-assertion, his
sweet temper, and his tactful consideration for others,
no matter how humble their rank, were irresistible. On
duty, indeed, his staff officers fared badly. Tireless himself, regardless of all personal comforts, he seemed to
think that others were fashioned in the same mould. After

a weary day's marching or fighting, it was no unusual thing for him to send them for a ride of thirty or forty miles through the night. And he gave the order with no more thought than if he were sending them with a message to the next tent. But off duty he was simply a personal friend, bent on making all things pleasant. 'Never,' says Dr. Hunter McGuire, ' can I forget his kindness and gentleness to me when I was in great sorrow and trouble. He came to my tent and spent hours with me, comforting me in his simple, kindly, Christian way, showing a depth of friendship and affection which can never be forgotten. There is no measuring the intensity with which the very soul of Jackson burned in battle. Out of it he was very gentle. Indeed, as I look back on the two years that I was daily, indeed hourly, with him, his gentleness as a man, his tenderness to those in trouble or affliction—the tenderness indeed of a woman—impress me more than his wonderful prowess as a warrior.'

It was with his generals and colonels that there was sometimes a lack of sympathy. Many of these were older than himself. Ewell and Whiting were his seniors in point of service, and there can be little doubt that it was sometimes a little hard to receive peremptory orders from a younger man. Jackson's secrecy was often irritating. Men who were over-sensitive thought it implied a want of confidence. Those overburdened with dignity objected to being treated like the private soldiers; and those over-conscious of superior wisdom were injured because their advice was not asked. Before the march to Richmond there was much discontent. General Whiting, on reaching Staunton with his division, rode at once to Port Republic to report. 'The distance,' says General Imboden, ' was twenty miles, and Whiting returned after midnight. He was in a towering passion, and declared that Jackson had treated him outrageously. I asked, "How is that possible, General ?—he is very polite to everyone."

' "Oh, hang him! he was polite enough. But he didn't say one word about his plans. I finally asked him for orders, telling him what troops I had. He simply told me to go back to Staunton, and he would send me orders to-morrow. I haven't the slightest idea what they will be. I believe he has no more sense than my horse."' [1]

The orders, when they came, simply directed him to take his troops by railway to Gordonsville, through which they had passed two days before, and gave no reason whatever for the movement.

General Whiting was not the only Confederate officer who was mystified. When the troops left the Valley not a single soul in the army, save Jackson alone, knew the object of their march. He had even gone out of his way to blind his most trusted subordinates.

'During the preceding afternoon,' says Major Hotchkiss, ' he sent for me to his tent, and asked me to bring maps of the country from Port Republic to Lexington (at the head of the Valley), as he wished to examine them. I took the maps to his tent, and for about half an hour we talked concerning the roads and streams, and points of offence and defence of that region, just as though he had in mind a march in that direction. After this interval had passed he thanked me and said that that would do. About half an hour later he sent for me again, and remarked that there had been some fighting down about Richmond, referring, of course, to the battle of Seven Pines, and that he would like to see the map of the field of the operations. I brought the maps of the district round Richmond, and we spent nearly twice as much time over those, talking about the streams, the roads, the condition of the country, and so forth. On retiring to my tent I said to myself, "Old Jack" is going to Richmond.' [2]

Even the faithful Dabney was left in the dark till the troops had reached Mechum's Station. There, calling him into a room in the hotel, the general locked the door and explained the object of his march. But it was under seal of secrecy; and Ewell, the second in command, complained to the chief of the staff that Jackson had gone off by train, leaving him without orders, or even a hint of what was in

¹ *Battles and Leaders*, p. 297.   ² Letter to the author.

the wind. In fact, a few days after the battle of Port Republic, Ewell had sent some of his staff on leave of absence, telling them that large reinforcements were coming up, and that the next move would be 'to beat up Banks' quarters about Strasburg.'

When Jackson was informed of the irritation of his generals he merely smiled, and said, 'If I can deceive my own friends I can make certain of deceiving the enemy.' Nothing shook his faith in Frederick the Great's maxim, which he was fond of quoting: 'If I thought my coat knew my plans, I would take it off and burn it.' An anecdote told by one of his brigadiers illustrates his reluctance to say more than necessary. Previous to the march to Richmond this officer met Jackson riding through Staunton. 'Colonel,' said the general, 'have you received the order?' 'No, sir.' 'Want you to march.' 'When, sir?' 'Now.' 'Which way?' 'Get in the cars—go with Lawton.' 'How must I send my train and the battery?' 'By the road.' 'Well, General, I hate to ask questions, but it is impossible to send my waggons off without knowing which road to send them.' 'Oh!'—laughing—'send them by the road the others go.'

At last, when they saw how constant fortune was to their reticent leader, his subordinates ceased to complain; but unfortunately there was another source of trouble. Jackson had no regard whatever for persons. Reversing the usual procedure, he held that the choleric word of the soldier was rank blasphemy in the captain; the higher the rank of the offender the more severe, in his opinion, should be the punishment. Not only did he hold that he who would rule others must himself set the example of punctiliousness, but that to whom much is given, from him much is to be expected. Honour and promotion fall to the lot of the officer. His name is associated in dispatches with the valorous deeds of his command, while the private soldier fights on unnoticed in the crowd. To his colonels, therefore, Jackson was a strict master, and stricter to his generals. If he had reason to believe that his subordinates were indolent or disobedient, he visited their shortcomings with a heavy hand. No excuse availed. Arrest and report followed immediately on detection, and if the cure was rude, the plague of incompetency was radically dealt with. Spirited young soldiers, proud of their high rank, and in no way underrating their own capacity, rebelled against such discipline; and the knowledge that they were closely watched, that their omissions would be visited on their heads with unfaltering severity, sometimes created a barrier between them and their commander.

But it was only wilful disobedience or actual insubordination that roused Jackson's wrath. 'If he found in an officer,' says Dabney, 'a hearty and zealous purpose to do all his duty, he was the most tolerant and gracious of superiors, overlooking blunders and mistakes with unbounded patience, and repairing them through his own exertions, without even a sign of vexation.' The delay at the bridge on the morning of Port Republic, so fatal to his design of crushing Frémont, caused no outburst of wrath. He received his adjutant-general's report with equanimity, regarding the accident as due to the will of Providence, and therefore to be accepted without complaint.[1]

Whether the nobler side of Jackson's character had a share in creating the confidence which his soldiers already placed in him must be matter of conjecture. It was well known in the ranks that he was superior to the frailties of human nature; that he was as thorough a Christian as he was a soldier; that he feared the world as little as he did the enemy.[2] In all things he was consistent; his sincerity was as clear as the noonday sun, and his faith as firmly rooted as the Massanuttons. Publicly and privately, in official dispatches and in ordinary conversation, the success of his army was ascribed to the Almighty. Every victory, as

[1] Dabney, *Southern Historical Society Papers*, vol. xi., p. 152.
[2] His devout habits were no secret in the camp. Jim, most faithful of servants, declared that he could always tell when there was going to be a battle. 'The general,' he said, 'is a great man for prayin'. He pray night and mornin'—all times. But when I see him git up several times in the night, an' go off an' pray, *den I know there is goin' to be somethin' to pay,* an' I go right away and pack his haversack!'

soon as opportunity offered, was followed by the order :
'The chaplains will hold divine service in their respective regiments.'   'The General Commanding,' ran the
order after Winchester, 'would warmly express to the
officers and men under his command his joy in their
achievements, and his thanks for their brilliant gallantry
in action, and their patient obedience under the hardships
of forced marches, often more painful to the brave soldier
than the danger of battle.   The explanation of the severe
exertions to which the commanding general called the
army, which were endured by them with such cheerful
confidence in him, is now given in the victory of yesterday.
He receives this proof of their confidence in the past with
pride and gratitude, and asks only a similar confidence in
the future.

'But his chief duty of to-day and that of the army is
to recognise devoutly the hand of a protecting Providence
in the brilliant successes of the last three days (which
have given us the results of a great victory without great
losses), and to make the oblation of our thanks to God for
His service to us and our country in heartfelt acts of religious
worship.   For this purpose the troops will remain in camp
to-day, suspending, as far as possible, all military exercises ;
and the chaplains of regiments will hold divine service in
their several charges at 4 o'clock P.M.' [1]

Whenever it was possible Sunday was always set apart
for a day of rest; and the claims of the day were seldom
altogether disregarded.[2]   On the morning of Cross Keys it
is related that a large portion of Elzey's brigade were at
service, and that the crash of the enemy's artillery interrupted the 'thirdly' of the chaplain's sermon.

It has been sometimes asserted that Jackson was of the
same type as the saints militant who followed Cromwell,
who, when they were not slaughtering their enemies,
would expound the harsh tenets of their unlovely creed to
the grim circle of belted Ironsides.   He has been described

[1] Dabney, vol. ii., pp. 114-5.
[2] Sometimes,' says Major Hotchkiss, 'Jackson would keep two or three
Sundays running, so as to make up arrears, and balance the account !'

as taking the lead at religious meetings, as distributing tracts from tent to tent, as acting as aide-de-camp to his chaplains, and as consigning to perdition all those 'whose doxy was not his doxy.'

Nothing is further from the truth. 'His views of each denomination,' says his wife, 'had been obtained from itself, not from its opponents. Hence he could see excellences in all. Even of the Roman Catholic Church he had a much more favourable impression than most Protestants, and he fraternised with all Evangelical denominations. During a visit to New York, one Sabbath morning, we chanced to find ourselves at the door of an Episcopal Church at the hour of worship. He proposed that we should enter ; and as it was a day for the celebration of the Communion, he remained for that service, and it was with the utmost reverence and solemnity that he walked up the chancel and knelt to receive the elements.'

Jackson, then, was by no means imbued with the belief that the Presbyterian was the one true Church, and that all others were in error. Nor did he attempt, in the very slightest degree, to usurp the functions of his chaplains. Although he invariably went to sleep during their sermons, he was deeply interested in their endeavours, and gave them all the assistance in his power. But he no more thought of taking their duties on himself than of interfering with the treatment of the men in hospital. He spoke no 'words in season,' even to his intimates. He had no 'message' for them. Where religion was concerned, so long as duly qualified instructors were available, he conceived it his business to listen and not to teach. Morning and evening prayers were the rule at his headquarters, but if any of his staff chose to remain absent, the general made no remark. Yet all suspicion of indifference to vice was effectually removed. Nothing ungenerous or unclean was said in his presence without incurring his displeasure, always unmistakably expressed, and although he made no parade of his piety he was far too manly to hide it.

Yet he was never a prominent figure at the camp services. Rather than occupy a conspicuous place he would seat himself amongst the privates; and the only share he took in directing the proceedings was to beckon men to the seats that respect had left empty beside him. Those who picture him as an enthusiastic fanatic, invading, like the Puritan dragoons, the pulpits of the chaplains, and leading the devotions of his troops with the same fervour that he displayed in battle, have utterly misread his character. The humblest soldier in the Confederate army was not more modest and unassuming than Stonewall Jackson.

NOTE

The Federal strength at M'Dowell.

Frémont's return of April 30 is as follows :—
        Milroy's Brigade 4,307
        Schenck's Brigade 3,335
of May 10 :—
        Milroy 3,694
        Schenck 3,335
of May 31 :—
        Milroy 2,914
        Schenck 3,335

Schenck reports that the total force *engaged* at M'Dowell was 1,768 of Milroy's brigade, and about 500 of his own, total 2,268 ; and that he himself brought to M'Dowell 1,300 infantry, a battery, and 250 cavalry—say, 1,600 men.

Milroy's command may fairly be estimated at 3,500 ; Schenck brought 1,600 men ; there were therefore available for action at M'Dowell 5,100 Federals.

Frémont's strength at Cross Keys.

The return of May 31 gives :—13,520 officers and men.

Frémont, in his report of the battle, says that on May 29 he had over 11,000 men, which, deducting guards, garrisons, working parties and stragglers, were reduced to 10,500 combatants at Cross Keys.

But he does not include in this last estimate Bayard's cavalry, which joined him at Strasburg.

On May 31 Bayard had 1,844 officers and men ; he had suffered some loss in fighting Ashby, and his strength at the battle may be put down as 1,750.

All garrisons, guards and working parties are included in the Confederate numbers, so they should be added to the Federal estimate. We may fairly say, then, that at Cross Keys the following troops were available :—

        Frémont 11,000
        Bayard 1,750
                                _____
                        Total . . 12,750

Strength of the Federals, May 17–25.

On April 30 Banks' 'effective' numbers were as follows:—

Donnelly's Brigade	2,747
Gordon's Brigade	3,005
Artillery (26 guns)	492
Cavalry (General Hatch)	2,834
Body-guard	70
	9,148

On May 23 he had :—

At Strasburg : Infantry . . .	4,476
„ Cavalry . . .	2,600
„ Artillery (18 guns) . .	350
At Front Royal, Buckton, &c. . . .	1,300
„ Body-guard	70

From the Harper's Ferry Garrison :—

At Strasburg : Cavalry	300
At Winchester : Infantry	856
„ Cavalry	600
	10,552

On May 31, after losing 2,019 men at Front Royal and Winchester, he had, the Harper's Ferry troops having been added to his command :—

Infantry	5,124
Cavalry	3,230
Artillery (16 guns)	286
Miscellaneous	82
	8,722
Add . .	2,019
	10,741

10,500 effectives on May 23 is therefore a fair estimate.

Geary's 2,000 at Rectortown, as they were acting under Mr. Stanton's orders, have not been included.

END OF THE FIRST VOLUME

Spottiswoode & Co. Ltd., Printers, New-street Square, London.

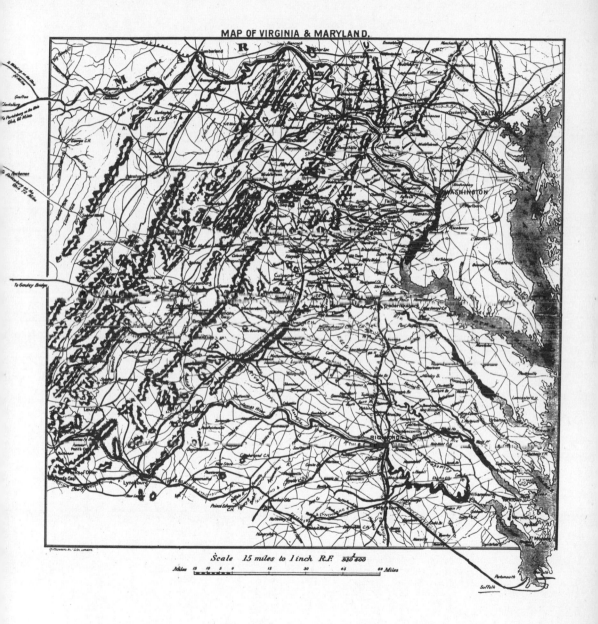

MAP OF VIRGINIA & MARYLAND.

Scale 15 miles to 1 inch R.F. $\frac{1}{950400}$

Miles

STONEWALL JACKSON

VOL. II.

STONEWALL JACKSON

AND THE

AMERICAN CIVIL WAR

BY

LIEUT.-COL. G. F. R. HENDERSON, C.B.

AUTHOR OF 'THE BATTLE OF SPICHEREN, A TACTICAL STUDY'
AND 'THE CAMPAIGN OF FREDERICKSBURG'

CONTENTS

OF

THE SECOND VOLUME

———

ILLUSTRATIONS IN VOL. II

MAPS

STONEWALL JACKSON

CHAPTER XIII

THE SEVEN DAYS. GAINES' MILL

THE region whither the interest now shifts is very different
from the Valley. From the terraced banks of the Rappahannock, sixty miles north of Richmond, to the
1862. shining reaches of the James, where the capital of
the Confederacy stands high on her seven hills, the lowlands
of Virginia are clad with luxuriant vegetation. The roads
and railways run through endless avenues of stately trees;
the shadows of the giant oaks lie far across the rivers, and
ridge and ravine are mantled with the unbroken foliage of
the primeval forest. In this green wilderness the main
armies were involved. But despite the beauty of broad
rivers and sylvan solitudes, gay with gorgeous blossoms and
fragrant with aromatic shrubs, the eastern, or 'tidewater,'
counties of Virginia had little to recommend them as a
theatre of war. They were sparsely settled. The wooden
churches, standing lonely in the groves where the congrega-
tions hitched their horses; the solitary taverns, half inns and
half stores; the court-houses of the county justices, with a few
wooden cottages clustered round them, were poor substi-
tutes for the market-towns of the Shenandoah. Here and
there on the higher levels, surrounded by coppice and
lawn, by broad acres of corn and clover, the manors of
the planters gave life and brightness to the landscape.
But the men were fighting in Lee's ranks, their families

had fled to Richmond, and these hospitable homes showed signs of poverty and neglect. Neither food nor forage was to be drawn from the country, and the difficulties of supply and shelter were not the worst obstacles to military operations. At this season of the year the climate and the soil were persistent foes. The roads were mere tracks, channels which served as drains for the interminable forest. The deep meadows, fresh and green to the eye, were damp and unwholesome camping-grounds. Turgid streams, like the Chickahominy and its affluents, winding sluggishly through rank jungles, spread in swamp and morass across the valleys, and the languid atmosphere, surcharged with vapour, was redolent of decay.

Through this malarious region the Federal army had been pushing its slow way forward for more than six weeks, June. and 105,000 men, accompanied by a large siege train, lay intrenched within sight of the spires of Richmond. 30,000 were north of the Chickahominy, covering the York River Railway and waiting the coming of McDowell. The remainder, from Woodbury's Bridge to the Charles City road, occupied the line of breastworks which stood directly east of the beleaguered city. So nearly was the prize within their grasp that the church bells, and even the clocks striking the hour, were heard in the camps; and at Mechanicsville Bridge, watched by a picket, stood a sign-post which bore the legend : ' To Richmond, 4½ miles.' The sentries who paced that beat were fortunate. For the next two years they could boast that no Federal soldier, except as a prisoner, had stood so close as they had to the rebel stronghold. But during these weeks in June not a single soul in McClellan's army, and few in the Confederacy, suspected that the flood of invasion had reached high-water mark. Richmond, gazing night after night at the red glow which throbbed on the eastern vault, the reflection of countless camp-fires, and listening with strained ears to the far-off call of hostile bugles, seemed in perilous case. No formidable position protected the approaches. Earthworks, indeed, were in process of construction; but, although the left flank at New Bridge was covered by the

Chickahominy, the right was protected by no natural obstacle, as had been the case at Yorktown; and the lines occupied no commanding site. Nor had the Government been able to assemble an army of a strength sufficient to man the whole front. Lee, until Jackson joined him, commanded no more than 72,500 men. Of these a large portion were new troops, and their numbers had been reduced by the 7,000 dispatched under Whiting to the Valley.

But if the Federal army was far superior in numbers, it was not animated by an energy in proportion to its strength. The march from the White House was more sluggish than the current of the Chickahominy. From May 17 to June 26 the Army of the Valley had covered four hundred miles. Within the same period the Army of the Potomac had covered twenty. It is true that the circumstances were widely different. McClellan had in front of him the lines of Richmond, and his advance had been delayed by the rising of the Chickahominy. He had fought a hard fight at Seven Pines; and the constant interference of Jackson had kept him waiting for McDowell. But, at the same time, he had displayed an excess of caution which was perfectly apparent to his astute opponent. He had made no attempt to use his superior numbers; and Lee had come to the conclusion that the attack on Richmond would take the same form as the attack on Yorktown,—the establishment of great batteries, the massing of heavy ordnance, and all the tedious processes of a siege. He read McClellan like an open book.

June 11.
He had personal knowledge both of his capacity and character, for they had served together on the same staff in the Mexican war. He knew that his young adversary was a man of undoubted ability, of fascinating address, and of courage that was never higher than when things were at their worst. But these useful qualities were accompanied by marked defects. His will was less powerful than his imagination. Bold in conception, he was terribly slow in execution. When his good sense showed him the opportunity, his imagination whispered, ' Suppose the enemy has reserves of which I know nothing! Is it not more prudent to wait until I receive more accurate information?' And so ' I dare not,'

B 2

inevitably waited on 'I would.' He forgot that in war it is impossible for a general to be absolutely certain. It is sufficient, according to Napoleon, if the odds in his favour are three to two; and if he cannot discover from the attitude of his enemy what the odds are, he is unfitted for supreme command.

Before Yorktown McClellan's five army corps had been held in check, first by 15,000 men, then by 53,000, protected by earthworks of feeble profile.[1] The fort at Gloucester Point was the key of the Confederate lines.[2] McClellan, however, although a division was actually under orders to move against it, appears to have been unwilling to risk a failure.[3] The channel of the York was thus closed both to his transports and the gunboats, and he did nothing whatever to interfere with Johnston's long line of communications, which passed at several points within easy reach of the river bank. Nor had he been more active since he had reached West Point. Except for a single expedition, which had dispersed a Confederate division near Hanover Court House, north of the Chickahominy, he had made no aggressive movement. He had never attempted to test the strength of the fortifications of Richmond, to hinder their construction, or to discover their weak points. His urgent demands for reinforcements had appeared in the Northern newspapers, and those newspapers had found their way to Richmond. From the same source the Confederates were made aware that he believed himself confronted by an army far larger than his own; and when, on the departure of Whiting's division for the Valley, he refused to take advantage of the opportunity to attack Lee's diminished force, it became abundantly clear, if further proof were wanting, that much might be ventured against so timid a commander.

From his knowledge of his adversary's character, and

[1] 'No one but McClellan would have hesitated to attack.' Johnston to Lee, April 22, 1862. O. R., vol. xi., part iii., p. 456.

[2] *Narrative of Military Operations*, General J. E. Johnston, pp. 112, 113

[3] The garrison consisted only of a few companies of heavy artillery, and the principal work was still unfinished when Yorktown fell. Reports of Dr. Comstock, and Colonel Cabell, C.S.A. O. R., vol. xi., part i.

still more from his attitude, Lee had little difficulty in discovering his intentions. McClellan, on the other hand, failed to draw a single correct inference. And yet the information at his disposal was sufficient to enable him to form a fair estimate of how things stood in the Confederate camp. He had been attacked at Seven Pines, but not by superior numbers; and it was hardly likely that the enemy had not employed their whole available strength in this battle; otherwise their enterprise was insensate. Furthermore, it was clearly to the interests of the Confederates to strike at his army before McDowell could join him. They had not done so, and it was therefore probable that they did not feel themselves strong enough to do so. It is true that he was altogether misled by the intelligence supplied as to the garrison of Richmond by his famous detective staff. 200,000 was the smallest number which the chief agent would admit. But that McClellan should have relied on the estimate of these untrained observers rather than on the evidence furnished by the conduct of the enemy is but a further proof that he lacked all power of deduction.[1]

It may well be questioned whether he was anxious at heart to measure swords with Lee. His knowledge of his adversary, whose reputation for daring, for ability, for strength of purpose, had been higher than any other in the old army, must needs have had a disturbing influence on his judgment. Against an enemy he did not know McClellan might have acted with resolution. Face to face with Lee, it can hardly be doubted that the weaker will was dominated by the stronger. Vastly different were their methods of war. McClellan made no effort whatever either to supplement or to corroborate the information supplied by his detectives. Since he had reached West Point his cavalry had done little.[2] Lee, on the other hand, had found

[1] In one sense McClellan was not far wrong in his estimate of the Confederate numbers. In assuming control of the Union armies Lincoln and Stanton made their enemies a present of at least 50,000 men.

[2] It must be admitted that his cavalry was very weak in proportion to the other arms. On June 20 he had just over 5,000 sabres (O. R., vol. xi., part iii., p. 238), of which 3,000 were distributed among the army corps. The

means to ascertain the disposition of his adversary's troops, and had acquired ample information of the measures which had been taken to protect the right wing, north of the Chickahominy, the point he had determined to attack.

Early on June 12, with 1,200 horsemen and a section of artillery, Stuart rode out on an enterprise of a June 12.   kind which at that time was absolutely unique, and which will keep his memory green so long as cavalry is used in war. Carefully concealing his march, he encamped that night near Taylorsville, twenty-two miles north of Richmond, and far beyond the flank of the Federal intrenchments. The next morning he turned June 13.   eastward towards Hanover Court House. Here he drove back a picket, and his advanced-guard, with the loss of one officer, soon afterwards charged down a squadron of regulars. A few miles to the south-east, near Old Church, the enemy's outposts were finally dispersed; and then, instead of halting, the column pushed on into the very heart of the district occupied by the Federals, and soon found itself in rear of their encampments. Stuart had already gained important information. He had learned that McClellan's right flank extended but a short way north of the Chickahominy, that it was not fortified, and that it rested on neither swamp nor stream, and this was what Lee had instructed him to discover. But it was one thing to obtain the information, another to bring it back. If he returned by the road he had come, it was probable he would be cut off, for the enemy was thoroughly roused, and the South Anna River, unfordable from recent rains, rendered a *détour* to the north impracticable. To the south and west of him lay the Federal army, some of the infantry camps not five miles distant. It was about

Confederates appear to have had about 3,000, but of superior quality, familiar, more or less, with the country, and united under one command. It is instructive to notice how the necessity for a numerous cavalry grew on the Federal commanders. In 1864 the Army of the Potomac was accompanied by a cavalry corps over 13,000 strong, with 32 guns. It is generally the case in war, even in a close country, that if the cavalry is allowed to fall below the usual proportion of one trooper to every six men of the other arms the army suffers.

four o'clock in the afternoon. He could hardly reach Hanover Court House before dark, and he might find it held by the enemy. To escape from the dilemma he determined on a plan of extraordinary daring, which involved nothing less than the passage of the Chickahominy in rear of the enemy, and a circuit of the entire Federal army.

The audacity of the design proved the salvation of his command. The enemy had assembled a strong force of both cavalry and infantry at Hanover Court House, under Stuart's father-in-law, General Cooke; but, misled by the reports brought in, and doubtless perplexed by the situation, the latter pursued but slowly and halted for the night at Old Church. Stuart, meanwhile, had reached Tunstall's Station on the York River Railway, picking up prisoners at every step. Here, routing the guard, he tore up the rails, destroyed a vast amount of stores and many waggons, broke down the telegraph and burnt the railway bridge, his men regaling themselves on the luxuries which were found in the well-stored establishments of the sutlers. Two squadrons, despatched to Garlick's Landing on the Pamunkey, set fire to two transports, and rejoined with a large number of prisoners, horses, and mules. Then, led by troopers who were natives of the country, the column marched south-east by the Williamsburg road, moving further and still further away from Richmond. The moon was full, and as the troops passed by the forest farms, the women, running to the wayside, wept with delight at the unexpected apparition of the grey jackets, and old men showered blessings on the heads of their gallant countrymen. At Talleysville, eight miles east, Stuart halted for three hours; and shortly after midnight, just as a Federal infantry brigade reached Tunstall's Station in hot pursuit, he turned off by a country road to the Chickahominy. At Forge Bridge, where he arrived at daylight, he should have found a ford;

June 14.

but the river had overflowed its banks, and was full of floating timber. Colonel Fitzhugh Lee, not the least famous member of a famous family, accompanied by a few men, swam his horse at imminent peril over to the

other bank ; but, although he re-crossed the swollen waters
in the same manner, the daring young officer had to report
that the passage was impracticable.   It was already light.
The enemy would soon be up, and the capture of the whole
column seemed absolutely certain.   Hitherto the men,
exhilarated by the complete success of the adventure, had
borne themselves as gaily as if they were riding through
the streets of Richmond.   But the danger of their situation
was now forcibly impressed upon them, and the whole
command became grave and anxious.   Stuart alone was
unmoved, and at this juncture one of his scouts informed
him that the skeleton of an old bridge spanned the stream
about a mile below.   An abandoned warehouse furnished
the materials for a footway, over which the troopers
passed, holding the bridles of their horses as they swam
alongside. Half the column thus crossed, while the remainder strengthened the bridge so as to permit the passage of
the artillery.   By one o'clock the whole force was over
the Chickahominy, unmolested by the enemy, of whom only
small parties, easily driven back by the rear-guard, had
made their appearance.

Thirty-five miles now to Richmond, in rear of the left
wing of the Northern army, and within range, for some
portion of the march, of the gunboats on the James River !
Burning the bridge, with a wave of the hand to the
Federal horsemen who covered the heights above Stuart
plunged into the woods, and without further misadventure
brought his troops at sunset to the neighbourhood of
Charles City Court House. Leaving his men sleeping,
after thirty-six hours in the saddle, he rode to Richmond to
June 15.   report to Lee.   Before dawn on the 15th, after
            covering another thirty miles, over a road which
was patrolled by the enemy, he reached head-quarters.   His
squadrons followed, marching at midnight, and bringing
with them 165 prisoners and 260 captured horses and mules.

This extraordinary expedition, which not only effected
the destruction of a large amount of Federal property,
and broke up, for the time being, their line of supplies, but
acquired information of the utmost value, and shook the con-

fidence of the North in McClellan's generalship, was accomplished with the loss of one man. These young Virginia soldiers marched one hundred and ten miles in less than two days. 'There was something sublime,' says Stuart, 'in the implicit confidence and unquestioning trust of the rank and file in a leader guiding them straight, apparently, into the very jaws of the enemy, every step appearing to them to diminish the hope of extrication.'[1] Nor was the influence of their achievement on the *moral* of the whole Confederate army the least important result attained. A host of over 100,000 men, which had allowed a few squadrons to ride completely round it, by roads which were within hearing of its bugles, was no longer considered a formidable foe.

On receiving Stuart's information, Lee drew up the plan of operations which had been imparted to Jackson on the 22nd.

It was a design which to all appearance was almost foolhardy. The Confederate army was organised as follows :—

Longstreet.	9,000
A. P. Hill .	14,000
Magruder .	13,000
Huger	9,000
Holmes	6,500
D. H. Hill .	10,000
Jackson	18,500
Cavalry .	3,000
Reserve Artillery	3,500
	86,500 [2]

On the night of June 24 the whole of these troops, with the exception of the Valley army, were south of the Chickahominy, holding the earthworks which protected Richmond. Less than two miles eastward, strongly intrenched, lay four of McClellan's army corps, in round numbers 75,000 officers and men.[3]

To attack this force, even after Jackson's arrival,

June 24.

[1] Stuart's Report, O. R., vol. xi., part i.

[2] This estimate is rather larger than that of the Confederate historians (Allan, W. H. Taylor, &c., &c.), but it has been arrived at after a careful examination of the strength at different dates and the losses in the various engagements.

[3] Return of June 20, O. R., vol. xi., part i., p. 238.

was to court disaster. The right was protected by the
Chickahominy, the left rested on White Oak Swamp, a
network of sluggish streams and impassable swamps,
screened everywhere by tangled thickets.   It needed not
the presence of the siege ordnance, placed on the most
commanding points within the lines, to make such a position absolutely impregnable.

North of the Chickahominy, however, the Federals were
less favourably situated. The Fifth Army Corps, 25,000
strong,[1] under General FitzJohn Porter, had been pushed
forward, stretching a hand to McDowell and protecting the
railway, in the direction of Mechanicsville; and although
the tributaries of the Chickahominy, running in from the
north, afforded a series of positions, the right flank of
these positions, resting, as Stuart had ascertained, on
no natural obstacle, was open to a turning movement.
Furthermore, in rear of the Fifth Corps, and at an oblique
angle to the front, ran the line of supply, the railway to
West Point. If Porter's right were turned, the Confederates, threatening the railway, would compel McClellan to
detach largely to the north bank of the Chickahominy in
order to recover or protect the line.

On the north bank of the Chickahominy, therefore,
Lee's attention had been for some time fixed. Here was
his adversary's weak point, and a sudden assault on Porter,
followed up, if necessary, by an advance against the
railway, would bring McClellan out of his intrenchments,
and force him to fight at a disadvantage. To ensure
success, however, in the attack on Porter it was necessary
to concentrate an overwhelming force on the north bank;
and this could hardly be done without so weakening the force
which held the Richmond lines that it would be unable
to resist the attack of the 75,000 men who faced it. If
McClellan, while Lee was fighting Porter, boldly threw
forward the great army he had on the south bank, the rebel
capital might be the reward of his resolution.   The danger

---

[1] The Fifth Army Corps included McCall's division, which had but
recently arrived by water from Fredericksburg.   Report of June 20, O. R.,
vol. xi., part i., p. 238.

was apparent to all, but Lee resolved to risk it, and his audacity has not escaped criticism. It has been said that he deliberately disregarded the contingency of McClellan either advancing on Richmond, or reinforcing Porter. The truth is, however, that neither Lee, nor those generals about him who knew McClellan, were in the least apprehensive that their over-cautious adversary, if the attack were sudden and well sustained, would either see or utilise his opportunity.

From Hannibal to Moltke there has been no great captain who has neglected to study the character of his opponent, and who did not trade on the knowledge thus acquired, and it was this knowledge which justified Lee's audacity.

The real daring of the enterprise lay in the inferiority of the Confederate armament. Muskets and shot-guns, still carried by a large part of the army, were ill-matched against rifles of the most modern manufacture; while the smooth-bore field-pieces, with which at least half the artillery was equipped, possessed neither the range nor the accuracy of the rifled ordnance of the Federals.

That Lee's study of the chances had not been patient and exhaustive it is impossible to doubt. He was no hare-brained leader, but a profound thinker, following the highest principles of the military art. That he had weighed the disconcerting effect which the sudden appearance of the victorious Jackson, with an army of unknown strength, would produce upon McClellan, goes without saying. He had omitted no precaution to render the surprise complete, and although the defences of Richmond were still too weak to resist a resolute attack, Magruder, the same officer who had so successfully imposed upon McClellan at Yorktown, was such a master of artifice that, with 28,000 men and the reserve artillery,[1] he might be relied upon to hold Richmond until Porter had been dis-

[1] Magruder's division, 13,000; Huger's division, 9,000; reserve artillery, 3,000; 5 regiments of cavalry, 2,000. Holmes' division, 6,500, was still retained on the south bank of the James.

posed of. The remainder of the army, 2,000 of Stuart's cavalry, the divisions of Longstreet and the two Hills, 35,000 men all told, crossing to the north bank of the Chickahominy and combining with the 18,500 under Jackson, would be sufficient to crush the Federal right.

The initial operations, however, were of a somewhat complicated nature. Four bridges [1] crossed the river on Lee's left. A little more than a mile and a half from Mechanicsville Bridge, up stream, is Meadow Bridge, and five and a half miles further up is another passage at the Half Sink, afterwards called Winston's Bridge. Three and a half miles below Mechanicsville Bridge is New Bridge. The northern approaches to Mechanicsville, Meadow, and New Bridge, were in possession of the Federals; and it was consequently no simple operation to transfer the troops before Richmond from one bank of the Chickahominy to the other. Only Mechanicsville and Meadow Bridges could be used. Winston's Bridge was too far from Richmond, for, if Longstreet and the two Hills were to cross at that point, not only would Magruder be left without support during their march, but McClellan, warned by his scouts, would receive long notice of the intended blow and have ample time for preparation. To surprise Porter, to give McClellan no time for reflection, and at the same time to gain a position which would bring the Confederates operating on the north bank into close and speedy communication with Magruder on the south, another point of passage must be chosen. The position would be the one commanding New Bridge, for the Confederate earthworks, held by Magruder, ran due south from that point. But Porter was already in possession of the coveted ground, with strong outposts at Mechanicsville. To secure, then, the two centre bridges was the first object. This, it was expected, would be achieved by the advance of the Valley army, aided by a brigade from the Half Sink, against the flank and rear of the Federals at Mechanicsville. Then, as soon

[1] Lee's bridge, shown on the map, had either been destroyed or was not yet built.

as the enemy fell back, Longstreet and the two Hills would cross the river by the Meadow and Mechanicsville Bridges, and strike Porter in front, while Jackson attacked his right. A victory would place the Confederates in possession of New Bridge, and the troops north of the Chickahominy would be then in close communication with Magruder.

Lee's orders were as follows :—' Headquarters, Army of Northern Virginia, June 24, 1862. General Orders, No. 75.

'I.—General Jackson's command will proceed to-morrow (June 25) from Ashland towards the Slash (Merry Oaks) Church, and encamp at some convenient point west of the Central Railroad. Branch's brigade of A. P. Hill's division will also, to-morrow evening, take position on the Chickahominy, near Half Sink. At three o'clock Thursday morning, 26th instant, General Jackson will advance on the road leading to Pole Green Church, communicating his march to General Branch, who will immediately cross the Chickahominy, and take the road leading to Mechanicsville. As soon as the movements of these columns are discovered, General A. P. Hill, with the rest of his division, will cross the Chickahominy at Meadow Bridge, and move direct upon Mechanicsville. To aid his advance the heavy batteries on the Chickahominy will at the proper time open upon the batteries at Mechanicsville. The enemy being driven from Mechanicsville and the passage of the bridge being opened, General Longstreet, with his division and that of General D. H. Hill, will cross the Chickahominy at or near that point ; General D. H. Hill moving to the support of General Jackson, and General Longstreet supporting General A. P. Hill ; the four divisions keeping in communication with each other, and moving *en échelon* on separate roads if practicable ; the left division in advance, with skirmishers and sharp-shooters extending in their front, will sweep down the Chickahominy, and endeavour to drive the enemy from his position above New Bridge, General Jackson bearing well to his left, turning Beaver Dam Creek, and taking the direction towards

Cold Harbour. They will then press forward towards the
York River Railroad, closing upon the enemy's rear, and
forcing him down the Chickahominy. An advance of the
enemy towards Richmond will be prevented by vigorously
following his rear, and crippling and arresting his
progress.

'II.—The divisions under Generals Huger and Magruder
will hold their position in front of the enemy against
attack, and make such demonstrations, Thursday, as to
discover his operations. Should opportunity offer, the
feint will be converted into a real attack. . . . .

'IV.—General Stuart, with the 1st, 4th, and 9th
Virginia Cavalry, the cavalry of Cobb's Legion, and the
Jeff Davis Legion, will cross the Chickahominy to-morrow
(Wednesday, June 25), and take position to the left of
General Jackson's line of march. The main body will be
held in reserve, with scouts well extended to the front and
left. General Stuart will keep General Jackson informed
of the movements of the enemy on his left, and will co-
operate with him in his advance. . . . .'

On the 25th Longstreet and the two Hills moved
towards the bridges; and although during the movement
June 25. McClellan drove back Magruder's pickets to their
trenches, and pushed his own outposts nearer
Richmond, Lee held firmly to his purpose. As a matter
of fact, there was little to be feared from McClellan.
With a profound belief in the advantages of defensive and
in the strength of a fortified position, he expected nothing
less than that the Confederates would leave the earthworks
they had so laboriously constructed, and deliberately risk
the perils of an attack. He seems to have had little
idea that in the hands of a skilful general intrenchments
may form a 'pivot of operations,'[1] the means whereby he
covers his most vulnerable point, holds the enemy in front,
and sets his main body free for offensive action. Yet

[1] 'The meaning of this term is clearly defined in Lee's report. 'It was
therefore determined to construct defensive lines, so as to enable a part of
the army to defend the city, and leave the other part free to operate on the
north bank.' O. R., vol. xi., part i., p. 490.

McClellan was by no means easy in his mind. He knew Jackson was approaching. He knew his communications were threatened. Fugitive negroes, who, as usual, either exaggerated or lied, had informed him that the Confederates had been largely reinforced, and that Beauregard, with a portion of the Western army, had arrived in Richmond. But that his right wing was in danger he had not the faintest suspicion. He judged Lee by himself. Such a plan as leaving a small force to defend Richmond, and transferring the bulk of the army to join Jackson, he would have at once rejected as overdaring. If attack came at all, he expected that it would come by the south bank ; and he was so far from anticipating that an opportunity for offensive action might be offered to himself that, on the night of the 25th, he sent word to his corps commanders that they were to regard their intrenchments as ' the true field of battle.' [1]

Lee's orders left much to Jackson. The whole operation which Lee had planned hinged upon his movements. On the morning of the 24th he was at Beaver Dam Station. The same night he was to reach Ashland, eighteen miles distant as the crow flies. On the night of the 25th he was to halt near the Slash Church, just west of the Virginia Central Railway, and six miles east of Ashland. At three o'clock,

June 26. however, on the morning of the 26th, the Army of 3 A.M. the Valley was still at Ashland, and it was not till nine that it crossed the railroad. Branch, on hearing 10.30 A.M. that Jackson was at last advancing, passed the Chickahominy by Winston's Bridge, and driving the Federal pickets before him, moved on Mechanicsville. General A. P. Hill was meanwhile near Meadow Bridge, waiting until the advance of Jackson and Branch should turn the flank of the Federal force which blocked his 3 P.M. passage. At 3 P.M., hearing nothing from his colleagues, and apprehensive that longer delay might hazard the failure of the whole plan, he ordered his advanced-guard to seize the bridge. The enemy, already threatened in rear by Branch, at once fell back. Hill followed

[1] O. R., vol. xi., part iii., p. 252.

the retiring pickets towards Beaver Dam Creek, and after a short march of three miles found himself under fire of the Federal artillery. Porter had occupied a position about two miles above New Bridge.

The rest of the Confederate army was already crossing the Chickahominy; and although there was no sign of Jackson, and the enemy's front was strong, protected by a long line of batteries, Hill thought it necessary to order an attack. A message from Lee, ordering him to postpone all further movement, arrived too late.[1] There was no artillery preparation, and the troops, checked unexpectedly by a wide abattis, were repulsed with terrible slaughter, the casualties amounting to nearly 2,000 men.[2] The Union loss was 360.[3]

Jackson, about 4.30 P.M., before this engagement had begun, had reached Hundley's Corner, three miles north
4.30 P.M. of the Federal position, but separated from it by dense forest and the windings of the creek. On the opposite bank was a detachment of Federal infantry, supported by artillery. Two guns, accompanied by the
6 P.M. advanced-guard, sufficed to drive this force to the shelter of the woods; and then, establishing his outposts, Jackson ordered his troops to bivouac.

It has been asserted by more than one Southern general that the disaster at Beaver Dam Creek was due to Jackson's indifferent tactics; and, at first sight, the bare facts would seem to justify the verdict. He had not reached his appointed station on the night of the 25th, and on the 26th he was five hours behind time. He should have crossed the Virginia Central Railway at sunrise, but at nine o'clock he was still three miles distant. His advance against the Federal right flank and rear should have been made in co-operation with the remainder of the army. But his whereabouts was unknown when Hill attacked; and although the cannonade was distinctly heard at Hundley's Corner, he made no effort to lend assistance, and his troops were encamping when their comrades, not three miles

[1] Letter from Capt. T. W. Sydnor, 4th Va. Cavalry, who carried the message.
[2] So General Porter. *Battles and Leaders*, vol. ii., p. 331.
[3] O. R., vol. xi., part i., pp. 38, 39.

away, were rushing forward to the assault. There would seem to be some grounds, then, for the accusation that his delay thwarted General Lee's design; some reason for the belief that the victor of the Valley campaign, on his first appearance in combination with the main army, had proved a failure, and that his failure was in those very qualities of swiftness and energy to which he owed his fame.

General D. H. Hill has written that 'Jackson's genius never shone when he was under the command of another. It seemed then to be shrouded or paralysed. . . . MacGregor on his native heath was not more different from MacGregor in prison than was Jackson his own master from Jackson in a subordinate position. This was the keynote to his whole character. The hooded falcon cannot strike the quarry.' [1]

The reader who has the heart to follow this chronicle to the end will assuredly find reason to doubt the acumen, however he may admire the eloquence, of Jackson's brother-in-law. When he reads of the Second Manassas, of Harper's Ferry, of Sharpsburg and of Chancellorsville, he will recall this statement with astonishment; and it will not be difficult to show that Jackson conformed as closely to the plans of his commander at Mechanicsville as elsewhere.

The machinery of war seldom runs with the smoothness of clockwork. The course of circumstances can never be exactly predicted. Unforeseen obstacles may render the highest skill and the most untiring energy of no avail; and it may be well to point out that the task which was assigned to Jackson was one of exceeding difficulty. In the first place, his march of eight-and-twenty miles, from Frederickshall to Ashland, on June 23, 24, and 25, was made over an unmapped country, unknown either to himself or to his staff, which had lately been in occupation of the Federals. Bridges had been destroyed and roads obstructed. The Valley army had already marched far and fast; and although Dabney hints that inexperienced and sluggish subordinates were the chief cause of delay,

[1] *Battles and Leaders*, vol. ii., pp. 389, 390.

there is hardly need to look so far for excuse.[1]   The march
from Ashland to Hundley's Corner, sixteen miles, was little
less difficult.   It was made in two columns, Whiting and the
Stonewall division, now under Winder, crossing the railway
near Merry Oaks Church, Ewell moving by Shady Grove
Church ; but this distribution did not accelerate the march.
The midsummer sun blazed fiercely down on the dusty
roads ; the dense woods on either hand shut out the air, and
interruptions were frequent.   The Federal cavalry held a
line from Atlee's Station to near Hanover Court House.
The 8th Illinois, over 700 strong, picketed all the woods
between the Chickahominy and the Totopotomoy Creek.
Two other regiments prolonged the front to the Pamunkey,
and near Hundley's Corner and Old Church were posted
detachments of infantry.   Skirmishing was constant.   The
Federal outposts contested every favourable position.   Here
and there the roads were obstructed by felled trees ; a
burned bridge over the Totopotomoy delayed the advance for
a full hour, and it was some time before the enemy's force
at Hundley's Corner was driven behind Beaver Dam Creek.

At the council of war, held on the 23rd, Lee had left
it to Jackson to fix the date on which the operation against
the Federal right should begin, and on the latter deciding on
the 26th, Longstreet had suggested that he should make
more ample allowance for the difficulties that might be presented by the country and by the enemy, and give himself
more time.[2]   Jackson had not seen fit to alter his decision,
and it is hard to say that he was wrong.

Had McClellan received notice that the Valley army
was approaching, a day's delay would have given him a
fine opportunity.   More than one course would have been
open to him.   He might have constructed formidable intrenchments on the north bank of the Chickahominy and

---

[1] Dr. White, in his excellent *Life of Lee*, states that the tardiness of the
arrival of the provisions sent him from Richmond had much to do with the
delay of Jackson's march.

[2] 'Lee's Attacks North of the Chickahominy.' By General D. H. Hill.
Battles and Leaders, vol. ii., p. 347.   General Longstreet, however, *From
Manassas to Appomattox*, says Jackson appointed the morning of the 25th,
but, on Longstreet's suggestion, changed the date to the 26th.

have brought over large reinforcements of men and guns; or he might have turned the tables by a bold advance on Richmond. It was by no means inconceivable that if he detected Lee's intention and was given time to prepare, he might permit the Confederates to cross the Chickahominy, amuse them there with a small force, and hurl the rest of his army on the works which covered the Southern capital. It is true that his caution was extreme, and to a mind which was more occupied with counting the enemy's strength than with watching for an opportunity, the possibility of assuming the offensive was not likely to occur. But, timid as he might be when no enemy was in sight, McClellan was constitutionally brave; and when the chimeras raised by an over-active imagination proved to be substantial dangers, he was quite capable of daring resolution. Time, therefore, was of the utmost importance to the Confederates. It was essential that Porter should be overwhelmed before McClellan realised the danger; and if Jackson, in fixing a date for the attack which would put a heavy tax on the marching powers of his men, already strained to the utmost, ran some risks, from a strategical point of view those risks were fully justified.

In the second place, an operation such as that which Lee had devised is one of the most difficult manœuvres which an army can be called upon to execute. According to Moltke, to unite two forces on the battle-field, starting at some distance apart, at the right moment, is the most brilliant feat of generalship. The slightest hesitation may ruin the combination. Haste is even more to be dreaded. There is always the danger that one wing may attack, or be attacked, while the other is still far distant, and either contingency may be fatal. The Valley campaign furnishes more than one illustration. In their pursuit of Jackson, Shields and Frémont failed to co-operate at Strasburg, at Cross Keys, and at Port Republic. And greater generals than either Shields or Frémont have met with little better success in attempting the same manœuvre. At both Eylau and Bautzen Napoleon was deprived of decisive victory by his failure to ensure the co-operation of his widely separated columns.

Jackson and A. P. Hill, on the morning of the 26th, were nearly fifteen miles apart. Intercommunication at the outset was ensured by the brigade under Branch; but as the advance progressed, and the enemy was met with, it became more difficult. The messengers riding from one force to the other were either stopped by the Federals, or were compelled to make long *détours*; and as they approached the enemy's position, neither Hill nor Jackson was informed of the whereabouts of the other.

The truth is, that the arrangements made by the Confederate headquarter staff were most inadequate. In the first place, the order of the 24th, instructing Jackson to start from Slash Church at 3 A.M. on the 26th, and thus leading the other generals to believe that he would certainly be there at that hour, should never have been issued. When it was written Jackson's advanced-guard was at Beaver Dam Station, the rear brigades fifteen miles behind; and to reach Slash Church his force had to march forty miles through an intricate country, in possession of the enemy, and so little known that it was impossible to designate the route to be followed. To fix an hour of arrival so long in advance was worse than useless, and Jackson cannot be blamed if he failed to comply with the exact letter of a foolish order. As it was, so many of the bridges were broken, and so difficult was it to pass the fords, that if Dr. Dabney had not found in his brother, a planter of the neighbourhood, an efficient substitute for the guide headquarters should have provided, the Valley army would have been not hours but days too late. In the second place, the duty of keeping up communications should not have been left to Jackson, but have been seen to at headquarters. Jackson had with him only a few cavalry, and these few had not only to supply the necessary orderlies for the subordinate generals, and the escorts for the artillery and trains, but to form his advanced-guard, for Stuart's squadrons were on his left flank, and not in his front. Moreover, his cavalry were complete strangers to the country, and there were no maps. In such circumstances the only means of ensuring constant communication was to have detached two of Stuart's squadrons, who knew the ground, to establish a series of posts between Jackson's line of march and the Chickahominy; and to have detailed a staff officer, whose sole duty would have been to furnish the Commander-in-Chief with hourly reports of the progress made, to join the Valley army.[1] It may be remarked, too, that Generals Branch and Ewell, following converging roads, met near Shady Grove Church about 3 P.M. No report appears to have been sent by the latter to General A. P. Hill; and although Branch a little later received a message to the effect that Hill had crossed the Chickahominy and was moving on Mechanics-ville,[2] the information was not passed on to Jackson.

Neglect of these precautions made it impracticable to arrange a simultaneous attack, and co-operation depended solely on the judgment of Hill and Jackson. In the action which ensued on Beaver Dam Creek there was no co-operation whatever. Hill attacked and was repulsed. Jackson had halted at Hundley's Corner, three miles distant from the battle-field. Had the latter come down on the Federal rear while Hill moved against their front an easy success would in all probability have been the result.

Nevertheless, the responsibility for Hill's defeat cannot be held to rest on Jackson's shoulders. On August 18, 1870, the Prussian Guards and the Saxon Army Corps

---

[1] Of the events of June 26 Dr. Dabney, in a letter to the author, writes as follows:—' Here we had a disastrous illustration of the lack of an organised and intelligent general staff. Let my predicament serve as a specimen. As chief of Jackson's staff, I had two assistant adjutant-generals, two men of the engineer department, and two clerks. What did I have for orderlies and couriers? A detail from some cavalry company which happened to bivouac near. The men were sent to me without any reference to their local knowledge, their intelligence, or their courage; most probably they were selected for me by their captain on account of their lack of these qualities. Next to the Commander-in-Chief, the Chief of the General Staff should be the best man in the country. The brains of an army should be in the General Staff. The lowest orderlies attached to it should be the very best soldiers in the service, for education, intelligence, and courage. Jackson had to find his own guide for his march from Beaver Dam Station. He had not been furnished with a map, and not a single orderly or message reached him during the whole day.'

[2] Branch's Report, O. R., vol. xi., part ii., p. 882.

were ordered to make a combined attack on the village
of St. Privat, the Guards moving against the front, the
Saxons against the flank.   When the order was issued the
two corps were not more than two miles apart.   The tract
of country which lay between them was perfectly open, the
roads were free, and inter-communication seemed easy in
the extreme.   Yet, despite their orders, despite the facilities
of communication, the Guards advanced to the attack an
hour and a half too soon ; and from six o'clock to nearly
seven their shattered lines lay in front of the position,
at the mercy of a vigorous counterstroke, without a single
Saxon regiment coming to their aid.   But the Saxons were
not to blame.   Their march had been unchecked ; they had
moved at speed.   On their part there had been no hesitation ; but on the part of the commander of the Guards
there had been the same precipitation which led to the premature attack on the Federal position at Beaver Dam
Creek.   It was the impatience of General Hill, not the
tardiness of Jackson, which was the cause of the Confederate repulse.

We may now turn to the question whether Jackson was
justified in not marching to the sound of the cannon.
Referring to General Lee's orders, it will be seen that as soon
as Longstreet and D. H. Hill had crossed the Chickahominy
the four divisions of the army were to move forward *in communication with each other* and drive the enemy from his
position, Jackson, in advance upon the left, 'turning Beaver
Dam Creek, and taking the direction of Cold Harbour.'

When Jackson reached Hundley's Corner, and drove the
Federal infantry behind the Creek, the first thing to do, as
his orders indicated, was to get touch with the rest of the
army.   It was already near sunset ; between Hundley's
Corner and Mechanicsville lay a dense forest, with no roads
in the desired direction ; and it was manifestly impossible, under ordinary conditions, to do more that evening
than to establish connection ; the combined movement
against the enemy's position must be deferred till the
morning.   But the sound of battle to the south-west introduced a complication.   'We distinctly heard,' says Jackson,

'the rapid and continued discharges of cannon.'[1] What did this fire portend? It might proceed, as was to be inferred from Lee's orders, from the heavy batteries on the Chickahominy covering Hill's passage. It might mean a Federal counterstroke on Hill's advanced-guard; or, possibly, a premature attack on the part of the Confederates. General Whiting, according to his report, thought it 'indicated a severe battle.'[2] General Trimble, marching with Ewell, heard both musketry and artillery; and in his opinion the command should have moved forward;[3] and whatever may have been Jackson's orders, it was undoubtedly his duty, if he believed a hot engagement was in progress, to have marched to the assistance of his colleagues. He could not help them by standing still. He might have rendered them invaluable aid by pressing the enemy in flank. But the question is, What inference did the cannonade convey to Jackson's mind? Was it of such a character as to leave no doubt that Hill was in close action, or might it be interpreted as the natural accompaniment of the passage of the Chickahominy? The evidence is conflicting. On the one hand we have the evidence of Whiting and Trimble, both experienced soldiers; on the other, in addition to the indirect evidence of Jackson's inaction, we have the statement of Major Dabney. 'We heard no signs,' says the chief of the staff, 'of combat on Beaver Dam Creek until a little while before sunset. The whole catastrophe took place in a few minutes about that time; and in any case our regiments, who had gone into bivouac, could not have been reassembled, formed up, and moved forward in time to be of any service. A night attack through the dense, pathless, and unknown forest was quite impracticable.'[4] It seems probable, then—and the Federal reports are to the same effect[5]—that the firing was only really heavy for a very short period, and that Jackson believed it

[1] Jackson's Report, O. R., vol. xi., part i., p. 553.
[2] Whiting's Report, O. R., vol. xi., part i., p. 562.
[3] Trimble's Report, O. R., vol. xi., part i., p. 614.
[4] Letter to the author.
[5] Porter's Report, O. R., vol. xi., part i., p. 222. *Battles and Leaders*, vol. ii., p. 330.

to be occasioned by Hill's passage of the Chickahominy, and the rout of the Federals from Mechanicsville. Neither Trimble nor Whiting were aware that Lee's orders directed that the operation was to be covered by a heavy cannonade.

Obeying orders very literally himself, Jackson found it difficult to believe that others did not do the same. He knew that the position he had taken up rendered the line of Beaver Dam Creek untenable by the Federals. They would never stand to fight on that line with a strong force established in their rear and menacing their communications, nor would they dare to deliver a counterstroke through the trackless woods. It might confidently be assumed, therefore, that they would fall back during the night, and that the Confederate advance would then be carried out in that concentrated formation which Lee's orders had dictated. Such, in all probability, was Jackson's view of the situation; and that Hill, in direct contravention of those orders, would venture on an isolated attack before that formation had been assumed never for a moment crossed his mind.[1]

Hill, on the other hand, seems to have believed that if the Federals were not defeated on the evening of the 26th they would make use of the respite, either to bring up reinforcements, or to advance on Richmond by the opposite bank of the Chickahominy. It is not impossible that he thought the sound of his cannon would bring Jackson to his aid. That it would have been wiser to establish communication, and to make certain of that aid before attacking, there can be no question. It was too late to defeat Porter the same evening. Nothing was to be gained by immediate attack, and much would be risked. The last assault, in which the heaviest losses were incurred, was made just as night fell. It was a sacrifice of life as unnecessary as that of the Prussian Guard before St. Privat. At the same time, that General Hill did wrong in crossing the Chickahominy before he heard of his colleague's approach is not a fair

---

[1] Longstreet, on p. 124 of his *From Manassas to Appomattox*, declares that 'Jackson marched by the fight without giving attention, and went into camp at Hundley's Corner, *half a mile in rear* of the enemy's position. A reference to the map is sufficient to expose the inaccuracy of this statement.

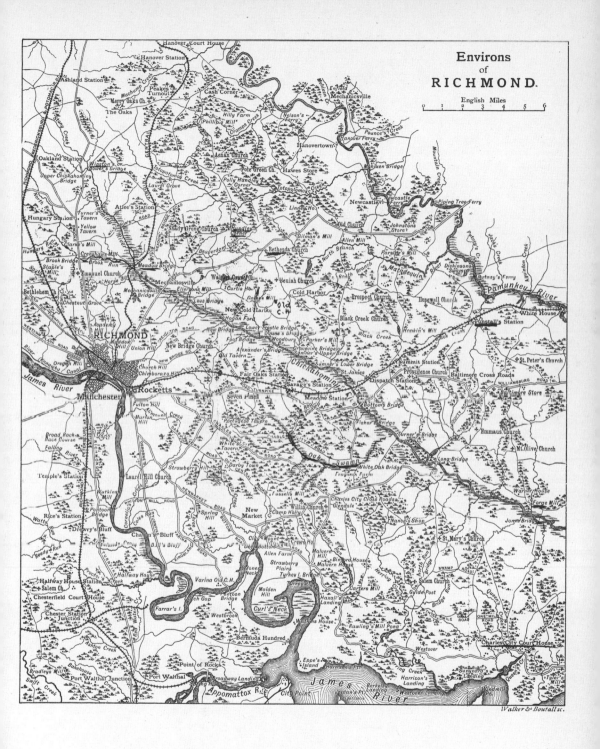

Environs
of
RICHMOND.

English Miles
0 1 2 3 4 5 6

Walker & Boutall sc.

accusation. To have lingered on the south bank would have
been to leave Jackson to the tender mercies of the Federals
should the turn against him in the forest. Moreover,
it was Hill's task to open a passage for the remaining
divisions, a.d if that passage had been deferred to a later
hour, it is improbable that the Confederate army would
have been concentrated on the north bank of the Chickahominy until the next morning. It must be admitted,
too, that the situation in which Hill found himself,
after crossing the river, was an exceedingly severe
test of his self-control. His troops had driven in the
Federal outposts; infantry, cavalry, and artillery were
retiring before his skirmishers. The noise of battle filled
the air. From across the Chickahominy thundered the
heavy guns, and his regiments were pressing forward with
the impetuous ardour of young soldiers. If he yielded to the
excitement of the moment, if eagerness for battle overpowered his judgment, if his brain refused to work calmly
in the wild tumult of the conflict, he is hardly to be blamed.
The patience which is capable of resisting the eagerness
of the troops, the imperturbable judgment which, in the
heat of action, weighs with deliberation the necessities of
the moment, the clear vision which forecasts the result of
every movement—these are rare qualities indeed.

During the night Porter fell back on Gaines' Mill.
While the engagement at Beaver Dam Creek was still in
progress vast clouds of dust, rising above the forests to the
north-west and north, had betrayed the approach of
Jackson, and the reports of the cavalry left no doubt
that he was threatening the Federal rear.

The retreat was conducted in good order, a strong
rear-guard, reinforced by two batteries of horse-artillery,
holding the Confederates in check, and before morning a
second position, east of Powhite Creek, and covering two
bridges over the Chickahominy, Alexander's and Grapevine,
was occupied by the Fifth Army Corps.

New Bridge was now uncovered, and Lee's army was in
motion shortly after sunrise, Jackson crossing Beaver Dam
Creek and moving due south in the direction of Walnut

Grove Church.[1] The enemy, however, had already passed
June 27, eastward ; and the Confederates, well concentrated
5 A.M. and in hand, pushed forward in pursuit ; A. P. Hill,
with Longstreet on his right, moving on Gaines' Mill, while
Jackson, supported by D. H. Hill, and with Stuart covering
his left, marched by a more circuitous route to Old Cold
Harbour. Near Walnut Grove Church Jackson met the
Commander-in-Chief, and it is recorded that the staff officers
of the Valley army, noting the eagerness displayed by
General Lee's suite to get a glimpse of ' Stonewall,' then for
the first time realised the true character and magnitude
of the Valley campaign.

About noon, after a march of seven miles, A. P. Hill's
scouts reported that the Federals had halted behind
12 noon. Powhite Creek. The leading brigade was sent
across the stream, which runs past Gaines'
Mill, and pressing through the thick woods found the
enemy in great strength on a ridge beyond. Hill formed
his division for attack, and opened fire with his four
batteries. The enemy's guns, superior in number, at
once responded, and the skirmish lines became actively
engaged. The Confederate general, despite urgent messages from his subordinates, requesting permission to
attack, held his troops in hand, waiting till he should be
supported, and for two and a half hours the battle was no
more than an affair of ' long bowls.'

The position held by the defence was emphatically one
to impose caution on the assailants. To reach it the
Confederates were confined to three roads, two from
Mechanicsville, and one from Old Cold Harbour. These
roads led each of them through a broad belt of forest,
and then, passing through open fields, descended into a

---

[1] Jackson's division—so-called in Lee's order—really consisted of three
divisions:

		Whiting's Division {	Hood's Brigade	
			Law's	,,
Jackson's	{ Stonewall Brigade			B. T. Johnson's Brigade
[Winder]	Cunningham's ,,	Ewell's	Elzey's	,,
Division	Fulkerson's ,,	Division	Trimble's	,,
	Lawton's ,,		Taylor's	,,

winding valley, from five hundred to a thousand yards
in breadth. Rising near McGehee's House, due south
of Old Cold Harbour, a sluggish creek, bordered by
swamps and thick timber, and cutting in places a deep
channel, filtered through the valley to the Chickahominy.
Beyond this stream rose an open and undulating plateau,
admirably adapted to the movement of all arms, and with
a slight command of the opposite ridge. On the plateau,
facing west and north, the Federals were formed up. A
fringe of trees and bushes along the crest gave cover and
concealment to the troops. 60 feet below, winding darkly
through the trees, the creek covered the whole front; and
in the centre of the position, east of New Cold Harbour, the
valley was completely filled with tangled wood.

Towards Old Cold Harbour the timber on the Confederate side of the ravine was denser than elsewhere. On
the Federal left flank the valley of the Chickahominy was
open ground, but it was swept by heavy guns from
the right bank of the river, and at this point the creek
became an almost impassable swamp.

Porter, who had been reinforced by 9,000 men under
General Slocum, now commanded three divisions of
infantry, four regiments of cavalry, and twenty-two
batteries, a total of 36,000 officers and men. The *moral*
of the troops had been strengthened by their easy victory
of the previous day. Their commander had gained
their confidence; their position had been partially intrenched, and they could be readily supported by way of
Alexander's and Grapevine Bridges from the south bank of
the Chickahominy.

The task before the Confederates, even with their
superior numbers, was formidable in the extreme. The
wooded ridge which encircled the position afforded scant
room for artillery, and it was thus impracticable to prepare
the attack by a preliminary bombardment. The ground
over which the infantry must advance was completely
swept by fire, and the centre and left were defended by
three tiers of riflemen, the first sheltered by the steep
banks of the creek, the second halfway up the bluff,

covered by a breastwork, the third on the crest, occupying
a line of shelter-trenches; and the riflemen were supported by a dozen batteries of rifled guns.[1]

But Lee had few misgivings. In one respect the
Federal position seemed radically defective. The line of
retreat on White House was exposed to attack from Old
Cold Harbour. In fact, with Old Cold Harbour in possession of the Confederates, retreat could only be effected by
one road north of the Chickahominy, that by Parker's
Mill and Dispatch Station; and if this road were threatened,
Porter, in order to cover it, would be compelled to bring
over troops from his left and centre, or to prolong his line
until it was weak everywhere. There was no great reason to
fear that McClellan would send Porter heavy reinforcements.
To do so he would have to draw troops from his intrenchments
on the south bank of the Chickahominy, and Magruder had
been instructed to maintain a brisk demonstration against
this portion of the line. It was probable that the Federal
commander, with his exaggerated estimate of the numbers
opposed to him, would be induced by this means to anticipate a general attack against his whole front, and would
postpone moving his reserves until it was too late.

While Hill was skirmishing with the Federals, Lee was
anxiously awaiting intelligence of Jackson's arrival at Old
Cold Harbour. Longstreet was already forming up for
battle, and at 2.30 Hill's regiments were slipped to the
2.30 P.M.   attack. A fierce and sanguinary conflict now
ensued. Emerging in well-ordered lines from the
cover of the woods, the Confederates swept down the open
slopes. Floundering in the swamps, and struggling
through the abattis which had been placed on the banks
of the stream, they drove in the advanced line of hostile
riflemen, and strove gallantly to ascend the slope which
lay beyond. 'But brigade after brigade,' says General
Porter, 'seemed almost to melt away before the concentrated fire of our artillery and infantry; yet others pressed
on, followed by supports daring and brave as their predecessors, despite their heavy losses and the disheartening

[1] The remainder of the guns were in reserve.

effect of having to clamber over many of their disabled and
dead, and to meet their surviving comrades rushing back
in great disorder from the deadly contest.' [1] For over
an hour Hill fought on without support. There were
no signs of Jackson, and Longstreet, whom it was not
intended to employ until Jackson's appearance should have
caused the Federals to denude their left, was then sent in to
save the day.

As on the previous day, the Confederate attack had
failed in combination. Jackson's march had been again
delayed. The direct road from Walnut Grove Church to
Old Cold Harbour, leading through the forest, was found
to be obstructed by felled timber and defended by sharp-
shooters, and to save time Jackson's division struck off
into the road by Bethesda Church. This threw it in rear of
D. H. Hill, and it was near 2 P.M. when the latter's
advanced-guard reached the tavern at the Old Cold Harbour cross roads. No harm, however, had been done.
A. P. Hill did not attack till half an hour later. But when
he advanced there came no response from the left. A battery
of D. H. Hill's division was brought into action, but was soon
silenced, and beyond this insignificant demonstration the
Army of the Valley made no endeavour to join the battle.
The brigades were halted by the roadside. Away to the right,
above the intervening forest, rolled the roar of battle, the
crash of shells and the din of musketry, but no orders
were given for the advance.

Nor had Jackson's arrival produced the slightest consternation in the Federal ranks. Although from his
position at Cold Harbour he seriously threatened their line
of retreat to the White House, they had neither denuded
their left nor brought up their reserves. Where he was
now established he was actually nearer White House than
any portion of Porter's army corps, and yet that general
apparently accepted the situation with equanimity.

Lee had anticipated that Jackson's approach would
cause the enemy to prolong their front in order to cover
their line of retreat to the White House, and so weaken

---

[1] *Battles and Leaders of the Civil War*, vol. ii., p. 337.

that part of the position which was to be attacked by
Longstreet; and Jackson had been ordered [1] to draw
up his troops so as to meet such a contingency. 'Hoping,'
he says in his report, 'that Generals A. P. Hill
and Longstreet would soon drive the Federals towards
me, I directed General D. H. Hill to move his division to
the left of the wood, so as to leave between him and the
wood on the right an open space, across which I hoped
that the enemy would be driven.' But Lee was deceived.
The Federal line of retreat ran not to the White House,
but over Grapevine Bridge. McClellan had for some time
foreseen that he might be compelled to abandon the York
River Railway, and directly he suspected that Jackson was
marching to Richmond had begun to transfer his line of
operations from the York to the James, and his base of
supply from the White House to Harrison's Landing.

So vast is the amount of stores necessary for the
subsistence, health, and armament of a host like
McClellan's that a change of base is an operation which
can only be effected under the most favourable circumstances.[2] It is evident, then, that the possibility of the
enemy shifting his line of operations to the James,
abandoning the York River Railroad, might easily have

[1] This order was verbal; no record of it is to be found, and Jackson
never mentioned, either at the time or afterwards, what its purport
was. His surviving staff officers, however, are unanimous in declaring
that he must have received direct instructions from General Lee. 'Is it
possible,' writes Dr. McGuire, 'that Jackson, who knew nothing of the
country, and little of the exact situation of affairs, would have taken the
responsibility of stopping at Old Cold Harbour for an hour or more, unless
he had had the authority of General Lee to do so? I saw him that
morning talking to General Lee. General Lee was sitting on a log, and
Jackson standing up. General Lee was evidently giving him instructions
for the day.' In his report (O. R., vol. xi., part i., p. 492) Lee says: 'The
arrival of Jackson on our left was momentarily expected; it was supposed
that his approach would cause the enemy's extension in that direction.'

[2] The Army of the Potomac numbered 105,000 men, and 25,000
animals. 600 tons of ammunition, food, forage, medical and other supplies
had to be forwarded each day from White House to the front; and at one
time during the operations from fifty to sixty days' rations for the
entire army, amounting probably to 25,000 tons, were accumulated at the
depôt. 5 tons daily per 1,000 men is a fair estimate for an army operating
in a barren country.

escaped the penetration of either Lee or Jackson. They were not behind the scenes of the Federal administrative system. They were not aware of the money, labour, and ingenuity which had been lavished on the business of supply. They had not seen with their own eyes the fleet of four hundred transports which covered the reaches of the York. They had not yet realised the enormous advantage which an army derives from the command of the sea.

Nor were they enlightened by the calmness with which their immediate adversaries on the field of battle regarded Jackson's possession of Old Cold Harbour. Still, one fact was manifest : the Federals showed no disposition whatever to weaken or change their position, and it was clear that the success was not to be attained by mere manœuvre. Lee, seeing Hill's division roughly handled, ordered Longstreet forward, while Jackson, judging from the sound and direction of the firing that the original plan had failed, struck in with vigour. Opposed to him was Sykes' division of regulars, supported by eighteen guns, afterwards increased to twenty-four ; and in the men of the United States Army the Valley soldiers met a stubborn foe. The position, moreover, occupied by Sykes possessed every advantage which a defender could desire. Manned even by troops of inferior mettle it might well have proved impregnable. The valley was wider than further west, and a thousand yards intervened between the opposing ridges. From either crest the cornfields sloped gently to the marshy sources of the creek, hidden by tall timber and dense undergrowth. The right and rear of the position were protected by a second stream, running south to the Chickahominy, and winding through a swamp which Stuart, posted on Jackson's left, pronounced impassable for horsemen. Between the head waters of these two streams rose the spur on which stands McGehee's house, facing the road from Old Cold Harbour, and completely commanding the country to the north and north-east. The flank, therefore, was well secured ; the front was strong, with a wide field of fire ; the Confederate artillery, even if it could make its way through the thick woods on the opposite crest, would have to unlimber under fire at effective range, and the marsh below, with its tangled undergrowth and abattis, could hardly fail to throw the attacking infantry into disorder. Along the whole of Sykes' line only two weak points were apparent. On his left, as already described, a broad tract of woodland, covering nearly the whole valley, and climbing far up the slope on the Federal side, afforded a covered approach from one crest to the other; on his right, a plantation of young pines skirted the crest of McGehee's Hill, and ran for some distance down the slope. Under shelter of the timber it was possible that the Confederate infantry might mass for the assault; but once in the open, unaided by artillery, their further progress would be difficult. Under ordinary circumstances a thorough reconnaissance, followed by a carefully planned attack, would have been the natural course of the assailant. The very strength of the position was in favour of the Confederates. The creek which covered the whole front rendered a counterstroke impracticable, and facilitated a flank attack. Holding the right bank of the creek with a portion of his force, Jackson might have thrown the remainder against McGehee's Hill, and, working round the flank, have repeated the tactics of Kernstown, Winchester, and Port Republic.

But the situation permitted no delay. A. P. Hill was hard pressed. The sun was already sinking. McClellan's reserves might be coming up, and if the battle was to be won, it must be won by direct attack. There was no time for further reconnaissance, no time for manœuvre.

Jackson's dispositions were soon made. D. H. Hill, eastward of the Old Cold Harbour road, was to advance against McGehee's Hill, overlapping, if possible, the enemy's line. Ewell was to strike in on Hill's right, moving through the tract of woodland; Lawton, Whiting, and Winder, in the order named, were to fill the gap between Ewell's right and the left of A. P. Hill's division, and the artillery was ordered into position opposite McGehee's Hill.

D. H. Hill, already in advance, was the first to move. Pressing forward from the woods, under a heavy fire of

artillery, his five brigades, the greater part in first line,
4 P.M. descended to the creek, already occupied by his skirmishers.   In passing through the marshy thickets,
where the Federal shells were bursting on every hand, the
confusion became great.   The brigades crossed each other's
march.   Regiments lost their brigades, and companies their
regiments.   At one point the line was so densely crowded that
whole regiments were forced to the rear ; at others there were
wide intervals, and effective supervision became impossible.
Along the edge of the timber the fire was fierce, for the Union
regulars were distant no more than four hundred yards ; the
smoke rolled heavily through the thickets, and on the right
and centre, where the fight was hottest, the impetuosity of
both officers and men carried them forward up the slope.   An
attempt to deliver a charge with the whole line failed in combination, and such portion of the division as advanced,
scourged by both musketry and artillery, fell back before
the fire of the unshaken Federals.

In the wood to the right Ewell met with even fiercer
opposition. So hastily had the Confederate line been formed,
and so difficult was it for the brigades to maintain touch and
direction in the thick covert, that gaps soon opened along
the front ; and of these gaps, directly the Southerners gained
the edge of the timber, the Northern brigadiers took
quick advantage.   Not content with merely holding their
ground, the regular regiments, changing front so as to
strike the flanks of the attack, came forward with the
bayonet, and a vigorous counterstroke, delivered by five
battalions, drove Ewell across the swamp.   Part of Trimble's
brigade still held on in the wood, fighting fiercely ; but
the Louisiana regiments were demoralised, and there were
no supports on which they might have rallied.

Jackson, when he ordered Hill to the front, had sent
verbal instructions—always dangerous—for the remainder
of his troops to move forward in line of battle.[1]   The young

---

[1] The instructions, according to Dr. Dabney, ran as follows :—
' The troops are standing at ease along our line of march. Ride back
rapidly along the line and tell the commanders to advance instantly *en
échelon* from the left.   Each brigade is to follow as a guide the right

staff officer to whom these instructions were entrusted, misunderstanding the intentions of his chief, communicated the message to the brigadiers with the addition that 'they were to await further orders before engaging the enemy.' Partly for this reason, and partly because the rear regiments of his division had lost touch with the leading brigades, Ewell was left without assistance. For some time the error was undiscovered. Jackson grew anxious. From his station near Old Cold Harbour little could be seen of the Confederate troops. On the ridge beyond the valley the dark lines of the enemy's infantry were visible amongst the trees, with their well-served batteries on the crests above. But in the valley immediately beneath, and as well as in the forest to the right front, the dense smoke and the denser timber hid the progress of the fight. Yet the sustained fire was a sure token that the enemy still held his own; and for the first time and the last his staff beheld their leader riding restlessly to and fro, and heard his orders given in a tone which betrayed the storm within.[1] 'Unconscious,' says Dabney, ' that his veteran brigades were but now reaching the ridge of battle, he supposed that all his strength had been put forth, and (what had never happened before) the enemy was not crushed.'[2] Fortunately, the error of the aide-de-camp had already been corrected by the vigilance of the chief of the staff, and the remainder of the Valley army was coming up.

Their entry into battle was not in accordance with the

regiment of the brigade on the left, and to keep within supporting distance. Tell the commanders that if this formation fails at any point, to form line of battle and move to the front, pressing to the sound of the heaviest firing and attack the enemy vigorously wherever found. As to artillery, each commander must use his discretion. If the ground will at all permit tell them to take in their field batteries and use them. If not, post them in the rear.' Letter to the author.

[1] It may be noted that Jackson's command had now been increased by two divisions, Whiting's and D. H. Hill's, but there had been no increase in the very small staff which had sufficed for the Valley army. The mistakes which occurred at Gaines' Mill, and Jackson's ignorance of the movements and progress of his troops, were in great part due to his lack of staff officers. A most important message, writes Dr. Dabney, involving tactical knowledge, was carried by a non-combatant.

[2] Dabney, vol. ii., p. 194.

intentions of their chief. Whiting should have come in
on Ewell's right, Lawton on the right of Whiting, and
Jackson's division on the right of Lawton. Whiting led
the way; but he had advanced only a short distance
through the woods when he was met by Lee, who directed
him to support General A. P. Hill.[1] The brigades of Law
and of Hood were therefore diverted to the right, and,
deploying on either side of the Gaines' Mill road, were
ordered to assault the commanding bluff which marked the
angle of the Federal position. Lawton's Georgians, 3,500
strong, moved to the support of Ewell; Cunningham and Fulkerson, of Winder's division, losing direction in the thickets,
eventually sustained the attack of Longstreet, and the
Stonewall Brigade reinforced the shattered ranks of D. H.
Hill. Yet the attack was strong, and in front of Old Cold
Harbour six batteries had forced their way through the forest.

As this long line of guns covered McGehee's Hill with
a storm of shells, and the louder crash of musketry told
him that his lagging brigades were coming into line,
Jackson sent his last orders to his divisional commanders:
'Tell them,' he said, 'this affair must hang in suspense no
longer; let them sweep the field with the bayonet.' But
there was no need for further urging. Before the messengers arrived the Confederate infantry, in every quarter of
the battlefield, swept forward from the woods, and a vast wave
of men converged upon the plateau. Lee, almost at the same
moment as Jackson, had given the word for a general
advance. As the supports came thronging up the shout was
carried down the line, ' The Valley men are here!' and with
the cry of ' Stonewall Jackson!' for their slogan, the Southern
army dashed across the deep ravine. Whiting, with the eight
regiments of Hood and Law, none of which had been yet
engaged, charged impetuously against the centre. The
brigades of A. P. Hill, spent with fighting but clinging stubbornly to their ground, found strength for a final effort.
Longstreet threw in his last reserve against the triple line
which had already decimated his division. Lawton's
Georgians bore back the regulars. D. H. Hill, despite the

[1] Whiting's Report, O. R., vol. xi., part i., p. 563.

D 2

fire of the batteries on McGehee's Hill, which, disregarding
the shells of Jackson's massed artillery, turned with canister
on the advancing infantry, made good his footing on the
ridge; and as the sun, low on the horizon, loomed blood-red
through the murky atmosphere, the Confederate colours
waved along the line of abandoned breastworks.

As the Federals retreated, knots of brave men, hastily
collected by officers of all ranks, still offered a fierce resistance, and, supported by the batteries, inflicted terrible losses
on the crowded masses which swarmed up from the ravine;
but the majority of the infantry, without ammunition and
with few officers, streamed in disorder to the rear. For a
time the Federal gunners stood manfully to their work.
Porter's reserve artillery, drawn up midway across the
upland, offered a rallying point to the retreating infantry.
Three small squadrons of the 5th United States Cavalry
made a gallant but useless charge, in which out of seven
officers six fell; and on the extreme right the division of
regulars, supported by a brigade of volunteers, fell back
fighting to a second line. As at Bull Run, the disciplined
soldiers alone showed a solid front amid the throng of
fugitives. Not a foot of ground had they yielded till their
left was exposed by the rout of the remainder. Of the
four batteries which supported them only two guns were
lost, and on their second position they made a determined effort to restore the fight. But their stubborn
valour availed nothing against the superior numbers which
Lee's fine strategy had concentrated on the field of battle.

Where the first breach was made in the Federal line is
a matter of dispute. Longstreet's men made a magnificent charge on the right, and D. H. Hill claimed to have
turned the flank of the regulars; but it is abundantly
evident that the advent of Jackson's fresh troops, and the
vigour of their assault, broke down the resistance of the
Federals.[1] When the final attack developed, and along the
whole front masses of determined men, in overwhelming

---

[1] Porter himself thought that the first break in his line was made by
Hood, ' at a point where he least expected it.'—*Battles and Leaders*, vol. ii.,
pp. 335 and 340.

numbers, dashed against the breastworks, Porter's troops were well-nigh exhausted, and not a single regiment remained in reserve. Against the very centre of his line the attack was pushed home by Whiting's men with extraordinary resolution. His two brigades, marching abreast, were formed in two lines, each about 2,000 strong. Riding along the front, before they left the wood, the general had enjoined his men to charge without a halt, in double time, and without firing. 'Had these orders,' says General Law, 'not been strictly obeyed the assault would have been a failure. No troops could have stood long under the withering storm of lead and iron that beat in their faces as they became fully exposed to view from the Federal line.'[1] The assault was met with a courage that was equally admirable.[2] But the Confederate second line reinforced the first at exactly the right moment, driving it irresistibly forward; and the Federal regiments, which had been hard pressed through a long summer afternoon, and had become scattered in the thickets, were ill-matched with the solid and ordered ranks of brigades which had not yet fired a shot. It was apparently at this point that the Southerners first set foot on the plateau, and sweeping over the intrenchments, outflanked the brigades which still held out to right and left, and compelled them to fall back. Inspired by his soldierly enthusiasm for a gallant deed, Jackson himself has left us a vivid description of the successful charge. 'On my extreme right,' he says in his report, 'General Whiting advanced his division through the dense forest and swamp, emerging from the wood into the field near the public road and at the head of the deep ravine which covered the enemy's left. Advancing thence through a number of retreating and disordered regiments he came within range of the enemy's fire, who, concealed in an open wood and protected by breastworks, poured a destructive fire for a quarter of a mile into his advancing

[1] *Battles and Leaders*, vol. ii., p. 363.

[2] 'The Confederates were within ten paces when the Federals broke cover, and leaving their log breastworks, swarmed up the hill in rear, carrying the second line with them in their rout.'—General Law, *Battles and Leaders*, vol. ii., p. 363.

line, under which many brave officers and men fell.
Dashing on with unfaltering step in the face of these
murderous discharges of canister and musketry, General
Hood and Colonel Law, at the heads of their respective
brigades, rushed to the charge with a yell. Moving down
a precipitous ravine, leaping ditch and stream, clambering
up a difficult ascent, and exposed to an incessant and
deadly fire from the intrenchments, those brave and
determined men pressed forward, driving the enemy from
his well-selected and fortified position. In this charge,
in which upwards of 1,000 men fell killed and wounded
before the fire of the enemy, and in which 14 pieces of
artillery and nearly a whole regiment were captured, the
4th Texas, under the lead of General Hood, was the first
to pierce these strongholds and seize the guns.' [1]

How fiercely the Northern troops had battled is told in
the outspoken reports of the Confederate generals. Before
Jackson's reserves were thrown in the first line of the Confederate attack had been exceedingly roughly handled.
A. P. Hill's division had done good work in preparing the
way for Whiting's assault, but a portion of his troops had
become demoralised. Ewell's regiments met the same fate;
and we read of them ' skulking from the front in a shameful
manner; the woods on our left and rear full of troops in
safe cover, from which they never stirred; ' of ' regiment
after regiment rushing back in utter disorder; ' of others
which it was impossible to rally; and of troops retiring in
confusion, who cried out to the reinforcements, ' You need
not go in; we are whipped, we can't do anything!' It is
only fair to say that the reinforcements replied, ' Get out of
our way, we will show you how to do it; ' [2] but it is not to
be disguised that the Confederates at one time came near
defeat. With another division in reserve at the critical
moment, Porter might have maintained his line unbroken.
His troops, had they been supported, were still capable of
resistance.

[1] Jackson's Report, O. R., vol. xi., part i., pp. 555, 556.
[2] Reports of Whiting, Trimble, Rodes, Bradley T. Johnson, O. R., vol. xi.,
part i.

McClellan, however, up to the time the battle was lost, had sent but one division (Slocum's) and two batteries to Porter's support. 66,000 Federals, on the south bank of the Chickahominy, had been held in their intrenchments, throughout the day, by the demonstrations of 28,000 Confederates. Intent on saving his trains, on securing his retreat to the river James, and utterly regardless of the chances which fortune offered, the 'Young Napoleon' had allowed his rearguard to be overwhelmed. He was not seen on the plateau which his devoted troops so well defended, nor even at the advanced posts on the further bank of the Chickahominy. So convinced was he of the accuracy of the information furnished by his detective staff that he never dreamt of testing the enemy's numbers by his own eyesight. Had he watched the development of Lee's attack, noted the small number of his batteries, the long delay in the advance of the supports, the narrow front of his line of battle, he would have discovered that the Confederate strength had been greatly exaggerated. There were moments, too, during the fight when a strong counterstroke, made by fresh troops, would have placed Lee's army in the greatest peril. But a general who thinks only of holding his lines and not of annihilating the enemy is a poor tactician, and McClellan's lack of enterprise, which Lee had so accurately gauged, may be inferred from his telegram to Lincoln : 'I have lost this battle because my force is too small.' [1]

Porter was perhaps a more than sufficient substitute for the Commander-in-Chief. His tactics, as fighting a waiting battle, had been admirable ; and, when his front was broken, strongly and with cool judgment he sought to hold back the enemy and cover the bridges. The line of batteries he established across the plateau—80 guns in all—proved at first an effective barrier. But the retreat of the infantry, the waning light, and the general dissolution of all order, had its effect upon the gunners. When the remnant of the 5th Cavalry was borne back in flight, the greater part of the batteries had already limbered up, and over the bare surface of the upland the Confederate infantry, shooting down

[1] Report of Committee on the Conduct of the War.

the terrified teams, rushed forward in hot pursuit. 22 guns, with a large number of ammunition waggons, were captured on the field, prisoners surrendered at every step, and the fight surged onward towards the bridges. But between the bridges and the battlefield, on the slopes falling to the Chickahominy, the dark forest covered the retreat of the routed army. Night had already fallen. The confusion in the ranks of the Confederates was extreme, and it was impossible to distinguish friend from foe. All direction had been lost. None knew the bearings of the bridges, or whether the Federals were retreating east or south. Regiments had already been exposed to the fire of their comrades, and in front of the forest a perceptible hesitation seized on both officers and men. At this moment, in front of D. H. Hill's division, which was advancing by the road leading directly to the bridges, loud cheers were heard. It was clear that Federal reinforcements had arrived; the general ordered his troops to halt, and along the whole line the forward movement came quickly to a standstill. Two brigades, French's and Meagher's, tardily sent over by McClellan, had arrived in time to stave off a terrible disaster. Pushing through the mass of fugitives with the bayonet, these fine troops had crossed the bridge, passed through the woods, and formed line on the southern crest of the plateau. Joining the regulars, who still presented a stubborn front, they opened a heavy fire, and under cover of their steadfast lines Porter's troops withdrew across the river.

Notwithstanding this strong reinforcement of 5,000 or 6,000 fresh troops, it is by no means impossible, had the Confederates pushed resolutely forward, that the victory would have been far more complete. 'Winder,' says General D. H. Hill, 'thought that we ought to pursue into the woods, on the right of the Grapevine Bridge road; but not knowing the position of our friends, nor what Federal reserves might be awaiting us in the woods, I thought it advisable not to move on. General Lawton concurred with me. I had no artillery to shell the woods in front, as mine had not got through the swamp. Winder,' he adds, 'was right; even a show of pressure must have been attended with great result.'[1] Had Jackson been at hand the pressure would in all probability have been applied. The contagion of defeat soon spreads; and whatever reserves a flying enemy may possess, if they are vigorously attacked whilst the fugitives are still passing through their ranks, history tells us, however bold their front, that, unless they are intrenched, their resistance is seldom long protracted. More than all, when night has fallen on the field, and prevents all estimate of the strength of the attack, a resolute advance has peculiar chances of success. But when his advanced line halted Jackson was not yet up; and before he arrived the impetus of victory had died away; the Federal reserves were deployed in a strong position, and the opportunity had already passed.

It is no time, when the tide of victory bears him forward, for a general 'to take counsel of his fears.' It is no time to count numbers, or to conjure up the phantoms of possible reserves; the sea itself is not more irresistible than an army which has stormed a strong position, and which has attained, in so doing, the exhilarating consciousness of superior courage. Had Stuart, with his 2,000 horsemen, followed up the pursuit towards the bridges, the Federal reserves might have been swept away in panic. But Stuart, in common with Lee and Jackson, expected that the enemy would endeavour to reach the White House, and when he saw that their lines were breaking he had dashed down a lane which led to the river road, about three miles distant. When he reached that point, darkness had already fallen, and finding no traces of the enemy, he had returned to Old Cold Harbour.

On the night of the battle the Confederates remained where the issue of the fight had found them. Across the Grapevine road the pickets of the hostile forces were in close proximity, and men of both sides, in search of water, or carrying messages, strayed within the enemy's lines. Jackson himself, it is said, came near capture. Riding forward in the darkness, attended by only a few staff

[1] *Battles and Leaders*, vol. ii., p. 357.

officers, he suddenly found himself in presence of a Federal picket. Judging rightly of the enemy's *moral*, he set spurs to his horse, and charging into the midst, ordered them to lay down their arms; and fifteen or twenty prisoners, marching to the rear, amused the troops they met on the march by loudly proclaiming that they had the honour of being captured by Stonewall Jackson. These men were not without companions. 2,830 Federals were reported either captured or missing; and while some of those were probably among the dead, a large proportion found their way to Richmond; 4,000, moreover, had fallen on the field of battle.[1]

The Confederate casualties were even a clearer proof of the severity of the fighting. So far as can be ascertained, 8,000 officers and men were killed or wounded.

Longstreet	1,850
A. P. Hill	2,450
Jackson	3,700

Jackson's losses were distributed as follows :—

Jackson's own Division	600
Ewell	650
Whiting	1,020
D. H. Hill	1,430

The regimental losses, in several instances, were exceptionally severe. Of the 4th Texas, of Hood's brigade, the first to pierce the Federal line, there fell 20 officers and 230 men. The 20th North Carolina, of D. H. Hill's division, which charged the batteries on McGehee's Hill, lost 70 killed and 200 wounded; of the same division the 3rd Alabama lost 200, and the 12th North Carolina 212; while two of Lawton's regiments, the 31st and the 38th Georgia, had each a casualty list of 170. Almost every single regiment north of the Chickahominy took part in the action. The cavalry did nothing, but at least 48,000 infantry were engaged, and seventeen batteries are mentioned in the reports as having participated in the battle.

[1] O. R., vol. xi., part i., pp. 40–2.

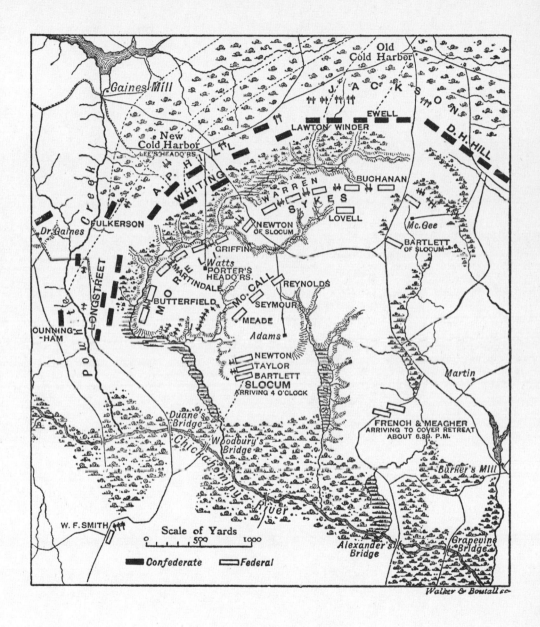

Old Cold Harbor

Gaines Mill

J A C K S O N

New Cold Harbor
LEE'S HEAD'RS.

EWELL

LAWTON WINDER

D. H. HILL

A. P. HILL

WHITING

W A R R E N

S Y K E S

BUCHANAN

FULKERSON

Dr. Gaines

NEWTON OF SLOCUM

LOVELL

Mc.Gee

BARTLETT OF SLOCUM

GRIFFIN

Watts PORTER'S HEAD'RS.

M O R E L L

MARTINDALE

P O W H I T E

L O N G S T R E E T

BUTTERFIELD

McCALL

REYNOLDS

SEYMOUR

OUNNING -HAM

MEADE

Adams

NEWTON
TAYLOR
BARTLETT
SLOCUM
ARRIVING 4 O'CLOCK

Martin

FRENCH & MEAGHER
ARRIVING TO COVER RETREAT
ABOUT 6.30 P.M.

Duane's Bridge

Woodbury's Bridge

Chickahominy River

Barker's Mill

W. F. SMITH

Scale of Yards
0   500   1000

Alexander's Bridge

Grapevine Bridge

■ Confederate   □ Federal

Walker & Boutall sc.

CHAPTER XIV

THE SEVEN DAYS.   FRAYSER'S FARM AND MALVERN HILL

THE battle of Gaines' Mill, although the assailants suffered heavier losses than they inflicted, was a long step towards accomplishing the deliverance of Richmond. One of McClellan's five army corps had been disposed of, a heavy blow had been struck at the *moral* of his whole army, and his communications with the White House and the Pamunkey were at the mercy of his enemies.   Still the Confederate outlook was not altogether clear.   It is one thing to win a victory, but another to make such use of it as to annihilate the enemy. Porter's defeat was but a beginning of operations; and although Lee was convinced that McClellan would retreat, he was by no means so certain that his escape could be prevented.   Yet this was essential.   If the Federal army were suffered to fall back without incurring further loss, it would be rapidly reinforced from Washington, and resuming the advance, this time with still larger numbers, might render Gaines' Mill a barren victory.   How to compass the destruction of McClellan's host was the problem that now confronted the Confederate leader; and before a plan could be devised it was necessary to ascertain the direction of the retreat.

On the morning of June 28 it was found that no formed body of Federal troops remained north of the Chickahominy. French, Meagher, and Sykes, the regulars forming the rear-guard, had fallen back during the night and destroyed the bridges.   Hundreds of stragglers were picked up, and one of the most gallant of the Northern

June 28, 1862.

brigadiers[1] was found asleep in the woods, unaware that his troops had crossed the stream. No further fighting was to be expected on the plateau. But it was possible that the enemy might still endeavour to preserve his communications, marching by the south bank of the river and recrossing by the railway and Bottom's Bridges. Stuart, supported by Ewell, was at once ordered to seize the former; but when the cavalry reached Dispatch Station, a small Federal detachment retreated to the south bank of the Chickahominy and fired the timbers.

Meanwhile, from the field of Gaines' Mill, long columns of dust, rising above the forests to the south, had been descried, showing that the enemy was in motion; and when the news came in that the railway bridge had been destroyed, and that the line itself was unprotected, it was at once evident that McClellan had abandoned his communications with White House.

This was valuable information, but still the line of retreat had not yet been ascertained. The Federals might retreat to some point on the James River, due south, there meeting their transports, or they might march down the Peninsula to Yorktown and Fortress Monroe. 'In the latter event,' says Lee, ' it was necessary that our troops should continue on the north bank of the river, and until the intention of General McClellan was discovered it was deemed injudicious to change their disposition. Ewell was therefore ordered to proceed to Bottom's Bridge, and the cavalry to watch the bridges below. No certain indications of a retreat to the James River were discovered by our forces (Magruder) on the south side of the Chickahominy, and late in the afternoon the enemy's works were reported to be fully manned. Below (south of) the enemy's works the country was densely wooded and intersected by impassable swamps, at once concealing his movements and precluding reconnaissances except by the regular roads, all of which were strongly guarded. The bridges over the Chickahominy in rear of the enemy were destroyed, and their reconstruction impracticable in the presence of

[1] General Reynolds.

his whole army and powerful batteries. We were therefore compelled to wait until his purpose should be developed.'[1]

During the day, therefore, the Confederate army remained on the battle-field, waiting for the game to bolt. In the evening, however, signs of a general movement were reported in rear of the intrenchments at Seven Pines; and as nothing had been observed by the cavalry on the Chickahominy, Lee, rightly concluding that McClellan was retreating to the James, issued orders for the pursuit to be taken up the next morning.

But to intercept the enemy before he could fortify a position, covered by the fire of his gunboats, on the banks of the James, was a difficult operation. The situation demanded rapid marching, close concert, and delicate manœuvres. The Confederate army was in rear of the Federals, and separated from them by the Chickahominy, and, to reach the James, McClellan had only fourteen miles to cover. But the country over which he had to pass was still more intricate, and traversed by even fewer roads, than the district which had hitherto been the theatre of operations. Across his line of march ran the White Oak Swamp, bordered by thick woods and a wide morass, and crossed by only one bridge. If he could transfer his whole army south of this stream, without molestation, he would find himself within six miles of his gunboats; and as his left flank was already resting on the Swamp, it was not easy for Lee's army to prevent his passage.

But 28,000 Confederates were already south of the Chickahominy, on the flank of McClellan's line of march, and it was certainly possible that this force might detain the Federals until A. P. Hill, Longstreet, and Jackson should come up. Magruder and Huger were therefore ordered to advance early on the 29th, and moving, the one by the Williamsburg, the other by the Charles City road, to strike the enemy in flank.

A. P. Hill and Longstreet, recrossing the Chickahominy at New Bridge, were to march by the Darbytown road in the

[1] Lee's Report, O. R., vol. xi., part i., pp. 493, 494.

direction of Charles City cross roads, thus turning the head
waters of the White Oak Swamp, and threatening the
Federal rear.

Jackson, crossing Grapevine Bridge, was to move down
the south bank of the Chickahominy, cross the Swamp by
the bridge, and force his way to the Long Bridge road.

The Confederate army was thus divided into four
columns, moving by four different roads; each column at
starting was several miles distant from the others, and a
junction was to be made upon the field of battle. The
cavalry, moreover, with the exception of a few squadrons,
was far away upon the left, pursuing a large detachment
which had been observed on the road to the White
House.[1]

McClellan had undoubtedly resolved on a most hazardous manœuvre. His supply and ammunition train
consisted of over five thousand waggons. He was encumbered with the heavy guns of the siege artillery. He
had with him more than fifty field batteries; his army was
still 95,000 strong; and this unwieldy multitude of men,
horses, and vehicles, had to be passed over White Oak
Swamp, and then to continue its march across the front
of a powerful and determined enemy.

But Lee also was embarrassed by the nature of the
country.[2] If McClellan's movements were retarded by the
woods, swamps, and indifferent roads, the same obstacles
would interfere with the combination of the Confederate
columns; and the pursuit depended for success on their
close co-operation.

[1] This detachment, about 3,500 strong, consisted of the outposts that had
been established north and north-east of Beaver Dam Creek on June 27, of
the garrison of the White House, and of troops recently disembarked.

[2] Strange to say, while the Confederates possessed no maps whatever,
McClellan was well supplied in this respect. 'Two or three weeks before
this,' says General Averell (*Battles and Leaders*, vol. ii., p. 431), 'three
officers of the 3rd Pennsylvania Cavalry, and others, penetrated the region
between the Chickahominy and the James, taking bearings and making
notes. Their fragmentary sketches, when put together, made a map which
exhibited all the roadways, fields, forests, bridges, the streams, and houses,
so that our commander knew the country to be traversed far better than
any Confederate commander.'

The first day's work was hardly promising. The risks of unconnected manœuvres received abundant illustration. Magruder, late in the afternoon, struck the enemy's rear-guard near Savage's Station, but was heavily repulsed by two Federal army corps. Huger, called by Magruder to his
June 29. assistance, turned aside from the road which had been assigned to him, and when he was recalled by an urgent message from Lee, advanced with the timidity which almost invariably besets the commander of an isolated force in the neighbourhood of a large army. Jackson, whose line of march led him directly on Savage's Station, was delayed until after nightfall by the necessity of rebuilding the Grapevine Bridge.[1] Stuart had gone off to the White House, bent on the destruction of the enemy's supply depôt. Longstreet and Hill encamped south-west of Charles City cross roads, but saw nothing of the enemy. Holmes, with 6,500 men, crossed the James during the afternoon and encamped on the north bank, near Laurel Hill Church. During the night the Federal rear-guard fell back, destroying the bridge over White Oak Swamp; and although a large quantity of stores were either destroyed or abandoned, together with a hospital containing 2,500 wounded, the whole of McClellan's army, men, guns, and trains, effected the passage of this dangerous obstacle.

The next morning Longstreet, with Hill in support, moved forward, and found a Federal division in position
June 30. near Glendale. Bringing his artillery into action, he held his infantry in hand until Huger should come up on his left, and Jackson's guns be heard at White Oak Bridge. Holmes, followed by Magruder, was marching up the Newmarket road to Malvern House; and when the sound of Jackson's artillery became audible to the northwards, Lee sent Longstreet forward to the attack. A sanguinary conflict, on ground covered with heavy timber, and cut up by deep ravines, resulted in the Federals holding

[1] Jackson had with him a gang of negroes who, under the superin-tendence of Captain Mason, a railroad contractor of long experience, per-formed the duties which in regular armies appertain to the corps of engineers. They had already done useful service in the Valley.

their ground till nightfall; and although many prisoners
and several batteries were captured by the Confederates,
McClellan, under cover of the darkness, made good his
escape.

The battle of Glendale or Frayser's Farm was the
crisis of the 'Seven Days.' Had Lee been able to concentrate his whole strength against the Federals it is
probable that McClellan would never have reached the
James. But Longstreet and Hill fought unsupported.
As the former very justly complained, 50,000 men were
within hearing of the guns but none came to co-operate,
and against the two Confederate divisions fought the
Third Federal Army Corps, reinforced by three divisions from the Second, Fifth, and Sixth. Huger's
march on the Charles City road was obstructed by felled
trees. When he at last arrived in front of the enemy, he
was held in check by two batteries, and he does not
appear to have opened communication with either Lee or
Longstreet. Magruder had been ordered to march down
from Savage Station to the Darbytown road, and there to
await orders. At 4.30 P.M. he was ordered to move to Newmarket in support of Holmes. This order was soon
countermanded, but he was unable to join Longstreet until
the fight was over. Holmes was held in check by Porter's
Army Corps, minus McCall's division, on Malvern Hill; and
the cavalry, which might have been employed effectively
against the enemy's left flank and rear, was still north of
the Chickahominy, returning from a destructive but useless
raid on the depôt at the White House. Nor had the conduct
of the battle been unaffected by the complicated nature of
the general plan. Longstreet attacked alone, Hill being
held back, in order to be fresh for the pursuit when
Jackson and Huger should strike in. The attack was
successful, and McCall's division, which had shared the
defeat at Gaines' Mill, was driven from its position.
But McCall was reinforced by other divisions; Longstreet
was thrown on to the defensive by superior numbers, and
when Hill was at length put in, it was with difficulty that
the fierce counterblows of the Federals were beaten off.

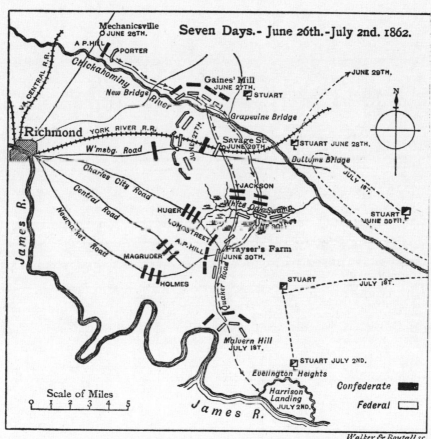

Seven Days.- June 26th.-July 2nd. 1862.

Mechanicsville
JUNE 26TH.
A.P. HILL
PORTER

Chickahominy
New Bridge River

Gaines' Mill
JUNE 27TH.
STUART

JUNE 29TH.

N

VA. CENTRAL R.R.

Richmond
YORK RIVER R.R.

Grapevine Bridge

STUART JUNE 28TH.

Savage St.
JUNE 29TH.

Bottoms Bridge

JULY 1ST.

W'msbg. Road

JUNE 27TH.

Charles City Road

Central Road

JACKSON

STUART
JUNE 30TH.

HUGER

White Oak Swamp

LONGSTREET

JUNE 30TH.

Newma ket Road

A.P. HILL

Frayser's Farm
JUNE 30TH.

STUART

JULY 1ST.

MAGRUDER

James R.

HOLMES

Quaker Road

Malvern Hill
JULY 1ST.

STUART JULY 2ND.

Evelington Heights

Scale of Miles
0 1 2 3 4 5

Confederate ▬
Federal ▭

Harrison
Landing
JULY 2ND.

James R.

Walker & Boutall sc.

Jackson had been unable to participate in the conflict. When night fell he was still north of the White Oak Swamp, seven miles distant from his morning bivouac, and hardly a single infantry man in his command had pulled a trigger. According to his own report his troops reached White Oak Bridge about noon. 'Here the enemy made a determined effort to retard our advance and thereby to prevent an immediate junction between General Longstreet and myself. We found the bridge destroyed, the ordinary place of crossing commanded by their batteries on the other side, and all approach to it barred by detachments of sharp-shooters concealed in a dense wood close by. . . . A heavy cannonading in front announced the engagement of General Longstreet at Frayser's Farm (Glendale) and made me eager to press forward ; but the marshy character of the soil, the destruction of the bridge over the marsh and creek, and the strong position of the enemy for defending the passage, prevented my advancing until the following morning.' [1]

Such are Jackson's reasons for his failure to co-operate with Longstreet. It is clear that he was perfectly aware of the importance of the part he was expected to play ; and he used every means which suggested itself as practicable to force a crossing. The 2nd Virginia Cavalry, under Colonel Munford, had now joined him from the Valley, and their commanding officer bears witness that Jackson showed no lack of energy.

'When I left the general on the preceding evening, he ordered me to be at the cross-roads (five miles from White Oak Bridge) at sunrise the next morning, ready to move in advance of his troops. The worst thunderstorm came up about night I ever was in, and in that thickly wooded country one could not see his horse's ears. My command scattered in the storm, and I do not suppose that any officer had a rougher time in any one night than I had to endure. When the first grey dawn appeared I started off my adjutant and officers to bring up the scattered regiment ; but at sunrise I had not more than fifty men,

[1] O. R., vol. xi., part i., pp. 556, 557.

and I was half a mile from the cross-roads. When I arrived, to my horror there sat Jackson waiting for me. He was in a bad humour, and said, " Colonel, my orders to you were to be here at sunrise." I explained my situation, telling him that we had no provisions, and that the storm and the dark night had conspired against me. When I got through he replied, " Yes, sir. But, Colonel, I ordered you to be here at sunrise. Move on with your regiment. If you meet the enemy drive in his pickets, and if you want artillery, Colonel Crutchfield will furnish you."

' I started on with my little handful of men. As others came straggling on to join me, Jackson noticed it, and sent two couriers to inform me that " my men were straggling badly." I rode back and went over the same story, hoping that he would be impressed with my difficulties. He listened to me, but replied as before, " Yes, sir. But I ordered you to be here at sunrise, and I have been waiting for you for a quarter of an hour."

' Seeing that he was in a peculiar mood, I determined to make the best of my trouble, sent my adjutant back, and made him halt the stragglers and form my men as they came up ; and with what I had, determined to give him no cause for complaint. When we came upon the enemy's picket we charged, and pushed the picket every step of the way into their camp, where there were a large number of wounded and many stores. It was done so rapidly that the enemy's battery on the other side of White Oak Swamp could not fire on us without endangering their own friends.

' When Jackson came up he was smiling, and he at once (shortly after noon) ordered Colonel Crutchfield to bring up the artillery, and very soon the batteries were at work. After the lapse of about an hour my regiment had assembled, and while our batteries were shelling those of the enemy, Jackson sent for me and said, " Colonel, move your regiment over the creek, and secure those guns. I will ride with you to the Swamp. When we reached the crossing we found that the enemy had torn up the bridge, and had thrown the timbers into the stream, forming a tangled mass which seemed to prohibit a crossing. I said to General Jackson that I did not think that we could cross. He looked at me, waved his hand, and replied, " Yes, Colonel, try it." In we went and floundered over, and before I formed the men, Jackson cried out to me to move on at the guns. Colonel Breckenridge started out with what we had over, and I soon got over the second squadron, and moved up the hill. We reached the guns, but they had an infantry support which gave us a volley; at the same time a battery on our right, which we had not seen, opened on us, and back we had to come. I moved down the Swamp about a quarter of a mile, and re-crossed with great difficulty by a cow-path.' [1]

The artillery did little better than the cavalry. The ground on the north bank of the Swamp by no means favoured the action of the guns. To the right of the road the slopes were clear and unobstructed, but the crest was within the forest; while to the left a thick pine wood covered both ridge and valley. On the bank held by the Federals the ground was open, ascending gently to the ridge; but the edge of the stream, immediately opposite the cleared ground on the Confederate right, was covered by a belt of tall trees, in full leaf, which made observation, by either side, a matter of much difficulty. This belt was full of infantry, while to the right rear, commanding the ruined bridge, stood the batteries which had driven back the cavalry.

After some time spent in reconnaissance, it was determined to cut a track through the wood to the right of the road. This was done, and thirty-one guns, moving forward simultaneously ready-shotted, opened fire on the position. The surprise was complete. One of the Federal batteries dispersed in confusion; the other disappeared, and the infantry supports fell back. Jackson immediately ordered two guns to advance down the road, and shell the belt of trees which harboured the

---

[1] ' Jackson himself,' writes Dr. McGuire, ' accompanied by three or four members of his staff, of whom I was one, followed the cavalry across the Swamp. The ford was miry and deep, and impracticable for either artillery or infantry.'

enemy's skirmishers. These were driven back; the divisions of D. H. Hill and Whiting were formed up in the pine wood on the left, and a working party was sent forward to repair the bridge. Suddenly, from the high ground behind the belt of trees, by which they were completely screened, two fresh Federal batteries—afterwards increased to three—opened on the line of Confederate guns. Under cover of this fire their skirmishers returned to the Swamp, and their main line came forward to a position whence it commanded the crossing at effective range. The two guns on the road were sent to the right-about. The shells of the Federal batteries fell into the stream, and the men who had been labouring at the bridge ran back and refused to work. The artillery duel, in which neither side could see the other, but in which both suffered some loss, continued throughout the afternoon.

Meantime a Confederate regiment, fording the stream, drove in the hostile skirmishers, and seized the belt of trees; Wright's brigade, of Huger's division, which had joined Jackson as the guns came into action, was sent back to force a passage at Brackett's Ford, a mile up stream; and reconnaissances were pushed out to find some way of turning the enemy's position. Every road and track, however, was obstructed by felled trees and abattis, and it was found that a passage was impracticable at Brackett's Ford. Two companies were pushed over the creek, and drove back the enemy's pickets. 'I discovered,' says Wright, 'that the enemy had destroyed the bridge, and had completely blockaded the road through the Swamp by felling trees in and across it. . . . I ascertained that the road debouched from the Swamp into an open field (meadow), commanded by a line of high hills, all in cultivation and free from timber. Upon this ridge of hills the enemy had posted heavy batteries of field-artillery, strongly supported by infantry, which swept the meadow by a direct and cross fire, and which could be used with terrible effect upon my column while struggling through the fallen timber in the wood through the Swamp.' [1]

[1] O R., vol. xi., part i., pp. 810, 811.

Having ascertained that the enemy was present in great strength on the further bank, that every road was obstructed, and that there was no means of carrying his artillery over the creek, or favourable ground on which his infantry could act, Jackson gave up all hope of aiding Longstreet.

That the obstacles which confronted him were serious there can be no question. His smooth-bore guns, although superior in number, were unable to beat down the fire of the rifled batteries. The enemy's masses were well hidden. The roads were blocked, the stream was swollen, the banks marshy, and although infantry could cross them, the fords which had proved difficult for the cavalry would have stopped the artillery, the ammunition waggons, and the ambulances ; while the Federal position, on the crest of a long open slope, was exceedingly strong. Jackson, as his report shows, maturely weighed these difficulties, and came to the conclusion that he could do no good by sending over his infantry alone. It was essential, it is true, to detain as many as possible of the enemy on the banks of the Swamp, while Longstreet, Hill, Huger, and Magruder dealt with the remainder ; and this he fully realised, but it is by no means improbable that he considered the heavy fire of his guns and the threatening position of his infantry would have this effect.

It is interesting to note how far this hope, supposing that he entertained it, was fulfilled. Two divisions of Federal infantry and three batteries—a total of 22,000 men—defended the passage at White Oak Bridge against 27,000 Confederates, including Wright; and a detached force of infantry and guns was posted at Brackett's Ford.[1] On the Confederate artillery opening fire, two

[1] General Heintzleman, commanding the Federal 3rd Corps, reports that he had placed a force at Brackett's Ford (O. R., vol. xi., part ii., p. 100). General Slocum (6th Corps) sent infantry and a 12-pounder howitzer (O. R., vol. xi., part ii., p. 435) to the same point ; and Seeley's battery of the 3rd Corps was also engaged here (O. R., vol. xi., part ii., p. 106). The force at White Oak Bridge was constituted as follows :—

Smith's Division	of the	6th Corps.
Richardson's Division	„	2nd Corps.
Dana's Brigade } Sedgwick's Division Sully's Brigade	„	2nd Corps.
Naglee's Brigade, Peck's Division	„	4th Corps.

brigades were sent up from near Glendale, but when it was found that this fire was not followed up by an infantry attack, these brigades, with two others in addition, were sent over to reinforce the troops which were engaged with Longstreet. When these facts became known; when it was clear that had Jackson attacked vigorously, the Federals would hardly have dared to weaken their line along White Oak Swamp, and that, in these circumstances, Longstreet and A. P. Hill would probably have seized the Quaker road, his failure to cross the creek exposed him to criticism. Not only did his brother-generals complain of his inaction, but Franklin, the Federal commander immediately opposed to him, writing long afterwards, made the following comments :—

'Jackson seems to have been ignorant of what General Lee expected of him, and badly informed about Brackett's Ford. When he found how strenuous was our defence at the bridge, he should have turned his attention to Brackett's Ford also. A force could have been as quietly gathered there as at the bridge ; a strong infantry movement at the ford would have easily overrun our small force there, placing our right at Glendale, held by Slocum's division, in great jeopardy, and turning our force at the bridge by getting between it and Glendale. In fact, it is likely that we should have been defeated that day had General Jackson done what his great reputation seems to make it imperative he should have done.'[1] But General Franklin's opinion as to the ease with which Brackett's Ford might have been passed is not justified by the facts. In the first place, General Slocum, who was facing Huger, and had little to do throughout the day, had two brigades within easy distance of the crossing ; in the second place, General Wright reported the ford impassable ; and in the third place, General Franklin himself admits that directly Wright's scouts were seen near the ford two brigades of Sedgwick's division were sent to oppose their passage.

General Long, in his life of Lee, finds excuse for Jackson in a story that he was utterly exhausted, and that

[1] *Battles and Leaders*, vol. ii., p. 381.

his staff let him sleep until the sun was high. Apart from the unlikelihood that a man who seems to have done without sleep whenever the enemy was in front should have permitted himself to be overpowered at such a crisis, we have Colonel Munford's evidence that the general was well in advance of his columns at sunrise, and the regimental reports show that the troops were roused at 2.30 A.M.

Jackson may well have been exhausted. He had certainly not spared himself during the operations. On the night of the 27th, after the battle of Gaines' Mill, he went over to Stuart's camp at midnight, and a long conference took place. At 3.30 on the morning of the 29th he visited Magruder, riding across Grapevine Bridge from McGehee's House, and his start must have been an early one. In a letter to his wife, dated near the White Oak Bridge, he says that in consequence of the heavy rain he rose 'about midnight' on the 30th. Yet his medical director, although he noticed that the general fell asleep while he was eating his supper the same evening, says that he never saw him more active and energetic than during the engagement;[1] and Jackson himself, neither in his report nor elsewhere, ever admitted that he was in any way to blame.

It is difficult to conceive that his scrupulous regard for truth, displayed in every action of his life, should have yielded in this one instance to his pride. He was perfectly aware of the necessity of aiding Longstreet; and if, owing to the obstacles enumerated in his report, he thought the task impossible, his opinion, as that of a man who as difficulties accumulated became the more determined to overcome them, must be regarded with respect. The critics, it is possible, have forgotten for the moment that the condition of the troops is a factor of supreme importance in military operations. General D. H. Hill has told us that 'Jackson's own corps was worn out by long and exhausting marches, and reduced in numbers by numerous sanguinary battles;'[2] and he records his conviction that pity for his

[1] Letter from Dr. Hunter McGuire to the author.
[2] *Battles and Leaders*, vol. ii., p. 389.

troops had much to do with the general's inaction. Hill would have probably come nearer the truth if he had said that the tired regiments were hardly to be trusted in a desperate assault, unsupported by artillery, on a position which was even stronger than that which they had stormed with such loss at Gaines' Mill.

Had Jackson thrown two columns across the fords—which the cavalry, according to Munford, had not found easy, —and attempted to deploy on the further bank, it was exceedingly probable that they would have been driven back with tremendous slaughter. The refusal of the troops to work at the bridge under fire was in itself a sign that they had little stomach for hard fighting.

It may be argued that it was Jackson's duty to sacrifice his command in order to draw off troops from Glendale. But on such unfavourable ground the sacrifice would have been worse than useless. The attack repulsed—and it could hardly have gone otherwise—Franklin, leaving a small rear-guard to watch the fords, would have been free to turn nearly his whole strength against Longstreet. It is quite true, as a tactical principle, that demonstrations, such as Jackson made with his artillery, are seldom to be relied upon to hold an enemy in position. When the first alarm has passed off, and the defending general becomes aware that nothing more than a feint is intended, he will act as did the Federals, and employ his reserves elsewhere. A vigorous attack is, almost invariably, the only means of keeping him to his ground. But an attack which is certain to be repulsed, and to be repulsed in quick time, is even less effective than a demonstration. It may be the precursor of a decisive defeat.

But it is not so much for his failure to force the passage at White Oak Swamp that Jackson has been criticised, as for his failure to march to Frayser's Farm on finding that the Federal position was impregnable. 'When, on the forenoon of the 30th,' writes Longstreet, 'Jackson found his way blocked by Franklin, he had time to march to the head of it (White Oak Swamp), and across to the Charles City road, in season for the engagement at

Frayser's Farm [Glendale], the distance being about four miles.' [1]

Without doubt this would have been a judicious course to pursue, but it was not for Jackson to initiate such a movement. He had been ordered by General Lee to move along the road to White Oak Swamp, to endeavour to force his way to the Long Bridge road, to guard Lee's left flank from any attack across the fords or bridges of the lower Chickahominy, and to keep on that road until he received further orders. These further orders he never received; and it was certainly not his place to march to the Charles City road until Lee, who was with Longstreet, sent him instructions to do so. 'General Jackson,' says Dr. McGuire, 'demanded of his subordinates implicit, blind obedience. He gave orders in his own peculiar, terse, rapid way, and he did not permit them to be questioned. He obeyed his own superiors in the same fashion. At White Oak Swamp he was looking for some message from General Lee, but he received none, and therefore, as a soldier, he had no right to leave the road which had been assigned to him. About July 13, 1862, the night before we started to Gordonsville, Crutchfield, Pendleton (assistant-adjutant-general), and myself were discussing the campaign just finished. We were talking about the affair at Frayser's Farm, and wondering if it would have been better for Jackson with part of his force to have moved to Longstreet's aid. The general came in while the discussion was going on, and curtly said : " If General Lee had wanted me he could have sent for me." It looked the day after the battle, and it looks to me now, that if General Lee had sent a staff officer, who could have ridden the distance in forty minutes, to order Jackson with three divisions to the cross roads, while D. H. Hill and the artillery watched Franklin, we should certainly have crushed McClellan's army. If Lee had wanted Jackson to give direct support to Longstreet, he could have had him there in under three hours. The staff officer was not sent, and the evidence is that General Lee believed Longstreet strong enough to defeat the Federals without

[1] *From Manassas to Appomattox*, p. 150.

direct aid from Jackson.'[1] Such reasoning appears in-
controvertible.   Jackson, be it remembered, had been
directed to guard the left flank of the army 'until further
orders.'   Had these words been omitted, and he had been
left free to follow his own judgment, it is possible that he
would have joined Huger on the Charles City road with
three divisions.   But in all probability he felt himself tied
down by the phrase which Moltke so strongly reprobates.
Despite Dr. McGuire's statement Jackson knew well that
disobedience to orders may sometimes be condoned.   It
may be questioned whether he invariably demanded 'blind'
obedience.   'General,' said an officer, 'you blame me for
disobedience of orders, but in Mexico you did the same
yourself.'   'But I was successful,' was Jackson's reply; as
much as to say that an officer, when he takes upon himself
the responsibility of ignoring the explicit instructions of
his superior, must be morally certain that he is doing what
that superior, were he present, would approve.   Apply
this rule to the situation at White Oak Swamp.   For anything Jackson knew it was possible that Longstreet and
Hill might defeat the Federals opposed to them without his
aid.   In such case, Lee, believing Jackson to be still on the
left flank, would have ordered him to prevent the enemy's
escape by the Long Bridge.   What would Lee have said
had his 'further orders' found Jackson marching to the
Charles City road, with the Long Bridge some miles in
rear?   The truth is that the principle of 'marching to
the sound of the cannon,' though always to be borne in
mind, cannot be invariably followed.   The only fair
criticism on Jackson's conduct is that he should have
informed Lee of his inability to force the passage across
the Swamp, and have held three divisions in readiness
to march to Glendale.   This, so far as can be ascertained,
was left undone, but the evidence is merely negative.

Except for this apparent omission, it cannot be fairly
said that Jackson was in the slightest degree responsible
for the failure of the Confederate operations.   If
the truth be told, Lee's design was by no means

[1] Letter to the author.

perfect. It had two serious defects. In the first
place, it depended for success on the co-operation of
several converging columns, moving over an intricate
country, of which the Confederates had neither accurate
maps nor reliable information. The march of the columns
was through thick woods, which not only impeded inter-
communication, but provided the enemy with ample
material for obstructing the roads, and Jackson's line of
march was barred by a formidable obstacle in White Oak
Swamp, an admirable position for a rear-guard. In the
second place, concentration at the decisive point was not
provided for. The staff proved incapable of keeping the divisions in hand. Magruder was permitted to wander to and
fro after the fashion of D'Erlon between Quatre Bras
and Ligny. Holmes was as useless as Grouchy at
Waterloo. Huger did nothing, although some of his
brigades, when the roads to the front were found to be
obstructed, might easily have been drawn off to reinforce
Longstreet. The cavalry had gone off on a raid to the
White House, instead of crossing the Chickahominy and
harassing the enemy's eastward flank; and at the decisive
point only two divisions were assembled, 20,000 men all
told, and these two divisions attacked in succession instead
of simultaneously. Had Magruder and Holmes, neither
of whom would have been called upon to march more
than thirteen miles, moved on Frayser's Farm, and had
part of Huger's division been brought over to the same
point, the Federals would in all probability have been
irretrievably defeated. It is easy to be wise after the
event. The circumstances were extraordinary. An army
of 75,000 men was pursuing an army of 95,000, of which
65,000, when the pursuit began, were perfectly fresh troops.
The problem was, indeed, one of exceeding difficulty; but,
in justice to the reputation of his lieutenants, it is only
fair to say that Lee's solution was not a masterpiece.

During the night which followed the battle of Frayser's
Farm the whole Federal army fell back on Malvern Hill—a
strong position, commanding the country for many miles,
and very difficult of access, on which the reserve artillery,

supported by the Fourth and Fifth Corps, was already posted.

July 1.   The Confederates, marching at daybreak, passed over roads which were strewn with arms, blankets, and equipments. Stragglers from the retreating army were picked up at every step. Scores of wounded men lay untended by the roadside. Waggons and ambulances had been abandoned ; and with such evidence before their eyes it was difficult to resist the conviction that the enemy was utterly demoralised. That McClellan had seized Malvern Hill, and that it was strongly occupied by heavy guns, Lee was well aware. But, still holding to his purpose of annihilating his enemy before McDowell could intervene from Fredericksburg, he pushed forward, determined to attack ; and with his whole force now well in hand the result seemed assured. Three or four miles south of White Oak Swamp Jackson's column, which was leading the Confederate advance, came under the fire of the Federal batteries. The advanced-guard deployed in the woods on either side of the road, and Lee, accompanied by Jackson, rode forward to reconnoitre.

Malvern Hill, a plateau rising to the height of 150 feet above the surrounding forests, possessed nearly every requirement of a strong defensive position. The open ground on the top, undulating and unobstructed, was a mile and a half in length by half a mile in breadth. To the north, north-west, and north-east it fell gradually, the slopes covered with wheat, standing or in shock, to the edge of the woods, which are from eight to sixteen hundred yards distant from the commanding crest. The base of the hill, except to the east and south-east, was covered with dense forest ; and within the forest, at the foot of the declivity, ran a tortuous and marshy stream. The right flank was partially protected by a long mill-dam. The left, more open, afforded an excellent artillery position overlooking a broad stretch of meadows, drained by a narrow stream and deep ditches, and flanked by the fire of several gunboats. Only three approaches, the Quaker and the river roads, and a track from the north-west, gave access to the heights.

The reconnaissance showed that General Porter, commanding the defence, had utilised the ground to the best advantage. A powerful artillery, posted just in rear of the crest, swept the entire length of the slopes, and under cover in rear were dense masses of infantry, with a strong line of skirmishers pushed down the hill in front.

Nevertheless, despite the formidable nature of the Federal preparations, orders were immediately issued for attack. General Lee, who was indisposed, had instructed Longstreet to reconnoitre the enemy's left, and to report whether attack was feasible. Jackson was opposed to a frontal attack, preferring to turn the enemy's right. Longstreet, however, was of a different opinion. 'The spacious open,' he says, 'along Jackson's front appeared to offer a field for play of a hundred or more guns. . . . I thought it probable that Porter's batteries, under the cross-fire of the Confederates' guns posted on his left and front, could be thrown into disorder, and thus make way for the combined assaults of the infantry. I so reported, and General Lee ordered disposition accordingly, sending the pioneer corps to cut a road for the right batteries.'[1]

It was not till four o'clock that the line of battle was formed. Jackson was on the left, with Whiting to the left of the Quaker road, and D. H. Hill to the right; Ewell's and Jackson's own divisions were in reserve. Nearly half a 4 P.M. mile beyond Jackson's right came two of Huger's brigades, Armistead and Wright, and to Huger's left rear was Magruder. Holmes, still on the river road, was to assail the enemy's left. Longstreet and A. P. Hill were in reserve behind Magruder, on the Long Bridge road.

The deployment of the leading divisions was not effected without loss, for the Federal artillery swept all the roads and poured a heavy fire into the woods; but at length D. H. Hill's infantry came into line along the edge of the timber.

The intervening time had been employed in bringing the artillery to the front; and now were seen the tremendous difficulties which confronted the attack. The swamps

[1] *From Manassas to Appomattox*, p. 143.

and thickets through which the batteries had to force their way were grievous impediments to rapid or orderly movement, and when they at last emerged from the cover, and unlimbered for action, the concentrated fire of the Federal guns overpowered them from the outset. In front of Huger four batteries were disabled in quick succession, the enemy concentrating fifty or sixty guns on each of them in turn; four or five others which Jackson had ordered to take post on the left of his line, although, with two exceptions, they managed to hold their ground, were powerless to subdue the hostile fire. 'The obstacles,' says Lee in his report, 'presented by the woods and swamp made it impracticable to bring up a sufficient amount of artillery to oppose successfully the extraordinary force of that arm employed by the enemy, while the field itself afforded us few positions favourable for its use and none for its proper concentration.'

According to Longstreet, when the inability of the batteries to prepare the way for the infantry was demonstrated by their defeat, Lee abandoned the original plan of attack. 'He proposed to me to move "round to the left with my own and A. P. Hill's division, and turn the Federal right." I issued my orders accordingly for the two divisions to go around and turn the Federal right, when in some way unknown to me the battle was drawn on.'[1]

Unfortunately, through some mistake on the part of Lee's staff, the order of attack which had been already issued was not rescinded. It was certainly an extraordinary production. 'Batteries,' it ran, 'have been established to rake the enemy's line. If it is broken, as is probable, Armistead, who can witness the effect of the fire, has been ordered to charge with a yell. Do the same.'[2] This was to D. H. Hill and to Magruder, who had under his command Huger's and McLaws' divisions as well as his own.

So, between five and six o'clock, General D. H. Hill, 5.30 P.M. believing that he heard the appointed signal, broke forward from the timber, and five brigades, in one irregular line, charged full against the enemy's front. The

[1] *Battles and Leaders*, vol. ii., p. 403.
[2] O. R., vol. xi., part i., p. 677.

Federals, disposed in several lines, were in overwhelming strength. Their batteries were free to concentrate on the advancing infantry. Their riflemen, posted in the interval between the artillery masses, swept the long slopes with a grazing fire, while fence, bank, and ravine, gave shelter from the Confederate bullets. Nor were the enormous difficulties which confronted the attack in any way mitigated by careful arrangement on the part of the Confederate staff. The only hope of success, if success were possible, lay in one strong concentrated effort; in employing the whole army; in supporting the infantry with artillery, regardless of loss, at close range; and in hurling a mass of men, in several successive lines, against one point of the enemy's position. It is possible that the Federal army, already demoralised by retreat, might have yielded to such vigorous pressure. But in the Confederate attack there was not the slightest attempt at concentration. The order which dictated it gave an opening to misunderstanding; and, as is almost invariably the case when orders are defective, misunderstanding occurred. The movement was premature. Magruder had only two brigades of his three divisions, Armistead's and Wright's, in position. Armistead, who was well in advance of the Confederate right, was attacked by a strong body of skirmishers. D. H. Hill took the noise of this conflict for the appointed signal, and moved forward. The divisions which should have supported him had not yet crossed the swamp in rear; and thus 10,500 men, absolutely unaided, advanced against the whole Federal army. The blunder met with terrible retribution. On that midsummer evening death reaped a fearful harvest. The gallant Confederate infantry, nerved by their success at Gaines' Mill, swept up the field with splendid determination. 'It was the onset of battle,' said a Federal officer present, 'with the good order of a review.' But the iron hail of grape and canister, laying the ripe wheat low as if it had been cut with a sickle, and tossing the shocks in air, rent the advancing lines from end to end. Hundreds fell, hundreds swarmed back to the woods, but still the brigades pressed on, and through the smoke of battle

F 2

the waving colours led the charge. But the Federal
infantry had yet to be encountered. Lying behind their
shelter they had not yet fired a shot; but as the Confederates
reached close range, regiment after regiment, springing to
their feet, poured a devastating fire into the charging
ranks. The rush was checked. Here and there small
bodies of desperate men, following the colours, still pressed
onward, but the majority lay down, and the whole front of
battle rang with the roar of musketry. But so thin was
the Confederate line that it was impossible to overcome
the sustained fire of the enemy. The brigade reserves
had already been thrown in; there was no further support
at hand; the Federal gunners, staunch and resolute, held
fast to their position, and on every part of the line Porter's
reserves were coming up. As one regiment emptied its
cartridge-boxes it was relieved by another. The volume of
fire never for a moment slackened; and fresh batteries,
amongst which were the 32-prs. of the siege train, unlimbering on the flanks, gave further strength to a front
which was already impregnable.

　　Jackson, meanwhile, on receiving a request for reinforcements, had sent forward three brigades of his own
division and a brigade of Hill's. But a mistake had been
committed in the disposition of these troops. The order
for attack had undoubtedly named only D. H. Hill's
division. But there was no good reason that it should
have been so literally construed as to leave the division unsupported. Whiting was guarding the left flank, and was
not available; but Ewell and Winder were doing nothing,
and there can be no question but that they should have
advanced to the edge of the woods directly D. H. Hill
moved forward, and have followed his brigades across the
open, ready to lend aid directly his line was checked. As
it was, they had been halted within the woods and beyond
the swamp, and the greater part, in order to avoid the
random shells, had moved even further to the rear. It
thus happened that before the reinforcements arrived
Hill's division had been beaten back, and under the tremendous fire of the Federal artillery it was with difficulty
that the border of the forest was maintained.

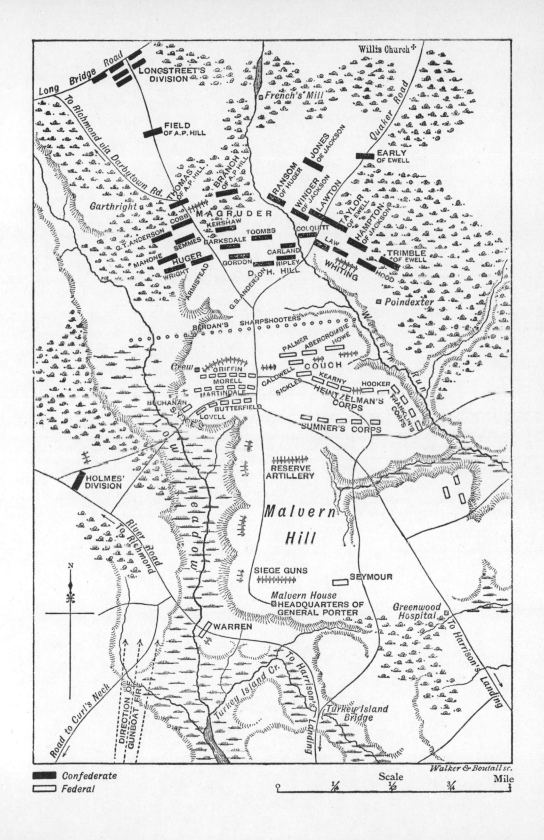

Willis Church

Long Bridge Road

LONGSTREET'S DIVISION

To Richmond via Darbytown Rd.

FIELD OF A.P. HILL

French's Mill

Quaker Road

THOMAS OF A.P. HILL

BRANCH OF A.P. HILL

RANSOM OF HUGER

JONES OF JACKSON

WINDER OF JACKSON

EARLY OF EWELL

LAWTON

TAYLOR OF EWELL

HAMPTON OF JACKSON

Garthright

G.T. ANDERSON

COBB

MAGRUDER

KERSHAW

TOOMBS

COLQUITT

LAW

TRIMBLE OF EWELL

SEMMES

BARKSDALE

CARLAND

MAHONE

HUGER

GORDON

RIPLEY

WHITING

HOOD

WRIGHT

ARMISTEAD

D.H. HILL

Poindexter

G.B. ANDERSON

BERDAN'S   SHARPSHOOTERS

Crew

PALMER

ABERCROMBIE

HOWE

GRIFFIN

COUCH

MORELL

CALDWELL

KEARNY

HOOKER

MARTINDALE

SICKLES

HEINTZELMAN'S CORPS

FRANKLIN'S CORPS

BUCHANAN

BUTTERFIELD

LOVELL

SUMNER'S CORPS

HOLMES' DIVISION

RESERVE ARTILLERY

River Road

To Richmond

Malvern Hill

SIEGE GUNS

SEYMOUR

Malvern House
HEADQUARTERS OF GENERAL PORTER

Greenwood Hospital

To Harrison's Landing

N

WARREN

To Harrison's Landing

Road to Curl's Neck

DIRECTION OF GUNBOAT FIRE

Turkey Island Cr.

Turkey Island Bridge

Walker & Boutall sc.

■ Confederate
□ Federal

Scale

0   1/4   1/2   3/4   Mile

While Hill was retiring, Huger, and then Magruder, came into action on the right. It had been reported to Lee that the enemy was beginning to fall back. This report originated, there can be little doubt, in the withdrawal of the Federal regiments and batteries which had exhausted their ammunition and were relieved by others; but, in any case, it was imperative that D. H. Hill should be supported, and the other divisions were ordered forward with all speed. Huger's and Magruder's men attacked with the same determination as had been displayed by Hill's, but no better success attended their endeavours. The brigades were not properly formed when the order arrived, but scattered over a wide front, and they went in piecemeal. Magruder's losses were even greater than Hill's; and with his defeat the battle ceased.

Had the Federals followed up the repulse with a strong counter-attack the victory of Malvern Hill might have been more decisive than that of Gaines' Mill. It is true that neither Longstreet nor A. P. Hill had been engaged, and that three of Jackson's divisions, his own, Whiting's and Ewell's, had suffered little. But Magruder and D. H. Hill, whose commands included at least 30,000 muskets, one half of Lee's infantry, had been completely crushed, and Holmes on the river road was too far off to lend assistance. The fatal influence of a continued retreat had paralysed, however, the initiative of the Federal generals. Intent only on getting away unscathed, they neglected, like McClellan at Gaines' Mill, to look for opportunities, forgetting that when an enemy is pursuing in hot haste he is very apt to expose himself. Jackson had acted otherwise at Port Republic.

The loss of over 5,000 men was not the worst which had befallen the Confederates. 'The next morning by dawn,' says one of Ewell's brigadiers, 'I went off to ask for orders, when I found the whole army in the utmost disorder— thousands of straggling men were asking every passer-by for their regiments; ambulances, waggons, and artillery obstructing every road, and altogether, in a drenching rain, presenting a scene of the most woeful and disheartening

confusion.'[1]   The reports of other officers corroborate
General Trimble's statement, and there can be no question
that demoralisation had set in.   Whether, if the Federals
had used their large reserves with resolution, and, as the
Confederates fell back down the slopes, had followed with
the bayonet, the demoralisation would not have increased
and spread, must remain in doubt.   Not one of the
Southern generals engaged has made public his opinion.
There is but one thing certain, that with an opponent so
blind to opportunity as McClellan a strong counterstroke
was the last thing to be feared.   After witnessing the
opening of the attack, the Federal commander, leaving the
control of the field to Porter, had ridden off to Harrison's
Landing, eight miles down the James, whither his trains,
escorted by the Fourth Army Corps, had been directed,
and where he had determined to await reinforcements.
The Federal troops, moreover, although they had withstood the charge of the Confederate infantry with
unbroken ranks, had not fought with the same spirit as
they had displayed at Gaines' Mill.   General Hunt,
McClellan's chief of artillery, to whose admirable disposition of the batteries the victory was largely due, wrote
that ' the battle was desperately contested, and frequently
trembled in the balance.   The last attack . . . was nearly
successful; but we won from the fact that we had kept
our reserves in hand.'[2]   Nor had McClellan much confidence in his army.   'My men,' he wrote to Washington
on the morning of the battle, ' are completely exhausted,
and I dread the result if we are attacked to-day by fresh
troops.   If possible, I shall retire to-night to Harrison's
Landing, where the gunboats can render more aid in
covering our position.   Permit me to urge that not an
hour should be lost in sending me fresh troops.   More
gunboats are much needed. . . . I now pray for time.   My

<hr/>

[1] Trimble's Report, O. R., vol. xi., part i., p. 619.

[2] Three horse-batteries and eight 32-pr. howitzers were ' brought up to
the decisive point at the close of the day, thus bringing every gun of this
large artillery force (the artillery reserve) into the most active and decisive
use.   Not a gun remained unemployed: not one could have been safely
spared. —Hunt's Report, O. R., vol. xi., part ii., p. 239.

men have proved themselves the equals of any troops in the world, but they are worn out. Our losses have been very great, we have failed to win only because overpowered by superior numbers.' [1]

Surely a more despairing appeal was never uttered. The general, whose only thought was 'more gunboats and fresh troops,' whatever may have been the condition of his men, had reached the last stage of demoralisation.

The condition to which McClellan was reduced seems to have been realised by Jackson. The crushing defeat of his own troops failed to disturb his judgment. Whilst the night still covered the battle-field, his divisional generals came to report the condition of their men and to receive instructions. 'Every representation,' says Dabney, ' which they made was gloomy.' At length, after many details of losses and disasters, they concurred in declaring that McClellan would probably take the aggressive in the morning, and that the Confederate army was in no condition to resist him. Jackson had listened silently, save when he interposed a few brief questions, to all their statements; but now he replied : 'No; he will clear out in the morning.'

The forecast was more than fulfilled. When morning dawned, grey, damp, and cheerless, and the Confederate sentinels, through the cold mist which rose from the sodden July 2.   woods, looked out upon the battle-field, they saw that Malvern Hill had been abandoned. Only a few cavalry patrols rode to and fro on the ground which had been held by the Federal artillery, and on the slopes below, covered with hundreds of dead and dying men, the surgeons were quietly at work. During the night the enemy had fallen back to Harrison's Landing, and justification for Lee's assault at Malvern Hill may be found in the story of the Federal retreat. The confusion of the night march, following on a long series of fierce engagements, told with terrible effect on the *moral* of the men, and stragglers increased at every step. 'It was like the retreat,' said one of McClellan's generals, ' of a whipped army. We retreated like a parcel of sheep, and a

[1] O. R., vol. xi., part iii., p. 282.

few shots from the rebels would have panic-stricken the
whole command.'[1]   At length, through blinding rain, the
flotilla of gunboats was discovered, and on the long
peninsula between Herring Run and the James the exhausted army reached a resting-place.   But so great was
the disorder, that during the whole of that day nothing
was done to prepare a defensive position ; a ridge to the
north, which commanded the whole camp, was unoccupied ;
and, according to the Committee of Congress which took
evidence on the conduct of the war, ' nothing but a heavy
rain, thereby preventing the enemy from bringing up their
artillery, saved the army from destruction.'[2]   McClellan's
own testimony is even more convincing.   ' The army,' he
wrote on July 3, the second day after the battle, ' is
thoroughly worn out and requires rest and very heavy
reinforcements. . . . I am in hopes that the enemy is as
completely worn out as we are. . . . The roads are now
very bad ; for these reasons I hope we shall have enough
breathing space to reorganise and rest the men, and get
them into position before the enemy can attack again. . . .
It is of course impossible to estimate as yet our losses, but
I doubt whether there are to-day more than 50,000 men
with the colours.'[3]

As his army of 105,000 men, during the whole of the
Seven Days, lost only 16,000, the last admission, if accurate,
is most significant.   Nearly half the men must either have
been sick or straggling.

It was not because the Confederates were also worn out
that the Federals were given time to reorganise and to
establish themselves in a strong position.   Jackson, the
moment it was light, rode through the rain to the front.
Learning that the enemy had evacuated their position, he
ordered his chief of staff to get the troops under arms,
to form the infantry in three lines of battle, and then to
allow the men to build fires, cook their rations, and dry
their clothes.   By 11 o'clock the ammunition had been

[1] Report on the Conduct of the War, p. 580.   General Hooker's evidence.
[2] Report on the Conduct of the War, p. 27.
[3] O. R., vol. xi., part i., pp. 291, 292.

replenished, and his four divisions were formed up. Longstreet's brigades had pushed forward a couple of miles, but no orders had reached the Valley troops, and Major Dabney rode off to find his general. 'I was told,' he writes, 'that he was in the Poindexter House, a large mansion near Willis' Church. Lee, Jackson, Dr. McGuire, and Major Taylor of Lee's staff, and perhaps others, were in the dining-room. Asking leave to report to General Jackson that his orders had been fulfilled, I was introduced to General Lee, who, with his usual kindness, begged me to sit by the fire and dry myself. Here I stayed much of the day, and witnessed some strange things. Longstreet, wet and muddy, was the first to enter. He had ridden round most of the battle-field, and his report was not particularly cheerful. Jackson was very quiet, never volunteering any counsel or suggestion, but answering when questioned in a brief, deferential tone. His countenance was very serious, and soon became very troubled. After a time the clatter of horses' hoofs was heard, and two gentlemen came in, dripping. They were the President and his nephew. Davis and Lee then drew to the table, and entered into an animated military discussion. Lee told the President the news which the scouts were bringing in, of horrible mud, and of abandoned arms and baggage-waggons. They then debated at length what was to be done next. McClellan was certainly retiring, but whether as beaten or as only manœuvring was not apparent, nor was the direction of his retreat at all clear. Was he aiming for some point on the lower James where he might embark and get away? or at some point on the upper James—say Shirley, or Bermuda Hundred—where he could cross the river (he had pontoons and gunboats) and advance on Richmond from the south? Such were the questions which came up, and at length it was decided that the army should make no movement until further information had been received. The enemy was not to be pursued until Stuart's cavalry, which had arrived the previous evening at Nance's Shop, should obtain reliable information.

'Jackson, meanwhile, sat silent in his corner. I

watched his face. The expression, changing from surprise to dissent, and lastly to intense mortification, showed clearly the tenor of his thoughts. He knew that McClellan was defeated, that he was retreating and not manœuvring. He knew that his troops were disorganised, that sleeplessness, fasting, bad weather, and disaster must have weakened their *moral*. He heard it said by General Lee that the scouts reported the roads so deep in mud that the artillery could not move, that our men were wet and wearied. But Jackson's mind reasoned that where the Federals could march the Confederates could follow, and that a decisive victory was well worth a great effort.' [1]

The decision of the council of war was that the army should move the next morning in the direction of Harrison's Landing. Longstreet, whose troops had not been engaged at Malvern Hill, was to lead the way. But the operations of this day were without result. The line of march was by Carter's Mill and the river road. But after the troops had been set in motion, it was found that the river road had been obstructed by the enemy, and Lee directed Longstreet to countermarch to the Charles City cross roads and move on Evelington Heights.[2] But ignorance of the country and inefficient guides once more played into the enemy's hands, and when night closed the troops were still some distance from the Federal outposts.

July 3.

The delay had been exceedingly unfortunate. At 9 A.M. Stuart's cavalry had occupied the Evelington Heights, and, believing that Longstreet was close at hand, had opened fire with a single howitzer on the camps below. The consternation caused by this unlooked-for attack was great. But the Federals soon recovered from their surprise, and, warned as to the danger of their situation, sent out infantry and artillery to drive back the enemy and secure the heights. Stuart, dismounting his troopers, held on for some time; but at two o'clock, finding that the Confederate infantry was still six or seven miles distant,

---

[1] Letter to the author. Dr. McGuire writes to the same effect.
[2] Evelington Heights are between Rawling's Mill Pond and Westover.

and that his ammunition was failing, he gave up the Heights, which were immediately fortified by the enemy. Had the cavalry commander resisted the temptation of spreading panic in the enemy's ranks, and kept his troops under cover, infantry and artillery might possibly have been brought up to the Heights before they were occupied by the Federals. In any case, it was utterly useless to engage a whole army with one gun and a few regiments of cavalry, and in war, especially in advanced-guard operations, silence is often golden.[1] It was not till they were warned by the fire of Stuart's howitzer that the Federals realised the necessity of securing and intrenching the Evelington Heights, and it is within the bounds of possibility, had they been left undisturbed, that they might have neglected them altogether. McClellan, according to his letters already quoted, believed that the condition of the roads would retard the advance of the enemy; and, as is evident from a letter he wrote the same morning, before the incident took place, he was of opinion that there was no immediate need for the occupation of a defensive position.[2]

During this day the Valley divisions, crawling in rear of Longstreet, had marched only three miles; and such sluggish progress, at so critical a moment, put the climax to Jackson's discontent. His wrath blazed forth with unwonted vehemence. 'That night,' says Dabney,[3] 'he was quartered in a farmhouse a mile or two east of Willis' Church. The soldier assigned to him as a guide made a most stupid report, and admitted that he knew nothing of the road. Jackson turned on him in fierce anger, and ordered him from his presence with threats of the severest punishment. On retiring, he said to his staff, " Now, gentlemen, Jim will have breakfast for you punctually at dawn. I expect you to be up, to eat immediately, and be in the saddle without delay. We must burn no more daylight." About daybreak I heard him tramping down the stairs. I alone went out to meet him. All the rest were asleep. He addressed me in

---

[1] The military student will compare the battles of Weissembourg, Vion-ville, and Gravelotte in 1870, all of which began with a useless surprise.
[2] O. R., vol. xi., part iii., pp. 291-2.   [3] Letter to the author.

stern tones : " Major, how is it that this staff never will be punctual ? " I replied : " I am in time ; I cannot control the others."   Jackson turned in a rage to the servant : " Put back that food into the chest, have that chest in the waggon, and that waggon moving in two minutes."   I suggested, very humbly, that he had better at least take some food himself.   But he was too angry to eat, and repeating his orders, flung himself into the saddle, and galloped off. Jim gave a low whistle, saying : " My stars, but de general is just mad dis time ; most like lightnin' strike him ! " '

With the engagement on the Evelington Heights the fighting round Richmond came to an end.   When Lee

July 4.   came up with his advanced divisions on the morning of the 4th, he found the pickets already engaged, and the troops formed up in readiness for action. He immediately rode forward with Jackson, and the two, dismounting, proceeded without staff or escort to make a careful reconnaissance of the enemy's position.   Their inspection showed them that it was practically impregnable.   The front, facing westward, was flanked from end to end by the fire of the gunboats, and the Evelington Heights, already fortified, and approached by a single road, were stronger ground than even Malvern Hill.   The troops were therefore withdrawn to the forest, and for the next three days, with the exception of those employed in collecting the arms and

July 8.   stores which the Federals had abandoned, they remained inactive.   On July 8, directing Stuart to watch McClellan, General Lee fell back to Richmond.

The battles of the Seven Days cost the Confederates 20,000 men. The Federals, although defeated, lost no more than 16,000, of whom 10,000, nearly half of them wounded, were prisoners.   In addition, however, 52 guns and 35,000 rifles became the prize of the Southerners ; and vast as was the quantity of captured stores, far greater was the amount destroyed.

But the defeat of McClellan's army is not to be measured by a mere estimate of the loss in men and in *matériel*. The discomfited general sought to cover his failure by a lavish employment of strategic phrases. The retreat to the James, he declared, had been planned before the battle of Mechanicsville. He had merely manœuvred to get quit of an inconvenient line of supply, and to place his army in a more favourable position for attacking Richmond. He congratulated his troops on their success in changing the line of operations, always regarded as the most hazardous of military expedients. Their conduct, he said, ranked them among the most celebrated armies of history. Under every disadvantage of numbers, and necessarily of position also, they had in every conflict beaten back their foes with enormous slaughter. They had reached the new base complete in organisation and unimpaired in spirit.[1]

It is possible that this address soothed the pride of his troops. It certainly deluded neither his own people nor the South. The immediate effect of his strategic manœuvre was startling.

5,000 men, the effective remnant of Shields' division, besides several new regiments, were sent to the Peninsula from the army protecting Washington. General Burnside, who had mastered a portion of the North Carolina coast, was ordered to suspend operations, to leave a garrison in New Berne, and to bring the remainder of his army to Fortress Monroe. Troops were demanded from General Hunter, who had taken the last fort which defended Savannah, the port of Georgia.[2] The Western army of the Union was asked to reinforce McClellan, and Lincoln called on the Northern States for a fresh levy. But although 300,000 men were promised him, the discouragement of the Northern people was so great that recruits showed no alacrity in coming forward. The South, on the other hand, ringing with the brilliant deeds of Lee and Jackson, turned with renewed vigour to the task of resisting the invader. Richmond, the beleaguered capital, although the enemy was in position not more than twenty miles away, knew that her agony was over. The city was one vast hospital. Many of the best and bravest of the Confederacy had fallen in the Seven Days, and the voice of mourning hushed all sound

[1] O. R., vol. xi., part iii., p. 299.
[2] The forces under Burnside and Hunter amounted to some 35,000 men.

of triumph. But the long columns of prisoners, the captured cannon, the great trains of waggons, piled high with spoil, were irrefragable proof of the complete defeat of the invader.

When the army once more encamped within sight of the city it was received as it deserved. Lee and Jackson were the special objects of admiration. All recognised the strategic skill which had wrought the overthrow of McClellan's host; and the hard marches and sudden blows of the campaign on the Shenandoah, crowned by the swift transfer of the Valley army from the Blue Ridge to the Chickahominy, took fast hold of the popular imagination. The mystery in which Jackson's operations were involved, the dread he inspired in the enemy, his reticence, his piety, his contempt of comfort, his fiery energy, his fearlessness, and his simplicity aroused the interest and enthusiasm of the whole community. Whether Lee or his lieutenant was the more averse to posing before the crowd it is difficult to say. Both succeeded in escaping all public manifestation of popular favour; both went about their business with an absolute absence of ostentation, and if the handsome features of the Commander-in-Chief were familiar to the majority of the citizens, few recognised in the plainly dressed soldier, riding alone through Richmond, the great leader of the Valley, with whose praises not the South only, but the whole civilised world, was already ringing.

CHAPTER XV

CEDAR RUN

THE victories in the Valley, the retreat of Banks, Shields, and Frémont, followed by the victory of Gaines' Mill, had raised the hopes of the South to the highest pitch.

When McClellan fell back to the James the capture or destruction of his army seemed a mere matter of time, and it was confidently expected that a disaster of such magnitude would assuredly bring the North to terms. But the slaughter of the Confederates at Malvern Hill, the unmolested retreat of the enemy to Harrison's Landing, the fortification of that strong position, induced a more sober mood. The Northern soldiers had displayed a courage for which the South had not yet given them credit. On the last of the Seven Days they had fought almost as stubbornly as on the first. Their losses had been heavy, but they had taught their adversaries that they were no longer the unmanageable levies of Bull Run, scattered by the first touch of disaster to the four winds. It was no frail barrier which stood now between the South and her independence, but a great army of trained soldiers, seasoned by experience, bound together by discipline, and capable of withstanding a long series of reverses. And when it became clear that McClellan, backed by the fleet, had no intention of losing his grip on Richmond; when the news came that Lincoln had asked for 300,000 fresh troops; and that the Federal Army of the West, undisturbed by Lee's victories, was still advancing through Tennessee,[1] the power and persistency of the North were revealed in all their huge proportions.

[1] After the repulse of the Confederates at Malvern Hill, and the unmolested retreat of the Army of the Potomac to Harrison's Landing, Lincoln cancelled his demand for troops from the West.

VOL. II.

G

But the disappointment of the Southern people in no way abated their gratitude. The troops drank their fill of praise. The deeds of the Valley regiments were on every tongue. The Stonewall Brigade was the most famous organisation in the Confederacy. To have marched with Jackson was a sure passport to the good graces of every citizen. Envied by their comrades, regarded as heroes by the admiring crowds that thronged the camps, the ragged soldiers of the Shenandoah found ample compensation for their labours. They had indeed earned the rest which was now given them. For more than two months they had been marching and fighting without cessation. Since they left Elk Run, on April 29, until they fell back to the capital on July 8, their camps had never stood in the same spot for more than four days in succession.

But neither they nor their general looked forward to a long sojourn within the works round Richmond. The men pined for the fresh breezes of their native highlands. The tainted atmosphere of a district which was one vast battle-ground told upon their health, and the people of Richmond, despite their kindness, were strangers after all. Nor was Jackson less anxious to leave the capital. The heavy rain which had deluged the bivouac on the Chicka-hominy had chilled him to the bone. During the whole of the pursuit, from White Oak Swamp to Westover, he had suffered from fever. But his longing for a move westward was dictated by other motives than the restoration of his health. No sooner had it become evident that McClellan's position was impregnable than he turned his thoughts to some more vulnerable point. He would allow the enemy no respite. In his opinion there should be no 'letting up' in the attack. The North should be given no leisure to reorganise the armies or to train recruits. A swift succession of fierce blows, delivered at a vital point, was the only means of bringing the colossus to its knees, and that vital point was far from Richmond.

Before the Confederate troops marched back to Richmond he laid his views before the member of Congress for the Winchester district, and begged Mr. Boteler to impress them on the Government. 'McClellan's army,' he said, 'was manifestly thoroughly beaten, incapable of moving until it had been reorganised and reinforced. There was danger,' he foresaw, 'that the fruits of victory would be lost, as they had been lost after Bull Run. The Confederate army should at once leave the malarious district round Richmond, and moving northwards, carry the horrors of invasion across the border. This,' he said, 'was the only way to bring the North to its senses, and to end the war. And it was within the power of the Confederates, if they were to concentrate their resources, to make a successful bid for victory. 60,000 men might march into Maryland and threaten Washington. But while he was anxious that these views should be laid before the President, he would earnestly disclaim the charge of self-seeking. He wished to follow, and not to lead. He was willing to follow anyone—Lee, or Ewell, or anyone who would fight.' 'Why do you not urge your views,' asked Mr. Boteler, 'on General Lee?' 'I have done so,' replied Jackson. 'And what does he say to them?' 'He says nothing,' was the answer; 'but do not understand that I complain of this silence; it is proper that General Lee should observe it. He is wise and prudent. He feels that he bears a fearful responsibility, and he is right in declining a hasty expression of his purpose to a subordinate like me.'[1]

Jackson was perfectly right in his estimate of the Federal army. McClellan had 90,000 men, but 16,000 were sick, and he was still under the delusion that he had been defeated by more than twice his numbers. His letters to the President, it is true, betrayed no misgiving. He was far from admitting that he had been defeated. His army, he wrote, was now so favourably placed that an advance on Richmond was easy. He was full of confidence. He was watching carefully for any fault committed by the enemy, and would take advantage of it. The spirit of his

[1] Dabney, vol. ii., pp. 230, 231.

army, he declared, was such that he felt unable to restrain it
from speedily assuming the offensive. He had determined
not to fall back unless he was absolutely forced to do so.
He was ready for a rapid and heavy blow at Richmond.
But to strike that blow he required heavy reinforcements,
and while waiting their arrival he was unwilling to leave
his strong position. [1]

Jackson's views were considered by Mr. Davis. For
the present, however, they were disregarded. The situation, in the opinion of the Government, was still critical.
McClellan might be reinforced by sea. He might be superseded by a more energetic commander, and the Federals
might then cross to the right bank of the James, cut the
railways which connected Richmond with the South,
and turn the line of fortifications. The losses of the
Seven Days had reduced the Confederate strength to
60,000. Under such circumstances it was not considered
safe to remove the army from the capital. Jackson,
however, was entrusted with a more congenial duty
than watching an enemy who, he was absolutely
convinced, had no intention of leaving his intrenchments. His longing for active work was gratified
July 13.   by an order to march westward. Lee, finding
            McClellan immovable, had recourse to his former
strategy. He determined to play once more on Lincoln's
fears. The Army of Virginia, under the command of
Pope, defended Washington. Would the Northern Government, when the news came that Stonewall Jackson
was returning to the Shenandoah, deem this force
sufficient to protect the capital? Would they not
rather think it necessary to recall McClellan? The
experiment was worth trying. After some delay in
recovering from the disorganisation caused by the
disasters in the Valley, Pope had assembled his army
east of the Blue Ridge, near the sources of the Rappahannock. Sperryville, his advanced post, was no more than
forty miles north of the Virginia Central Railway, and his
cavalry was already advancing. It was essential that

[1] O. R., vol. xi., part ii., p. 306.

the railway, the chief line of supply of the Confederate army, should be protected; and Jackson was instructed July 16. to halt near Gordonsville. On the 16th his leading brigades reached their destination. Their arrival was opportune. The Federal cavalry, with a strong infantry support, was already threatening Gordonsville. On learning, however, that the town was occupied they at once fell back.

Jackson, as soon as his command was up, and he had had time to ascertain the Federal strength, applied for reinforcements. His own numbers were very small. The divisions of D. H. Hill and Whiting had remained at Richmond. The Army of the Valley, reduced to its original elements, was no more than 11,000 strong. Pope's army consisted of 47,000 men.[1] But the Federals were scattered over a wide front. Sigel, a German who had succeeded Frémont, was near Sperryville, and Banks lay close to Sigel. Each of these officers commanded an army corps of two divisions. Of McDowell's army corps, Ricketts' division held Warrenton, twenty-five miles east of Banks; while King's division was retained at Fredericksburg, forty miles south-east of Ricketts'. Such dispersion seemed to invite attack. Lee, however, found it impossible to comply with his lieutenant's request for such aid as would enable him to assume the offensive. The army covering Richmond was much smaller than McClellan's, and the Confederates were aware that a large reinforcement for the latter, under General Burnside, had landed in the Peninsula. But assistance was promised in case Pope advanced so far south that troops could be detached without risk to Richmond. Pope, in fact, was too far off, and Jackson was to entice him forward.

A week, however, passed away without any movement on the part of McClellan. He knew that Lee's army was diminished; and it was believed at his headquarters that 'Jackson had started towards the Valley with 60,000 to 80,000 troops.'[2] He knew that there was no large force

[1] Sigel, 13,000; Banks, 11,000; McDowell, 18,000; Bayard's and Buford's cavalry, 5,000.

[2] O. R., vol. xi., part iii., p. 334.

within ten miles of his outposts, and if the President would send him 20,000 or 30,000 more men he said that he was ready to march on Richmond. But, as yet, he had not observed the opportunity for which, according to his own account, he was so carefully watching. Pope was far more enterprising. His cavalry had burned the railway depôt at Beaver Dam, destroyed some Confederate stores, cut the line at several points, and threatened Hanover Junction. Stuart, with his cavalry division, was immediately sent northwards, and Lee ordered A. P. Hill to Gordonsville.

Jackson's letters to headquarters at this period are missing. But Lee's answers indicate the tenor of the views therein expressed. On July 27 the Commander-in-Chief wrote :—

'I have received your dispatch of the 26th instant. I will send A. P. Hill's division and the Second Brigade of Louisiana volunteers to you. . . . I want Pope to be suppressed. . . . A. P. Hill you will, I think, find a good officer, with whom you can consult, and by advising with your division commanders as to your movements, much trouble will be saved you in arranging details, and they can act more intelligently. I wish to save you trouble from my increasing your command. *Cache* your troops as much as possible till you can strike your blow, and be prepared to return to me when done, if necessary. I will endeavour to keep General McClellan quiet till it is over, if rapidly executed.'

This letter, besides containing a delicate hint that extreme reticence is undesirable, evidently refers to some plan proposed by Jackson. Whatever this may have been, it is certain that both he and Lee were in close accord. They believed that the best method of protecting the railway was, in Lee's words, 'to find the main body of the enemy and drive it,' and they were agreed that there should be no more Malvern Hills. 'You are right,' says Lee on August 4, 'in not attacking them in their strong and chosen positions. They ought always to be turned as you propose, and thus force them on to more favourable ground.'

At the end of July, about the same time that Hill

joined Jackson, Pope, under instructions from Washington, moved forward. His cavalry occupied the line of Robertson River, within twenty miles of the Confederate lines, and it became clear that he intended advancing on Gordonsville. His infantry, however, had not yet crossed Hazel Run, and Jackson, carefully concealing his troops, remained on the watch for a few days longer. His anxiety, however, to bring his enemy to battle was even greater than usual. Pope had already gained an unenviable notoriety. On taking over command he had issued an extraordinary address. His bombast was only equalled by his want of tact. Not content with extolling the prowess of the Western troops, with whom he had hitherto served, he was bitterly satirical at the expense of McClellan and of McClellan's army. 'I have come to you,' he said to his soldiers, ' from the West, where we have always seen the backs of our enemies—from an army whose business it has been to seek the adversary, and beat him when found, whose policy has been attack and not defence. . . . I presume that I have been called here to pursue the same system, and to lead you against the enemy. It is my purpose to do so, and that speedily. . . . Meantime, I desire you to dismiss from your minds certain phrases, which I am sorry to find much in vogue amongst you. I hear constantly of taking strong positions and holding them—of lines of retreat and of bases of supplies. Let us discard such ideas. . . . Let us study the probable line of retreat of our opponents, and leave our own to take care of themselves. Let us look before and not behind. Success and glory are in the advance. Disaster and shame lurk in the rear.' [1]

Even the Northern press made sport of Pope's ' 'Ercles vein,' and the Confederates contrasted his noisy declamation with the modesty of Lee and Jackson. To the South the new commander was peculiarly obnoxious. He was the first of the Federal generals to order that the troops should subsist upon the country, and that the people should be held responsible for all damage done to roads, railways, and

[1] O. R., vol. xii., part iii., p. 474.

telegraphs by guerillas. His orders, it is true, were
warranted by the practice of war. But ' forced requisitions,'
unless conducted on a well-understood system, must inevitably degenerate into plunder and oppression ; and Pope,
in punishing civilians, was not careful to distinguish between
the acts of guerillas and those of the regular Confederate
cavalry. ' These orders,' says a Northern historian, ' were
followed by the pillaging of private property, and by insults
to females to a degree unknown heretofore during the war.'
But in comparison with a third edict they were mild
and humane. On July 23 Pope's generals were instructed
to arrest every Virginian within the limits of their
commands, to administer the oath of allegiance to the
Union, and to expel from their homes all those who
refused to take it. This order was preceded by one from
General von Steinwehr, a German brigadier, directing the
arrest of five prominent citizens, to be held as hostages,
and to suffer death in the event of any soldiers being shot
by bushwhackers. The Confederate Government retaliated
by declaring that Pope and his officers were not entitled to
be considered as soldiers. If captured they were to be
imprisoned so long as their orders remained unrepealed ;
and in the event of any unarmed Confederate citizens being
tried and shot, an equal number of Federal prisoners were
to be hanged. It need hardly be added that the operations
north of Gordonsville were watched with peculiar interest
by the South. ' This new general,' it was said to Jackson,
' claims your attention.' ' And, please God, he shall have
it,' was the reply.

Nevertheless, with all his peculiar characteristics,
Pope was no despicable foe. The Federal cavalry were
employed with a boldness which had not hitherto been
seen. Their outposts were maintained twenty miles in
advance of the army. Frequent reconnaissances were
made. A regiment of Jackson's cavalry was defeated
at Orange Court House, with a loss of 60 or 70 men,
and scouting parties penetrated to within a few miles of
Gordonsville. Even Banks was spurred to activity, and
learned at last that information is generally to be obtained

if it is resolutely sought.[1]   Very little that occurred within
the Confederate lines escaped the vigilance of the enemy;
and although Jackson's numbers were somewhat overestimated, Pope's cavalry, energetically led by two able young
officers, Generals Buford and Bayard, did far better service
than McClellan's detectives.   Jackson had need of all his
prudence.   Including the Light Division, his force amounted
to no more than 24,000 men; and if Pope handled his
whole army with as much skill as he used his cavalry, it
would go hard with Gordonsville.   24,000 men could
hardly be expected to arrest the march of 47,000 unless
the larger force should blunder.

During the first week in August events began to thicken.
Stuart made a strong reconnaissance towards Fredericksburg, and administered a check to the Federal scouting
parties in that quarter.   But McClellan threw forward a
division and occupied Malvern Hill, and it became evident
that Pope also was meditating a further advance.

Jackson, for the purpose of luring him forward, and
also of concealing Hill's arrival, had drawn back his cavalry,
and moved his infantry south of Gordonsville.   Pope was
warned from Washington that this was probably a ruse.
His confidence, however, was not to be shaken.   'Within
ten days,' he reported, 'unless the enemy is heavily reinforced from Richmond, I shall be in possession of Gordonsville and Charlottesville.'

Although such an operation would carry Pope far from
Washington there was no remonstrance from headquarters.
Lincoln and Stanton, mistrustful at last of their ability as
strategists, had called to their councils General Halleck,
who had shown some evidence of capacity while in command
of the Western armies.   The new Commander-in-Chief had
a difficult problem to work out.   It is impossible to determine how far Jackson's movement to Gordonsville influenced
the Federal authorities, but immediately on Halleck's arrival

[1] 'We must constantly feel the enemy, know where he is, and what he
is doing.   Vigilance, activity, and a precaution that has a considerable
mixture of audacity in it will carry you through many difficulties.'   Such
were his instructions to an officer of the regular army !   It was unfortunate
he had not acted on those sound principles in the Valley.

at Washington, about the same date that the movement was reported, he was urged, according to his own account, to withdraw McClellan from the Peninsula. 'I delayed my decision,' he says, ' as long as I dared delay it ; ' but on August 3 his mind was made up, and McClellan, just after Hill joined Jackson, was ordered to embark his army at Fortress Monroe, sail to Aquia Creek, near Fredericksburg, and join Pope on the Rappahannock. The proposed combination, involving the transfer by sea of 90,000 men, with all their artillery and trains, was a manœuvre full of danger.[1] The retreat and embarkation of McClellan's troops would take time, and the Confederates, possessing 'the interior lines,' had two courses open to them :—

1. Leaving Jackson to check Pope, they might attack McClellan as soon as he evacuated his intrenched position at Harrison's Landing.

2. They might neglect McClellan and concentrate against Pope before he could be reinforced.

Halleck considered that attack on McClellan was the more likely, and Pope was accordingly instructed to threaten Gordonsville, so as to force Lee to detach heavily from Richmond, and leave him too weak to strike the Army of the Potomac.

On August 6 Pope commenced his advance. Banks had pushed a brigade of infantry from Sperryville to Aug. 6.   Culpeper Court House, and Ricketts' division (of McDowell's corps) was ordered to cross the Rappahannock at Waterloo Bridge and march to the same spot. Jackson, whose spies had informed him of the enemy's dispositions, received early intelligence of Banks' movement, and the next afternoon his three divisions were ordered forward, marching by roads where there was no chance of their being seen. 'He hoped,' so he wrote to Lee, 'through the blessing of Providence, to defeat the advanced Federal detachment before reinforcements should arrive.' This detachment was

[1] McClellan had received no further reinforcements than those sent from Washington. Burnside, with 14,000 men, remained at Fortress Monroe until the beginning of August, when he embarked for Aquia Creek, concentrating on August 5. Hunter's troops were withheld.

his first objective; but he had long since recognised the strategic importance of Culpeper Court House. At this point four roads meet, and it was probable, from their previous dispositions, that the Federal army corps would use three of these in their advance. Pope's right wing at Sperryville would march by Woodville and Griffinsburg. His centre had already moved forward from Warrenton. His left wing at Falmouth, north of Fredericksburg, would march by Bealeton and Brandy Station, or by Richardsville and Georgetown. As all these roads were several miles apart, and the lateral communications were indifferent, the three columns, during the movement on Culpeper Court House, would be more or less isolated; and if the Confederates could seize the point at which the roads met, it might be possible to keep them apart, to prevent them combining for action, and to deal with them in detail. Pope, in fact, had embarked on a manœuvre which is always dangerous in face of a vigilant and energetic enemy. Deceived by the passive attitude which Jackson had hitherto maintained, and confident in the strength of his cavalry, which held Robertson River, a stream some ten miles south of Culpeper Court House, he had pushed a small force far in advance, and was preparing to cross Hazel Run in several widely separated columns. He had no apprehension that he might be attacked during the process. Most generals in Jackson's situation, confronted by far superior numbers, would have been content with occupying a defensive position in front of Gordonsville, and neither Pope nor Halleck had gauged as yet the full measure of their opponent's enterprise. So confident was the Federal Commander-in-Chief that General Cox, with 11,000 men, was ordered to march from Lewisburg, ninety miles southwest of Staunton, to join Pope at Charlottesville.[1]

Jackson's force was composed as follows:—

Jackson's Own Division (commanded by Winder)	3,000
Ewell	7,550
A. P. Hill (The Light Division)	12,000
Cavalry	1,200
	23,750

[1] *Battles and Leaders*, vol. ii., p. 281.

Jackson was by no means displeased when he learned who was in command of the Federal advance. 'Banks is in front of me,' he said to Dr. McGuire, 'he is always ready to fight;' and then, laughing, he added as if to himself, 'and he generally gets whipped.'

The Confederate regiments, as a rule, were very weak. The losses of the Seven Days, of Winchester, of Cross Keys, and of Port Republic had not yet been replaced. Companies had dwindled down to sections. Brigades were no stronger than full battalions, and the colonel was happy who could muster 200 muskets. But the waste of the campaign was not altogether an evil. The weak and sickly had been weeded out. The faint-hearted had disappeared, and if many of the bravest had fallen before Richmond, those who remained were hardy and experienced soldiers. The army that lay round Gordonsville was the best that Jackson had yet commanded. The horses, which had become almost useless in the Peninsula, had soon regained condition on the rich pastures at the foot of the South-west Mountains. Nearly every man had seen service. The officers were no longer novices. The troops had implicit confidence in their leaders, and their *moral* was high. They had not yet tasted defeat. Whenever they had met the enemy he had abandoned the field of battle. With such troops much might be risked, and if the staff was not yet thoroughly trained, the district in which they were now operating was far less intricate than the Peninsula. As the troops marched westward from Richmond, with their faces towards their own mountains, the country grew more open, the horizon larger, and the breezes purer. The dark forests disappeared. The clear streams, running swiftly over rocky beds, were a welcome change from the swamps of the Chickahominy. North of Gordonsville the spurs of the Blue Ridge, breaking up into long chains of isolated hills, towered high above the sunlit plains. The rude tracks of the Peninsula, winding through the woods, gave place to broad and well-trodden highways. Nor did the marches now depend upon the guidance of some casual rustic or terrified negro. There were many in the Confederate ranks who were familiar with the country; and the quick pencil of Captain Hotchkiss, Jackson's trusted engineer, who had rejoined from the Valley, was once more at his disposal. Information, moreover, was not hard to come by. The country was far more thickly populated than the region about Richmond, and, notwithstanding Pope's harsh measures, he was unable to prevent the people communicating with their own army. If the men had been unwilling to take the risk, the women were quite ready to emulate the heroines of the Valley, and the conduct of the Federal marauders had served only to inflame their patriotism. Under such circumstances Jackson's task was relieved of half its difficulties. He was almost as much at home as on the Shenandoah, and although there were no Massanuttons to screen his movements, the hills to the north, insignificant as they might be when compared with the great mountains which divide the Valley, might still be turned to useful purpose.

On August 7, starting late in the afternoon, the Confederates marched eight miles by a country track, and halted

Aug. 7. at Orange Court House. Culpeper was still twenty miles distant, and two rivers, the Rapidan and Robertson, barred the road. The Robertson was held by 5,000 or 6,000 Federal cavalry; five regiments, under General Buford, were near Madison Court House; four, under General Bayard, near Rapidan Station. East of the railway two more regiments held Raccoon Ford; others watched the Rappahannock as far as Fredericksburg, and on Thoroughfare Mountain, ten miles south-west of Culpeper, and commanding a view of the surrounding country as far as Orange Court House, was a signal station.

Aug. 8. Early on the 8th, Ewell's division crossed the Rapidan at Liberty Mills, while the other divisions were ordered to make the passage at Barnett's Ford, six miles below. A forced march should have carried the Confederates to within striking distance of Culpeper, and a forced march was almost imperative. The cavalry had been in contact; the advance must already have been reported to Pope, and within twenty-four hours

the whole of the Federal army, with the exception of the
division at Fredericksburg, might easily be concentrated in
a strong position.

Still there were no grounds for uneasiness. If the
troops made sixteen miles before nightfall, they would be
before Culpeper soon after dawn, and sixteen miles was no
extraordinary march for the Valley regiments. But to
accomplish a long march in the face of the enemy, something is demanded more than goodwill and endurance on
the part of the men. If the staff arrangements are faulty,
or the subordinate commanders careless, the best troops
in the world will turn sluggards. It was so on August 8.
Jackson's soldiers never did a worse day's work during the
whole course of his campaigns. Even his energy was
powerless to push them forward. The heat, indeed, was
excessive. Several men dropped dead in the ranks ; the
long columns dragged wearily through the dust, and the
Federal cavalry was not easily pushed back. Guns and
infantry had to be brought up before Bayard's dismounted
squadrons were dislodged. But the real cause of delay is
to be found elsewhere. Not only did General Hill mis-
understand his orders, but, apparently offended by Jackson's
reticence, he showed but little zeal. The orders were
certainly incomplete. Nothing had been said about the
supply trains, and they were permitted to follow their divisions, instead of moving in rear of the whole force.
Ewell's route, moreover, was changed without Hill being
informed. The lines of march crossed each other, and
Hill was delayed for many hours by a long column of
ambulances and waggons. So tedious was the march
that when the troops halted for the night, Ewell had
made eight miles, Hill only two, and the latter was still
eighteen miles from Culpeper. Chagrined by the delay,
Jackson reported to Lee that ' he had made but little progress, and that the expedition,' he feared, ' in consequence
of his tardy movements, would be productive of little
good.'

How the blame should be apportioned it is difficult to
say. Jackson laid it upon Hill, and that officer's conduct

was undoubtedly reprehensible. The absence of Major Dabney, struck down by sickness, is a possible explanation of the faulty orders. But that Jackson would have done better to have accepted Lee's hint, to have confided his intentions to his divisional commanders, and to have trusted something to their discretion, seems more than clear. In war, silence is not invariably a wise policy. It was not a case in which secresy was all-important. The movement had already been discovered by the Federal cavalry, and in such circumstances the more officers that understood the intention of the general-in-chief the better. Men who have been honoured with their leader's confidence, and who grasp the purpose of the efforts they are called upon to make, will co-operate, if not more cordially, at least more intelligently, than those who are impelled by the sense of duty alone.

As it was, so much time had been wasted that Jackson would have been fully warranted in suspending the movement, and halting on the Rapidan. The Federals were aware he was advancing. Their divisions were not so far apart that they could not be concentrated within a few hours at Culpeper, and, in approaching so close, he was entering the region of uncertainty. Time was too pressing to admit of waiting for the reports of spies. The enemy's cavalry was far more numerous than his own, and screened the troops in rear from observation. The information brought in by the country people was not to be implicitly relied on ; their estimate of numbers was always vague, and it would be exceedingly difficult to make sure that the force at Culpeper had not been strongly reinforced. It was quite on the cards that the whole of Pope's army might reach that point in the course of the next day, and in that case the Confederates would be compelled to retreat, followed by a superior army, across two bridgeless rivers.

Nevertheless, the consideration of these contingencies had no effect on Jackson's purpose. The odds, he decided, were in his favour; and the defeat of Pope's army in detail, with all the consequences that might follow, was worth risking much to bring about. It was still possible

that Pope might delay his concentration; it was still
possible that an opportunity might present itself; and,
as he had done at Winchester in March, when threatened
by a force sevenfold stronger than his own, he resolved to
look for that opportunity before he renounced his enterprise.

In speed and caution lay the only chance of success.
The start on the 9th was early. Hill, anxious to redeem
his shortcomings, marched long before daylight,
and soon caught up with Ewell and Winder.

Aug. 9.

Half of the cavalry covered the advance; the remainder,
screening the left flank, scouted west and in the direction
of Madison Court House. Two brigades of infantry, Gregg's
and Lawton's, were left in rear to guard the trains, for the
Federal horsemen threatened danger, and the army, dis-
embarrassed of the supply waggons, pressed forward across
the Rapidan. Pushing the Federal cavalry before them, the
troops reached Robertson River. The enemy's squadrons,
already worn out by incessant reconnaissance and picket
duty, were unable to dispute the passage, and forming a
single column, the three divisions crossed the Locustdale
Ford. Climbing the northern bank, the high-road to Culpeper, white with dust, lay before them, and to their right
front, little more than two miles distant, a long wooded
ridge, bearing the ominous name of Slaughter Mountain,
rose boldly from the plain.

Ewell's division led the march, and shortly before noon,
as the troops swept past the western base of Slaughter
Mountain, it was reported that the Federal cavalry, massed
in some strength, had come to a halt a mile or two north,
on the bank of a small stream called Cedar Run.

The Confederate guns opened, and the hostile cavalry
fell back; but from a distant undulation a Federal battery
came into action, and the squadrons, supported by this
fire, returned to their old position. Although Cedar Run
was distant seven miles from Culpeper, it was evident, from
the attitude of the cavalry, that the enemy was inclined to
make a stand, and that in all probability Banks' army corps
was in support.[1] Early's brigade, forming the advanced-

[1] This was the case. Banks had reached Culpeper on the 8th. On the

guard, which had halted in a wood by the roadside, was now ordered forward. Deploying to the right of the highway, it drove in the enemy's vedettes, and came out on the open ground which overlooks the stream. Across the shallow valley, covered with the high stalks and broad leaves of Indian corn, rose a loftier ridge, twelve hundred yards distant, and from more than one point batteries opened on the Confederate scouts. The regiments of the advanced-guard were immediately withdrawn to the reverse slope of the ridge, and Jackson galloped forward to the sound of the guns. His dispositions had been quickly made. A large force of artillery was ordered to come into action on either flank of the advanced-guard. Ewell's division was ordered to the right, taking post on the northern face of Slaughter Mountain; Winder was ordered to the left, and Hill, as soon as he came up, was to form the reserve, in rear of Winder. These movements took time. The Confederate column, 20,000 infantry and fifteen batteries, must have occupied more than seven miles of road; it would consequently take over two hours for the whole force to deploy for battle.

Before three o'clock, however, the first line was formed. On the right of the advanced-guard, near a clump of
2.45 P.M. cedars, were eight guns, and on Slaughter Mountain eight more. Along the high-road to the left six guns of Winder's division were soon afterwards
3 P.M. deployed, reinforced by four of Hill's. These twenty-six pieces, nearly the whole of the long-range ordnance which the Confederates possessed, were turned on the opposing batteries, and for nearly two hours the artillery thundered across the valley. The infantry, meanwhile, awaiting Hill's arrival, had come into line. Ewell's brigades, Trimble's, and the Louisianians (commanded by Colonel Forno) had halted in the woods on the extreme right, at the base of the mountain, threatening the enemy's flank. Winder had come up on the left, and had posted the Stonewall Brigade in rear of his guns; Campbell's

same day his advanced brigade was sent forward to Cedar Run, and was followed by the rest of the army corps on the 9th.

brigade, under Lieut.-Colonel Garnett, was stationed in front, west, and Taliaferro's brigade east, of the road.   The 10,000 men of the Light Division, however, were still some distance to the rear, and the position was hardly secure against a counterstroke.   The left of the line extended along a skirt of woodland, which ran at right angles to the road, overlooking a wheat-field but lately reaped, on the further side of which, and three hundred yards distant, was dense wood. This point was the most vulnerable, for there was no support at hand, and a great tract of forest stretched away westward, where cavalry was useless, but through which it was quite possible that infantry might force its way. Jackson ordered Colonel Garnett, commanding the brigade on this flank, 'to look well to his left, and to ask his divisional commander for rein- forcements.'   The brigadier sent a staff officer and an orderly to reconnoitre the forest to the left, and two officers were dispatched to secure the much-needed support.

But at this juncture General Winder was mortally wounded by a shell ; there was some delay in issuing orders, and before the weak place in the line could be strengthened the storm broke.   The enemy's batteries, five in number, although the concentrated fire of the Confederates had compelled them to change position, had not yet been silenced. No large force of Federal infantry had as yet appeared ; skirmishers only had pushed forward through the corn ; but the presence of so many guns was a clear indication that a strong force was not far off, and Jackson had no intention of attacking a position which had not yet been reconnoitred until his rear division had closed up, and the hostile artillery had lost its sting.   About five o'clock, however, General

5 P.M.   Banks, although his whole force, including Bayard's cavalry, did not exceed 9,000 officers and men,[1] and Ricketts' division, in support, was four miles distant, gave orders for a general attack.[2]   Two brigades, crossing the rise which formed the Federal position,

[1] 3,500 of Banks' army corps had been left at Winchester, and his sick were numerous.

[2] Banks had received an order from Pope which might certainly be under- stood to mean that he should take the offensive if the enemy ap- proached.—*Report of Committee of Congress*, vol. iii., p. 45.

bore down on the Confederate centre, and strove to cross the stream. Early was hard pressed, but, Taliaferro's brigade advancing on his left, he held his own; and on the highroad, raked by a Confederate gun, the enemy was unable to push forward. But within the wood to the left, at the very point where Jackson had advised precaution, the line of defence was broken through. On the edge of the timber commanding the wheat-field only two Confederate regiments were posted, some 500 men all told, and the 1st Virginia, on the extreme left, was completely isolated. The Stonewall Brigade, which should have been placed in second line behind them, had not yet received its orders; it was more than a half-mile distant, in rear of Winder's artillery, and hidden from the first line by the trees and undergrowth. Beyond the wheat-field 1,500 Federals, covered by a line of skirmishers, had formed up in the wood. Emerging from the covert with fixed bayonets and colours flying, their long line, overlapping the Confederate left, moved steadily across the three hundred yards of open ground. The shocks of corn, and some ragged patches of scrub timber, gave cover to the skirmishers, but in the closed ranks behind the accurate fire of the Southern riflemen made fearful ravages. Still the enemy pressed forward; the skirmishers darted from bush to bush; the regiments on the right swung round, enveloping the Confederate line; and the 1st Virginia, despite the entreaties of its officers, broke and scattered.[1] Assailed in front from the field and in flank from the forest, the men would stand no longer, and flying back through the woodland, left the way open to the very rear of the position. The 42nd Virginia, outflanked in turn, was compelled to give ground; and the Federals, without waiting to reform, swept rapidly through the wood, and bore down upon the flank of Taliaferro's brigade and Winder's batteries.

And now occurred a scene of terrible confusion. So swift was the onslaught that the first warning received by the Confederates on the highroad was a sudden storm

[1] O. R., vol. xii., part ii., p. 201.

of musketry, the loud cheers of the enemy, and the rush of fugitives from the forest. Attacked simultaneously in front, flank and rear, with the guns and limbers entangled among the infantry, Winder's division was subjected to an ordeal of which it was without experience. The batteries, by Jackson's order, were at once withdrawn, and not a gun was lost. The infantry, however, did not escape so lightly. The Federals, emboldened by the flight of the artillery, charged forward with reckless courage. Every regimental commander in Garnett's brigade was either killed or wounded. Taliaferro's brigade was driven back, and Early's left was broken. Some regiments attempted to change front, others retreated in disorder. Scattered groups, plying butt and bayonet, endeavoured to stay the rout. Officers rushed into the *mêlée*, and called upon those at hand to follow. Men were captured and recaptured, and, for a few moments, the blue and grey were mingled in close conflict amid the smoke. But the isolated efforts of the Confederates were of no avail. The first line was irretrievably broken; the troops were mingled in a tumultuous mass, through which the shells tore shrieking; the enemy's bayonets were surging forward on every side, and his well-served batteries, firing over the heads of their own infantry, played heavily on the road. But fortunately for the Virginians the Federal right wing was unsupported; and although the Light Division was still at some distance from the field, the Stonewall Brigade was already advancing. Breaking through the rout to the left of the highroad, these five staunch regiments, undismayed by the disaster, opened a heavy fire. The Federals, although still superior in numbers at the decisive point, had lost all order in their successful charge; to meet this fresh onset they halted and drew together, and then Jackson, with wonderful energy, restored the battle.

Sending orders for Ewell and A. P. Hill to attack at once, he galloped forward, unattended by either staff officer or orderly, and found himself in the midst of his own men, his soldiers of the Valley, no longer presenting the stubborn front of Bull Run or Kernstown, but an ungovernable mob, breaking rapidly to the rear, and on the very verge of panic. Drawing his sword, for the first time in the war, his voice pealed high above the din; the troops caught the familiar accents, instinct with resolution, and the presence of their own general acted like a spell. 'Rally, men,' he shouted, 'and follow me!' Taliaferro, riding up to him, emphatically insisted that the midst of the *mêlée* was no place for the leader of an army. He looked a little surprised, but with his invariable ejaculation of 'Good, good,' turned slowly to the rear. The impulse, however, had already been given to the Confederate troops. With a wild yell the remnant of the 21st Virginia rushed forward to the front, and received the pursuers with a sudden volley. The officers of other regiments, inspired by the example of their commander, bore the colours forward, and the men, catching the enthusiasm of the moment, followed in the path of the 21st. The Federals recoiled. Taliaferro and Early, reforming their brigades, again advanced upon the right; and Jackson, his front once more established, turned his attention to the counterstroke he had already initiated.

Ewell was ordered to attack the Federal left. Branch, leading the Light Division, was sent forward to support the Stonewall Brigade, and Lane to charge down the highroad. Thomas was to give aid to Early. Archer and Pender, following Branch, were to outflank the enemy's right, and Field and Stafford were to follow as third line.

Ewell was unable to advance at once, for the Confederate batteries on Slaughter Mountain swept the whole field, and it was some time before they could be induced to cease fire. But on the left the mass of fresh troops, directed on the critical point, exerted a decisive influence. The Federal regiments, broken and exhausted, were driven back into the wood and across the wheat-field by the charge of the Stonewall Brigade. Still they were not yet done with. Before Hill's troops could come into action, Jackson's old regiments, as they advanced into the open, were attacked in front and threatened on the flank. The 4th and 27th Virginia were immediately thrown back to meet the more pressing danger, forming to the left within

the wood; but assailed in the confusion of rapid movement, they gave way and scattered through the thickets.
But the rift in the line was rapidly closed up. Jackson,
riding in front of the Light Division, and urging the
men to hold their fire and use their bayonets, rallied
the 27th and led them to the front; while Branch's
regiments, opening their ranks for the fugitives to pass
through, and pressing forward with unbroken line, drove
back the Northern skirmishers, and moving into the wheat-
field engaged their main body in the opposite wood.

Lane, meanwhile, was advancing astride the road,
Archer and Pender, in accordance with Jackson's orders,
were sweeping round through the forest, and Field and
Stafford were in rear of Branch. A fresh brigade had come
up to sustain the defeated Federals; but gallantly as
they fought, the Northerners could make no head against
overwhelming numbers. Outflanked to both right and
left, for Early and Ewell were now moving forward,
they began to yield. Jackson rode forward to the
wheat-field, and just at this moment Banks made a
despairing effort to extricate his infantry. Two squadrons, hitherto concealed by the woods, appeared suddenly on
the road, and, deploying into two lines, charged full against
the Confederate centre. The skirmishers were ridden
down; but the troops in rear stood firm, and several
companies, running to a fence along the highway, poured
a devastating fire into the mass of horsemen. Out of 174
officers and men only 71 rode back.[1]

This brilliant but useless exploit brought no respite to
the Federals. Archer and Pender had turned their right;
6.30 P.M.   Ewell was pressing forward against their left,
scaling the ridge on which their batteries had been
posted; Early and Lane were pressing back their centre,
and their guns had already limbered up. Jackson, galloping
to the front, was received with the cheers of his victorious
troops. In every quarter of the field the enemy was in
full retreat, and as darkness began to fall the whole
Confederate line crossed Cedar Run and swept up the

[1] O. R., vol. xii., part ii., p. 141.

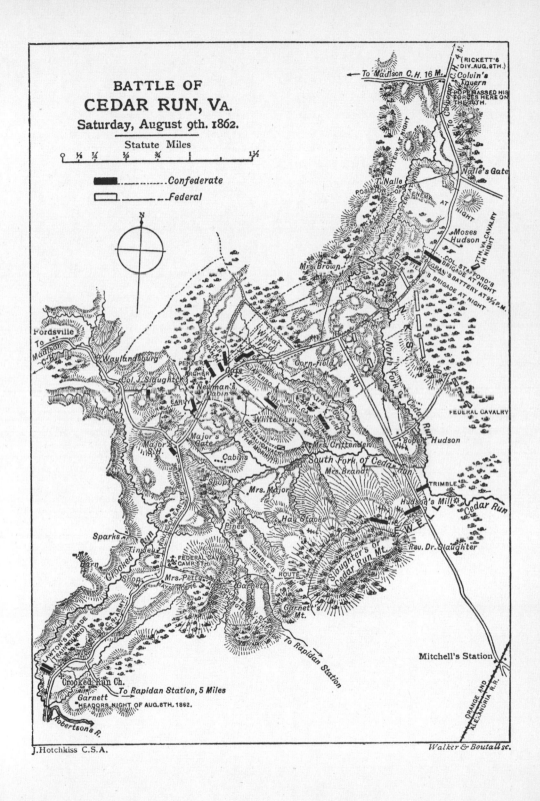

BATTLE OF
CEDAR RUN, VA.
Saturday, August 9th. 1862.

Statute Miles

Confederate
Federal

N

To Madison C.H. 16 M. →

(RICKETT'S DIV. AUG. 8TH.)
Colvin's Tavern
POPE MASSED HIS FORCES HERE ON THE 9TH.

Nalle's Gate

Moses Hudson

CEDAR BATTERY AT NIGHT
T. Nalle
POSITIONS OF ENEMY AT NIGHT
COL. STAFFORD'S BRIGADE AT NIGHT
PEGRAM'S BATTERY AT 9½ P.M.
FIELD'S BRIGADE AT NIGHT
7TH. VA. CAVALRY IN NIGHT

Mrs. Brown.

Wheat Field

Corn-field

North Fork of Cedar Run

FEDERAL CAVALRY

Fordsville
To Madison C.H.
Waylandsburg
Col. J. Slaughter
PENDER
ARCHER
Newman's Cabin
Gate
EARLY
TALIAFERRO
Whitebarn
THE MORNING
Cole's Ford
EARLY
Major's S.H.
Major's Gate
Cabins
SHOP
Mrs. Crittenden
Robert Hudson
Mrs. Brandt
South Fork of Cedar Run
TRIMBLE
Hudson's Mill
E W E L L
Cedar Run

Mrs. Major
Hay Stacks
Rev. Dr. Slaughter
Pines
Sparks
Crooked Run
Tinsley
EARLY
Shop
FEDERAL CAVALRY CAMP 8TH.
TRIMBLE'S ROUTE
Slaughter's or Cedar Run Mt.
Barn
Mrs. Petty
AYS ROUTE
HUNTER'S ROUTE
Garnett
Garnett's Mt.
LAWTON'S BRIGADE TRAIN 8TH(?)
EARLY'S ARMY
To Rapidan Station

Mitchell's Station

Crooked Run Ch.
Garnett
HEADQRS. NIGHT OF AUG. 8TH. 1862.
To Rapidan Station, 5 Miles →

Robertson's R.

ORANGE AND ALEXANDRIA R.R.

J. Hotchkiss C.S.A.   Walker & Boutall sc.

slopes beyond. Every yard of ground bore witness to the
severity of the fighting. The slaughter had been very
heavy. Within ninety minutes 3,000 men had fallen. The
woods were a shambles, and among the corn the dead
lay thick. Scores of prisoners surrendered themselves,
and hundreds of discarded muskets bore witness to the demoralisation of the Northerners. Nevertheless, the pursuit
was slow. The impetuosity of the Confederates, eager to
complete their triumph, was checked with a firm hand.
The infantry were ordered to reform before they entered
the dense forest which lay between them and Culpeper. The
guns, unable to cross Cedar Run except by the road, were
brought over in a single column, and two fresh brigades,
Field's and Stafford's, which had not yet fired a shot, were
brought forward as advanced-guard. Although Jackson had
been careful to bring guides who knew the woodland tracks,
there was need for prudence. The light was failing;
the cavalry could find no space to act; and, above all, the
whereabouts of Pope's main body was still uncertain. The
Federals had fought with fine courage. Their resolute attack,
pressed home with extraordinary dash, had rolled up the
choicest of the Valley regiments. And yet it was evident
that only a small portion of the Northern army had been
engaged. The stirring incidents of the battle had been
crowded into a short space of time. It was five o'clock when
the Federals left their covert. An hour and a half later
they had abandoned the field. Their precipitate retreat, the
absence of a strong rear-guard, were sure tokens that every
regiment had been employed in the attack, and it was
soon discovered by the Confederate soldiers that these regiments were old opponents of the Valley army. The men
who had surprised and outflanked Jackson's old division
were the same men that had been surprised at Front Royal
and outflanked at Winchester. But Banks' army corps
formed only a third part of Pope's army. Sigel and
McDowell were still to be accounted for.

It was possible, however, that no more formidable
enemies than the troops already defeated would be found
between Cedar Run and Culpeper, and Jackson, intent

upon securing that strategic point before morning,[1] pushed steadily forward.   Of the seven miles that intervened between the battle-field and the Court House only one-and-a-half had been passed, when the scouts brought information that the enemy was in position a few hundred yards to the front.   A battery was immediately sent forward to develop the situation.   The moon was full, and on the far side of the glade where the advanced-guard, acting under Jackson's orders, had halted and deployed, a strong line of fire marked the hostile front.   Once more the woodland avenues reverberated to the crash of musketry, and when the guns opened a portion of the Federal line was seen flying in disorder.   Pope himself had arrived upon the scene, but surprised by the sudden salvo of Jackson's guns, he was constrained to do what he had never done in the West—to turn his back upon the enemy, and seek a safer position.   Yet despite the disappearance of the staff the Union artillery made a vigorous reply.   Two batteries, hidden by the timber, concentrated on the four guns of the advanced-guard, and about the same moment the Confederate cavalry on the extreme right reported that they had captured prisoners belonging to Sigel's army corps.   'Believing it imprudent,' says Jackson, 'to continue to move forward during the darkness, I ordered a halt for the night.'

Further information appears to have come to hand after midnight; and early the next morning General Stuart, Aug. 10. who had arrived on a tour of inspection, having been placed in charge of the cavalry, ascertained beyond all question that the greater part of Pope's army had come up.   The Confederates were ordered to withdraw, and before noon nearly the whole force had regained their old position on Cedar Run.   They were not followed, save by the Federal cavalry; and for two days they remained in position, ready to receive attack.   The enemy, however, gave no sign of aggressive intentions.   Aug. 11. On the morning of the 11th a flag of truce was received, and Pope was permitted to bury the dead which had not already been interred.   The same

[1] Report.   O. R., vol. xii., part ii., p. 184.

night, his wounded, his prisoners, and the captured arms
having already been removed, Jackson returned
to his old camps near Gordonsville. His position on Cedar Run, tactically strong, was strategically
unsound. The intelligence he had obtained was sub-
stantially correct. With the exception of five regiments
of McDowell's cavalry, only Banks' army corps had been
engaged at Cedar Run. But during the evening both Sigel
and McDowell had reached the field, and it was their
troops which had checked the Confederate pursuit. In fact,
on the morning of the 10th, Pope, besides 5,000 cavalry,
had 22,000 fresh troops in addition to those which had
been defeated, and which he estimated at 5,000 effectives,
wherewith to bar the way to Culpeper. McDowell's second
division, 10,000 strong, on the march from Fredericksburg, was not more than twenty miles east of Slaughter
Mountain.

In front, therefore, Jackson was confronted by superior
numbers. At the least estimate, 32,000 men were posted
beyond Cedar Run, and 10,000 under King were coming
up from Fredericksburg. Nor was a preponderance
of numbers the only obstacle with which Jackson had to
deal. A direct attack on Pope was impossible, but a turning movement, by way of James City, might have found him
unprepared, or a swift advance might have crushed King.
But for the execution of either manœuvre a large force of
cavalry was absolutely essential. By this means alone
could the march be concealed and a surprise effected.
In view, however, of the superior strength of the Federal
horsemen such a project was unfeasible, and retreat
was manifestly the only alternative. Nevertheless, it
was not till he was assured that no further opportunity
would be given him that Jackson evacuated his position.
For two days he remained on Cedar Run, within two
miles of the Federal outposts, defying his enemy to
battle. If an attack on the Federals promised nothing
but defeat, it was not so sure that Pope with 27,000 infantry,
of whom a considerable number had just tasted defeat,
would be able to oust Jackson with 22,000 from a position

Aug. 12.

which the latter had selected ; and it was not till King's
approach gave the Federals an overwhelming superiority
that the Confederates withdrew behind the Rapidan.

With sublime audacity, as soon as his enemy had
disappeared, Pope claimed the battle of Cedar Run as a
Federal success.   Carried away by enthusiasm he ventured
to forecast the future.   'It is safe to predict,' he declared in a general order, 'that this is only the first of a
series of victories which shall make the Army of Virginia
famous in the land.'   That such language, however, was
the natural result of intense relief at Jackson's retreat
may be inferred from his telegrams, which, unfortunately
for his reputation, have been preserved in the archives of
Washington.   Nor was his attitude on the 10th and 11th
that of a victorious commander.   For two days he never
stirred from his position.   He informed Halleck that the
enemy was in very superior force, that Stuart and Longstreet had joined Jackson, and while the Confederates
were withdrawing he was telegraphing that he would
certainly be attacked the next morning.

Halleck's reply to Pope's final dispatch, which congratulated the defeated army corps on a ' hard-earned but brilliant
success,' must have astonished Banks and his hapless troops.
They might indeed be fairly considered to have 'covered
themselves with glory.'[1]   9,000 men, of which only 7,000
were infantry, had given an enemy of more than double
their strength a hard fight.   They had broken some of the
best troops in the Confederate army, under their most
famous leader ; and if they had been overwhelmed by
numbers, they had at least fought to the last man.   Jackson himself bore witness to the vigour of their onslaught,
to their 'temporary triumph,' and to the 'impetuous
valour' of their cavalry.   The Federal defeat was more
honourable than many victories.   But that it was a
crushing defeat can hardly be disputed.   The two divisions
which had been engaged were completely shattered, and
Pope reported that they were no longer fit for service.
The casualties amongst the infantry amounted to a third

[1] O. R., vol. xii., part ii., p. 135.

of the total strength. Of the brigade that had driven in the Confederate left the 28th New York lost the whole of its company officers; the 5th Connecticut 17 officers out of 20, and the 10th Maine had 170 killed or wounded. In two brigades nearly every field-officer and every adjutant was struck down. The 2nd Massachusetts, employed in the last effort to hold back Jackson's counterstroke, lost 16 officers out of 23, and 147 men out of 451. The Ohio regiments, which had been with Shields at Kernstown and Port Republic, and had crossed Cedar Run opposite the Confederate centre, were handled even more roughly. The 5th lost 118 men out of 275, the 7th 10 officers out of 14, and 170 men out of 293. Two generals were wounded and one captured. 400 prisoners, three stand of colours, 5,000 rifles and one gun were taken by the Southerners, and, including those suffered by Sigel and McDowell in the night action, the sum of losses reached 2,380. The Confederates by no means came off scatheless. General Winder died upon the field, and the two brigades that stood the brunt of the attack, together with Early's, suffered heavily. But the number of killed and wounded amounted to no more than 1,314, and many of the brigades had few losses to report. The spirit of the Valley troops was hardly to be tamed by such punishment as this. Nevertheless, Northern historians have not hesitated to rank Cedar Run as a battle unfavourable to the Confederates. Swinton declares that Jackson undertook the pursuit of Banks, *under the impression* that he had gained a victory.'[1] Southern writers, on the other hand, have classed Cedar Run amongst the most brilliant achievements of the war, and an unbiassed investigation goes far to support their view.

During the first week in August Jackson, protecting the Virginia Central Railroad, was confronted by a much superior force. He could expect no further reinforcements,

[1] I may here express my regret that in the first edition I should have classed Mr. Ropes amongst the adverse critics of Jackson's operations at this period. How I came to fall into the error I cannot explain. I should certainly have remembered that Mr. Ropes' writings are distinguished as much by impartiality as by ability.

for McClellan was still near Richmond, and according to the latest information was actually advancing. On the 7th he heard that Pope also was moving forward from Hazel Run, and had pushed a portion of his army as far as Culpeper. In face of the overwhelming strength of the Federal cavalry it was impossible, if he occupied a defensive position, that he could protect the railroad ; for while their infantry and artillery held him in front, their swarming squadrons would operate at their leisure on either flank. Nor could a defensive position have been long maintained. There were no natural obstacles, neither river nor mountains, to protect Jackson's flanks ; and the railroad—his line of supply—would have been parallel to his front. In a vigorous offensive, then, should opportunity offer, lay his best chance of success. That opportunity was offered by the unsupported advance of the Federal detachment under Banks. It is true that Jackson hoped to achieve more than the defeat of this comparatively small force. If he could have seized Culpeper he might have been able to deal with Pope's army in detail ; he saw before him another Valley campaign, and he was fully justified in believing that victory on the Rapidan would bring McClellan back to Washington.

His anticipations were not altogether realised. He crushed the detachment immediately opposed to him, but he failed to seize Culpeper, and McClellan had already been ordered, although this was unknown to the Confederates, to evacuate the Peninsula. But it cannot be fairly said that his enterprise was therefore useless. Strategically it was a fine conception. The audacity of his manœuvre was not the least of its merits. For an army of 24,000 men, weak in cavalry, to advance against an army of 47,000, including 5,000 horsemen, was the very height of daring. But it was the daring of profound calculation. As it was, Jackson ran little risk. He succeeded in his immediate object. He crushed Pope's advanced-guard, and he retreated unmolested, bearing with him the prisoners, the colours, and the arms which he had captured. If he did not succeed in occupying Culpeper, it was not his fault. Fortune was against

him. On the very day that he had moved forward Pope
had done the same. Banks and McDowell were at Culpeper on the 8th, and Sigel received orders to move the
same day.

Nevertheless the expedition was far from barren in result.
If Jackson failed to defeat Pope altogether, he at least
'singed his beard.' It was well worth the loss of 1,300
men to have destroyed two whole divisions under the very
eyes of the general commanding a superior army. A
few days later Pope was to feel the want of these gallant
regiments,[1] and the confidence of his troops in their commander was much shaken. Moreover, the blow was felt
at Washington. There was no more talk of occupying
Gordonsville. Pope was still full of ardour. But Halleck
forbade him to advance further than the Rapidan, where
Burnside would reinforce him ; and McClellan was ordered
to hasten the departure of his troops from the Peninsula.

Jackson's tactics have been criticised as severely as his
strategy. Because his first line was broken it is asserted
that he narrowly escaped a serious defeat, and that had the
two forces been equally matched Banks would have won a
decisive victory. This is hardly sound criticism. In the
first place, Jackson was perfectly well aware that the two
forces were not equally matched. If he had had no
more men than Banks, would he have disposed his forces
as he did? He would scarcely have occupied the same
extent of ground with 9,000 men that he did with 20,000.
His actual front, when Banks attacked, was two miles
long. With smaller numbers he would have occupied a
smaller front, and would have retained a sufficient force in
reserve. In the second place, it is generally possible for an
inferior force, if it puts every man into the fighting-line, to
win some measure of success. But such success, as was
shown at Kernstown, can seldom be more than temporary ;
and if the enemy makes good use of his reserves must end
in defeat.

[1] So late as August 23, Pope reported that Banks' troops were much
demoralised. O. R., vol. xii., part iii., p. 653.

So far from Jackson's tactics being indifferent, it is very easy to show that they were exactly the contrary. Immediately he came upon the field he sent Ewell to occupy Slaughter Mountain, a mile distant from his line of march; and the huge hill, with batteries planted on its commanding terraces, not only secured his flank, but formed a strong pivot for his attack on the Federal right. The preliminary operations were conducted with due deliberation. There was no rushing forward to the attack while the enemy's strength was still uncertain. The ridge occupied by the enemy, so far as possible, was thoroughly reconnoitred, and every rifled gun was at once brought up. The artillery positions were well selected, for, notwithstanding their superiority of ordnance, the Federal batteries suffered far more heavily than the Confederates. The one weak point was the extreme left, and to this point Jackson in person directed the attention of his subordinates. 'Had reinforcements,' says Colonel Garnett, who commanded the troops that first gave way, 'momentarily expected, arrived ten minutes sooner no disaster would have happened.'[1] That the point was not strengthened, that the Stonewall Brigade was not posted in second line behind the 1st Virginia, and that only a staff officer and an orderly were sent to patrol the forest to the westward, instead of several companies of infantry, was in no way due to the general-in-chief.

Nor was the position of A. P. Hill's division, which, in conjunction with the Stonewall Brigade, averted the disaster and won the victory, a fortuitous circumstance. Before the attack began it had been directed to this point, and the strong counterstroke which was made by these fresh troops was exactly the manœuvre which the situation demanded. At the time it was ordered the Confederate left and centre were hard pressed. The Stonewall Brigade had checked the troops which had issued from the forest, but the whole Confederate line was shaken. The normal, though less brilliant, course would have been to have re-established the front, and not

[1] O. R., vol. xii., part ii., p. 201.

till that had been done to have ventured on the counter-stroke. Jackson, with that quick intuition which is possessed by few, saw and seized his opportunity while the Federals were still pressing the attack. One of Hill's brigades was sent to support the centre, and, almost in the same breath, six others, a mass of 7,000 or 8,000 men, were ordered to attack the enemy's right, to outflank it, and to roll back his whole line upon Ewell, who was instructed at the same moment to outflank the left. Notwithstanding some delay in execution, Ewell's inability to advance, and the charge of the Federal cavalry, this vigorous blow changed the whole aspect of the battle within a short half-hour. Conceived in a moment, in the midst of wild excitement and fierce tumult, delivered with all the strength available, it cannot be judged otherwise than as the mark of a great captain. Few battles, indeed, bear the impress of a single personality more clearly than Cedar Run. From the first cannon-shot of the advanced-guard until the last volley in the midnight forest, one will directed every movement. The field was no small one. The fight was full of startling changes. It was no methodical conflict, but a fierce struggle at close quarters, the lines swaying to and fro, and the ground covered with confused masses of men and guns, with flying batteries and broken regiments. But the turmoil of battle found a master. The strong brain was never clearer than when the storm raged most fiercely. Wherever his presence was most needed there Jackson was seen, rallying the fugitives, reinforcing the centre, directing the counterstroke, and leading the pursuit. And he was well supported. His subordinate generals carried out their orders to the letter. But every order which bore upon the issue of the battle came from the lips of one man.

If Northern writers have overlooked the skill with which Jackson controlled the fight, they have at the same time misunderstood his action two days later. His retreat to Gordonsville has been represented as a flight. He is said to have abandoned many wounded and stragglers, and to have barely saved his baggage. In all this there is not one word

of truth.   We have, indeed, the report of the Federal officer
who conducted the pursuit.   ' The flight of the enemy after
Saturday's fight was most precipitate and in great confusion.   His old camp was strewn with dead men, horses,
and arms. . . . A good many (Federal) prisoners, wounded
in Saturday's fight, were found almost abandoned.   Major
Andrews, chief of artillery to General Jackson, was found,
badly wounded, at Crooked Run, in charge of an assistant
surgeon.'   It is hardly necessary to say that General Buford,
the officer thus reporting, had not been present at the battle.
He had been cut off with his four regiments by the advance
of the Confederate cavalry, and had retired on Sperryville.
He may accordingly be excused for imagining that a retreat
which had been postponed for two days was precipitate.
But dead men, dead horses, and old arms which the
Confederates had probably exchanged for those which
were captured, several wounded Federals, who had been
prisoners in the enemy's hands, and one wounded
Confederate, a major of horse-artillery and not a staff-
officer at all, are hardly evidences of undue haste or
great confusion.   Moreover, in the list of Confederate
casualties only thirty-one men were put down as missing.

   It is true that Jackson need not have retreated so far
as Gordonsville.   He might have halted behind the Rapidan,
where the bluffs on the south bank overlook the level
country to the north.   But Jackson's manœuvres, whether
in advance or retreat, were invariably actuated by some
definite purpose, and what that purpose was he explains in
his dispatches.[1]   ' I remained in position until the night of
the 11th, when I returned to the vicinity of Gordonsville,
in order to avoid being attacked by the vastly superior force
in front of me, *and with the hope that by thus falling back,
General Pope would be induced to follow me until I should
be reinforced.*'   That Pope, had he been left to his own
judgment, would have crossed the Rapidan is certain.
' The enemy,' he reported, ' has retreated to Gordonsville. . . . I shall move forward on Louisa Court House
as soon as Burnside arrives.'   He was restrained, however,

[1] O. R., vol. xii., part ii., p. 185.

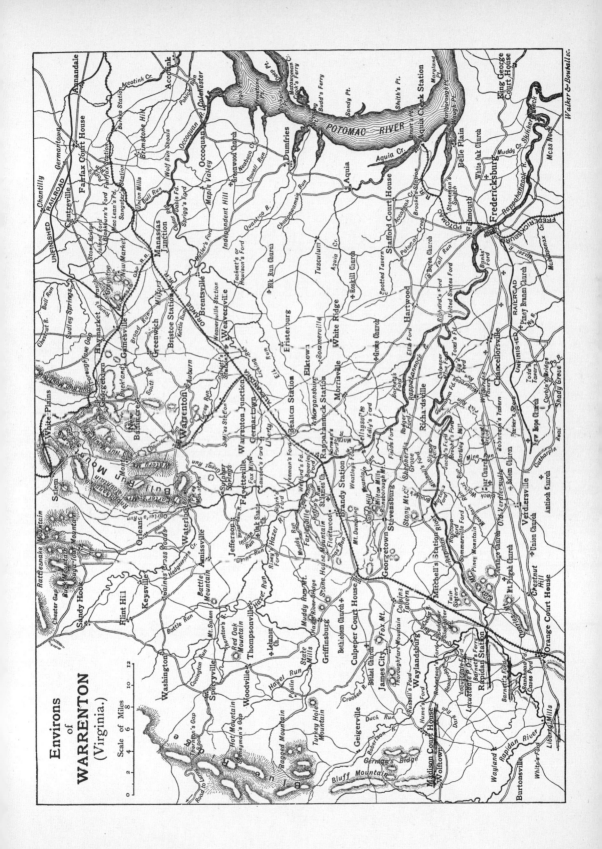

Environs
of
WARRENTON
(Virginia.)

Scale of Miles
0   2   4   6   8   10   12

Walker & Boutelle.

by the more wary Halleck. 'Beware of a snare,' wrote the Commander-in-Chief. 'Feigned retreats are "Secesh" tactics.' How wise was this warning, and what would have been the fate of Pope had he recklessly crossed the Rapidan, the next chapter will reveal.

CHAPTER XVI

GROVETON AND THE SECOND MANASSAS

DURING the summer of 1862 the stirring events in the Western hemisphere attracted universal attention. All eyes were fixed on Richmond. The fierce fighting on the Chickahominy, and the defeat of the invaders, excited Europe hardly less than it did the North. The weekly mails were eagerly awaited. The newspapers devoted many columns to narrative, criticism, and prediction. The strategy and tactics of the rival armies were everywhere discussed, and the fact that almost every single item of intelligence came from a Northern source served only as a whet to curiosity. The vast territory controlled by the Confederacy was so completely cut off from the outer world that an atmosphere of mystery enveloped the efforts of the defence. 'The Southern States,' it has been said, 'stood in the attitude of a beleaguered fortress. The war was in truth a great siege; the fortress covered an area of more than 700,000 square miles, and the lines of investment around it extended over more than 10,000 miles.' Within the circle of Federal cannon and Federal cruisers only the imagination could penetrate. At rare intervals some daring blockade-runner brought a budget of Southern newspapers, or an enterprising correspondent succeeded in transmitting a dispatch from Richmond. But such glimpses of the situation within the cordon did little more than tantalise. The news was generally belated, and had often been long discounted by more recent events. Still, from Northern sources alone, it was abundantly clear that the weaker of the two belligerents was making a splendid struggle. Great names and great achievements loomed large through the darkness. The war at the outset, waged by ill-trained and ill-disciplined volunteers, commanded by officers unknown to fame, had attracted small notice from professional soldiers. After the Seven Days' battles it assumed a new aspect. The men, despite their shortcomings, had displayed undeniable courage, and the strategy which had relieved Richmond recalled the master-strokes of Napoleon. It was evident that the Southern army was led by men of brilliant ability, and the names of Lee's lieutenants were on every tongue. Foremost amongst these was Stonewall Jackson. Even the Northern newspapers made no scruple of expressing their admiration, and the dispatches of their own generals gave them constant opportunities of expatiating on his skill. During the first weeks of August, the reports from the front, whether from Winchester, from Fredericksburg, or from the Peninsula, betrayed the fear and uneasiness he inspired. The overthrow of Pope's advanced-guard at Cedar Run, followed by the unaccountable disappearance of the victorious army, was of a piece with the manœuvres in the Valley. What did this disappearance portend? Whither had the man of mystery betaken himself? Where would the next blow fall? 'I don't like Jackson's movements,' wrote McClellan to Halleck; 'he will suddenly appear when least expected.' This misgiving found many echoes. While Jackson was operating against Pope, McClellan had successfully completed the evacuation of Harrison's Landing. Embarking his sick, he marched his five army corps to Fortress Monroe, observed by Lee's patrols, but otherwise unmolested. The quiescence of the Confederates, however, brought no relief to the North. Stocks fell fast, and the premium on gold rose to sixteen per cent. For some days not a shot had been fired along the Rapidan. Pope's army rested in its camps. Jackson had completely vanished. But the silence at the front was not considered a reassuring symptom.

If the Confederates had allowed McClellan to escape, it was very generally felt that they had done so only because they were preparing to crush Pope before he could be reinforced. 'It is the fear of this operation,' wrote the *Times* Special Correspondent in the Northern States, 'conducted by the redoubtable Stonewall Jackson, that has filled New York with uneasy forebodings. Wall Street does not ardently believe in the present good fortune or the future prospects of the Republic.'[1]

Neither the knowledge which McClellan possessed of his old West Point comrade, nor the instinct of the financiers, proved misleading. Jackson had already made his plans. Even before he had lured Pope forward to the Rapidan he had begun to plot his downfall. 'When we were marching back from Cedar Run,' writes Major Hotchkiss, 'and had passed Orange Court House on our way to Gordonsville, the general, who was riding in front of the staff, beckoned me to his side. He at once entered into conversation, and said that as soon as we got back to camp he wished me to prepare maps of the whole country between Gordonsville and Washington, adding that he required several copies—I think five. This was about noon on Sunday, and as we were near camp I asked him

Aug. 13. if the map was to be begun immediately, knowing his great antipathy to doing anything on Sunday which was not a work of necessity. He replied that it was important to have it done at once.'[2] The next day,

Aug. 14. August 14, the exact position of the Federal army was ascertained. The camps were north and east of Slaughter Mountain, and Jackson instructed Captain Boswell, his chief engineer, who had lived in the neighbourhood, to report on the best means of turning the enemy's left flank and reaching Warrenton, thus intervening between Pope and Washington, or between Pope and Aquia Creek. The line of march recommended by Boswell led through Orange Court House to Pisgah Church, and crossing the Rapidan at Somerville Ford, ran by Lime Church and Stevensburg to Brandy Station.

Aug. 15. On the night of the 15th, after two days' rest, the three divisions moved from Gordonsville to Pisgah Church, and there halted to await reinforcements.

[1] The *Times*, September 4, 1862.   [2] Letter to the author.

These were already on their way. On the 13th General Lee had learned that Burnside, who had already left the Peninsula for Aquia Creek on the Potomac, was preparing to join Pope, and it was reported by a deserter that part of McClellan's army had embarked on the transports at Harrison's Landing. Inferring that the enemy had relinquished all active operations in the Peninsula, and that Pope would soon be reinforced by the Army of the Potomac, Lee resolved to take the offensive without delay. The campaign which Jackson had suggested more than a month before, when McClellan was still reeling under the effects of his defeat, and Pope's army was not yet organised, was now to be begun. The same evening the railway conveyed Longstreet's advanced brigade to Gordonsville, and with the exception of D. H. Hill's and McLaws' divisions, which remained to watch McClellan, the whole army followed.

On the 15th Lee met his generals in council. The map drawn by Captain Hotchkiss was produced, and the manœuvre which had suggested itself to Jackson was definitely ordered by the Commander-in-Chief. The Valley army, at dawn on the 18th, was to cross the Rapidan at Somerville Ford. Longstreet, preceded by Stuart, who was to cut the Federal communications in rear of Culpeper Court House, was to make the passage at Raccoon Ford. Jackson's cavalry was to cover the left and front, and Anderson's division was to form a general reserve. The movement was intended to be speedy. Only ambulances and ammunition waggons were to follow the troops. Baggage and supply trains were to be parked on the south side of the Rapidan, and the men were to carry three days' cooked rations in their haversacks.

On Clark's Mountain, a high hill near Pisgah Church, Jackson had established a signal station. The view from the summit embraced an extensive landscape. The ravages of war had not yet effaced its tranquil beauty, nor had the names of its bright rivers and thriving villages become household words. It was still unknown to history, a peaceful and pastoral district, remote from the beaten tracks of trade and travel, and inhabited by a quiet and industrious people. To-day there are few regions which boast sterner or more heroic memories. To the right, rolling away in light and shadow for a score of miles, is the great forest of Spotsylvania, within whose gloomy depths lie the fields of Chancellorsville; where the breast-works of the Wilderness can still be traced; and on the eastern verge of which stand the grass-grown batteries of Fredericksburg. Northward, beyond the woods which hide the Rapidan, the eye ranges over the wide and fertile plains of Culpeper, with the green crest of Slaughter Mountain overlooking Cedar Run, and the dim levels of Brandy Station, the scene of the great cavalry battle,[1] just visible beyond. Far away to the north-east the faint outline of a range of hills marks the source of Bull Run and the Manassas plateau, and to the west, the long rampart of the Blue Ridge, softened by distance, stands high above the Virginia plains.

On the afternoon of August 17, Pope's forces seemed doomed to inevitable destruction. The Confederate army, Aug. 17. ready to advance the next morning, was con-centrated behind Clark's Mountain, and Lee and Jackson, looking toward Culpeper, saw the promise of victory in the careless attitude of the enemy. The day was hot and still. Round the base of Slaughter Mountain, fifteen miles northward, clustered many thousands of tents, and the blue smoke of the camp-fires rose straight and thin in the sultry air. Regiments of infantry, just discernible through the glare, were marching and countermarching in various directions, and long waggon-trains were creeping slowly along the dusty roads. Near at hand, rising above the tree-tops, the Union colours showed that the outposts still held the river, and the flash of steel at the end of some woodland vista betrayed the presence of scouting party or vedette. But there were no symptoms of unusual excitement, no sign of working parties, of reinforcements for the advanced posts, of the construction of earthworks or abattis. Pope's camps were scattered over a wide tract of

[1] June 9, 1863.

country, his cavalry was idle, and it seemed absolutely
certain that he was unconscious of the near neighbourhood
of the Confederate army.

The inference was correct. The march to Pisgah
Church had escaped notice. The Federals were unaware
that Lee had arrived at Gordonsville, and they had as yet
no reason to believe that there was the smallest danger of
attack.

Between Raccoon and Locustdale fords, and stretching
back to Culpeper Court House, 52,500 men—for Reno, with
two divisions of Burnside's army, 8,000 strong, had arrived
from Fredericksburg—were in camp and bivouac. The front
was protected by a river nearly a hundred yards wide, of
which every crossing was held by a detachment, and Pope
had reported that his position was so strong that it would
be difficult to drive him from it. But he had not made
sufficient allowance for the energy and ability of the Confederate leaders. His situation, in reality, was one of
extreme danger. In ordering Pope to the Rapidan, and bidding him 'fight like the devil' [1] until McClellan should come
up, Halleck made the same fatal error as Stanton, when
he sent Shields up the Luray Valley in pursuit of Jackson.
He had put an inferior force within reach of an enemy
who held the interior lines, and had ordered two armies,
separated by several marches, to effect their concentration
under the fire of the enemy's guns. And if Pope's strategical
position was bad, his tactical position was even worse. His
left, covering Raccoon and Somerville Fords, was very
weak. The main body of his army was massed on the
opposite flank, several miles distant, astride the direct road
from Gordonsville to Culpeper Court House, and he remained without the least idea, so late as the morning of
the 18th, that the whole Confederate army was concentrated
behind Clark's Mountain, within six miles of his most
vulnerable point. Aware that Jackson was based on
Gordonsville, he seems to have been convinced that if
he advanced at all, he would advance directly on Culpeper

[1] O. R., vol. xii., part ii., p. 57. 'It may have been fortunate for the Confederates,' says Longstreet, 'that he was not instructed to *fight like Jackson*.'

Court House; and the move to Pisgah Church, which left Gordonsville unprotected, never entered into his calculations. A sudden attack against his left was the last contingency that he anticipated; and had the Confederates moved as Lee intended, there can be no question but that the Federal army, deprived of all supplies, cut off from Washington, and forced to fight on ground where it was unprepared, would have been disastrously defeated.

But it was not to be. The design was thwarted by one of those petty accidents which play so large a part in war. Stuart had been instructed to lead the advance. The only brigade at his disposal had not yet come up into line, but a message had been sent to appoint a rendezvous, and it was expected to reach Verdiersville, five miles from Raccoon Ford, on the night of the 17th. Stuart's message, however, was not sufficiently explicit. Nothing was said of the exigencies of the situation; and the brigadier, General Fitzhugh Lee, not realising the importance of reaching Verdiersville on the 17th, marched by a circuitous route in order to replenish his supplies. At nightfall he was still absent, and the omission of a few words in a simple order cost the Confederates dear. Moreover, Stuart himself, who had ridden to Verdiersville with a small escort, narrowly escaped capture. His plumed hat, with which the whole army was familiar, as well as his adjutant-general and his dispatch-box, fell into the hands of a Federal reconnoitring party; and among the papers brought to Pope was found a letter from General Lee, disclosing the fact that Jackson had been strongly reinforced.

In consequence of the absence of Fitzhugh Lee's brigade, the movement was postponed until the morning of the 20th. The Commander-in-Chief was of opinion that the horses, exhausted by their long march, would require some rest before they were fit for the hard work he proposed for them. Jackson, for once in opposition, urged that the movement should go forward. His signal officer on Clark's Mountain reported that the enemy was quiet, and even extending his right up stream. The location of the Federal divisions had been already ascertained. The cavalry was not required to get information. There was no need, therefore, to wait till Fitzhugh Lee's brigade was fit for movement. Jackson had, with his own command, a sufficient number of squadrons to protect the front and flanks of the whole army ; and the main object was not to cut the enemy's communications, but to turn his left and annihilate him. Pope was still isolated, still unconscious of his danger, and the opportunity might never return.

The suggestion, however, was overruled, and ' it was fortunate,' says one of Pope's generals, ' that Jackson was not in command of the Confederates on the night of August 17 ; for the superior force of the enemy must have overwhelmed us, if we could not have escaped, and escape on that night was impossible.' [1]

It is probable, however, that other causes induced General Lee to hold his hand. There is good reason to believe that it was not only the cavalry that was unprepared. The movement from Richmond had been rapid, and both vehicles and supplies had been delayed. Nor were all the generals so avaricious of time as Jackson. It was impossible, it was urged, to move without some food in the waggons. Jackson replied that the enemy had a large magazine at Brandy Station, which might easily be captured, and that the intervening district promised an abundance of ripening corn and green apples. It was decided, however, that such fare, on which, it may be said, the Confederates learned afterwards to subsist for many days in succession, was too meagre for the work in hand. Jackson, runs the story, groaned so audibly when Lee pronounced in favour of postponement, that Longstreet called the attention of the Commander-in-Chief to his apparent disrespect.

Be this as it may, had it been possible to adopt Jackson's advice, the Federal army would have been caught in the execution of a difficult manœuvre. On the morning of the 18th, about the very hour that the advance should have begun, Pope was informed by a spy that the Confederate army was assembled behind Clark's

Aug. 18.

[1] General George H. Gordon. *The Army of Virginia*, p. 9.

Mountain and the neighbouring hills; that the artillery horses were harnessed, and that the troops were moment-arily expecting orders to cross the river and strike his rear. He at once made preparations for retreat. The trains moved off to seek shelter behind the Rappahannock, and the army followed, leaving the cavalry in position, and marching as follows :—

Reno by Stevensburg to Kelly's Ford.
Banks and McDowell by Culpeper Court House and Brandy Station
    to the Rappahannock railway bridge.
Sigel by Rixeyville to Sulphur Springs.

The march was slow and halts were frequent. The long lines of waggons blocked every road, and on the morning of August 19 the troops were still at some distance from the Rappahannock, in neither condition nor formation to resist a resolute attack.

Aug. 19.

The movement, however, was not discovered by the Con-federates until it had been more than four-and-twenty hours in progress. General Lee, on August 19, had taken his stand on Clark's Mountain, but the weather was unfavourable for observation. Late in the afternoon the haze lifted, and almost at the same moment the remaining tents of the Federal army, fifteen miles away to the north-west, sud-denly vanished from the landscape, and great clouds of dust, rising high above the woods, left it no longer doubtful that Pope had taken the alarm. It was too late to inter-fere, and the sun set on an army baffled of its prey. In the Confederate councils there was some dismay, among the troops much heart-burning. Every hour that was wasted brought nearer the junction of Pope and McClellan, and the soldiers were well aware that a most promising opportunity, which it was worth while living on green corn and apples to secure, had been allowed to slip. Nevertheless, the pursuit was prompt. By the light of the rising moon the advanced-guards plunged thigh-deep into the clear waters of the Rapidan, and the whole army crossed by Raccoon and Somerville Fords. Stuart, with Robertson's and Fitzhugh Lee's brigades, pressed forward on the traces

Aug. 20.

of the retreating foe. Near Brandy Station the Federal cavalry made a stubborn stand. The Confederates, covering a wide front, had become separated. Robertson had marched through Stevensburg, Fitzhugh Lee on Kelly's Ford, an interval of six miles dividing the two brigades; and when Robertson was met by Bayard's squadrons, holding a skirt of woods with dismounted men, it was several hours before a sufficient force could be assembled to force the road. Towards evening two of Fitzhugh Lee's regiments came up, and the Confederates were now concentrated in superior numbers. A series of vigorous charges, delivered by successive regiments on a front of fours, for the horsemen were confined to the road, hurried the retreating Federals across the Rappahannock; but the presence of infantry and guns near the railway bridge placed an effective barrier in the way of further pursuit. Before nightfall Jackson's advanced-guard reached Brandy Station, after a march of twenty miles, and Longstreet bivouacked near Kelly's Ford.

The Rappahannock, a broad and rapid stream, with banks high and well-timbered, now rolled between the hostile armies. Pope, by his timely retreat, had gained a position where he could be readily reinforced, and although the river, in consequence of the long drought, had much dwindled from its usual volume, his front was perfectly secure.

The situation with which the Confederate commander had now to deal was beset by difficulties. The delay from August 18 to August 20 had been most unfortunate. The Federals were actually nearer Richmond than the Army of Northern Virginia, and if McClellan, landing as Burnside had done at Aquia Creek, were to move due south through Fredericksburg, he would find the capital but feebly garrisoned. It was more probable, however, that he would reinforce Pope, and Lee held fast to his idea of crushing his enemies in detail. Aquia Creek was only thirty-five miles' march from the Rappahannock, but the disembarkation with horses, trains, and artillery must needs be a lengthy process, and it might still be possible, by skilful and swift

manœuvres, to redeem the time which had been already lost.
But the Federal position was very strong.   Early on the
21st it was ascertained that Pope's whole army was massed
Aug. 21.   on the left bank of the Rappahannock, extending
         from Kelly's Ford to Hazel Run, and that a
powerful artillery crowned the commanding bluffs.   To
turn the line of the river from the south was hardly
practicable.   The Federal cavalry was vigilant, and Pope
would have quietly fallen back on Washington.   A turning movement from the north was more promising, and
during the day Stuart, supported by Jackson, made
vigorous efforts to find a passage across the river.   Covered
by a heavy fire of artillery, the squadrons drove in a
regiment and a battery holding Beverley Ford, and
spread their patrols over the country on the left bank.   It
was soon evident, however, that the ground was unsuitable
for attack, and Stuart, menaced by a strong force of
infantry, withdrew his troopers across the stream.   Nothing
further was attempted.   Jackson went into bivouac near St.
James's Church, and Longstreet closed in upon his right.

The next morning, in accordance with Lee's orders to
' seek a more favourable place to cross higher up the river,
Aug. 22.   and thus gain the enemy's right,' Jackson, still
        preceded by Stuart, and concealing his march
as far as possible in the woods, moved towards the fords
near Warrenton Springs.   Longstreet, meanwhile, marched
towards the bridge at Rappahannock Station, where the
enemy had established a *tête-de-pont,* and bringing his guns
into action at every opportunity, made brisk demonstrations
along the river.

Late in the afternoon, after an attack on his rear-guard
at Welford's Mill had been repulsed by Trimble, reinforced
by Hood, Jackson, under a lowering sky, reached the ruined
bridge at the Sulphur Springs.   Only a few of the enemy's
cavalry had been descried, and he at once made preparations
to effect the passage of the Rappahannock.   The 13th
Georgia dashed through the ford, and occupied the
cottages of the little watering-place.   Early's brigade and
two batteries crossed by an old mill-dam, a mile below, and

took post on the ridge beyond. But heavy rain had begun to fall; the night was closing in; and the river, swollen by the storms in the mountains, was already rising. The difficulties of the passage increased every moment, and the main body of the Valley army was ordered into bivouac on the western bank. It was not, however, the darkness of the ford or the precarious footing of the mill-dam that held Jackson back from reinforcing his advanced-guard, but the knowledge that these dangerous roadways would soon be submerged by a raging torrent. Early was, indeed, in peril, but it was better that one brigade should take its chance of escape than that one half the column should be cut off from the remainder. Next morning the pioneers were ordered to repair the bridge, while Longstreet, feinting strongly against the *tête-de-pont*, gave Pope occupation. Early's troops, under cover of the woods, moved northward to the protection of a creek named Great Run, and although the Federal cavalry kept close watch upon him, no attack was made till nightfall. This was easily beaten back; and Jackson, anxious to keep the attention of the enemy fixed on this point, sent over another brigade. At dawn on the 24th, however, as the Federals were reported to be advancing in force, the detachment was brought back to the Confederate bank. The men had been for two days and a night without food or shelter. It was in vain that Early, after the bridge had been restored, had requested to be withdrawn. Jackson sent Lawton to reinforce him with the curt message: 'Tell General Early to hold his position;' and although the generals grumbled at their isolation, Pope was effectually deluded into the conviction that a serious attack had been repulsed, and that no further attempt to turn his right was to be immediately apprehended. The significance of Jackson's action will be seen hereafter.

While Jackson was thus mystifying the enemy, both Longstreet and Stuart had been hard at work. The former, after an artillery contest of several hours' duration, had driven the enemy from his *tête-de-pont* on the railway, and had burnt the bridge. The latter, on the morning of the

Aug. 23.

Aug. 24.

22nd, had moved northward with the whole of the cavalry, except two regiments, and had ridden round the Federal right.   Crossing the Rappahannock at Waterloo Bridge and Hart's Mills, he marched eastward without meeting a single hostile scout, and as evening fell the column of 1,500 men and two pieces of artillery clattered into Warrenton.   The troopers dismounted in the streets.   The horses were fed and watered, and while the officers amused themselves by registering their names, embellished with fantastic titles, at the hotel, Stuart's staff, questioning the throng of women and old men, elicited important information.   None of the enemy's cavalry had been seen in the vicinity for some days, and Pope's supply trains were parked at Catlett's Station, on the Orange and Alexandria Railway, ten miles south-east.   After an hour's rest the force moved on, and passing through Auburn village was caught by the same storm that had cut off Early.   The narrow roads became running streams, and the creeks which crossed the line of march soon rose to the horses' withers.   But this was the very condition of the elements most favourable for the enterprise.   The enemy's vedettes and patrols, sheltering from the fury of the storm, were captured, one after another, by the advanced-guard, and the two brigades arrived at Catlett's Station without the Federals receiving the least notice of their approach.

A moment's halt, a short consultation, a silent movement forward, and the astonished sentinels were overpowered.   Beyond were the encampments and the trains, guarded by 1,500 infantry and 500 horsemen.   The night was dark—the darkest, said Stuart, that he had ever known.   Without a guide concerted action seemed impossible.   The rain still fell in torrents, and the raiders, soaked to the skin, could only grope aimlessly in the gloom.   But just at this moment a negro was captured who recognised Stuart, and who knew where Pope's baggage and horses were to be found.   He was told to lead the way, and Colonel W. H. F. Lee, a son of the Commander-in-Chief, was ordered to follow with his regiment.   The guide led the column towards the headquarter tents. 'Then there mingled with the noise of the rain upon the canvas and the roar of the wind in the forest the rushing sound of many horsemen, of loud voices, and clashing sabres.' One of Pope's staff officers, together with the uniform and horses of the Federal commander, his treasure chest, and his personal effects, fell into the hands of the Confederates, and the greater part of the enemy's troops, suddenly alarmed in the deep darkness, dispersed into the woods. Another camp was quickly looted, and the 1st and 5th Virginia Cavalry were sent across the railway, riding without accident, notwithstanding the darkness, over a high embankment with deep ditches on either side. But the Federal guards had now rallied under cover, and the attack on the railway waggons had to be abandoned. Another party had taken in hand the main object of the expedition, the destruction of the railway bridge over Cedar Run. The force which should have defended it was surprised and scattered. The timbers, however, were by this time thoroughly saturated, and only a few axes had been discovered. Some Federal skirmishers maintained a heavy fire from the opposite bank, and it was impossible to complete the work. The telegraph was more easily dealt with; and shortly before daylight on the 23rd, carrying with him 300 prisoners, including many officers, Stuart withdrew by the light of the blazing camp, and after a march of sixty miles in six-and-twenty hours, reached the Sulphur Springs before evening.

The most important result of this raid was the capture of Pope's dispatch book, containing most detailed information as to his strength, dispositions, and designs; referring to the reinforcements he expected, and disclosing his belief that the line of the Rappahannock was no longer tenable. But the enterprise had an indirect effect upon the enemy's calculations, which was not without bearing on the campaign. Pope believed that Stuart's advance on Catlett's Station had been made in connection with Jackson's attempt to cross at Sulphur Springs; and the retreat of the cavalry, combined with that of Early, seemed to indicate that the movement to turn his right had been definitely abandoned.

The Federal commander was soon to be undeceived. Thrice had General Lee been baulked. The enemy, who should have been annihilated on August 19, had gained six days' respite. On the 20th he had placed himself behind the Rappahannock. On the 22nd the rising waters forbade Jackson's passage at the Sulphur Springs ; and now, on the afternoon of the 24th, the situation was still unchanged. Disregarding Longstreet's demonstrations, Pope had marched northward, keeping pace with Jackson, and his whole force was concentrated on the great road which runs from the Sulphur Springs through Warrenton and Gainesville to Washington and Alexandria. He had answered move by countermove. Hitherto, except in permitting Early to recross the river, he had made no mistake, and he had gained time. He had marched over thirty miles, and executed complicated manœuvres, without offering the Confederates an opening. His position near the Sulphur Springs was as strong as that which he had left on the lower reaches near the railway bridge. Moreover, the correspondence in his dispatch book disclosed the fact that a portion at least of McClellan's army had landed at Aquia Creek, and was marching to Bealtown ;[1] that a strong force, drawn from the Kanawha Valley and elsewhere, was assembling at Washington ; and that 150,000 men might be concentrated within a few days on the Rappahannock. Lee, on learning McClellan's destination, immediately asked that the troops which had been retained at Richmond should be sent to join him. Mr. Davis assented, but it was not till the request had been repeated and time lost that the divisions of D. H. Hill and McLaws', two brigades of infantry, under J. G. Walker, and Hampton's cavalry

[1] Between August 21 and 25 Pope received the following reinforcements for the Army of the Potomac, raising his strength to over 80,000 men :

Third Corps. Heintzleman .	{	Hooker's Division	} 10,000
		Kearney's „	
Fifth Corps. Porter . .	{	Morell's „	} 10,000
		Sykes' „	
Pennsylvania Reserves. Reynolds . . . 8,000			

brigade were ordered up. Yet these reinforcements only raised Lee's numbers to 75,000 men, and they were from eighty to a hundred miles distant by an indifferent railroad.

Nor was it possible to await their arrival. Instant action was imperative. But what action was possible? A defensive attitude could only result in the Confederate army being forced back by superior strength; and retreat on Richmond would be difficult, for the Federals held the interior lines. The offensive seemed out of the question. Pope's position was more favourable than before. His army was massed, and reinforcements were close at hand. His right flank was well secured. The ford at Sulphur Springs and the Waterloo Bridge were both in his possession; north of the Springs rose the Bull Run Mountains, a range covered with thick forest, and crossed by few roads; and his left was protected by the march of McClellan's army corps from Aquia Creek. Even the genius of a Napoleon might well have been baffled by the difficulties in the way of attack. But there were men in the Confederate army to whom overwhelming numbers and strong positions were merely obstacles to be overcome.

On August 24 Lee removed his headquarters to Jefferson, where Jackson was already encamped, and on the same evening, with Pope's captured correspondence before them, the two generals discussed the problem. What occurred at this council of war was never made public. To use Lee's words: 'A plan of operations was determined on;' but by whom it was suggested there is none to tell us. 'Jackson was so reticent,' writes Dr. McGuire, 'that it was only by accident that we ever found out what he proposed to do, and there is no staff officer living (1897) who could throw any light on this matter. The day before we started to march round Pope's army I saw Lee and Jackson conferring together. Jackson—for him—was very much excited, drawing with the toe of his boot a map in the sand, and gesticulating in a much more earnest way than he was in the habit of doing. General Lee was simply listening, and after Jackson had got through, he nodded his head, as if acceding to some proposal. I believe, from what occurred afterwards, that Jackson suggested the movement as it was made, but I have no further proof than the incident I have just mentioned.' [1] It is only certain that we have record of few enterprises of greater daring than that which was then decided on; and no matter from whose brain it emanated, on Lee fell the burden of the responsibility; on his shoulders, and on his alone, rested the honour of the Confederate arms, the fate of Richmond, the independence of the South; and if we may suppose, so consonant was the design proposed with the strategy which Jackson had already practised, that it was to him its inception was due, it is still to Lee that we must assign the higher merit. It is easy to conceive. It is less easy to execute. But to risk cause and country, name and reputation, on a single throw, and to abide the issue with unflinching heart, is the supreme exhibition of the soldier's fortitude.

Lee's decision was to divide his army. Jackson, marching northwards, was to cross the Bull Run Mountains at Thoroughfare Gap, ten miles as the crow flies from the enemy's right, and strike the railway which formed Pope's line of supply. The Federal commander, who would meanwhile be held in play by Longstreet, would be compelled to fall back in a north-easterly direction to save his communications, and thus be drawn away from McClellan. Longstreet would then follow Jackson, and it was hoped that the Federals, disconcerted by these movements, might be attacked in detail or forced to fight at a disadvantage. The risk, however, was very great.

An army of 55,000 men was about to march into a region occupied by 100,000,[2] who might easily be reinforced to 150,000; and it was to march in two wings,

---

[1] Letter to the author.

[2] Pope, 80,000; Washington and Aquia Creek, 20,000. Lee was well aware, from the correspondence which Stuart had captured, if indeed he had not already inferred it, that Pope had been strictly enjoined to cover Washington, and that he was dependent on the railway for supplies. There was not the slightest fear of his falling back towards Aquia Creek to join McClellan.

separated from each other by two days' march. If Pope
were to receive early warning of Jackson's march, he might
hurl his whole force on one or the other. Moreover, defeat,
with both Pope and McClellan between the Confederates
and Richmond, spelt ruin and nothing less. But as Lee
said after the war, referring to the criticism evoked by
manœuvres, in this as in other of his campaigns, which were
daring even to rashness, 'Such criticism is obvious, but
the disparity of force between the contending forces
rendered the risks unavoidable.' [1]   In the present case the
only alternative was an immediate retreat; and retreat, so
long as the enemy was not fully concentrated, and there was
a chance of dealing with him in detail, was a measure which
neither Lee nor Jackson was ever willing to advise.

On the evening of the 24th Jackson began his preparations for the most famous of his marches. His troops
were quietly withdrawn from before the Sulphur Springs,
and Longstreet's division, unobserved by the Federals, took
their place. Captain Boswell was ordered to report on the
most direct and hidden route to Manassas Junction, and
the three divisions—Ewell's, Hill's, and the Stonewall, now
commanded by Taliaferro—assembled near Jefferson. Three
days' cooked rations were to be carried in the haversacks,
and a herd of cattle, together with the green corn standing
in the fields, was relied upon for subsistence until requisition
could be made on the Federal magazines. The troops
marched light. Knapsacks were left behind. Tin cans and
a few frying-pans formed the only camp equipment, and
many an officer's outfit consisted of a few badly baked
biscuits and a handful of salt.

Long before dawn the divisions were afoot. The men
were hungry, and their rest had been short; but they were
old acquaintances of the morning star, and to march while
Aug. 25   the east was still grey had become a matter of
routine. But as their guides led northward, and
the sound of the guns, opening along the Rappahannock,
grew fainter and fainter, a certain excitement began to
pervade the column. Something mysterious was in the air.

[1] *The Army of Northern Virginia*, Colonel Allan, p. 200.

What their movement portended not the shrewdest of the
soldiers could divine ; but they recalled their marches in the
Valley and their inevitable results, and they knew instinctively that a surprise on a still larger scale was in contemplation. The thought was enough. Asking no questions, and
full of enthusiasm, they followed with quick step the leader
in whom their confidence had become so absolute. The flood
had subsided on the Upper Rappahannock, and the divisions
forded it at Hinson's Mill, unmolested and apparently unobserved. Without halting it pressed on, Boswell with a
small escort of cavalry leading the way. The march led first
by Amissville, thence north to Orleans, beyond Hedgeman's
River, and thence to Salem, a village on the Manassas Gap
Railroad. Where the roads diverged from the shortest line
the troops took to the fields. Guides were stationed by the
advanced-guard at each gap and gate which marked the
route. Every precaution was taken to conceal the movement.
The roads in the direction of the enemy were watched by
cavalry, and so far as possible the column was directed
through woods and valleys. The men, although they knew
nothing of their destination, whether Winchester, or
Harper's Ferry, or even Washington itself, strode on mile
after mile, through field and ford, in the fierce heat of the
August noon, without question or complaint. ' Old Jack '
had asked them to do their best, and that was enough to
command their most strenuous efforts.

Near the end of the day Jackson rode to the head of
the leading brigade, and complimented the officers on the
fine condition of the troops and the regularity of the
march. They had made more than twenty miles, and
we're still moving briskly, well closed up, and without
stragglers. Then, standing by the wayside, he watched
his army pass. The sun was setting, and the rays
struck full on his familiar face, brown with exposure,
and his dusty uniform. Ewell's division led the way,
and when the men saw their general, they prepared
to salute him with their usual greeting. But as they
began to cheer he raised his hand to stop them, and the
word passed down the column, ' Don't shout, boys, the

Yankees will hear us ; ' and the soldiers contented themselves with swinging their caps in mute acclamation. When the next division passed a deeper flush spread over Jackson's face. Here were the men he had so often led to triumph, the men he had trained himself, the men of the Valley, of the First Manassas, of Kernstown, and M'Dowell. The Stonewall regiments were before him, and he was unable to restrain them ; devotion such as theirs was not to be silenced at such a moment, and the wild battle-yell of his own brigade set his pulses tingling. For once a breach of discipline was condoned. ' It is of no use,' said Jackson, turning to his staff, ' you see I can't stop them ; ' and then, with a sudden access of intense pride in his gallant veterans, he added, half to himself, ' Who could fail to win battles with such men as these ? '

It was midnight before the column halted near Salem village, and the men, wearied outright with their march of six-and-twenty miles, threw themselves on the ground by the piles of muskets, without even troubling to unroll their blankets. So far the movement had been entirely successful. Not a Federal had been seen, and none appeared during the warm midsummer night. Yet the soldiers were permitted scant time for rest. Once more they were aroused while the stars were bright ; and, half awake, snatching what food they could, they stumbled forward through the darkness. As the cool breath of the morning rose about them, the dark forests of the Bull Run Mountains became gradually visible in the faint light of Aug. 26. the eastern sky, and the men at last discovered whither their general was leading them. With the knowledge, which spread quickly through the ranks, that they were making for the communications of the boaster Pope, the regiments stepped out with renewed energy. ' There was no need for speech, no breath to spare if there had been —only the shuffling tramp of marching feet, the rumbling of wheels, the creak and clank of harness and accoutrements, with an occasional order, uttered under the breath, and always the same : '' Close up, men ! Close up !'' ' [1]

[1] *Battles and Leaders*, vol. ii., p. 533.

Through Thoroughfare Gap, a narrow gorge in the Bull Run range, with high cliffs, covered with creepers and crowned with pines on either hand, the column wound steadily upwards; and, gaining the higher level, the troops looked down on the open country to the eastward. Over a vast area of alternate field and forest, bounded by distant uplands, the shadows of the clouds were slowly sailing. Issuing from the mouth of the pass, and trending a little to the south-east, ran the broad high-road, passing through two tiny hamlets, Haymarket and Gainesville, and climbing by gentle gradients to a great bare plateau, familiar to the soldiers of Bull Run under the name of Manassas Plains. At Gainesville this road was crossed by another, which, lost in dense woods, appeared once more on the open heights to the far north-east, where the white buildings of Centreville glistened in the sunshine. The second road was the Warrenton and Alexandria highway, the direct line of communication between Pope's army and Washington, and it is not difficult to divine the anxiety with which it was scrutinised by Jackson. If his march had been detected, a far superior force might already be moving to intercept him. At any moment the news might come in that the Federal army was rapidly approaching; and even were that not the case, it seemed hardly possible that the Confederate column, betrayed by the dust, could escape the observation of passing patrols or orderlies. But not a solitary scout was visible; no movement was reported from the direction of Warrenton; and the troops pressed on, further and further round the Federal rear, further and further from Lee and Longstreet. The cooked rations which they carried had been consumed or thrown away; there was no time for the slaughter and distribution of the cattle; but the men took tribute from the fields and orchards, and green corn and green apples were all the morning meal that many of them enjoyed. At Gainesville the column was joined by Stuart, who had maintained a fierce artillery fight at Waterloo Bridge the previous day; and then, slipping quietly away under cover of the darkness, had marched at two in the morning to cover

Jackson's flank. The sun was high in the heavens, and still the enemy made no sign. Munford's horsemen, forming the advanced-guard, had long since reached the Alexandria turnpike, sweeping up all before them, and neither patrols nor orderlies had escaped to carry the news to Warrenton.

So the point of danger was safely passed, and thirteen miles in rear of Pope's headquarters, right across the communications he had told his troops to disregard, the long column swung swiftly forward in the noonday heat. Not a sound, save the muffled roll of many wheels, broke the stillness of the tranquil valley; only the great dust cloud, rolling always eastward up the slopes of the Manassas plateau, betrayed the presence of war.

Beyond Gainesville Jackson took the road which led to Bristoe Station, some seven miles south of Manassas Junction. Neither the success which had hitherto accompanied his movement, nor the excitement incident on his situation, had overbalanced his judgment. From Gainesville the Junction might have been reached in little more than an hour's march; and prudence would have recommended a swift dash at the supply depôt, swift destruction, and swift escape. But it was always possible that Pope might have been alarmed, and the railroad from Warrenton Junction supplied him with the means of throwing a strong force of infantry rapidly to his rear. In order to obstruct such a movement Jackson had determined to seize Bristoe Station. Here, breaking down the railway bridge over Broad Run, and establishing his main body in an almost impregnable position behind the stream, he could proceed at his leisure with the destruction of the stores at Manassas Junction. The advantages promised by this manœuvre more than compensated for the increased length of the march.

The sun had not yet set when the advanced-guard arrived within striking distance of Bristoe Station. Munford's squadrons, still leading the way, dashed upon the village. Ewell followed in hot haste, and a large portion of the guard, consisting of two companies, one of cavalry and one of infantry, was immediately captured.

A train returning empty from Warrenton Junction to Alexandria darted through the station under a heavy fire.[1] The line was then torn up, and two trains which followed in the same direction as the first were thrown down a high embankment. A fourth, scenting danger ahead, moved back before it reached the break in the road. The column had now closed up, and it was already dark. The escape of the two trains was most unfortunate. It would soon be known, both at Alexandria and Warrenton, that Manassas Junction was in danger. The troops had marched nearly five-and-twenty miles, but if the object of the expedition was to be accomplished, further exertions were absolutely necessary. Trimble, energetic as ever, volunteered with two regiments, the 21st Georgia and 21st North Carolina, to move on Manassas Junction. Stuart was placed in command, and without a moment's delay the detachment moved northward through the woods. The night was hot and moonless. The infantry moved in order of battle, the skirmishers in advance; and pushing slowly forward over a broken country, it was nearly midnight before they reached the Junction. Half a mile from the depôt their advance was greeted by a salvo of shells. The Federal garrison, warned by the fugitives from Bristoe Station, were on the alert; but so harmless was their fire that Trimble's men swept on without a check. The two regiments, one on either side of the railroad, halted within a hundred yards of the Federal guns. The countersign was passed down the ranks, and the bugles sounded the charge. The Northern gunners, without waiting for the onset, fled through the darkness, and two batteries, each with its full complement of guns and waggons, became the prize of the Confederate infantry. Stuart, coming up on the flank, rode down the fugitives. Over 300 prisoners were taken, and the remainder of the garrison streamed northward through the deserted camps. The results of

---

[1] The report received at Alexandria from Manassas Junction ran as follows : ' No. 6 train, engine Secretary, was fired into at Bristoe by a party of cavalry, some 500 strong. They had piled ties on the track, but the engine threw them off. Secretary is completely riddled by bullets.'

this attack more than compensated for the exertions the troops had undergone. Only 15 Confederates had been wounded, and the supplies on which Pope's army, whether it was intended to move against Longstreet or merely to hold the line of the Rappahannock, depended both for food and ammunition were in Jackson's hands.

The next morning Hill's and Taliaferro's divisions joined Trimble. Ewell remained at Bristoe; cavalry patrols were sent out in every direction, and Jackson, riding to Manassas, saw before him the reward of his splendid march. Streets of warehouses, stored to overflowing, had sprung up round the Junction. A line of freight cars, two miles in length, stood upon the railway. Thousands of barrels, containing flour, pork, and biscuit, covered the neighbouring fields. Brand-new ambulances were packed in regular rows. Field-ovens, with the fires still smouldering, and all the paraphernalia of a large bakery, attracted the wondering gaze of the Confederate soldiery; while great pyramids of shot and shell, piled with the symmetry of an arsenal, testified to the profusion with which the enemy's artillery was supplied.

Aug. 27.

It was a strange commentary on war. Washington was but a long day's march to the north; Warrenton, Pope's headquarters, but twelve miles distant to the south-west; and along the Rappahannock, between Jackson and Lee, stood the tents of a host which outnumbered the whole Confederate army. No thought of danger had entered the minds of those who selected Manassas Junction as the depôt of the Federal forces. Pope had been content to leave a small guard as a protection against raiding cavalry. Halleck, concerned only with massing the whole army on the Rappahannock, had used every effort to fill the store-houses. If, he thought, there was one place in Virginia where the Stars and Stripes might be displayed in full security, that place was Manassas Junction; and here, as nowhere else, the wealth of the North had been poured out with a prodigality such as had never been seen in war. To feed, clothe, and equip the Union armies no expenditure was deemed extravagant. For the comfort and well-being of the individual soldier the purse-strings of the nation were freely loosed. No demand, however preposterous, was disregarded. The markets of Europe were called upon to supply the deficiencies of the States; and if money could have effected the re-establishment of the Union, the war would have already reached a triumphant issue. But the Northern Government had yet to learn that the accumulation of men, *matériel*, and supplies is not in itself sufficient for success. Money alone cannot provide good generals, a trained staff, or an efficient cavalry; and so on this August morning 20,000 ragged Confederates, the soldiers of a country which ranked as the poorest of nations, had marched right round the rear of the Federal army, and were now halted in undisturbed possession of all that made that army an effective force.

Few generals have occupied a position so commanding as did Jackson on the morning of August 27. His enemies would henceforward have to dance while he piped. It was Jackson, and not Pope, who was to dictate the movements of the Federal army. It was impossible that the latter could now maintain its position on the Rappahannock, and Lee's strategy had achieved its end. The capture of Manassas Junction, however, was only the first step in the campaign. Pope, to restore his communications with Alexandria, would be compelled to fall back; but before he could be defeated the two Confederate wings must be united, and the harder part of the work would devolve on Jackson. The Federals, at Warrenton, were nearer by five miles to Thoroughfare Gap, his shortest line of communication with Lee and Longstreet, than he was himself. Washington held a large garrison, and the railway was available for the transit of the troops. The fugitives from Manassas must already have given the alarm, and at any moment the enemy might appear.

If there were those in the Confederate ranks who considered the manœuvres of their leader overbold, their misgivings were soon justified.

A train full of soldiers from Warrenton Junction put back on finding Ewell in possession of Bristoe Station; but a more determined effort was made from the direction of Alexandria. So early as seven o'clock a brigade of infantry, accompanied by a battery, detrained on the north bank of Bull Run, and advanced in battle order against the Junction.[1] The Federals, unaware that the depôt was held in strength, expected to drive before them a few squadrons of cavalry. But when several batteries opened a heavy fire, and heavy columns advanced against their flanks, the men broke in flight towards the bridge. The Confederate infantry followed rapidly, and two Ohio regiments, which had just arrived from the Kanawha Valley, were defeated with heavy loss. Fitzhugh Lee, who had fallen back before the enemy's advance, was then ordered in pursuit. The cars and railway bridge were destroyed; and during the day the brigade followed the fugitives as far as Burke's Station, only twelve miles from Alexandria.

This feeble attack appears to have convinced Jackson that his danger was not pressing. It was evident that the enemy had as yet no idea of his strength. Stuart's cavalry watched every road; Ewell held a strong position on Broad Run, barring the direct approach from Warrenton Junction, and it was determined to give the wearied soldiers the remainder of the day for rest and pillage. It was impossible to carry away even a tithe of the stores, and when an issue of rations had been made, the bakery set working, and the liquor placed under guard, the regiments were let loose on the magazines. Such an opportunity occurs but seldom in the soldier's service, and the hungry Confederates were not the men to let it pass. 'Weak and haggard from their diet of green corn and apples, one can well imagine,' says Gordon, 'with what surprise their eyes opened upon the contents of the sutlers' stores, containing an amount and

---

[1] These troops were sent forward, without cavalry, by order of General Halleck. O. R., vol. xii., part iii., p. 680. The Federal Commander-in-Chief expected that the opposition would be slight. He had evidently no suspicion of the length to which the daring of Lee and Jackson might have carried them.

variety of property such as they had never conceived. Then
came a storming charge of men rushing in a tumultuous
mob over each other's heads, under each other's feet,
anywhere, everywhere, to satisfy a craving stronger
than a yearning for fame.   There were no laggards in
that charge, and there was abundant evidence of the fruits of
victory.   Men ragged and famished clutched tenaciously
at whatever came in their way, whether of clothing or
food, of luxury or necessity.   Here a long yellow-haired,
barefooted son of the South claimed as prizes a tooth-
brush, a box of candles, a barrel of coffee ; while another,
whose butternut homespun hung round him in tatters,
crammed himself with lobster salad, sardines, potted game
and sweetmeats, and washed them down with Rhenish
wine.   Nor was the outer man neglected.   From piles of
new clothing the Southerners arrayed themselves in the
blue uniforms of the Federals.   The naked were clad, the
barefooted were shod, and the sick provided with luxuries
to which they had long been strangers.' [1]

The history of war records many extraordinary scenes,
but there are few more ludicrous than this wild revel at
Manassas.   Even the chagrin of Northern writers gives
way before the spectacle ; and Jackson must have smiled
grimly when he thought of the maxim which Pope had
promulgated with such splendid confidence : ' Let us study
the probable lines of retreat of our opponents, and leave
our own to take care of themselves ! '

It was no time, however, to indulge in reflections on
the irony of fortune.   All through the afternoon, while the
sharp-set Confederates were sweeping away the profits
which the Northern sutlers had wrung from Northern
soldiers, Stuart's vigilant patrols sent in report on report
of the Federal movements.   From Warrenton heavy
columns were hurrying over the great highroad to Gainesville, and from Warrenton Junction a large force of all
arms was marching direct on Bristoe.   There was news,
too, from Lee.   Despite the distance to be covered, and the

[1] *The Army of Virginia*.   General George H. Gordon.

proximity of the enemy, a trooper of the 'Black Horse,' a regiment of young planters which now formed Jackson's escort, disguised as a countryman, made his way back from headquarters, and Jackson learned that Longstreet, who had started the previous evening, was following his own track by Orleans, Salem, and Thoroughfare Gap.[1]   It was evident, then, that the whole Federal army was in motion north-wards, and that Longstreet had crossed the Rappahannock. But Longstreet had many miles to march and Thorough-fare Gap to pass before he could lend assistance ; and the movement of the enemy on Gainesville threatened to intervene between the widely separated wings of the Confederate army.

It was no difficult matter for Jackson to decide on the course to be adopted.   There was but one thing to do, to retreat at once ; and only one line of escape still open, the roads leading north and north-west from Manassas Junction. To remain at Manassas and await Lee's arrival would have been to sacrifice his command.   20,000 men, even with the protection of intrenchments, could hardly hope to hold the whole Federal army at bay for two days ; and it was always possible that Pope, blocking Thoroughfare Gap with a portion of his force, might delay Lee for even longer than two days. Nor did it recommend itself to Jackson as sound strategy to move south, attack the Federal column approaching Bristoe, and driving it from his path to escape past the rear of the column moving to Gainesville.   The exact position of the Federal troops was far from clear.   Large forces might be encountered near the Rappahannock, and part of McClellan's army was known to be marching westward from Aquia Creek.   Moreover, such a movement would have ac-centuated the separation of the Confederate wings, and a local success over a portion of the hostile army would have been but a poor substitute for the decisive victory which Lee hoped to win when his whole force was once more concentrated.

---

[1] 'Up to the night of August 28 we received,' says Longstreet, 'reports from General Jackson at regular intervals, assuring us of his successful operation, and of confidence in his ability to baffle all efforts of the enemy till we should reach him.'—*Battles and Leaders*, vol. ii., p. 517.

About three in the afternoon the thunder of artillery was heard from the direction of Bristoe. Ewell had sent a brigade along the railroad to support some cavalry on reconnaissance, and to destroy a bridge over Kettle Run. Hardly had the latter task been accomplished when a strong column of Federal infantry emerged from the forest and deployed for action. Hooker's division of 5,500 men, belonging to McClellan's army, had joined Pope on the same day that Jackson had crossed the Rappahannock, and had been dispatched northwards from Warrenton Junction as soon as the news came in that Manassas Junction had been captured. Hooker had been instructed to ascertain the strength of the enemy at Manassas, for Pope was still under the impression that the attack on his rear was nothing more than a repetition of the raid on Catlett's Station. Striking the Confederate outposts at Kettle Run, he deployed his troops in three lines and pushed briskly forward. The batteries on both sides opened, and after a hot skirmish of an hour's duration Ewell, who had orders not to risk an engagement with superior forces, found that his flanks were threatened. In accordance with his instructions he directed his three brigades to retire in succession across Broad Run. This difficult manœuvre was accomplished with trifling loss, and Hooker, ascertaining that Jackson's whole corps, estimated at 30,000 men, was near at hand, advanced no further than the stream. Ewell fell back slowly to the Junction; and shortly after midnight the three Confederate divisions had disappeared into the darkness. The torch had already been set to the captured stores; warehouses, trains, camps, and hospitals were burning fiercely, and the dark figures of Stuart's troopers, still urging on the work, passed to and fro amid the flames. Of the value of property destroyed it is difficult to arrive at an estimate. Jackson, in his official report, enumerates the various items with an unction which he must have inherited from some moss-trooping ancestor. Yet the actual quantity mattered little, for the stores could be readily replaced. But the effect of their destruction on the Federal operations was for the time being overwhelming. And of this destruction Pope himself was a witness. The fight with Ewell had just ceased, and the troops were going into bivouac, when the Commander-in-Chief, anxious to ascertain with his own eyes the extent of the danger to which he was exposed, reached Bristoe Station. There, while the explosion of the piles of shells resembled the noise of a great battle, from the ridge above Broad Run he saw the sky to the north-east lurid with the blaze of a vast conflagration ; and there he learned for the first time that it was no mere raid of cavalry, but Stonewall Jackson, with his whole army corps, who stood between himself and Washington.

For the best part of three days the Union general had been completely mystified. Jackson had left Jefferson on the 25th. But although his march had been seen by the Federal signallers on the hills near Waterloo Bridge,[1] and the exact strength of his force had been reported, his destination had been unsuspected. When the column was last seen it was moving northward from Orleans, but the darkness had covered it, and the measure of prolonging the march to midnight bore good fruit. For the best part of two days Jackson had vanished from his enemy's view, to be found by Pope himself at Manassas Junction.[2] Nevertheless, although working in the dark, the Federal commander, up to the moment he reached Bristoe Station, had acted with sound judgment. He had inferred from the reports of his signalmen that Jackson was marching to Front Royal on the Shenandoah ; but in order to clear up the situation, on the 26th Sigel and McDowell were ordered to force the passage of the Rappahannock at Waterloo Bridge and the Sulphur Springs, and obtain information of the enemy's movements. Reno, at the same time, was to

---

[1] Five messages were sent in between 8.45 A.M. and 11 A.M., but evidently reached headquarters much later. O. R., vol. xii., part iii., pp. 654–5.

[2] There is a curious undated report on page 671, O. R., vol. xii., part iii., from Colonel Duffie, a French officer in the Federal service, which speaks of a column passing through Thoroughfare Gap ; but, although the compilers of the Records have placed it under the date August 26, it seems evident, as this officer (see p. 670) was at Rappahannock Station on the 26th and 27th (O. R., vol. xii., part. iii., p. 688), that the report refers to Longstreet's and not Jackson's troops, and was written on August 28.

cross below the railway bridge and make for Culpeper. The manœuvres, however, were not carried out as contemplated. Only McDowell advanced; and as Lee had replaced Longstreet, who marched to Orleans the same afternoon, by Anderson, but little was discovered.

It was evident, however, that the Confederates were trending steadily northwards, and on the night of the 26th Pope ordered his 80,000 Federals to concentrate in the neighbourhood of Warrenton. Reports had come in that hostile troops had passed through Salem, White Plains, and Thoroughfare Gap.[1] But it seemed improbable, both to Pope and McDowell, the second in command, that more was meant by this than a flank attack on Warrenton. McDowell expressed his opinion that a movement round the right wing in the direction of Alexandria was far too hazardous for the enemy to attempt. Pope appears to have acquiesced, and a line of battle near Warrenton, with a strong reserve at Greenwich, to the right rear, was then decided on. Franklin's army corps from the Peninsula, instead of proceeding to Aquia Creek, was disembarking at Alexandria, and Halleck had been requested to push these 10,000 men forward with all speed to Gainesville. The Kanawha regiments had also reached Washington, and Pope was under the impression that these too would be sent to join him. He had therefore but little apprehension for his rear. The one error of judgment into which both Pope and McDowell had been betrayed was in not giving Lee due credit for audacity or Jackson for energy. That Lee would dare to divide his army they had never conceived; that Jackson would march fifty miles in two days and place his single corps astride their communications was an idea which had they thought of they would have instantly dismissed. Like the Austrian generals when they first confronted Napoleon, they might well have complained that their enemy broke every rule of the military art; and like all generals who believe that war is a mere matter of precedent, they found themselves egregiously deceived.

[1] O. R., vol. xii., part iii., p. 672. Pope to Porter, p. 675. Pope to Halleck, p. 684.

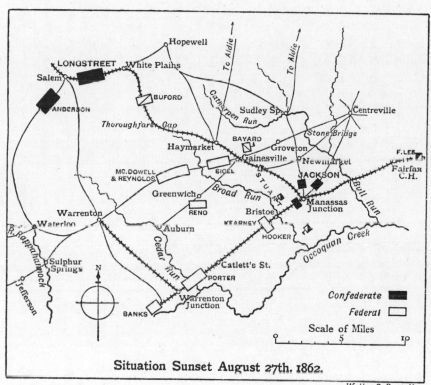

Hopewell

LONGSTREET   White Plains

Salem

ANDERSON

To Aldie   To Aldie

BUFORD

Catharpen Run

Sudley Sp.

Centreville

Thoroughfare Gap

BAYARD

Stone Bridge

Haymarket   Groveton

Gainesville

Newmarket

F. LEE

Fairfax C.H.

MC. DOWELL & REYNOLDS

SIGEL

STUART

JACKSON

Greenwich

RENO

Broad Run

Manassas Junction

Bristoe

Bull Run

Warrenton

Waterloo

KEARNEY

Cedar Run

Auburn

HOOKER

Occoquan Creek

R. Rappahannock

Sulphur Springs

Jefferson

N

Catlett's St.

PORTER

Warrenton Junction

BANKS

Confederate ▮

Federal ▯

Scale of Miles

0   5   10

Situation Sunset August 27th, 1862.

Walker & Boutall sc.

The capture of Manassas, to use Pope's own words, rendered his position at Warrenton no longer tenable, and early on the 27th, the army, instead of concentrating on Warrenton, was ordered to move to Gainesville (from Gainesville it was easy to block Thoroughfare Gap); Buford's cavalry brigade was thrown out towards White Plains to observe Longstreet, and Hooker was dispatched to clear up the situation at Manassas. This move, which was completed before nightfall, could hardly have been improved upon. The whole Federal army was now established on the direct line of communication between Jackson and Lee, and although Jackson might still escape, the Confederates had as yet gained no advantage beyond the destruction of Pope's supplies. It seemed impossible that the two wings could combine east of the Bull Run Mountains. But on the evening of the 27th, after the conclusion of the engagement at Bristoe Station, Pope lost his head. The view he now took of the situation was absolutely erroneous. Ewell's retreat before Hooker he interpreted as an easy victory, which fully compensated for the loss of his magazines. He imagined that Jackson had been surprised, and that no other course was open to him than to take refuge in the intrenchments of Manassas Junction and await Lee's arrival. Orders were at once issued for a manœuvre which should ensure the defeat of the presumptuous foe. The Federal army corps, marching in three columns, were called up to Manassas, a movement which would leave Thoroughfare Gap unguarded save by Buford's cavalry. Some were to move at midnight, others ' at the very earliest blush of dawn.' 'We shall bag the whole crowd, if they are prompt and expeditious,'[1] said Pope, with a sad lapse from the poetical phraseology he had just employed.

And so, on the morning of the 28th, a Federal army once more set out with the expectation of surrounding Jackson, to find once more that the task was beyond their powers.

Aug. 28.

The march was slow. Pope made no movement from

[1] O. R. vol. xii., part ii., p. 72.

Bristoe Station until Hooker had been reinforced by
Kearney and Reno; McDowell, before he turned east
from Gainesville, was delayed by Sigel's trains, which
crossed his line of march, and it was not till noon that
Hooker's advanced-guard halted amid the still smouldering
ruins on the Manassas plateau. The march had been
undisturbed. The redoubts were untenanted. The woods
to the north were silent. A few grey-coated vedettes
watched the operations from far-distant ridges; a few
stragglers, overcome perhaps by their Gargantuan meal of
the previous evening, were picked up in the copses, but
Jackson's divisions had vanished from the earth.

Then came order and counterorder. Pope was completely bewildered. By four o'clock, however, the news
arrived that the railway at Burke's Station, within twelve
miles of Alexandria, had been cut, and that the enemy was
in force between that point and Centreville. On Centreville, therefore, the whole army was now directed; Hooker,
Kearney, and Reno, forming the right wing, marched by
Blackburn's Ford, and were to be followed by Porter and
Banks; Sigel and Reynolds, forming the centre, took the
road by New Market and the Stone Bridge; McDowell
(King's and Ricketts' divisions), forming the left, was to
pass through Gainesville and Groveton. But when the right
wing reached Centreville, Pope was still at fault. There
were traces of a marching column, but some small patrols
of cavalry, who retreated leisurely before the Federal
advance, were the sole evidence of the enemy's existence.
Night was at hand, and as the divisions he accompanied
were directed to their bivouacs, Pope sought in vain for the
enemy he had believed so easy a prey.

Before his troops halted the knowledge came to him.
Far away to the south-west, where the great Groveton valley,
backed by the wooded mountains, lay green and beautiful,
rose the dull booming of cannon, swelling to a continuous
roar; and as the weary soldiers, climbing the slopes near
Centreville, looked eagerly in the direction of the sound, the
rolling smoke of a fierce battle was distinctly visible above the
woods which bordered the Warrenton-Alexandria highway.

Across Bull Run, in the neighbourhood of Groveton, and still further westward, where the cleft in the blue hills marked Thoroughfare Gap, was seen the flash of distant guns. McDowell, marching northwards through Gainesville, had evidently come into collision with the enemy. Jackson was run to earth at last; and it was now clear that while Pope had been moving northwards on Centreville, the Confederates had been moving westward, and that they were once more within reach of Lee. But by what means, Pope might well have asked, had a whole army corps, with its batteries and waggons, passed through the cordon which he had planned to throw around it, and passed through as if gifted with the secret of invisibility?

The explanation was simple. While his enemies were watching the midnight glare above Manassas, Jackson was moving north by three roads; and before morning broke A. P. Hill was near Centreville, Ewell had crossed Bull Run by Blackburn's Ford, and Taliaferro was north of Bald Hill, with a brigade at Groveton, while Stuart's squadrons formed a screen to front and flank. Then, as the Federals slowly converged on Manassas, Hill and Ewell, marching unobserved along the north bank of Bull Run, crossed the Stone Bridge; Taliaferro joined them, and before Pope had found that his enemy had left the Junction, the Confederates were in bivouac north of Groveton, hidden in the woods, and recovering from the fatigue of their long night march.[1]

Jackson's arrangements for deceiving his enemy, for concealing his line of retreat, and for drawing Pope northward on Centreville, had been carefully thought out. The march from Manassas was no hasty movement to the rear. Taliaferro, as soon as darkness fell, had moved by New Market on Bald Hill. At 1 A.M. Ewell followed Hill to Blackburn's Ford; but instead of continuing the march on Centreville, had crossed Bull Run, and moving up stream, had joined Taliaferro by way of the Stone Bridge. Hill, leaving Centreville at 10 A.M.,

[1] A. P. Hill had marched fourteen miles, Ewell fifteen, and Taliaferro, with whom were the trains, from eight to ten.

marched to the same rendezvous. Thus, while the attention of the enemy was attracted to Centreville, Jackson's
divisions were concentrated in the woods beyond Bull
Run, some five or six miles west. The position in
which his troops were resting had been skilfully selected.
South of Sudley Springs, and north of the Warrenton
turnpike, it was within twelve miles of Thoroughfare
Gap, and a line of retreat, in case of emergency,
as well as a line by which Lee could join him, should
Thoroughfare Gap be blocked, ran to Aldie Gap, the
northern pass of the Bull Run Mountains. Established
on his enemy's flank, he could avoid the full shock of his
force should Lee be delayed, or he could strike effectively
himself; and it was to retain the power of striking that
he had not moved further northward, and secured his front
by camping beyond Catharpen Run. It was essential that
he should be prepared for offensive action. The object with
which he had marched upon Manassas had only been half
accomplished. Pope had been compelled to abandon the
strong line of the Rappahannock, but he had not yet been
defeated; and if he were not defeated, he would combine
with McClellan, and advance in a few days in overwhelming
force. Lee looked for a battle with Pope before he could
be reinforced, and to achieve this end it was necessary that
the Federal commander should be prevented from retreating further; that Jackson should hold him by the
throat until Lee should come up to administer the *coup
de grâce*.

It was with this purpose in his mind that Jackson
had taken post near Groveton, and he was now awaiting
the information that should tell him the time had come to
strike. But, as already related, the march of the Federals
on Manassas was slow and toilsome. It was not till
the morning was well on that the brigade of Taliaferro's
division near Groveton, commanded by Colonel Bradley
Johnson, was warned by the cavalry that the enemy was
moving through Gainesville in great strength. A skirmish
took place a mile or two north of that village, and Johnson,
finding himself menaced by far superior numbers, fell back

to the wood near the Douglass House. He was not followed. The Union generals, Sigel and Reynolds, who had been ordered to Manassas to ' bag' Jackson, had received no word of his departure from the Junction; and believing that Johnson's small force was composed only of cavalry, they resumed the march which had been temporarily interrupted.

The situation, however, was no clearer to the Confederates. The enemy had disappeared in the great woods south-west of Groveton, and heavy columns were still reported coming up from Gainesville. During the afternoon, however, the cavalry captured a Federal courier, carrying McDowell's orders for the movement of the left and centre, which had been placed under his command, to Manassas Junction,[1] and this important document was immediately forwarded to Jackson.

' Johnson's messenger,' says General Taliaferro, ' found the Confederate headquarters established on the shady side of an old-fashioned worm-fence, in the corner of which General Jackson and his division commanders were profoundly sleeping after the fatigues of the preceding night, notwithstanding the intense heat of the August day. There was not so much as an ambulance at headquarters. The headquarters' train was back beyond the Rappahannock, at Jefferson, with remounts, camp equipage, and all the arrangements for cooking and serving food. All the property of the general, the staff, and the headquarters' bureau was strapped to the pommels and cantels of the saddles, and these formed the pillows of their weary owners. The captured dispatch roused Jackson like an electric shock. He was essentially a man of action. He rarely, if ever, hesitated. He never asked advice. He called no council to discuss the situation disclosed by this

[1] The order, dated 2 A.M., August 28, was to the following effect:—

' 1. Sigel's Corps to march from Gainesville to Manassas Junction, the right resting on the Manassas railroad.

' 2. Reynolds to follow Sigel.

' 3. King to follow Reynolds.

' 4. Ricketts to follow King; but to halt at Thoroughfare Gap if the enemy threatened the pass.'

King was afterwards, while on the march, directed to Centreville by the Warrenton-Alexandria road.

communication, although his ranking officers were almost at his side. He asked no conference of opinion. He made no suggestion, but simply, without a word, except to repeat the language of the message, turned to me and said: "Move your division and attack the enemy;" and to Ewell, "Support the attack." The slumbering soldiers sprang from the earth at the first murmur. They were sleeping almost in ranks; and by the time the horses of their officers were saddled, the long lines of infantry were moving to the anticipated battle-field.

'The two divisions, after marching some distance to the north of the turnpike, were halted and rested, and the prospect of an engagement on that afternoon seemed to disappear with the lengthening shadows. The enemy did not come. The Warrenton turnpike, along which it was supposed he would march, was in view, but it was as free from Federal soldiery as it had been two days before, when Jackson's men had streamed along its highway.' [1]

Jackson, however, was better informed than his subordinate. Troops were still moving through Gainesville, and, instead of turning off to Manassas, were marching up the turnpike on which so many eyes were turned from the neighbouring woods. King's division, while on the march to Manassas, had been instructed to countermarch and make for Centreville, by Groveton and the Stone Bridge. Ricketts, who had been ordered by McDowell to hold Thoroughfare Gap, was already engaged with Longstreet's advanced-guard, and of this Jackson was aware; for Stuart, in position at Haymarket, three miles north of Gainesville, had been skirmishing all day with the enemy's cavalry, and had been in full view of the conflict at the Gap.[2]

Jackson, however, knew not that one division was all that was before him. The Federal movements had covered

---

[1] *Battles and Leaders*, vol. ii., pp. 507, 508.

[2] Longstreet had been unable to march with the same speed as Jackson. Leaving Jefferson on the afternoon of August 26, he did not reach Thoroughfare Gap until 'just before night' on August 28. He had been delayed for an hour at White Plains by the Federal cavalry, and the trains of the army, such as they were, may also have retarded him. In two days he covered only thirty miles.

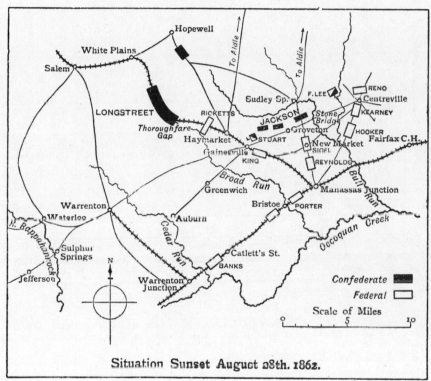

Hopewell

White Plains

Salem

To Aldie

To Aldie

Sudley Sp.

F. LEE

RENO

Centreville

LONGSTREET

RICKETTS

JACKSON

Stone Bridge

KEARNEY

Thoroughfare Gap

Groveton

Haymarket

STUART

HOOKER

Fairfax C.H.

Gainesville

New Market

SIGEL

KING

REYNOLDS

Broad Run

Greenwich

Manassas Junction

Bull Run

Warrenton

Waterloo

Bristoe

PORTER

Occoquan Creek

R. Rappahannock

Auburn

Cedar Run

Sulphur Springs

N

Catlett's St.

BANKS

Jefferson

Warrenton Junction

Confederate

Federal

Scale of Miles

0   5   10

Situation Sunset August 28th. 1862.

Walker & Boutall sc.

so wide an extent of country, and had been so well concealed by the forests, that it was hardly possible for Stuart's patrols, enterprising as they were, to obtain accurate information. Unaccustomed to such disjointed marches as were now in progress across his front, Jackson believed that King's column was the flank-guard of McDowell's army corps. But, although he had been compelled to leave Hill near the Stone Bridge, in order to protect his line of retreat on Aldie, he had still determined to attack. The main idea which absorbed his thoughts is clear enough. The Federal army, instead of moving direct from Warrenton on Alexandria, as he had anticipated, had apparently taken the more circuitous route by Manassas, and if Pope was to be fought in the open field before he could be reinforced by McClellan, he must be induced to retrace his steps. To do this, the surest means was a resolute attack on King's division, despite the probability that it might be strongly reinforced ; and it is by no means unlikely that Jackson deferred his attack until near sunset in order that, if confronted by superior numbers, he might still be able to hold on till nightfall, and obtain time for Longstreet to come up.

Within the wood due north of the Dogan House, through which ran an unfinished railroad, Ewell's and Taliaferro's divisions, awaiting the propitious moment for attack, were drawn up in order of battle. Eight brigades, and three small batteries, which had been brought across country with great difficulty, were present, and the remainder of the artillery was not far distant.[1] Taliaferro, on the right, had two brigades (A. G. Taliaferro's and the Stonewall) in first line ; Starke was in second line, and Bradley Johnson near Groveton village. Ewell, on the left, had placed Lawton and Trimble in front, while Early and Forno formed a general reserve. This force numbered in all about 8,000 men, and even the skirmishers, thrown out well to the front, were concealed by the undulations of the ground.

---

[1] Twenty pieces had been ordered to the front soon after the infantry moved forward. The dense woods, however, proved impenetrable to all but three horse-artillery guns, and one of these was unable to keep up.

The Federal division commanded by General King, although unprovided with cavalry and quite unsupported, was no unworthy enemy. It was composed of four brigades of infantry, led by excellent officers, and accompanied by four batteries. The total strength was 10,000 men. The absence of horsemen, however, placed the Northerners at a disadvantage from the outset.

The leading brigade was within a mile of Groveton, a hamlet of a few houses at the foot of a long descent, and the advanced-guard, deployed as skirmishers, was searching the woods in front. On the road in rear, with the batteries between the columns, came the three remaining brigades— Gibbon's, Doubleday's, and Patrick's—in the order named.

The wood in which the Confederates were drawn up was near a mile from the highway, on a commanding ridge, overlooking a broad expanse of open ground, which fell gently in successive undulations to the road. The Federals were marching in absolute unconsciousness that the enemy, whom the last reports had placed at Manassas, far away to the right, was close at hand. No flank-guards had been thrown out. General King was at Gainesville, sick, and a regimental band had just struck up a merry quickstep. On the open fields to the left, bathed in sunshine, there was not a sign of life. The whitewashed cottages, surrounded by green orchards, which stood upon the slopes, were lonely and untenanted, and on the edge of the distant wood, still and drooping in the heat, was neither stir nor motion. The troops trudged steadily forward through the dust; regiment after regiment disappeared in the deep copse which stands west of Groveton, and far to the rear the road was still crowded with men and guns. Jackson's time had come.

Two Confederate batteries, trotting forward from the wood, deployed upon the ridge. The range was soon found, and the effect was instantaneous. But the confusion in the Northern ranks was soon checked; the troops found cover inside the bank which lined the road, and two batteries, one with the advanced-guard and one from the centre of the column, wheeling into the fields to the left, came quickly into action. About the same moment Bradley Johnson became engaged with the skirmishers near Groveton.

The Confederate infantry, still hidden by the rolling ground, was forming for attack, when a Federal brigade, led by General Gibbon, rapidly deploying on the slopes, moved forward against the guns. It was Stuart's horse-artillery, so the Northerners believed, which had fired on the column, and a bold attack would soon drive back the cavalry. But as Gibbon's regiments came forward the Southern skirmishers, lying in front of the batteries, sprang to their feet and opened with rapid volleys; and then the grey line of battle, rising suddenly into view, bore down upon the astonished foe. Taliaferro, on the right, seized a small farmhouse near Gainesville, and occupied the orchard; the Stonewall Brigade advanced upon his left, and Lawton and Trimble prolonged the front towards the Douglass House. But the Western farmers of Gibbon's brigade were made of stubborn stuff. The Wisconsin regiments held their ground with unflinching courage. Both flanks were protected by artillery, and strong reinforcements were coming up. The advanced-guard was gradually falling back from Groveton; the rear brigades were hurrying forward up the road. The two Confederate batteries, over-powered by superior metal, had been compelled to shift position; only a section of Stuart's horse-artillery under Captain Pelham had come to their assistance, and the battle was confined to a frontal attack at the closest range. In many places the lines approached within a hundred yards, the men standing in the open and blazing fiercely in each other's faces. Here and there, as fresh regiments came up on either side, the grey or the blue gave way for a few short paces; but the gaps were quickly filled, and the wave once more surged forward over the piles of dead. Men fell like leaves in autumn. Ewell was struck down, and Taliaferro, and many of their field officers, and still the Federals held their ground. Night was settling on the field, and although the gallant Pelham, the boy soldier, brought a gun into action within seventy paces of Gibbon's line, yet

the front of fire, flashing redly through the gloom, neither
receded nor advanced.   A flank attack on either side would
have turned the scale, but the fight was destined to end as
it had begun.   The Federal commander, ignorant of the
enemy's strength, and reaching the field when the fight
was hottest, was reluctant to engage his last reserves.
Jackson had ordered Early and Forno, moving through
the wood west of the Douglass House, to turn the enemy's
right; but within the thickets ran the deep cuttings and
high embankments of the unfinished railroad; and the
regiments, bewildered in the darkness, were unable to
advance.   Meanwhile the fight to the front had gradually
died away.   The Federals, outflanked upon the left, and
far outnumbered, had slowly retreated to the road.   The
Confederates had been too roughly handled to pursue.

The reports of the engagement at Groveton are singularly meagre.   Preceded and followed by events of still
greater moment, it never attracted the attention it deserved.
On the side of the Union 2,800 men were engaged, on the
side of the Southerners 4,500, and for more than an hour
and a half the lines of infantry were engaged at the
very closest quarters.   The rifled guns of the Federals undoubtedly gave them a marked advantage.   But the men
who faced each other that August evening fought with a
gallantry that has seldom been surpassed.   The Federals,
surprised and unsupported, bore away the honours.   The
Western brigade, commanded by General Gibbon, displayed
a coolness and a steadfastness worthy of the soldiers
of Albuera.   Out of 2,000 men the four Wisconsin and
Indiana regiments lost 750, and were still unconquered.
The three regiments which supported them, although it was
their first battle, lost nearly half their number, and the
casualties must have reached a total of 1,100.   The Confederate losses were even greater.   Ewell, who was shot
down in the first line, and lay long on the field, lost 725
out of 3,000.   The Stonewall Brigade, which had by this time
dwindled to 600 muskets, lost over 200, including five field
officers; the 21st Georgia, of Trimble's brigade, 173
men out of 242; and it is probable that the Valley army on

this day was diminished by more than 1,200 stout soldiers. The fall of Ewell was a terrible disaster. Zealous and indefatigable, a stern fighter and beloved by his men, he was the most able and the most loyal of Jackson's generals. Taliaferro, peculiarly acceptable to his Virginia regiments as a Virginian himself, had risen from the rank of colonel to the command of a division, and his spurs had been well won. The battle of Groveton left gaps in Jackson's ranks which it was hard to fill, and although the men might well feel proud of their stubborn fight, they could hardly boast of a brilliant victory.

Strategically, however, the engagement was decisive. Jackson had brought on the fight with the view of drawing the whole Federal army on himself, and he was completely successful. The centre, marching on the Stone Bridge from Manassas Junction, heard the thunder of the cannon and turned westward; and before nightfall A. P. Hill's artillery became engaged with Sigel's advanced-guard. Pope himself, who received the intelligence of the engagement at 9.20 P.M., immediately issued orders for an attack on Jackson the next morning, in which the troops who had already reached Centreville were to take part. 'McDowell,' ran the order, 'has intercepted the retreat of the enemy, Sigel is immediately in his front, and I see no possibility of his escape.'

But Pope, full of the idea that Jackson had been stopped in attempting to retreat through Thoroughfare Gap, altogether misunderstood the situation. He was badly informed. He did not know even the position of his own troops. His divisions, scattered over a wide extent of country, harassed by Stuart's cavalry, and ignorant of the topography, had lost all touch with the Commander-in-Chief. Important dispatches had been captured. Messages and orders were slow in arriving, if they arrived at all. Even the generals were at a loss to find either the Commander-in-Chief or the right road. McDowell had ridden from Gainesville to Manassas in order to consult with Pope, but Pope had gone to Centreville. McDowell thereupon set out to rejoin his troops, but lost his way in the forest and went back to Manassas. From Ricketts Pope received no information whatever.[1] He was not aware that after a long skirmish at Thoroughfare Gap, Longstreet had opened the pass by sending his brigades over the mountains on either hand, threatening both flanks of the Federals, and compelling them to retire. He was not aware that King's division, so far from intercepting Jackson's retreat, had abandoned the field of Groveton at 1 A.M., and, finding its position untenable in face of superior numbers, had fallen back on Manassas; or that Ricketts, who had by this time reached Gainesville, had in consequence continued his retreat in the same direction.

Seldom have the baneful effects of dispersion been more strikingly illustrated, and the difficulty, under such circumstances, of keeping the troops in the hand of the Commander-in-Chief. On the morning of the 28th Pope had ordered his army to march in three columns on Manassas, one column starting from Warrenton Junction, one from Greenwich, and one from Buckland Mills, the roads which they were to follow being at their furthest point no more than seven miles apart. And yet at dawn on the 29th he was absolutely ignorant of the whereabouts of McDowell's army corps; he was but vaguely informed of what had happened during the day; and while part of his army was at Bald Hill, another part was at Centreville, seven miles north-east, and a third at Manassas and at Bristoe, from seven to twelve miles south-east. Nor could the staff be held to blame for the absence of communication between the columns. In peace it is an easy matter to assume that a message sent to a destination seven miles distant by a high-road or even country lanes arrives in good time. Seven miles in peace are very short. In war, in the neigh-bourhood of the enemy, they are very long. In peace, roads are easy to find. In war, it is the exception that they are found, even when messengers are provided with good maps

---

[1] Ricketts' report would have been transmitted through McDowell, under whose command he was, and as McDowell was not to be found, it naturally went astray.

and the country is thickly populated; and it is from war that the soldier's trade is to be learned.

Jackson's army corps bivouacked in the position they had held when the fierce musketry of Groveton died away. It was not till long after daybreak on the 29th that his cavalry patrols discovered that King's troops had disappeared, and that Longstreet's advanced-guard was already through Thoroughfare Gap. Nor was it till the sun was high that Lee learned the events of the previous evening, and these threw only a faint light on the general situation. But had either the Commander-in-Chief or his lieutenant, on the night of the 28th, known the true state of affairs, they would have had reason to congratulate themselves on the success of the plan which had been hatched on the Rappahannock. They had anticipated that should Jackson's movement on Manassas prove successful, Pope would not only fall back, but that he would fall back in all the confusion which arises from a hastily conceived plan and hastily executed manœuvres. They had expected that in his hurried retreat his army corps would lose touch and cohesion; that divisions would become isolated; that the care of his *impedimenta*, suddenly turned in a new direction, would embarrass every movement; and that the general himself would become demoralised.

The orders and counterorders, the marches and counter-marches of August 28, and the consequent dispersion of the Federal army, are sufficient in themselves to prove the deep insight into war possessed by the Confederate leaders.

Nevertheless, the risk bred of separation which, in order to achieve great results, they had deliberately accepted had not yet passed away. Longstreet had indeed cleared the pass, and the Federals who guarded it had retreated; but the main body of the Confederate army had still twelve miles to march before it could reach Jackson, and Jackson was confronted by superior numbers. On the plateau of Bull Run, little more than two miles from the field of Groveton, were encamped over 20,000 Federals, with the same number at Manassas. At Centreville, a seven miles' march, were 18,000; and at Bristoe Station, about the same distance, 11,000.

M 2

It was thus possible for Pope to hurl a superior force against Jackson before Lee could intervene ; and although it would have been sounder strategy, on the part of the Federal commander, to have concentrated towards Centreville, and have there awaited reinforcements, now fast coming up, he had some reason for believing that he might still, unaided, deal with the enemy in detail. The high virtue of patience was not his. Ambition, anxiety to retrieve his reputation, already blemished by his enforced retreat, the thought that he might be superseded by McClellan, whose operations in the Peninsula he had contemptuously criticised, all urged him forward. An unsuccessful general who feels instinctively that his command is slipping from him, and who sees in victory the only hope of retaining it, seldom listens to the voice of prudence.

So on the morning of the 29th Jackson had to do with an enemy who had resolved to overwhelm him by weight of numbers. Nor could he expect immediate help. The Federal cavalry still stood between Stuart and Thoroughfare Gap, and not only was Jackson unaware that Longstreet had broken through, but he was unaware whether he *could* break through. In any case, it would be several hours before he could receive support, and for that space of time his three divisions, worn with long marching and the fierce fight of the previous evening, would have to hold their own unaided. The outlook, to all appearance, was anything but bright. But on the opposite hills, where the Federals were now forming in line of battle, the Valley soldiers had already given proof of their stubborn qualities on the defensive. The sight of their baptismal battle-field and the memories of Bull Run must have gone far to nerve the hearts of the Stonewall regiments, and in preparing once more to justify their proud title the troops were aided by their leader's quick eye for a position. While it was still dark the divisions which had been engaged at Groveton took ground to their left, and passing north of the hamlet, deployed on the right of A. P. Hill. The long, flat-topped ridge, covered with scattered copses and rough undergrowth, which stands north of the War-

Aug. 29.

renton-Centreville road, commands the approaches from the south and east, and some five hundred yards below the crest ran the unfinished railroad.

Behind the deep cuttings and high embankments the Confederate fighting-line was strongly placed. The left, slightly thrown back, rested on a rocky spur near Bull Run, commanding Sudley Springs Ford and the road to Aldie Gap. The front extended for a mile and three-quarters south-west. Early, with two brigades and a battery, occupied a wooded knoll where the unfinished railroad crosses the highroad, protecting the right rear, and stretching a hand to Longstreet.

The infantry and artillery were thus disposed :—

Infantry.

Left.—A. P. Hill's Division. First and Second line : Three brigades. (Field, Thomas, Gregg.) Third line : Three brigades. (Branch, Pender, Archer.)

Centre.—Two brigades of Ewell's Division (now commanded by Lawton). (Trimble's and Lawton's.)

Right.—Taliaferro's Division (now commanded by Starke). First and Second line : Two brigades. Third line : Two brigades.

Force detached on the right : Two brigades of Ewell's Division (Early and Forno), and one battery.

Artillery.

16 guns behind the left,   } On the ridge, five hundred yards
24 guns behind the right centre, }   in rear of the fighting-line.

The flanks were secured by Stuart. A portion of the cavalry was placed at Haymarket to communicate as soon as possible with Longstreet. A regiment was pushed out towards Manassas, and on the left bank of Bull Run Fitzhugh Lee's brigade watched the approaches from Centreville and the north. Jackson's strength, deducting the losses of the previous day, and the numerous stragglers left behind during his forced marches, can hardly have exceeded 18,000 muskets, supported by 40 guns, all that there was room for, and some 2,500 cavalry. These numbers, however, were ample for the defence of the position which had been selected. Excluding the detached force on the extreme right, the line occupied was three thousand yards in length, and to every yard of this line there were more than five muskets, so that half the force could be retained in third line or reserve. The position was thus strongly held and strong by nature. The embankments formed stout parapets, the cuttings deep ditches.

Before the right and the right centre the green pastures, shorn for thirteen hundred yards of all obstacles save a few solitary cottages, sloped almost imperceptibly to the brook which is called Young's Branch. The left centre and left, however, were shut in by a belt of timber, from four hundred to six hundred yards in width, which we may call the Groveton wood. This belt closed in upon, and at one point crossed, the railroad, and, as regards the field of fire, it was the weakest point. In another respect, however, it was the strongest, for the defenders were screened by the trees from the enemy's artillery. The rocky hill on the left, facing north-east, was a point of vantage, for an open corn-field lay between it and Bull Run. Within the position, behind the copses and undulations, there was ample cover for all troops not employed on the fighting-line; and from the ridge in rear the general could view the field from commanding ground.

Shortly after 5 A.M., while the Confederates were still taking up their positions, the Federal columns were seen 5.15 A.M. moving down the heights near the Henry House. Jackson had ridden round his lines, and ordering Early to throw forward two regiments east of the turnpike, had then moved to the great battery forming in rear of his right centre. His orders had already been issued. The troops were merely to hold their ground, no general counterstroke was intended, and the divisional commanders were to confine themselves to repulsing the attack. The time for a strong offensive return had not yet come.

The enemy advanced slowly in imposing masses. Shortly after seven o'clock, hidden to some extent by the woods, four divisions of infantry deployed in several lines at the foot of the Henry Hill, and their skirmishers became engaged with the Confederate pickets. At the same moment three batteries came into action on a rise north-east of Groveton, opposite the Confederate centre, and Sigel, supported by Reynolds, prepared to carry out his instructions, and hold Jackson until the remainder of Pope's army should arrive upon the field. At the end of July, Sigel's army corps had numbered 13,000 men. Allowing for stragglers and for casualties on the Rappahannock, where it had been several times engaged, it must still have mustered 11,000. It was accompanied by ten batteries, and Reynolds' division was composed of 8,000 infantry and four batteries. The attack was thus no stronger than the defence, and as the Federal artillery positions were restricted by the woods, there could be little doubt of the result. In other respects, moreover, the combatants were not evenly matched. Reynolds' Pennsylvanians were fine troops, already seasoned in the battles on the Peninsula, and commanded by such officers as Meade and Seymour. But Sigel, who had been an officer in the Baden army, had succeeded Frémont, and his corps was composed of those same Germans whom Ewell had used so hardly at Cross Keys. Many of them were old soldiers, who had borne arms in Europe; but the stern discipline and trained officers of conscript armies were lacking in America, and the Confederate volunteers had little respect for these foreign levies. Nor were Sigel's dispositions a brilliant example of offensive tactics. His three divisions, Schurz', Schenck's, and Steinwehr's, supported by Milroy's independent brigade, advanced to the attack along a wide front. Schurz, with two brigades, moving into the Groveton wood, assailed the Confederate left, while Milroy and Schenck advanced over the open meadows which lay in front of the right. Steinwehr was in reserve, and Reynolds, somewhat to the rear, moved forward on the extreme left. The line was more than two miles long; the artillery, hampered by the ground, could render but small assistance; and at no single point were the troops disposed in sufficient depth to break through the front of the defence. The attack, too, was piecemeal. Advancing through the wood, Schurz' division was at once met by a sharp counterstroke, delivered by the left brigade (Gregg's South Carolina) of A. P. Hill's division, which drove the two Federal brigades apart. Reinforcements were sent in by Milroy, who had been checked on the open ground by the heavy fire of Jackson's guns, and the Germans rallied; but, after some hard fighting, a fresh counterstroke, in which Thomas' brigade took part, drove them in disorder from the wood; and the South Carolinians, following to the edge, poured heavy volleys into their retreating masses. Schenck, meanwhile, deterred by the batteries on Jackson's right, had remained inactive; the Federal artillery, such as had been brought into action, had produced no effect; Reynolds, who had a difficult march, had not yet come into action; and in order to support the broken troops Schenck was now ordered to close in upon the right. But the opportunity had already passed.

It was now 10.30 A.M., and Jackson had long since learned that Lee was near at hand. Longstreet's advanced-guard had passed through Gainesville, and the main body 10.15 A.M. was closing up. Not only had time been gained, but two brigades alone had proved sufficient to hold the enemy at arm's length, and the rough counter-strokes had disconcerted the order of attack. A fresh Federal force, however, was already approaching. The troops from Centreville, comprising the divisions of Hooker, Kearney, and Reno, 17,000 or 18,000 men, were hurrying over the Stone Bridge; and a second and more vigorous attack was now to be withstood. Sigel, too, was still capable of further effort. Bringing up Steinwehr's division, and demanding reinforcements from Reno, he threw his whole force against the Confederate front. Schenck, however, still exposed to the fire of the massed artillery, was unable to advance, and Milroy in the centre was hurled back. But through the wood the attack was vigorously pressed, and the fight raged fiercely at close quarters along the railway. Between Gregg's and Thomas' brigades a gap of over a hundred yards, as the men closed in upon the centre, had gradually opened. Opposite the gap was a deep cutting, and the Federals, covered by the wood, massed here unobserved in heavy force. Attack from this quarter was unexpected, and for a moment Hill's first line was in jeopardy. Gregg, however, had still a regiment in second line, and throwing it quickly forward he drove the enemy across the railroad. Then Hill, bringing up Branch from the third line, sent this fresh brigade to Gregg's support, and cleared the front.

The Germans had now been finally disposed of. But although Longstreet had arrived upon the ground, and was deploying in the woods on Jackson's right, thus relieving Early, who at once marched to support the centre, Jackson's men had not yet finished with the enemy. Pope had now taken over command; and besides the troops from Centreville, who had already reached the field, McDowell and Porter, with 27,000 men, were coming up from Manassas, and Reynolds had not yet been engaged. But it is one thing to assemble large numbers on the battle-field, another to give them the right direction.

In the direction of Gainesville high woods and rolling ridges had concealed Longstreet's approach, and the Federal patrols had been everywhere held in check by Stuart's squadrons. In ignorance, therefore, that the whole Confederate army was concentrated before him, Pope, anticipating an easy victory, determined to sweep Jackson from the field. But it was first necessary to relieve Sigel. Kearney's division had already deployed on the extreme right of the Federal line, resting on Bull Run. Hooker was on the left of Kearney and a brigade of Reno's on the left of Hooker. While Sigel assembled his shattered forces, these 10,000 fresh troops, led by some of the best officers of the Army of the Potomac, were ordered to advance against A. P. Hill. Reynolds, under the impression that he was fighting Jackson, was already in collision with Longstreet's advanced-guard; and McDowell and Porter, marching along the railway from Manassas, might be expected to strike the Confederate right rear at any moment. It was then with good hope of victory that Pope rode along his line and explained the situation to his generals.

But the fresh attack was made with no better concert than those which preceded it.   Kearney, on the right, near
1 P.M.   Bull Run, was held at bay by Jackson's guns, and Hooker and Reno advanced alone.

As the Federals moved forward the grey skirmishers fell back through the Groveton wood, and scarcely had they reached the railroad before the long blue lines came crashing through the undergrowth.   Hill's riflemen, lying down to load, and rising only to fire, poured in their deadly volleys at point-blank range.   The storm of bullets, shredding leaves and twigs, stripped the trees of their verdure, and the long dry grass, ignited by the powder sparks, burst into flames between the opposing lines.   But neither flames nor musketry availed to stop Hooker's onset.   Bayonets flashed through the smoke, and a gallant rush placed the stormers on the embankment.   The Confederates reeled back in confusion, and men crowded round the colours to protect them.   But assistance was at hand.   A fierce yell and a heavy volley, and the regiments of the second line surged forward, driving back the intruders, and closing the breach.   Yet the Federal ranks reformed; the wood rang with cheers, and a fresh brigade advanced to the assault.   Again the parapet was carried; again the Southern bayonets cleared the front. Hooker's leading brigade, abandoning the edge of the wood, had already given ground.   Reno's regiments, suffering fearful slaughter, with difficulty maintained their place; and Hill, calling once more upon his reserves, sent in Pender to the counterstroke.   Passing by the right of Thomas, who, with Field, had borne the brunt of the last attack, Pender crossed the railroad, and charged into the wood.   Many of the men in the fighting-line joined in the onward movement. The Federals were borne back; the brigades in rear were swept away by the tide of fugitives; the wood was cleared, and a battery near by was deserted by the gunners.

Then Pender, received with a heavy artillery fire from the opposite heights, moved boldly forward across the open. But the counterstroke had been pushed too far.   The line

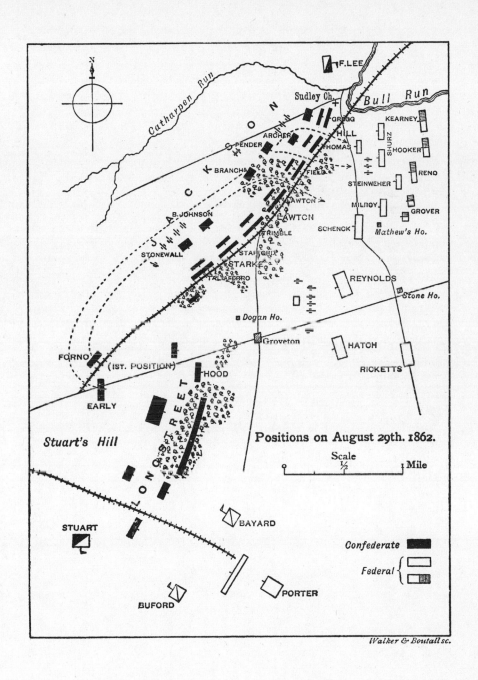

N

Catharpen Run

Bull Run

F. LEE

Sudley Ch.

GREGG

KEARNEY

ARCHER

PENDER

HILL

SCHURZ

HOOKER

THOMAS

BRANCH

FIELD

STEINWEHER

RENO

J A C K S O N

LAWTON

MILROY

GROVER

B. JOHNSON

LAWTON

TRIMBLE

SCHENCK

Mathew's Ho.

STONEWALL

STAFFORD

STARKE

TALIAFERRO

REYNOLDS

Stone Ho.

Dogan Ho.

HATCH

Groveton

FORNO

RICKETTS

(1ST. POSITION)

HOOD

EARLY

Stuart's Hill

L O N G S T R E E T

Positions on August 29th. 1862.

Scale

0   ½   Mile

STUART

BAYARD

Confederate ▬

Federal { □ ▦

BUFORD

PORTER

Walker & Boutall sc.

faltered; hostile infantry appeared on either flank, and as
the Confederates fell back to the railroad, the enemy came
forward in pursuit. Grover's brigade of Hooker's division
had hitherto been held in reserve, sheltered by a roll of the
land opposite that portion of the front which was held by
3 P.M. Thomas. It was now directed to attack. 'Move
slowly forward,' were the orders which Grover
gave to his command, 'until the enemy opens fire. Then
advance rapidly, give them one volley, and then the bayonet.'
The five regiments moved steadily through the wood in a
single line. When they reached the edge they saw immediately before them the red earth of the embankment, at this
point ten feet high and lined with riflemen. There was a
crash of fire, a swift rush through the rolling smoke, and the
Federals, crossing the parapet, swept all before them. Hill's
second line received them with a scattered fire, turned in confusion, and fled back upon the guns. Then beckoned victory
to him who had held his reserves in hand. Jackson had
seen the charge, and Forno's Louisianians, with a regiment
of Lawton's, had already been sent forward with the bayonet.

In close order the counterstroke came on. The thinned
ranks of the Federals could oppose no resolute resistance.
Fighting they fell back, first to the embankment, where
for a few moments they held their own, and then to the
wood. But without supports it was impossible to rally.
Johnson's and Starke's brigades swept down upon their
flank, the Louisianians, supported by Field and Archer,
against their front, and in twenty minutes, with a loss of
one-fourth his numbers, Grover in his turn was driven
beyond the Warrenton turnpike.

Four divisions, Schurz', Steinwehr's, Hooker's, and
Reno's, had been hurled in succession against Jackson's
front. Their losses had been enormous. Grover's brigade
had lost 461 out of 2,000, of which one regiment, 283 strong,
accounted for 6 officers and 106 men; three regiments of
Reno's lost 530; and it is probable that more than 4,000
men had fallen in the wood which lay in front of Hill's
brigades.

The fighting, however, had not been without effect on

the Confederates. The charges to which they had been
exposed, impetuous as they were, were doubtless less trying
than a sustained attack, pressed on by continuous waves of
fresh troops, and allowing the defence no breathing space.
Such steady pressure, always increasing in strength, saps
the *moral* more rapidly than a series of fierce assaults,
delivered at wide intervals of time. But such pressure
implies on the part of the assailant an accumulation of
superior force, and this accumulation the enemy's generals
had not attempted to provide. In none of the four attacks
which had shivered against Hill's front had the strength of
the assailants been greater than that of his own division ;
and to the tremendous weight of such a stroke as had won
the battles of Gaines' Mill or Cedar Run, to the closely
combined advance of overwhelming numbers, Jackson's men
had not yet been subjected.

The battle, nevertheless, had been fiercely contested, and
the strain of constant vigilance and close-range fighting
had told on the Light Division. The Federal skirmishers,
boldly advancing as Pender's men fell back, had once more
filled the wood, and their venomous fire allowed the defenders
no leisure for repose.[1] Ammunition had already given out ;
many of the men had but two or three cartridges remaining,
and the volunteers who ran the gauntlet to procure fresh
supplies were many of them shot down. Moreover, nine
hours' fighting, much of it at close range, had piled the
corpses thick upon the railroad, and the ranks of Hill's
brigades were terribly attenuated. The second line had
already been brought up to fill the gaps, and every brigade
had been heavily engaged.

It was about four o'clock, and for a short space the
pressure on the Confederate lines relaxed. The continuous

---

[1] 'The Federal sharpshooters at this time,' says Colonel McCrady, of the
Light Division, ' held possession of the wood, and kept up a deadly fire of
single shots whenever any one of us was exposed. Every lieutenant who
had to change position did so at the risk of his life. What was my
horror, during an interval in the attack, to see General Jackson himself
walking quickly down the railroad cut, examining our position, and calmly
looking into the wood that concealed the enemy ! Strange to say, he was
not molested.'—*Southern Historical Society Papers*, vol. xiii., p. 27.

roar of the artillery dwindled to a fitful cannonade ; and along the edge of the wood, drooping under the heat, where the foliage was white with the dust of battle, the skirmishers let their rifles cool. But the Valley soldiers knew that their respite would be short. The Federal masses were still marching and countermarching on the opposite hills ; from the forest beyond long columns streamed steadily to the front, and near the Warrenton turnpike fresh batteries were coming into action.

4 P.M.

Pope had ordered Kearney and Reno to make a fresh attack. The former, one of the most dashing officers in the Federal army, disposed his division in two lines. Reno, in the same formation, deployed upon Kearney's right, and with their flank resting on Bull Run the five brigades went forward to the charge. The Confederate batteries, posted on the ridge in rear, swept the open ground along the stream ; but, regardless of their fire, the Federals came rapidly to close quarters, and seized the railroad. When Hill saw this formidable storm bursting on his lines he felt that the supreme moment had arrived. Would Gregg, on whose front the division of Reno was bearing down, be able to hold his own ? That gallant soldier, although more than one half of his command lay dead or wounded, replied, in answer to his chief's enquiry, that his ammunition was almost expended, but that he had still the bayonet. Nevertheless, the pressure was too heavy for his wearied troops. Foot by foot they were forced back, and, at the same moment, Thomas, Field, and Branch, still fighting desperately, were compelled to yield their ground. Hill, anxiously looking for succour, had already called on Early. The enemy, swarming across the railroad, had penetrated to a point three hundred yards within the Confederate position. But the grey line was not yet shattered. The men of the Light Division, though borne backwards by the rush, still faced towards the foe ; and Early's brigade, supported by two regiments of Lawton's division, advanced with levelled bayonets, drove through the tumult, and opposed a solid line to the crowd of Federals.

4.30 P.M.

Once more the fresh reserve, thrown in at the propitious

moment, swept back numbers far superior to itself. Once more order prevailed over disorder, and the cold steel asserted its supremacy. The strength of the assailants was already spent. The wave receded more swiftly than it had risen, and through the copses and across the railroad the Confederates drove their exhausted foe. General Hill had instructed Early that he was not to pass beyond the original front; but it was impossible to restrain the troops, and not till they had advanced several hundred yards was the brigade halted and brought back. The counterstroke was as completely successful as those 5.15 P.M. that had preceded it. Early's losses were comparatively slight, those inflicted on the enemy very heavy, and Hill's brigades were finally relieved. Pope abandoned all further efforts to crush Jackson. Five assaults had failed. 30,000 infantry had charged in vain through the fatal wood; and of the 8,000 Federal casualties reported on this day, by far the larger proportion was due to the deadly fire and dashing counterstrokes of Jackson's infantry.

While Pope was hurling division after division against the Confederate left, Lee, with Longstreet at his side, observed the conflict from Stuart's Hill, the wooded eminence which stands south-west of Groveton. On this wing, though a mile distant from Jackson's battle, both Federals and Confederates were in force. At least one half of Pope's army had gradually assembled on this flank. Here were Reynolds and McDowell, and on the Manassas road stood two divisions under Porter.

Within the woods on Stuart's Hill, with the cavalry on his flank, Longstreet had deployed his whole force, with the exception of Anderson, who had not yet passed Thoroughfare Gap. But although both Pope and Lee were anxious to engage, neither could bring their subordinates to the point. Pope had sent vague instructions to Porter and McDowell, and when at length he had substituted a definite order it was not only late in arriving, but the generals found that it was based on an absolutely incorrect view of the situation. The Federal commander had no knowledge that Longstreet, with 25,000 men, was already in position beyond his left. So close lay the Confederates that under the impression that Stuart's Hill was still untenanted, he desired Porter to move across it and envelop Jackson's right. Porter, suspecting that the main body of the Southern army was before him, declined to risk his 10,000 men until he had reported the true state of affairs. A peremptory reply to attack at once was received at 6.30, but it was then too late to intervene.

Nor had Lee been more successful in developing a counterstroke. Longstreet, with a complacency it is difficult to understand, has related how he opposed the wishes of the Commander-in-Chief. Three times Lee urged him forward. The first time he rode to the front to reconnoitre, and found that the position, in his own words, was not inviting. Again Lee insisted that the enemy's left might be turned. While the question was under discussion, a heavy force (Porter and McDowell) was reported advancing from Manassas Junction. No attack followed, however, and Lee repeated his instructions. Longstreet was still unwilling. A large portion of the Federal force on the Manassas road now marched northward to join Pope, and Lee, for the last time, bade Longstreet attack towards Groveton. 'I suggested,' says the latter, 'that the day being far spent, it might be as well to advance before night on a forced reconnaissance, get our troops into the most favourable positions, and have all things ready for battle the next morning. To this General Lee reluctantly gave consent, and orders were given for an advance to be pursued under cover of night, until the main position could be carefully examined. It so happened that an order to advance was issued on the other side at the same time, so that the encounter was something of a surprise on both sides.' [1] Hood, with his two Texan brigades, led the Confederates, and King's division, now commanded by Hatch, met him on the slopes of Stuart's Hill. Although the Federals, since 1 A.M. the same morning, had marched to Manassas and back again, the fight was spirited. Hood, however, was strongly supported, and the Texans pushed forward

[1] *Battles and Leaders*, vol. ii., p. 519.

a mile and a half in front of the position they had held
since noon. Longstreet had now full leisure to make
his reconnaissance. The ground to which the enemy
had retreated was very strong. He believed it strongly
manned, and an hour after midnight Hood's brigades
were ordered to withdraw.

The firing, even of the skirmishers, had long since
died away on the opposite flank. The battle was over,
and the Valley army had been once more victorious.
But when Jackson's staff gathered round him in the
bivouac, 'their triumph,' says Dabney, 'bore a solemn
hue.' Their great task had been accomplished, and Pope's
army, harassed, starving, and bewildered, had been brought
to bay. But their energies were worn down. The incessant
marching, by day and night, the suspense of the past week,
the fierce strife of the day that had just closed, pressed
heavily on the whole force. Many of the bravest were gone.
Trimble, that stout soldier, was severely wounded, Field
and Forno had fallen, and in Gregg's brigade alone 40
officers were dead or wounded. Doctor McGuire, fresh
from the ghastly spectacle of the silent battle-field, said,
'General, this day has been won by nothing but stark and
stern fighting.' 'No,' replied Jackson, very quietly, 'it
has been won by nothing but the blessing and protection of Providence.' And in this attitude of acknowledg-
ment general and soldiers were as one. When the pickets
had been posted, and night had fallen on the forest, officers
and men, gathered together round their chaplains, made
such preparations for the morrow's battle as did the host of
King Harry on the eve of Agincourt.

NOTE

Students of war will note with interest the tactical details of the passage of the Rappahannock by the Army of Northern Virginia.

August 21.—FEDERALS.

In position behind the river from Kelly's Ford to Freeman's Ford. *Tête de pont* covering the railway bridge, occupied by a brigade.

CONFEDERATES.

Longstreet to Kelly's Ford.
Jackson to Beverley Ford.
Stuart to above Beverley Ford.
        Constant skirmishing and artillery fire.

August 22.—FEDERALS.

In position from Kelly's Ford to Freeman's Ford.
Bayard's cavalry brigade on right flank.
Buford's cavalry brigade at Rappahannock Station.

CONFEDERATES.

Jackson to Sulphur Springs.   Early crosses the river.
Longstreet to Beverley Ford and railway.
        Constant skirmishing and artillery fire.

August 23.—FEDERALS.

Pope abandons *tête de pont* and burns railway bridge.
Sigel moves against Early, but his advance is repulsed.
Army to a position about Warrenton, with detachments along the
    river, and a strong force at Kelly's Ford.

CONFEDERATES.

Early moves north to Great Run, and is reinforced by Lawton.
Stuart to Catlett's Station.
Longstreet demonstrates against railway bridge.

N 2

August 24.—Federals.

Buford's and Bayard's cavalry to Waterloo.
Army to Waterloo and Sulphur Springs.

Confederates.

Jackson in the evening retires to Jefferson, and is relieved after
  dark opposite Sulphur Springs and Waterloo by Longstreet.
Anderson relieves Longstreet on the railway.
    Constant skirmishing and artillery fire all along the line.

August 25.—Federals.

Pope extends his left down the river to Kelly's Ford, determining
  to receive attack at Warrenton should the Confederates cross.

Confederates.

Jackson moves north and crosses the river at Hinson's Mills.
Longstreet demonstrates at Waterloo, and Anderson at the Sulphur
  Springs.

August 26.—Federals.

A reconnaissance in force, owing to bad staff arrangements, comes
  to nothing. At nightfall the whole army is ordered to concentrate at Warrenton.

Confederates.

2 A.M. Stuart follows Jackson.
Late in the afternoon, Longstreet, having been relieved by
  Anderson, marches to Hinson's Mills.
Jackson captures Manassas Junction.
    Skirmishing all day along the Rappahannock.

August 27.—Federals.

7 A.M. Hooker's division from Warrenton Junction to Bristoe
  Station.
8.30 A.M. Army ordered to concentrate at Gainesville, Buckland
  Mills, and Greenwich. Porter and Banks at Warrenton
  Junction.
3 P.M. Action at Bristoe Station.
6.30 P.M. Pope arrives at Bristoe Station.
Army ordered to march to Manassas Junction at dawn.

Confederates.

Jackson at Manassas Junction.
Longstreet to White Plains.

CHAPTER XVII

THE SECOND MANASSAS (*continued*)

DURING the night of August 30 the long line of camp-fires
on the heights above Bull Run, and the frequent skirmishes
along the picket line, told General Lee that his enemy had
no intention of falling back behind the stream. And
when morning broke the Federal troops were observed upon
every ridge.

The Confederate leader, eager as he had been to force
the battle to an issue on the previous afternoon, had now
abandoned all idea of attack. The respite which
the enemy had gained might have altogether
changed the situation. It was possible that the Federals
had been largely reinforced. Pope and McClellan had
been given time, and the hours of the night might have
been utilised to bring up the remainder of the Army of
the Potomac. Lee resolved, therefore, to await events.
The Federal position was strong; their masses were
well concentrated; there was ample space, on the ridges
beyond Young's Branch, for the deployment of their
numerous artillery, and it would be difficult to outflank
them. Moreover, a contingent of fresh troops from
Richmond, the divisions of D. H. Hill, McLaws, and Walker,
together with Hampton's brigade of cavalry, and part of the
reserve artillery, 20,350 men in all, had crossed the
Rappahannock.[1] Until this force should join him he deter-

Aug. 30.

[1] D. H. Hill	7,000
McLaws	6,850
Walker	4,000
Hampton	1,500
Artillery	1,000
	20,350

mined to postpone further manœuvres, and to rest his army. But he was not without hope that Pope might assume the initiative and move down from the heights on which his columns were already forming. Aware of the sanguine and impatient temper of his adversary, confident in the *moral* of his troops, and in the strength of his position, he foresaw that an opportunity might offer for an overwhelming counterstroke.

Meanwhile, the Confederate divisions, still hidden in the woods, lay quietly on their arms. Few changes were made in the dispositions of the previous day. Jackson, despite his losses, had made no demand for reinforcements; and the only direct support afforded him was a battery of eighteen guns, drawn from the battalion of Colonel S. D. Lee, and established on the high ground west of the Douglass House, at right angles to his line of battle. These guns, pointing north-east, overlooked the wide tract of undulating meadow which lay in front of the Stonewall and Lawton's divisions, and they commanded a field of fire over a mile long. The left of the battery was not far distant from the guns on Jackson's right, and the whole of the open space was thus exposed to the cross-fire of a formidable artillery.

To the right of the batteries, Stuart's Hill was strongly occupied by Longstreet, with Anderson's division as general reserve; and this wing of the Confederate army was gradually wheeled up, but always under cover, until it was almost perpendicular to the line of the unfinished railroad. The strength of Lee's army at the battle of Manassas was hardly more than 50,000 of all arms. Jackson's command had been reduced by battle and forced marches to 17,000 men. Longstreet mustered 30,000, and the cavalry 2,500.

But numbers are of less importance than the confidence of the men in their ability to conquer,[1] and the spirit of the Confederates had been raised to the highest pitch. The keen

---

[1] Hood's Texans had a hymn which graphically expressed this truism :

'The race is not to him that's got
The longest legs to run,
Nor the battle to those people
That shoot the biggest gun.'

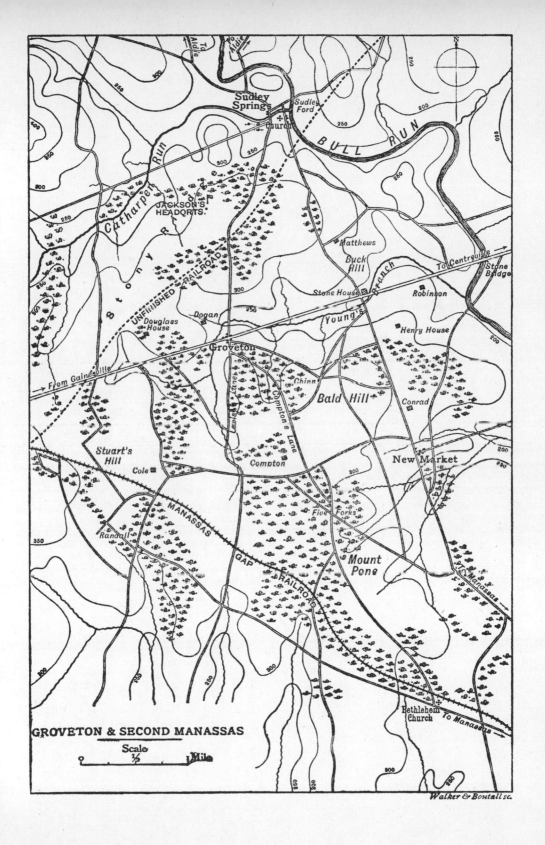

GROVETON & SECOND MANASSAS

Scale
1/2 — 1 Mile

Walker & Boutall sc.

critics in Longstreet's ranks, although they had taken
no part in the Manassas raid, or in the battles of August 28
and 29, fully appreciated the daring strategy which had
brought them within two short marches of Washington. The
junction of the two wings, in the very presence of the
enemy, after many days of separation, was a manœuvre
after their own hearts. The passage of Thoroughfare
Gap revealed the difficulties which had attended the
operations, and the manner in which the enemy had been
outwitted appealed with peculiar force to their quick intelligence. Their trust in Lee was higher than ever; and
the story of Jackson's march, of the capture of Manassas,
of the repulse of Pope's army, if it increased their contempt for the enemy, inspired them with an enthusiastic
determination to emulate the achievements of their comrades. The soldiers of the Valley army, who, unaided
by a single bayonet, had withstood the five successive
assaults which had been launched against their position,
were supremely indifferent, now Longstreet was in line,
to whatever the enemy might attempt. It was noticed
that notwithstanding the heavy losses they had experienced Jackson's troops were never more light-hearted
than on the morning of August 30. Cartridge-boxes
had been replenished, rations had been issued, and for
several hours the men had been called on neither to march
nor fight. As they lay in the woods, and the pickets,
firing on the enemy's patrols, kept up a constant skirmish
to the front, the laugh and jest ran down the ranks, and
the unfortunate Pope, who had only seen ' the backs of his
enemies,' served as whetstone for their wit.

By the troops who had revelled in the spoils of Winchester Banks had been dubbed ' Old Jack's Commissary
General.' By universal acclamation, after the Manassas
foray, Pope was promoted to the same distinction; and had
it been possible to penetrate to the Federal headquarters, the
mirth of those ragged privates would hardly have diminished. Pope was in an excellent humour, conversing
affably with his staff, and viewing with pride the martial
aspect of his massed divisions. Nearly his whole force

was concentrated on the hills around him, and Porter, who had been called up from the Manassas road, was already marching northwards through the woods.   Banks still was absent at Bristoe Station, in charge of the trains and stores which had been removed from Warrenton ; but, shortly after ten o'clock, 65,000 men, with eight-and-twenty batteries, were at Pope's disposal.   He had determined to give battle, although Franklin and Sumner, who had already reached Alexandria, had not yet joined him ; and he anticipated an easy triumph. He was labouring, however, under an extraordinary delusion. The retreat of Hood's brigades the preceding night, after their reconnaissance, had induced him to believe that Jackson had been defeated, and he had reported to Halleck at daybreak : ' We fought a terrific battle here yesterday with the combined forces of the enemy, which lasted with continuous fury from daylight until dark, by which time the enemy was driven from the field, which we now occupy. The enemy is still in our front, but badly used up.   We lost not less than 8,000 men killed and wounded, but from the appearance of the field the enemy lost at least two to one.   The news has just reached me from the front that the enemy is retreating towards the mountains.'

10.15 A.M.

If, in these days of long-range weapons, Napoleon's dictum still stands good, that the general who is ignorant of his enemy's strength and dispositions is ignorant of his trade, then of all generals Pope was surely the most incompetent.   At ten o'clock on the morning of August 30, and for many months afterwards, despite his statement that he had fought ' the combined forces of the enemy ' on the previous day, he was still under the impression, so skilfully were the Confederate troops concealed, that Longstreet had not yet joined Jackson, and that the latter was gradually falling back on Thoroughfare Gap. His patrols had reported that the enemy's cavalry had been withdrawn from the left bank of Bull Run.   A small reconnaissance in force, sent to test Jackson's strength, had ascertained that the extreme left was not so far forward as it had been yesterday ; while two of the Federal generals, reconnoitring beyond the turn-

pike, observed only a few skirmishers. On these negative
reports Pope based his decision to seize the ridge
which was held by Jackson. Yet the woods along the
unfinished railroad had not been examined, and the information from other sources was of a different colour
and more positive. Buford's cavalry had reported on
the evening of the 29th that a large force had passed
through Thoroughfare Gap. Porter declared that the
enemy was in great strength on the Manassas road.
Reynolds, who had been in close contact with Longstreet
since the previous afternoon, reported that Stuart's Hill
was strongly occupied. Ricketts, moreover, who had fought
Longstreet for many hours at Thoroughfare Gap, was
actually present on the field. But Pope, who had made up
his mind that the enemy ought to retreat, and that therefore
he must retreat, refused credence to any report whatever
which ran counter to these preconceived ideas. Without
making the slightest attempt to verify, by personal observation, the conclusions at which his subordinates had
12 noon. arrived, at midday, to the dismay of his best
officers, his army being now in position, he issued
orders for his troops to be ' immediately thrown forward in
pursuit of the enemy, and to press him vigorously.'

Porter and Reynolds formed the left of the Federal
army. These generals, alive to the necessity of examining
the woods, deployed a strong skirmish line before them as
they formed for action. Further evidence of Pope's hal-
lucination was at once forthcoming. The moment Reynolds
moved forward against Stuart's Hill he found his front
overlapped by long lines of infantry, and, riding back, he
informed Pope that in so doing he had had to run the
gauntlet of skirmishers who threatened his rear. Porter,
too, pushing his reconnaissance across the meadows west
of Groveton, drew the fire of several batteries. But at this
juncture, unfortunately for the Federals, a Union prisoner,
recaptured from Jackson, declared that he had ' heard the
rebel officers say that their army was retiring to unite with
Longstreet.' So positively did the indications before him
contradict this statement, that Porter, on sending the man

to Pope, wrote : ' In duty bound I send him, but I regard him as either a fool or designedly released to give a wrong impression. No faith should be put in what he says.' If Jackson employed this man to delude his enemy, the ruse was eminently successful. Porter received the reply : ' General Pope believes that soldier, and directs you to attack; ' Reynolds was dismissed with a message that cavalry would be sent to verify his report ; and McDowell was ordered to put in the divisions of Hatch and Ricketts on Porter's right.

During the whole morning the attention of the Confederates had been directed to the Groveton wood. Beyond the timber rose the hill north-east, and on this hill three or four Federal batteries had come into action at an early hour, firing at intervals across the meadows. The Confederate guns, save when the enemy's skirmishers approached too close, hardly deigned to reply, reserving their ammunition for warmer work. That such work was to come was hardly doubtful. Troops had been constantly in motion near the hostile batteries, and the thickets below 12.15 P.M. were evidently full of men. Shortly after noon the enemy's skirmishers became aggressive, swarming over the meadows, and into the wood which had seen such heavy slaughter in the fight of yesterday. As Jackson's pickets, extended over a wide front, gave slowly back, his guns opened in earnest, and shell and shrapnel flew fast over the open space. The strong force of skirmishers betrayed the presence of a line of battle not far in rear, and ignoring the fire of the artillery, the Confederate batteries concentrated on the covert behind which they knew the enemy's masses were forming for attack. But, except the pickets, not a single man of either the Stonewall or Lawton's division was permitted to expose himself. A few companies held the railroad, the remainder were carefully concealed. The storm was not long in breaking. Jackson had just ridden along his lines, examining with his own eyes the stir in the Groveton wood, when, in rear of the skirmishers, advancing over the highroad, appeared the serried ranks of the line of battle. 20,000 bayonets, on a front which extended from Groveton to near Bull Run, swept forward against his front ; 40,000, formed in dense masses on the slopes in rear, stood in readiness to support them; and numerous batteries, coming into action on every rising ground, covered the advance with a heavy fire.

Pope, standing on a knoll near the Stone House, saw victory within his grasp. The Confederate guns had been pointed out to his troops as the objective of the attack. Unsupported, as he believed, save by the scattered groups of skirmishers who were already retreating to the railroad, and assailed in front and flank, these batteries, he expected, would soon be flying to the rear, and the Federal army, in possession of the high ground, would then sweep down in heavy columns towards Thoroughfare Gap. Suddenly his hopes fell. Porter's masses, stretching far to right and left, had already passed the Dogan House ; Hatch was entering the Groveton wood ; Ricketts was moving forward along Bull Run, and the way seemed clear before them ; when loud and clear above the roar of the artillery rang out the Confederate bugles, and along the whole length of the ridge beyond the railroad long lines of infantry, streaming forward from the woods, ran down to the embankment. 'The effect,' said an officer who witnessed this unexpected apparition, 'was not unlike flushing a covey of quails.'

Instead of the small rear-guard which Pope had thought to crush by sheer force of overwhelming numbers, the whole of the Stonewall division, with Lawton on the left, stood across Porter's path.

Reynolds, south of the turnpike, and confronting Longstreet, was immediately ordered to fall back and support the attack, and two small brigades, Warren's and Alexander's, were left alone on the Federal left. Pope had committed his last and his worst blunder. Sigel with two divisions was in rear of Porter, and for Sigel's assistance Porter had already asked. But Pope, still under the delusion that Longstreet was not yet up, preferred rather to weaken his left than grant the request of a subordinate.

Under such a leader the courage of the troops, however vehement, was of no avail, and in Porter's attack the soldiers displayed a courage to which the Confederates paid a willing tribute. Morell's division, with the two brigades abreast, arrayed in three lines, advanced across the meadows. Hatch's division, in still deeper formation, pushed through the wood on Morell's right. Nearer Bull Run were two brigades of Ricketts; and to Morell's left rear the division of regulars moved forward under Sykes.

Morell's attack was directed against Jackson's right. In the centre of the Federal line a mounted officer, whose gallant bearing lived long in the memories of the Stonewall division, rode out in front of the column, and, drawing his sabre, led the advance over the rolling grass-land. The Confederate batteries, with a terrible cross-fire, swept the Northern ranks from end to end. The volleys of the infantry, lying behind their parapet, struck them full in face. But the horse and his rider lived through it all. The men followed close, charging swiftly up the slope, and then the leader, putting his horse straight at the embankment, stood for a moment on the top. The daring feat was seen by the whole Confederate line, and a yell went up from the men along the railroad, 'Don't kill him! don't kill him!' But while the cry went up horse and rider fell in one limp mass across the earthwork, and the gallant Northerner was dragged under shelter by his generous foes.

With such men as this to show the way what soldiers would be backward? As the Russians followed Skobeleff's grey up the bloody slopes of Plevna, so the Federals followed the bright chestnut of this unknown hero, and not till the colours waved within thirty paces of the parapet did the charge falter. But, despite the supports that came thronging up, Jackson's soldiers, covered by the earthwork, opposed a resistance which no mere frontal attack could break. Three times, as the lines in rear merged with the first, the Federal officers brought their men forward to the assault, and three times were they hurled back, leaving hundreds of their number dead and wounded on the blood-

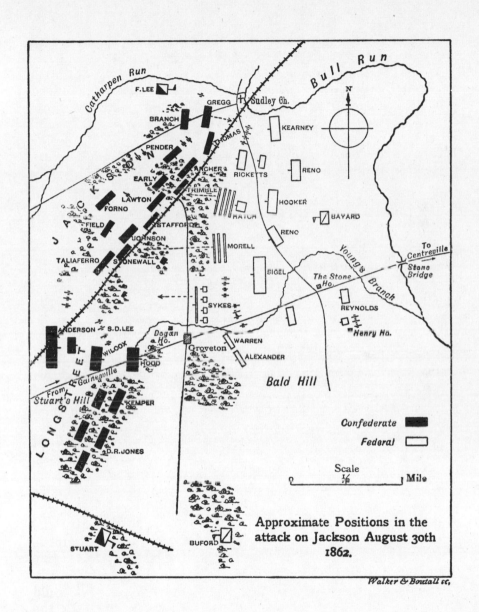

Catharpen Run

Bull Run

F. LEE

GREGG · Sudley Ch.

BRANCH

KEARNEY

N

PENDER

THOMAS

ARCHER

RICKETTS

RENO

EARLY

TRIMBLE

HATCH

HOOKER

LAWTON

FORNO

BAYARD

FIELD

STAFFORD

RENO

JOHNSON

MORELL

TALIAFERRO

STONEWALL

SIGEL

To Centreville

Young's Branch

The Stone Ho.

Stone Bridge

SYKES

ANDERSON · S.D.LEE

Dogan Ho.

WARREN

REYNOLDS

WILCOX

Groveton

HOOD

ALEXANDER

Henry Ho.

From Stuart's Hill

Gainesville

KEMPER

Bald Hill

D.R.JONES

Confederate

Federal

Scale
0   ½   Mile

STUART

BUFORD

**Approximate Positions in the
attack on Jackson August 30th
1862.**

Walker & Boutall sc.

soaked turf.   One regiment of the Stonewall division, posted
in a copse beyond the railroad, was driven in ; but others,
when cartridges failed them, had recourse, like the Guards at
Inkermann, to the stones which lay along the railway-bed ;
and with these strange weapons, backed up by the bayonet,
more than one desperate effort was repulsed.   In arresting
Garnett after Kernstown, because when his ammunition
was exhausted he had abandoned his position, Jackson had
lost a good general, but he had taught his soldiers a useful
lesson.   So long as the cold steel was left to them, and their
flanks were safe, they knew that their indomitable leader
expected them to hold their ground, and right gallantly they
responded.   For over thirty minutes the battle raged along
the front at the closest range.   Opposite a deep cutting the
colours of a Federal regiment, for nearly half an hour, rose
and fell, as bearer after bearer was shot down, within ten
yards of the muzzles of the Confederate rifles, and after the
fight a hundred dead Northerners were found where the flag
had been so gallantly upheld.

Hill, meanwhile, was heavily engaged with Hatch. Every
brigade, with the exception of Gregg's, had been thrown into
the fighting-line; and so hardly were they pressed, that Jackson, turning to his signallers, demanded reinforcements from
his colleague.   Longstreet, in response to the call, ordered
two more batteries to join Colonel Stephen Lee ; and Morell's
division, penned in that deadly cockpit between Stuart's
Hill and the Groveton wood, shattered by musketry in front
and by artillery at short range in flank, fell back across the
meadows.   Hatch soon followed suit, and Jackson's artillery, which during the fight at close quarters had turned its
fire on the supports, launched a storm of shell on the
defeated Federals.   Some batteries were ordered to change
position so as to rake their lines ; and the Stonewall
division, reinforced by a brigade of Hill's, was sent forward to
the counter-attack.   At every step the losses of the Federals
increased, and the shattered divisions, passing through
two regiments of regulars, which had been sent forward to
support them, sought shelter in the woods.   Then Porter
and Hatch, under cover of their artillery, withdrew their

infantry. Ricketts had fallen back before his troops arrived within decisive range. Under the impression that he was about to pursue a retreating enemy, he had found on advancing, instead of a thin screen of skirmishers, a line of battle, strongly established, and backed by batteries to which he was unable to reply. Against such odds attack would only have increased the slaughter.

It was after four o'clock. Three hours of daylight yet remained, time enough still to secure a victory. But the Federal army was in no condition to renew the attack. Worn with long marches, deprived of their supplies, and oppressed by the consciousness that they were ill-led, both officers and men had lost all confidence. Every single division on the field had been engaged, and every single division had been beaten back. For four days, according to General Pope, they had been following a flying foe. 'We were sent forward,' reported a regimental commander with quiet sarcasm, 'to pursue the enemy, who was said to be retreating; we found the enemy, but did not see them retreat.'

4.15 P.M.

Nor, had there been a larger reserve in hand, would a further advance have been permitted. The Stonewall division, although Porter's regiments were breaking up before its onset, had been ordered to fall back before it became exposed to the full sweep of the Federal guns. But the woods to the south, where Longstreet's divisions had been lying for so many hours, were already alive with bayonets. The grey skirmishers, extending far beyond Pope's left, were moving rapidly down the slopes of Stuart's Hill, and the fire of the artillery, massed on the ridge in rear, was increasing every moment in intensity. The Federals, just now advancing in pursuit, were suddenly thrown on the defensive; and the hand of a great captain snatched control of the battle from the grasp of Pope.

As Porter reeled back from Jackson's front, Lee had seen his opportunity. The whole army was ordered to advance to the attack. Longstreet, prepared since dawn for the counterstroke, had moved before the message

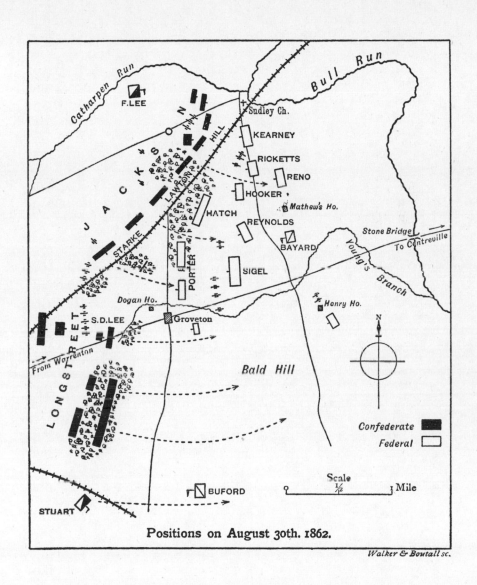

Catharpen Run

F. LEE

Bull Run

Sudley Ch.

KEARNEY

RICKETTS

RENO

HOOKER

Mathew's Ho.

HATCH

REYNOLDS

Stone Bridge

To Centreville

BAYARD

SIGEL

Young's Branch

Dogan Ho.

S.D. LEE

Groveton

Henry Ho.

From Warrenton

N

Bald Hill

Confederate

Federal

BUFORD

Scale
½
Mile

STUART

Positions on August 30th. 1862.

Walker & Boutall sc.

o 2

reached him, and the exulting yells of his soldiers were
now resounding through the forest. Jackson was desired
to cover Longstreet's left; and sending Starke and
Lawton across the meadows, strewn with the bloody *débris*
of Porter's onslaught, he instructed Hill to advance *en
échelon* with his left 'refused.' Anticipating the order,
the commander of the Light Division was already sweeping
through the Groveton wood.

The Federal gunners, striving valiantly to cover the
retreat of their shattered infantry, met the advance of the
Southerners with a rapid fire. Pope and McDowell exerted
themselves to throw a strong force on to the heights above
Bull Run; and the two brigades upon the left, Warren's
and Alexander's, already overlapped, made a gallant effort
to gain time for the occupation of the new position.

But the counterstroke of Lee was not to be withstood
by a few regiments of infantry. The field of Bull Run
had seen many examples of the attack as executed by
indifferent tacticians. At the first battle isolated brigades
had advanced at wide intervals of time. At the second
battle the Federals had assaulted by successive divisions.
Out of 50,000 infantry, no more than 20,000 had been
simultaneously engaged, and when a partial success had
been achieved there were no supports at hand to complete the victory. When the Confederates came forward it
was in other fashion; and those who had the wit to understand were now to learn the difference between mediocrity
and genius, between the half-measures of the one and
the resolution of the other. Lee's order for the advance embraced his whole army. Every regiment, every battery, and
every squadron was employed. No reserves save the artillery were retained upon the ridge, but wave after wave of
bayonets followed closely on the fighting-line. To drive
the attack forward by a quick succession of reinforcements, to push it home by weight of numbers, to pile
blow on blow, to keep the defender occupied along his
whole front, and to provide for retreat, should retreat be
necessary, not by throwing in fresh troops, but by leaving the enemy so crippled that he would be powerless

to pursue—such were the tactics of the Confederate leader.

The field was still covered with Porter's and Hatch's disordered masses when Lee's strong array advanced, and the sight was magnificent. As far as the eye could reach the long grey lines of infantry, with the crimson of the colours gleaming like blood in the evening sun, swept with ordered ranks across the Groveton valley. Batteries galloped furiously to the front; far away to the right fluttered the guidons of Stuart's squadrons, and over all the massed artillery maintained a tremendous fire. The men drew fresh vigour from this powerful combination. The enthusiasm of the troops was as intense as their excitement. With great difficulty, it is related, were the gunners restrained from joining in the charge, and the officers of the staff could scarcely resist the impulse to throw themselves with their victorious comrades upon the retreating foe.

The advance was made in the following order:

Wilcox' division, north of the turnpike, connected with Jackson's right. Then came Evans, facing the two brigades which formed the Federal left, and extending across the turnpike. Behind Evans came Anderson on the left and Kemper on the right. Then, in prolongation of Kemper's line, but at some interval, marched the division of D. R. Jones, flanked by Stuart's cavalry, and on the further wing, extending towards Bull Run, were Starke, Lawton, and A. P. Hill. 50,000 men, including the cavalry, were thus deployed over a front of four miles; each division was formed in at least two lines; and in the centre, where Anderson and Kemper supported Evans, were no less than eight brigades one in rear of the other.

The Federal advanced line, behind which the troops which had been engaged in the last attack were slowly rallying, extended from the Groveton wood to a low hill, south of the turnpike and east of the village. This hill was quickly carried by Hood's brigade of Evans's division. The two regiments which defended it, rapidly outflanked, and assailed by overwhelming numbers, were routed with the loss of nearly half their muster. Jackson's attack through the Groveton wood was equally successful, but on the ridge in rear were posted the regulars under Sykes ; and, further east, on Buck Hill, had assembled the remnants of four divisions.

Outflanked by the capture of the hill upon their left, and fiercely assailed in front, Sykes's well-disciplined regiments, formed in lines of columns and covered by a rear-guard of skirmishers, retired steadily under the tremendous fire, preserving their formation, and falling back slowly across Young's Branch. Then Jackson, reforming his troops along the Sudley road, and swinging round to the left, moved swiftly against Buck Hill. Here, in addition to the infantry, were posted three Union batteries, and the artillery made a desperate endeavour to stay the counterstroke.

But nothing could withstand the vehement charge of the Valley soldiers. 'They came on,' says the correspondent of a Northern journal, 'like demons emerging from the earth.' The crests of the ridges blazed with musketry, and Hill's infantry, advancing in the very teeth of the canister, captured six guns at the bayonet's point. Once more Jackson reformed his lines ; and, as twilight came down upon the battle-field, from position after position, in the direction of the Stone Bridge, the divisions of Stevens, Ricketts, Kearney, and Hooker, were gradually pushed back.

On the Henry Hill, the key of the Federal position, a fierce conflict was meanwhile raging. From the high ground to the south Longstreet had driven back several brigades which, in support of the artillery, Sigel and McDowell had massed upon Bald Hill. But this position had not been occupied without a protracted struggle. Longstreet's first line, advancing with over-impetuosity, had outstripped the second ; and before it could be supported was compelled to give ground under the enemy's fire, one of the brigades losing 62 officers and 560 men. Anderson and Kemper were then brought up ; the flank of the defenders was turned ; a counterstroke was beaten back, ridge after ridge was mastered, the edge of every wood was stormed ; and as the sun set

behind the mountains Bald Hill was carried.   During
this fierce action the division of D. R. Jones, leaving
the Chinn House to the left, had advanced against the
Henry Hill.   On the very ground which Jackson had
held in his first battle the best troops of the Federal
army were rapidly assembling.   Here were
6 P.M. Sykes' regulars and Reynolds' Pennsylvanians ;
where the woods permitted batteries had been established ;
and Porter's Fifth Army Corps, who at Gaines' Mill and
Malvern Hill had proved such stubborn fighters, opposed
a strong front once more to their persistent foes.

Despite the rapid fire of the artillery the Southerners
swept forward with unabated vigour.   But as the attack was
pressed the resistance of the Federals grew more stubborn,
and before long the Confederate formation lost its strength.
The lines in rear had been called up.   The assistance of the
strong centre had been required to rout the defenders of Bald
Hill ; and although Anderson and Wilcox pressed forward
on his left, Jones had not sufficient strength to storm the
enemy's last position.   Moreover, the Confederate artillery
had been unable to follow the infantry over the broken
ground ; the cavalry, confronted by Buford's squadrons
and embarrassed by the woods, could lend no active aid,
and the Federals, defeated as they were, had not yet lost all
heart.   Whatever their guns could do, in so close a country,
to relieve the infantry had been accomplished ; and the
infantry, though continually outflanked, held together
with unflinching courage.   Stragglers there were, and
stragglers in such large numbers that Bayard's cavalry
brigade had been ordered to the rear to drive them back ;
but the majority of the men, hardened by months of discipline and constant battle, remained staunch to the
colours. The conviction that the battle was lost was no longer
a signal for ' the thinking bayonets ' to make certain of their
individual safety ; and the regulars, for the second time on
the same field, provided a strong nucleus of resistance.

Thrown into the woods along the Sudley-Manassas
road, five battalions of the United States army held the extreme left, the most critical point of the Federal line, until

a second brigade relieved them. To their right Meade and his Pennsylvanians held fast against Anderson and Wilcox; and although six guns fell into the hands of the Confederate infantry, and four of Longstreet's batteries, which had accompanied the cavalry, were now raking their left, Pope's soldiers, as twilight descended upon the field, redeemed as far as soldiers could the errors of their general. Stuart, on the right flank of the Confederate line, charged down the opposing cavalry [1] and crossed Bull Run at Lewis' Ford; but the dark masses on the Henry Hill, increased every moment by troops ascending from the valley, still held fast, with no hope indeed of victory, but with a stern determination to maintain their ground. Had the hill been lost, nothing could have saved Pope's army. The crest commanded the crossings of Bull Run. The Stone Bridge, the main point of passage, was not more than a mile northward, within the range of artillery, and Jackson was already in possession of the Matthew Hill, not fourteen hundred yards from the road by which the troops must pass in their retreat.

The night, however, put an end to the battle. Even the Valley soldiers were constrained to halt. It was impossible in the obscurity to distinguish friend from foe. The 7.30 P.M. Confederate lines presented a broken front, here pushed forward, and here drawn back; divisions, brigades, and regiments had intermingled; and the thick woods, intervening at frequent intervals, rendered combination impracticable. During the darkness, which was accompanied by heavy rain, the Federals quietly withdrew, leaving thousands of

---

[1] This was one of the most brilliant cavalry fights of the war. Colonel Munford, of the 2nd Virginia, finding the enemy advancing, formed line and charged, the impetuosity of the attack carrying his regiment through the enemy's first line, with whom his men were thoroughly intermingled in hand-to-hand conflict. The Federals, however, who had advanced at a trot, in four successive lines, were far superior in numbers; but the 7th and 12th Virginia rapidly came up, and the charge of the 12th, constituting as it were a last reserve, drove the enemy from the field. The Confederates lost 5 killed and 40 wounded. Munford himself, and the commander of the First Michigan (Union) cavalry were both wounded by sabre-cuts, the latter mortally. 300 Federals were taken prisoners, 19 killed, and 80 wounded. Sabre, carbine, and revolver were freely used.

wounded on the field, and morning found them in position on the heights of Centreville, four miles beyond Bull Run.

Pope, with an audacity which disaster was powerless to tame, reported to Halleck that, on the whole, the results of the battle were favourable to the Federal army. 'The enemy,' he wrote, 'largely reinforced, assailed our position early to-day. We held our ground firmly until 6 o'clock P.M., when the enemy, massing very heavy forces on our left, forced that wing back about half a mile. At dark we held that position. Under all the circumstances, with horses and men having been two days without food, and the enemy greatly outnumbering us, I thought it best to move back to this place at dark. The movement has been made in perfect order and without loss. The battle was most furious for hours without cessation, and the losses on both sides very heavy. The enemy is badly whipped, and we shall do well enough. Do not be uneasy. We will hold our own here.'

Pope's actions, however, were invariably at variance with Pope's words. At 6 P.M. he had ordered Franklin, who was approaching Bull Run from Alexandria with 10,000 fresh troops, to occupy with his own command and whatever other troops he could collect, the fortifications round Centreville, and hold them 'to the last extremity.' Banks, still at Bristoe Station, was told to destroy all the supplies of which he was in charge, as well as the railway, and to march on Centreville; while 30 guns and more than 2,000 wounded were left upon the field. Nor were Pope's anticipations as to the future to be fulfilled. The position at Centreville was strong. The intrenchments constructed by the Confederates during the winter of 1861 were still standing. Halleck had forwarded supplies; there was ammunition in abundance, and 20,000 infantry under Franklin and Sumner—for the latter also had come up from Washington—more than compensated for the casualties of the battle. But formidable earthworks, against generals who dare manœuvre, are often a mere trap for the unwary.

Before daylight Stuart and his troopers were in the saddle;

and, picking up many stragglers as they marched, came
Aug. 31. within range of the guns at Centreville. Lee, accompanied by Jackson, having reconnoitred the position, determined to move once more upon the Federal rear. Longstreet remained on the battle-field to engage the attention of the enemy and cover the removal of the wounded ; while Jackson, crossing not by the Stone Bridge, but by Sudley Ford, was entrusted with the work of forcing Pope from his strong position.

The weather was inclement, the roads were quagmires, and the men were in no condition to make forced marches. Yet before nightfall Jackson had pushed ten miles through the mud, halting near Pleasant Valley, on the Little River turnpike, five miles north-west of Centreville. During the afternoon Longstreet, throwing a brigade across Bull Run to keep the enemy on the *qui vive*, followed the same route. Of these movements Pope received no warning, and Jackson's proclivity for flank manœuvres had evidently made no impression on him, for, in blissful unconsciousness that his line of retreat was already threatened, he ordered all waggons to be unloaded at Centreville, and to return to Fairfax Station for forage and rations.

But on the morning of September 1, although his whole army, including Banks, was closely concentrated
Sept. 1. behind strong intrenchments, Pope had conceived a suspicion that he would find it difficult to fulfil his promise to Halleck that ' he would hold on.' The previous night Stuart had been active towards his right and rear, capturing his reconnoitring parties, and shelling his trains. Before noon suspicion became certainty. Either stragglers or the country people reported that Jackson was moving down the Little River turnpike, and Centreville was at once evacuated, the troops marching to a new position round Fairfax Court House.

Jackson, meanwhile, covered by the cavalry, was advancing to Chantilly—a fine old mansion which the Federals had gutted—with the intention of seizing a position whence he could command the road. The day was sombre, and a tempest was gathering in the mountains. Late in the

afternoon, Stuart's patrols near Ox Hill were driven in by
hostile infantry, the thick woods preventing the scouts from
ascertaining the strength or dispositions of the Federal force.
Jackson at once ordered two brigades of Hill's to feel the
enemy.   The remainder of the Light Division took ground
to the right, followed by Lawton; Starke's division held
the turnpike, and Stuart was sent towards Fairfax Court
House to ascertain whether the Federal main body was
retreating or advancing.

Reno, who had been ordered to protect Pope's flank, came
briskly forward, and Hill's advanced-guard was soon brought
to a standstill.   Three fresh brigades were rapidly deployed ;
as the enemy pressed the attack a fourth was sent in, and
the Northerners fell back with the loss of a general and
many men.   Lawton's first line became engaged at the same
time, and Reno, now reinforced by Kearney, made a vigorous
effort to hold the Confederates in check.   Hays' brigade of
Lawton's division, commanded by an inexperienced officer,
was caught while 'clubbed' during a change of formation, and driven back in disorder ; and Trimble's brigade,
now reduced to a handful, became involved in the confusion.   But a vigorous charge of the second line restored
the battle.   The Federals were beginning to give way.
General Kearney, riding through the murky twilight into
the Confederate lines, was shot by a skirmisher.   The
hostile lines were within short range, and the advent
of a reserve on either side would have probably ended
the engagement.   But the rain was now falling in
torrents ; heavy peals of thunder, crashing through the
forest, drowned the discharges of the two guns which
Jackson had brought up through the woods, and the red
flash of musketry paled before the vivid lightning.   Much
of the ammunition was rendered useless, the men were
unable to discharge their pieces, and the fierce wind
lashed the rain in the faces of the Confederates.   The
night grew darker and the tempest fiercer ; and as if by
mutual consent the opposing lines drew gradually apart.[1]

[1] It was at this time, probably, that Jackson received a message from a
brigade commander, reporting that his cartridges were so wet that he

On the side of the Confederates only half the force had been engaged. Starke's division never came into action, and of Hill's and Lawton's there were still brigades in reserve. 500 men were killed or wounded; but although the three Federal divisions are reported to have lost 1,000, they had held their ground, and Jackson was thwarted in his design. Pope's trains and his whole army reached Fairfax Court House without further disaster. But the persistent attacks of his indefatigable foe had broken down his resolution. He had intended, he told Halleck, when Jackson's march down the Little River turnpike was first announced, to attack the Confederates the next day, or

Sept. 2. 'certainly the day after.' The action at Chantilly, however, induced a more prudent mood; and, on the morning of the 2nd, he reported that 'there was an intense idea among the troops that they must get behind the intrenchments [of Alexandria]; that there was an undoubted purpose, on the part of the enemy, to keep on slowly turning his position so as to come in on the right, and that the forces under his command were unable to prevent him doing so in the open field. Halleck must decide what was to be done.' The reply was prompt, Pope was to bring his forces, 'as best he could,' under the shelter of the heavy guns.

Whatever might be the truth as regards the troops, there could be no question but that the general was demoralised; and, preceded by thousands of stragglers, the army fell back without further delay to the Potomac. It was not followed except by Stuart. 'It was found,' says Lee, in his official dispatch, 'that the enemy had conducted his retreat so rapidly that the attempt to interfere with him was abandoned. The proximity of the fortifications around Alexandria and Washington rendered further pursuit useless.'

On the same day General McClellan was entrusted with the defence of Washington, and Pope, permitted to resign, was soon afterwards relegated to an obscure

feared he could not maintain his position. 'Tell him,' was the quick reply, ' to hold his ground; if his guns will not go off, neither will the enemy's.'

command against the Indians of the North-west. His
errors had been flagrant. He can hardly be charged with
want of energy, but his energy was spasmodic; on the
field of battle he was strangely indolent, and yet he distrusted
the reports of others. But more fatal than his neglect
of personal reconnaissance was his power of self-deception.
He was absolutely incapable of putting himself in his
enemy's place, and time after time he acted on the supposition that Lee and Jackson would do exactly what he
most wished them to do. When his supplies were destroyed, he concentrated at Manassas Junction, convinced
that Jackson would remain to be overwhelmed. When he
found Jackson near Sudley Springs, and Thoroughfare Gap
open, he rushed forward to attack him, convinced that Longstreet could not be up for eight-and-forty hours. When he
sought shelter at Centreville, he told Halleck not to be uneasy, convinced that Lee would knock his head against his
fortified position. Before the engagement at Chantilly he
had made up his mind to attack the enemy the next
morning. A few hours later he reported that his troops
were utterly untrustworthy, although 20,000 of them,
under Franklin and Sumner, had not yet seen the enemy.
In other respects his want of prudence had thwarted
his best endeavours. His cavalry at the beginning of the
campaign was effectively employed. But so extravagant
were his demands on the mounted arm, that before the battle
of Manassas half his regiments were dismounted. It is true
that the troopers were still indifferent horsemen and bad
horse-masters, but it was the fault of the commander that
the unfortunate animals had no rest, that brigades were
sent to do the work of patrols, and that little heed was paid
to the physical wants of man and beast. As a tactician
Pope was incapable. As a strategist he lacked imagination,
except in his dispatches. His horizon was limited, and
he measured the capacity of his adversaries by his own.
He was familiar with the campaign in the Valley, with the
operations in the Peninsula, and Cedar Run should have
enlightened him as to Jackson's daring. But he had no
conception that his adversaries would cheerfully accept

great risks to achieve great ends; he had never dreamt of a general who would deliberately divide his army, or of one who would make fifty-six miles in two marches.

Lee, with his extraordinary insight into character, had played on Pope as he had played on McClellan, and his strategy was justified by success. In the space of three weeks he had carried the war from the James to the Potomac. With an army that at no time exceeded 55,000 men he had driven 80,000 into the fortifications of Washington.[1] He had captured 30 guns, 7,000 prisoners, 20,000 rifles, and many stand of colours; he had killed or wounded 13,500 Federals, destroyed supplies and material of enormous value; and all this with a loss to the Confederates of 10,000 officers and men.

So much had he done for the South; for his own reputation he had done more. If, as Moltke avers, the junction of two armies on the field of battle is the highest achievement of military genius,[2] the campaign against Pope has seldom been surpassed; and the great counterstroke at Manassas is sufficient in itself to make Lee's reputation as a tactician. Salamanca was perhaps a more brilliant example of the same manœuvre, for at Salamanca Wellington had no reason to anticipate that Marmont would blunder, and the mighty stroke which beat 40,000 French in forty minutes was conceived in a few moments. Nor does Manassas equal Austerlitz. No such subtle manœuvres were employed as those by which Napoleon induced the Allies to lay bare their centre, and drew them blindly to their doom. It was not due to the skill of Lee that Pope weakened his left at the crisis of the battle.[3]

[1] Sumner and Franklin had become involved in Pope's retreat.

[2] Tried by this test alone Lee stands out as one of the greatest soldiers of all times. Not only against Pope, but against McClellan at Gaines' Mill, against Burnside at Fredericksburg, and against Hooker at Chancellorsville, he succeeded in carrying out the operations of which Moltke speaks; and in each case with the same result of surprising his adversary. None knew better how to apply that great principle of strategy, 'to march divided but to fight concentrated.'

[3] It may be noticed, however, that the care with which Longstreet's troops were kept concealed for more than four-and-twenty hours had much to do with Pope's false manœuvres.

But in the rapidity with which the opportunity was seized, in the combination of the three arms, and in the vigour of the blow, Manassas is in no way inferior to Austerlitz or Salamanca. That the result was less decisive was due to the greater difficulties of the battle-field, to the stubborn resistance of the enemy, to the obstacles in the way of rapid and connected movement, and to the inexperience of the troops. Manassas was not, like Austerlitz and Salamanca, won by veteran soldiers, commanded by trained officers, perfect in drill and inured to discipline.

Lee's strategic manœuvres were undoubtedly hazardous. But that an antagonist of different calibre would have met them with condign punishment is short-sighted criticism. Against an antagonist of different calibre, against such generals as he was afterwards to encounter, they would never have been attempted. ' He studied his adversary,' says his Military Secretary, ' knew his peculiarities, and adapted himself to them. His own methods no one could foresee—he varied them with every change in the commanders opposed to him. He had one method with McClellan, another with Pope, another with Hooker, another with Meade, and yet another with Grant.' Nor was the dangerous period of the Manassas campaign so protracted as might be thought. Jackson marched north from Jefferson on August 25. On the 26th he reached Bristoe Station. Pope, during these two days, might have thrown himself either on Longstreet or on Jackson. He did neither, and on the morning of the 27th, when Jackson reached Sudley Springs, the crisis had passed. Had the Federals blocked Thoroughfare Gap that day, and prevented Longstreet's passage, Lee was still able to concentrate without incurring defeat. Jackson, retreating by Aldie Gap, would have joined Longstreet west of the mountains; Pope would have escaped defeat, but the Confederates would have lost nothing.

Moreover, it is well to remember that the Confederate cavalry was in every single respect, in leading, horsemanship, training, and knowledge of the country, superior to the Federal. The whole population, too, was staunchly

Southern. It was always probable, therefore, that information would be scarce in the Federal camps, and that if some items did get through the cavalry screen, they would be so late in reaching Pope's headquarters as to be practically useless. There can be no question that Lee, in these operations, relied much on the skill of Stuart. Stuart was given a free hand. Unlike Pope, Lee issued few orders as to the disposition of his horsemen. He merely explained the manœuvres he was about to undertake, pointed out where he wished the main body of the cavalry should be found, and left all else to their commander. He had no need to tell Stuart that he required information of the enemy, or to lay down the method by which it was to be obtained. That was Stuart's normal duty, and right well was it performed. How admirably the young cavalry general co-operated with Jackson has already been described. The latter suggested, the former executed, and the combination of the three arms, during the whole of Jackson's operations against Pope, was as close as when Ashby led his squadrons in the Valley.

Yet it was not on Stuart that fell, next to Lee, the honours of the campaign. Brilliant as was the handling of the cavalry, impenetrable the screen it formed, and ample the information it procured, the breakdown of the Federal horse made the task comparatively simple. Against adversaries whose chargers were so leg-weary that they could hardly raise a trot it was easy to be bold. One of Stuart's brigadiers would have probably done the work as well as Stuart himself. But the handling of the Valley army, from the time it left Jefferson on the 25th until Longstreet reached Gainesville on the 29th, demanded higher qualities than vigilance and activity. Throughout the operations Jackson's endurance was the wonder of his staff. He hardly slept. He was untiring in reconnaissance, in examination of the country and in observation of the enemy, and no detail of the march escaped his personal scrutiny. Yet his muscles were much less hardly used than his brain. The intellectual problem was more difficult than the physical. To march his army fifty-six miles in two days was far simpler than to maintain it on Pope's flank until Longstreet came into line. The direction of his marches, the position of his bivouacs, the distribution of his three divisions, were the outcome of long premeditation. On the night of the 25th he disappeared into the darkness on the road to Salem, leaving the Federals under the conviction that he was making for the Valley. On the 26th he moved on Bristoe Station, rather than on Manassas Junction, foreseeing that he might be interrupted from the south-west in his destruction of the stores. On the 27th he postponed his departure till night had fallen, moving in three columns, of which the column marching on Centre-ville, whither he desired that the enemy should follow, was the last to move. Concentrating at Sudley Springs on the 28th, he placed himself in the best position to hold Pope fast, to combine with Longstreet, or to escape by Aldie Gap; and on the 29th the ground he had selected for battle enabled him to hold out against superior numbers.

Neither strategically nor tactically did he make a single mistake. His attack on King's division at Groveton, on the evening of the 28th, was purely frontal, and his troops lost heavily. But he believed King to be the flank-guard of a larger force, and under such circumstances turning move-ments were over-hazardous. The woods, too, prevented the deployment of his artillery; and the attack, in its wider aspect, was eminently successful, for the aim was not to defeat King, but to bring Pope back to a position where Lee could crush him. On the 29th his dispositions were admirable. The battle is a fine example of defensive tactics. The position, to use a familiar illustration, 'fitted the troops like a glove.' It was of such strength that, while the front was adequately manned, ample reserves remained in rear. The left, the most dangerous flank, was secured by Bull Run, and massed batteries gave protection to the right. The distribution of the troops, the orders, and the amount of latitude accorded to subordinate leaders, followed the best models. The front was so apportioned that each brigadier on the fighting-line had his own reserve, and each divisional general half his force in third line. The orders indicated that counterstrokes were not to be pushed so far as to involve the troops in an engagement with the enemy's reserves, and the subordinate generals were encouraged, without waiting for orders, and thus losing the occasion, to seize all favourable opportunities for counter-stroke. The methods employed by Jackson were singu-larly like those of Wellington. A position was selected which gave cover and concealment to the troops, and against which the powerful artillery of a more numerous enemy was prac-tically useless. These were the characteristics of Vimiera, Busaco, Talavera, and Waterloo. Nor did Jackson's orders differ from those of the great Englishman.

The Duke's subordinates, when placed in position, acted on a well-established rule. Within that position they had unlimited power. They could defend the first line, or they could meet the enemy with a counter-attack from a position in rear, and in both cases they could pursue. But the pursuit was never to be carried beyond certain defined limits. Moreover, Wellington's views as to the efficacy of the counterstroke were identical with those of Jackson, and he had the same predilection for cold steel. 'If they attempt this point again, Hill,' were his orders to that general at Busaco, 'give them a volley and charge bayonets; but don't let your people follow them too far.'

But it was neither wise strategy nor sound tactics which was the main element in Pope's defeat; neither the strong effort of a powerful brain, nor the judicious devo-lution of responsibility. A brilliant military historian, more conversant perhaps with the War of Secession than the wars of France, concludes his review of this cam-paign with a reference to Jackson as 'the Ney of the Confederate army.'[1] The allusion is obvious. So long as the victories of Napoleon are remembered, the name of his lieutenant will always be a synonym for heroic valour. But the valour of Ney was of a different type from that of Jackson. Ney's valour was animal, Jackson's was moral, and between the two there is a vast distinction. Before the

[1] Swinton. *Campaigns of the Army of the Potomac.*

enemy, when his danger was tangible, Ney had few rivals. But when the enemy was unseen and his designs were doubtful, his resolution vanished. He was without confidence in his own resources. He could not act without direct orders, and he dreaded responsibility. At Bautzen his timidity ruined Napoleon's combinations ; in the campaign of Leipsic he showed himself incapable of independent command ; and he cannot be acquitted of hesitation at Quatre Bras.

It was in the same circumstances that Ney's courage invariably gave way that Jackson's courage shone with the brightest lustre. It might appear that he had little cause for fear in the campaign of the Second Manassas, that he had only to follow his instructions, and that if he had failed his failure would have been visited upon Lee. The instructions which he received, however, were not positive, but contingent on events. If possible, he was to cut the railway, in order to delay the reinforcements which Pope was expecting from Alexandria ; and then, should the enemy permit, he was to hold fast east of the Bull Run Mountains until Lee came up. But he was to be guided in everything by his own discretion. He was free to accept battle or refuse it, to attack or to defend, to select his own line of retreat, to move to any quarter of the compass that he pleased. For three days, from the morning of August 26 to the morning of August 29, he had complete control of the strategic situation ; on his movements were dependent the movements of the main army ; the bringing the enemy to bay and the choice of the field of battle were both in his hands. And during those three days he was cut off from Lee and Longstreet. The mountains, with their narrow passes, lay between ; and, surrounded by three times his number, he was abandoned entirely to his own resources.

Throughout the operations he had been in unusually high spirits. The peril and responsibility seemed to act as an elixir, and he threw off much of his constraint. But as the day broke on August 29 he looked long and earnestly in the direction of Thoroughfare Gap, and when a messenger from Stuart brought the intelligence that Longstreet was through the pass, he drew a long breath and uttered a sigh of relief.[1] The period of suspense was over, but even on that unyielding heart the weight of anxiety had pressed with fearful force. For three days he had only received news of the main army at long and uncertain intervals. For two of these days his information of the enemy's movements was very small. While he was marching to Bristoe Station, Pope, for all he knew, might have been marching against Longstreet with his whole force. When he attacked King on the 28th the Federals, in what strength he knew not, still held Thoroughfare Gap ; when he formed for action on the 29th he was still ignorant of what had happened to the main body, and it was on the bare chance that Longstreet would force the passage that he accepted battle with far superior numbers.

It is not difficult to imagine how a general like Ney, placed in Jackson's situation, would have trimmed and hesitated : how in his march to Manassas, when he had crossed the mountains and left the Gap behind him, he would have sent out reconnaissances in all directions, halting his troops until he learned the coast was clear ; how he would have dashed at the Junction by the shortest route ; how he would have forced his weary troops northward when the enemy's approach was reported ; how, had he reached Sudley Springs, he would have hugged the shelter of the woods and let King's division pass unmolested ; and, finally, when Pope's columns converged on his position, have fallen back on Thoroughfare or Aldie. Nor would he have been greatly to blame. Unless gifted with that moral fortitude which Napoleon ranks higher than genius or experience, no general would have succeeded in carrying Lee's design to a successful issue. In his unhesitating march to Manassas Junction, in his deliberate sojourn for four-and-twenty hours astride his enemy's communications, in his daring challenge to Pope's whole army at Groveton, Jackson displayed the indomitable courage characteristic of the greatest soldiers.

[1] Letter from Dr. Hunter McGuire.

As suggested in the first volume, it is too often overlooked, by those who study the history of campaigns, that war is the province of uncertainty. The reader has the whole theatre of war displayed before him. He notes the exact disposition of the opposing forces at each hour of the campaign, and with this in his mind's eye he condemns or approves the action of the commanders. In the action of the defeated general he usually often sees much to blame; in the action of the successful general but little to admire. But his judgment is not based on a true foundation. He has ignored the fact that the information at his disposal was not at the disposal of those he criticises; and until he realises that both generals, to a greater or less degree, must have been groping in the dark, he will neither make just allowance for the errors of the one, nor appreciate the genius of the other.

It is true that it is difficult in the extreme to ascertain how much or how little those generals whose campaigns have become historical knew of their enemy at any particular moment. For instance, in the campaign before us, we are nowhere told whether Lee, when he sent Jackson to Manassas Junction, was aware that a portion of McClellan's army had been shipped to Alexandria in place of Aquia; or whether he knew, on the second day of the battle of Manassas, that Pope had been reinforced by two army corps from the Peninsula. He had certainly captured Pope's dispatch book, and no doubt it threw much light on the Federal plans, but we are not aware how far into the future this light projected. We do know, however, that, in addition to this correspondence, such knowledge as he had was derived from reports. But reports are never entirely to be relied on; they are seldom full, they are often false, and they are generally exaggerated. However active the cavalry, however patriotic the inhabitants, no general is ever possessed of accurate information of his enemy's dispositions, unless the forces are very small, or the precautions to elude observation very feeble. On August 28 Stuart's patrols covered the whole country round Jackson's army, and during the whole day the Federal columns were converging on Manassas. Sigel and Reynolds' four divisions passed through Gainesville, not five miles from Sudley Springs, and for a time were actually in contact with Jackson's outposts ; and yet Sigel and Reynolds mistook Jackson's outposts for reconnoitring cavalry. Again, when King's single division, the rear-guard of Pope's army, appeared upon the turnpike, Jackson attacked it with the idea that it was the flank-guard of a much larger force. Nor was this want of accurate intelligence due to lack of vigilance or to the dense woods. As a matter of fact the Confederates were more amply provided with information than is usually the case in war, even in an open country and with experienced armies.

But if, in the most favourable circumstances, a general is surrounded by an atmosphere which has been most aptly named ' the fog of war,' his embarrassments are intensified tenfold when he commands a portion of a divided army. Under ordinary conditions a general is at least fully informed of the dispositions of his own forces. But when between two widely separated columns a powerful enemy, capable of crushing each in turn, intervenes ; when the movements of that enemy are veiled in obscurity ; when anxiety has taken possession of the troops, and the soldiers of either column, striving hopelessly to penetrate the gloom, reflect on the fate that may have overtaken their comrades, on the obstacles that may delay them, on the misunderstandings that may have occurred—it is at such a crisis that the courage of their leader is put to the severest test.

His situation has been compared to a man entering a dark room full of assailants, never knowing when or whence a blow may be struck against him. The illustration is inadequate. Not only has he to contend with the promptings of his own instincts, but he has to contend with the instincts and to sustain the resolution of his whole army. It is not from the enemy that he has most to fear. A time comes in all protracted operations when the nervous energy of the best troops becomes exhausted, when the most daring shrink from further sacrifice, when the desire of self-preservation infects the stoutest veterans, and the will of the mass opposes a tacit resistance to all further effort. 'Then,' says Clausewitz, 'the spark in the breast of the commander must rekindle hope in the hearts of his men, and so long as he is equal to this he remains their master. When his influence ceases, and his own spirit is no longer strong enough to revive the spirit of others, the masses, drawing him with them, sink into that lower region of animal nature which recoils from danger and knows not shame. Such are the obstacles which the brain and courage of the military commander must overcome if he is to make his name illustrious.' And the obstacles are never more formidable than when his troops see no sign of the support they have expected. Then, if he still moves forward, although his peril increase at every step, to the point of junction ; if he declines the temptation, although overwhelming numbers threaten him, of a safe line of retreat ; if, as did Jackson, he deliberately confronts and challenges the hostile masses, then indeed does the soldier rise to the highest level of moral energy.

Strongly does Napoleon inveigh against operations which entail the division of an army into two columns unable to communicate ; and especially does he reprobate the strategy which places the point of junction under the very beard of a concentrated enemy. Both of these maxims Lee violated. The last because he knew Pope, the first because he knew Jackson. It is rare indeed that such strategy succeeds. When all has depended on a swift and unhesitating advance, generals renowned for their ardent courage have wavered and turned aside. Hasdrubal, divided from Hannibal by many miles and a Consular army, fell back to the Metaurus, and Rome was saved. Two thousand years later, Prince Frederick Charles, divided by a few marches and two Austrian army corps from the Crown Prince, lingered so long upon the Iser that the supremacy of Prussia trembled in the balance. But the character of the Virginian soldier was of loftier type. It has been remarked that after Jackson's death Lee never again attempted those great turning movements which had achieved his most brilliant victories. Never again did he divide his army to unite it again on the field of battle. The reason is not far to seek. There was now no general in the Confederate army to whom he dared confide the charge of the detached wing, and in possessing one such general he had been more fortunate than Napoleon.[1]

[1] It is noteworthy that Moltke once, at Königgrätz, carried out the operation referred to ; Wellington twice, at Vittoria and Toulouse ; Napoleon, although he several times attempted it, and against inferior numbers, never, except at Ulm, with complete success.

CHAPTER XVIII

HARPER'S FERRY

THE Confederate operations in Virginia during the spring and summer of 1862 had been successful beyond expectation

Sept. 1862.

and almost beyond precedent. Within six months two great armies had been defeated; McClellan had been driven from the Peninsula, and Pope from the Rappahannock. The villages of Virginia no longer swarmed with foreign bayonets. The hostile camps had vanished from her inland counties. Richmond was free from menace; and in the Valley of the Shenandoah the harvest was gathered in without let or hindrance. Except at Winchester and Martinsburg, where the garrisons, alarmed by the news of Pope's defeat, were already preparing to withdraw; in the vicinity of Norfolk, and at Fortress Monroe, the invaders had no foothold within the boundaries of the State they had just now overrun; and their demoralised masses, lying exhausted behind the fortifications of Washington and Alexandria, were in no condition to resume the offensive. The North had opened the campaign in the early spring with the confident hope of capturing the rebel capital; before the summer was over it was questionable whether it would be able to save its own. Had the rival armies been equally matched in numbers and equipment this result would have hardly been remarkable. The Federals had had great difficulties to contend with—an unknown country, bad roads, a hostile population, natural obstacles of formidable character, statesmen ignorant of war, and generals at loggerheads with the Administration. Yet so superior were their numbers, so ample their resources, that even these disadvantages might have been overcome had the strategy of the Southern leaders been less admirable. Lee, Jackson, and Johnston had played the *rôle* of the defender to perfection. No attempt had been made to hold the frontier. Mobility and not earthworks was the weapon on which they had relied. Richmond, the only fortress, had been used as a 'pivot of operations,' and not merely as a shelter for the army. The specious expedient of pushing forward advanced-guards to harass or delay the enemy had been avoided; and thus no opportunity had been offered to the invaders of dealing with the defence in detail, or of raising their own *moral* by victory over isolated detachments. The generals had declined battle until their forces were concentrated and the enemy was divided. Nor had they fought except on ground of their own choice. Johnston had refused to be drawn into decisive action until McClellan became involved in the swamps of the Chickahominy. Jackson, imitating like his superior the defensive strategy of Wellington and Napoleon, had fallen back to a 'zone of manœuvre' south of the Massanuttons. By retreating to the inaccessible fastness of Elk Run Valley he had drawn Banks and Frémont up the Shenandoah, their lines of communication growing longer and more vulnerable at every march, and requiring daily more men to guard them. Then, rushing from his stronghold, he had dealt his blows, clearing the Valley from end to end, destroying the Federal magazines, and threatening Washington itself; and when the overwhelming masses he had drawn on himself sought to cut him off, he had selected his own battle-field, and crushed the converging columns which his skill had kept apart. The hapless Pope, too, had been handled in the same fashion as McClellan, Banks, Shields, and Frémont. Jackson had lured him forward to the Rapidan; and although his retreat had been speedy, Lee had completed his defeat before he could be efficiently supported. But, notwithstanding all that had been done, much yet remained to do.

It was doubtless within the bounds of probability that a second attempt to invade Virginia would succeed no better than the first. But it was by no means certain that the resolution of the North was not sufficient to withstand a long series of disasters so long as the war was confined to Southern territory; and, at the same time, it might well be questioned whether the South could sustain, without foreign aid, the protracted and exhausting process of a purely defensive warfare. If her tactics, as well as her strategy, could be confined to the defensive; that is, if her generals could await the invaders in selected and prepared positions, and if no task more difficult should devolve upon her troops than shooting down their foes as they moved across the open to the assault of strong intrenchments, then the hope might reasonably be entertained that she might tire out the North. But the campaign, so far as it had progressed, had shown, if indeed history had not already made it sufficiently clear, that opportunities for such tactics were not likely to occur. The Federal generals had consistently refused to run their heads against earthworks. Their overwhelming numbers would enable them to turn any position, however formidable; and the only chance of success lay in keeping these numbers apart and in preventing them from combining.

It was by strategic and tactical counterstrokes that the recent victories had been won. Although it had awaited attack within its own frontier, the Army of Northern Virginia had but small experience of defensive warfare. With the exception of the actions round Yorktown, of Cross Keys, and of the Second Manassas, the battles had been entirely aggressive. The idea that a small army, opposed to one vastly superior, cannot afford to attack because the attack is costly, and that it must trust for success to favourable ground, had been effectually dispelled. Lee and Jackson had taught the Southerners that the secret of success lies not in strong positions, but in the concentration, by means of skilful strategy, of superior numbers on the field of battle. Their tactics had been essentially offensive, and it is noteworthy that their victories had not been dearly purchased. If we compare them with those of the British in the Peninsula, we shall find that with no greater loss than Wellington incurred in the defensive engagements of three years, 1810, 1811, 1812, the Confederates had attacked and routed armies far larger in proportion than those which Wellington had merely repulsed.[1]

But if they had shown that the best defence lies in a vigorous offensive, their offensive had not yet been applied at the decisive point. To make victory complete it is the sounder policy to carry the war into hostile territory. A nation endures with comparative equanimity defeat beyond its own borders. Pride and prestige may suffer, but a high-spirited people will seldom be brought to the point of making terms unless its army is annihilated in the heart of its own country, unless the capital is occupied and the hideous sufferings of war are brought directly home to the mass of the population. A single victory on Northern soil, within easy reach of Washington, was far more likely to bring about the independence of the South than even a succession of victories in Virginia. It was time, then, for a strategic counterstroke on a larger scale than had hitherto been attempted. The opportunity was ripe. No great risk would be incurred by crossing the Potomac. There was no question of meeting a more powerful enemy. The Federals, recruited by fresh levies, would undoubtedly be numerically the stronger; and the Confederate equipment, despite the large captures of guns and rifles, was still deficient. But for deficiencies in numbers and in *matériel* the higher *moral* and the more skilful leading would make ample compensation. It might safely be inferred that the Northern soldiers would no longer display the cool confidence of Gaines' Mill or even of Malvern Hill. The places of the brave and seasoned soldiers who had fallen would

[1] Wellington's losses in the battles of these three years were 33,000. The Confederates lost 23,000 in the Valley and the Seven Days and 10,000 in the campaign against Pope. It is not to be understood, however, that the Duke's strategy was less skilful or less audacious than Lee's and Jackson's. During these three years his army, largely composed of Portuguese and Spaniards, was incapable of offensive tactics against his veteran enemies, and he was biding his time. It was the inefficiency of his allies and the miserable support he received from the English Government that prevented him, until 1813, from adopting a bolder policy.

be filled by recruits ; and generals who had been out-manœuvred on so many battle-fields might fairly be expected, when confronted once more with their dreaded opponents, to commit even more egregious errors than those into which they had already fallen.

Such were the ideas entertained by Lee and accepted by the President, and on the morning of September 2, as soon
Sept. 2.   as it was found that the Federals had sought
shelter under the forts of Alexandria, Jackson was instructed to cross the Potomac, and form the advanced-guard of the army of invasion. It may be imagined with what feelings he issued his orders for the march on Leesburg, above which lay an easy ford. For more than twelve months, since the very morrow of Bull Run, he had persistently advocated an aggressive policy.[1] The fierce battles round Richmond and Manassas he had looked upon as merely the prelude to more resolute efforts. After he had defeated Banks at Winchester he had urged his friend Colonel Boteler to inform the authorities that, if they would reinforce him, he would undertake to capture Washington. The message had been conveyed to Lee. ‘ Tell General Jackson,’ was the reply of the Commander-in-Chief, ‘ that he must first help me to drive these people away from Richmond.’ This object had been now thoroughly accomplished, and General Lee’s decision to redeem his promise was by none more heartily approved than by the leader of the Valley army. And yet, though the risks of the venture were small, the prospects of complete success were dubious. The opportunity had come, but the means of seizing it were feeble. Lee himself was buoyed up by no certain expectation of great results. In

[1] In Mrs. Jackson’s Memoirs of her husband a letter is quoted from her brother-in-law, giving the substance of a conversation with General Jackson on the conduct of the war. This letter I have not felt justified in quoting. In the first place, it lacks corroboration ; in the second place, it contains a very incomplete statement of a large strategical question ; in the third place, the opinions put in Jackson’s mouth are not only contradictory, but altogether at variance with his practice ; and lastly, it attributes certain ideas to the general—raising ‘ the black flag,’ &c.—which his confidential staff officers declare that he never for a moment entertained.

advocating invasion he confessed to the President that his troops were hardly fit for service beyond the frontier. ' The army,' he wrote, ' is not properly equipped for an invasion of the enemy's territory. It lacks much of the material of war, is feeble in transportation, the animals being much reduced, and the men are poorly provided with clothes, and in thousands of instances are destitute of shoes. . . . What concerns me most is the fear of getting out of ammunition.' [1]

This description was by no means over-coloured. As a record of military activity the campaign of the spring and summer of 1862 has few parallels. Jackson's division, since the evacuation of Winchester at the end of February, that is, in six months, had taken part in no less than eight battles and innumerable minor engagements; it had marched nearly a thousand miles, and it had long ago discarded tents. The remainder of the army had been hardly less severely tasked. The demands of the outpost service in front of Richmond had been almost as trying as the forced marches in the Valley, and the climate of the Peninsula had told heavily on the troops. From the very first the army had been indifferently equipped ; the ill effects of hasty organisation were still glaring ; the regimental officers had not yet learned to study the wants and comfort of their men ; the troops were harassed by the ignorance of a staff that was still half-trained, and the commissariat officials were not abreast of their important duties. More than all, the operations against Pope, just brought to a successful issue, had been most arduous ; and the strain on the endurance of the troops, not yet recovered from their exertions in the Peninsula, had been so great that a period of repose seemed absolutely necessary. It was not only that battle and sickness had thinned the ranks, but that those whose health had been proof against continued hardships, and whose strength and spirit were still equal to further efforts, were so badly shod that a few long marches over indifferent roads were certain to be more productive of casualties than a pitched battle. The want of

[1] O. R., vol. xix., part ii., pp. 590, 591.

boots had already been severely felt.[1] It has been said that the route of the Confederate army from the Rappahannock to Chantilly might have been traced by the stains of bloody feet along the highways; and if the statement is more graphic than exact, yet it does not fall far short of the truth. Many a stout soldier, who had hobbled along on his bare feet until Pope was encountered and defeated, found himself utterly incapable of marching into Maryland. In rear of the army the roads were covered with stragglers. Squads of infantry, banding together for protection, toiled along painfully by easy stages, unable to keep pace with the colours, but hoping to be up in time for the next fight; and amongst these were not a few officers. But this was not the worst. Lax discipline and the absence of soldierly habits asserted themselves with the same pernicious effect as in the Valley. Not all the stragglers had their faces turned towards the enemy, not all were incapacitated by physical suffering. Many, without going through the formality of asking leave, were making for their homes, and had no idea that their conduct was in any way peculiar. They had done their duty in more than one battle, they had been long absent from their farms, their equipment was worn out, the enemy had been driven from Virginia, and they considered that they were fully entitled to some short repose. And amongst these, whose only fault was an imperfect sense of their military obligations, was the residue of cowards and malingerers shed by every great army engaged in protracted operations.

Lee had been joined by the divisions of D. H. Hill, McLaws, Walker, and by Hampton's cavalry, and the strength of his force should have been 65,000 effectives.[2] But it was evident that these numbers could not be long

---

[1] '1,000 pairs of shoes were obtained in Fredericktown, 250 pairs in Williamsport, and about 400 pairs in this city (Hagerstown). They will not be sufficient to cover the bare feet of the army.' Lee to Davis, September 12, 1862. O. R., vol. xix., part ii., p. 605.

[2] Calculated on the basis of the Field Returns dated July 20, 1862, with the addition of Jackson's and Ewell's divisions, and subtracting the losses (10,000) of the campaign against Pope.

maintained. The men were already accustomed to half-rations of green corn, and they would be no worse off in Maryland and Pennsylvania, untouched as yet by the ravages of war, than in the wasted fields of Virginia. The most ample commissariat, however, would not compensate for the want of boots and the want of rest, and a campaign of invasion was certain to entail an amount of hard marching to which the strength of the troops was hardly equal. Not only had the South to provide from her seven millions of white population an army larger than that of Imperial France, but from a nation of agriculturists she had to provide another army of craftsmen and mechanics to enable the soldiers to keep the field. For guns and gun-carriages, powder and ammunition, clothing and harness, gunboats and torpedoes, locomotives and railway plant, she was now dependent on the hands of her own people and the resources of her own soil; the organisation of those resources, scattered over a vast extent of territory, was not to be accomplished in the course of a few months, nor was the supply of skilled labour sufficient to fill the ranks of her industrial army. By the autumn of 1862, although the strenuous efforts of every Government department gave the lie to the idea, not uncommon in the North, that the Southern character was shiftless and the Southern intellect slow, so little real progress had been made that if the troops had not been supplied from other sources they could hardly have marched at all. The captures made in the Valley, in the Peninsula, and in the Second Manassas campaign proved of inestimable value. Old muskets were exchanged for new, smooth-bore cannon for rifled guns, tattered blankets for good overcoats. 'Mr. Commissary Banks,' his successor Pope, and McClellan himself, had furnished their enemies with the material of war, with tents, medicines, ambulances, and ammunition waggons. Even the vehicles at Confederate headquarters bore on their tilts the initials U.S.A.; many of Lee's soldiers were partially clothed in Federal uniforms, and the bad quality of the boots supplied by the Northern contractors was a very general subject of complaint in the

Southern ranks. Nor while the men were fighting were the women idle. The output of the Government factories was supplemented by private enterprise. Thousands of spinning-wheels, long silent in dusty lumber-rooms, hummed busily in mansion and in farm; matrons and maids, from the wife and daughters of the Commander-in-Chief to the mother of the drummer-boy, became weavers and seamstresses; and in every household of the Confederacy, although many of the necessities of life—salt, coffee and sugar—had become expensive luxuries, the needs of the army came before all else.

But notwithstanding the energy of the Government and the patriotism of the women, the troops lacked everything but spirit. Nor, even with more ample resources, could their wants have been readily supplied. In any case this would have involved a long halt in a secure position, and in a few weeks the Federal strength would be increased by fresh levies, and the *moral* of their defeated troops restored. But even had time been given the Government would have been powerless to render substantial aid. Contingents of recruits were being drilled into discipline at Richmond; yet they hardly exceeded 20,000 muskets; and it was not on the Virginia frontier alone that the South was hard pressed. The Valley of the Mississippi was beset by great armies; Alabama was threatened, and Western Tennessee was strongly occupied; it was already difficult to find a safe passage across the river for the supplies furnished by the prairies of Texas and Louisiana, and communication with Arkansas had become uncertain. If the Mississippi were lost, not only would three of the most fertile States, as prolific of hardy soldiers as of fat oxen, be cut off from the remainder, but the enemy, using the river as a base, would push his operations into the very heart of the Confederacy. To regain possession of the great waterway seemed of more vital importance than the defence of the Potomac or the secession of Maryland, and now that Richmond had been relieved, the whole energy of the Government was expended on the operations in Kentucky and

Tennessee. It may well be questioned whether a vigorous endeavour, supported by all the means available, and even by troops drawn from the West, to defeat the Army of the Potomac and to capture Washington, would not have been a more efficacious means to the same end ; but Davis and his Cabinet consistently preferred dispersion to concentration, and, indeed, the situation of the South was such as might well have disturbed the strongest brains. The sea-power of the Union was telling with deadly effect. Although the most important strategic points on the Mississippi were still held by Confederate garrisons, nearly every mile of the great river, from Cairo to New Orleans, was patrolled by the Federal gunboats ; and in deep water, from the ports of the Atlantic to the road-steads of the Gulf, the frigates maintained their vigilant blockade.

Even on the northern border there was hardly a gleam of light across the sky. The Federal forces were still formidable in numbers, and a portion of the Army of the Potomac had not been involved in Pope's defeat. It was possible, therefore, that more skilful generalship than had yet been displayed by the Northern commanders might deprive the Confederates of all chance of winning a decisive victory. Yet, although the opportunity of meeting the enemy with a prospect of success might never offer, an inroad into Northern territory promised good results.

1. Maryland, still strong in sympathy with the South, might be induced by the presence of a Southern army to rise against the Union.

2. The Federal army would be drawn off westward from its present position ; and so long as it was detained on the northern frontier of Virginia nothing could be attempted against Richmond, while time would be secured for improving the defences of the Confederate capital.

3. The Shenandoah Valley would be most effectively protected, and its produce transported without risk of interruption both to Lee's army and to Richmond.

To obtain such advantages as these was worth an effort, and Lee, after careful consideration, determined to cross the

Q 2

Potomac. The movement was made with the same speed which had characterised the operations against Pope. It was of the utmost importance that the passage of the river should be accomplished before the enemy had time to discover the design and to bar the way. Stuart's cavalry formed the screen. On the morning after the battle of Chantilly, Fitzhugh Lee's brigade followed the retreating Federals in the direction of Alexandria. Hampton's brigade was pushed forward to Dranesville by way of Hunter's Mill. Robertson's brigade made a strong demonstration towards Washington, and Munford, with the 2nd Virginia, cleared out a Federal detachment which occupied Leesburg. Behind the cavalry the army marched unmolested and unobserved.[1] D. H. Hill's division was pushed forward as advanced-guard; Jackson's troops, who had been granted a day's rest, brought up the rear, and on the morning of the 6th reached White's Ford on the Potomac.

Sept. 6.

Through the silver reaches of the great river the long columns of men and waggons, preceded by Fitzhugh Lee's brigade, splashed and stumbled, and passing through the groves of oaks which overhung the water, wound steadily northward over the green fields of Maryland.

[1] The Army of Northern Virginia was thus organised during the Maryland campaign :—

Longstreet's	McLaws' Division . . . . R. H. Anderson's Division . . . . D. R. Jones' Division . . . . J. G. Walker's Division . . . . Evans' Brigade . . . . Washington Artillery . . . . S. D. Lee's Artillery battalion . .	= 35,600
Jackson's	Ewell's (Lawton) Division . . . The Light (A. P. Hill) Division . . . Jackson's own (J. R. Jones) Division . .	= 16,800
	D. H. Hill's Division	7,000
Pendleton's Reserve Artillery, 4 battalions		1,000
Stuart	Hampton's Brigade . . . . Fitzhugh Lee's Brigade . . . . Robertson's Brigade . . . . 3 H. A. batteries, Captain Pelham	= 4,000
	Total	64,400

No allowance has been made for straggling. It is doubtful if more than 55.000 men entered Maryland.

The next day Frederick was occupied by Jackson, who was once more in advance; the cavalry at Urbanna watched the roads to Washington, and every city in the North was roused by the tidings that the grey jackets had crossed the border. But although the army had entered Maryland without the slightest difficulty, the troops were not received with the enthusiasm they had anticipated. The women, indeed, emulating their Virginia sisters, gave a warm welcome to the heroes of so many victories. But the men, whether terrorised by the stern rule of the Federal Government, or mistrusting the power of the Confederates to secure them from further punishment, showed little disposition to join the ranks. It is possible that the appearance of the Southern soldiery was not without effect. Lee's troops, after five months' hard marching and hard fighting, were no delectable objects. With torn and brimless hats, strands of rope for belts, and raw-hide moccasins of their own manufacture in lieu of boots; covered with vermin, and carrying their whole kit in Federal haversacks, the ragged scarecrows who swarmed through the streets of Frederick presented a pitiful contrast to the trim battalions which had hitherto held the Potomac. Their conduct indeed was exemplary. They had been warned that pillage and depredations would be severely dealt with, and all requisitions, even of fence-rails, were paid for on the spot. Still recruits were few. The war-worn aspect and indifferent equipment of the 'dirty darlings,' as more than one fair Marylander spoke of Jackson's finest soldiers, failed to inspire confidence, and it was soon evident that the western counties of Maryland had small sympathy with the South.

There were certainly exceptions to the general absence of cordiality. The troops fared well during their sojourn in Frederick. Supplies were plentiful; food and clothing were gratuitously distributed, and Jackson was presented with a fine but unbroken charger. The gift was timely, for 'Little Sorrel,' the companion of so many marches, was lost for some days after the passage of the Potomac; but the Confederacy was near paying a heavy price for the 'good grey mare.' When Jackson first mounted her a band struck up close by, and as she reared the girth broke, throwing her rider to the ground. Fortunately, though stunned and severely bruised, the general was only temporarily disabled, and, if he appeared but little in public during his stay in Frederick, his inaccessibility was not due to broken bones. 'Lee, Longstreet, and Jackson, and for a time Jeb Stuart,' writes a staff officer, 'had their headquarters near one another in Best's Grove. Hither in crowds came the good people of Frederick, especially the ladies, as to a fair. General Jackson, still suffering from his hurt, kept to his tent, busying himself with maps and official papers, and declined to see visitors. Once, however, when he had been called to General Lee's tent, two young girls waylaid him, paralysed him with smiles and questions, and then jumped into their carriage and drove off rapidly, leaving him there, cap in hand, bowing, blushing, speechless. But once safe in his tent, he was seen no more that day.'[1] The next evening (Sunday) he went with his staff to service in the town, and slept soundly, as he admitted to his wife, through the sermon of a minister of the German Reformed Church.[2]

But it was not for long that the Confederates were permitted to repose in Frederick. The enemy had made no further reply to the passage of the Potomac beyond concentrating to the west of Washington. McClellan, who had superseded Pope, was powerless, owing to the inefficiency of his cavalry, to penetrate the cordon of Stuart's pickets, and to ascertain, even approximately, the dispositions of the invading force. He was still in doubt if the whole or only part of Lee's army had crossed

---

[1] 'Stonewall Jackson in Maryland.' Colonel H. K. Douglas. *Battles and Leaders*, vol. ii., p. 621.

[2] 'The minister,' says Colonel Douglas, 'was credited with much loyalty and courage, because he had prayed for the President of the United States in the very presence of Stonewall Jackson. Well, the general didn't hear the prayer, and if he had he would doubtless have felt like replying as General Ewell did, when asked at Carlisle, Pennsylvania, if he would permit the usual prayer for President Lincoln—"Certainly; I'm sure he needs it."'

into Maryland; and whether his adversary intended to
attack Washington by the left bank of the Potomac,
to move on Baltimore, or to invade Pennsylvania, were
questions which he had no means of determining. This
uncertainty compelled him to move cautiously, and on
September 9 his advanced-guard was still twenty miles
east of Frederick.

Nevertheless, the situation of the Confederates had
become suddenly complicated. When the march into
Maryland was begun, three towns in the Valley were
held by the Federals. 3,000 infantry and artillery occupied Winchester. 3,000 cavalry were at Martinsburg;
and Harper's Ferry, in process of conversion into an
intrenched camp, had a garrison of 8,000 men. Lee
was well aware of the presence of these forces when he
resolved to cross the Potomac, but he believed that immediately his advance threatened to separate them from
the main army, and to leave them isolated, they would
be ordered to insure their safety by a timely retreat.
Had it depended upon McClellan this would have been
done. Halleck, however, thought otherwise; and the officer
commanding at Harper's Ferry was ordered to hold his
works until McClellan should open communication with
him.

On arrival at Frederick, therefore, the Confederates,
contrary to anticipation, found 14,000 Federals still established in their rear, and although Winchester had been
evacuated,[1] it was clear that Harper's Ferry was to be
defended. The existence of the intrenched camp was
a serious obstacle to the full development of Lee's designs.
His line of communication had hitherto run from Rapidan
Station to Manassas Junction, and thence by Leesburg
and Point of Rocks to Frederick. This line was within
easy reach of Washington, and liable to be cut at any
moment by the enemy's cavalry. Arrangements had
therefore been already made to transfer the line to the
Valley. There, sheltered by the Blue Ridge, the convoys of

[1] On the night of September 2. Lee's Report, O. R., vol. xix., part i.,
p. 139.

sick and wounded, of arms, clothing, and ammunition, could move in security from Staunton to Shepherdstown, and the recruits which were accumulating at Richmond be sent to join the army in Northern territory. But so long as Harper's Ferry was strongly garrisoned this new line would be liable to constant disturbance, and it was necessary that the post should either be masked by a superior force, or carried by a *coup de main*. The first of these alternatives was at once rejected, for the Confederate numbers were too small to permit any permanent detachment of a considerable force, and without hesitation Lee determined to adopt the bolder course. 25,000 men, he considered, would be no more than sufficient to effect his object. But 25,000 men were practically half the army, and the plan, when laid before the generals, was not accepted without remonstrance. Longstreet, indeed, went so far as to refuse command of the detachment. 'I objected,' he writes, 'and urged that our troops were worn with marching and were on short rations, and that it would be a bad idea to divide our forces while we were in the enemy's country, where he could get information, in six or eight hours, of any movement we might make. The Federal army, though beaten at the Second Manassas, was not disorganised, and it would certainly come out to look for us, and we should guard against being caught in such a condition. Our army consisted of a superior quality of soldiers, but it was in no condition to divide in the enemy's country. I urged that we should keep it in hand, recruit our strength, and get up supplies, and then we could do anything we pleased. General Lee made no reply to this, and I supposed the Harper's Ferry scheme was abandoned.'[1]

Jackson, too, would have preferred to fight McClellan first, and consider the question of communications afterwards;[2] but he accepted with alacrity the duty which his colleague had declined. His own divisions, reinforced by

---

[1] *Battles and Leaders*, vol. ii., p. 662.   [2] Dabney, vol. ii., p. 302.

those of McLaws, R. H. Anderson,[1] and Walker, were detailed for the expedition; Harper's Ferry was to be invested on three sides, and the march was to begin at daybreak on September 10. Meanwhile, the remainder of the army was to move north-west to Hagerstown, five-and-twenty miles from Frederick, where it would alarm Lincoln for the safety of Pennsylvania, and be protected from McClellan by the parallel ranges of the Catoctin and South Mountains.

Undoubtedly, in ordinary circumstances, General Longstreet would have been fully justified in protesting against the dispersion of the army in the presence of the enemy. Hagerstown and Harper's Ferry are five-and-twenty miles apart, and the Potomac was between them. McClellan's advanced-guard, on the other hand, was thirty miles from Harper's Ferry, and forty-five from Hagerstown. Tho Federals were advancing, slowly and cautiously it is true, but still pushing westward, and it was certainly possible, should they receive early intelligence of the Confederate movements, that before Harper's Ferry fell a rapid march might enable them to interpose between Lee and Jackson. But both Lee and Jackson calculated the chances with a surer grasp of the several factors. Had the general in command of the Federal army been bold and enterprising, had the Federal cavalry been more efficient, or Stuart less skilful, they would certainly have hesitated before running the risk of defeat in detail. But so long as McClellan controlled the movements of the enemy, rapid and decisive action was not to be apprehended; and it was exceedingly improbable that the scanty and unreliable information which he might obtain from civilian sources would induce him to throw off his customary caution. Moreover, only a fortnight previously the Federal army had been heavily defeated.[2]

Lee had resolved to woo fortune while she was in the

[1] Anderson was placed under McLaws' command.
[2] 'Are you acquainted with McClellan?' said Lee to General Walker on September 8, 1862. 'He is an able general but a very cautious one. His enemies among his own people think him too much so. His army is in a very demoralised and chaotic condition, and will not be prepared for offensive operations—or he will not think it so—for three or four weeks.'—*Battles and Leaders*, vol. ii., pp. 605 and 606.

mood.   The movement against Harper's Ferry once determined, it was essential that it should be carried out with the utmost speed, and Jackson marched with even more than ordinary haste, but without omitting his usual precautions.   Before starting he asked for a map of the Pennsylvania frontier, and made many inquiries as to roads and localities to the north of Frederick, whereas his route lay in the opposite direction. 'The cavalry, which preceded the column,' says Colonel Douglas, 'had instructions to let no civilian go to the front, and we entered each village we passed before the inhabitants knew of our coming.   In Middletown two very pretty girls, with ribbons of red, white, and blue floating from their hair, and small Union flags in their hands, rushed out of a house as we passed, came to the kerbstone, and with much laughter waved their flags defiantly in the face of the general.   He bowed, raised his hat, and turning with his quiet smile to the staff, said, "We evidently have no friends in this town."   Having crossed South Mountain at Turner's Gap, the command encamped for the night within a mile of Boonsboro' (fourteen miles from Frederick).   Here General Jackson must determine whether he would go to Williamsport or turn towards Shepherdstown.   I at once rode into the village with a cavalryman to make some inquiries, but we ran into a Federal squadron, who without ceremony proceeded to make war upon us.   We retraced our steps, and although we did not stand upon the order of our going, a squad of them escorted us out of the town with great rapidity.   Reaching the top of the hill, we discovered, just over it, General Jackson, walking slowly towards us, leading his horse. There was but one thing to do.   Fortunately the chase had become less vigorous, and with a cry of command to unseen troops, we turned and charged the enemy.   They, suspecting trouble, turned and fled, while the general quickly galloped to the rear.   As I returned to camp I picked up the gloves which he had dropped in mounting, and took them to him.   Although he had sent a regiment of infantry to the front as soon as he went back, the only

Sept. 10.

Sept. 11.

allusion he made to the incident was to express the opinion that I had a very fast horse.

'The next morning, having learned that the Federal troops still occupied Martinsburg, General Jackson took the direct road to Williamsport. He then forded the Potomac, the troops singing, the bands playing "Carry me back to ole Virginny!" We marched on Martinsburg. General A. P. Hill took the direct turnpike, while Jackson, with the rest of his command, followed a side road, so as to approach Martinsburg from the west, and encamped four miles from the town. His object was to drive

Sept. 12.

General White, who occupied Martinsburg, towards Harper's Ferry, and thus "corral" all the Federal troops in that military pen. As the Comte de Paris puts it, he "organised a grand hunting match through the lower Valley, driving all the Federal detachments before him and forcing them to crowd into the blind alley of Harper's Ferry."

'The next morning the Confederates entered Martinsburg. Here the general was welcomed with enthusiasm, and a great crowd hastened to the hotel to greet him. At first he shut himself up in a room to write dispatches, but the demonstration became so persistent that he ordered the door to be opened. The crowd, chiefly ladies, rushed in and embarrassed the general with every possible outburst of affection, to which he could only reply, "Thank you, you are very kind." He gave them his autograph in books and on scraps of paper, cut a button from his coat for a little girl, and then submitted patiently to an attack by the others, who soon stripped the coat of nearly all the remaining buttons. But when they looked beseechingly at his hair, which was thin, he drew the line, and managed to close the interview. These blandishments did not delay his movements, however, for in the afternoon he was off again, and his troops bivouacked on the banks of the Opequon.'[1]

[1] *Battles and Leaders*, vol. ii., pp. 622, 623. Major Hotchkiss relates that the ladies of Martinsburg made such desperate assaults on the mane and tail of the general's charger that he had at last to post a sentry over the stable.

On the 13th Jackson passed through Halltown and halted a mile north of that village,[1] throwing out pickets to hold the roads which lead south and west from Harper's Ferry. Meanwhile, McLaws and Walker had taken possession of the heights to the north and east, and the intrenched camp of the Federals, which, in addition to the garrison, now held the troops who had fled from Martinsburg, was surrounded on every side. The Federal officer in command had left but one brigade and two batteries to hold the Maryland Heights, the long ridge, 1,000 feet high, on the north shore of the Potomac, which looks down on the streets of the little town. This detachment, although strongly posted, and covered by breastworks and abattis, was driven off by General McLaws ; while the Loudoun Heights, a portion of the Blue Ridge, east of the Shenandoah, and almost equally commanding, were occupied without opposition by General Walker. Harper's Ferry was now completely surrounded. Lee's plans had been admirably laid and precisely executed, and the surrender of the place was merely a question of hours.

Nor had matters progressed less favourably elsewhere. In exact accordance with the anticipations of Lee and Jackson, McClellan, up till noon on the 13th, had received no inkling whatever of the dangerous manœuvres which Stuart so effectively concealed, and his march was very slow. On the 12th, after a brisk skirmish with the Confederate cavalry, his advanced-guard had occupied Frederick, and discovered that the enemy had marched off in two columns, one towards Hagerstown, the other towards Harper's Ferry, but he was uncertain whether Lee intended to recross the Potomac or to move northwards into Pennsylvania. On the morning of the 13th, although General Hooker, commanding the First Army Corps, took the liberty of reporting that, in his opinion, ' the rebels had no more intention of going to Pennsylvania than they had

Sept. 13.

---

[1] On September 10 he marched fourteen miles, on September 11 twenty, on September 12 sixteen, and on September 13 twelve, arriving at Halltown at 11 A.M.

of going to heaven,' the Federal Commander-in-Chief was still undecided, and on the Boonsboro' road only his cavalry was pushed forward. In four days McClellan had marched no more than five-and-twenty miles; he had been unable to open communication with Harper's Ferry, and he had moved with even more than his usual caution. But at noon on the 13th he was suddenly put into possession of the most ample information. A copy of Lee's order for the investment of Harper's Ferry, in which the exact position of each separate division of the Confederate army was laid down, was picked up in the streets of Frederick, and chance had presented McClellan with an opportunity unique in history.[1] He was within twenty miles of Harper's Ferry. The Confederates were more than that distance apart. The intrenched camp still held out, for the sound of McLaws' battle on the Maryland Heights was distinctly heard during the afternoon, and a resolute advance would have either compelled the Confederates to raise the siege, or have placed the Federal army between their widely separated wings.

But, happily for the South, McClellan was not the man for the opportunity. He still hesitated, and during the afternoon of the 13th only one division was pushed forward. In front of him was the South Mountain, the name given to the continuation of the Blue Ridge north of the Potomac, and the two passes, Turner's and Crampton's Gaps, were held by Stuart. No Confederate infantry, as Lee's order indicated, with the exception, perhaps, of a rear-guard, were nearer the passes than

---

[1] General Longstreet, in his *From Manassas to Appomattox*, declares that the lost order was sent by General Jackson to General D. H. Hill, ' but was not delivered. The order,' he adds, ' that was sent to General Hill from general headquarters was carefully preserved.' General Hill, however, in *Battles and Leaders*, vol. ii., p. 570 (note), says : ' It was proper that I should receive that order through Jackson, and not through Lee. I have now before me (1888) the order received from Jackson. My adjutant-general swore affidavit, twenty years ago, that no order was received at our office from General Lee.' Jackson was so careful that no one should learn the contents of the order that the copy he furnished to Hill was written by his own hand. The copy found by the Federals was wrapped round three cigars, and was signed by Lee's adjutant-general.

the Maryland Heights and Boonsboro'.[1] The roads
were good and the weather fine, and a night march of
twelve miles would have placed the Federal advanced-
guards at the foot of the mountains, ready to force the
Gaps at earliest dawn.   McClellan, however, although his
men had made no unusual exertions during the past few
days, preferred to wait till daylight.

Nevertheless, on the night of the 13th disaster
threatened the Confederates.   Harper's Ferry had not
yet fallen, and, in addition to the cavalry, D. H. Hill's
division was alone available to defend the passes. Lee,
however, still relying on McClellan's irresolution, determined to hold South Mountain, thus gaining time for
the reduction of Harper's Ferry, and Longstreet was
ordered back from Hagerstown, thirteen miles west of
Boonsboro', to Hill's assistance.

On the same night Jackson, at Halltown, opened communications with McLaws and Walker, and on the next
Sept. 14. morning (Sunday) he made the necessary arrangements to ensure combination in the attack.   The
Federal lines, although commanded by the Maryland and
Loudoun Heights to the north and east, opposed a strong
front to the south and west.   The Bolivar Heights, an open
plateau, a mile and a quarter in length, which has the
Potomac on the one flank and the Shenandoah on the other,
was defended by several batteries and partially intrenched.
Moreover, it was so far from the summits occupied by
McLaws and Walker that their guns, although directed
against the enemy's rear, could hardly render effective aid ;
only the extremities of the plateau were thoroughly exposed to fire from the heights.

In order to facilitate communication across the two
great rivers Jackson ordered a series of signal stations to
be established, and while his own batteries were taking up
their ground to assail the Bolivar Heights he issued his
instructions to his colleagues.   At ten o'clock the flags on
the Loudoun Heights signalled that Walker had six rifled
guns in position.   He was ordered to wait until McLaws,

---

[1] For the lost order, see Note at end of chapter.

who was employed in cutting roads through the woods, should have done the same, and the following message explained the method of attack :—

'General McLaws,—If you can, establish batteries to drive the enemy from the hill west of Bolivar and on which Barbour's House is, and from any other position where he may be damaged by your artillery. Let me know when you are ready to open your batteries, and give me any suggestions by which you can operate against the enemy. Cut the telegraph line down the Potomac if it is not already done. Keep a good look-out against a Federal advance from below. Similar instructions will be sent to General Walker. I do not desire any of the batteries to open until all are ready on both sides of the river, except you should find it necessary, of which you must judge for yourself. I will let you know when to open all the batteries.

'T. J. JACKSON,

'*Major-General Commanding.*' [1]

About half-past two in the afternoon McLaws reported that his guns were up, and a message 'to fire at such positions of the enemy as will be most effective,' followed the formal orders for the co-operation of the whole force.

'Headquarters, Valley District,
Sept. 14, 1862.

'1. To-day Major-General McLaws will attack so as to sweep with his artillery the ground occupied by the enemy, take his batteries in reverse, and otherwise operate against him as circumstances may justify.

'2. Brigadier-General Walker will take in reverse the battery on the turnpike, and sweep with his artillery the ground occupied by the enemy, and silence the batteries on the island of the Shenandoah should he find a battery (*sic*) there.

'3. Major-General A. P. Hill will move along the left bank of the Shenandoah, and thus turn the enemy's left flank and enter Harper's Ferry.

[1] Report of Signal Officer, O. R., vol. xix., part i., p. 958.

'4. Brigadier-General Lawton will move along the turnpike for the purpose of supporting General Hill, and otherwise operating against the enemy to the left of General Hill.

'5. Brigadier-General Jones will, with one of his brigades and a battery of artillery, make a demonstration against the enemy's right; the remaining part of his division will constitute the reserve and move along the turnpike.

'By order of Major-General Jackson,

'Wm. L. Jackson,

'*Acting Assistant Adjutant-General.*'[1]

Jackson, it appears, was at first inclined to send a flag of truce, for the purpose of giving the civilian population time to get away, should the garrison refuse to surrender; but during the morning heavy firing was heard to the northward, and McLaws reported that he had been obliged to detach troops to guard his rear against McClellan. The batteries were therefore ordered to open fire on the Federal works without further delay.

According to General Walker, Jackson, although he was aware that McClellan had occupied Frederick, not over twenty miles distant, could not bring himself to believe that his old classmate had overcome his prudential instincts, and attributed the sounds of battle to a cavalry engagement. It is certain that he never for a single moment anticipated a resolute attempt to force the passages of the South Mountain, for, in reply to McLaws, he merely instructed him to ask General D. H. Hill to protect his rear, and to communicate with Lee at Hagerstown. Had he entertained the slightest suspicion that McClellan was advancing with his whole force against the passages of the South Mountain, he would hardly have suggested that Hill should be asked to defend Crampton's as well as Turner's Gap.

With full confidence, therefore, that he would have time to enforce the surrender of Harper's Ferry and to join Lee on the further bank of the Potomac, the progress of

[1] Report of Signal Officer, O. R., vol xix., part i., p. 659.

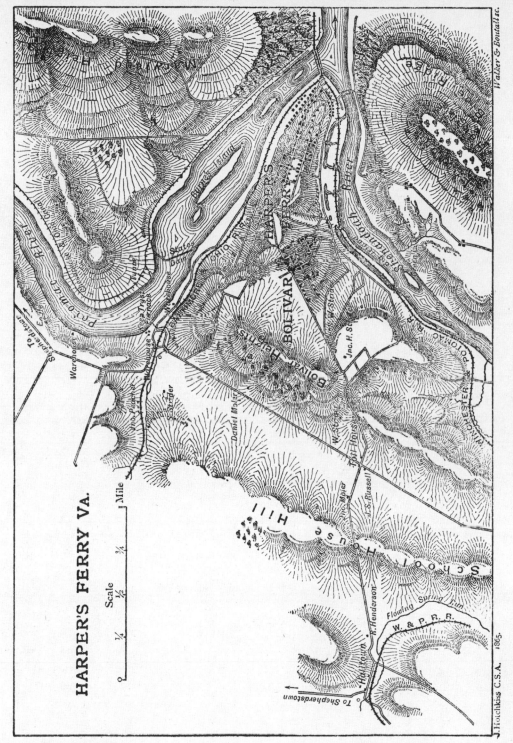

HARPER'S FERRY VA.

Scale

0   ¼   ½   ¾   1 Mile

Walker & Boutall sc.

J. Hotchkiss C.S.A. 1865.

To Shepherdstown

Loudoun Heights

Maryland Heights

Potomac River

Shenandoah River

Byrnes Island

HARPER'S FERRY

BOLIVAR

Bolivar Heights

School House Hill

W. & P. R. R.

Flowing Spring Run

R. Henderson

Halltown

J. S. Russell

Jno. Moler

Fort House

Jno. H. St.

Daniel Moler

WINCHESTER & POTOMAC R. R.

To Sleepers Ess.

Warehouse

his attack was cautious and methodical. 'The position in front of me,' he wrote to McLaws, 'is a strong one, and I desire to remain quiet, and let you and Walker draw attention from Furnace Hill (west of Bolivar Heights), so that I may have an opportunity of getting possession of the hill without much loss.' It was not, then, till the artillery had been long in action, and the fire of the enemy's guns had been in some degree subdued, that the infantry was permitted to advance. Although the Federal batteries opened vigorously on the lines of skirmishers, the casualties were exceedingly few. The troops found cover in woods and broken ground, and before nightfall Hill had driven in the enemy's pickets, and had secured a knoll on their left flank which afforded an admirable position for artillery. Lawton, in the centre, occupied a ridge over which ran the Charlestown turnpike, brought his guns into action, and formed his regiments for battle in the woods. Jones' division held the Shepherdstown road on Lawton's left, seized Furnace Hill, and pushed two batteries forward.

No attempt was made during this Sunday evening to storm the Bolivar Heights; and yet, although the Confederate infantry had been hardly engaged, the enemy had been terribly shaken. From every point of the compass, from the lofty crests which looked down upon the town, from the woods towards Charlestown, from the hill to westward, a ceaseless hail of shells had swept the narrow neck to which the garrison was confined. Several guns had been dismounted. More than one regiment of raw troops had dispersed in panic, and had been with difficulty rallied. The roads were furrowed with iron splinters. Many buildings had been demolished, and although the losses among the infantry, covered by their parapets, had been insignificant, the batteries had come almost to their last round.

During the night Jackson made preparations for an early assault. Two of A. P. Hill's brigades, working their way along the bank of the Shenandoah, over ground which the Federal commander had considered impassable, established themselves to the left rear of the Bolivar Heights. Guns were brought up to the knoll which Hill had seized during the afternoon; and ten pieces, which Jackson had ordered to be taken across the Shenandoah by Keyes' Ford, were placed in a position whence they could enfilade the enemy's works at effective range. Lawton and Jones pushed forward their lines until they could hear voices in the intrenchments; and a girdle of bayonets, closely supported by many batteries, encircled the hapless Federals. The assault was to be preceded by a heavy bombardment, and the advance was to be made as soon as Hill's guns ceased fire.

All night long the Confederates slept upon their arms, waiting for the dawn. When day broke, a soft silver mist, rising from the broad Potomac, threw its protecting folds over Harper's Ferry. But the Southern gunners knew the direction of their targets; the clouds were rent by the passage of screaming shells, and as the sun, rising over the Loudoun Heights, dispersed the vapours, the whole of Jackson's artillery became engaged. The Federal batteries, worked with stubborn courage, and showing a bold front to every fresh opponent, maintained the contest for an hour; but, even if ammunition had not failed them, they could not have long withstood the terrible fire which took them in front, in flank, and in reverse.[1] Then, perceiving that the enemy's guns were silenced, Hill ordered his batteries to cease fire, and threw forward his brigades against the ridge. Staunch to the last, the Federal artillerymen ran their pieces forward, and opened on the Confederate infantry. Once more the long line of Jackson's guns crashed out in answer, and two batteries, galloping up to within four hundred yards of the ridge, poured in a destructive fire over the heads of their own troops. Hill's brigades, when the artillery duel recommenced, had halted at the foot of the slope. Beyond, over the bare fields, the way was obstructed by felled timber, the lopped branches of which were closely interlaced, and above the abattis rose the line of breastworks. But before the charge was sounded

Sept. 15.

_____
[1] The ten guns which had been carried across the Shenandoah were specially effective. Report of Colonel Crutchfield, Jackson's chief of artillery. O. R., vol. xix., part i., p. 962.

the Confederate gunners completed the work they had so
well begun.   At 7.30 A.M. the white flag was hoisted,
and with the loss of no more than 100 men Jackson had
captured Harper's Ferry with his artillery alone.

The general was near the church in the wood on the
Charlestown road, and Colonel Douglas was sent forward
to ascertain the enemy's purpose. ' Near the top of the
hill,' he writes, ' I met General White (commanding the
Federals), and told him my mission. Just then General
Hill came up from the direction of his line, and on his
request I conducted them to General Jackson, whom I
found sitting on his horse where I had left him. He
was not, as the Comte de Paris says, leaning against a
tree asleep, but exceedingly wide-awake. . . . The surrender was unconditional, and then General Jackson turned
the matter over to General A. P. Hill, who allowed General
White the same liberal terms that Grant afterwards gave
Lee at Appomattox. The fruits of the surrender were
12,520 prisoners, 13,000 small arms, 73 pieces of artillery,
and several hundred waggons.

'General Jackson, after a brief dispatch to General
Lee announcing the capitulation, rode up to Bolivar and
down into Harper's Ferry. The curiosity in the Union
army to see him was so great that the soldiers lined the
sides of the road. Many of them uncovered as he passed,
and he invariably returned the salute. One man had an
echo of response all about him when he said aloud:
" Boys, he's not much for looks, but if we'd had him we
wouldn't have been caught in this trap." ' [1]

The completeness of the victory was marred by the
escape of the Federal cavalry. Under cover of the night
1,200 horsemen, crossing the pontoon bridge, and passing
swiftly up the towpath under the Maryland Heights, had
ridden boldly beneath the muzzles of McLaws' batteries,
and, moving north-west, had struck out for Pennsylvania.
Yet the capture of Harper's Ferry was a notable exploit,
although Jackson seems to have looked upon it as a mere
matter of course.

[1] *Battles and Leaders*, vol. ii., pp. 625-7.

' Through God's blessing,' he reported to Lee at eight o'clock, ' Harper's Ferry and its garrison are to be surrendered. As Hill's troops have borne the heaviest part of the engagement, he will be left in command until the prisoners and public property shall be disposed of, unless you direct otherwise. The other forces can move off this evening so soon as they get their rations. To what point shall they move? I write at this time in order that you may be apprised of the condition of things. You may expect to hear from me again to-day, after I get more information respecting the number of prisoners, &c.' [1]

Lee, with D. H. Hill, Longstreet, and Stuart, was already falling back from the South Mountain to Sharpsburg, a little village on the right bank of the Antietam Creek; and late in the afternoon Jackson, Walker, and McLaws were ordered to rejoin without delay.[2] September 14 had been an anxious day for the Confederate Commander-in-Chief. During the morning D. H. Hill, with no more than 5,000 men in his command, had seen the greater part of McClellan's army deploy for action in the wide valley below and to the eastward of Turner's Gap. Stuart held the woods below Crampton's Gap, six miles south, with Robertson's brigade, now commanded by the gallant Munford; and on the heights above McLaws had posted three brigades, for against this important pass, the shortest route by which the Federals could interpose between Lee and Jackson, McClellan's left wing, consisting of 20,000 men under General Franklin, was steadily advancing.

The positions at both Turner's and Crampton's Gaps were very strong. The passes, at their highest points, are at least 600 feet above the valley, and the slopes steep, rugged, and thickly wooded. The enemy's artillery had

[1] O. R., vol. xix., part i., p. 951. General Longstreet (*From Manassas to Appomattox*, p. 233) suggests that Jackson, after the capitulation of Harper's Ferry, should have moved east of South Mountain against McClellan's rear. Jackson, however, was acquainted neither with McClellan's position nor with Lee's intentions, and nothing could have justified such a movement except the direct order of the Commander-in-Chief.

[2] ' The Invasion of Maryland,' General Longstreet, *Battles and Leaders*, vol. ii., p. 666.

little chance. Stone walls, running parallel to the crest, gave much protection to the Southern infantry, and loose boulders and rocky scarps increased the difficulties of the ascent. But the numbers available for defence were very small; and had McClellan marched during the night he would probably have been master of the passes before mid-day. As it was, Crampton's Gap was not attacked by Franklin until noon; and although at the same hour the advanced-guard of the Federal right wing had gained much ground, it was not till four in the evening that a general attack was made on Turner's Gap. By this time Long-street, after a march of thirteen miles, had reached the battle-field;[1] and despite the determination with which the attack was pressed, Turner's Gap was still held when darkness fell.

The defence of Crampton's Gap had been less successful. Franklin had forced the pass before five o'clock, and driving McLaws' three brigades before him, had firmly established himself astride the summit. The Confederate losses were larger than those which they had inflicted. McClellan reports 1,791 casualties on the right, Franklin 533 on the left. McLaws' and Munford's loss was over 800, of whom 400 were captured. The number of killed and wounded in Hill's and Longstreet's commands is unknown; it probably reached a total of 1,500, and 1,100 of their men were marched to Frederick as prisoners. Thus the day's fighting had cost the South 3,400 men. Moreover, Long-street's ammunition column, together with an escort of 600 men, had been cut up by the cavalry which had escaped from Harper's Ferry, and which had struck the Hagerstown road as it marched northward into Pennsyl-

[1] The order for the march had been given the night before ('The Invasion of Maryland,' General Longstreet, *Battles and Leaders*, vol. ii., p. 666), and there seems to have been no good reason, even admitting the heat and dust, that Longstreet's command should not have joined Hill at noon. The troops marched 'at daylight' (5 A.M.), and took ten hours to march thirteen miles. As it was, only four of the brigades took part in the action, and did so, owing to their late arrival, in very disjointed fashion. Not all the Confederate generals appear to have possessed the same 'driving power' as Jackson.

vania. Yet, on the whole, Lee had no reason to be chagrined with the result of his operations. McClellan had acted with unexpected vigour. But neither in strategy nor in tactics had he displayed improvement on his Peninsular methods. He should have thrown the bulk of his army against Crampton's Gap, thus intervening between Lee and Jackson; but instead of doing so he had directed 70,000 men against Turner's Gap. Nor had his attack on Hill and Longstreet been characterised by resolution. The advanced-guard was left unsupported until 2 P.M., and not more than 30,000 men were employed throughout the day. Against this number 8,000 Confederates had held the pass. Cobb, one of McLaws' brigadiers, who commanded the defence at Crampton's Gap, though driven down the mountain, had offered a stout resistance to superior forces; and twenty-four hours had been gained for Jackson. On the other hand, in face of superior numbers, the position at Turner's Gap had become untenable; and during the night Hill and Longstreet marched to Sharpsburg.

This enforced retreat was not without effect on the *moral* of either army. McClellan was as exultant as he was credulous. 'I have just learned,' he reported to Halleck at

Sept. 15.   8 A.M. on the 15th, 'from General Hooker, in advance, that the enemy is making for Shepherdstown in a perfect panic; and that General Lee last night stated publicly that he must admit they had been shockingly whipped. I am hurrying forward to endeavour to press their retreat to the utmost.' Then, two hours later: 'Information this moment received completely confirms the rout and demoralisation of the rebel army. It is stated that Lee gives his losses as 15,000. We are following as rapidly as the men can move.'[1] Nor can it be doubted that McClellan's whole army, unaccustomed to see their antagonists give ground before them, shared the general's mood.[2] Amongst the Confederates, on the other hand, there was some depression. It could not be disguised that

[1] O. R. vol. xix., pp. 294, 295.
[2] 'The *moral* of our men is now restored.' McClellan to Halleck after South Mountain. O. R., vol. xix., part ii., p. 294.

a portion of the troops had shown symptoms of demoralisation. The retreat to the Antietam, although effectively
screened by Fitzhugh Lee's brigade of cavalry, was not
effected in the best of order. Many of the regiments had
been broken by the hard fighting on the mountain ; men
had become lost in the forest, or had sought safety to the
rear ; and the number of stragglers was very large. It
was not, then, with its usual confidence that the army
moved into position on the ridge above the Antietam Creek.
General Longstreet, indeed, was of opinion that the army
should have recrossed the Potomac at once. 'The moral
effect of our move into Maryland had been lost by our
discomfiture at South Mountain, and it was evident we
could not hope to concentrate in time to do more than
make a respectable retreat, whereas by retiring before the
battle [of Sharpsburg] we could have claimed a very successful campaign.'[1] So spake the voice of prudence. Lee,
however, so soon as he was informed of the fall of Harper's
Ferry, had ordered Jackson to join him, resolving to hold
his ground, and to bring McClellan to a decisive battle on
the north bank of the Potomac.

Although 45,000 men—for Lee at most could count on
no more than this number, so great had been the straggling—were about to receive the attack of over 90,000,
Jackson, when he reached Sharpsburg on the morning
of the 16th, heartily approved the Commander-in-Chief's
decision, and it is worth while to consider the reasons
which led them to disagree with Longstreet.

1. Under ordinary conditions, to expect an army of
45,000 to wrest decisive victory from one of 90,000 well-
armed enemies would be to demand an impossibility. The
defence, when two armies are equally matched, is physically
stronger than the attack, although we have Napoleon's
word for it that the defence has the harder task. But that
the inherent strength of the defence is so great as to
enable the smaller force to annihilate its enemy is contrary
to all the teaching of history. By making good use of
favourable ground, or by constructing substantial works,

[1] *Battles and Leaders*, vol. ii., pp. 666, 667.

the smaller force may indeed stave off defeat and gain
time.   But it can hope for nothing more.   The records of
warfare contain no instance, when two armies were of
much the same quality, of the smaller army bringing the
campaign to a decisive issue by defensive tactics.   Wellington and Lee both fought many defensive battles with inferior
forces.   But neither of them, under such conditions, ever
achieved the destruction of their enemy.   They fought
such battles to gain time, and their hopes soared no
higher.   At Talavera, Busaco, Fuentes d'Onor, where
the French were superior to the allies, Wellington repulsed
the attack, but he did not prevent the defeated armies
taking the field again in a few days.   At the Wilderness,
Spotsylvania, the North Anna, and Cold Harbour, the great
battles of 1864, Lee maintained his ground, but he did
not prevent Grant moving round his flank in the direction
of Richmond.   At the Second Manassas, Jackson stood fast
for the greater part of two days, but he would never have
driven Pope across Bull Run without the aid of Longstreet.
Porter at Gaines' Mill held 55,000 men with 35,000 for
more than seven hours, but even if he had maintained his
position, the Confederate army would not have become a
mob of fugitives.   No; except on peculiarly favourable
ground, or when defending an intrenched camp, an army
matched with one of equal efficiency and numerically
superior, can never hope for decisive success.   So circumstanced, a wise general will rather retreat than fight, and
thus save his men for a more favourable opportunity.[1]

But Lee and Jackson had not to deal with ordinary
conditions.   Whatever may have been the case in the
Peninsula and in the Valley, there can be no question but
that the armies in Maryland were by no means equal in

---

[1] Before Salamanca, for instance, because Marmont, whose strength was
equal to his own, was about to be reinforced by 4,000 cavalry, Wellington
had determined to retreat.   It is true, however, that when weaker than Mas-
séna, whom he had already worsted, by 8,000 infantry and 3,800 sabres, but
somewhat stronger in artillery, he stood to receive attack at Fuentes
d'Onor.   Yet Napier declares that it was a very audacious resolution.   The
knowledge and experience of the great historian told him that to pit 32,000
infantry against 40,000 was to trust too much to fortune.

quality.   The Federals were far more accustomed to
retreat than advance.   For several months, whether they
were engaged on the Shenandoah, on the Chickahominy,
on the Rappahannock, or on Bull Run, they had been
invariably outmanœuvred.   Their losses had been exceedingly severe, not only in battle, but from sickness
and straggling.   Many of their bravest officers and men
had fallen.   With the exception of the Second and Sixth
Army Corps, commanded by Sumner and by Franklin,
by far the greater part of the troops had been involved
in Pope's defeat, and they had not that trust in their
leaders which promises a strong offensive.   While at
Washington the army had been reinforced by twenty-four
regiments of infantry, but the majority of these troops
had been but lately raised ; they knew little of drill ;
they were commanded by officers as ignorant as themselves, and they had never fired a musket.   Nor were
the generals equal in capacity to those opposing them.
' If a student of history,' says a Northern officer, ' familiar
with the characters who figured in the War of Secession, but happening to be ignorant of the battle of
Antietam, should be told the names of the men who
held high commands there, he would say that with anything like equality of forces the Confederates must have
won, for their leaders were men who made great names
in the war, while the Federal leaders were, with few
exceptions, men who never became conspicuous, or
became conspicuous only through failure.' [1]   And the difference in military capacity extended to the rank and file.
When the two armies met on the Antietam, events had
been such as to confer a marked superiority on the
Southerners.   They were the children of victory, and every
man in the army had participated in the successes of Lee
and Jackson.   They had much experience of battle.   They
were supremely confident in their own prowess, for the fall
of Harper's Ferry had made more than amends for the
retreat from South Mountain, and they were supremely
confident in their leaders.   No new regiments weakened

[1] *The Antietam and Fredericksburg*, General Palfrey, p. 53.

the stability of their array. Every brigade and every regiment could be depended on. The artillery, which had been but lately reorganised in battalions, had, under the fostering care of General Pendleton, become peculiarly efficient, although the *matériel* was still indifferent; and against Stuart's horsemen the Federal cavalry was practically useless.

In every military attribute, then, the Army of Northern Virginia was so superior to the Army of the Potomac that Lee and Jackson believed that they might fight a defensive battle, outnumbered as they were, with the hope of annihilating their enemy. They were not especially favoured by the ground, and time and means for intrenching were both wanting; but they were assured that not only were their veterans capable of holding the position, but, if favoured by fortune, of delivering a counterstroke which should shiver the Army of the Potomac into a thousand fragments.

2. By retreating across the Potomac, in accordance with General Longstreet's suggestion, Lee would certainly have avoided all chances of disaster. But, at the same time, he would have abandoned a good hope of ending the war. The enemy would have been fully justified in assuming that the retrograde movement had been made under the compulsion of his advance, and the balance of *moral* have been sensibly affected in favour of the Federals. If the Potomac had once been placed between the opposing forces, McClellan would have had it in his power to postpone an encounter until his army was strongly reinforced, his raw regiments trained, and his troops rested. The passage of the river, it is true, had been successfully forced by the Confederates on September 5. But it by no means followed that it could be forced for the second time in face of a concentrated enemy, who would have had time to recover his *moral* and supply his losses. McClellan, so long as the Confederates remained in Maryland, had evidently made up his mind to attack. But if Maryland was evacuated he would probably content himself with holding the line of the Potomac; and, in view of the relative strength of the two armies, it would be an

extraordinary stroke of fortune which should lay him open to assault. Lee and Jackson were firmly convinced that it was the wiser policy to give the enemy no time to reorganise and recruit, but to coerce him to battle before he had recovered from the defeat which he had sustained on the heights above Bull Run. To recross the Potomac would be to slight the favours of fortune, to abandon the initiative, and to submit, in face of the vast numbers of fresh troops which the North was already raising, to a defensive warfare, a warfare which might protract the struggle, but which must end in the exhaustion of the Confederacy. McClellan's own words are the strongest justification of the views held by the Southern leaders :—

'The Army of the Potomac was thoroughly exhausted and depleted by the desperate fighting and severe marching in the unhealthy regions of the Chickahominy and afterwards, during the second Bull Run campaign ; its trains, administrative services and supplies were disorganised or lacking in consequence of the rapidity and manner of its removal from the Peninsula, as well as from the nature of its operations during the second Bull Run campaign.

'Had General Lee remained in front of Washington (south of the Potomac) it would have been the part of wisdom to hold our own army quiet until its pressing wants were fully supplied, its organisation was restored, and its ranks were filled with recruits—in brief, until it was prepared for a campaign. But as the enemy maintained the offensive, and crossed the Upper Potomac to threaten or invade Pennsylvania, it became necessary to meet him at any cost, notwithstanding the condition of the troops, to put a stop to the invasion, to save Baltimore and Washington, and throw him back across the Potomac. Nothing but sheer necessity justified the advance of the Army of the Potomac to South Mountain and Antietam in its then condition. The purpose of advancing from Washington was simply to meet the necessities of the moment by frustrating Lee's invasion of the Northern States, and when that was accomplished, to push with the

utmost rapidity the work of reorganisation and supply, so
that a new campaign might be promptly inaugurated with
the army in condition to prosecute it to a successful termination without intermission.' [1]

And in his official report, showing what the result of a
Confederate success might well have been, he says : ' One
battle lost and almost all would have been lost.   Lee's army
might have marched as it pleased on Washington, Baltimore, Philadelphia, or New York.   It could have levied its
supplies from a fertile and undevastated country, extorted
tribute from wealthy and populous cities, and nowhere
east of the Alleghanies was there another organised force
to avert its march.' [2]

3. The situation in the West was such that even a
victory in Maryland was exceedingly desirable.   Confederate
movements in Tennessee and Kentucky had won a measure
of success which bade fair to open up a brilliant opportunity.   Should the Federals be defeated in both the theatres
of war, the blow would be felt throughout the length
and breadth of the Northern States ; and, in any case, it
was of the utmost importance that all McClellan's troops
should be retained in the East.

So, when the tidings came of Jackson's victory at
Harper's Ferry, both armies braced themselves for the
coming battle, the Confederates in the hope that it would be
decisive of the war, the Federals that it would save the
capital.   But the Confederates had still a most critical time
before them, and Lee's daring was never more amply illustrated than when he made up his mind to fight on the
Antietam.   McClellan's great army was streaming through
the passes of the South Mountain. At Rohrersville, six miles
east of the Confederate bivouacs, where he had halted as
soon as the cannonade at Harper's Ferry ceased, Franklin
was still posted with 20,000 men.   From their battle-field at
Turner's Gap, ten miles from Sharpsburg, came the 70,000
which composed the right and centre ; and on the banks of
the Antietam but 15,000 Southerners were in position. Jack-

[1] *Battles and Leaders*, vol. ii., p. 554.
[2] O. R., vol. xix., part i., p. 65.

son had to get rid of his prisoners, to march seventeen miles, and to ford the Potomac before he could reach the ground. Walker was twenty miles distant, beyond the Shenandoah; and McLaws, who would be compelled by Franklin's presence near Rohrersville to cross at Harper's Ferry and follow Jackson, over five-and-twenty. Would they be up before McClellan attacked? Lee, relying on McClellan's caution and Jackson's energy, answered the question in the affirmative.

The September day wore on. The country between the South Mountain and Sharpsburg, resembling in every characteristic the Valley of the Shenandoah, is open and gently undulating. No leagues of woodland, as in Eastern Virginia, block the view. The roads run through wide corn-fields and rolling pastures, and scattered copses are the only relics of the forest. It was not yet noon when the Federal scouts appeared among the trees which crown the left bank of the Antietam Creek. 'The number increased, and larger and larger grew the field of blue until it seemed to stretch as far as the eye could see. It was an awe-inspiring spectacle,' adds Longstreet, ' as this grand force settled down in sight of the Confederates, shattered by battles and scattered by long and tedious marches.'[1] But when night fell upon the field the only interchange of hostilities had been a brief engagement of artillery. McClellan's advance, owing to the difficulty of passing his great army through the mountains, and to the scarcity of roads, had been slow and tedious; in some of the divisions there had been unnecessary delay; and Lee had so disposed his force that the Federal commander, unenlightened as to the real strength of his adversary, believed that he was opposed by 50,000 men.

Nor was the next morning marked by any increase of activity. McClellan, although he should have been well aware Sept. 16. that a great part of the Confederate army was still west of the Potomac, made no attack. ' It was discovered,' he reports, ' that the enemy had changed the position of some of his batteries. The masses of

[1] *Battles and Leaders*, vol. ii., p. 667.

his troops, however, were still concealed behind the opposite heights. It was afternoon before I could move the troops to their positions for attack, being compelled to spend the morning in reconnoitring the new position taken up by the enemy, examining the ground, and finding fords, clearing the approaches, and hurrying up the ammunition and supply trains.' [1]

Considering that McClellan had been in possession of the left bank of the Antietam since the forenoon of the previous day, all these preliminaries might well have been completed before daylight on the 16th. That a change in the dispositions of a few batteries, a change so unimportant as to pass unnoticed in the Confederate reports, should have imposed a delay, when every moment was precious, of many hours, proves that Lee's and Jackson's estimate of their opponent's character was absolutely correct. While McClellan was reconnoitring, and the guns were thundering across the Antietam, Jackson and Walker crossed the Potomac, and reported to Lee in Sharpsburg.[2] Walker had expected to find the Commander-in-Chief anxious and careworn. 'Anxious no doubt he was; but there was nothing in his look or manner to indicate it. On the contrary, he was calm, dignified, and even cheerful. If he had had a well-equipped army of a hundred thousand veterans at his back, he could not have appeared more composed and confident. On shaking hands with us, he simply expressed his satisfaction with the result of our operations at Harper's Ferry, and with our timely arrival at Sharpsburg; adding that with our reinforcements he felt confident of being able to hold his ground until the arrival of the divisions of R. H. Anderson, McLaws, and A. P. Hill, which were still behind, and which did not arrive till next day.' [3]

Yet the reinforcements which Jackson and Walker had brought up were no considerable addition to Lee's

[1] O. R., vol. xix., part i., p. 55.

[2] According to Jackson's staff officers he himself reported shortly after daylight.

[3] *Battles and Leaders*, vol. ii., p. 675.

strength. Jones' division consisted of no more than 1,600 muskets, Lawton's of less than 3,500. Including officers and artillery, therefore, the effectives of these divisions numbered about 5,500. A. P. Hill's division appears to have mustered 5,000 officers and men, and we may add 1,000 for men sick or on detached duties. The total should undoubtedly have been larger. After the battle of Cedar Run, Jackson had 22,450 effectives in his ranks. His losses in the operations against Pope, and the transfer of Robertson's cavalry to Stuart, had brought his numbers down by 5,787 ; but on September 16, including 70 killed or wounded at Harper's Ferry, they should have been not less than 16,800. In reality they were only 11,500. We have not far to look for the cause of this reduction. Many of the men had absented themselves before the army crossed into Maryland ; and if those who remained with the colours had seen little fighting since Pope's defeat, they had had no reason to complain of inactivity. The operations which resulted in the capture of Harper's Ferry had been arduous in the extreme. Men who had taken part in the forced marches of the Valley campaign declared that the march from Frederick to Harper's Ferry surpassed all their former experiences. In three-and-a-half days they had covered over sixty miles, crossing two mountain ranges, and fording the Potomac. The weather had been intensely hot, and the dust was terrible. Nor had the investment of Harper's Ferry been a period of repose. They had been under arms during the night which preceded the surrender, awaiting the signal to assault within a few hundred yards of the enemy's sentries. As soon as the terms of capitulation were arranged they had been hurried back to the bivouac, had cooked two days' rations, and shortly after midnight had marched to the Potomac, seventeen miles away. This night march, coming on the top of their previous exertions, had taxed the strength of many beyond endurance. The majority were badly shod. Many were not shod at all. They were ill-fed, and men ill-fed are on the highroad to hospital. There were stragglers, then, from every company in the command. Even the Stonewall

Brigade, though it had still preserved its five regiments, was reduced to 300 muskets ; and the other brigades of Jackson's division were but little stronger. Walker's division, too, although less hardly used in the campaign than the Valley troops, had diminished under the strain of the night march, and mustered no more than 3,500 officers and men at Sharpsburg. Thus the masses of troops which McClellan conceived were hidden in rear of D. H. Hill and Longstreet amounted in reality to some 10,000 effective soldiers.

It was fortunate, indeed, that in their exhausted condition there was no immediate occasion for their services on September 16. The shadows grew longer, but yet the Federals made no move ; even the fire of the artillery died away, and the men slept quietly in the woods to north and west of the little town. Meanwhile, in an old house, one of the few which had any pretensions to comfort in Sharpsburg, the generals met in council. Staff officers strolled to and fro over the broad brick pavement; the horses stood lazily under the trees which shaded the dusty road ; and within, Lee, Jackson, and Longstreet pored long and earnestly over the map of Maryland during the bright September afternoon. But before the glow of a lovely sunset had faded from the sky the artillery once more opened on the ridge above, and reports came in that the Federals were crossing the Antietam near Pry's Mill. Lee at once ordered Longstreet to meet this threat with Hood's division, and Jackson was ordered into line on the left of Hood. No serious collision, however, took place during the evening. The Confederates made no attempt to oppose the passage of the Creek. Hood's pickets were driven in, but a speedy reinforcement restored the line, and except that the batteries on both sides took part the fighting was little more than an affair of outposts. At eleven o'clock Hood's brigades were withdrawn to cook and eat. Jackson's division filled their place; and the night, although broken by constant alarms, passed away without further conflict. The Federal movements had clearly exposed their intention of attacking, and had even revealed the point which they would first assail.

McClellan had thrown two army corps, the First under Hooker, and the Twelfth under Mansfield, across the Antietam; and they were now posted, facing southward, a mile and a half north of Sharpsburg, concealed by the woods beyond Jackson's left.

NOTE

The essential paragraphs of the lost order ran as follows :—

' The army will resume its march to-morrow, taking the Hagerstown road. General Jackson's command will form the advance, and after passing Middletown, with such portions as he may select, take the route towards Sharpsburg, cross the Potomac at the most convenient point, and by Friday night (September 12) take possession of the Baltimore and Ohio Railroad, capture such of the enemy as may be at Martinsburg, and intercept such as may attempt to escape from Harper's Ferry.

' General Longstreet's command will pursue the same road as far as Boonsboro', where it will halt with the reserve, supply, and baggage trains of the army.

' General McLaws, with his own division and that of General Anderson, will follow General Longstreet; on reaching Middletown he will take the route to Harper's Ferry, and by Friday morning (September 12) possess himself of the Maryland Heights and endeavour to capture the enemy at Harper's Ferry and vicinity.

' General Walker with his division . . . will take possession of the Loudoun Heights, if practicable by Friday morning (September 12), . . . He will as far as practicable co-operate with General McLaws and General Jackson in intercepting the retreat of the enemy.

' General D. H. Hill's division will form the rear-guard of the army, pursuing the road taken by the main body.

' General Stuart will detach a squadron of cavalry to accompany the commands of Generals Longstreet, Jackson, and McLaws, and, with the main body of the cavalry, will cover the route of the army and bring up all stragglers.

' The commands of Generals Jackson, McLaws and Walker, after accomplishing the objects for which they have been detached, will join the main body at Boonsboro' or Hagerstown.'

The second paragraph was afterwards modified by General Lee so as to place Longstreet at Hagerstown.

CHAPTER XIX

SHARPSBURG

IT is a curious coincidence that not only were the numbers of the opposing armies at the battle of Sharpsburg almost identical with those of the French and Germans at the
1862. battle of Wörth, but that there is no small resem-
Sept. 17. blance between the natural features and surrounding scenery of the two fields. Full in front of the Confederate position rises the Red Hill, a spur of the South Mountain, wooded, like the Vosges, to the very crest, and towering high above the fields of Maryland, as the Hochwald towers above the Rhineland. The Antietam, however, is a more difficult obstacle than the Sauerbach, the brook which meanders through the open meadows of the Alsatian valley. A deep channel of more than sixty feet in width is overshadowed by forest trees; and the ground on either bank ascends at a sharp gradient to the crests above. Along the ridge to the west, which parts the Antietam from the Potomac, and about a mile distant from the former stream, runs the Hagerstown turnpike, and in front of this road there was a strong position. Sharpsburg, a village of a few hundred inhabitants, lies on the reverse slope of the ridge, extending in the direction of the Potomac, and only the church steeples were visible to the Federals. Above the hamlet was the Confederate centre. Here, near a limestone boulder, which stood in a plot which is now included in the soldiers' cemetery, was Lee's station during the long hours of September 17, and from this point he overlooked the whole extent of his line of battle. A mile northward, on the Hagerstown pike, his left centre was marked by a square white building, famous

under the name of the Dunkard Church, and backed by a
long dark wood. To the right, a mile southward, a bold
spur, covered with scattered trees, forces the Antietam westward, and on this spur, overlooking the stream, he had
placed his right.

Between the Hagerstown pike and the Antietam the open
slopes, although not always uniform, but broken, like those
on the French side of the Sauerbach, by long ravines, afforded
an admirable field of fire. The lanes which cross them are
sunk in many places below the surface : in front of Sharpsburg the fields were divided by low stone walls ; and these
natural intrenchments added much to the strength of the
position. Nor were they the only advantages. The belt
of oaks beyond the Dunkard Church, the West Wood,
was peculiarly adapted for defence. Parallel ledges of
outcropping limestone, both within the thickets and
along the Hagerstown road, rising as high as a man's
waist, gave good cover from shot and shell ; the trees
were of old growth, and there was little underwood. To
the north-east, however, and about five hundred yards
distant across the fields, lay the East Wood, covering
the slopes to the Antietam, with Poffenberger's Wood
beyond ; while further to the left, the North Wood,
extending across the Hagerstown pike, approached the Confederate flank. The enemy, if he advanced to the attack
in this quarter of the field, would thus find ample protection during his march and deployment ; and in case of
reverse he would find a rallying-point in the North and
Poffenberger's Woods, of which Hooker was already in
possession. In the space between the woods were several
small farms, surrounded by orchards and stone fences ;
and on the slope east of the Dunkard Church stood a few
cottages and barns.

Access to the position was not easy. Only a single
ford, near Snaveley's house, exists across the Antietam,
and this was commanded by the bluff on the Confederate
right. The stone bridges, however, for want of time and
means to destroy them, had been left standing. That
nearest the confluence of the Antietam and the Potomac,

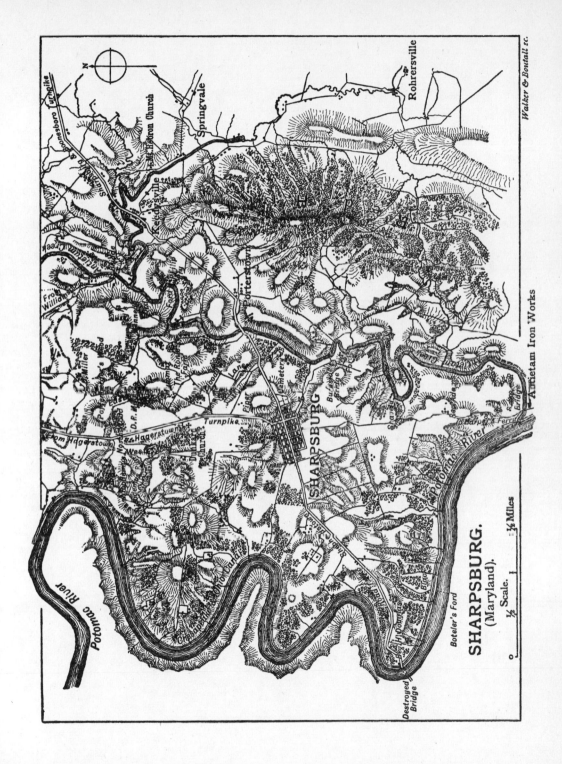

SHARPSBURG.
(Maryland).
Scale.
0   ½   ½ Miles

Walker & Boutall sc.

at the Antietam Iron-works, by which A. P Hill was expected, was defended by rifle-pits and enfiladed by artillery. The next, known as the Burnside Bridge, was completely overlooked by the heights above. That opposite Lee's centre could be raked throughout its length; but the fourth, at Pry's Mill, by which Hooker and Mansfield had already crossed, was covered both from view and fire. Roads within the position were numerous. The Hagerstown turnpike, concealed for some distance on either side of Sharpsburg by the crest of the ridge, was admirably adapted for the movement of reserves, and another broad highway ran through Sharpsburg to the Potomac.

The position, then, in many respects, was well adapted to Lee's purpose. The flanks were reasonably secure. The right rested on the Antietam. The left was more open; but the West Wood formed a strong *point d'appui*, and beyond the wood a low ridge, rising above Nicodemus Run, gave room for several batteries; while the Potomac was so close that the space available for attack on this flank was much restricted. The ground could thus be held by a comparatively small number of men, and a large reserve set free for the counterstroke. The great drawback was that the ridge east of the Antietam, although commanded by the crest which the Confederates occupied, would permit McClellan to deploy the whole of his powerful artillery, and in no place did the range exceed two thousand yards. In case of retreat, moreover, the Potomac, two hundred yards from shore to shore, would have to be crossed by a few deep fords,[1] of which only one was practicable for waggons. These disadvantages, however, it was impossible to avoid; and if the counterstroke were decisive, they would not be felt.

The left of the position was assigned to Jackson, with Hood in third line. Next in order came D. H. Hill. Longstreet held the centre and the right, with Walker in reserve behind the flank. Stuart, with Fitzhugh Lee's

---

[1] Two fords, behind the left and centre, were examined by Major Hotchkiss during the battle by Jackson's order, and were reported practicable for infantry.

brigade and his four guns, was between the West Wood and the Potomac. Munford's two regiments of cavalry, reinforced by a battery, held the bridge at the Antietam Iron-works, and kept open the communication with Harper's Ferry; and twenty-six rifled pieces of the reserve artillery were with D. H. Hill. From the Nicodemus Run to the bluff overhanging the Burnside Bridge is just three miles, and for the occupation of this front the following troops were at Lee's disposal :—

		Men	Guns
Jackson {	Jones' Division	} 5,500	16[1]
	Ewell's Division (General Lawton)		
Longstreet {	D. R. Jones' Division	} 8,000	50
	Hood's Division (detached to Jackson)		
	Evans' Brigade		
	D. H. Hill's Division	5,000	26
	Walker's Division	3,500	12
Stuart {	Fitzhugh Lee's Brigade	} 2,500	4
	Munford's Brigade		
Reserve Artillery		1,000	26
		25,500	134

On the far side of the Potomac the Shepherdstown Ford was protected by the remainder of the reserve artillery, with an infantry escort; but so small was the force whose retreat was thus secured that nearly every man was required in the fighting-line. Except the divisions of Hood and Walker, 5,500 men all told, there was no immediate reserve.

But at daybreak on the 17th the troops which had been left at Harper's Ferry were rapidly coming up. McLaws and Anderson, who had started before midnight, were already nearing the Potomac; Hampton's cavalry brigade was not far behind, and orders had been dispatched to A. P. Hill. But could these 13,000 bayonets be up in time—before Hooker and Mansfield received strong support, or before the Burnside Bridge was heavily attacked? The question was indeed momentous. If the Federals were to put forth their whole strength without

[1] The majority of Jackson's guns appear to have been left behind, the teams having broken down, at Harper's Ferry.

delay, bring their numerous artillery into action, and
press the battle at every point, it seemed hardly possible that
defeat could be averted. McClellan, however, who had
never yet ventured on a resolute offensive, was not likely,
in Lee's judgment, to assault so strong a position as that
held by the Confederates with whole-hearted energy, and it
was safe to calculate that his troops would be feebly
handled. Yet the odds were great. Even after the arrival
of the absent divisions [1] no more than 35,000 infantry,
4,000 cavalry, and 194 guns would be in line, and the
enemy's numbers were far superior. McClellan had
called in Franklin from Rohrersville, and his muster roll
was imposing.

	Men	Guns
First Corps—Hooker	14,856	40
Second Corps—Sumner	18,813	42
Fifth Corps—Porter	12,930	70
Sixth Corps—Franklin	12,300	36
Ninth Corps—Burnside	13,819	35
Twelfth Corps—Mansfield	10,126	36
Cavalry—Pleasanton	4,920	16
	87,164	275

In comparison with the masses arrayed between the
Red Hill and the Antietam, the Confederate army was but
a handful.

Notwithstanding McClellan's caution, the opening of the
battle was not long delayed. Before sunrise the desultory
firing of the pickets had deepened to the roar of
5 A.M. battle. Hooker, who had been ordered to begin
the attack, forming his troops behind the North Wood,
directed them on the Dunkard Church, which, standing on rising ground, appeared the key of the position.
Jackson had already thrown back his two divisions at
nearly a right angle to the Confederate front. His

	Men	Guns
[1] A. P. Hill's Division	5,000	18
McLaws' Division	4,500	24
R. H. Anderson's Division	3,500	18
Hampton's Cavalry Brigade	1,500	—
	14,500	60

right, which connected with the left of D. H. Hill, and resting on the western edge of the East Wood extended as far as the Miller House, was held by Lawton, with two brigades in front and one in second line. West of the Hagerstown turnpike, and covering the ground as far as the Nicodemus Farm, was Jones' division ; the Stonewall and Jones' brigades in front, Taliaferro's and Starke's along the edge of the wood in rear. Three guns stood upon the turnpike; the remainder of the artillery (thirteen) guns was with Stuart on the high ground north of Nicodemus Run. Hood, in third line, stood near the Dunkard Church ; and on Hood's right were three of Longstreet's batteries under Colonel Stephen Lee.

The ground which Jackson had been ordered to occupy was not unfavourable for defence, although the troops had practically no cover except the rail-fences and the rocky ledges. There was a wide and open field of fire, and when the Federal skirmishers appeared north of the Miller House the Confederate batteries, opening with vigour at a range of eight hundred yards, struck down sixteen men at the first salvo. This fire, and the stubborn resistance of the pickets, held the enemy for some time in check ; but Hooker deployed six batteries in reply, and after a cannonade of nearly an hour his infantry advanced. From the cover of the woods, still veiled by the morning mist, the Federals came forward in strong force. Across the dry ploughed land in Lawton's front the fight grew hot, and on the far side of the turnpike the meadows round the Nicodemus Farm became the scene of a desperate struggle. Hooker had sent in two divisions, Meade on the left and Doubleday on the right, while a third under Ricketts acted in close support of Meade.[1] The attack was waged with the dash and energy which had earned for Hooker the sobriquet of ' Fighting Joe,' and the troops he commanded had already proved their mettle on many murderous fields. Meade's Pennsylvanians, together with the Indiana and Wisconsin

[1] Doubleday's Division consisted of Phelps', Wainwright's, Patrick's, and Gibbon's brigades ; Rickett's Division of Duryea's, Lyle's, and Hartsuff's ; and Meade's Pennsylvania Division of Seymour's, Magilton's, and Anderson's.

regiments, which had wrought such havoc in Jackson's ranks at Grovetown, were once more bearing down upon his line.   Nor were the tactics of the leaders ill-calculated to second the valour of the troops.   Hooker's whole army corps of 12,500 men was manœuvred in close combination. The second line was so posted as to render quick support. No portion of the front was without an adequate reserve in rear.   The artillery was used in mass, and the flanks were adequately guarded.

The conflict between soldiers so well matched was not less fierce than when they had met on other fields. Hooker's troops had won a large measure of success at South Mountain three days previously, and their blood was up.   Meade, Gibbon, and Ricketts were there to lead them, and the battle opened with a resolution which, if it had infected McClellan, would have carried the Sharpsburg ridge ere set of sun.   Stubborn was the resistance of Jackson's regiments, unerring the aim of his seasoned riflemen ; but the opposing infantry, constantly rein-forced, pressed irresistibly forward, and the heavy guns beyond the Antietam, finding an opening between the woods, swept the thin grey line from end to end.   Jones' division, after fighting for three-quarters of an hour on the meadows, fell back to the West Wood ; General Jones was carried wounded from the field, and the guns on the turnpike were abandoned.   So tremendous was

6.30 A.M.   the fire, that the corn, said Hooker, over thirty acres was cut as close by the bullets as if it had been reaped with the sickle, and the dead lay piled in regular ranks along the whole Confederate front. Never, he added, had been seen a more bloody or dismal battle-field.   To the east of the turnpike Lawton's division, strengthened at the critical moment by the brigade in second line, held Meade in check, and with a sharp counter-stroke drove the Pennsylvanians back upon their guns. But Gibbon, fighting fiercely in the centre by the Miller House, brought up a battery in close support of his first line, and pressed heavily on the West Wood until the Confederate skirmishers, creeping through the maize, shot down the gunners and the teams;[1] and Starke, who had succeeded Jones, led the Valley regiments once more into the open field. The battle swayed backwards and forwards under the clouds of smoke; the crash of musketry, reverberating in the woods, drowned the roar of the artillery; and though hundreds were shot down at the shortest range neither Federal nor Confederate flinched from the dreadful fray. Hooker sent in a fresh brigade, and Patrick, reinforcing Gibbon with four regiments, passed swiftly to the front, captured two colours, and made some headway. But again the Virginians rallied, and Starke, observing that the enemy's right had become exposed, led his regiments forward to the charge. Doubleday's division, struck fiercely in front and flank, reeled back in confusion past the Miller House, and although the gallant Starke fell dead, the Confederates recovered the ground which they had lost. Jackson's men had not been left unaided. Colonel Lee's guns had themselves to look to, for along the whole course of the Antietam McClellan's batteries were now in action, sweeping the Sharpsburg ridge with a tremendous fire; but Stuart, west of the Nicodemus Farm, had done much to embarrass Hooker's operations. Bringing his artillery into action, for the ground was unsuited to cavalry, he had distracted the aim of the Federal gunners, and, assailing their infantry in flank, had compelled Doubleday to detach a portion of his force against him. Jackson, with supreme confidence in the ability of his men to hold their ground, had not hesitated to reinforce Stuart with Early's brigade, the strongest in his command; but before Doubleday was beaten back, Early had been recalled.

It was now half-past seven. The battle had been in progress nearly three hours, and Hooker's attack had 7.30 A.M. been repulsed. But fresh troops were coming into action from the north and north-east, and Lawton's and Jones' divisions were in no condition to withstand a renewed assault. No less than three officers in succession had led the latter. Not one single brigade in either

---

[1] This battery of regulars, 'B' 4th U. S. Artillery, lost 40 officers and men killed and wounded, besides 33 horses. O. R., vol. xix., part i., p. 229.

division was still commanded by the officer who brought it
into action, and but few regiments. Of 4,200 infantry,[1]
1,700 had already fallen. Never had Jackson's soldiers displayed a spirit more akin to that of their intrepid leader, and
their fierce courage was not to be wasted. Reinforcements
were close at hand. Early's brigade, 1,100 strong,[2] was
moving across from Nicodemus Run into the West Wood.
Hood brought his Texans, 1,800 muskets, to the relief of
Lawton; and on Hood's right, but facing eastward, for
Ricketts was working round Jackson's right, three of
D. H. Hill's brigades, hitherto hidden under cover, came
rapidly into line. Lawton's division, nearly half the command being killed or wounded, was withdrawn to the
Dunkard Church; but on the skirt of the West Wood the
heroic remnant of the Valley regiments still held fast
among the limestone ledges.

The 8,500 infantry which McClellan had sent to
Hooker's assistance formed the Twelfth Army Corps, commanded by Mansfield; and with these men, too, Jackson's
soldiers were well acquainted.[3] They were the men who had
followed Banks and Shields from Kernstown to Winchester,
from Port Republic to Cedar Run; and the Valley army had
not yet encountered more determined foes. Their attack
was delivered with their wonted vigour. Several regiments,
moving west of the turnpike, bore down on the West
Wood. But coming into action at considerable intervals,
they were roughly handled by Jones' division, now commanded by Colonel Grigsby, and protected by the rocks;
and Stuart's artillery taking them in flank they were
rapidly dispersed. East of the highroad the battle
raged with still greater violence. Hood and his Texans, as
Lawton's brigades passed to the rear, dashed across the
corn-field against Meade and Ricketts, driving back
the infantry on the batteries, and shooting down the

[1] Early's brigade had not yet been engaged.
[2] One small regiment was left with Stuart.
[3] Mansfield's corps consisted of two divisions, commanded by Crawford
(two brigades) and Greene (three brigades). The brigadiers were Knipe,
Gordon, Tynedale, Stainbrook, Goodrich.

gunners.   But the Federal line remained unbroken, and
Mansfield's troops were already moving forward.   Crawford's brigade, and then Gordon's, struck the Texans in
front, while Greene, working round the East Wood, made
a resolute onslaught on D. H. Hill.   The struggle was
long and bloody.   The men stood like duellists, firing and
receiving the fire at fifty or a hundred paces.   Crawford
lost 1,000 men without gaining a foot of ground; but
Gordon turned the scale, and Hood's brigades were
gradually forced back through the corn-field to the
Dunkard Church. A great gap had now opened in Jackson's
line.   Jones' division, its flank uncovered by Hood's
retreat, found itself compelled to seek a new position.
D. H. Hill's brigades, in the same plight, gave ground
towards Sharpsburg; and Greene, following in pursuit,
actually crossed the turnpike, and penetrated the West
Wood; but neither Hooker nor Mansfield were able to
support him, and unassisted he could make no progress.

At this moment, as if by common consent, the firing
ceased on this flank of the battle; and as McClellan's
9 A.M.   Second Army Corps, led by Sumner, advanced
          to sustain the First and Twelfth, we may stand
by Jackson near the Dunkard Church, and survey the
field after four hours' fighting.

Assailed in front by superior numbers, and enfiladed
by the batteries beyond the Antietam, the Confederate
left had everywhere given back.   The East Wood was in
possession of the enemy.   Their right occupied the Miller
House; their centre, supported by many batteries, stood
across the corn-field; while the left, thrust forward,
was actually established on the edge of the West Wood,
some five hundred yards to northward of the church.
But if Jackson had yielded ground, he had exacted a fearful
price.   The space between the woods was a veritable
slaughter-pen, reeking under the hot September sun, where
the blue uniforms lay thicker than the grey.   The First
Army Corps had been cut to pieces.   It had been beaten
in fair fight by Jackson's two divisions, counting at the
outset less than half its numbers, and aided only by

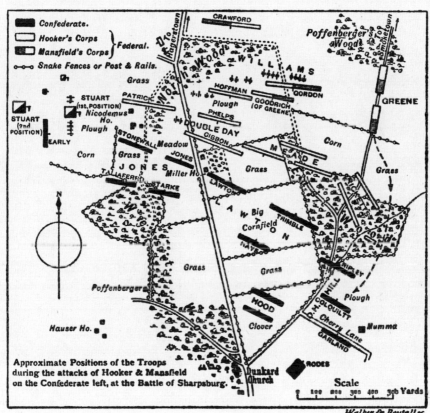

Confederate.

Hooker's Corps } Federal.
Mansfield's Corps }

Snake Fences or Post & Rails.

CRAWFORD

Poffenberger's Wood

To Hagerstown

NORTH WOOD
WILLIAMS
GRASS

To Keedysville

GREENE

STUART
(1st POSITION)
Nicodemus Ho.
Plough

PATRICK
HOFFMAN
Plough
PHELPS
GORDON
GOODRICH
(OF GREENE)

STUART
(2nd POSITION)

EARLY

DOUBLE DAY
GIBBON
MEADE

Corn

Grass

STONEWALL Meadow
JONES
Corn
Grass
JONES
Miller Ho.
TALIAFERRO
STARKE
Grass

LAWTON

LAW
Big
Cornfield
TRIMBLE
HAYS

Corn

Grass
Grass

Grass

HILL
RIPLEY
Plough

Poffenberger's

Grass

WOOD
Clover

D. H. COLQUITT
Cherry Lane
GARLAND
Humma

Hauser Ho.

Approximate Positions of the Troops
during the attacks of Hooker & Mansfield
on the Confederate left, at the Battle of Sharpsburg.

Dunkard
Church

RODES

Scale
100 200 300 400 500 Yards

Walker & Boutall sc.

the cavalry. It had lost in killed and wounded over 100 officers and 2,400 men. Hooker himself had been struck down, and as far as the Antietam the field was covered with his stragglers. The Twelfth Corps had suffered hardly less severely; and Mansfield himself, an old man and a gallant soldier, was dying of his wounds. His batteries indeed remained in action, pouring shot and shell on the West Wood and the Dunkard Church; but his infantry, reduced by more than 1,500 rifles, could do no more than hold their ground.

Nor was the exhaustion of the enemy the only advantage which the Confederates had gained by the slaughter of 4,000 men. The position to which Jackson had retired was more favourable than that from which he had been driven. The line, no longer presenting a weak angle, was almost straight, and no part of the front was open to enfilade. Stuart and his artillery, withdrawn to a more favourable position, secured the left. D. H. Hill on the right, though part of his force had given way, still held the Roulette House and the sunken road, and the troops in the West Wood were well protected from the Northern batteries. The one weak point was the gap occupied by Greene's Federals, which lay between Grigsby's regiments in the northern angle of the West Wood and Hood's division at the Dunkard Church. The enemy, however, showed no signs of making good his opportunity; Early's brigade was close at hand, and Lee had promised further reinforcements.

A glance southward showed that there was no reason for despair. Over all the field lay the heavy smoke of a great artillery battle. From near the Dunkard Church to the bluff overhanging the Antietam, a distance of two miles, battery on battery was in line. Here were Longstreet's artillery under Stephen Lee, together with the six-and-twenty guns of Cutts' reserve battalion, forty-eight guns in all; the divisional batteries of D. H. Hill, and the Washington artillery of New Orleans,[1] and in addition to these eighty guns others were in action above the Burnside Bridge. An array even more formidable crowned the opposite

---

[1] Both D. H. Hill and the Washington artillery had sixteen guns each.

crest; but although the Confederate batteries, opposed by larger numbers and heavier metal, had suffered terribly, both in men and in *matériel*, yet the infantry, the main strength of the defence, was still intact.[1] The cliffs of the Red Hill, replying to the rolling thunder of near 300 guns, gave back no echo to the sharper crack of musketry.   Save a few skirmishers, who had crossed the Sharpsburg Bridge, not one company of McClellan's infantry had been sent into action south of the Dunkard Church.   Beyond the Antietam, covering the whole space between the river and the hills, the blue masses were plainly to be seen through the drifting smoke; some so far in the distance that only the flash of steel in the bright sunshine distinguished them from the surrounding woods; others moving in dense columns towards the battle:

> Standards on standards, men on men;
> In slow succession still.

But neither by the Sharpsburg nor yet by the Burnside Bridge had a single Federal regiment crossed the stream; Lee's centre and right were not even threatened, and it was evident his reserves might be concentrated without risk at whatever point he pleased.

Walker's division was therefore withdrawn from the right, and McLaws, who had reached Sharpsburg shortly after sunrise, was ordered to the front.   G. T. Anderson's brigade was detached from D. H. Hill; and the whole force was placed at Jackson's disposal.   These fresh troops, together with Early's regiments, not yet engaged, gave 10,000 muskets for the counterstroke, and had Hooker and Mansfield been alone upon the field the Federal right wing would have been annihilated.   But as the Confederate reserves approached the Dunkard Church, Sumner, whom McClellan

---

[1] 'Our artillery,' says General D. H. Hill, ' could not cope with the superior weight, calibre, range, and number of the Yankee guns; hence it ought only to have been used against masses of infantry.   On the contrary, our guns were made to reply to the Yankee guns, and were smashed up or withdrawn before they could be effectually turned against massive columns of attack.'   After Sharpsburg Lee gave orders that there were to be no more ' artillery duels ' so long as the Confederates fought defensive battles

had ordered to cross Pry's Bridge with the Second Army Corps, threw three divisions against the West Wood and the Roulette House.   In three lines, up the slope from the Antietam, at sixty yards distance and covering a wide front, came Sedgwick on the right, French on the left, and Richardson to the left rear.   So orderly was the advance of those 18,000 Northerners, and so imposing their array, that even the Confederate officers watched their march with admiration, and terrible was the shock with which they renewed the conflict.

Sedgwick, emerging from the East Wood, moved directly over the corn-field, crossed the turnpike, and entering the West Wood to northward of the point still held by Greene, swept through the timber, and with a portion of his advanced brigade reached the further edge.   Greene, at the same moment, moved upon the Dunkard Church, and Early, who with the fragments of Jones' division was alone within the wood, marched rapidly in the same direction. Attacked suddenly in flank from behind a ridge of rock Greene's regiments were driven back; and then Early, observing Sedgwick's third line pushing across the turnpike, reformed his troops for further action.   Greene, for the moment, had been disposed of, but a more formidable attack was threatening.   Sedgwick's 6,000 muskets, confronted only by some 600[1] of the Valley soldiers under Grigsby, were thronging through the wood, and a change of front southward would have sent them sweeping down the Confederate line.   Early could hardly have withstood their onset; Hood was incapable of further effort, and D. H. Hill was heavily pressed by French.   But Jackson's hand still held the reins of battle.   During the fierce struggle of the morning he had remained on the edge of the West Wood, leaving, as was his wont, the conduct of the divisions to his subordinates, but watching his enemy with a glance that saw beyond the numbers arrayed against him.   He had already demanded reinforcements from General Lee; and in anticipation of their speedy arrival

[1] Letter of Jackson's Adjutant-General. *Memoirs of W. N. Pendleton, D.D.*, p. 216.

their orders had been already framed. They had not been called for to sustain his front, or to occupy a new position. Despite the thronging masses of the Federals, despite the fact that his line was already broken, attack, and attack only, was in Jackson's mind, and the reserves and the opportunity arrived together. A staff officer was dispatched to direct Walker, on the left, to sustain the Texans, to clear the West Wood, and to place a detachment in the gap between the Dunkard Church and the batteries of Colonel Lee;[1] while Jackson himself, riding to meet McLaws, ordered him 'to drive the enemy back and turn his right.' Anderson's brigade was sent to support McLaws, and Semmes' brigade of McLaws' division was detached to strengthen Stuart.

Forming into line as they advanced, McLaws and Walker, leaving the Dunkard Church on their right, and moving swiftly through the wood, fell suddenly on Sedgwick's flank. Early joined in the *mêlée*, and 'the result,' says Palfrey, a Northern general who was present on the field, 'was not long doubtful. Sedgwick's fine division was at the mercy of their enemy. Change of front was impossible. In less time than it takes to tell it the ground was strewn with the bodies of the dead and wounded, while the unwounded were moving off rapidly to the north. Nearly 2,000 men were disabled in a moment.'[2] And the impetus of the counterstroke was not yet spent. Gordon's brigade of the Twelfth Corps had been dispatched to Sedgwick's help, but McLaws had reformed his troops, and after a short struggle the Confederates drove all before them.

Confusion reigned supreme in the Federal ranks. In vain their powerful artillery, firing case and canister with desperate energy, strove to arrest the rush of the pursuing infantry. Out from the West Wood and across the cornfield the grey lines of battle, preceded by clouds of skirmishers, pressed forward without a check, and the light batteries, plying whip and spur, galloped to the front in

---

[1] Sharpsburg. By Major-General J. G. Walker, C.S.A. *Battles and Leaders*, vol. ii., pp. 677, 678.

[2] *Memoirs*, p. 572. *The Antietam and Fredericksburg*, p. 87.

close support. Hope rose high. The Southern yell, pealing from ten thousand throats, rang with a wild note of anticipated triumph, and Jackson, riding with McLaws, followed with kindling gaze the progress of his counterstroke attack. 'God,' he said to his companion, as the shells fell round them and the masses of the enemy melted away like the morning mist, ' has been very kind to us this day.'

But the end was not yet. Sedgwick's brigades, flying to the north-east, rallied under the fire of their batteries, and as the Confederates advanced upon the East Wood, they found it already occupied by a fresh brigade. Smith's division of the Sixth Corps had been sent forward by McClellan to sustain the battle, and its arrival saved his army from defeat. Once more the corn-field became the scene of a furious struggle, the Southerners fighting for decisive victory, the Federals for existence. So impetuous was McLaws' attack that the regiments on his left, although checked by the fences, drove in a battery and dashed back the enemy's first line; but the weight of the artillery in front of the North Wood, supported by a portion of Smith's division, prevented further advance, and a Federal brigade, handled with rare judgment, rushed forward to meet the assailants in the open. Sharp was the conflict, for McLaws, a fine soldier, as daring as he was skilful, strove fiercely to complete the victory; but the fight within the woods and the swift pursuit had broken the order of his division. Brigade had mingled with brigade, regiment with regiment. There were no supports; and the broken ranks, scourged by the terrible cross-fire of many batteries, were unable to withstand the solid impact of the Federal reserve. Slowly and sullenly the troops fell back from the deadly strife. The enemy, no less exhausted, halted and lay down beyond the turnpike; and while the musketry once more died away to northward of the Dunkard Church, Jackson, rallying his brigades, re-established his line along the edge of the West Wood.

Near the church was a portion of Walker's division. Further north were two of McLaws' brigades; then Armistead, who had been sent forward from Sharpsburg, and

then Early. A brigade of McLaws' division formed the
second line, and Anderson was sent back to D. H. Hill.
Hood also was withdrawn, and the survivors of Jones'
division, many of whom had shared in the counter-
attack, were permitted to leave the front. Their rifles
10.30 A.M. were no longer needed, for from half-past ten
onwards, so far as the defence of the Confederate left was concerned, the work was done. For many
hours the West Wood was exposed to the concentrated fire
of the Federal artillery; but this fire, although the range
was close, varying from six to fifteen hundred yards, had
little effect. The shattered branches fell incessantly among
the recumbent ranks, and the shells, exploding in the foliage,
sent their hissing fragments far and wide; yet the losses,
so more than one general reported, were surprisingly small.

But although the enemy's infantry had been repulsed,
no immediate endeavour was made by the Confederates to
initiate a fresh counterstroke. When Lee sent McLaws
and Walker to Jackson's aid, he sent in his last reserve, for
A. P. Hill had not yet reached the field, and R. H. Anderson's
division had already been taken to support the centre.
Thus no fresh troops were available, and the Federal right
was strong. At least fifteen batteries of artillery were in
position along the edge of the North Wood, and they were
powerfully supported by the heavy guns beyond the stream.

Yet the infantry so effectively protected was only
formidable by reason of its numbers. The First Corps and
the Twelfth no longer existed as organised bodies.[1] Sedgwick's division of the Second Corps was still more shattered.
Only Smith's division was effective, and General McClellan,
acting on the advice of Sumner, forbade all further
attack. Slocum's division of the Sixth Corps, which
reached the East Wood at twelve o'clock, was ordered
to remain in rear as support to Smith. The Confederate
left wing, then, had offered such strenuous resistance that
eight divisions of infantry, more than half of McClellan's
army, lay paralysed before them for the remainder of

[1] It was not until two o'clock that even Meade's Pennsylvanians were
reformed.

the day. 30,500 infantry, at the lowest calculation,[1] and probably 100 guns, besides those across the Antietam, had been massed by the Federals in this quarter of the field. Jackson's numbers, even after he had been reinforced by McLaws and Walker, at no time approached those arrayed against him, and 19,400 men, including Stuart and three brigades of Hill, and 40 guns, is a liberal estimate of his strength.[2] The losses on both sides had been exceedingly heavy. Nearly 13,000 men,[3] including no less than fifteen generals and brigadiers, had fallen within six hours. But although the Confederate casualties were not greatly exceeded by those of the enemy, and were much larger in proportion to their strength, the Federals had lost more than mere numbers. The *moral* of the troops had suffered, and still more the *moral* of the leaders. Even

[1] Hooker	11,000
Mansfield	8,500
Sedgwick	6,000
Smith	5,000
	30,500
[2] Lawton	3,600
Jones	1,800
Hood	2,000
Stuart	1,500
G. T. Anderson	1,000
Walker	3,500
McLaws	4,500
D. H. Hill (3 brigades)	1,500
	19,400

[3] The Federals engaged against Jackson lost in five and a half hours 7,000 officers and men. During the seven hours they were engaged at Gravelotte the Prussian Guard and the Saxon Army Corps lost 10,349; but 50,000 infantry were in action. The percentage of loss (20) was about the same in both cases. The Confederate losses up to 10.30 A.M. were as follows:

Jones	700
Lawton	1,334
Hood	1,002
McLaws	1,119
Walker	1,012
Anderson	87
D. H. Hill (estimate)	500
	5,754 (29 p.c.)

Sumner, bravest of men, had been staggered by the fierce assault which had driven Sedgwick's troops like sheep across the corn-field, nor was McClellan disposed to push matters to extremity.

Over in the West Wood, on the other hand, discouragement had no place. Jackson had not yet abandoned hope of sweeping the enemy from the field. He was disappointed with the partial success of McLaws' counterstroke. It had come too late. The fortuitous advance of Smith's division, at the very crisis of the struggle, had, in all human probability, rescued the Federal right from a terrible defeat. Had McLaws been able to reach the East Wood he would have compelled the hostile batteries to retreat; the Federal infantry, already shattered and disorganised, could hardly have held on, and the line would have been broken through. But although one opportunity had been lost, and he was once more thrown on the defensive, Jackson's determination to make the battle decisive of the war was still unshaken. His judgment was never clearer. Shortly before eleven o'clock his medical director, appalled by the number of wounded men sent back from the front, and assured that the day was going badly, rode to the West Wood in order to discuss the advisability of transferring the field hospitals across the Potomac. Dr. McGuire found Jackson sitting quietly on 'Little Sorrel' behind the line of battle, and some peaches he had brought with him were gratefully accepted. He then made his report, and his apprehensions were not made less by the weakness of the line which held the wood. The men, in many places, were lying at intervals of several yards; for support there was but one small brigade, and over in the corn-fields the overwhelming strength of the Federal masses was terribly apparent. Yet his imperturbable commander, apparently paying more attention to the peaches than to his subordinate's suggestions, replied by pointing to the enemy and saying quietly, 'Dr. McGuire, they have done their worst.'

Meanwhile, the tide of battle, leaving Jackson's front and setting strongly southwards, threatened to submerge the Confederate centre. French's division of Sumner's corps, two brigades of Franklin's, and afterwards Richardson's division, made repeated efforts to seize the Dunkard Church, the Roulette Farm, and the Piper House. From before ten until one o'clock the battle raged fiercely about

1 P.M.   the sunken road which was held by D. H. Hill, and which witnessed on this day such pre-eminence of slaughter that it has since been known by the name of the 'Bloody Lane.' Here, inspired by the unyielding courage of their leaders, fought the five brigades of D. H. Hill, with R. H. Anderson's division and two of Walker's regiments; and here Longstreet, confident as always, controlled the battle with his accustomed skill. The Confederate artillery was by this time overpowered, for on each battery in turn the enemy's heavy ordnance had concentrated an overwhelming fire, and the infantry were supported by no more than a dozen guns. The attack was strong, but the sunken road, fortified by piles of fence-rails, remained inviolable. Still the Confederate losses were enormous, and defeat appeared a mere question of time; at one moment, the enemy under French had actually seized the wood near the Dunkard Church, and was only dispossessed by a desperate counterstroke. Richardson, who advanced on French's right, and at an appreciable interval of time, was even more successful than his colleague. The 'Bloody Lane,' already piled with dead, and enfiladed from a height to the north-west, was carried by a brilliant charge; and when the Roulette Farm, a strong defensive post, was stormed, Longstreet fell back to the turnpike through the wreck of the artillery. But at this critical juncture the Federals halted. They had not been supported by their batteries. Richardson had received a mortal wound, and a succession of rough counterstrokes had thinned their ranks. Here, too, the musketry dwindled to a spattering fire, and the opposing forces, both reduced to the defensive, lay watching each other through the long hours of the afternoon. A threat of a Federal advance from the Sharpsburg Bridge came to nothing. Four batteries of regulars, preceded by a force of infantry, pushed across the stream and came into action on either side of

the Boonsboro' road; but on the slopes above, strongly
protected by the walls, Evans' brigade stood fast; Lee sent
up a small support, and the enemy confined his movements
to a demonstration.

Still further to the south, however, the battle blazed out
at one o'clock with unexpected fury. The Federal attack,
recoiling first from Jackson and then from Longstreet,
swung round to the Confederate right; and it seemed
as if McClellan's plan was to attempt each section of
Lee's line in succession. Burnside had been ordered
to force the passage of the bridge at nine o'clock, but
either the difficulty of the task, or his inexperience in
handling troops on the offensive, delayed his movements;
and when the attack was made, it was fiercely met by four
Confederate brigades. At length, well on in the afternoon,
three Federal divisions crowned the spur, and, driving
Longstreet's right before them, made good their footing on the ridge. Sharpsburg was below them; the Southern
infantry, outflanked and roughly handled, was falling back
in confusion upon the town; and although Lee had assembled
a group of batteries in the centre, and regiments were
hurrying from the left, disaster seemed imminent. But
strong assistance was at hand. A. P. Hill, who had forded
the Potomac and crossed the Antietam by the lower bridge,
after a forced march of seventeen miles in eight hours from
Harper's Ferry,[1] attacked without waiting for orders, and
struck the Federals in flank with 3,000 bayonets. By this
brilliant counterstroke Burnside was repulsed and the
position saved.

Northern writers have laid much stress on this attack.
Had Burnside displayed more, or A. P. Hill less, energy,
the Confederates, they assert, could hardly have escaped
defeat. It is certainly true that Longstreet's four
brigades had been left to bear the brunt of Burnside's
assault without further support than could be rendered by
the artillery. They were not so left, however, because it
was impossible to aid them. Jackson's and Longstreet's

---

[1] Hill received his orders at 6.30 A.M. and marched an hour later,
reaching the battle-field about 3.30 P.M.

troops, despite the fiery ordeal through which they had passed, were not yet powerless, and the Confederate leaders were prepared for offensive tactics. A sufficient force to sustain the right might have been withdrawn from the left and centre ; but Hill's approach was known, and it was considered inadvisable to abandon all hold of the means for a decisive counterstroke on the opposite flank. Early in the afternoon Longstreet had given orders for an advance. Hood's division, with full cartridge-boxes, had reappeared upon the field. Jones' and Lawton's divisions were close behind; the batteries had replenished their ammunition, and if Longstreet was hardly warranted in arranging a general counter-attack on his own responsibility, he had at least full confidence in the ability of the troops to execute it. ' It seemed probable,' he says, ' that by concealing our movements under cover of the (West) wood, we could draw our columns so near to the enemy to the front that we would have but a few rods to march to mingle our ranks with his ; that our columns, massed in goodly numbers, and pressing heavily upon a single point, would give the enemy much trouble and might cut him in two, breaking up his battle arrangements at Burnside Bridge.' [1]

The stroke against the centre was not, however, to be tried. Lee had other views, and Jackson had been already ordered to turn the Federal right. Stuart, reinforced by a regiment of infantry and several light batteries, was instructed to reconnoitre the enemy's position, and if favourable ground were found, he was to be supported by all the infantry available. 'About half-past twelve,' says General Walker, ' I sought Jackson to report that from the front of my position in the wood I thought I had observed a movement of the enemy, as if to pass through the gap where I had posted Colonel Cooke's two regiments. I found Jackson in rear of Barksdale's brigade, under an apple tree, sitting on his horse, with one leg thrown carelessly over the pommel of his saddle, plucking and eating the fruit. Without making any reply to my report, he asked me abruptly: " Can you spare me a

[1] *From Manassas to Appomattox*, pp. 256, 257.

regiment and a battery?" . . . adding that he wished to
make up, from the different commands on our left, a force
of four or five thousand men, and give them to Stuart,
with orders to turn the enemy's right and attack him
in the rear; that I must give orders to my division to
advance to the front, and attack the enemy as soon as I
should hear Stuart's guns, and that our whole left wing
would move to the attack at the same time. Then,
replacing his foot in the stirrup, he said with great
emphasis, "We'll drive McClellan into the Potomac."

'Returning to my command, I repeated General Jackson's order to my brigade commanders and directed them
to listen to the sound of Stuart's guns. We all confidently
expected to hear the welcome sound by two o'clock at
least, and as that hour approached every ear was on the
alert. Napoleon at Waterloo did not listen more intently
for the sound of Grouchy's fire than did we for Stuart's.
Two o'clock came, but nothing was heard of Stuart. Half-
past two, and then three, and still Stuart made no sign.

'About half-past three a staff officer of General Longstreet's brought me an order to advance and attack the
enemy in my front. As the execution of this order would
have materially interfered with Jackson's plans, I thought
it my duty before beginning the movement to communicate
with General Longstreet personally. I found him in rear
of the position in which I had posted Cooke in the morning,
and upon informing him of Jackson's intentions, he withdrew his order.

'While we were discussing this subject, Jackson himself joined us with the information of Stuart's failure to
turn the Federal right, for the reason that he found it
securely posted on the Potomac. Upon my expressing surprise at this statement, Jackson replied that he also had
been surprised, as he had supposed the Potomac much
further away; but he remarked that Stuart had an excellent
eye for topography, and it must be as he represented.
"It is a great pity," he added; "we should have driven
McClellan into the Potomac." '[1]

[1] *Battles and Leaders*, vol. ii., pp. 679, 680.

That a counterstroke which would have combined a frontal and flank attack would have been the best chance of destroying the Federal army can hardly be questioned. The front so bristled with field artillery, and the ridge beyond the Antietam was so strong in heavier ordnance, that a purely frontal attack, such as Longstreet suggested, was hardly promising; but the dispositions which baffled Stuart were the work of a sound tactician. Thirty rifled guns had been assembled in a single battery a mile north of the West Wood, where the Hagerstown turnpike ascends a commanding ridge, and the broad channel of the Potomac is within nine hundred yards. Here had rallied such portions of Hooker's army corps as had not dispersed, and here Mansfield's two divisions had reformed; and although the infantry could hardly have opposed a resolute resistance the guns were ready to repeat the lesson of Malvern Hill. Against the rifled pieces the light Confederate smooth-bores were practically useless. Stuart's caution was fully justified, and the sun sank on an indecisive battle.

'The blessed night came, and brought with it sleep and forgetfulness and refreshment to many; but the murmur of the night wind, breathing over fields of wheat and clover, was mingled with the groans of the countless sufferers of both armies. Who can tell, who can even imagine, the horrors of such a night, while the unconscious stars shone above, and the unconscious river went rippling by?'[1] Out of 130,000 men upon the ground, 21,000 had been killed or wounded, more than sixteen per cent.; and 25,000 of the Federals can hardly be said to have been engaged.

The losses of the Confederate left have already been enumerated. Those of the centre and the right, although A. P. Hill reported only 350 casualties, had hardly been less severe. In all 9,500 officers and men, one-fourth of the total strength, had fallen, and many of the regiments had almost disappeared.[2] The 17th Virginia, for in-

[1] General Palfrey. *The Antietam and Fredericksburg.*
[2] 'One does not look for humour in a stern story like this, but the *Charleston Courier* account of the battle contains the following statement:

stance, of Longstreet's command, took into battle 9 officers and 46 men; of these 7 officers and 24 men were killed or wounded, and 10 taken prisoners, leaving 2 officers and 12 men to represent a regiment which was over 1,000 strong at Bull Run. Yet as the men sank down to rest on the line of battle, so exhausted that they could not be awakened to eat their rations; as the blood cooled and the tension on the nerves relaxed, and even the officers, faint with hunger and sickened with the awful slaughter, looked forward with apprehension to the morrow, from one indomitable heart the hope of victory had not yet vanished. In the deep silence of the night, more oppressive than the stunning roar of battle, Lee, still mounted, stood on the highroad to the Potomac, and as general after general rode in wearily from the front, he asked quietly of each, 'How is it on your part of the line?' Each told the same tale: their men were worn out; the enemy's numbers were overwhelming; there was nothing left but to retreat across the Potomac before daylight. Even Jackson had no other counsel to offer. His report was not the less impressive for his quiet and respectful tone. He had had to contend, he said, against the heaviest odds he had ever met. Many of his divisional and brigade commanders were dead or wounded, and his loss had been severe. Hood, who came next, was quite unmanned. He exclaimed that he had no men left. 'Great God!' cried Lee, with an excitement he had not yet displayed, 'where is the splendid division you had this morning?' 'They are lying on the field, where you sent them,' was the reply, 'for few have straggled. My division has been almost wiped out.'

After all had given their opinion, there was an appalling silence, which seemed to last for several minutes, and then General Lee, rising erect in his stirrups, said, 'Gentlemen, we will not cross the Potomac to-night. You will go to your respective commands, strengthen your lines; send

"They [the Confederates] fought until they were cut to pieces, and then retreated only because they had fired their last round!"' General Palfrey, *The Antietam and Fredericksburg*.

two officers from each brigade towards the ford to collect
your stragglers and get them up. Many have come in. I
have had the proper steps taken to collect all the men who
are in the rear. If McClellan wants to fight in the morning, I will give him battle again. Go!' Without a word
of remonstrance the group broke up, leaving their great
commander alone with his responsibility, and, says an eye-
witness, 'if I read their faces aright, there was not one but
considered that General Lee was taking a fearful risk.'[1]
So the soldiers' sleep was undisturbed. Through the
September night they lay beside their arms, and from the
dark spaces beyond came the groans of the wounded and
the nameless odours of the battle-field. Not often has the
night looked down upon a scene more terrible. The moon,
rising above the mountains, revealed the long lines of men
and guns, stretching far across hill and valley, waiting for
the dawn to shoot each other down, and between the armies
their dead lay in such numbers as civilised war has seldom
seen. So fearful had been the carnage, and comprised
within such narrow limits, that a Federal patrol, it is
related, passing into the corn-field, where the fighting had
been fiercest, believed that they had surprised a whole
Confederate brigade. There, in the shadow of the woods,
lay the skirmishers, their muskets beside them, and there, in
regular ranks, lay the line of battle, sleeping, as it seemed,
the profound sleep of utter exhaustion. But the first man
that was touched was cold and lifeless, and the next, and
the next; it was the bivouac of the dead.

When the day dawned the Confederate divisions, reinforced by some 5,000 or 6,000 stragglers, held the same
position as the previous evening, and over
Sept. 18. against them, seen dimly through the mist, lay
the Federal lines. The skirmishers, crouching behind the
shattered fences, confronted each other at short range; the
guns of both armies were unlimbered, and the masses of
infantry, further to the rear, lay ready for instant conflict.
But not a shot was fired. The sun rose higher in the

[1] Communicated by General Stephen D. Lee, who was present at the
conference.

heavens; the warm breath of the autumn morning rustled in the woods, but still the same strange silence prevailed. The men spoke in undertones, watching intently the movements of staff officers and orderlies; but the ranks lay as still as the inanimate forms, half hidden by the trodden corn, which lay so thickly between the lines; and as the hours passed on without stir or shot, the Southern generals acknowledged that Lee's daring in offering battle was fully justified. The enemy's aggressive strength was evidently exhausted; and then arose the question, Could the Confederates attack? It would seem that the possibility of a great counterstroke had already been the subject of debate, and that Lee, despite the failure of the previous evening, and Jackson's adverse report, believed that the Federal right might be outflanked and overwhelmed. 'During the morning,' writes General Stephen D. Lee, 'a courier from headquarters came to my battalion of artillery with a message that the Commander-in-Chief wished to see me. I followed the courier, and on meeting General Lee, he said, "Colonel Lee, I wish you to go with this courier to General Jackson, and say that I sent you to report to him." I replied, "General, shall I take my batteries with me?" He said, "No, just say that I told you to report to him, and he will tell you what he wants." I soon reached General Jackson. He was dismounted, with but few persons round him. He said to me, "Colonel Lee, I wish you to take a ride with me," and we rode to the left of our lines with but one courier, I think. We soon reached a considerable hill and dismounted. General Jackson then said, "Let us go up this hill, and be careful not to expose yourself, for the Federal sharpshooters are not far off." The hill bore evidence of fierce fight the day before.[1] A battery of artillery had been on it, and there were wrecked caissons, broken wheels, dead bodies, and dead horses around. General Jackson said: "Colonel, I wish you to take your glasses and carefully examine the Federal line of battle." I did so, and saw a remarkably strong line of battle, with more troops than I knew General Lee had. After locating the

---

[1] Evidently the ridge which had been held by Stuart on the 17th.

different batteries, unlimbered and ready for action, and noting the strong skirmish line, in front of the dense masses of infantry, I said to him, "General, that is a very strong position, and there is a large force there.' He said, "Yes. I wish you to take fifty pieces of artillery and crush that force, which is the Federal right. Can you do it?" I can scarcely describe my feelings as I again took my glasses, and made an even more careful examination. I at once saw such an attempt must fail. More than fifty guns were unlimbered and ready for action, strongly supported by dense lines of infantry and strong skirmish lines, advantageously posted. The ground was unfavourable for the location of artillery on the Confederate side, for, to be effective, the guns would have to move up close to the Federal lines, and that, too, under fire of both infantry and artillery. I could not bring myself to say all that I felt and knew. I said, "Yes, General; where will I get the fifty guns?" He said, "How many have you?" I replied, "About twelve out of the thirty I carried into the action the day before." (My losses had been very great in men, horses, and carriages.) He said, "I can furnish you some, and General Lee says he can furnish some." I replied, "Shall I go for the guns?" "No, not yet," he replied. "Colonel Lee, can you crush the Federal right with fifty guns?" I said, "General, I can try. I can do it if anyone can." He replied, "That is not what I asked you, sir. If I give you fifty guns, can you crush the Federal right?" I evaded the question again and again, but he pressed it home. Finally I said, "General, you seem to be more intent upon my giving you my technical opinion as an artillery officer, than upon my going after the guns and making the attempt." "Yes, sir," he replied, "and I want your positive opinion, yes or no." I felt that a great crisis was upon me, and I could not evade it. I again took my glasses and made another examination. I waited a good while, with Jackson watching me intently.

' I said, "General, it cannot be done with fifty guns and the troops you have near here." In an instant he said, "Let us ride back, Colonel." I felt that I had positively shown a lack of nerve, and with considerable emotion begged that I might be allowed to make the attempt, saying, " General, you forced me to say what I did unwillingly. If you give the fifty guns to any other artillery officer, I am ruined for life. I promise you I will fight the guns to the last extremity, if you will only let me command them." Jackson was quiet, seemed sorry for me, and said, " It is all right, Colonel. Everybody knows you are a brave officer and would fight the guns well," or words to that effect. We soon reached the spot from which we started. He said, " Colonel, go to General Lee, and tell him what has occurred since you reported to me. Describe our ride to the hill, your examination of the Federal position, and my conversation about your crushing the Federal right with fifty guns, and my forcing you to give your opinion."

'With feelings such as I never had before, nor ever expect to have again, I returned to General Lee, and gave a detailed account of my visit to General Jackson, closing with the account of my being forced to give my opinion as to the possibility of success. I saw a shade come over General Lee's face, and he said, " Colonel, go and join your command."

'For many years I never fully understood my mission that day, or why I was sent to General Jackson. When Jackson's report was published of the battle, I saw that he stated, that on the afternoon of September 17, General Lee had ordered him to move to the left with a view of turning the Federal right, but that he found the enemy's numerous artillery so judiciously posted in their front, and so near the river, as to render such an attempt too hazardous to undertake. I afterwards saw General J. E. B. Stuart's report, in which he says that it was determined, the enemy not attacking, to turn the enemy's right on the 18th. It appears General Lee ordered General Jackson, on the evening of the 17th, to turn the enemy's right, and Jackson said that it could not be done. It also appears from Stuart's report, and from the incident I relate, that General Lee reiterated the order on the 18th, and told Jackson to take fifty guns, and crush the Federal right. Jackson having reported against such attempt on the 17th, no doubt said that if an artillerist, in whom General Lee had confidence, would say the Federal right could be crushed with fifty guns, he would make the attempt.

'I now have the satisfaction of knowing that the opinion which I was forced to give on September 18 had already been given by Jackson on the evening of September 17, and that the same opinion was reiterated by him on September 18, and confirmed by General J. E. B. Stuart on the same day. I still believe that Jackson, Stuart, and myself were right, and that the attempt to turn the Federal right either on the 17th or on the 18th would have been unwise.

'The incident shows General Lee's decision and boldness in battle, and General Jackson's delicate loyalty to his commanding general, in convincing him of the inadvisability of a proposed movement, which he felt it would be hazardous to undertake.' [1]

The Federal left, protected by the Antietam, was practically inaccessible; and on receiving from the artillery officers' lips the confirmation of Jackson's report, Lee was fain to relinquish all hope of breaking McClellan's line. The troops, however, remained in line of battle; but during the day information came in which made retreat imperative. The Federals were being reinforced. Humphreys' division, hitherto held back at Frederick by orders from Washington, had marched over South Mountain; Couch's division, which McClellan had left to observe Harper's Ferry, had been called in; and a large force of militia was assembling on the Pennsylvania border. Before evening, therefore, Lee determined to evacuate his position, and during the night the Army of Northern Virginia, with all its trains and artillery, recrossed the Potomac at Boteler's Ford.

[1] Communicated to the author. The difficulties in the way of the attack, of which Jackson was aware on the night of the 17th, probably led to his advising retreat when Lee asked his opinion at the conference (ante, pp. 259, 260).

Such was the respect which the hard fighting of the Confederates had imposed upon the enemy, that although the rumbling of heavy vehicles, and the tramp of the long columns, were so distinctly audible in the Federal lines that they seemed to wakeful ears like the steady flow of a river, not the slightest attempt was made to interfere. It was not till the morning of the 19th that a Federal battalion, reconnoitring towards Sharpsburg, found the ridge and the town deserted; and although Jackson, who was one of the last, except the cavalry scouts, to cross the river, did not reach the Virginia shore till eight o'clock, not a shot was fired at him.

Nor were the trophies gathered by the Federals considerable. Several hundred badly wounded men were found in Sharpsburg, and a number of stragglers were picked up, but neither gun nor waggon had been left upon the field. The retreat, despite many obstacles, was as successfully as skilfully executed. The night was very dark, and a fine rain, which had set in towards evening, soon turned the heavy soil into tenacious mud; the ford was wide and beset with boulders, and the only approach was a narrow lane. But the energetic quartermaster of the Valley army, Major Harman, made light of all difficulties, and under the immediate supervision of Lee and Jackson, the crossing was effected without loss or misad-

Sept. 19. venture. Just before nightfall, however, under cover of a heavy artillery fire, the Federals pushed a force of infantry across the ford, drove back the two brigades, which, with thirty pieces of artillery, formed the Confederate rear-guard, and captured four guns. Emboldened by this partial success, McClellan ordered Porter to put three brigades of the Fifth Army Corps across the river the next morning, and reconnoitre towards Winchester.

The news of the disaster to his rear-guard was long in reaching Lee's headquarters. His army had not yet recovered from the confusion and fatigue of the retreat. The bivouacs of the divisions were several miles from the river, and were widely scattered. The generals were ignorant of each other's dispositions. No arrangements had been made to support the rear-guard in case of emergency. The greater part of the cavalry had been sent off to Williamsport, fifteen miles up stream, with instructions to cross the Potomac and delay the enemy's advance by demonstration. The brigadiers had no orders; many of the superior generals had not told their subordinates where they would be found; and the commander of the rear-guard, General Pendleton, had not been informed of the strength of the infantry placed at his disposal. On the part of the staff, worn out by the toils and anxieties of the past few days, there appears to have been a general failure; and had McClellan, calculating on the chances invariably offered by an enforced retreat, pushed resolutely forward in strong force, success might possibly have followed.

Lee, on receiving Pendleton's report, long after midnight, sent off orders for Jackson to drive the enemy back.

Sept. 20. When the messenger arrived, Jackson had already ridden to the front. He, too, had received news of the capture of the guns; and ordering A. P. Hill and Early,[1] who were in camp near Martinsburg, to march at once to Shepherdstown, he had gone forward to reconnoitre the enemy's movements. When Lee's courier found him he was on the Shepherdstown road, awaiting the arrival of his divisions, and watching, unattended by a single aide-de-camp, the advance of Porter's infantry. He had at once grasped the situation. The Confederates were in no condition to resist an attack in force. The army was not concentrated. The cavalry was absent. No reconnaissance had been made either of lines of march or of positions. The roads were still blocked by the trains. The men were exhausted by their late exertions, and depressed by their retreat, and the straggling was terrible. The only chance of safety lay in driving back the enemy's advanced-guard across the river before it could be reinforced; and the chance was seized without an instant's hesitation.

The Federals advanced leisurely, for the cavalry which

[1] Commanding Ewell's division, *vice* Lawton, wounded at Sharpsburg.

should have led the way had received its orders too late to
reach the rendezvous at the appointed hour, and the infantry,
compelled to reconnoitre for itself, made slow progress.
Porter's leading brigade was consequently not more than a
mile and a half from the river when the Light Division
reported to Jackson. Hill was ordered to form his troops
in two lines, and with Early in close support to move at
once to the attack. The Federals, confronted by a large
force, and with no further object than to ascertain the
whereabouts of the Confederate army, made no attempt to
hold their ground. Their left and centre, composed mainly
of regulars, withdrew in good order. The right, hampered
by broken country, was slow to move; and Hill's soldiers,
who had done much at Sharpsburg with but little loss, were
confident of victory. The Federal artillery beyond the river
included many of their heavy batteries, and when the long
lines of the Southerners appeared in the open, they were
met by a storm of shells. But without a check, even to
close the gaps in the ranks, or to give time to the
batteries to reply to the enemy's fire, the Light Division
pressed forward to the charge. The conflict was short.
The Northern regulars had already passed the ford, and
only a brigade of volunteers was left on the southern bank.
Bringing up his reserve regiment, the Federal general made
a vain effort to prolong his front. Hill answered by calling
up a brigade from his second line; and then, outnumbered
and outflanked, the enemy was driven down the bluffs and
across the river. The losses in this affair were comparatively
small. The Federals reported 340 killed and wounded, and
of these a raw regiment, armed with condemned Enfield
rifles, accounted for no less than 240. Hill's casualties were
271. Yet the engagement was not without importance.
Jackson's quick action and resolute advance convinced the
enemy that the Confederates were still dangerous; and
McClellan, disturbed by Stuart's threat against his rear,
abandoned all idea of crossing the Potomac in pursuit
of Lee.

The losses at Sharpsburg may be here recorded.

JONES' DIVISION—1,800.

The Stonewall Brigade, 250 strong . . .	88
Taliaferro's Brigade	173
Starke's Brigade	287
Jones' Brigade	152

700 (38 p.c.)

EWELL'S (LAWTON) DIVISION—3,600.

Lawton's Brigade, 1,150 strong . . .	567
Early's Brigade, 1,200 strong	194
Trimble's Brigade, 700 strong	237
Hays' Brigade, 550 strong . . .	336

1,334 (47 p.c.)

THE LIGHT DIVISION—3,000.

Branch's Brigade	104
Gregg's Brigade	165
Archer's Brigade	105
Pender's Brigade	30
Field's Brigade (not engaged)	—
Thomas' Brigade (at Harper's Ferry) . .	—

404
Artillery (Estimated) 50

Total, 2,488 (209 officers).

D. H. HILL'S DIVISION—3,500.

Rodes' Brigade	203
Garland's Brigade (estimated) . . .	300
Anderson's Brigade	302
Ripley's Brigade (estimated) . . .	300
Colquitt's Brigade (estimated) . .	300

1,405

McLAWS' DIVISION—4,500.

Kershaw's Brigade	355
Cobb's Brigade	156
Semmes' Brigade	314[1]
Barksdale's Brigade	294

1,119

---

[1] Semmes' four regiments, engaged in Jackson's counterstroke, reported the following percentage of loss. 53rd Georgia, 30 p.c.; 32nd Virginia, 45 p.c.; 10th Georgia, 57 p.c; 15th Virginia, 58 p.c.

D. R. Jones' Division—3,500.

Toombs' Brigade (estimated)	125
Drayton's Brigade (estimated). . . .	400
Anderson's Brigade	87
Garnett's Brigade	99
Jenkins' Brigade	210
Kemper's Brigade (estimated) . . .	120
	1,041

Walker's Division—3,500.

Walker's Brigade	825
Ransom's Brigade	187
	1,012

Hood's Division—2,000.

Laws' Brigade	454
Hood's Brigade	548
	1,002
Evans' Brigade, 250 strong	200

R. H. Anderson's Division—3,500.

Featherston's Brigade	304
Mahone's Brigade	76
Pryor's Brigade	182
Armistead's Brigade	35
Wright's Brigade	203
Wilcox' Brigade	221
	1,021

Artillery.

Colonel S. D. Lee's Battalion . . .	85
Washington Artillery	34
Cavalry, &c. &c. (estimated) . . .	143
	262

Grand total, 9,550.

Army of the Potomac.

First Corps—Hooker	2,590
Second Corps—Sumner	5,138
Fifth Corps—Porter	109
Sixth Corps—Franklin	439
Ninth Corps—Burnside	2,349
Twelfth Corps—Mansfield	1,746
Cavalry Division, &c.	39
(2,108 killed)	12,410 [1]

[1] For the losses in various great battles, see Note at end of volume.

With Porter's repulse the summer campaign of 1862 was closed. Begun on the Chickahominy, within thirty miles of Richmond, it ended on the Potomac, within seventy miles of Washington; and six months of continuous fighting had brought both belligerents to the last stage of exhaustion. Falling apart like two great battleships of the older wars,

> The smoke of battle drifting slow a-lee,

hulls rent by roundshot, and scuppers awash with blood, but with the colours still flying over shattered spars and tangled shrouds, the armies drew off from the tremendous struggle. Neither Confederates nor Federals were capable of further effort. Lee, gathering in his stragglers, left Stuart to cover his front, and fell back towards Winchester. McClellan was content with seizing the Maryland Heights at Harper's Ferry, and except the cavalry patrols, not a single Federal soldier was sent across the river.

Reorganisation was absolutely imperative. The Army of the Potomac was in no condition to undertake the invasion of Virginia. Not only had the losses in battle been very large, but the supply train, hurriedly got together after Pope's defeat, had broken down; in every arm there was great deficiency of horses; the troops, especially those who had been engaged in the Peninsula, were half-clad and badly shod; and, above all, the army was very far from sharing McClellan's conviction that Sharpsburg was a brilliant victory. The men in the ranks were not so easily deceived as their commander. McClellan, relying on a return drawn up by General Banks, now in command at Washington, estimated the Confederate army at 97,000 men, and his official reports made frequent mention of Lee's overwhelming strength.[1]

[1] Mr. Lincoln had long before this recognised the tendency of McClellan and others to exaggerate the enemy's strength. As a deputation from New England was one day leaving the White House, a delegate turned round and said : 'Mr. President, I should much like to know what you reckon to be the number the rebels have in arms against us.' Without a moment's hesitation Mr. Lincoln replied : 'Sir, I have the best possible reason for knowing the number to be one million of men, for whenever one of our generals engages

The soldiers knew better.   They had been close enough to
the enemy's lines to learn for themselves how thin was the
force which manned them.   They were perfectly well aware
that they had been held in check by inferior numbers, and
that the battle on the Antietam, tactically speaking, was no
more of a victory for the North than Malvern Hill had been
for the South.   From dawn to dark on September 18 they
had seen the tattered colours and bright bayonets of the
Confederates still covering the Sharpsburg ridge ; they had
seen the grey line, immovable and defiant, in undisputed
possession of the battle-ground, while their own guns were
silent and their own generals reluctant to renew the fight.
Both the Government and the people expected McClellan to
complete his success by attacking Lee in Virginia.   The Confederates, it was said—and men based their opinions on
McClellan's reports—had been heavily defeated, not only at
Antietam, but also at South Mountain ; and although the
Army of the Potomac might be unfit for protracted operations, the condition of the enemy must necessarily be far
worse.

Such arguments, however, were entirely inapplicable to
the situation.   The Confederates had not been defeated at
all, either at South Mountain or Sharpsburg ; and although
they had eventually abandoned their positions they had
suffered less than their opponents.   The retreat, however,
across the Potomac had undoubtedly shaken their *moral*.
' In a military point of view,' wrote Lee to Davis on September 25, ' the best move, in my opinion, the army could
make would be to advance upon Hagerstown and endeavour
to defeat the enemy at that point.   I would not hesitate
to make it even with our diminished numbers did the
army exhibit its former temper and condition, but, as
far as I am able to judge, the hazard would be great and
reverse disastrous.' [1]   But McClellan was not more cheerful.   ' The army,' he said on the 27th, ' is not now in a

a rebel army he reports that he has encountered a force twice his strength.
Now I know we have half a million soldiers, so I am bound to believe that
the rebels have twice that number.'
    [1] O. R., vol. xix., part ii., p. 627.

condition to undertake another campaign nor to bring on another battle, unless great advantages are offered by some mistake of the enemy, or pressing military exigencies render it necessary.' So far from thinking of pursuit, he thought only of the defence of the Potomac, apprehending a renewed attempt to enter Maryland, and by no means over-confident that the two army corps which he had at last sent to Harper's Ferry would be able to maintain their position if attacked.[1] Nor were the soldiers more eager than their commander to cross swords with their formidable enemy. 'It would be useless,' says General G. H. Gordon, who now commanded a Federal division, ' to deny that at this period there was a despondent feeling in the army,' and the Special Correspondents of the New York newspapers, the 'World' and 'Tribune,' confirm the truth of this statement. But the clearest evidence as to the condition of the troops is furnished in the numerous reports which deal with straggling. The vice had reached a pitch which is almost inconceivable. Thousands and tens of thousands, Federals as well as Confederates, were absent from their commands.

'The States of the North,' wrote McClellan, 'are flooded with deserters and absentees. One corps of this army has 13,000 men present and 15,000 absent; of this 15,000, 8,000 probably are at work at home.'[2] On September 23, General Meade, who had succeeded to the command of Hooker's corps, reported that over 8,000 men, including 250 officers, had quitted the ranks either before or during the battle of Antietam; adding that ' this terrible and serious evil seems to pervade the whole body.'[3] The Confederates, although the privations of the troops during the forced marches, their indifferent equipment, and the deficiencies of the commissariat were contributory causes, had almost as much reason to complain. It is said that in the vicinity of Leesburg alone over 10,000 men were living on the citizens. Jackson's own division, which took into action 1,600 effectives on September 17 and lost 700, had 3,900 present for duty on September 30; Lawton's

---

[1] O. R., vol. xix., part i., p. 70.
[2] Ibid., part ii., p. 365. [3] Ibid., p. 348.

division rose from 2,500 to 4,450 during the same period; and the returns show that the strength of Longstreet's and Jackson's corps was only 37,992 on September 22, but 52,019 on October 1.[1]   It is thus evident that in eight days the army was increased by more than 14,000 men, yet only a few conscripts had been enrolled.   Lee's official reports and correspondence allude in the strongest terms to the indiscipline of his army.   'The absent,' he wrote on September 23, 'are scattered broadcast over the land;' and in the dispatches of his subordinates are to be found many references to the vagrant tendencies of their commands.[2]   A strong provost guard was established at Winchester for the purpose of collecting stragglers. Parties of cavalry were sent out to protect the farms from pillage, and to bring in the marauders as prisoners.   The most stringent regulations were issued as to the preservation of order on the march, the security of private property, and the proper performance of their duties by regimental and commissariat officers.   On September 23, General Jones reported from Winchester that the country was full of stragglers, that he had already sent back 5,000 or 6,000, and that the numbers of officers amongst them was astonishing.[3]   The most earnest representations were made to the President, suggesting trial of the offenders by drumhead court-martial, and ordinary police duties became the engrossing occupation of every general officer.

It can hardly be said, then, that the Confederates had drawn much profit from the invasion of Maryland.   The capture of Harper's Ferry made but small amends for

[1] O. R., vol. xix., part ii., pp. 621, 639.

[2] General orders, Sept. 4; Lee to Davis, Sept. 7; Lee to Davis, Sept. 13; special orders, Sept. 21; circular order, Sept. 22; Lee to Davis, Sept. 23; Lee to Secretary of War, Sept. 23; Lee to Pendleton, Sept. 24; Lee to Davis, Sept. 24; Lee to Davis, Sept. 28; Lee to Davis, Oct. 2; O. R., vol. xix., part ii. *See also* Report of D. H. Hill, O. R., vol. xix., part i., p. 1026. Stuart to Secretary of War, Oct. 13. On Sept. 21, Jackson's adjutant-general wrote, 'We should have gained a victory and routed them, had it not been for the straggling. We were twenty-five thousand short by this cause.' *Memoirs of W. N. Pendleton, D.D.*, p. 217. It is but fair to say that on September 13 there was a camp of 900 barefooted men at Winchester, and 'a great many more with the army.' Lee to Quarter-Master-General, O. R., vol. xix., part ii., p. 614.

[3] O. R., vol. xix., part ii., p. 629.

the retreat into Virginia; and the stubborn endurance of Sharpsburg, however remarkable in the annals of war, had served no useful purpose beyond crippling for the time being the Federal army. The battle must be classed with Aspern and Talavera; Lee's soldiers saved their honour, but no more. The facts were not to be disguised. The Confederates had missed their mark. Only a few hundred recruits had been raised in Maryland, and there had been no popular outbreak against the Union Government. The Union army had escaped defeat; Lincoln had been able to announce to the Northern people that Lee's victorious career had at length been checked; and 12,000 veteran soldiers, the flower of the Southern army, had fallen in battle. Had General Longstreet's advice been taken, and the troops withdrawn across the Potomac after the fall of Harper's Ferry, this enormous loss, which the Confederacy could so ill afford, would certainly have been avoided. Yet Lee was not ill-satisfied with the results of the campaign, nor did Jackson doubt the wisdom of accepting battle on the Antietam.

The hazard was great, but the stake was greater. To achieve decisive success in war some risk must be run. 'It is impossible,' says Moltke, 'to forecast the result of a pitched battle;' but this is no reason that pitched battles, if there is a fair prospect of success, should be shirked. And in the Sharpsburg campaign the Confederates had un-doubtedly fair prospects of success. If the lost order had not fallen into McClellan's hands, Lee in all probability would have had ample time to select his battlefield and concentrate his army; there would have been no need of forced marches, and consequently much less straggling. Both Lee and Jackson counted on the caution of their opponent. Both were surprised by the unwonted vigour he displayed, especially at South Mountain and in the march to Sharpsburg. Such resolution in action, they were aware, was foreign to his nature. 'I cannot understand this move of McClellan's,' was Jackson's remark, when it was reported that the Federal general had boldly advanced against the strong position on South Mountain. But neither Lee nor Jackson was aware that McClellan had exact information of their dispositions, and that the carelessness of a Confederate staff officer had done more for the Union than all the Northern scouts and spies in Maryland. Jackson had been disposed to leave a larger margin for accidents than his commander. He would have left Harper's Ferry alone, and have fought the Federals in the mountains;[1] and he was probably right, for in the Gettysburg campaign of the following year, when Lee again crossed the Potomac, Harper's Ferry was ignored, although occupied by a strong garrison, and neither in advance nor retreat were the Confederate communications troubled. But as to the wisdom of giving battle on the Antietam, after the fall of Harper's Ferry, there was no divergence of opinion between Lee and his lieutenant. They had no reason to respect the Union army as a weapon of offence, and very great reason to believe that McClellan was incapable of wielding it. Their anticipations were well founded. The Federal attack was badly designed and badly executed. If it be compared with the German attack at Wörth, the defects of McClellan, the defects of his subordinates, the want of sound training throughout the whole army, become at once apparent. On August 6, 1870, there was certainly, early in the day, much disjointed fighting, due in great part to the difficulties of the country, the absence of the Crown Prince, and the anxiety of the generals to render each other loyal support. But when once the Commander-in-Chief appeared upon the field, and, assuming direction of the battle, infused harmony into the operations, the strength and unity of the attack could hardly have been surpassed. Almost at the same moment 30,000 men were launched against McMahon's front, 25,000 against his right, and 10,000 against his left. Every battalion within sound of the cannon participated in the forward movement; and numerous batteries, crossing the stream which corresponds with the Antietam, supported the infantry at the closest range. No general hesitated to act on his own responsibility. Everywhere there was

[1] Dabney, vol. ii., p. 302

co-operation, between infantry and artillery, between division and division, between army corps and army corps; and such co-operation, due to a sound system of command, is the characteristic mark of a well-trained army and a wise leader. At Sharpsburg, on the other hand, there was no combination whatever, and even the army corps commanders dared not act without specific orders. There was nothing like the close concert and the aggressive energy which had carried the Southerners to victory at Gaines' Mill and the Second Manassas. The principle of mutual support was utterly ignored. The army corps attacked in succession and not simultaneously, and in succession they were defeated. McClellan fought three separate battles, from dawn to 10 A.M. against Lee's left; from 10 A.M. to 1 P.M. against his centre; from 1 to 4 P.M. against his right. The subordinate generals, although, with a few exceptions, they handled their commands skilfully, showed no initiative, and waited for orders instead of improving the opportunity. Only two-thirds of the army was engaged; 25,000 men hardly fired a shot, and from first to last there was not the slightest attempt at co-operation. McClellan was made aware by his signallers on the Red Hill of every movement that took place in his opponent's lines, and yet he was unable to take advantage of Lee's weakness. He had still to grasp the elementary rule that the combination of superior numbers and of all arms against a single point is necessary to win battles.

The Northern infantry, indeed, had not fought like troops who own their opponents as the better men. Rather had they displayed an elasticity of spirit unsuspected by their enemies; and the Confederate soldiers, who knew with what fierce courage the attack had been sustained, looked on the battle of Sharpsburg as the most splendid of their achievements. No small share of the glory fell to Jackson. Since the victory of Cedar Run, his fame, somewhat obscured by Frayser's Farm and Malvern Hill, had increased by leaps and bounds, and the defence of the West Wood was classed with the march to Manassas Junction, the three days' battle about Groveton, and the swift seizure of Harper's Ferry. On October 2, Lee proposed to the President that the Army of Northern Virginia should be organised in two army corps, for the command of which he recommended Longstreet and Jackson. 'My opinion,' wrote Lee, 'of General Jackson has been greatly enhanced during this expedition. He is true, honest, and brave; has a single eye to the good of the service, and spares no exertion to accomplish his object.'[1] On October 11, Jackson received his promotion as Lieutenant-General, and was appointed to the Second Army Corps, consisting at that date of his own division, the Light Division, Ewell's, and D. H. Hill's, together with Colonel Brown's battalion of artillery; a force of 1,917 officers, 25,000 men, and 126 guns.

Jackson does not appear to have been unduly elated by his promotion, for two days after his appointment he wrote to his wife that there was no position in the world equal to that of a minister of the Gospel, and his letter was principally concerned with the lessons he had learned from the sermon of the previous Sunday.[2] The soldiers of

[1] O. R., vol. xix., part ii., p. 643.

[2] About this time he made a successful appearance in a new *rôle*. In September, General Bradley T. Johnson was told off to accompany Colonel Garnet Wolseley, the Hon. Francis Lawley, Special Correspondent to the *Times*, and Mr. Vizetelly, Special Correspondent of the *Illustrated London News*, round the Confederate camps. 'By order of General Lee,' he says, 'I introduced the party to General Jackson. We were all seated in front of General Jackson's tent, and he took up the conversation. He had been to England, and had been greatly impressed with the architecture of Durham Cathedral and with the history of the bishopric. The Bishops had been Palatines from the date of the Conquest, and exercised semi-royal authority over their bishopric.

'There is a fair history of the Palatinate of Durham in Blackstone and Coke, but I can hardly think that General Jackson derived his information from those two fountains of the law. Anyhow, he cross-examined the Englishmen in detail about the cathedral and the close and the rights of the bishops, &c. &c. He gave them no chance to talk, and kept them busy answering questions, for he knew more about Durham than they did.

'As we rode away, I said: "Gentlemen, you have disclosed Jackson in a new character to me, and I've been carefully observing him for a year and a half. You have made him exhibit *finesse*, for he did all the talking to keep you from asking too curious or embarrassing questions. I never saw anything like it in him before." We all laughed, and agreed that the general had been too much for the interviewers.'—*Memoirs*, pp. 530–1.

the Second Army Corps, however, did not allow him to forget his greatness. In their bivouacs by the clear waters of the Opequon, with abundance of supplies and with ample leisure for recuperation, the troops rapidly regained their strength and spirit. The reaction found vent in the most extravagant gaiety. No circumstance that promised entertainment was permitted to pass without attention, and the jest started at the expense of some unfortunate wight, conspicuous for peculiarity of dress or demeanour, was taken up by a hundred voices. None were spared. A trim staff officer was horrified at the irreverent reception of his nicely twisted moustache, as he heard from behind innumerable trees : ' Take them mice out o' your mouth ! take 'em out—no use to say they ain't there, see their tails hanging out ! ' Another, sporting immense whiskers, was urged ' to come out o' that bunch of hair ! I know you're in there ! I see your ears a-working ! ' So the soldiers chaffed the dandies, and the camp rang with laughter ; fun and frolic were always in the air, and the fierce fighters of Sharpsburg behaved like schoolboys on a holiday. But when the general rode by the men remembered the victories they had won and to whom they owed them, the hardships they had endured, and who had shared them ; and the appearance of ' Little Sorrel ' was the sure precursor of a scene of the wildest enthusiasm. The horse soon learned what the cheers implied, and directly they began he would break into a gallop, as if to carry his rider as quickly as possible through the embarrassing ordeal. But the soldiers were not to be deterred by their commander's modesty, and whenever he was compelled to pass through the bivouacs the same tribute was so invariably offered that the sound of a distant cheer, rolling down the lines of the Second Army Corps, always evoked the exclamation : ' Boys, look out ! here comes old Stonewall or an old hare ! ' ' These being the only individuals,' writes one of Jackson's soldiers, ' who never failed to bring down the whole house.'

Nothing could express more clearly the loyalty of the soldiers to their general than this quaint estimate of his popularity. The Anglo-Saxon is averse to the unrestrained display of personal affection; and when his natural reluctance is overborne by irrepressible emotion, he attempts to hide it by a jest. So Jackson's veterans laughed at his peculiarities, at his dingy uniform, his battered cap, his respect for clergymen, his punctilious courtesy, and his blushes. They delighted in the phrase, when a distant yell was heard, 'Here's "Old Jack" or a rabbit!' They delighted more in his confusion when he galloped through the shouting camp. 'Here he comes,' they said, 'we'll make him take his hat off.' They invented strange fables of which he was the hero. 'Stonewall died,' ran one of the most popular, 'and two angels came down from heaven to take him back with them. They went to his tent. He was not there. They went to the hospital. He was not there. They went to the outposts. He was not there. They went to the prayer-meeting. He was not there. So they had to return without him; but when they reported that he had disappeared, they found that he had made a flank march and reached heaven before them.' Another was to the effect that whereas Moses took forty years to get the children of Israel through the wilderness, ' " Old Jack " would have double-quicked them through in three days on half rations ! '

But, nevertheless, beneath this affectation of hilarity lay a deep and passionate devotion; and two incidents which occurred at this time show the extent of this feeling, and at least one reason for its existence. 'On October 8th,' writes Major Heros von Borcke, adjutant-general of the cavalry division, 'I was honoured with the pleasing mission of presenting to Stonewall, as a slight token of Stuart's high regard, a new uniform coat, which had just arrived from the hands of a Richmond tailor. Starting at once, I reached the simple tent of our great general just in time for dinner. I found him in his old weather-stained coat, from which all the buttons had been clipped by the fair hands of patriotic ladies, and which, from exposure to sun, rain, and powder-smoke, and by reason of many rents and patches, was in a very unseemly condition. When I had despatched more important matters, I produced General Stuart's present in all its magnificence of gilt buttons and sheeny facings and gold lace, and I was heartily amused at the modest confusion with which the hero of many battles regarded the fine uniform, scarcely daring to touch it, and at the quiet way in which at last he folded it up carefully and deposited it in his portmanteau, saying to me, "Give Stuart my best thanks, Major ; the coat is much too handsome for me, but I shall take the best care of it, and shall prize it highly as a souvenir. And now let us have some dinner." But I protested emphatically against the summary disposition of the matter of the coat, deeming my mission indeed but half executed, and remarked that Stuart would certainly ask how the coat fitted, and that I should take it as a personal favour if he would put it on. To this with a smile he readily assented, and having donned the garment, he escorted me outside the tent to the table where dinner had been served in the open air. The whole of the staff were in a perfect ecstasy at their chief's brilliant appearance, and the old negro servant, who was bearing the roast turkey to the board, stopped in mid career with a most bewildered expression, and gazed in such wonderment at his master as if he had been transfigured before him. Meanwhile, the rumour of the change ran like electricity through the neighbouring camps, the soldiers came running by hundreds to the spot, desirous of seeing their beloved Stonewall in his new attire ; and the first wearing of a new robe by Louis XIV., at whose morning toilette all the world was accustomed to assemble, never created half the excitement at Versailles that was roused in the woods of Virginia by the investment of Jackson in the new regulation uniform.'[1]

The second incident is less amusing, but was not less appreciated by the rank and file. Riding one morning near Front Royal, accompanied by his staff, Jackson was stopped by a countrywoman, with a chubby child on either side, who inquired anxiously for her son Johnnie, serving, she said, 'in Captain Jackson's company.' The

[1] *Memoirs of the Confederate War*, vol. i.

general, with the deferential courtesy he never laid
aside, introduced himself as her son's commanding officer,
but begged for further information as to his regiment.
The good dame, however, whose interest in the war
centred on one individual, appeared astonished that
'Captain Jackson' did not know her particular 'Johnnie,'
and repeated her inquiries with such tearful emphasis that
the young staff officers began to smile.   Unfortunately
for themselves, Jackson heard a titter, and turning on them
with a scathing rebuke for their want of manners, he sent
them off in different directions to discover Johnnie,
giving them no rest until mother and son were brought
together.

But if the soldiers loved Jackson for his simplicity, and
respected him for his honesty, beyond and above was the
sense of his strength and power, of his indomitable will,
of the inflexibility of his justice, and of the unmeasured resources of his vigorous intellect.   It is curious even after
the long lapse of years to hear his veterans speak of
their commander. Laughter mingles with tears ; each
has some droll anecdote to relate, each some instance
of thoughtful sympathy or kindly deed ; but it is still
plain to be seen how they feared his displeasure, how
hard they found his discipline, how conscious they were of
their own mental inferiority.   The mighty phantom of
their lost leader still dominates their thoughts ; just as in
the battles of the Confederacy his earthly presentment
dominated the will of the Second Army Corps.   In the
campaign which had driven the invaders from Virginia,
and carried the Confederate colours to within sight of
Washington, his men had found their master.   They had
forgotten how to criticise.   His generals had learned to
trust him.   Success and adulation had not indeed made
him more expansive.   He was as reticent as ever, and
his troops—'the foot-cavalry' as they were now called—
were still marched to and fro without knowing why or
whither.   But men and officers, instead of grumbling when
they were roused at untimely hours, or when their marches
were prolonged, without apparent necessity, obeyed with

alacrity, and amused themselves by wondering what new surprise the general was preparing. 'Where are you going?' they were asked as they were turned out for an unexpected march: 'We don't know, but "Old Jack" does,' was the laughing reply. And they had learned something of his methods. They had discovered the value of time, of activity, of mystery, of resolution. They discussed his stratagems, gradually evolving, for they were by no means apparent at the time, the object and aim of his manœuvres; and the stirring verses, sung round every camp-fire, show that the soldiers not only grasped his principles of warfare, but that they knew right well to whom their victories were to be attributed.

STONEWALL JACKSON'S WAY

Come, stack arms, men, pile on the rails;
   Stir up the camp-fires bright;
No matter if the canteen fails,
   We'll make a roaring night.
Here Shenandoah brawls along,
There lofty Blue Ridge echoes strong,
To swell the Brigade's roaring song
   Of Stonewall Jackson's way.

We see him now—the old slouched hat,
   Cocked o'er his eye askew;
The shrewd dry smile—the speech so pat,
   So calm, so blunt, so true.
The 'Blue-Light Elder' knows them well:
Says he, 'That's Banks—he's fond of shell;
Lord save his soul! we'll give him——' well,
   That's Stonewall Jackson's way.

Silence! ground arms! kneel all! caps off!
   Old Blue-Light's going to pray;
Strangle the fool that dares to scoff!
   Attention! it's his way!
Appealing from his native sod,
In formâ pauperis to God,
' Lay bare thine arm—stretch forth thy rod,
   Amen!' That's Stonewall's way.

He's in the saddle now !   Fall in !
  Steady, the whole Brigade !
Hill's at the Ford, cut off !—we'll win
  His way out, ball and blade.
What matter if our shoes are worn ?
What matter if our feet are torn ?
Quick step ! we're with him before morn !
  That's Stonewall Jackson's way.

The sun's bright lances rout the mists
  Of morning—and, by George !
There's Longstreet struggling in the lists,
  Hemmed in an ugly gorge.
Pope and his columns whipped before—
' Bayonets and grape ! ' hear Stonewall roar ;
' Charge, Stuart ! pay off Ashby's score ! '
  That's Stonewall Jackson's way.

Ah ! maiden, wait and watch and yearn
  For news of Stonewall's band ;
Ah ! widow, read with eyes that burn
  The ring upon thy hand.
Ah ! wife, sew on, pray on, hope on,
Thy life shall not be all forlorn ;
The foe had better ne'er been born
  That gets in Stonewall's way.

NOTE

Jackson's Strength and Losses, August–September 1862.

Strength at Cedar Run, August 9 :

Winder's (Jackson's own) Division (estimate) . . .	3,000
Ewell's Division [1]	5,350
Lawton's Brigade [2]	2,200
A. P. Hill's (the Light) Division [3]	12,000
Robertson's Cavalry Brigade [4] (estimate)	1,200
	23,750

Losses at Cedar Run :

Winder's Division	718
Ewell's Division	195
The Light Division	381
Cavalry, &c.	20

1,314

22,436

Losses on the Rappahannock, August 20–24 . . .	100
Losses at Bristoe Station and Manassas Junction, August 26, 27	300
Losses at Groveton, August 28 :	
Stonewall Division (estimate) . . . 441	1,200
Ewell's Division 759	
Stragglers and sick (estimate)	1,200
Cavalry transferred to Stuart	1,200

4,000

Strength at Second Manassas, August 29 and 30 . . . 18,436

Losses :

Taliaferro's Division	416
Ewell's Division	364
The Light Division	1,507

2,387

Loss at Chantilly, September 1	500

Should have marched into Maryland 15,549

---

[1] Report of July 31, O. R., vol. xii., part iii., p. 965.
[2] Report of August 20, O. R., vol. xii., part iii., p. 966. (Not engaged at Cedar Run.)
[3] Report of July 20, O. R., vol. xi., part iii., p. 645. (3½ regiments had been added.)
[4] Four regiments.

Strength at Sharpsburg:

Jones' Division 2,000	
Ewell's Division 4,000	11,800 [1]
The Light Division 5,000	
(1 Brigade left at Harper's Ferry) 800	

Loss at Harper's Ferry 62

Losses at Sharpsburg:

Jones' Division 700	
Ewell's Division 1,334	2,438
The Light Division 404	

Strength on September 19 9,300

The Report of September 22, O. R., vol. xiv., part ii., p. 621, gives :

Jackson's own Division 2,553
Ewell's Division 3,290
The Light Division 4,777
                                   ————
                                  10,620 [2]

---

[1] 3,866 sick and straggling since August 28 = 21 p.c.
[2] Over 1,300 stragglers had rejoined.

CHAPTER XX

FREDERICKSBURG

WHILE the Army of Northern Virginia was resting in the Valley, McClellan was preparing for a winter campaign.

1862. October. He was unable, however, to keep pace with the impatience of the Northern people. Not only was he determined to postpone all movement until his army was properly equipped, his ranks recruited, his cavalry remounted, and his administrative services reorganised, but the military authorities at Washington were very slow in meeting his demands. Notwithstanding, then, the orders of the President, the remonstrances of Halleck, and the clamour of the press, for more than five weeks after the battle of Sharpsburg he remained inactive on the Potomac. It may be that in the interests of the army he was perfectly right in resisting the pressure brought to bear upon him. He was certainly the best judge of the temper of his troops, and could estimate more exactly than either Lincoln or Halleck the chances of success if he were to encounter Lee's veterans on their native soil. However this may be, his inaction was not in accordance with the demands of the political situation. The President, immediately the Confederates retired from Maryland, had taken a step which changed the character of the war. Hitherto the Northerners had fought for the restoration of the Union on the basis of the Constitution, as interpreted by themselves. Now, after eighteen months of conflict, the Constitution was deliberately violated. For the clause which forbade all interference with the domestic institutions of the several States, a declaration that slavery should no longer exist within the boundaries

of the Republic was substituted, and the armies of the
Union were called upon to fight for the freedom of the
negro.

In the condition of political parties this measure was
daring. It was not approved by the Democrats, and many
of the soldiers were Democrats; or by those—and they
were not a few—who believed that compromise was the
surest means of restoring peace; or by those—and they
were numerous—who thought the dissolution of the Union
a smaller evil than the continuance of the war. The opposition was very strong, and there was but one means of
reconciling it—vigorous action on the part of the army,
the immediate invasion of Virginia, and a decisive victory.
Delay would expose the framers of the measure to the
imputation of having promised more than they could
perform, of wantonly tampering with the Constitution, and
of widening the breach between North and South beyond
all hope of healing.

In consequence, therefore, of McClellan's refusal to move
forward, the friction between the Federal Government and
their general-in-chief, which, so long as Lee remained in
Maryland, had been allayed, once more asserted its baneful
influence; and the aggressive attitude of the Confederates
did not serve to make matters smoother. Although the
greater part of October was for the Army of Northern
Virginia a period of unusual leisure, the troops were not
altogether idle. As soon as the stragglers had been
brought in, and the ranks of the divisions once more
presented a respectable appearance, various enterprises
were undertaken. The Second Army Corps was entrusted with the destruction of the Baltimore and Ohio
Railway, a duty carried out by Jackson with characteristic thoroughness. The line from Harper's Ferry
to Winchester, as well as that from Manassas Junction to Strasburg, were also torn up; and the spoils of the
late campaign were sent south to Richmond and Staunton.
These preparations for defensive warfare were not, however,
so immediately embarrassing to the enemy as the action
of the cavalry. Stuart's three brigades, after the affair at

Boteler's Ford, picketed the line of the Potomac from the North Mountain to the Shenandoah, a distance of forty miles : Hampton's brigade at Hedgesville, Fitzhugh Lee's at Shepherdstown, Munford's at Charlestown, and head-quarters near Leetown.

On October 8 General Lee, suspecting that McClellan was meditating some movement, ordered the cavalry to cross the Potomac and reconnoitre. Selecting 600 men from each of his brigades, with General Hampton, Colonels W. H. F. Lee and W. E. Jones in command, and accompanied by four horse-artillery guns, Stuart ren-
Oct. 9. dezvoused on the night of the 9th at Darkes-ville. As the day dawned he crossed the Potomac at McCoy's Ford, drove in the Federal pickets, and broke up a signal station near Fairview. Marching due north, he reached Mercersburg at noon, and Chambersburg, forty-six miles from Darkesville, at 7 P.M. on October 10. Chambersburg, although a Federal supply depôt of some importance, was without a garrison, and here 275 sick and
Oct. 10. wounded were paroled, 500 horses requisitioned, the wires cut, and the railroad obstructed ; while the machine shops, several trains of loaded cars, and a large quantity of small arms, ammunition, and clothing was de-
Oct. 11. stroyed. At nine the next morning the force marched in the direction of Gettysburg, moving round the Federal rear. Then, crossing the mountains, it turned south through Emmittsburg, passed the Monocacy near Frederick, and after a march of ninety miles since leaving Chambersburg reached Hyattstown at daylight on the
Oct. 12. 12th. Here, on the road which formed McClellan's line of communication with Washington, a few waggons were captured, and information came to hand that 4,000 or 5,000 Federal troops were near Poolesville, guarding the fords across the Potomac. Moving at a trot through the woods, the column, leaving Poolesville two or three miles to the left, made for the mouth of the Monocacy. About a mile and a half from that river an advanced-guard of hostile cavalry, moving eastward, was encountered and driven in. Colonel Lee's men were dis-

mounted, a gun was brought into action, and under cover of
this screen, posted on a high crest, the main body made a
dash for White's Ford. The point of passage, although
guarded by about 100 Federal riflemen, was quickly seized,
and Stuart's whole force, together with the captured horses,
had completed the crossing before the enemy, advancing
in large force from the Monocacy, was in a position to
interfere.

This brilliantly conducted expedition was as fruitful of
results as the ride round McClellan's army in the previous
June. The information obtained was most important.
Lee, besides being furnished with a sufficiently full report
of the Federal dispositions, learned that no part of McClellan's army had been detached to Washington, but that
it was being reinforced from that quarter, and that therefore no over-sea expedition against Richmond was to be
apprehended. Several hundred fine horses from the farms
of Pennsylvania furnished excellent remounts for the
Confederate troopers. Prominent officials were brought
in as hostages for the safety of the Virginia citizens who
had been thrown into Northern prisons. Only a few scouts
were captured by the enemy, and not a man was killed.
The distance marched by Stuart, from Darkesville to White's
Ford, was one hundred and twenty-six miles, of which the
last eighty were covered without a halt. Crossing the
Potomac at McCoy's Ford about 6 A.M. on October 10,
he had recrossed it at White's Ford, between 1 and 2 P.M. on
October 12 ; he was thus for fifty-six hours inside the enemy's
lines, and during the greater part of his march within thirty
miles of McClellan's headquarters near Harper's Ferry.

It is often the case in war that a well-planned and
boldly executed enterprise has a far greater effect than
could possibly have been anticipated. Neither Lee nor
Stuart looked for larger results from this raid than a
certain amount of plunder and a good deal of intelligence.
But skill and daring were crowned with a more ample reward
than the attainment of the immediate object.

In the first place, the expedition, although there was
little fighting, was most destructive to the Federal cavalry.

McClellan had done all in his power to arrest the raiders. Directly the news came in that they had crossed the Potomac, troops were sent in every direction to cut off their retreat. Yet so eminently judicious were Stuart's precautions, so intelligent the Maryland soldiers who acted as his guides, and so rapid his movements, that although constant reports were received by the Federal generals as to the progress and direction of his column, the information came always too late to serve any practical purpose, and his pursuers were never in time to bar his march. General Pleasanton, with such cavalry as could be spared from the picket line, marched seventy-eight miles in four-and-twenty hours, and General Averell's brigade, quartered on the Upper Potomac, two hundred miles in four days. The severity of the marches told heavily on these commands, already worn out by hard work on the outposts ; and so many of the horses broke down that a period of repose was absolutely necessary to refit them for the field. Until his cavalry should have recovered it was impossible for McClellan to invade Virginia.

In the second place, neither the Northern Government nor the Northern people could forget that this was the second time that McClellan had allowed Stuart to ride at will round the Army of the Potomac. Public confidence in the general-in-chief was greatly shaken ; and a handle was given to his opponents in the ranks of the abolitionists, who, because he was a Democrat, and had much influence with the army, were already clamouring for his removal.

The respite which Stuart had gained for Virginia was not, however, of long duration. On October 26, McClellan, having ascertained by means of a strong reconnaissance in force that the Confederate army was still in the vicinity of Winchester, commenced the passage of the Potomac. The principal point of crossing was Oct. 26. near Berlin, and so soon as it became evident that the Federal line of operations lay east of the Blue Ridge, Lee ordered Longstreet to Culpeper Court House. Jackson, taking post on the road between Berryville and Charlestown, was to remain in the Valley.

On November 7 the situation was as follows :—

ARMY OF THE POTOMAC.

First Corps	Warrenton.
Second Corps . . .	Rectortown.
Third Corps	{ Between Manassas Junction and Warrenton.
Fifth Corps	White Plains.
Ninth Corps	Waterloo.
Eleventh Corps . . .	New Baltimore.
Cavalry Division . . .	{ Rappahannock Station and Sperryville.
Line of Supply . . .	{ Orange and Alexandria and Manassas Railways.
Twelfth Corps . . .	Harper's Ferry and Sharpsburg.

ARMY OF NORTHERN VIRGINIA.

First Corps	Culpeper Court House.
Second Corps	Headquarters, Millwood.
Cavalry Division . . .	{ Hampton's and Fitzhugh Lee's Brigades on the Rappahannock. Munford's Brigade with Jackson.
Lines of Supply . . .	{ Staunton—Strasburg. Staunton—Culpeper Court House. Richmond—Gordonsville.

Nov. 7.　　On this date the six corps of the Army of the Potomac which were assembled between the Bull Run Mountains and the Blue Ridge numbered 125,000 officers and men present for duty, together with 320 guns.

The returns of the Army of Northern Virginia give the following strength :—

		Guns	
First Army Corps .	. 31,939	112	(54 short-range smooth-bores)
Second Army Corps .	. 31,794	123	(53　　　,,　　　　　,,　　)
Cavalry Division .	. 7,176	4	
Reserve Artillery .	. 900	36	(20　　　,,　　　　　,,　　)
	71,809	275	

The Confederates were not only heavily outnumbered by the force immediately before them, but along the Potomac, from Washington westward, was a second hostile army, not indeed so large as that commanded by McClellan, but larger by several thousands than that commanded by

Lee. The Northern capital held a garrison of 80,000; at Harper's Ferry were 10,000; in the neighbourhood of Sharpsburg over 4,000; along the Baltimore and Ohio Railroad 8,000. Thus the total strength of the Federals exceeded 225,000 men. Yet in face of this enormous host, and with Richmond only weakly garrisoned behind him, Lee had actually separated his two wings by an interval of sixty miles. He was evidently playing his old game, dividing his army with a view to a junction on the field of battle.

Lincoln, in a letter of advice with which he had favoured McClellan a few days previously, had urged the importance of making Lee's line of supply the first objective of the invading army. 'An advance east of the Blue Ridge,' he said, 'would at once menace the enemy's line of communications, and compel him to keep his forces together; and if Lee, disregarding this menace, were to cut in between the Army of the Potomac and Washington, McClellan would have nothing to do but to attack him in rear.' He suggested, moreover, that by hard marching it might be possible for McClellan to reach Richmond first.

The Confederate line of communications, so the President believed, ran from Richmond to Culpeper Court House, and McClellan's advanced-guards, on November 7, were within twenty miles of that point. Lee, however, had altogether failed to respond to Mr. Lincoln's strategical pronouncements. Instead of concentrating his forces he had dispersed them; and instead of fearing for his own communications, he had placed Jackson in a position to interfere very seriously with those of his enemy.

Mr. Lincoln's letter to McClellan shows that the lessons of the war had not been altogether lost upon him. Generals Banks and Pope, with some stimulus from Stonewall Jackson, had taught him what an important part is played by lines of supply. He had mastered the strategical truism that an enemy's communications are his weakest point. But there were other considerations which had not come home to him. He had overlooked the possibility that Lee might threaten McClellan's communications before McClellan could threaten his; and he had yet to learn that an army operating in its own country, if proper forethought be exercised, can establish an alternative line of supply, and provide itself with a double base, thus gaining a freedom of action of which an invader, bound, unless he has command of the sea, to a single line, is generally deprived.

The President appears to have thought that, if Lee were cut off from Richmond, the Army of Northern Virginia would be reduced to starvation, and become absolutely powerless. It never entered his head that the astute commander of that army had already, in anticipation of the very movement which McClellan was now making, established a second base at Staunton, and that his line of supply, in case of necessity, would not run over the open country between Richmond and Gordonsville, but from Staunton to Culpeper, behind the ramparts of the Blue Ridge.

Lee, in fact, accepted with equanimity the possibility of the Federals intervening between himself and Richmond. He had already, in the campaign against Pope, extricated himself from such a situation by a bold stroke against his enemy's communications; and the natural fastness of the Valley, amply provided with food and forage, afforded facilities for such a manœuvre which had been altogether absent before the Second Manassas. Nor was he of Mr. Lincoln's opinion, that if the Army of Northern Virginia cut in between Washington and McClellan it would be a simple operation for the latter to about face and attack the Confederates in rear. He knew, and Mr. Lincoln, if he had studied Pope's campaign, should have known it too, that the operation of countermarching, if the line of communication has been cut, is not only apt to produce great confusion and great suffering, but has the very worst effect on the *moral* of the troops. But Lee had that practical experience which Mr. Lincoln lacked, and without which it is but waste of words to dogmatise on strategy. He was well aware that a large army is a cumbrous machine, not readily deflected from the original

direction of the line of march ;[1] and, more than all, he had
that intimate acquaintance with the soldier in the ranks,
that knowledge of the human factor, without which no
military problem, whether of strategy, tactics, or organisation, can be satisfactorily solved. McClellan's task, therefore, so long as he had to depend for his supplies on a
single line of railway, was not quite so simple as Mr.
Lincoln imagined.

Nevertheless, on November 7 Lee decided to unite
his army. As soon as the enemy advanced from Warrenton, Jackson was to ascend the Valley, and crossing the
Blue Ridge at Fisher's Gap, join hands with Longstreet, who would retire from Madison Court House to the
vicinity of Gordonsville. The Confederates would then be
concentrated on McClellan's right flank should he march on
Richmond, ready to take advantage of any opportunity for
attack ; or, if attack were considered too hazardous, to
threaten his communications, and compel him to fall back
to the Potomac.

The proposed concentration, however, was not immediately carried out. In the first place, the Federal advance
came to a sudden standstill ; and, in the second place,
Jackson was unwilling to abandon his post of vantage behind
the Blue Ridge. It need hardly be said that the policy of
manœuvring instead of intrenching, of aiming at the
enemy's flank and rear instead of barring his advance
directly, was in full agreement with his views of war ; and
it appears that about this date he had submitted proposals
for a movement against the Federal communications. It
would be interesting indeed to have the details of his design,
but Jackson's letter-book for this period has unfortunately
disappeared, nor did he communicate his ideas to any of his
staff. Letters from General Lee, however, indicate that
the manœuvre proposed was of the same character as

[1] On November 1 the Army of the Potomac (not including the Third
Corps) was accompanied by 4,818 waggons and ambulances, 8,500 transport
horses, and 12,000 mules. O. R., vol. xix., part i., pp. 97–8. The train of
each army corps and of the cavalry covered eight miles of road, or fifty
miles for the whole.

that which brought Pope in such hot haste from the Rappahannock to Bull Run, and that it was Jackson's suggestion which caused the Commander-in-Chief to reconsider his determination of uniting his army.

'As long as General Jackson,' wrote Lee to the Secretary of War on November 10, 'can operate with safety, and secure his retirement west of the Massanutton Mountains, I think it advantageous that he should be in a position to threaten the enemy's flank and rear, and thus prevent his advance southward on the east side of the Blue Ridge. General Jackson has been directed accordingly, and should the enemy descend into the Valley, General Longstreet will attack his rear, and cut off his communications. The enemy apparently is so strong in numbers that I think it preferable to baffle his designs by manœuvring, rather than resist his advance by main force. To accomplish the latter without too great a risk and loss would require more than double our present numbers.' [1]

His letter to Jackson, dated November 9, ran as follows: 'The enemy seems to be massing his troops along the Manassas Railroad in the vicinity of Piedmont, which gives him great facilities for bringing up supplies from Alexandria. It has occurred to me that his object may be to seize upon Strasburg with his main force, to intercept your ascent of the Valley. . . . This would oblige you to cross into the Lost River Valley, or west of it, unless you could force a passage through the Blue Ridge; hence my anxiety for your safety. If you can prevent such a movement of the enemy, and operate strongly on his flank and rear through the gaps of the Blue Ridge, you would certainly in my opinion effect the object you propose. A demonstration of crossing into Maryland would serve the same purpose, and might call him back to the Potomac. As my object is to retard and baffle his designs, if it can be accomplished by manœuvring your corps as you propose, it will serve my purpose as well as if effected in any other way. With this understanding, you can use your discretion, which I know I can rely upon, in remaining or advancing up the

[1] O. R., vol. xix., part ii., p. 711.

Valley. Keep me advised of your movements and intentions; and you must keep always in view the probability of an attack upon Richmond from either north or south, when a concentration of force will become necessary.'[1]

Jackson's plan, however, was not destined to be tried. McClellan had issued orders for the concentration of his army at Warrenton. His troops had never been in better condition. They were in good spirits, well supplied and admirably equipped. Owing to the activity of his cavalry, coupled with the fact that the Confederate horses were at this time attacked by a disease which affected both tongue and hoof, his information was more accurate than usual. He knew that Longstreet was at Culpeper, and Jackson in the Valley. He saw the possibility of separating the two wings of the enemy's forces, and of either defeating Longstreet or forcing him to fall back to Gordonsville, and he had determined to make the attempt.

On the night of November 7, however, at the very moment when his army was concentrating for an advance against Longstreet, McClellan was ordered to hand over his command to General Burnside. Lincoln had yielded to the insistence of McClellan's political opponents, to the rancour of Stanton, and the jealousy of Halleck. But in sacrificing the general who had saved the Union at Sharpsburg he sacrificed the lives of many thousands of his soldiers. A darker day than even the Second Manassas was in store for the Army of the Potomac. McClellan was not a general of the first order. But he was the only officer in the United States who had experience of handling large masses of troops, and he was improving every day. Stuart had taught him the use of cavalry, and Lee the value of the initiative. He was by no means deficient in resolution, as his march with an army of recently defeated men against Lee in Maryland conclusively proves; and although he had never won a decisive victory, he possessed, to a degree which was never attained by any of his successors, the confidence and affection of his troops. But deplorable

[1] O. R., vol. xix., part ii., p. 705.

as was the weakness which sanctioned his removal on the eve of a decisive manœuvre, the blunder which put Burnside in his place was even more so. The latter appears to have been the *protégé* of a small political faction. He had many good qualities. He was a firm friend, modest, generous, and energetic. But he was so far from being distinguished for military ability that in the Army of the Potomac it was very strongly questioned whether he was fit to command an army corps. His conduct at Sharpsburg, where he had been entrusted with the attack on the Confederate right, had been the subject of the severest criticism, and by not a few of his colleagues he was considered directly responsible for the want of combination which had marred McClellan's plan of attack. More than once Mr. Lincoln infringed his own famous aphorism, ' Never swap horses when crossing a stream,' but when he transferred the destinies of the Army of the Potomac from McClellan to Burnside he did more— he selected the weakest of his team of generals to bear the burden.

At the same time that McClellan was superseded, General FitzJohn Porter, the gallant soldier of Gaines' Mill and Malvern Hill, probably the best officer in the Army of the Potomac, was ordered to resign command of the Fifth Army Corps, and to appear before a court-martial on charges of incompetency and neglect of duty at the Second Manassas. The fact that those charges were preferred by Pope, and that Porter had been allowed to retain his command through the campaign in Maryland, were hardly calculated to inspire the army with confidence in either the wisdom or the justice of its rulers ; and it was the general opinion that his intimate friendship with McClellan had more to say to his trial than his alleged incompetency.

Burnside commenced his career by renouncing the enterprise which McClellan had contemplated. Longstreet was left unmolested at Culpeper ; and, in order to free the communications from Jackson, the Federal army was marched eastward along the Rappahannock to Falmouth, a new line of supply being established between that village and Aquia Creek, the port on the Potomac, six hours' sail from Washington.

Lee had already foreseen that Jackson's presence in the Valley might induce the Federals to change their line of operations. Fredericksburg, on the south side of the Rappahannock, and the terminus of the Richmond and Potomac Railroad, had consequently been garrisoned by an infantry regiment and a battery, while three regiments of cavalry patrolled the river. This force, however, was not posted on the Rappahannock with a view of retarding the enemy's advance, but merely for observation. Lee, at this date, had no intention of concentrating at Fredericksburg. The Federals, if they acted with resolution, could readily forestall him, and the line of the North Anna, a small but difficult stream, thirty-six miles south, offered peculiar advantages to the defence.

The Federal march was rapid. On November 15 the Army of the Potomac left Warrenton, and the advanced-guard reached Falmouth on the afternoon of the Nov. 17. 17th. General Sumner, in command, observing the weakness of the Confederate garrison, requested permission from Burnside to cross the Rappahannock and establish himself on the further bank. Although two army corps were at hand, and the remainder were rapidly closing up, Burnside refused, for the bridges had been broken, and he was unwilling to expose part of his forces on the right bank with no means of retreat except a difficult and uncertain ford. The same day, part of Longstreet's corps and a brigade of cavalry were sent to Fredericksburg; and on the 19th, Lee, finding that the Federals had left Warrenton, ordered Longstreet to concentrate his whole force at Fredericksburg, and summoned Jackson from the Valley to Orange Court House.

Jackson, meanwhile, had moved to Winchester, probably with the design of threatening the enemy's garrisons on the Potomac, and this unexpected movement had caused much perturbation in the North. Pennsylvania and Maryland expected nothing less than instant invasion. The merchant feared for his strong-box, the farmer for

his herds; plate was once more packed up; railway
presidents demanded further protection for their lines;
generals begged for reinforcements, and, according to the
'Times' Correspondent, it was 'the universal belief that
Stonewall Jackson was ready to pounce upon Washington from the Shenandoah, and to capture President,
Secretaries, and all.' But before apprehension increased
to panic, before Mr. Lincoln had become infected by the
prevailing uneasiness, the departure of the Confederates
from the Valley brought relief to the affrighted citizens.

On November 22 Jackson bade farewell to Winchester.
His headquarters were not more than a hundred yards
from Dr. Graham's manse, and he spent his last evening
with his old friends. 'He was in fine health and fine
spirits,' wrote the minister's wife to Mrs. Jackson. 'The
children begged to be permitted to sit up to see "General
Jackson," and he really seemed overjoyed to see them,
played with them and fondled them, and they were
equally pleased. I have no doubt it was a great recreation
to him. He seemed to be living over last winter again,
and talked a great deal about the hope of getting back
to spend this winter with us, in the old room, which I
told him I was keeping for you and him. He certainly
has had adulation enough to spoil him, but it seems not
to affect or harm him at all. He is the same humble,
dependent Christian, desiring to give God all the glory,
looking to Him alone for a blessing, and not thinking of
himself.'

So it was with no presage that this was the last time
he would look upon the scenes he loved that Jackson
moved southward by the Valley turnpike. Past Kernstown
his columns swept, past Middletown and Strasburg, and all
the well-remembered fields of former triumphs; until the
peaks of the Massanuttons threw their shadows across the
highway, and the mighty bulk of the noble mountains,
draped in the gold and crimson of the autumn, once more re-
echoed to the tramp of his swift-footed veterans. Turning
east at New Market, he struck upwards by the familiar
road; and then, descending the narrow pass, he forded the

Shenandoah, and crossing the Luray valley vanished in the forests of the Blue Ridge. Through the dark pines of Fisher's Gap he led his soldiers down to the Virginia plains, and the rivers and the mountains knew him no more until their dead returned to them.

On the 26th the Second Army Corps was at Madison Court House. The next day it was concentrated at Orange Court House, six-and-thirty miles from Fredericksburg. In Nov. 27. eight days, two being given to rest, the troops had marched one hundred and twenty miles, and with scarce a straggler, for the stern measures which had been taken to put discipline on a firmer basis, and to make the regimental officers do their duty, had already produced a salutary effect.

On Jackson's arrival at Orange Court House he found the situation unchanged. Burnside, notwithstanding that heavy snow-storms and sharp frosts betokened the approach of winter, the season of impassable roads and swollen rivers, was still encamped near Falmouth. The difficulty of establishing a new base of supplies at Aquia Creek, and some delay on the part of the Washington authorities in furnishing him with a pontoon train, had kept him idle; but he had not relinquished his design of marching upon Richmond. His quiescence, however, together with the wishes of the President, had induced General Lee to change his plans. The Army of Northern Virginia, 78,500 strong, although, in order to induce the Federals to attack, it was not yet closely concentrated, was ready to oppose in Nov. 29. full force the passage of the Rappahannock, and all thought of retiring to the North Anna had been abandoned. On November 29, therefore, Jackson was ordered forward, and while the First Army Corps occupied a strong position in rear of Fredericksburg, with an advanced detachment in the town, the Second was told off to protect the lower reaches of the Rappahannock. Ewell's division, still commanded by Early, was posted at Skinker's Neck, twelve miles south-east of Fredericksburg, a spot which afforded many facilities for crossing; D. H. Hill's at Port Royal, already menaced by Federal gunboats, six miles further down stream; A. P. Hill's and Taliaferro's (Jackson's own) at Yerby's House and Guiney's Station, five and nine miles respectively from Longstreet's right; and Stuart, whose division was now increased to four brigades, watched both front and flanks.

The Rappahannock was undoubtedly a formidable obstacle. Navigable for small vessels as far as Fredericksburg, the head of the tide water, it is two hundred yards wide in the neighbourhood of the city, and it increases in width and depth as it flows seaward. But above Falmouth there are several easy fords; the river banks, except near Fredericksburg, are clad with forest, hiding the movements of troops; and from Falmouth downward, the left bank, under the name of the Stafford Heights, so completely commands the right that it was manifestly impossible for the Confederates to prevent the enemy, furnished with a far superior artillery, from making good the passage of the stream. A mile west of Fredericksburg, however, extending from Beck's Island to the heights beyond the Massaponax Creek, runs a long low ridge, broken by ravines and partially covered with timber, which with some slight aid from axe and spade could be rendered an exceedingly strong position. Longstreet, who occupied this ridge, had been ordered to intrench himself; gun-pits had been dug on the bare crest, named Marye's Hill, which immediately faces Fredericksburg; a few shelter-trenches had been thrown up, natural defences improved, and some slight breastworks and abattis constructed along the outskirts of the woods. These works were at extreme range from the Stafford Heights; and the field of fire, extending as far as the river, a distance varying from fifteen hundred to three thousand yards, needed no clearing. Over such ground a frontal attack, even if made by superior numbers, had little chance of success.

But notwithstanding its manifest advantages the position found no favour in the eyes of Jackson. It could be easily turned by the fords above Falmouth—Banks', United States, Ely's, and Germanna. This, however, was a minor disqualification compared with the restrictions in the way of offensive action. If the enemy should cross at Fredericksburg, both his flanks would be protected by the river, while his numerous batteries, arrayed on the Stafford Heights, and commanding the length and the breadth of the battle-field, would make counterstroke difficult and pursuit impossible. To await attack, moreover, was to allow the enemy to choose his own time and place, and to surrender the advantages of the initiative. Burnside's communications were protected by the Rappahannock, and it was thus impracticable to manœuvre against his most vulnerable point, to inflict on him a surprise, to compel him to change front, and, in case he were defeated, to cut him off from his base and deprive him of his supplies. The line of the North Anna, in Jackson's opinion, promised far greater results. The Federals, advancing from Fredericksburg, would expose their right flank and their communications for a distance of six-and-thirty miles; and if they were compelled to retreat, the destruction of their whole army was within the bounds of possibility. 'I am opposed,' he said to General D. H. Hill, 'to fighting on the Rappahannock. We will whip the enemy, but gain no fruits of victory. I have advised the line of the North Anna, but have been overruled.'[1]

So the days passed on. The country was white with snow. The temperature was near zero, and the troops, their blankets as threadbare as their uniforms, without greatcoats, and in many instances without boots, shivered beneath the rude shelters of their forest bivouacs. Fortunately there was plenty of work. Roads were cut through the woods, and existing tracks improved. The river banks were incessantly patrolled. Fortifications were constructed at Port Royal and Skinker's Neck, and the movements of the Federals, demonstrating now here and now there, kept the whole army on the alert. Nor were Jackson's men deprived of all excitement. He had the satisfaction of reporting to General Lee that D. H. Hill, with the aid of Stuart's horse-artillery, had frustrated two attempts of the Federal gunboats to pass up the river at Port Royal;

[1] Dabney, vol. ii., p. 355. From *Manassas to Appomattox*, p. 299.

and that the vigilance of Early at Skinker's Neck had caused the enemy to abandon the design which he had apparently conceived of crossing at that point.

But more vigorous operations were not long postponed. On December 10, General Burnside, urged by the impatience of the Northern press, determined to advance, and the next morning, at 3 A.M., the signal guns of the Confederates gave notice that the enemy was in motion. One hundred and forty Federal guns, many of large calibre, placed in epaulments on the Stafford Heights, frowned down upon Fredericksburg, and before the sun rose the Federal bridge builders were at work on the opposite shore. The little city, which had been deserted by the inhabitants, was held by Barksdale's Mississippi brigade of McLaws' division, about 1,600 strong, and the conduct of this advanced detachment must have done much to inspirit the troops who watched their prowess from the ridge in rear. A heavy fog hung upon the water, and not until the bridge was two-thirds completed, and shadowy figures became visible in the mist, did the Mississippians open fire. At such close quarters the effect was immediate, and the builders fled. Twice, at intervals of half an hour, they ventured again upon the deserted bridge, and twice were they driven back. Strong detachments were now moved forward by the Federals to cover the working parties, and artillery began to play upon the town. The Southerners, however, securely posted in rifle-pits and cellars, were not to be dislodged ; and at ten o'clock Burnside ordered the heavy batteries into action. Every gun which could be brought to bear on Fredericksburg discharged fifty rounds of shot and shell. To this bombardment, which lasted upwards of an hour, Longstreet's artillery could make no reply. Yet though the effect on the buildings was appalling, and flames broke out in many places, the defenders not only suffered little loss, but at the very height of the cannonade repelled another attempt to complete the bridge.

After a delay of several hours General Hooker, commanding the advance, called for volunteers to cross the river in boats. Four regiments came forward. The pon-

Dec. 11.

toons were manned, and though many lives were lost during
the transit, the gallant Federals pushed quickly across;
others followed, and Barksdale, who had no orders to hold
the place against superior strength, withdrew his men from
the river bank. About 4.30 P.M., three bridges being at
last established, the enemy pushed forward, and the Mississippians, retiring in good order, evacuated Fredericksburg.
A mile below, near the mouth of Hazel Run, the Confederate
outposts had been driven in, and three more bridges had
been thrown across. Thus on the night of the 11th the
Federals, who were now organised in three Grand Divisions,
each of two army corps, had established their advanced-
guards on the right bank of the Rappahannock, and, under
cover of the batteries on the Stafford Heights, could rapidly
and safely pass over their great host of 120,000 men.[1]

Burnside had framed his plan of attack on the assumption that Lee's army was dispersed along the Rappahannock. His balloon had reported large Confederate
bivouacs below Skinker's Neck, and he appears to have
believed that Lee, alarmed by his demonstrations near
Port Royal, had posted half his army in that neighbourhood. Utterly unsuspicious that a trap had been laid
for him, he had resolved to take advantage of this
apparently vicious distribution, and, crossing rapidly at
Fredericksburg, to defeat the Confederate left before the
right could lend support. Port Royal is but eighteen miles
from Fredericksburg, and in prompt action, therefore,
lay his only hope of success. Burnside, however, after the
successful establishment of his six bridges, evinced the
same want of resolution which had won him so unenviable
a reputation at Sharpsburg. The long hours of darkness
slipped peacefully away; no unusual sound broke the silence
of the night, and all was still along the Rappahannock. It
was not till the next morning, December 12, that
the army began to cross, and the movement,
made difficult by a dense fog, was by no means energetic.
Four of the six army corps were transferred during the

Dec. 12.

[1] The three Grand Divisions were commanded by Sumner, Hooker, and
Franklin.

day to the southern bank; but beyond a cavalry reconnaissance, which was checked by Stuart, there was no
fighting, and to every man in the Federal ranks it was
perfectly plain that the delay was fatal.

Lee, meanwhile, with ample time at his disposal and
full confidence in the wisdom of his dispositions, calmly
awaited the development of his adversary's plans. Jackson
brought up A. P. Hill and Taliaferro at noon, and posted
them on Longstreet's right; but it was not till that hour,
when it had at last become certain that the whole Federal
army was crossing, that couriers were dispatched to call
in Early and D. H. Hill. Once more the Army of Northern
Virginia was concentrated at exactly the right moment on
the field of battle.[1]

Like its predecessor, December 13 broke dull and calm,
and the mist which shrouded river and plain hid from each
Dec. 13. other the rival hosts. Long before daybreak the
Federal divisions still beyond the stream began
to cross; and as the morning wore on, and the troops near
Hazel Run moved forward from their bivouacs, the rumbling of artillery on the frozen roads, the loud words of
command, and the sound of martial music came, muffled
by the fog, to the ears of the Confederates lying expectant
on the ridge. Now and again the curtain lifted for a
moment, and the Southern guns assailed the long dark
columns of the foe. Very early had the Confederates taken
up their position. The ravine of Deep Run, covered with
tangled brushwood, was the line of demarcation between
Jackson and Longstreet. On the extreme right of the
Second Corps, and half a mile north of the marshy valley
of the Massaponax, where a spur called Prospect Hill juts
down from the wooded ridge, were fourteen guns under
Colonel Walker. Supported by two regiments of Field's
brigade, these pieces were held back for the present within
the forest which here clothed the ridge. Below Prospect
Hill, and running thence along the front of the position,
the embankment of the Richmond and Potomac Railroad
formed a tempting breastwork. It was utilised, however,

[1] Lord Wolseley. *North American Review*, vol. 149, p. 282.

only by the skirmishers of the defence. The edge of the forest, one hundred and fifty to two hundred yards in rear, looked down upon an open and gentle slope, and along the brow of this natural glacis, covered by the thick timber, Jackson posted his fighting-line. To this position it was easy to move up his supports and reserves without exposing them to the fire of artillery; and if the assailants should seize the embankment, he relied upon the deadly rifles of his infantry to bar their further advance up the ascent beyond.

The Light Division supplied both the first and second lines of Jackson's army corps. To the left of Walker's guns, posted in a shelter-trench within the skirts of the wood, was Archer's brigade of seven regiments, including two of Field's, the left resting on a coppice that projected beyond the general line of forest. On the further side of this coppice, but nearer the embankment, lay Lane's brigade, an unoccupied space of six hundred yards intervening between his right and Archer's left. Between Lane's right and the edge of the coppice was an open tract two hundred yards in breadth. Both of these brigades had a strong skirmish line pushed forward along and beyond the railroad. Five hundred yards in rear, along a road through the woods which had been cut by Longstreet's troops, Gregg's South Carolina brigade, in second line, covered the interval between Archer and Lane. To Lane's left rear lay Pender's brigade, supporting twelve guns posted in the open, on the far side of the embankment, and twenty-one massed in a field to the north of a small house named Bernard's Cabin. Four hundred yards in rear of Lane's left and Pender's right was stationed Thomas's brigade of four regiments.[1]

It is necessary to notice particularly the shape, size, and position of the projecting tongue of woodland which

[1] The dispositions were as follows:—

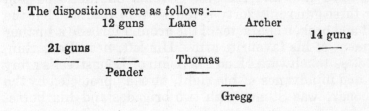

broke the continuity of Hill's line. A German officer on Stuart's staff had the day previous, while riding along the position, remarked its existence, and suggested the propriety of razing it; but, although Jackson himself predicted that there would be the scene of the severest fighting, the ground was so marshy within its depths, and the undergrowth so dense and tangled, that it was judged impenetrable and left unoccupied—an error of judgment which cost many lives. General Lane had also recognised the danger of leaving so wide a gap between Archer and himself, and had so reported, but without effect, to his divisional commander.

The coppice was triangular in shape, and extended nearly six hundred yards beyond the embankment. The base, which faced the Federals, was five hundred yards long. Beyond the apex the ground was swampy and covered with scrub, and the ridge, depressed at this point to a level with the plain, afforded no position from which artillery could command the approach to or issue from this patch of jungle. A space of seven hundred yards along the front was thus left undefended by direct fire.

Early, who with D. H. Hill had marched in shortly after daybreak, formed the right of the third line, Taliaferro the left. The division of D. H. Hill, with several batteries, formed the general reserve, and a portion of Early's artillery was posted about half a mile in rear of his division, in readiness, if necessary, to relieve the guns on Prospect Hill.

Jackson's line was two thousand six hundred yards in length, and his infantry 30,000 strong, giving eleven rifles to the yard; but nearly three-fourths of the army corps, the divisions of Early, Taliaferro, and D. H. Hill, were in third line and reserve. Of his one hundred and twenty-three guns only forty-seven were in position, but the wooded and broken character of the ground forbade a further deployment of his favourite arm. His left, near Deep Run, was in close touch with Hood's division of Longstreet's army corps; and in advance of his right, already protected by the Massaponax, was Stuart with two brigades and his horse-

THE FIELD OF FREDERICKSBURG.

Scale of Miles

0   ½   1   2

N

Scott's Ford

Falmouth
Scott's

Beck I.

Dr. Taylor

Banks Ford

Taylor's Hill

River Road

Canal

Stansbury Hill

Chatham

Phillips

Lady Hansor

White Oak Church Road

Cemetery Hill

Cemetery

FREDERICKSBURG

Stansbury Plank

White Cabins

Toll House

Marye

Marye's Hill

Salem Church

Dam Spring Mill

Hazel Run

Lee's Hill

Howison

A. Bernard

Rappahannock River

Hazel Run

Deep Run

Mansfield

Pollock's Mill

Smithfield

White Chimney

MEADE'S ATTACK

Bernard's Cabins

Military

Dr. Reynolds

Massaponax Hill

Telegraph Road

Prospect Hill

Hamilton's Crossing

River Road

Wm. Yerby

John Yerby

Massaponax

Massaponax Creek

Walker & Boutall sc.

artillery.   One Whitworth gun, a piece of great range and large calibre, was posted on the wooded heights beyond the Massaponax, north-east of Yerby's House.

Jackson's dispositions were almost identical with those which he had adopted at the Second Manassas.   His whole force was hidden in the woods; every gun that could find room was ready for action, and the batteries were deployed in two masses.   Instead, however, of giving each division a definite section of the line, he had handed over the whole front to A. P. Hill.   This arrangement, however, had been made before D. H. Hill and Early came up, and with the battle imminent a change was hazardous.   In many respects, moreover, the ground he now occupied resembled that which he had so successfully defended on August 29 and 30.   There was the wood opposite the centre, affording the enemy a covered line of approach; the open fields, pasture and stubble, on either hand; the stream, hidden by timber and difficult of passage, on the one flank, and Longstreet on the other.   But the position at Fredericksburg was less strong for defence than that at the Second Manassas, for not only was Jackson's line within three thousand yards—a long range but not ineffective—of the heavy guns on the Stafford Heights, but on the bare plain between the railway and the river there was ample room for the deployment of the Federal field-batteries.   At the Second Manassas, on the other hand, the advantages of the artillery position had been on the side of the Confederates.

Nevertheless, with the soldiers of Sharpsburg, ragged indeed and under-fed, but eager for battle and strong in numbers, there was no reason to dread the powerful artillery of the foe; and Jackson's confidence was never higher than when, accompanied by his staff, he rode along his line of battle.   He was not, however, received by his soldiers with their usual demonstrations of enthusiastic devotion.   In honour of the day he had put on the uniform with which Stuart had presented him; the old cadet cap, which had so often waved his men to victory, was replaced by a head-dress resplendent with gold lace; 'Little Sorrel' had been deposed in favour of a more imposing charger; and

z 2

the veterans failed to recognise their commander until
he had galloped past them.   A Confederate artillery-man
has given a graphic picture of his appearance when the
fight was at its hottest :—

'A general officer, mounted upon a superb bay horse
and followed by a single courier, rode up through our guns.
Looking neither to the right nor the left, he rode straight to
the front, halted, and seemed gazing intently on the enemy's
line of battle.   The outfit before me, from top to toe, cap,
coat, top-boots, horse and furniture, were all of the new
order of things.   But there was something about the man
that did not look so new after all.   He appeared to be an
old-time friend of all the turmoil around him.   As he had
done us the honour to make an afternoon call on the
artillery, I thought it becoming in someone to say something on the occasion.   No one did, however, so, although
a somewhat bashful and weak-kneed youngster, I plucked
up courage enough to venture to remark that those big
guns over the river had been knocking us about pretty
considerably during the day.   He quickly turned his head,
and I knew in an instant who it was before me.   The
clear-cut, chiselled features ; the thin, compressed and determined lips ; the calm, steadfast eye ; the countenance to
command respect, and in time of war to give the soldier
that confidence he so much craves from a superior officer,
were all there.   He turned his head quickly, and looking me
all over, rode up the line and away as quickly and silently
as he came, his little courier hard upon his heels; and
this was my first sight of Stonewall Jackson.'

From his own lines Jackson passed along the front,
drawing the fire of the Federal skirmishers, who were
creeping forward, and proceeded to the centre of the
position, where, on the eminence which has since borne
the name of Lee's Hill, the Commander-in-Chief, surrounded by his generals, was giving his last instructions.   It
was past nine o'clock.   The sun, shining out with almost
September warmth, was drawing up the mist which
hid the opposing armies ; and as the dense white folds
dissolved and rolled away, the Confederates saw the broad

plain beneath them dark with more than 80,000 foes. Of these the left wing, commanded by Franklin, and composed of 55,000 men and 116 guns, were moving against the Second Corps; 30,000, under Sumner, were forming for attack on Longstreet, and from the heights of Stafford, where the reserves were posted in dense masses, a great storm of shot and shell burst upon the Confederate lines. 'For once,' says Dabney, 'war unmasked its terrible proportions with a distinctness hitherto unknown in the forest-clad landscapes of America, and the plain of Fredericksburg presented a panorama that was dreadful in its grandeur.' It was then that Longstreet, to whose sturdy heart the approach of battle seemed always welcome, said to Jackson, 'General, do not all those multitudes of Federals frighten you?' 'We shall very soon see whether I shall not frighten them;' and with this grim reply the commander of the Second Corps rode back to meet Franklin's onset.

The Federals were already advancing. From Deep Run southward, for more than a mile and a half, three great lines of battle, accompanied by numerous 9 A.M. batteries, moved steadily forward, powerful enough, to all appearance, to bear down all opposition by sheer weight of numbers. 'On they came,' says an eye-witness, 'in beautiful order, as if on parade, their bayonets glistening in the bright sunlight; on they came, waving their hundreds of regimental flags, which relieved with warm bits of colouring the dull blue of the columns and the russet tinge of the wintry landscape, while their artillery beyond the river continued the cannonade with unabated fury over their heads, and gave a background of white fleecy smoke, like midsummer clouds, to the animated picture.'

And yet that vast array, so formidable of aspect, lacked that moral force without which physical power, even in its most terrible form, is but an idle show. Not only were the strength of the Confederate position, the want of energy in the preliminary movements, the insecurity of their own situation, but too apparent to the intelligence of the regimental officers and men, but they mistrusted their commander. Northern writers have recorded that the Army of the Potomac never went down to battle with less alacrity than on this day at Fredericksburg.

Nor was the order of attack of such a character as to revive the confidence of the troops. Burnside, deluded by the skill with which Jackson had hidden his troops into the belief that the Second Army Corps was still at Port Royal, had instructed Franklin to seize the ridge with a single division, and Meade's 4,500 Pennsylvanians were sent forward alone, while the remainder of the Grand Division, over 50,000 strong, stood halted on the plain, awaiting the result of this hopeless manœuvre.[1] Meade advanced in three lines, each of a brigade, with skirmishers in front and on the flank, and his progress was soon checked. No sooner had his first line crossed the Richmond road than the left was assailed by a well-directed and raking artillery fire.

Captain Pelham, commanding Stuart's horse-artillery, had galloped forward by Jackson's orders with his two rifled guns, and, escorted by a dismounted squadron, had come into action beyond a marshy stream which ran through a tangled ravine on the Federal flank. So telling was his fire that the leading brigade wavered and gave ground; and though Meade quickly brought up his guns and placed his third brigade *en potence* in support, he was unable to continue his forward movement until he had brushed away his audacious antagonist. The four Pennsylvania batteries were reinforced by two others; but rapidly changing his position as often as the Federal gunners found his range, for more than half an hour Pelham defied their efforts, and for that space of time arrested the advance of Meade's 4,500 infantry. One of his pieces was soon disabled; but with the remaining gun, captured from the enemy six months before, he maintained the unequal fight until his limbers were empty, and he received peremptory orders from Stuart to withdraw.

On Pelham's retirement, Franklin, bringing several batteries forward to the Richmond road, for more than

---

[1] Franklin's Grand Division consisted of the 42,800 men, and 12,000 of Hooker's Grand Division had reinforced him.

half an hour subjected the woods before him to a heavy
cannonade, in which the guns on the Stafford Heights
played a conspicuous part. Hidden, however, by the thick
timber, Jackson's regiments lay secure, unharmed by the
tempest that crashed above them through the leafless
branches ; and, reserving their fire for the hostile infantry,
his guns were silent. The general, meanwhile, according
to his custom, had walked far out into the fields to reconnoitre for himself, and luck favoured the Confederacy
on this day of battle. Lieutenant Smith was his only
companion, and a Federal sharpshooter, suddenly rising
from some tall weeds two hundred paces distant, levelled
his rifle and fired. The bullet whistled between their
heads, and Jackson, turning with a smile to his aide-
de-camp, said cheerfully : ' Mr. Smith, had you not better
go to the rear ? They may shoot you.' Then, having
deliberately noted the enemy's arrangements, he returned
to his station on Prospect Hill. It was past
11.15 A.M. eleven before Meade resumed his advance.
Covered by the fire of the artillery, his first line was within
eight hundred yards of Jackson's centre, when suddenly
the silent woods awoke to life. The Confederate batteries,
pushing forward from the covert, came rapidly into action,
and the flash and thunder of more than fifty guns revealed
to the astonished Federals the magnitude of the task they
had undertaken. From front and flank came the scathing
fire ; the skirmishers were quickly driven in, and on the closed
ranks behind burst the full fury of the storm. Dismayed
and decimated by this fierce and unexpected onslaught,
Meade's brigades broke in disorder and fell back to the
Richmond road.

For the next hour and a half an artillery duel, in which
over 400 guns took part, raged over the whole field, and the
Confederate batteries, their position at last revealed, engaged
with spirit the more numerous and powerful ordnance
of the enemy. Then Franklin brought up three divisions
to Meade's support ; and from the smouldering ruins of
Fredericksburg, three miles to the northward, beyond the
high trees of Hazel Run, the deep columns of Sumner's

Grand Division deployed under the fire of Longstreet's
guns. Sumner's attack had been for some time in progress
before Franklin was in readiness to co-operate.   The
battle was now fully developed, and the morning mists
had been succeeded by dense clouds of smoke, shrouding
hill and plain, through which the cannon flashed redly, and
the defiant yells of Longstreet's riflemen, mingled with their
rattling volleys, stirred the pulses of Jackson's veterans.
As the familiar sounds were borne to their ears, it was seen
that the dark lines beyond the Richmond road were moving
forward, and the turn of the Second Corps had come.

It was one o'clock, and Jackson's guns had for the
moment ceased their fire. Meade's Pennsylvanians had
rallied. Gibbon's division had taken post on their right;
Birney and Newton were in support; and Doubleday, facing
south, was engaged with Stuart's dismounted
troopers.   Twenty-one guns on the right, and
thirty on the left, stationed on the Richmond road, a
thousand yards from the Confederate position, formed a
second tier to the heavier pieces on the heights, and
fired briskly on the woods. Preceded by clouds of skirmishers, Meade and Gibbon advanced in column of brigades
at three hundred paces distance, the whole covering
a front of a thousand yards ; and the supporting divisions
moved up to the Richmond road.

1 P.M.

When the Federals reached the scene of their former
repulse, Jackson's guns again opened ; but without the
same effect, for they were now exposed to the fire of the
enemy's batteries at close range. Even Pelham could do
but little ; and the artillery beyond the railroad on Hill's
left was quickly driven in.

Meade's rear brigade was now brought up and deployed
on the left of the first, in the direction of the Massaponax,
thus further extending the front.

The leading brigade made straight for the tongue of
woodland which interposed between Lane and Archer. As
they neared the Confederate line, the Pennsylvanians,
masked by the trees, found that they were no longer
exposed to fire, and that the coppice was unoccupied.

Quickly crossing the border, through swamp and undergrowth they pushed their way, and, bursting from the
covert to the right, fell on the exposed flank of Lane's
brigade. The fight was fierce, but the Southerners were
compelled to give ground, for neither Archer nor Gregg
was able to lend assistance.

Meade's second brigade, though following close upon
the first, had, instead of conforming to the change of
direction against Lane's flank, rushed forward through the
wood. Two hundred paces from the embankment it came
in contact with Archer's left, which was resting on the very
edge of the coppice. The Confederates were taken by surprise. Their front was secured by a strong skirmish line ;
but on the flank, as the thickets appeared impenetrable,
neither scouts nor pickets had been thrown out, and the
men were lying with arms piled. Two regiments, leaping
to their feet and attempting to form line to the left, were
broken by a determined charge, and gave way in disorder.
The remainder, however, stood firm, for the Federals,
instead of following up their success in this direction,
left Archer to be dealt with by the third brigade of
the division, which had now reached the railroad, and
swept on towards the military road, where Gregg's brigade
was drawn up within the forest. So thick was the cover,
and so limited the view, that General Gregg, taking the
advancing mass for part of Archer's line retiring, restrained the fire of his men. The Federals broke upon his
right. He himself fell mortally wounded. His flank regiment, a battalion of conscripts, fled, except one company,
without firing a shot. The two regiments on the opposite
flank, however, were with great readiness turned about, and
changing front inwards, arrested the movement of the
enemy along the rear.

The Federals had now been joined by a portion of the
first brigade, inspirited by their victory over Lane, and the
moment, to all appearance, seemed critical in the extreme
for the Confederates. To the left rear of the attacking
column, Meade's third brigade was held in check by
Walker's batteries and the sturdy Archer, who, notwith-

standing that a strong force had passed beyond his flank, and had routed two of his regiments, still resolutely held his ground, and prevented his immediate opponents from joining the intruding column.   To the right rear, opposite Pender, Gibbon's division had been checked by the fire of the great battery near Bernard's Cabin ; two of his brigades had been driven back, and the third had with difficulty gained the shelter of the embankment.   So from neither left nor right was immediate support to be expected by Meade's victorious regiments.   But on the Richmond road were the divisions of Birney and Newton, with Doubleday's and Sickles' not far in rear, and 20,000 bayonets might have been thrown rapidly into the gap which the Pennsylvanians had so vigorously forced.   Yet Jackson's equanimity was undisturbed. The clouds of smoke and the thick timber hid the fighting in the centre from his post of observation on Prospect Hill, and the first intimation of the enemy's success was brought by an aide-de-camp, galloping wildly up the slope.   ' General,' he exclaimed in breathless haste, ' the enemy have broken through Archer's left, and General Gregg says he must have help, or he and General Archer will both lose their position.'   Jackson turned round quietly, and without the least trace of excitement in either voice or manner, sent orders to Early and Taliaferro, in third line, to advance with the bayonet and clear the front.   Then, with rare self-restraint, for the fighting instinct was strong within him, and the danger was so threatening as to have justified his personal interference, he raised his field-glasses and resumed his scrutiny of the enemy's reserves on the Richmond road. His confidence in his lieutenants was not misplaced. Early's division, already deployed in line, came forward with a rush, and the Stonewall Brigade, responding with alacrity to Jackson's summons, led the advance of Taliaferro.

1.45 P.M.

The counterstroke was vigorous.   Meade's brigades had penetrated to the heart of the Confederate position, but their numbers were reduced to less than 2,000 bayonets ; in the fierce fighting and dense thickets they had lost all semblance of cohesion, and not a single regiment had supported them. The men looked round in vain for help, and the forest around them resounded with the yells of the Confederate reinforcements. Assailed in front and flank by a destructive fire, the Pennsylvanians were rapidly borne back. Hill's second line joined in Early's advance. Gibbon was strongly attacked. Six brigades, sweeping forward from the forest, dashed down the slopes, and in a few moments the broken remnants of the Federal divisions were dispersing in panic across the plain. As the enemy fled the Confederate gunners, disregarding the shells of Franklin's batteries, poured a heavy fire into the receding mass; and although instructions had been given that the counterstroke was not to pass the railroad, Hoke's and Atkinson's brigades,[1] carried away by success and deaf to all orders, followed in swift pursuit. Some of Birney's regiments, tardily coming forward to Meade's support, were swept away, and the yelling line of grey infantry, shooting down the fugitives and taking many prisoners, pressed on towards the Richmond road. There the remainder of Birney's division was drawn up, protected by the breast-high bank, and flanked by artillery; yet it seemed for a moment as if the two Confederate brigades would carry all before them.

The troops of Meade and Gibbon were streaming in confusion to the rear. Two batteries had been abandoned, and before Hoke's onset the left of Birney's infantry gave ground for fifty yards. But the rash advance had reached its climax. Unsupported, and with empty cartridge-boxes, the Southerners were unable to face the fire from the road; sixteen guns had opened on them with canister; and after suffering heavy losses in killed, wounded, and prisoners, they withdrew in disorder but unpursued.

The success of the Second Army Corps was greater than even Jackson realised. Meade and Gibbon had lost 4,000 officers and men; and it was not till late in the afternoon that they were rallied on the river bank. The casualties in Birney's division swelled the total to 5,000, and the Confederate counterstroke had inflicted a

[1] Of Early's Division.

heavier blow than the tale of losses indicates. Not only
the troops which had been engaged, but those who had
witnessed their defeat, who had seen them enter the
enemy's position, and who knew they should have been
supported, were much disheartened. At 2.30 P.M.,
2.30 P.M. soon after the repulse of Hoke and Atkinson,
Burnside, having just witnessed the signal failure of a fourth
assault on Longstreet, sent an urgent order to Franklin to
renew his attack. Franklin made no response. He had
lost all confidence both in his superior and his men, and
he took upon himself to disobey.

On the Confederate side Taliaferro and Early, with part
of the Light Division, now held the railway embankment
and the skirt of the woods. D. H. Hill was brought up
into third line, and the shattered brigades of A. P. Hill
were withdrawn to the rear. During the rest of the afternoon the skirmishers were actively engaged, but although
Jackson's victorious soldiery long and eagerly expected a
renewal of the assault, the enemy refused to be again
tempted to close quarters.

On the left, meanwhile, where the battle still raged, the
Confederates were equally successful. Against an impregnable position 40,000 Northerners were madly hurled
by the general of Mr. Lincoln's choice. By those
hapless and stout-hearted soldiers, sacrificed to incompetency, a heroism was displayed which won the praise
and the pity of their opponents. The attack was insuffi-
ciently prepared, and feebly supported, by the artillery.
The troops were formed on a narrow front. Marye's Hill,
the strongest portion of the position, where the Confederate
infantry found shelter behind a stout stone wall, and
numerous batteries occupied the commanding ground in
rear, was selected for assault. Neither feint nor demonstration, the ordinary expedients by which the attacker
seeks to distract the attention and confuse the efforts of
the defence, was made use of; and yet division after
division, with no abatement of courage, marched in good
order over the naked plain, dashed forward with ever-
thinning ranks, and then, receding sullenly before the

storm of fire, left, within a hundred yards of the stone wall, a long line of writhing forms to mark the limit of their advance.

Two army corps had been repulsed by Longstreet with fearful slaughter when Meade and Gibbon gave way before
3 P.M. Jackson's counterstroke, and by three o'clock nearly one-half of the Federal army was broken and demoralised. The time appeared to have come for a general advance of the Confederates. Before Fredericksburg, the wreck of Sumner's Grand Division was still clinging to such cover as the ground afforded. On the Richmond road, in front of Jackson, Franklin had abandoned all idea of the offensive, and was bringing up his last reserves to defend his line. The Confederates, on the other hand, were in the highest spirits, and had lost but few.

General Lee's arrangements, however, had not included preparation for a great counterstroke, and such a movement is not easily improvised. The position had been occupied for defensive purposes alone. There was no general reserve, no large and intact force which could have moved to the attack immediately the opportunity offered. 'No skill,' says Longstreet, 'could have marshalled our troops for offensive operations in time to meet the emergency. My line was long and over broken country, so much so that the troops could not be promptly handled in offensive operations. Jackson's corps was in mass, and could he have anticipated the result of my battle, he would have been justified in pressing Franklin to the river when the battle of the latter was lost. Otherwise, pursuit would have been as unwise as the attack he had just driven off. It is well known that after driving off attacking forces, if immediate pursuit can be made, so that the victors can go along with the retreating forces pell-mell, it is well enough to do so; but the attack should be immediate. To follow a success by counter-attack against the enemy in position is problematical.' [1]

Moreover, so large was the battle-field, so limited the view by reason of the woods, and with such ease had the

[1] *Battles and Leaders*, vol. iii., pp. 82-3.

Federal attacks been repulsed, that General Lee was unaware of the extent of his success. Ignorant, too, as he necessarily was, of the mistrust and want of confidence in its leaders with which the Federal army was infected, he was far from suspecting what a strong ally he had in the hearts of his enemies; while, on the other hand, the inaccessible batteries on the Stafford Heights were an outward and visible token of unabated strength.

Jackson, however, although the short winter day was already closing in, considered that the attempt was worth making. About 3 P.M. he had seen a feeble attack on the Confederate centre repulsed by Hood and Pender, and about the same time he received information of Longstreet's success.

Franklin, meanwhile, was reforming his lines behind the high banks of the Richmond road, and the approach of his reserves, plainly visible from the Confederate position, seemed to presage a renewed attack. ' I waited some time,' says Jackson, ' to receive it, but he making no forward movement, I determined, if prudent, to do so myself. The artillery of the enemy was so judiciously posted as to make an advance of our troops across the plain very hazardous ; yet it was so promising of good results, if successfully executed, as to induce me to make preparations for the attempt. In order to guard against disaster, the infantry was to be preceded by artillery, and the movement postponed until late in the afternoon, so that if compelled to retire, it would be under cover of the night.' [1]

Jackson's decision was not a little influenced by Stuart, or rather by the reports which Stuart, who had sent out staff officers to keep the closest watch on the enemy's movements, had been able to furnish of the demoralised condition of a great part of Franklin's force. The cavalry general, as soon as he verified the truth of these reports in person, galloped off to confer with Jackson on Prospect Hill, and a message was at once sent to Lee, requesting permission for an advance. A single cannon shot was to be the signal for a general attack, which Stuart, striking the

[1] *Jackson's Reports*, O. R., vol. xxi., p. 634.

enemy in flank, was to initiate with his two brigades and the lighter guns.

'Returning to our position,' to quote Stuart's chief of staff, 'we awaited in anxious silence the desired signal; but minute after minute passed by, and the dark veil of the winter night began to envelop the valley, when Stuart, believing that the summons agreed upon had been given, issued the order to advance. Off we went into the gathering darkness, our sharpshooters driving their opponents easily before them, and Pelham with his guns, pushing ahead at a trot, giving them a few shots whenever the position seemed favourable, and then again pressing forward. This lasted about twenty minutes, when the fire of the enemy's infantry began to be more and more destructive, and other fresh batteries opened upon us. Still all remained silent upon our main line. Our situation had become, indeed, a critical one, when a courier from General Jackson galloped up at full speed, bringing the order for Stuart to retreat as quickly as he could to his original position.'

Under cover of the night this retrograde movement was effected without loss; and the cavalry, as they marched back, saw the camp-fires kindling on the skirts of the forest, and the infantry digging intrenchments by the fitful glare.

The Second Corps had not come into action. Jackson had issued orders that every gun, of whatever calibre or range, which was not disabled should be brought to the front and open fire at sunset; and that as soon as the enemy showed signs of wavering, the infantry should charge with fixed bayonets, and sweep the invaders into the river. Hood's division, which had been temporarily placed at his disposal, was instructed to co-operate.[1] It appears, however, that it had not been easy, in the short space of daylight still available, to remedy the confusion into which the Confederates had been thrown by Meade's attack and their own counterstroke. The divisions were to some extent mixed up. Several regiments had been broken, and the ammunition of both infantry and artillery needed replenishment.

Advance and Retreat. Lieutenant-General J. B. Hood, p. 50.

Moreover, it was difficult in the extreme to bring the batteries forward through the forest; and, when they eventually arrived, the strength of the Federal position was at once revealed. Franklin's line was defended by a hundred and sixteen field pieces, generally of superior metal to those of the Confederates, and the guns on the Stafford Heights, of which at least thirty bore upon Jackson's front, were still in action. As the first Confederate battery advanced, this great array of artillery, which had been for some time comparatively quiet, reopened with vigour, and, to use Jackson's words, 'so completely swept our front as to satisfy me that the proposed movement should be abandoned.'

But he was not yet at the end of his resources. A strong position, which cannot be turned, is not always impregnable. If the ground be favourable, and few obstacles exist, a night attack with the bayonet, especially if the enemy be exhausted or half-beaten, has many chances of success; and during the evening Jackson made arrangements for such a movement. 'He asked me,' says Dr. McGuire, 'how many yards of bandaging I had, and when I replied that I did not know the exact number, but that I had enough for another fight, he seemed a little worried at my lack of information and showed his annoyance. I repeated rather shortly, "I have enough for another battle," meaning to imply that this was all that it was necessary for him to know. I then asked him: "Why do you want to know how much bandaging I have?" He said: "I want a yard of bandaging to put on the arm of every soldier in this night's attack, so that the men may know each other from the enemy." I told him I had not enough cotton cloth for any such purpose, and that he would have to take a piece of the shirt tail of each soldier to supply the cloth, but, unfortunately, half of them had no shirts! The expedient was never tried. General Lee decided that the attack would be too hazardous.' [1]

That night both armies lay on their arms. Burnside,

[1] Letter to the author.

notwithstanding that he spent several hours amongst the troops before Fredericksburg, and found that both officers and men were opposed to further attack, decided to renew the battle the next day.   His arrangements became known to Lee, an officer or orderly carrying dispatches having strayed within the Confederate outposts,[1] and the Southern generals looked forward, on the morning of the 14th, to a fresh attack, a more crushing repulse, and a general counterstroke.

Such cheerful anticipations, however, so often entertained by generals holding a strong defensive position, are but seldom realised, and Fredericksburg was no exception. The Confederates spent the night in diligent preparation. Supplies of ammunition were brought up and distributed, the existing defences were repaired, abattis cut and laid, and fresh earthworks thrown up.   Jackson, as usual on the eve of battle, was still working while others rested.   Until near midnight he sat up writing and dispatching orders ; then, throwing himself, booted and spurred, on his camp bed, he slept for two or three hours, when he again arose, lighted his candle, and resumed his writing.   Before four o'clock he sent to his medical director to inquire as to the condition of General Gregg. Dr. McGuire reported that his case was hopeless, and Jackson requested that he would go over and see that he had everything he wished.   Somewhat against his will, for there were many wounded who required attention, the medical officer rode off, but scarcely had he entered the farmhouse where Gregg was lying, than he heard the tramp of horses, and Jackson himself dismounted on the threshold.   The brigadier, it appears, had lately fallen under the ban of his displeasure ; but from the moment his condition was reported, Jackson forgot everything but the splendid services he had rendered on so many hard-fought fields ; and in his anxiety that every memory should be effaced which might embitter his last moments, he had followed Dr. McGuire to his bedside.

The interview was brief, and the dying soldier was

[1] *From Manassas to Appomattox*, p. 316.

the happier for it ; but the scene in that lonely Virginian homestead, where, in the dark hours of the chill December morning, the life of a strong man, of a gallant comrade, of an accomplished gentleman, and of an unselfish patriot—for Gregg was all these—was slowly ebbing, made a deeper impression on those who witnessed it than the accumulated horrors of the battle-field. Sadly and silently the general and his staff officer rode back through the forest, where the troops were already stirring round the smouldering camp-fires. Their thoughts were sombre. The Confederacy, with a relatively slender population, could ill spare such men as Gregg. And yet Jackson, though yielding to the depression of the moment, and deploring the awful sacrifices which the defence of her liberties imposed upon the South, was in no melting mood. Dr. McGuire, when they reached headquarters, put a question as to the best means of coping with the overwhelming numbers of the enemy. 'Kill them, sir ! kill every man !' was the reply of the stern soldier who but just now, with words of tender sympathy and Christian hope, had bade farewell to his dying comrade.

But on December 14, as on the morrow of Sharpsburg, the Confederates were doomed to disappointment. 'Darkness still prevailed,' writes Stuart's chief of the staff, 'when we mounted our horses and again hastened to Prospect Hill, the summit of which we reached just in time

Dec. 14.   to see the sun rising, and unveiling, as it dispersed the haze, the long lines of the Federal army, which once more stood in full line of battle between our own position and the river. I could not withhold my admiration as I looked down upon the well-disciplined ranks of our antagonists, astonished that these troops now offering so bold a front should be the same whom not many hours since I had seen in complete flight and disorder. The skirmishers of the two armies were not much more than a hundred yards apart, concealed from each other's view by the high grass in which they were lying, and above which, from time to time, rose a small cloud of blue smoke, telling that a shot had been fired. As the boom of artillery began to sound from different parts of the line, and the attack might be expected every minute, each hastened to his post.'

But though the skirmishing at times grew hotter, and the fire of the artillery more rapid, long intervals of silence succeeded, until it at length became apparent to the Confederates that the enemy, though well prepared to resist attack, was determined not to fight outside his breastworks. Burnside, indeed, giving way to the remonstrances of his subordinates, had abandoned all idea of further aggressive action, and unless Lee should move forward, had determined to recross the Potomac.

The next morning saw the armies in the same positions, and the Federal wounded, many of whom had been struck down nearly forty-eight hours before, still lying untended between the hostile lines. It was not till now that Burnside admitted his defeat by sending a flag of truce with a request that he might be allowed to bury his dead.[1]

Dec. 15.

The same night a fierce storm swept the valley of the Rappahannock, and the Army of the Potomac repassed the bridges, evading, under cover of the elements, the observation of the Confederate patrols.

The retreat was effected with a skill which did much credit to the Federal staff. Within fourteen hours 100,000 troops, with the whole of their guns, ambulances, and ammunition waggons, were conveyed across the Rappahan-

---

[1] 'When the flag of truce,' says Major Hotchkiss, 'was received by General Jackson, he asked me for paper and pencil, and began a letter to be sent in reply; but after writing a few lines he handed the paper back, and sent a personal message by Captain Smith.'

Captain Smith writes: 'The general said to me, before I went out to meet Colonel Sumner, representing the Federals: "If you are asked who is in command of your right, do not tell them I am, and be guarded in your remarks." It so happened that Colonel Sumner was the brother-in-law of Colonel Long, an officer on General Lee's staff. While we were together, another Federal officer named Junkin rode up. He was the brother or cousin of Jackson's first wife, and I had known him before the war. After some conversation, Junkin asked me to give his regards to General Jackson, and to deliver a message from the Rev. Dr. Junkin, the father of his first wife. I replied, "I will do so with pleasure when I meet General Jackson." Junkin smiled and said: "It is not worth while for you to try to deceive us. We know that General Jackson is in front of us."

nock; but there remained on the south bank sufficient
evidence to show that the Army of the Potomac had not
escaped unscathed. When the morning broke the dead lay
thick upon the field; arms and accoutrements, the *débris*
of defeat, were strewed in profusion on every hand, and the
ruined houses of Fredericksburg were filled with wounded.
Burnside lost in the battle 12,647 men.

LEFT ATTACK—FRANKLIN.

First Corps	Meade's Division	1,853
	Gibbon's Division	1,267
	Doubleday's Division	214
Third Corps	Birney's Division	950
	Sickles' Division	100
Sixth Corps	Newton's Division	63
	Total . .	4,447

CENTRE.

Brook's Division	197
Howe's Division	186
Total . .	383

RIGHT ATTACK—SUMNER AND HOOKER.

Second Corps	Hancock's Division	2,032
	Howard's Division.	914
	French's Division	1,160
Ninth Corps	Burns' Division	27
	Sturgis' Division	1,007
	Getty's Division	296
Third Corps	Whipple's Division	129
Fifth Corps	Griffin's Division	926
	Sykes' Division	228
	Humphrey's Division . . .	1,019
Engineers and Reserve Artillery, &c.		79
	Total . .	7,817
Grand Total (including 877 officers) . .		12,647
		(589 prisoners).

The Confederates showed 5,309 casualties out of less
than 30,000 actually engaged.

Left Wing—Longstreet.

First Corps	{ Ransom's Division	535
	McLaws' Division	858
	Anderson's Division	159
Artillery .	. . . .	37
(1,224 on December 12.)	Total . .	1,589

Centre.

First Corps	{ Pickett's Division	54
	Hood's Division	251
	Total . .	305

Right Wing—Jackson.

Light Division	2,120
Early's Division	932
D. H. Hill's Division	173
Taliaferro's Division	190
Total (including 500 captured) . .	3,415

No attempt was made by the Confederates to follow the enemy across the Rappahannock. The upper fords were open; but the river was rising fast, and the Army of the Potomac, closely concentrated and within a few miles of Aquia Creek, was too large to be attacked, and too close to its base to permit effective manœuvres, which might induce it to divide, against its line of communications. The exultation of the Southern soldiers in their easy victory was dashed by disappointment. Burnside's escape had demonstrated the fallacy of one of the so-called rules of war. The great river which lay behind him during the battle of Fredericksburg had proved his salvation instead of—as it theoretically should—his ruin. Over the six bridges his troops had more lines of retreat than is usually the case when roads only are available; and these lines of retreat were secure, protected from the Confederate cavalry by the river, and from the infantry and artillery by the batteries on the Stafford Heights. Had the battle been fought on the North Anna, thirty-six miles from Fredericksburg, the result might have been very different. A direct counterstroke would possibly have been no more practicable than on the Rappahannock, for the superior numbers of the enemy, and his powerful artillery, could not have been disregarded. Nor would a direct pursuit have been a certain means of making success decisive ; the rear of a retreating army, as the Confederates had found to their cost at Malvern Hill, is usually its strongest part. But a pursuit directed against the flanks, striking the line of retreat, cutting off the supply and ammunition trains, and blocking the roads, a pursuit such as Jackson had organised when he drove Banks from the Valley, if conducted with vigour, seldom fails in its effect. And who would have conducted such an operation with greater skill and energy than Stuart, at the head of his 9,000 horsemen ? Who would have supported Stuart more expeditiously than the ' foot-cavalry ' of the Second Army Corps ?

Lee's position at Fredericksburg, strong as it might appear, was exceedingly disadvantageous. A position which an army occupies with a view to decisive battle should fulfil four requirements :—

1. It should not be too strong, or the enemy will not attack it.

2. It should give cover to the troops both from view and fire from artillery, and have a good field of fire.

3. It should afford facilities for counterstroke.

4. It should afford facilities for pursuit.

Of these Lee's battle-field fulfilled but the first and second. It would have been an admirable selection if the sole object of the Confederates had been to gain time, or to prevent the enemy establishing himself south of the Rappahannock; but to encompass the destruction of the enemy's whole army it was as ill adapted as Wellington's position at Torres Vedras, at Busaco, or at Fuentes d'Onor. But while Wellington in taking up these positions had no further end in view than holding the French in check, the situation of the Confederacy was such that a decisive victory was eminently desirable. Nothing was to be gained by gaining time. The South could furnish Lee with no further reinforcements. Every able-bodied man was in the service of his country; and it was perfectly certain that the Western armies, although they had been generally successful during the past year, would never be permitted by Mr. Davis to leave the valley of the Mississippi.

The Army of Northern Virginia was not likely to be stronger or more efficient. Equipped with the spoils of many victories, it was more on a level with the enemy than had hitherto been the case. The ranks were full. The men were inured to hardships and swift marches; their health was proof against inclement weather, and they knew their work on the field of battle. The artillery had recently been reorganised. During the Peninsular campaign the batteries had been attached to the infantry brigades, and the indifferent service they had often rendered had been attributed to the difficulty of collecting the scattered units, and in handling them in combination. Formed into battalions of four or six batteries a large number of guns was now attached to each of the divisions, and each army corps had a strong reserve; so that the concentration of a heavy force of artillery on any part of a position became a feasible operation. The cavalry, so admirably commanded by Stuart, Hampton, and the younger Lees, was not less hardy or efficient than the infantry, and the *moral* of the soldiers of every arm, founded on confidence in themselves not less than on confidence in their leaders, was never higher.

'After the truce had been agreed upon,' says Captain Smith, 'litter-bearers to bring away the dead and wounded were selected from the command of General Rodes. When they had fallen in, General Rodes said to them : " Now, boys, those Yankees are going to ask you questions, and you must not tell them anything. Be very careful about this." At this juncture one of the men spoke up, and said, " General, can't we tell them that we whipped them yesterday ? " Rodes replied, laughing : " Yes, yes ! you can tell them that." Immediately another man spoke up : " General, can't we tell them that we can whip them to-morrow and the day after ? " Rodes again laughed, and sent those incorrigible jokers off with : " Yes, yes ! go on, go on ! Tell them what you please." '

The Army of the Potomac, on the other hand, was not

likely to become weaker or less formidable if time were allowed it to recuperate. It had behind it enormous reserves. 60,000 men had been killed, wounded, or captured since the battle of Kernstown, and yet the ranks were as full as when McClellan first marched on Richmond. Many generals had disappeared; but those who remained were learning their trade; and the soldiers, although more familiar with defeat than victory, showed little diminution of martial ardour. Nor had the strain of the war sapped the resources of the North. Her trade, instead of dwindling, had actually increased; and the gaps made in the population by the Confederate bullets were more than made good by a constant influx of immigrants from Europe.

It was not by partial triumphs, not by the slaughter of a few brigades, by defence without counterstroke, by victories without pursuit, that a Power of such strength and vitality could be compelled to confess her impotence. Whether some overwhelming disaster, a Jena or a Waterloo, followed by instant invasion, would have subdued her stubborn spirit is problematical. Rome survived Cannæ, Scotland Flodden, and France Sedan. But in some such 'crowning mercy' lay the only hope of the Confederacy, and had the Army of the Potomac, ill-commanded as it was, been drawn forward to the North Anna, it might have been utterly destroyed. Half-hearted strategy, which aims only at repulsing the enemy's attack, is not the path to 'king-making victory;' it is not by such feeble means that States secure or protect their independence. To occupy a position where Stuart's cavalry was powerless, where the qualities which made Lee's infantry so formidable—the impetuosity of their attack, the swiftness of their marches—had no field for display, and where the enemy had free scope for the employment of his artillery, his strongest arm, was but to postpone the evil day. It had been well for the Confederacy if Stonewall Jackson, whose resolute strategy had but one aim, and that aim the annihilation of the enemy, had been the supreme director of her councils. To paraphrase Mahan: 'The strategic mistake (in occupying a position for which pursuit was impracticable) neutralised the tactical advantage gained, thus confirming the military maxim that a strategic mistake is more serious and far-reaching in its effects than an error in tactics.'

Lee, however, was fettered by the orders of the Cabinet; and Mr. Davis and his advisers, more concerned with the importance of retaining an area of country which still furnished supplies than of annihilating the Army of the Potomac, and relying on European intervention rather than on the valour of the Southern soldier, were responsible for the occupation of the Fredericksburg position. In extenuation of their mistake it may, however, be admitted that the advantages of concentration on the North Anna were not such as would impress themselves on the civilian mind, while the surrender of territory would undoubtedly have embarrassed both the Government and the supply department. Moreover, at the end of November, it might have been urged that if Burnside were permitted to possess himself of Fredericksburg, it was by no means certain that he would advance on Richmond; establishing himself in winter quarters, he might wait until the weather improved, controlling, in the meantime, the resources and population of that portion of Virginia which lay within his reach.

Nevertheless, as events went far to prove, Mr. Davis would have done wisely had he accepted the advice of the soldiers on the spot. His strategical glance was less comprehensive than that of Lee and Jackson. In the first place, they knew that if Burnside proposed going into winter quarters, he would not deliberately place the Rappahannock between himself and his base, nor halt with the great forest of Spotsylvania on his flank. In the second place, there could be no question but that the Northern Government and the Northern people would impel him forward. The tone of the press was unmistakable; and the very reason that Burnside had been appointed to command was because McClellan was so slow to move. In the third place, both Lee and Jackson saw the need of decisive victory. With them questions of strategic dispositions, offering chances of such victory, were of more importance than questions of supply or internal politics. They knew with what rapidity the Federal soldiers recovered their *moral*; and they realised but too keenly the stern determination which inspired the North. They had seen the hosts of invasion retire in swift succession, stricken and exhausted, before their victorious bayonets. Thousands of prisoners had been marched to Richmond; thousands of wounded, abandoned on the battle-field, had been paroled; guns, waggons and small arms, enough to equip a great army, had been captured; and general after general had been reduced to the ignominy that awaits a defeated leader. Frémont and Shields had disappeared; Banks was no longer in the field; Porter was waiting trial; McDowell had gone; Pope had gone, and McClellan; and yet the Army of the Potomac still held its ground, the great fleets still kept their stations, the capture of Richmond was still the objective of the Union Government, and not for a single moment had Lincoln wavered from his purpose.

It will not be asserted that either Lee or Jackson fathomed the source of this unconquerable tenacity. They had played with effect on the fears of Lincoln; they had recognised in him the motive power of the Federal hosts; but they had not yet learned, for the Northern people themselves had not yet learned it, that they were opposed by an adversary whose resolution was as unyielding as their own, who loved the Union even as they loved Virginia, and who ruled the nation with the same tact and skill that they ruled their soldiers.

In these pages Mr. Lincoln has not been spared. He made mistakes, and he himself would have been the last to claim infallibility. He had entered the White House with a rich endowment of common-sense, a high sense of duty, and an extraordinary knowledge of the American character; but his ignorance of statesmanship directing arms was great, and his military errors were numerous. Putting these aside, his tenure of office during the dark days of '61 and '62 had been marked by the very highest political sagacity; his courage and his patriotism had sustained the nation in its distress; and in spite of every obstacle he was gradually bringing into being a unity of sympathy and of purpose, which in the early days of the war had seemed an impossible ideal. Not the least politic of his measures was the edict of emancipation, published after the battle of Sharpsburg. It was not a measure without flaw. It contained paragraphs which might fairly be interpreted, and were so interpreted by the Confederates, as inciting the negroes to rise against their masters, thus exposing to all the horrors of a servile insurrection, with its accompaniments of murder and outrage, the farms and plantations where the women and children of the South lived lonely and unprotected. But if the edict served only to embitter the Southerners, to bind the whole country together in a still closer league of resistance, and to make peace except by conquest impossible, it was worth the price. The party in the North which fought for the re-establishment of the Union had carried on the war with but small success. The tale of reverses had told at last upon recruiting. Men were unwilling to come forward; and those who were bribed by large bounties to join the armies were of a different character to the original volunteer. Enthusiasm in the cause was fast diminishing when Lincoln, purely on his own initiative, proclaimed emancipation, and, investing the war with the dignity of a crusade, inspired the soldier with a new incentive, and appealed to a feeling which had not yet been stirred. Many Northerners had not thought it worth while to fight for the re-establishment of the Union on the basis of the Constitution. If slavery was to be permitted to continue they preferred separation; and these men were farmers and agriculturists, the class which furnished the best soldiers, men of American birth, for the most part abolitionists, and ready to fight for the principle they had so much at heart. It is true that the effect of the edict was not at once apparent. It was not received everywhere with acclamation. The army had small sympathy with the coloured race, and the political opponents of the President accused him vehemently of unconstitutional action. Their denunciations, however, missed the mark. The letter of the Constitution, as Mr. Lincoln clearly saw, had ceased to be regarded, at least by the great bulk of the people, with superstitious reverence.

They had learned to think more of great principles than of political expedients; and if the defence of their hereditary rights had welded the South into a nation, the assertion of a still nobler principle, the liberty of man, placed the North on a higher plane, enlisted the sympathy of Europe, and completed the isolation of the Confederacy.

But although Lee and Jackson had not yet penetrated the political genius of their great antagonist, they rated at its true value the vigour displayed by his Administration, and they saw that something more was wanting to wrest their freedom from the North than a mere passive resistance to the invader's progress. Soon after the battle of Fredericksburg, Lee went to Richmond and laid proposals for an aggressive campaign before the President. 'He was assured, however,' says General Longstreet, 'that the war was virtually over, and that we need not harass our troops by marches and other hardships. Gold had advanced in New York to two hundred premium, and we were told by those in the Confederate capital that in thirty or forty days we would be recognised (by the European Powers) and peace proclaimed. General Lee did not share this belief.' [1]

So Jackson, who had hoped to return to Winchester, was doomed to the inaction of winter quarters on the Rappahannock, for with Burnside's repulse operations practically ceased. The Confederate cavalry, however, did not at once abandon hostilities. On December Dec. 18. 18, Hampton marched his brigade as far as the village of Occoquan, bringing off 150 prisoners and capturing a convoy; and on December 26 Stuart closed Dec. 26. his record for 1862 by leading 1,800 troopers far to the Federal rear. After doing much damage in the district about Occoquan and Dumfries, twenty miles from Burnside's headquarters, he marched northward in the direction of Washington, and penetrated as far as Burke's Station, fifteen miles from Alexandria. Sending a telegraphic

[1] *Battles and Leaders*, vol. iii., p. 84.

message to General Meigs, Quartermaster-General at Washington, to the effect that the mules furnished to Burnside's army were of such bad quality that he was embarrassed in taking the waggons he had captured into the Confederate lines, and requesting that a better class of animal might be supplied in future, he returned by long marches through Warrenton to Culpeper Court House, escaping pursuit, and bringing with him a large amount of plunder and many prisoners. From the afternoon of December 26 to nightfall on December 31 he rode one hundred and fifty miles, losing 28 officers and men in skirmishes with detachments of the Federal cavalry. He had contrived to throw a great part of the troops sent to meet him into utter confusion by intercepting their telegrams, and answering them himself in a manner that scattered his pursuers and broke down their horses.

Near the end of January, Burnside made a futile attempt to march his army round Lee's flank by way of Ely's and Germanna Fords. The weather, however, was inclement ; the roads were in a fearful condition, and the troops experienced such difficulty in movement, that the operation, which goes by the name of the 'Mud Campaign,' was soon abandoned.

On January 26, Burnside, in consequence of the strong 1863. representations made by his lieutenants to the Jan. 26. President, was superseded. General Hooker, the dashing fighter of the Antietam, replaced him in command of the Army of the Potomac, and the Federal troops went into winter quarters about Falmouth, where, on the opposite shore of the Rappahannock, within full view of the sentries, stood a row of finger-posts, on which the Confederate soldiers had painted the taunting legend, 'This way to Richmond !'

CHAPTER XXI

THE ARMY OF NORTHERN VIRGINIA

' IN war men are nothing ; it is the man who is everything. The general is the head, the whole of an army. It was not the Roman army that conquered Gaul, but Cæsar ; it was not the Carthaginian army that made Rome tremble in her gates, but Hannibal ; it was not the Macedonian army that reached the Indus, but Alexander ; it was not the French army that carried the war to the Weser and the Inn, but Turenne ; it was not the Prussian army which, for seven years, defended Prussia against the three greatest Powers of Europe, but Frederick the Great.' So spoke Napoleon, reiterating a truth confirmed by the experience of successive ages, that a wise direction is of more avail than overwhelming numbers, sound strategy than the most perfect armament ; a powerful will, invigorating all who come within its sphere, than the spasmodic efforts of ill-regulated valour.

Even a professional army of long standing and old traditions is what its commander makes it ; its character sooner or later becomes the reflex of his own ; from him the officers take their tone ; his energy or his inactivity, his firmness or vacillation, are rapidly communicated even to the lower ranks ; and so far-reaching is the influence of the leader, that those who record his campaigns concern themselves but little as a rule with the men who followed him. The history of famous armies is the history of great generals, for no army has ever achieved great things unless it has been well commanded. If the general be second-rate the army also will be second-rate. Mutual confidence is the basis of

success in war, and unless the troops have implicit trust in
the resolution and resources of their chief, hesitation and
half-heartedness are sure to mark their actions. They
may fight with their accustomed courage; but the eagerness for the conflict, the alacrity to support, the determination to conquer, will not be there. The indefinable quality
which is expressed by the word *moral* will to some degree
be affected. The history of the Army of the Potomac is a
case in point.

Between the soldiers of the North and South there was
little difference. Neither could claim a superiority of martial qualities. The Confederates, indeed, at the beginning
of the war possessed a larger measure of technical skill; they
were the better shots and the finer riders. But they were
neither braver nor more enduring, and while they probably
derived some advantage from the fact that they were defending their homes, the Federals, defending the integrity of
their native land, were fighting in the noblest of all causes.
But Northerner and Southerner were of the same race, a
race proud, resolute, independent; both were inspired by
the same sentiments of self-respect; *noblesse oblige*—the
noblesse of a free people—was the motto of the one as of
the other. It has been asserted that the Federal armies
were very largely composed of foreigners, whose motives
for enlisting were purely mercenary. At no period of
the war, however, did the proportion of native Americans
sink below seventy per cent.,[1] and at the beginning of
1863 it was much greater. As a matter of fact, the Union
army was composed of thoroughly staunch soldiers.[2]

[1] See Note at end of chapter.

[2] 'Throughout New England,' wrote the Special Correspondent of an
English newspaper, ' you can scarcely enter a door without being aware that
you are in a house of mourning. Whatever may be said of Irish and German
mercenaries, I must bear witness that the best classes of Americans have
bravely come forth for their country. I know of scarcely a family more than
one member of which has not been or is not in the ranks of the army. The
maimed and crippled youths I meet on the highroad certainly do not for the
most part belong to the immigrant rabble of which the Northern regiments
are said to consist; and even the present conscription is now in many splendid
instances most promptly and cheerfully complied with by the wealthy people
who could easily purchase exemption, but who prefer to set a good example.'
Letter from Rhode Island, the *Times*, August 8, 1863.

Nor was the alien element at this time a source of weakness. Ireland and Germany supplied the greater number of those who have been called 'Lincoln's hirelings;' and, judging from the official records, the Irish regiments at least were not a whit less trustworthy than those purely American. Moreover, even if the admixture of foreigners had been greater, the Army of the Potomac, for the reason that it was always superior in numbers, contained in its ranks many more men bred in the United States than the Army of Northern Virginia.[1] For the consistent ill-success of the Federals the superior marksmanship and finer horsemanship of the Confederates cannot, therefore, be accepted as sufficient explanation.

In defence the balance of endurance inclined neither to one side nor the other. Both Southerner and Northerner displayed that stubborn resolve to maintain their ground which is the peculiar attribute of the Anglo-Saxon. To claim for any one race a pre-eminence of valour is repugnant alike to good taste and to sound sense. Courage and endurance are widely distributed over the world's surface, and political institutions, the national conception of duty, the efficiency of the corps of officers, and love of country, are the foundation of vigour and staunchness in the field. Yet it is a fact which can hardly be ignored, that from Crecy to Inkermann there have been exceedingly few instances where an English army, large or small, has been driven from a position. In the great struggle with France, neither Napoleon nor his marshals, although the armies of every other European nation had fled before them, could boast of having broken the English infantry; and no soldiers have ever received a prouder tribute than the admission of a generous enemy, 'They never know when they are beaten.' In America, the characteristics of the parent race were as prominent in the Civil War as they had been in the Revolution. In 1861–65, the side that stood on the defensive, unless hopelessly outnumbered, was almost

---

[1] John Mitchell, the Irish Nationalist, said in a letter to the Dublin *Nation* that there were 40,000 Irishmen in the Southern armies. The *Times*, February 7, 1863.

invariably successful, just as it had been in 1776-82.
' My men,' said Jackson, ' sometimes fail to drive the
enemy from his position, but to hold one, never ! '   The
Federal generals might have made the same assertion with
almost equal truth.   Porter had indeed been defeated at
Gaines' Mill, but he could only set 35,000 in line against
55,000; Banks had been overwhelmed at Winchester, but
6,500 men could hardly have hoped to resist more than
twice their strength ; and Shields' advanced-guard at Port
Republic was much inferior to the force which Jackson
brought against it ; yet these were the only offensive victories
of the '62 campaign.   But if in defence the armies were
well matched, it must be conceded that the Northern attack
was not pressed with the same concentrated vigour as the
Southern.   McClellan at Sharpsburg had more than twice
as many men as Lee ; Pope, on the first day of the Second
Manassas, twice as many as Jackson ; yet on both occasions the smaller force was victorious.   But, in the first
place, the Federal tactics in attack were always feeble.
Lincoln, in appointing Hooker to command the Army
of the Potomac, warned him ' to put in all his men.'
His sharp eye had detected the great fault which had
characterised the operations of his generals.   Their
assaults had been piecemeal, like those of the Confederates
at Malvern Hill, and they had been defeated in detail by
the inferior numbers.   The Northern soldiers were strangers
to those general and combined attacks, pressed with unyielding resolution, which had won Winchester, Gaines'
Mill, and the Second Manassas, and which had nearly
won Kernstown.   The Northern generals invariably kept
large masses in reserve, and these masses were never used.
They had not yet learned, as had Lee, Jackson, and Longstreet, that superior numbers are of no avail unless they
are brought into action, impelling the attack forward by
sheer weight, at the decisive point. In the second place, none
of the Federal leaders possessed the entire confidence either
of their generals or their troops.   With all its affection
for McClellan, it may strongly be questioned whether his
army gave him credit for dash or resolution.   Pope was

defeated in his first action at Cedar Run.   Banks at
Winchester, Frémont west of Staunton, had both been out-
manœuvred.   Burnside had against him his feeble conduct
at Sharpsburg.   Hence the Federal soldiers fought most of
their offensive battles under a terrible disadvantage.   They
were led by men who had known defeat, and who owed
their defeat, in great measure, to the same fault—neglect to
employ their whole force in combination.   Brave and unyielding as they were, the troops went into battle mistrustful
of their leader's skill, and fearful, from the very outset, that
their efforts would be unsupported; and when men begin
to look over their shoulders for reinforcements, demoralisation is not far off.   It would be untrue to say that a
defeated general can never regain the confidence of
his soldiers; but unless he has previous successes to
set off against his failure, to permit him to retain
his position is dangerous in the extreme.   Such was
the opinion of Jackson, always solicitous of the *moral* of his
command.   ' To his mind nothing ever fully excused failure,
and it was rarely that he gave an officer the opportunity of
failing twice.   "The service," he said, "cannot afford to
keep a man who does not succeed."   Nor was he ever
restrained from a change by the fear of making matters
worse.   His motto was, get rid of the unsuccessful man at
once, and trust to Providence for finding a better.'

Nor was the presence of discredited generals the only
evil which went to neutralise the valour of the Federal
soldiers.   The system of command was as rotten in the
Army of the Potomac as in the Armies of Northern Virginia
and of the Valley it was sound; and the system of command plays a most important part in war.   The natural
initiative of the American, the general fearlessness of responsibility, were as conspicuous among the soldiers as in
the nation at large.   To those familiar with the Official
Records, where the doings of regiments and even companies
are preserved, it is perfectly apparent that, so soon as the
officers gained experience, the smaller units were as boldly
and efficiently handled as in the army of Germany under
Moltke.   But while Lee and Jackson, by every means in

their power, fostered the capacity for independent action, following therein the example of Napoleon,[1] of Washington, of Nelson, and of Wellington, and aware that their strength would thus be doubled, McClellan and Pope did their best to stifle it; and in the higher ranks they succeeded. In the one case the generals were taught to wait for orders, in the other to anticipate them. In the one case, whether troops were supported or not depended on the word of the commanding general; in the other, every officer was taught that to sustain his colleagues was his first duty. It thus resulted that while the Confederate leaders were served by scores of zealous assistants, actively engaged in furthering the aim of their superiors, McClellan, Pope, and Frémont, jealous of power reduced their subordinates, with few exceptions, to the position of machines, content to obey the letter of their orders, oblivious of opportunity, and incapable of co-operation. Lee and Jackson appear to have realised the requirements of battle far more fully than their opponents. They knew that the scope of the commander is limited; that once his troops are committed to close action it is impossible for him to exert further control, for his orders can no longer reach them; that he cannot keep the whole field under observation, much less observe every fleeting opportunity. Yet it is by utilising opportunities that the enemy's strength is sapped. For these reasons the Confederate generals were exceedingly careful not to chill the spirit of enterprise. Errors of judgment were never considered in the light of crimes; while the officer who, in default of orders, remained inactive, or who, when his orders were manifestly inapplicable to a suddenly changed situation, and there was no time to have them altered, dared not act for himself, was not long retained in responsible command. In the Army of the Potomac, on the other hand, centralisation was the rule. McClellan

[1] In the opinion of the author, the charge of centralisation preferred against Napoleon can only be applied to his leading in his later campaigns. In his earlier operations he gave his generals every latitude, and he maintained that loose but effective system of tactics, in which much was left to the individual, adopted by the French army just previous to the wars of the Revolution.

expected blind obedience from his corps commanders, and nothing more, and Pope brought Porter to trial for using his own judgment, on occasions when Pope himself was absent, during the campaign of the Second Manassas. Thus the Federal soldiers, through no fault of their own, laboured for the first two years of the war under a disadvantage from which the wisdom of Lee and Jackson had relieved the Confederates. The Army of the Potomac was an inert mass, the Army of Northern Virginia a living organism, endowed with irresistible vigour.

It is to be noted, too, as tending to prove the equal courage of North and South, that on the Western theatre of war the Federals were the more successful. And yet the Western armies of the Confederacy were neither less brave, less hardy, nor less disciplined than those in Virginia. They were led, however, by inferior men, while, on the other hand, many of the Northern generals opposed to them possessed unquestionable ability, and understood the value of a good system of command.

We may say, then, without detracting an iota from the high reputation of the Confederate soldiers, that it was not the Army of Northern Virginia that saved Richmond in 1862, but Lee; not the Army of the Valley which won the Valley campaign, but Jackson.

It is related that a good priest, once a chaplain in Taylor's Louisiana brigade, concluded his prayer at the unveiling of the Jackson monument in New Orleans with these remarkable words: 'When in Thine inscrutable decree it was ordained that the Confederacy should fail, it became necessary for Thee to remove Thy servant Stonewall Jackson.'[1] It is unnecessary, perhaps, to lay much forcible emphasis on the personal factor, but, at the same time, it is exceedingly essential that it should never be overlooked.

The Government which, either in peace or war, commits the charge of its armed forces to any other than the ablest and most experienced soldier the country can produce is but laying the foundation of national disaster. Had the

[1] *Bright Skies and Dark Shadows*, p. 294. H. M. Field, D.D.

importance of a careful selection for the higher commands been understood in the North as it was understood in the South, Lee and Jackson would have been opposed by foes more formidable than Pope and Burnside, or Banks and Frémont. The Federal Administration, confident in the courage and intelligence of their great armies, considered that any ordinary general, trained to command, and supported by an efficient staff, should be able to win victories. Mr. Davis, on the other hand, himself a soldier, who, as United States Secretary of War, had enjoyed peculiar opportunities of estimating the character of the officers of the old army, made no such mistake. He was not always, indeed, either wise or consistent; but, with few exceptions, his appointments were the best that could be made, and he was ready to accept the advice, as regarded selections for command, of his most experienced generals.

But however far-reaching may be the influence of a great leader, in estimating his capacity the temper of the weapon that he wielded can hardly be overlooked. In the first place, that temper, to a greater or less degree, must have been of his own forging,—it is part of his fame. ' No man,' says Napier, ' can be justly called a great captain who does not know how to organise and form the character of an army, as well as to lead it when formed.' In the second place, to do much with feeble means is greater than to do more with large resources. Difficulties are inherent in all military operations, and not the least may be the constitution of the army. Nor would the story of Stonewall Jackson be more than half told without large reference to those tried soldiers, subalterns and private soldiers as they were, whom he looked upon as his comrades, whose patriotism and endurance he extolled so highly, and whose devotion to himself, next to the approval of his own conscience, was the reward that most he valued.

He is blind indeed who fails to recognise the unselfish patriotism displayed by the citizen-soldiers of America, the stern resolution with which the war was waged; the tenacity of the Northerner, ill-commanded and con-

stantly defeated, fighting in a most difficult country and
foiled on every line of invasion; the tenacity of the
Southerner, confronting enormous odds, ill-fed, ill-armed,
and ill-provided, knowing that if wounded his sufferings
would be great—for drugs had been declared contraband of
war, the hospitals contained no anæsthetics to relieve the
pain of amputation, and the surgical instruments, which
were only replaced when others were captured, were worn
out with constant usage; knowing too that his women-folk
and children were in want, and yet never yielding to
despair nor abandoning hope of ultimate victory. Neither
Federal nor Confederate deemed his life the most precious
of his earthly possessions. Neither New Englander nor Virginian ever for one moment dreamt of surrendering, no matter
what the struggle might cost, a single acre of the territory,
a single item of the civil rights, which had been handed
down to him. ' I do not profess,' said Jackson, ' any romantic
sentiments as to the vanity of life. Certainly no man has
more that should make life dear to him than I have, in the
affection of my home; but I do not desire to survive the
independence of my country.' And Jackson's attitude was
that of his fellow-countrymen. The words of Naboth,
' Jehovah forbid that I should give to thee the inheritance of
my forefathers,' were graven on the heart of both North and
South ; and the unknown and forgotten heroes who fought
in the ranks of either army, and who fought for a principle,
not on compulsion or for glory, are worthy of the highest
honours that history can bestow.

Nor can a soldier withhold his tribute of praise to the
capacity for making war which distinguished the American
citizen. The intelligence of the rank and file played an
important *rôle* in every phase of a campaign. As skirmishers,—and modern battles, to a very great extent, are
fought out by lines of skirmishers—their work was admirable ; and when the officers were struck down, or when
command, by reason of the din and excitement, became impossible, the self-dependence of the individual asserted itself
with the best effect.[1] The same quality which the German

[1] The historical student may profitably compare with the American

training had sought to foster, and which, according to Moltke,[1] had much to do with the victories of 1870, was inborn in both Northerner and Southerner. On outpost and on patrol, in seeking information and in counteracting the ruses of the enemy, the keen intelligence of the educated volunteer was of the utmost value. History has hitherto overlooked the achievements of the ' scouts,' whose names so seldom occur in the Official Records, but whose daring was unsurpassed, and whose services were of vast importance. In the Army of Northern Virginia every commanding general had his own party of scouts, whose business it was to penetrate the enemy's lines, to see everything and to hear everything, to visit the base of operations, to inspect the line of communications, and to note the condition and the temper of the hostile troops. Attracted by a pure love of adventure, these private soldiers did exactly the same work as did the English Intelligence officers in the Peninsula, and did it with the same thoroughness and acuteness. Wellington, deploring the capture of Captain Colquhoun Grant, declared that the gallant Highlander was worth as much to the army as a brigade of cavalry; Jackson had scouts who were more useful to him than many of his brigadiers. Again, in constructing hasty intrenchments, the soldiers needed neither assistance nor impulsion. The rough cover thrown up by the men when circumstances demanded it, on their own volition, was always adapted to the ground, and generally fulfilled the main principles of fortification. For bridge-building, for road-making, for the destruction, the repair, and even the making, of railroads, skilled labour was always forthcoming from the ranks; and the soldiers stamped the impress of their individuality on the tactics of the infantry. Modern formations, to a very large extent, had their origin on American battle-fields. The men realised very quickly the advantages of shelter; the advance by rushes from one cover to another, and the gradually working up, by this method, of the firing-line to effective range—

soldier the Armies of Revolutionary France, in which education and intelligence were also conspicuous.

[1] *Official Account of the Franco-German War*, vol. ii., p. 168.

the method which all experience shows to be the true one —became the general rule.

That the troops had faults, however, due in great part to the fact that their intelligence was not thoroughly trained, and to the inexperience of their officers, it is impossible to deny.

' I agree with you,' wrote Lee in 1863, ' in believing that our army would be invincible if it could be properly organised and officered. There were never such men in an army before. They will go anywhere and do anything if properly led. But there is the difficulty—proper commanders. Where can they be obtained? But they are improving—constantly improving. Rome was not built in a day, nor can we expect miracles in our favour.' [1] Yet, taking them all in all, the American rank and file of 1863, with their native characteristics, supplemented by a great knowledge of war, were in advance of any soldiers of their time.

In the actual composition of the Confederate forces no marked change had taken place since the beginning of the war. But the character of the army, in many essential respects, had become sensibly modified. The men encamped on the Rappahannock were no longer the raw recruits who had blundered into victory at the First Manassas ; nor were they the unmanageable divisions of the Peninsula. They were still, for the most part, volunteers, for conscripts in the Army of Northern Virginia were not numerous, but they were volunteers of a very different type from those who had fought at Kernstown or at Gaines' Mill. Despite their protracted absence from their homes, the wealthy and well-born privates still shouldered the musket. Though many had been promoted to commissions, the majority were content to set an example of self-sacrifice and sterling patriotism, and the regiments were thus still leavened with a large admixture of educated and intelligent men. It is a significant fact that during those months of 1863 which were spent in winter quarters Latin, Greek, mathematical, and even Hebrew classes were instituted by the soldiers. But all trace of social distinction had long since vanished. Between the rich planter

[1] Lee to Hood, May 21, 1863; *Advance and Retreat*, p. 53.

and the small farmer or mechanic there was no difference
either in aspect or habiliments. Tanned by the hot
Virginia sun, thin-visaged and bright-eyed, gaunt of frame
and spare of flesh, they were neither more nor less than
the rank and file of the Confederate army ; the product of
discipline and hard service, moulded after the same pattern, with the same hopes and fears, the same needs, the
same sympathies. They looked at life from a common
standpoint, and that standpoint was not always elevated.
Human nature claimed its rights. When his hunger was
satisfied and, to use his own expression, ' he was full of hog
and hominy,' the Confederate soldier found time to discuss
the operations in which he was engaged. Pipe in mouth,
he could pass in review the strategy and tactics of both
armies, the capacity of his generals, and the bearing of his
enemies, and on each one of these questions, for he was the
shrewdest of observers, his comments were always to the
point. He had studied his profession in a practical school.
The more delicate moves of the great game were topics of
absorbing interest. He cast a comprehensive glance over
the whole theatre ; he would puzzle out the reasons for
forced marches and sudden changes of direction ; his
curiosity was great, but intelligent, and the groups round
the camp-fires often forecast with surprising accuracy the
manœuvres that the generals were planning. But far more
often the subjects of conversation were of a more immediate
and personal character. The capacity of the company
cook, the quality of the last consignment of boots, the
merits of different bivouacs, the prospect of the supply
train coming up to time, the temper of the captain and
subaltern—such were the topics which the Confederate
privates spent their leisure in discussing. They had long
since discovered that war is never romantic and seldom
exciting, but a monotonous round of tiresome duties,
enlivened at rare intervals by dangerous episodes. They
had become familiar with its constant accompaniment of
privations—bad weather, wet bivouacs, and wretched roads,
wood that would not kindle, and rations that did not
satisfy. They had learned that a soldier's worst enemy

may be his native soil, in the form of dust or mud ; that
it is possible to march for months without firing a shot
or seeing a foe ; that a battle is an interlude which breaks in
at rare intervals on the long round of digging, marching,
bridge-building, and road-making ; and that the time of
the fiercest fire-eater is generally occupied in escorting mule-
trains, in mounting guard, in dragging waggons through
the mud, and in loading or unloading stores.   Volunteering
for perilous and onerous duties, for which hundreds had
eagerly offered themselves in the early days, ere the
glamour of the soldier's life had vanished, had ceased
to be popular.   The men were now content to wait
for orders ; and as discipline crystallised into habit, they
became resigned to the fact that they were no longer
volunteers, masters of their own actions, but the paid
servants of the State, compelled to obey and powerless to
protest.

　　To all outward appearance, then, in the spring of 1863
the Army of Northern Virginia bore an exceedingly close
resemblance to an army of professional soldiers.   It is true
that military etiquette was not insisted on ; that more
license, both in quarters and on the march, was permitted
than would be the case in a regular army ; that officers
were not treated with the same respect ; and that tact,
rather than the strict enforcement of the regulations, was
the key-note of command.   Nevertheless, taken as a whole,
the Confederate soldiers were exceedingly well-conducted.
The good elements in the ranks were too strong for those
who were inclined to resist authority, and the amount of
misbehaviour was wonderfully small.   There was little
neglect of duty. Whatever the intelligence of the men
told them was necessary for success, for safety, or for
efficiency, was done without reluctance.   The outposts
were seldom caught napping.   Digging and tree-felling—
for the men had learned the value of making fortifications
and good roads—were taken as a matter of course.   Nor
was the Southern soldier a grumbler.   He accepted half-
rations and muddy camping-grounds without remonstrance ;
if his boots wore out he made shift to march without

them ; and when his uniform fell to pieces he waited for
the next victory to supply himself with a new outfit. He
was enough of a philosopher to know that it is better to
meet misery with a smile than with a scowl. Mark Tapley
had many prototypes in the Confederate ranks, and the men
were never more facetious than when things were at their
worst. 'The very intensity of their sufferings became a
source of merriment. Instead of growling and deserting,
they laughed at their own bare feet, ragged clothes, and
pinched faces ; and weak, hungry, cold, wet and dirty, with
no hope of reward or rest, they marched cheerfully to meet
the warmly clad and well-fed hosts of the enemy.'[1] Indomitable indeed were the hearts that beat beneath the
grey jackets, and a spirit rising superior to all misfortune,

> That ever with a frolic welcome took
> The thunder and the sunshine,

was a marked characteristic of the Confederate soldier.
Nor was it only in camp or on the march that the
temper of the troops betrayed itself in reckless gaiety.[2]
The stress of battle might thin their ranks, but it was
powerless to check their laughter. The dry humour of the
American found a fine field in the incidents of a fierce
engagement. Nothing escaped without remark : the
excitement of a general, the accelerated movements of the
non-combatants, the vagaries of the army mule, the bad
practice of the artillery—all afforded entertainment. And
when the fight became hotter and the Federals pressed

[1] *Soldier Life in the Army of Northern Virginia.*
[2] General Longstreet relates an amusing story :—' One of the soldiers,
during the investment of Suffolk (April 1863), carefully constructed
and equipped a full-sized man, dressed in a new suit of improved
"butternut" clothing ; and christening him Julius Cæsar, took him to a
signal platform which overlooked the works, adjusted him to a graceful
position, and made him secure to the framework by strong cords. A
little after sunrise "Julius Cæsar" was discovered by some of the Federal
battery officers, who prepared for the target so inviting to skilful practice.
The new soldier sat under the hot fire with irritating indifference until the
Confederates, unable to restrain their hilarity, exposed the joke by calling
for " Three cheers for Julius Cæsar ! " The other side quickly recognised the
situation, and good-naturedly added to ours their cheers for the old hero.'—
From Manassas to Appomattox.

resolutely to the attack, the flow of badinage took a
grim and peculiar turn. It has already been related that
the Confederate armies depended, to a large degree, for
their clothing and equipments on what they captured.
So abundant was this source of supply, that the soldier had
come to look upon his enemy as a movable magazine of
creature comforts; and if he marched cheerfully to battle,
it was not so much because he loved fighting, but that
he hoped to renew his wardrobe. A victory was much, but
the spoils of victory were more. No sooner, then, did the
Federals arrive within close range, than the wild yells of
the Southern infantry became mingled with fierce laughter
and derisive shouts. 'Take off them boots, Yank!' 'Come
out of them clothes; we're gwine to have them!' 'Come on,
blue-bellies, we want them blankets!' 'Bring them rations
along! You've got to leave them!'—such were the cries,
like the howls of half-famished wolves, that were heard along
Jackson's lines at Fredericksburg.[1] And they were not raised
in mockery. The battle-field was the soldier's harvest, and
as the sheaves of writhing forms, under the muzzles of their
deadly rifles, increased in length and depth, the men listened
with straining ears for the word to charge. The counterstroke was their opportunity. The rush with the bayonet
was never so speedy but that deft fingers found time to rifle
the haversacks of the fallen, and such was the eagerness for
booty that it was with the greatest difficulty that the troops
were dragged off from the pursuit. It is said that at Fredericksburg, some North Carolina regiments, which had re-

---

[1] 'During the truce on the second day of Fredericksburg,' says Captain
Smith, 'a tall, fine-looking Alabama soldier, who was one of the litter-bearers,
picked up a new Enfield rifle on the neutral ground, examined it, tested the
sights, shouldered it, and was walking back to the Confederate lines, when
a young Federal officer, very handsomely dressed and mounted, peremptorily
ordered him to throw it down, telling him he had no right to take it. The
soldier, with the rifle on his shoulder, walked very deliberately round the officer,
scanning him from head to foot, and then started again towards our lines.
On this the Federal lieutenant, drawing his little sword, galloped after him,
and ordered him with an oath to throw down the rifle. The soldier halted,
then walked round the officer once again, very slowly, looking him up and
down, and at last said, pointing to his fine boots: "I shall shoot you to-
morrow, and get them boots;" then strode away to his command. The
lieutenant made no attempt to follow.'

pulsed and followed up a Federal brigade, were hardly to be restrained from dashing into the midst of the enemy's reserves, and when at length they were turned back their complaints were bitter. The order to halt and retire seemed to them nothing less than rank injustice. Half-crying with disappointment, they accused their generals of favouritism! 'They don't want the North Car'linians to git anything,' they whined. 'They wouldn't hev' stopped Hood's " Texicans "—they'd hev' let *them* go on ! '

But if they relieved their own pressing wants at the expense of their enemies, if they stripped the dead, and exchanged boots and clothing with their prisoners, seldom getting the worst of the bargain, no armies—to their lasting honour be it spoken, for no armies were so destitute—were ever less formidable to peaceful citizens, within the border or beyond it, than those of the Confederacy. It was exceedingly seldom that wanton damage was laid to the soldier's charge. The rights of non-combatants were religiously respected, and the farmers of Pennsylvania were treated with the same courtesy and consideration as the planters of Virginia. A village was none the worse for the vicinity of a Confederate bivouac, and neither man nor woman had reason to dread the half-starved tatterdemalions who followed Lee and Jackson. As the grey columns, in the march through Maryland, swung through the streets of those towns where the Unionist sentiment was strong, the women, standing in the porches, waved the Stars and Stripes defiantly in their faces. But the only retort of ' the dust brown ranks ' was a volley of jests, not always unmixed with impudence. The personal attributes of their fair enemies did not escape observation. The damsel whose locks were of conspicuous hue was addressed as ' bricktop ' until she screamed with rage, and threatened to fire into the ranks ; while the maiden of sour visage and uncertain years was saluted as ' Ole Miss Vinegar ' by a whole division of infantry. But this was the limit of the soldier's resentment. At the same time, when in the midst of plenty he was not impeccable. For highway robbery and housebreaking he had no inclination, but he was by no means above petty larceny. Pigs and poultry, fruit, corn, vegetables and fence-rails, he looked upon as his lawful perquisites.

He was the most cunning of foragers, and neither stringent orders nor armed guards availed to protect a field of maize or a patch of potatoes; the traditional negro was not more skilful in looting a fowl-house;[1] he had an unerring scent for whisky or 'apple-jack;' and the address he displayed in compassing the destruction of the unsuspecting porker was only equalled, when he was caught *flagrante delicto*, by the ingenuity of his excuses. According to the Confederate private, the most inoffensive animals, in the districts through which the armies marched, developed a strange pugnacity, and if bullet and bayonet were used against them, it was solely in self-defence.

But such venial faults, common to every army, and almost justified by the deficiencies of the Southern commissariat, were more than atoned for when the enemy was met. Of the prowess of Lee's veterans sufficient has been said. Their deeds speak for themselves. But it was not the battle-field alone that bore witness to their fortitude. German soldiers have told us that in the war of 1870, when their armies, marching on Paris, found, to their astonishment, the great city strongly garrisoned, and hosts gathering in every quarter for its relief, a singular apathy took possession of the troops. The explanation offered by a great military writer is that ' after a certain period even the victor becomes tired of war;' and 'the more civilised,' he adds, 'a people is, the more quickly will this weakness become apparent.'[2] Whether this explanation be adequate is not easy to decide. The fact remains, however, that the Confederate volunteer was able to overcome that longing for home which chilled the enthusiasm of the German conscript. And this is the more remarkable, inasmuch as his career was not one of unchequered victory. In the spring of 1863, the Army of the Potomac, more numerous than ever, was still before

---

[1] Despite Lee's proclamations against indiscriminate foraging, 'the hens,' he said, 'had to roost mighty high when the Texans were about.'

[2] *The Conduct of War.* Von der Goltz.

him, firmly established on Virginian soil; hope of foreign intervention, despite the assurances of the politicians, was gradually fading, and it was but too evident that the war was far from over. Yet at no time during their two years of service had the soldiers shown the slightest sign of that discouragement which seized the Germans after two months. And who shall dare to say that the Southerner was less highly civilised than the Prussian or the Bavarian? Political liberty, freedom of speech and action, are the real elements of civilisation, and not merely education. But let the difference in the constitution of the two armies be borne in mind. The Confederates, with few exceptions, were volunteers, who had become soldiers of their own choice, who had assumed arms deliberately and without compulsion, and who by their own votes were responsible that war had been declared. The Germans were conscripts, a dumb, powerless, irresponsible multitude, animated, no doubt, by hereditary hatred of the enemy, but without that sense of moral obligation which exists in the volunteer. We may be permitted, then, to believe that this sense of moral obligation was one reason why the spirit of the Southerners rose superior to human weakness, and that the old adage, which declares that 'one volunteer is better than three pressed men,' is not yet out of date. Nor is it an unfair inference that the armies of the Confederacy, allied by the 'crimson thread of kinship' to those of Wellington, of Raglan, and of Clyde, owed much of their enduring fortitude to 'the rock whence they were hewn.'

And yet, with all their admirable qualities, the Southern soldiers had not yet got rid of their original defects. Temperate, obedient, and well-conducted, small as was the percentage of bad characters and habitual misdoers, their discipline was still capable of improvement. The assertion, at first sight, seems a contradiction in terms. How could troops, it may be asked, who so seldom infringed the regulations be other than well-disciplined? For the simple reason that discipline in quarters is an absolutely different quality from discipline in battle. No large body of

intelligent men, assembled in a just cause and of good
character, is likely to break out into excesses, or, if obedience
is manifestly necessary, to rebel against authority.   Subordination to the law is the distinguishing mark of all
civilised society.   But such subordination, however praise-
worthy, is not the discipline of the soldier, though it is often
confounded with it.   A regiment of volunteers, billeted in
some country town, would probably show a smaller list of
misdemeanours than a regiment of regulars.   Yet the latter
might be exceedingly well-disciplined, and the former have
no real discipline whatever.   Self-respect—for that is the
discipline of the volunteer—is not battle discipline, the
discipline of the cloth, of habit, of tradition, of constant
association and of mutual confidence.   Self-respect, excellent in itself, and by no means unknown amongst regular
soldiers, does not carry with it a mechanical obedience to
command, nor does it merge the individual in the mass, and
give the tremendous power of unity to the efforts of large
numbers.

It will not be pretended that the discipline of regular
troops always rises superior to privation and defeat.   It
is a notorious fact that the number of deserters from
Wellington's army in Spain and Portugal, men who
wilfully absented themselves from the colours and wandered over the country, was by no means inconsiderable ;
while the behaviour of the French regulars in 1870, and
even of the Germans, when they rushed back in panic
through the village of Gravelotte, deaf to the threats
and entreaties of their aged sovereign, was hardly in
accordance with military tradition.   Nevertheless, it is not
difficult to show that the Southerners fell somewhat short
of the highest standard.   They were certainly not incapable
of keeping their ranks under a hot fire, or of holding
their ground to the last extremity.   Pickett's charge at
Gettysburg is one of the most splendid examples of disciplined valour in the annals of war, and the endurance of
Lee's army at Sharpsburg has seldom been surpassed.   Nor
was the disorder into which the attacking lines were sooner
or later thrown a proof of inferior training.   Even in the

days of flint-lock muskets, the admixture of not only companies and battalions, but even of brigades and divisions, was a constant feature of fierce assaults over broken ground. If, under such conditions, the troops still press forward, and if, when success has been achieved, order is rapidly restored, then discipline is good ; and in neither respect did the Confederates fail. But to be proof against disorder is not everything in battle. It is not sufficient that the men should be capable of fighting fiercely ; to reap the full benefit of their weapons and their training they must be obedient to command. The rifle is a far less formidable weapon when every man uses it at his own discretion than when the fire of a large body of troops is directed by a single will. Precision of movement, too, is necessary for the quick concentration of superior forces at the decisive point, for rapid support, and for effective combination. But neither was the fire of the Confederate infantry under the complete control of their officers, nor were their movements always characterised by order and regularity. It was seldom that the men could be induced to refrain from answering shot with shot ; there was an extraordinary waste of ammunition, there was much unnecessary noise, and the regiments were very apt to get out of hand. It is needless to bring forward specific proof ; the admissions of superior officers are quite sufficient. General D. H. Hill, in an interesting description of the Southern soldier, speaks very frankly of his shortcomings. ' Self-reliant always, obedient when he chose to be, impatient of drill and discipline, he was unsurpassed as a scout or on the skirmish line. Of the shoulder-to-shoulder courage, bred of drill and discipline, he knew nothing and cared less. Hence, on the battle-field, he was more of a free lance than a machine. Who ever saw a Confederate line advancing that was not crooked as a ram's horn ? Each ragged rebel yelling on his own hook and aligning on himself ! But there is as much need of the machine-made soldier as of the self-reliant soldier, and the concentrated blow is always the most effective blow. The erratic effort of the Confederate, heroic though it was, yet failed to achieve the maximum result just because it was erratic. Moreover, two serious evils attended that excessive egotism and individuality which came to the Confederate through his training, association, and habits. He knew when a movement was false and a position untenable, and he was too little of a machine to give in such cases the whole-hearted service which might have redeemed the blunder. The other evil was an ever-growing one. His disregard of discipline and independence of character made him often a straggler, and by straggling the fruit of many a victory was lost.'[1]

General Lee was not less outspoken. A circular issued to his troops during the last months of the war is virtually a criticism on their conduct. 'Many opportunities,' he wrote, 'have been lost and hundreds of valuable lives uselessly sacrificed for want of a strict observance of discipline. Its object is to enable an army to bring promptly into action the largest possible number of men in good order, and under the control of their officers. Its effects are visible in all military history, which records the triumph of discipline and courage far more frequently than that of numbers and resources. The importance and utility of thorough discipline should be impressed on officers and men on all occasions by illus-trations taken from the experience of the instructor or from other sources of information. They should be made to understand that discipline contributes no less to their safety than to their efficiency. Disastrous surprises and those sudden panics which lead to defeat and the greatest loss of life are of rare occurrence among disciplined troops. It is well known that the greatest number of casualties occur when men become scattered, and especially when they retreat in confusion, as the fire of the enemy is then more deliberate and fatal. The experience of every officer shows that those troops suffer least who attack most vigorously, and that a few men, retaining their organisation and acting in concert, accomplish far more with smaller loss than a larger number scattered and disorganised.

[1] *Southern Historical Society Papers*, vol. xiii., p. 261.

'The appearance of a steady, unbroken line is more formidable to the enemy, and renders his aim less accurate and his fire less effective. Orders can be readily transmitted, advantage can be promptly taken of every opportunity, and all efforts being directed to a common end, the combat will be briefer and success more certain.

'Let officers and men be made to feel that they will most effectually secure their safety by remaining steadily at their posts, preserving order, and fighting with coolness and vigour. . . . Impress upon the officers that discipline cannot be attained without constant watchfulness on their part. They must attend to the smallest particulars of detail. Men must be habituated to obey or they cannot be controlled in battle, and the neglect of the least important order impairs the proper influence of the officer.'[1]

That such a circular was considered necessary after the troops had been nearly four years under arms establishes beyond all question that the discipline of the Confederate army was not that of the regular troops with whom General Lee had served under the Stars and Stripes; but it is not to be understood that he attributed the deficiencies of his soldiers to any spirit of resistance on their part to the demands of subordination. Elsewhere he says: 'The greatest difficulty I find is in causing orders and regulations to be obeyed. This arises not from a spirit of disobedience, but from ignorance.'[2] And here, with his usual perspicacity, he goes straight to the root of the evil. When the men in the ranks understand all that discipline involves, safety, health, efficiency, victory, it is easily maintained; and it is because experience and tradition have taught them this that veteran armies are so amenable to control. 'Soldiers,' says Sir Charles Napier, 'must obey in all things. They may and do laugh at foolish orders, but they nevertheless obey, not because they are blindly obedient, but because they know that to disobey is to break the backbone of their profession.'

[1] *Memoirs of General Robert E. Lee.* By A. L. Long, Military Secretary and Brigadier-General, pp. 685–6.
[2] *Memoirs, &c.*, p. 619. Letter dated March 21, 1863.

Such knowledge, however, is long in coming, even to the regular, and it may be questioned whether it ever really came home to the Confederates.

In fact, the Southern soldier, ignorant, at the outset, of what may be accomplished by discipline, never quite got rid of the belief that the enthusiasm of the individual, his goodwill and his native courage, was a more than sufficient substitute. 'The spirit which animates our soldiers,' wrote Lee, 'and the natural courage with which they are so liberally endowed, have led to a reliance upon those good qualities, to the neglect of measures which would increase their efficiency and contribute to their safety.'[1] Yet the soldier was hardly to blame. Neither he nor his regimental officers had any previous knowledge of war when they were suddenly launched against the enemy, and there was no time to instil into them the habits of discipline. There was no regular army to set them an example; no historic force whose traditions they would unconsciously have adopted; the exigencies of the service forbade the retention of the men in camps of instruction, and trained instructors could not be spared from more important duties.

Such ignorance, however, as that which prevailed in the Southern ranks is not always excusable. It would be well if those who pose as the friends of the private soldier, as his protectors from injustice, realised the mischief they may do by injudicious sympathy. The process of being broken to discipline is undoubtedly galling to the instincts of free men, and it is beyond question that among a multitude of superiors, some will be found who are neither just nor considerate. Instances of hardship must inevitably occur. But men and officers—for discipline presses as hardly on the officers as on the men—must obey, no matter at what cost to their feelings, for obedience to orders, instant and unhesitating, is not only the life-blood of armies but the security of States; and the doctrine that under any conditions whatever deliberate disobedience can be justified is treason to the commonwealth. It is to be remembered that the

[1] *Memoirs, &c.*, p. 684. By A. L. Long.

end of the soldier's existence is not merely to conduct himself as a respectable citizen and earn his wages, but to face peril and privations, not of his own free will, but at the bidding of others; and, in circumstances where his natural instincts assert themselves most strongly, to make a complete surrender of mind and body. If he has been in the habit of weighing the justice or the wisdom of orders before obeying them, if he has been taught that disobedience may be a pardonable crime, he will probably question the justice of the order that apparently sends him to certain death; if he once begins to think; if he once contemplates the possibility of disobedience; if he permits a single idea to enter his head beyond the necessity of instant compliance, it is unlikely that he will rise superior to the promptings of his weaker nature. '*Men must be habituated to obey or they cannot be controlled in battle;*' and the slightest interference with the habit of subordination is fraught, therefore, with the very greatest danger to the efficiency of an army.

It has been asserted, and it would appear that the idea is widespread, that patriotism and intelligence are of vastly more importance than the habit of obedience, and it was certainly a very general opinion in America before the war. This idea should have been effectually dissipated, at all events in the North, by the battle of Bull Run. Nevertheless, throughout the conflict a predilection existed in favour of what was called the 'thinking bayonet;' and the very term 'machine-made soldier,' employed by General D. H. Hill, proves that the strict discipline of regular armies was not held in high esteem.

It is certainly true that the 'thinking bayonet' is by no means to be decried. A man can no more be a good soldier without intelligence and aptitude for his profession than he can be a successful poacher or a skilful jockey. But it is possible, in considering the value of an armed force, to rate too highly the natural qualities of the individual in the ranks. In certain circumstances, especially in irregular warfare, where each man fights for his own hand, they doubtless play a con-

spicuous part. A thousand skilled riflemen, familiar with
the ' moving accidents by flood and field,' even if they have
no regular training and are incapable of precise manœuvres,
may prove more than a match for the same number of
professional soldiers. But when large numbers are in
question, when the concentration of superior force at a
single point, and the close co-operation of the three arms,
infantry, artillery, and cavalry, decide the issue, then the
force that can manœuvre, that moves like a machine at the
mandate of a single will, has a marked advantage ; and
the power of manœuvring and of combination is conferred
by discipline alone. ' Two Mamelukes,' said Napoleon,
' can defeat three French horsemen, because they are better
armed, better mounted, and more skilful. A hundred
French horse have nothing to fear from a hundred
Mamelukes, three hundred would defeat a similar number,
and a thousand French would defeat fifteen hundred
Mamelukes. So great is the influence of tactics, order,
and the power of manœuvring.'

It may be said, moreover, that whatever may have been
the case in past times, the training of the regular soldier
to-day neither aims at producing mere machines nor has it
that effect. As much attention is given to the development
of self-reliance in the rank and file as to making them subordinate. It has long been recognised that there are many
occasions in war when even the private must use his wits ;
on outpost, or patrol, as a scout, an orderly, or when his
immediate superiors have fallen, momentous issues may
hang on his judgment and initiative ; and in a good army
these qualities are sedulously fostered by constant instruction in field duties. Nor is the fear justified that the
strict enforcement of exact obedience, whenever a superior is present, impairs, under this system of training, the
capacity for independent action when such action becomes
necessary. In the old days, to drill and discipline the
soldier into a machine was undoubtedly the end of all his
training. To-day his officers have the more difficult task
of stimulating his intelligence, while, at the same time,
they instil the habits of subordination ; and that such task

may be successfully accomplished we have practical proof.
The regiments of the Light Brigade, trained by Sir John
Moore nearly a century ago on the system of to-day,
proved their superiority in the field over all others. As
skirmishers, on the outpost, and in independent fighting,
they were exceedingly efficient; and yet, when they marched
shoulder to shoulder, no troops in Wellington's army showed
a more solid front, manœuvred with greater precision, or
were more completely under the control of their officers.

Mechanical obedience, then, is perfectly compatible with
the freest exercise of the intelligence, provided that the
men are so trained that they know instinctively when to
give the one and to use the other; and the Confederates,
had their officers and non-commissioned officers been trained
soldiers, might easily have acquired this highest form of
discipline. As it was, and as it always will be with improvised troops, the discipline of battle was to a great
degree purely personal. The men followed those officers
whom they knew, and in whom they had confidence; but
they did not always obey simply because the officer had the
right to command; and they were not easily handled when
the wisdom of an order or the necessity of a movement was
not apparent. The only way, it was said by an Englishman
in the Confederacy, in which an officer could acquire
influence over the Southern soldiers was by his personal
conduct under fire. 'Every ounce of authority,' was his
expression, 'had to be purchased by a drop of my blood.'[1]
Such being the case, it is manifest that Jackson's methods
of discipline were well adapted to the peculiar constitution
of the army in which he served. With the officers he was
exceedingly strict. He looked to them to set an example
of unhesitating obedience and the precise performance of
duty. He demanded, too—and in this respect his own
conduct was a model—that the rank and file should be
treated with tact and consideration. He remembered that
his citizen soldiers were utterly unfamiliar with the forms
and customs of military life, that what to the regular would

[1] *Three Months in the Southern States.* General Sir Arthur Fremantle,
G.C.B.

be a mere matter of course, might seem a gross outrage to the man who had never acknowledged a superior. In his selection of officers, therefore, for posts upon his staff, and in his recommendations for promotion, he considered personal characteristics rather than professional ability. He preferred men who would win the confidence of others— men not only strong, but possessing warm sympathies and broad minds—to mere martinets, ruling by regulation, and treating the soldier as a machine. But, at the same time, he was by no means disposed to condone misconduct in the volunteers. Never was there a more striking contrast than between Jackson the general and Jackson off duty. During his sojourn at Moss Neck, Mr. Corbin's little daughter, a child of six years old, became a special favourite. ' Her pretty face and winsome ways were so charming that he requested her mother that she might visit him every afternoon, when the day's labours were over. He had always some little treat in store for her—an orange or an apple—but one afternoon he found that his supply of good things was exhausted. Glancing round the room his eye fell on a new uniform cap, ornamented with a gold band. Taking his knife, he ripped off the braid, and fastened it among the curls of his little playfellow.' A little later the child was taken ill, and after his removal from Moss Neck he heard that she had died. ' The general,' writes his aide-de-camp, ' wept freely when I brought him the sad news.' Yet in the administration of discipline Jackson was far sterner than General Lee, or indeed than any other of the generals in Virginia. ' Once on the march, fearing lest his men might stray from the ranks and commit acts of pillage, he had issued an order that the soldiers should not enter private dwellings. Disregarding the order, a soldier entered a house, and even used insulting language to the women of the family. This was reported to Jackson, who had the man arrested, tried by drum-head court-martial, and shot in twenty minutes.'[1] He never failed to confirm the sentences of death passed by courts-martial on deserters. It was in vain that his oldest

[1] *Bright Skies and Dark Shadows.* Rev. H. M. Field, D.D., p. 286.

friends, or even the chaplains, appealed for a mitigation of the extreme penalty. 'While he was in command at Winchester, in December 1861, a soldier who was charged with striking his captain was tried by court-martial and sentenced to be shot. Knowing that the breach of discipline had been attended with many extenuating circumstances, some of us endeavoured to secure his pardon. Possessing ourselves of all the facts, we waited upon the general, who evinced the deepest interest in the object of our visit, and listened with evident sympathy to our plea. There was moisture in his eyes when we repeated the poor fellow's pitiful appeal that he be allowed to die for his country as a soldier on the field of battle, and not as a dog by the muskets of his own comrades. Such solicitude for the success of our efforts did he manifest that he even suggested some things to be done which we had not thought of. At the same time he warned us not to be too hopeful. He said: " It is unquestionably a case of great hardship, but a pardon at this juncture might work greater hardship. Resistance to lawful authority is a grave offence in a soldier. To pardon this man would be to encourage insubordination throughout the army, and so ruin our cause. Still," he added, " I will review the whole case, and no man will be happier than myself if I can reach the same conclusions as you have done." The soldier was shot.' [1]

On another occasion four men were to be executed for desertion to the enemy. The firing party had been ordered to parade at four o'clock in the afternoon, and shortly before the hour a chaplain, not noted for his tact, made his way to the general's tent, and petitioned earnestly that the prisoners might even now be released. Jackson, whom he found pacing backwards and forwards, in evident agitation, watch in hand, listened courteously to his arguments, but made no reply, until at length the worthy minister, in his most impressive manner, said, 'General, consider your responsibility before the Lord. You are sending these men's souls to hell!' With a look of intense

[1] Communicated by the Rev. Dr. Graham.

disgust at such empty cant, Jackson made one stride forward, took the astonished divine by his shoulders, and saying, in his severest tones, 'That, sir, is my business— do you do yours!' thrust him forcibly from the tent.

His severity as regards the more serious offences did not, however, alienate in the smallest degree the confidence and affection of his soldiers. They had full faith in his justice. They were well aware that to order the execution of some unfortunate wretch gave him intense pain. But they recognised, as clearly as he did himself, that it was sometimes expedient that individuals should suffer. They knew that not all men, nor even the greater part, are heroes, and that if the worthless element had once reason to believe that they might escape the legitimate consequences of their crimes, desertion and insubordination would destroy the army. By some of the senior officers, however, his rigorous ideas of discipline were less favourably considered. They were by no means disposed to quarrel with the fact that the sentences of courts-martial in the Second Army Corps were almost invariably confirmed; but they objected strongly to the same measure which they meted out to the men being consistently applied to themselves. They could not be brought to see that neglect of duty, however trivial, on the part of a colonel or brigadier was just as serious a fault as desertion or insubordination on the part of the men; and the conflict of opinion, in certain cases, had unfortunate results.

To those whose conduct he approved he was more than considerate. General Lane, who was under him as a cadet at Lexington, writes as follows :—

'When in camp at Bunker Hill, after the battle of Sharpsburg, where the gallant Branch was killed, I, as colonel commanding the brigade, was directed by General A. P. Hill to hold my command in readiness, with three days' rations, for detached service, and to report to General Jackson for further orders. That was all the information that Hill could give me. I had been in Jackson's corps since the battles round Richmond, and had been very derelict in not paying my respects to my old professor.

As I rode to his headquarters I wondered if he would recognise me. I certainly expected to receive his orders in a few terse sentences, and to be promptly dismissed with a military salute. He knew me as soon as I entered his tent, though we had not met for years. He rose quickly, with a smile on his face, took my hand in both of his in the warmest manner, expressed his pleasure at seeing me, chided me for not having been to see him, and bade me be seated. His kind words, the tones of his voice, his familiarly calling me Lane, whereas it had always been Mr. Lane at the Institute, put me completely at my ease. Then, for the first time, I began to love that reserved man whom I had always honoured and respected as my professor, and whom I greatly admired as my general.

'After a very pleasant and somewhat protracted conversation, he ordered me to move at once, and as rapidly as possible, to North Mountain Depôt, tear up the Baltimore and Ohio Railroad, and put myself in communication with General Hampton (commanding cavalry brigade), who would cover my operations. While we were there General Jackson sent a member of his staff to see how we were progressing. That night I received orders to move at once and quickly to Martinsburg, as there had been heavy skirmishing near Kerneysville. Next morning, when I reported to General Jackson, he received me in the same cordial, warm-hearted manner, complimented me on the thoroughness of my work, told me that he had recommended me for promotion to take permanent charge of Branch's brigade, and that as I was the only person recommended through military channels, I would be appointed in spite of the two aspirants who were trying to bring political influence to bear in Richmond in their behalf. When I rose to go he took my hand in both of his, looked me steadily in the face, and in the words and tones of friendly warmth, which can never be forgotten, again expressed his confidence in my promotion, and bade me good-bye, with a " God bless you, Lane ! " ' [1]

On the other hand, Jackson's treatment of those who

[1] *Memoirs*, pp. 536–7.

failed to obey his orders was very different. No matter how high the rank of the offender, Jackson never sought to screen the crime.[1] No thought that the public rebuke of his principal subordinates might impair their authority or destroy their cordial relations with himself ever stayed his hand; and it may well be questioned whether his disregard of consequences was not too absolutely uncompromising. Men who live in constant dread of their chief's anger are not likely to render loyal and efficient service, and the least friction in the higher ranks is felt throughout the whole command. When the troops begin taking sides and unanimity disappears, the power of energetic combination at once deteriorates. That Jackson was perfectly just is not denied; the misconduct of his subordinates was sometimes flagrant; but it may well be questioned whether to keep officers under arrest for weeks, or even months, marching without their swords in rear of the column, was wholly wise. There is but one public punishment for a senior officer who is guilty of serious misbehaviour, and that is instant dismissal. If he is suffered to remain in the army his presence will always be a source of weakness. But the question will arise, Is it possible to replace him? If he is trusted by his men they will resent his removal, and give but half-hearted support to his successor; so in dealing with those in high places tact and consideration are essential. Even Dr. Dabney admits that in this respect Jackson's conduct is open to criticism.

As already related, he looked on the blunders of his officers, if those blunders were honest, and due simply to misconception of the situation, with a tolerant eye. He knew too much of war and its difficulties to expect that their judgment would be unerring. He never made the mistake of reprehending the man who had done his best to succeed, and contented himself with pointing out, quietly and courteously, how failure might have been avoided. 'But if he believed,' says his chief of the

[1] The five regimental commanders of the Stonewall Brigade were once placed under arrest at the same time for permitting their men to burn fence-rails; they were not released until they had compensated the farmer.

staff, 'that his subordinates were self-indulgent or con-
tumacious, he became a stern and exacting master ; . . .
and during his career a causeless friction was produced
in the working of his government over several gallant
and meritorious officers who served under him. This
was almost the sole fault of his military character :
that by this jealousy of intentional inefficiency he
diminished the sympathy between himself and the
general officers next his person by whom his orders were
to be executed. Had he been able to exercise the same
energetic authority, through the medium of a zealous
personal affection, he would have been a more perfect
leader of armies.' [1]

This system of command was in all probability the outcome of deliberate calculation. No officer, placed in permanent charge of a considerable force, least of all a man who
never acted except upon reflection, and who had a wise regard
for human nature, could fail to lay down for himself certain
principles of conduct towards both officers and men. It may
be, then, that Jackson considered the course he pursued the
best adapted to maintain discipline amongst a number of
ambitious young generals, some of whom had been senior
to himself in the old service, and all of whom had been
raised suddenly, with probably some disturbance to their
self-possession, to high rank. It is to be remembered,
too, that during the campaigns of 1862 his pre-eminent
ability was only by degrees made clear. It was not everyone who, like General Lee, discerned the great qualities of
the silent and unassuming instructor of cadets, and other
leaders, of more dashing exterior, with a well-deserved
reputation for brilliant courage, may well have doubted
whether his capacity was superior to their own.

Such soaring spirits possibly needed a tight hand ; and,
in any case, Jackson had much cause for irritation. With
Wolfe and Sherman he shared the distinguished honour
of being considered crazy by hundreds of self-sufficient
mediocrities. It was impossible that he should have been
ignorant, although not one word of complaint ever passed

[1] Dabney, vol. ii. pp. 519-20.

his lips, how grossly he was misrepresented, how he was caricatured in the press, and credited with the most extravagant and foolhardy ideas of war. Nor did his subordinates, in very many instances, give him that loyal and ungrudging support which he conceived was the due of the commanding general. More than one of his enterprises fell short of the full measure of success owing to the shortcomings of others; and these shortcomings, such as Loring's insubordination at Romney, Steuart's refusal to pursue Banks after Winchester, Garnett's retreat at Kernstown, A. P. Hill's tardiness at Cedar Run, might all be traced to the same cause—disdain of his capacity, and a misconception of their own position. In such circumstances it is hardly to be wondered at if his wrath blazed to a white heat. He was not of a forgiving nature. Once roused, resentment took possession of his whole being, and it may be questioned whether it was ever really appeased. At the same time, the fact that Jackson lacked the fascination which, allied to lofty intellect, wins the hearts of men most readily, and is pre-eminently the characteristic of the very greatest warriors, can hardly be denied. His influence with men was a plant of slow growth. Yet the glamour of his great deeds, the gradual recognition of his unfailing sympathy, his modesty and his truth, produced in the end the same result as the personal charm of Napoleon, of Nelson, and of Lee. His hold on the devotion of his troops was very sure : ' God knows,' said his adjutant-general, weeping the tears of a brave man, ' I would have died for him ! ' and few commanders have been followed with more implicit confidence or have inspired a deeper and more abiding affection. Long years after the war a bronze statue, in his habit as he lived, was erected on his grave at Lexington. Thither, when the figure was unveiled, came the survivors of the Second Army Corps, the men of Manassas and of Sharpsburg, of Fredericksburg and Chancellorsville, and of many another hard-fought field ; and the younger generation looked on the relics of an army whose peer the world has seldom seen. When the guns had fired a salute, the wild rebel yell, the music which the great Virginian had loved so well, rang loud above his grave, and as the last reverberations died away across the hill, the grey-haired ranks stood still and silent. 'See how they loved him!' said one, and it was spoken with deepest reverence. Two well-known officers, who had served under Jackson, were sitting near each other on their horses. Each remarked the silence of the other, and each saw that the other was in tears. 'I'm not ashamed of it, Snowden!' 'Nor I, old boy,' replied the other, as he tried to smile.

When, after the unveiling, the columns marched past the monument, the old fellows looked up, and then bowed their uncovered heads and passed on. But one tall, gaunt soldier of the Stonewall Brigade, as he passed out of the cemetery, looked back for a moment at the life-like figure of his general, and waving his old grey hat towards it, cried out, 'Good-bye, old man, good-bye; we've done all we could for you; good-bye!'

It is not always easy to discern why one general is worshipped, even by men who have never seen him, while another, of equal or even superior capacity, fails to awaken the least spark of affection, except in his chosen friends. Grant was undoubtedly a greater soldier than McClellan, and the genius of Wellington was not less than that of Nelson. And yet, while Nelson and McClellan won all hearts, not one single private had either for Wellington or Grant any warmer sentiment than respect. It would be as unfair, however, to attribute selfishness or want of sympathy to either Wellington or Grant, as to insinuate that Nelson and McClellan were deliberate bidders for popularity. It may be that in the two former the very strength of their patriotism was at fault. To them the State was everything, the individual nothing. To fight for their country was merely a question of duty, into which the idea of glory or recompense hardly entered, and, indifferent themselves either to praise or blame, they considered that the victory of the national arms was a sufficient reward for the soldier's toils. Both were generous and open-handed, exerting themselves incessantly to provide for the comfort and well-being of their troops.

Neither was insensible to suffering, and both were just as capable of self-sacrifice as either Nelson or McClellan. But the standpoint from which they looked at war was too exalted. Nelson and McClellan, on the other hand, recognised that they commanded men, not stoics. Sharing with Napoleon the rare quality of captivating others, a quality which comes by nature or comes not at all, they made allowance for human nature, and identified themselves with those beneath them in the closest *camaraderie*. And herein, to a great extent, lay the secret of the enthusiastic devotion which they inspired.

If the pitiless dissectors of character are right we ought to see in Napoleon the most selfish of tyrants, the coldest and most crafty of charlatans. It is difficult, however, to believe that the hearts of a generation of hardy warriors were conquered merely by ringing phrases and skilful flattery. It should be remembered that from a mercenary force, degraded and despised, he transformed the Grand Army into the terror of Europe and the pride of France. During the years of his glory, when the legions controlled the destinies of their country, none was more honoured than the soldier. His interests were always the first to be considered. The highest ranks in the peerage, the highest offices of State, were held by men who had carried the knapsack, and when thrones were going begging their claims were preferred before all others. The Emperor, with all his greatness, was always ' the Little Corporal ' to his grenadiers. His career was their own. As they shared his glory, so they shared his reward. Every upward step he made towards supreme power he took them with him, and their relations were always of the most cordial and familiar character. He was never happier than when, on the eve of some great battle, he made his bivouac within a square of the Guard ; never more at ease than when exchanging rough compliments with the veterans of Rivoli or Jena. He was the representative of the army rather than of the nation. The men knew that no civilian would be preferred before them ; that their gallant deeds were certain of his recognition ; that their claims to the cross, to pension, and to promotion, would be as carefully considered as the claims of their generals. They loved Napoleon and they trusted him; and whatever may have been his faults, he was 'the Little Corporal,' the friend and comrade of his soldiers, to the end.

It was by the same hooks of steel that Stonewall Jackson grappled the hearts of the Second Army Corps to his own. His men loved him, not merely because he was the bravest man they had ever known, the strongest, and the most resolute, not because he had given them glory, and had made them heroes whose fame was known beyond the confines of the South, but because he was one of themselves, with no interests apart from their interests; because he raised them to his own level, respecting them not merely as soldiers, but as comrades, the tried comrades of many a hard fight and weary march. Although he ruled them with a rod of iron, he made no secret, either officially or privately, of his deep and abiding admiration for their self-sacrificing valour. His very dispatches showed that he regarded his own skill and courage as small indeed when compared with theirs. Like Napoleon's, his congratulatory orders were conspicuous for the absence of all reference to himself; it was always 'we,' not 'I,' and he was among the first to recognise the worth of the rank and file. 'One day,' says Dr. McGuire, 'early in the war, when the Second Virginia Regiment marched by, I said to General Johnston, "If these men will not fight, you have no troops that will." He expressed the prevalent opinion of the day in his reply, saying, "I would not give one company of regulars for the whole regiment." When I returned to Jackson I had occasion to quote General Johnston's opinion. "Did he say that?" he asked, "and of those splendid men?" And then he added: "The patriot volunteer, fighting for his country and his rights, makes the most reliable soldier upon earth." And his veterans knew more than that their general believed them to be heroes. They knew that this great, valiant man, beside whom all others, save Lee himself, seemed small and feeble, this mighty captain, who held the hosts of the enemy in the hollow of his hand, was the

kindest and the most considerate of human beings. To them
he was " Old Jack " in the same affectionate sense as he had
been " Old Jack " to his class-mates at West Point. They
followed him willingly, for they knew that the path he trod
was the way to victory; but they loved him as children
do their parents, because they were his first thought and his
last.

In season and out of season he laboured for their welfare.
To his transport and commissariat officers he was a hard
master. The unfortunate wight who had neglected to bring
up supplies, or who ventured to make difficulties, discovered,
to his cost, that his quiet commander could be very
terrible ; but those officers who did their duty, in whatever
branch of the service they might be serving, found that
their zeal was more than appreciated. For himself
he asked nothing ; on behalf of his subordinates he was a
constant and persistent suitor. He was not only ready to
support the claims to promotion of those who deserved
it, but in the case of those who displayed special merit he
took the initiative himself : and he was not content with
one refusal. His only difference with General Lee, if difference it can be called, was on a question of this nature. The
Commander-in-Chief, it appears, soon after the battle of
Fredericksburg, had proposed to appoint officers to the
Second Army Corps who had served elsewhere. After
some correspondence Jackson wrote as follows :—' My rule
has been to recommend such as were, in my opinion, best
qualified for filling vacancies. The application of this rule
has prevented me from even recommending for the
command of my old brigade one of its officers, because I
did not regard any of them as competent as another of
whose qualifications I had a higher opinion. This rule has
led me to recommend Colonel Bradley T. Johnson for the
command of Taliaferro's brigade. . . . I desire the interest
of the service, and no other interest, to determine who
shall be selected to fill the vacancies. Guided by this
principle, I cannot go outside of my command for persons
to fill vacancies in it, unless by so doing a more competent
officer is secured. This same principle leads me to oppose

having officers who have never served with me, and of whose qualifications I have no knowledge, forced upon me by promoting them to fill vacancies in my command, and advancing them over meritorious officers well qualified for the positions, and of whose qualifications I have had ample opportunities of judging from their having served with me.

'In my opinion, the interest of the service would be injured if I should quietly consent to see officers with whose qualifications I am not acquainted promoted into my command to fill vacancies, regardless of the merits of my own officers who are well qualified for the positions. The same principle leads me, when selections have to be made outside of my command, to recommend those (if there be such) whose former service with me proved them well qualified for filling the vacancies. This induced me to recommend Captain Chew, who does not belong to this army corps, but whose well-earned reputation when with me has not been forgotten.'

And as he studied the wishes of his officers, working quietly and persistently for their advancement, so he studied the wishes of the private soldiers. It is well known that artillerymen come, after a time, to feel a personal affection for their guns, especially those which they have used in battle. When in camp near Fredericksburg Jackson was asked to transfer certain field-pieces, which had belonged to his old division, to another portion of the command. The men were exasperated, and the demand elicited the following letter :—

'December 3, 1862.

'General R. E. LEE,
'Commanding Army of Northern Virginia.

'General,—Your letter of this date, recommending that I distribute the rifle and Napoleon guns "so as to give General D. H. Hill a fair proportion" has been received. I respectfully request, if any such distribution is to be made, that you will direct your chief of artillery or some other officer to do it ; but I hope that none of the guns which belonged to the Army of the Valley before it became part of the Army of Northern Virginia, after the battle of Cedar Run, will be taken from it. If since that time any artillery has improperly come into my command, I trust that it will be taken away, and the person in whose possession it may be found punished, if his conduct requires it. So careful was I to prevent an improper distribution of the artillery and other public property captured at Harper's Ferry, that I issued a written order directing my staff officers to turn over to the proper chiefs of staff of the Army of Northern Virginia all captured stores. A copy of the order is herewith enclosed.

'General D. H. Hill's artillery wants existed at the time he was assigned to my command, and it is hoped that the artillery which belonged to the Army of the Valley will not be taken to supply his wants.

'I am, General, your obedient servant,
'T. J. JACKSON, *Lieutenant-General.*'

No further correspondence is to be found on the subject, so it may be presumed that the protest was successful.

Jackson's relations with the rank and file have already been referred to, and although he was now commander of an army corps, and universally acknowledged as one of the foremost generals of the Confederacy, his rise in rank and reputation had brought no increase of dignity. He still treated the humblest privates with the same courtesy that he treated the Commander-in-Chief. He never repelled their advances, nor refused, if he could, to satisfy their curiosity; and although he seldom went out of his way to speak to them, if any soldier addressed him, especially if he belonged to a regiment recruited from the Valley, he seldom omitted to make some inquiry after those he had left at home. Never, it was said, was his tone more gentle or his smile more winning than when he was speaking to some ragged representative of his old brigade. How his heart went out to them may be inferred from the following. Writing to a friend at Richmond he said : ' Though I have been relieved from command in the Valley, and may never again be assigned to that important trust, yet I feel deeply when I see the patriotic people of that region under the heel of a hateful military despotism. There are all the hopes of those who have been with me from the commencement of the war in Virginia, who have repeatedly left their homes and families in the hands of the enemy, to brave the dangers of battle and disease; and there are those who have so devotedly laboured for the relief of our suffering sick and wounded.'

NOTE

Table showing the Nationality and Average Measurements of 346,744
Federal Soldiers examined for Military Service after March 6,
1863.

	Number.	Height. ft.	Height. in.	Chest at Inspiration. in.
United States (69 per cent.)	237,391	5	7·40	35·61
Germany	35,935	5	5·54	35·88
Ireland .	32,473	5	5·54	35·24
Canada .	15,507	5	5·51	35·42
England	11,479	5	6·02	35·41
France .	2,630	5	5·81	35·29
Scotland	2,127	5	6·13	35·97
Other nationalities, including Wales and five British Colonies .	9,202	—		—
	346,744			

Report of the Provost Marshal General, 1866, p. 698.

The Roll of the 35th Massachusetts, which may be taken as a typical Northern regiment, shows clearly enough at what period the great influx of foreigners took place. Of 104 officers the names of all but four—and these four joined in 1864—are pure English. Of the 964 rank and file of which the regiment was originally composed, only 50 bore foreign names. In 1864, however, 495 recruits were received, and of these over 400 were German immigrants.—*History of the 35th Regiment, Mass. Volunteers, 1862–65.*

CHAPTER XXII

WINTER QUARTERS

DURING the long interval which intervened between the battle of Fredericksburg and the next campaign, Jackson employed himself in preparing the reports of his battles, which had been called for by the Commander-in-Chief. They were not compiled in their entirety by his own hand. He was no novice at literary composition, and his pen, as his letter-book shows, was not that of an unready writer. He had a good command of language, and that power of clear and concise expression which every officer in command of a large force, a position naturally entailing a large amount of confidential correspondence, must necessarily possess. But the task now set him was one of no ordinary magnitude. Since the battle of Kernstown, the report of which had been furnished in April 1862, the time had been too fully occupied to admit of the crowded events being placed on record, and more than one-half of the division, brigade, and regimental commanders who had been engaged in the operations of the period had been killed. Nor, even now, did his duties permit him the necessary leisure to complete the work without assistance. On his requisition, therefore, Colonel Charles Faulkner, who had been United States Minister to France before the war, was attached to his staff for the purpose of collecting the reports of the subordinate commanders, and combining them in the proper form. The rough drafts were carefully gone over by the general. Every sentence was weighed; and everything that might possibly convey a wrong impression was at once rejected; evidence was called to clear up disputed points;

<small>1863.</small>

no inferences or suppositions were allowed to stand ; truth was never permitted to be sacrificed to effect; superlatives were rigorously excluded,[1] and the narratives may be unquestionably accepted as an accurate relation of the facts. Many stirring passages were added by the general's own pen; and the praise bestowed upon the troops, both officers and men, is couched in the warmest terms. Yet much was omitted. Jackson had a rooted objection to represent the motives of his actions, or to set forth the object of his movements. In reply to a remonstrance that those who came after him would be embarrassed by the absence of these explanations, and that his fame would suffer, he said: ' The men who come after me must act for themselves; and as to the historians who speak of the movements of my command, I do not concern myself greatly as to what they may say.' To judge, then, from the reports, Jackson himself had very little to do with his success ; indeed, were they the only evidence available, it would be difficult to ascertain whether the more brilliant manœuvres were ordered by himself or executed on the initiative of others. But in this he was perfectly consistent. When the publisher of an illustrated periodical wrote to him, asking him for his portrait and some notes of his battles as the basis of a sketch, he replied that he had no likeness of himself, and had done nothing worthy of mention. It is not without interest, in this connection, to note that the Old Testament supplied him with a pattern for his reports, just as it supplied him, as he often declared, with precepts and principles applicable to every military emergency. After he was wounded, enlarging one morning on his favourite topic of practical religion, he turned to the staff officer in attendance, Lieutenant Smith, and asked him with a smile: ' Can you tell me where the Bible gives generals a model for their official reports of battles ? ' The aide-de-camp answered, laughing, that it never entered his mind to think of looking for such a thing

---

[1] The report of Sharpsburg, which Jackson had not yet revised at the time of his death, is not altogether free from exaggeration.

in the Scriptures. ' Nevertheless,' said the general, ' there are such ; and excellent models, too. Look, for instance, at the narrative of Joshua's battles with the Amalekites ; there you have one. It has clearness, brevity, modesty ; and it traces the victory to its right source, the blessing of God.'

The early spring of 1863 was undoubtedly one of the happiest seasons of a singularly happy life. Jackson's ambition, if the desire for such rank that would enable him to put the powers within him to the best use may be so termed, was fully gratified. The country lad who, one-and-twenty years ago, on his way to West Point, had looked on the green hills of Virginia from the Capitol at Washington, could hardly have anticipated a higher destiny than that which had befallen him. Over the hearts and wills of thirty thousand magnificent soldiers, the very flower of Southern manhood, his empire was absolute ; and such dominion is neither the heritage of princes nor within the reach of wealth. The most trusted lieutenant of his great commander, the strong right arm with which he had executed his most brilliant enterprises, he shared with him the esteem and admiration not only of the army but of the whole people of the South. The name he had determined, in his lonely boyhood, to bring back to honour already ranked with those of the Revolutionary heroes. Even his enemies, for the brave men at the front left rancour to the politicians, were not proof against the attraction of his great achievements. A friendly intercourse, not always confined to a trade of coffee for tobacco, existed between the outposts; 'Johnnies' and 'Yanks' often exchanged greetings across the Rappahannock ; and it is related that one day when Jackson rode along the river, and the Confederate troops ran together, as was their custom, to greet him with a yell, the Federal pickets, roused by the sudden clamour, crowded to the bank, and shouted across to ask the cause. ' General Stonewall Jackson,' was the proud reply of the grey-coated sentry. Immediately, to his astonishment, the cry, ' Hurrah for Stonewall Jackson ! ' rang out from the Federal ranks, and the voices of North

and South, prophetic of a time to come, mingled in acclamation of a great American.

The situation of the army, although the winter was unusually severe, was not without its compensations. The
country was covered with snow, and storms were frequent;
rations were still scarce,[1] for the single line of badly laid
rails, subjected to the strain of an abnormal traffic, formed
a precarious means of transport; every spring and pond
was frozen; and the soldiers shivered beneath their scanty
coverings.[2] Huts, however, were in process of erection, and
the goodwill of the people did something to supply the deficiencies of the commissariat.[3] The homes of Virginia
were stripped, and many—like Jackson himself, whose
blankets had already been sent from Lexington to his
old brigade—ordered their carpets to be cut up into
rugs and distributed amongst the men. But neither
cold nor hunger could crush the spirit of the troops.
The bivouacs were never merrier than on the bare hills
and in the dark pine-woods which looked down on the
ruins and the graves of Fredericksburg. Picket duty was

---

[1] On January 23 the daily ration was a quarter of a pound of beef, and
one-fifth of a pound of sugar was ordered to be issued in addition, but there
was no sugar! Lee to Davis, O. R., vol. xxi., p. 1110. In the Valley, during
the autumn, the ration had been one and one-eighth pound of flour, and one
and a quarter pounds of beef. On March 27 the ration was eighteen ounces
of flour, and four ounces of indifferent bacon, with occasional issues of rice,
sugar, or molasses. Symptoms of scurvy were appearing, and to supply
the place of vegetables each regiment was directed to send men daily to
gather sassafras buds, wild onions, garlic, &c., &c. Still 'the men are
cheerful,' writes Lee, 'and I receive no complaints.' O. R., vol. xxv.,
part ii., p. 687. On April 17 the ration had been increased by ten pounds of
rice to every 100 men about every third day, with a few peas and dried
fruits occasionally. O. R., vol. xxv., part ii., p. 730.

[2] On January 19, 1,200 pairs of shoes and 400 or 500 pairs of blankets
were forwarded for issue to men without either in D. H. Hill's division.
O. R., vol. xxi., p. 1097. In the Louisiana brigade on the same date, out
of 1,500 men, 400 had no covering for their feet whatever. A large number
had not a particle of underclothing, shirts, socks, or drawers; overcoats were
so rare as to be a curiosity; the 5th Regiment could not drill for want of
shoes; the 8th was almost unfit for duty from the same cause; the condition of the men's feet, from long exposure, was horrible, and the troops
were almost totally unprovided with cooking utensils. O. R., vol. xxi.,
p. 1098.

[3] O. R., vol. xxi., p. 1098.

light, for the black waters of the great river formed a secure barrier against attack ; and if the men's stomachs were empty, they could still feast their eyes on a charming landscape. 'To the right and left the wooded range extended towards Fredericksburg on the one hand, and Port Royal on the other ; in front, the far-stretching level gave full sweep to the eye ; and at the foot of its forest-clad bluffs, or by the margin of undulating fields, the Rappahannock flowed calmly to the sea. Old mansions dotted this beautiful land—for beautiful it was in spite of the chill influences of winter, with its fertile meadows, its picturesque woodlands, and its old roads skirted by long lines of shadowy cedars.' [1]

The headquarters of the Second Army Corps were established at Moss Neck, on the terrace above the Rappahannock, eleven miles below Fredericksburg. After the retreat of the Federals to Falmouth, the Confederate troops had reoccupied their former positions, and every point of passage between Fredericksburg and Port Royal was strongly intrenched and closely watched. At Moss Neck Jackson was not only within easy reach of his divisions, but was more comfortably housed than had usually been the case. A hunting-lodge which stood on the lawn of an old and picturesque mansion-house, the property of a gentleman named Corbin, was placed at his disposal—he had declined the offer of rooms in the house itself lest he should trespass on the convenience of its inmates ; and to show the peculiar constitution of the Confederate army, an anecdote recorded by his biographers is worth quoting. After his first interview with Mrs. Corbin, he passed out to the gate, where a cavalry orderly who had accompanied him was holding his horse. 'Do you approve of your accommodation, General ?' asked the courier. 'Yes, sir, I have decided to make my quarters here.' 'I am Mr. Corbin, sir,' said the soldier, 'and I am very pleased.'

The lower room of the lodge, hung with trophies of the chase, was both his bedroom and his office ; while a large tent, pitched on the grass outside, served as a mess-

[1] Cooke, p. 389.

room for his military family; and here for three long
months, until near the end of March, he rested from the
labour of his campaigns. The Federal troops, on the
snow-clad heights across the river, remained idle in their
camps, slowly recovering from the effects of their defeat
on the fields of Fredericksburg; the pickets had ceased to
bicker; the gunboats had disappeared, and 'all was quiet
on the Rappahannock.' Many of the senior officers in the
Confederate army took advantage of the lull in operations
to visit their homes; but, although his wife urged him to
do the same, Jackson steadfastly refused to absent himself
even for a few days from the front. In November, to his
unbounded delight, a daughter had been born to him. 'To
a man of his extreme domesticity, and love for children,'
says his wife, 'this was a crowning happiness; and yet, with
his great modesty and shrinking from publicity, he requested that he should not receive the announcement by
telegraph, and when it came to him by letter he kept the
glad tidings to himself—leaving his staff and those around
him in the camp to hear of it from others. This was to
him " a joy with which a stranger could not intermeddle,"
and from which even his own hand could not lift the veil
of sanctity. His letters were full of longing to see his little
Julia; for by this name, which had been his mother's, he
had desired her to be christened, saying, " My mother was
mindful of me when I was a helpless, fatherless child, and
I wish to commemorate her now." '

'How thankful I am,' he wrote, ' to our kind Heavenly
Father for having spared my precious wife and given us a
little daughter ! I cannot tell how gratified I am, nor how
much I wish I could be with you and see my two darlings.
But while this pleasure is denied me, I am thankful it is
accorded to you to have the little pet, and I hope it may be
a great deal of company and comfort to its mother. Now,
don't exert yourself to write to me, for to know that you
were exerting yourself to write would give me more pain
than the letter would pleasure, *so you must not do it*. But
you must love your *esposo* in the mean time. . . . I expect
you are just now made up with that baby. Don't you wish

your husband wouldn't claim any part of it, but let you have the sole ownership? Don't you regard it as the most precious little creature in the world? Do not spoil it, and don't let anybody tease it. Don't permit it to have a bad temper. How I would love to see the darling little thing! Give her many kisses from her father.

'At present I am fifty miles from Richmond, and eight miles from Guiney's Station, on the railroad from Richmond to Fredericksburg. Should I remain here, I do hope you and baby can come to see me before spring, as you can come on the railway. Wherever I go, God gives me kind friends. The people here show me great kindness. I receive invitation after invitation to dine out and spend the night, and a great many provisions are sent me, including cakes, tea, loaf-sugar, &c., and the socks and gloves and handkerchiefs still come!

'I am so thankful to our over-kind Heavenly Father for having so improved my eyes as to enable me to write at night. He continually showers blessings upon me; and that you should have been spared, and our darling little daughter given us, fills my heart with overflowing gratitude. If I know my unworthy self, my desire is to live entirely and unreservedly to God's glory. Pray, my darling, that I may so live.'

Again to his sister-in-law: 'I trust God will answer the prayers offered for peace. Not much comfort is to be expected until this cruel war terminates. I haven't seen my wife since last March, and never having seen my child, you can imagine with what interest I look to North Carolina.'

But the tender promptings of his deep natural affection were stilled by his profound faith that 'duty is ours, consequences are God's.' The Confederate army, at this time as at all others, suffered terribly from desertion; and one of his own brigades reported 1,200 officers and men absent without leave.

'Last evening,' he wrote to his wife on Christmas Day, 'I received a letter from Dr. Dabney, saying, "one of the highest gratifications both Mrs. Dabney and I could enjoy would be another visit from Mrs. Jackson," and he invites me to meet you there. He and Mrs. Dabney are very kind, but it appears to me that it is better for me to remain with my command so long as the war continues. . . . If all our troops, officers and men, were at their posts, we might, through God's blessing, expect a more speedy termination of the war. The temporal affairs of some are so deranged as to make a strong plea for their returning home for a short time; but our God has greatly blessed me and mine during my absence, and whilst it would be a great comfort to see you and our darling little daughter, and others in whom I take a special interest, yet duty appears to require me to remain with my command. It is important that those at headquarters set an example by remaining at the post of duty.'

So business at headquarters went on in its accustomed course. There were inspections to be made, the deficiencies of equipment to be made good, correspondence to be conducted—and the control of 30,000 men demanded much office-work—the enemy to be watched, information to be sifted, topographical data to be collected, and the reports of the battles to be written. Every morning, as was his invariable habit during a campaign, the general had an interview with the chiefs of the commissariat, transport, ordnance, and medical departments, and he spent many hours in consultation with his topographical engineer. The great purpose for which Virginia stood in arms was ever present to his mind, and despite his reticence, his staff knew that he was occupied, day and night, with the problems that the future might unfold. Existence at headquarters to the young and high-spirited officers who formed the military family was not altogether lively. Outside there was abundance of gaiety. The Confederate army, even on those lonely hills, managed to extract enjoyment from its surroundings. The hospitality of the plantations was open to the officers, and wherever Stuart and his brigadiers pitched their tents, dances and music were the order of the day. Nor were the men behindhand. Even the heavy snow afforded them entertainment. Whenever a thaw took place they set themselves to making snowballs; and great battles, in which one division was arrayed against another, and which were carried through with the pomp and circumstance of war, colours flying, bugles sounding, and long lines charging elaborately planned intrenchments, were a constant source of amusement, except to unpopular officers. Theatrical and musical performances enlivened the tedium of the long evenings; and when, by the glare of the camp-fires, the band of the 5th Virginia broke into the rattling quick-step of 'Dixie's Land,' not the least stirring of national anthems, and the great concourse of grey-jackets took up the chorus, closing it with a yell

> That shivered to the tingling stars,

the Confederate soldier would not have changed places with the President himself.

There was much social intercourse, too, between the different headquarters. General Lee was no unfrequent visitor to Moss Neck, and on Christmas Day Jackson's aides-de-camp provided a sumptuous entertainment, at which turkeys and oysters figured, for the Commander-in-Chief and the senior generals. Stuart, too, often invaded the quarters of his old comrade, and Jackson looked forward to the merriment that was certain to result just as much as the youngest of his staff. 'Stuart's exuberant cheerfulness and humour,' says Dabney, 'seemed to be the happy relief, as they were the opposites, to Jackson's serious and diffident temper. While Stuart poured out his " quips and cranks," not seldom at Jackson's expense, the latter sat by, sometimes unprepared with any repartee, sometimes blushing, but always enjoying the jest with a quiet and merry laugh. The ornaments on the wall of the general's quarters gave Stuart many a topic of badinage. Affecting to believe that they were of General Jackson's selection, he pointed now to the portrait of some famous race-horse, and now to the print of some celebrated rat-terrier, as queer revelations of his private tastes, indicating a great decline in his moral character, which would be a grief and disappointment to the pious old ladies of the South. Jackson, with a quiet smile, replied that perhaps he had had more to do with race-horses than his friends suspected. It was in the midst of such a scene as this that dinner was announced, and the two generals passed to the mess-table. It so happened that Jackson had just received, as a present from a patriotic lady, some butter, upon the adornment of which the fair donor had exhausted her housewife's skill. The servants, in honour of General Stuart's presence, had chosen this to grace the centre of the board. As his eye fell upon it, he paused, and with mock gravity pointed to it, saying, "There, gentlemen! If that is not the crowning evidence of our host's sporting tastes. He even has his favourite game-cock stamped on his butter!" The dinner, of course, began with great laughter, in which Jackson joined, with as much enjoyment as any.'

Visitors, too, from Europe, attracted by the fame of the army and its leaders, had made their way into the Confederate lines, and were received with all the hospitality that the camps afforded. An English officer has recorded his experiences at Moss Neck :—

'I brought from Nassau a box of goods (a present from England) for General Stonewall Jackson, and he asked me when I was at Richmond to come to his camp and see him. I left the city one morning about seven o'clock, and about ten landed at a station distant some eight or nine miles from Jackson's (or, as his men called him, "Old Jack's") camp. A heavy fall of snow had covered the country for some time before to the depth of a foot, and formed a crust over the Virginian mud, which is quite as villainous as that of Balaclava. The day before had been mild and wet, and my journey was made in a drenching shower, which soon cleared away the white mantle of snow. You cannot imagine the slough of despond I had to pass through. Wet to the skin, I stumbled through mud, I waded through creeks, I passed through pine-woods, and at last got into camp about two o'clock. I then made my way to a small house occupied by the general as his headquarters. I wrote down my name, and gave it to the orderly, and I was immediately told to walk in.

'The general rose and greeted me warmly. I expected

to see an old, untidy man, and was most agreeably surprised and pleased with his appearance. He is tall, handsome, and powerfully built, but thin. He has brown hair and a brown beard. His mouth expresses great determination. The lips are thin and compressed firmly together; his eyes are blue and dark, with keen and searching expression. I was told that his age was thirty-eight, and he looks forty. The general, who is indescribably simple and unaffected in all his ways, took off my wet overcoat with his own hands, made up the fire, brought wood for me to put my feet on to keep them warm while my boots were drying, and then began to ask me questions on various subjects. At the dinner hour we went out and joined the members of his staff. At this meal the general said grace in a fervent, quiet manner, which struck me very much. After dinner I returned to his room, and he again talked for a long time. The servant came in and took his mattress out of a cupboard and laid it on the floor.

'As I rose to retire, the general said, " Captain, there is plenty of room on my bed, I hope you will share it with me?" I thanked him very much for his courtesy, but said "Good-night," and slept in a tent, sharing the blankets of one of his aides-de-camp. In the morning at breakfast-time I noticed that the general said grace before the meal with the same fervour I had remarked before. An hour or two afterwards it was time for me to return to the station; on this occasion, however, I had a horse, and I returned to the general's headquarters to bid him adieu. His little room was vacant, so I slipped in and stood before the fire. I then noticed my greatcoat stretched before it on a chair. Shortly afterwards the general entered the room. He said: "Captain, I have been trying to dry your greatcoat, but I am afraid I have not succeeded very well." That little act illustrates the man's character. With the care and responsibilities of a vast army on his shoulders he finds time to do little acts of kindness and thoughtfulness.'

With each of his staff officers he was on most friendly

terms; and the visitors to his camp, such as the English officer quoted above, found him a most delightful host, discussing with the ease of an educated gentleman all manner of topics, and displaying not the slightest trace of that awkwardness and extreme diffidence which have been attributed to him. The range and accuracy of his information surprised them. 'Of military history,' said another English soldier, 'he knew more than any other man I met in America; and he was so far from displaying the somewhat grim characteristics that have been associated with his name, that one would have thought his tastes lay in the direction of art and literature.' 'His chief delight,' wrote the Hon. Francis Lawley, who knew him well, 'was in the cathedrals of England, notably in York Minster and Westminster Abbey. He was never tired of talking about them, or listening to details about the chapels and cloisters of Oxford.'[1]

'General Jackson,' writes Lord Wolseley, 'had certainly very little to say about military operations, although he was intensely proud of his soldiers, and enthusiastic in his devotion to General Lee; and it was impossible to make him talk of his own achievements. Nor can I say that his speech betrayed his intellectual powers. But his manner, which was modesty itself, was most attractive. He put you at your ease at once, listening with marked courtesy and attention to whatever you might say; and when the subject of conversation was congenial, he was a most interesting companion. I quite endorse the statement as to his love for beautiful things. He told me that in all his travels he had seen nothing so beautiful as the lancet windows in York Minster.'

In his daily intercourse with his staff, however, in his office or in the mess-room, he showed to less advantage than in the society of strangers. His gravity of demeanour seldom wholly disappeared, his intense earnestness was in itself oppressive, and he was often absent and preoccupied. 'Life at headquarters,' says one of his staff officers, 'was decidedly dull. Our meals were often very

[1] *The Times*, June 11, 1863.

dreary. The general had no time for light or trivial conversation, and he sometimes felt it his duty to rebuke our thoughtless and perhaps foolish remarks. Nor was it always quite safe to approach him. Sometimes he had a tired look in his eyes, and although he never breathed a word to one or another, we knew that he was dissatisfied with what was being done with the army.' [1]

Intense concentration of thought and purpose, in itself an indication of a powerful will, had distinguished Jackson from his very boyhood. During his campaigns he would pace for hours outside his tent, his hands clasped behind his back, absorbed in meditation; and when the army was on the march, he would ride for hours without raising his eyes or opening his lips. It was unquestionably at such moments that he was working out his plans, step by step, forecasting the counter-movements of the enemy, and providing for every emergency that might occur. And here the habit of keeping his whole faculties fixed on a single object, and of imprinting on his memory the successive processes of complicated problems, fostered by the methods of study which, both at West Point and Lexington, the weakness of his eyes had made compulsory, must have been an inestimable advantage. Brilliant strategical manœuvres, it cannot be too often repeated, are not a matter of inspiration and of decision on the spur of the moment. The problems presented by a theatre of war, with their many factors, are not to be solved except by a vigorous and sustained intellectual effort. 'If,' said Napoleon, 'I always appear prepared, it is because, before entering on an undertaking, I have meditated for long and have foreseen what may occur. It is not genius which reveals to me suddenly and secretly what I should do in circumstances unexpected by others; it is thought and meditation.'

The proper objective, speaking in general terms, of all military operations is the main army of the enemy, for a campaign can never be brought to a successful conclusion until the hostile forces in the field have become demoralised

[1] Letter from Dr. Hunter McGuire.

by defeat; but, to ensure success, preponderance of numbers is usually essential, and it may be said, therefore, that the proper objective is the enemy's main army when it is in inferior strength.

Under ordinary conditions, the first step, then, towards victory must be a movement, or a series of movements, which will compel the enemy to divide his forces, and put it out of his power to assemble even equal strength on the battle-field.

This entails a consideration of the strategic points upon the theatre of war, for it is by occupying or threatening some point which the enemy cannot afford to lose that he will be induced to disperse his army, or to place himself in a position where he can be attacked at a disadvantage. While his main army, therefore, is the ultimate objective, certain strategic points become the initial objectives, to be occupied or threatened either by the main body or detached forces. It is seldom, however, that these initial objectives are readily discovered; and it is very often the case that even the ultimate objective may be obscured.

These principles are well illustrated by the operations in the Valley of Virginia during the month of May and the first fortnight of June, 1862. After the event it is easy to see that Banks' army was Jackson's proper objective—being the principal force in the secondary theatre of war. But at the time, before the event, Lee and Jackson alone realised the importance of overwhelming Banks and thus threatening Washington. It was not realised by Johnston, a most able soldier, for the whole of his correspondence goes to show that he thought a purely defensive attitude the best policy for the Valley Army. It was not realised by Jackson's subordinates, for it was not till long after the battle of Winchester that the real purport of the operations in which they had been engaged began to dawn on them. It was not realised by Lincoln, by Stanton, or even by McClellan, for to each of them the sudden attack on Front Royal was as much of a surprise as to Banks himself; and we may be perfectly confident that none but a trained strategist, after a prolonged study of the map and the situation, would realise it now.

It is to be noted, too, that Jackson's initial objectives— the strategical points in the Valley—were invariably well selected. The Luray Gap, the single road which gives access across the Massanuttons from one side of the Valley to the other, was the most important. The flank position on Elk Run, the occupation of which so suddenly brought up Banks, prevented him interposing between Jackson and Edward Johnson, and saved Staunton from capture, was a second; Front Royal, by seizing which he threatened Banks at Strasburg in flank and rear, compelling him to a hasty retreat, and bringing him to battle on ground which he had not prepared, a third; and the position at Port Republic, controlling the only bridge across the Shenandoah, and separating Shields from Frémont, a fourth. The bearing of all these localities was overlooked by the Federals, and throughout the campaign we cannot fail to notice a great confusion on their part as regards objectives. They neither recognised what the aim of their enemy would be, nor at what they should aim themselves. It was long before they discovered that Lee's army, and not Richmond, was the vital point of the Confederacy. Not a single attempt was made to seize strategic points, and if we may judge from the orders and dispatches in the Official Records, their existence was never recognised. To this oversight the successive defeats of the Northern forces were in great part due. From McClellan to Banks, each one of their generals appears to have been blind to the advantages that may be derived from a study of the theatre of war. Not one of them hit upon a line of operations which embarrassed the Confederates, and all possessed the unhappy knack of joining battle on the most unfavourable terms. Moreover, when it at last became clear that the surest means of conquering a country is to defeat its armies, the true objective was but vaguely realised. The annihilation of the enemy's troops seems to have been the last thing dreamt of. Opportunities of crushing him in detail were neither sought for nor created. As General

Sheridan said afterwards: 'The trouble with the commanders of the Army of the Potomac was that they never marched out to "lick" anybody; all they thought of was to escape being "licked" themselves.'

But it is not sufficient, in planning strategical combinations, to arrive at a correct conclusion as regards the objective. Success demands a most careful calculation of ways and means: of the numbers at disposal; of food, forage, and ammunition; and of the forces to be detached for secondary purposes. The different factors of the problem—the strength and dispositions of the enemy, the roads, railways, fortresses, weather, natural features, the *moral* of the opposing armies, the character of the opposing general, the facilities for supply—have each and all of them to be considered, their relative prominence assigned to them, and their conflicting claims to be brought into adjustment.

For such mental exertion Jackson was well equipped. He had made his own the experience of others. His knowledge of history made him familiar with the principles which had guided Washington and Napoleon in the selection of objectives, and with the means by which they attained them. It is not always easy to determine the benefit, beyond a theoretical acquaintance with the phenomena of the battle-field, to be derived from studying the campaigns of the great masters of war. It is true that no successful general, whatever may have been his practical knowledge, has neglected such study; but while many have borne witness to its efficacy, none have left a record of the manner in which their knowledge of former campaigns influenced their own conduct.

In the case of Stonewall Jackson, however, we have much evidence, indirect, but unimpeachable, as to the value to a commander of the knowledge thus acquired. The Maxims of Napoleon, carried in his haversack, were constantly consulted throughout his campaigns, and this little volume contains a fairly complete exposition, in Napoleon's own words, of the grand principles of war. Moreover, Jackson often quoted principles which are not to be found in the Maxims, but on which Napoleon consistently acted. It is clear, therefore, that he had studied the campaigns of the great Corsican in order to discover the principles on which military success is based ; that having studied and reflected on those principles, and the effect their application produced, in numerous concrete cases, they became so firmly imbedded in his mind as to be ever present, guiding him into the right path, or warning him against the wrong, whenever he had to deal with a strategic or tactical situation.

It may be noted, moreover, that these principles, especially those which he was accustomed to quote, were concerned far more with the moral aspect of war than with the material. It is a fair inference, therefore, that it was to the study of human nature as affected by the conditions of war, by discipline, by fear, by the want of food, by want of information, by want of confidence, by the weight of responsibility, by political interests, and, above all, by surprise, that his attention was principally directed. He found in the campaigns of Jena and of Austerlitz not merely a record of marches and manœuvres, of the use of intrenchments, or of the general rules for attack and defence ; this is the mechanical and elementary part of the science of command. What Jackson learned was the truth of the famous maxim that the moral is to the physical—that is, to armament and numbers—as three to one. He learned, too, to put himself into his adversary's place and to realise his weakness. He learned, in a word, that war is a struggle between two intellects rather than the conflict of masses ; and it was by reason of this knowledge that he played on the hearts of his enemies with such extraordinary skill.

It is not to be asserted, however, that the study of military history is an infallible means of becoming a great or even a good general. The first qualification necessary for a leader of men is a strong character, the second, a strong intellect. With both Providence had endowed Jackson, and the strong intellect illuminates and explains the page that to others is obscure and meaningless. With its innate faculty for discerning what is essential and for discarding unimportant details, it discovers most valuable lessons where ordinary men see neither light nor leading. Endowed with the power of analysis and assimilation, and accustomed to observe and to reflect upon the relations between cause and effect, it will undoubtedly penetrate far deeper into the actual significance and practical bearing of historical facts than the mental vision which is less acute.

Jackson, by reason of his antecedent training, was eminently capable of the sustained intellectual efforts which strategical conceptions involve. Such was his self-command that under the most adverse conditions, the fatigues and anxieties of a campaign, the fierce excitement of battle, his brain, to use the words of a great Confederate general, 'worked with the precision of the most perfect machinery.'[1] But it was not only in the field, when the necessity for action was pressing, that he was accustomed to seclude himself with his own thoughts. Nor was he content with considering his immediate responsibilities. His interest in the general conduct of the war was of a very thorough-going character. While in camp on the Rappahannock, he followed with the closest attention the movements of the armies operating in the Valley of the Mississippi, and made himself acquainted, so far as was possible, not only with the local conditions of the war, but also with the character of the Federal leaders. It was said that, in the late spring of 1862, it was the intention of Mr. Davis to transfer him to the command of the Army of the Tennessee, and it is possible that some inkling of this determination induced him to study the Western theatre.[2] Be this as it may, the general situation, military and political, was always in his mind, and despite the victory of Fredericksburg, the future was dark and the indications ominous.

According to the Official Records, the North, at the beginning of April, had more than 900,000 soldiers under

---

[1] General G. B. Gordon. *Introduction to Memoirs of Stonewall Jackson,* p. xiv.

[2] In April he wrote to his wife: 'There is increasing probability that I may be elsewhere as the season advances.' That he said no more is characteristic.

arms ; the South, so far as can be ascertained, not more than 600,000. The Army of the Potomac was receiving constant reinforcements, and at the beginning of April, 130,000 men were encamped on the Stafford Heights. In the West, the whole extent of the Mississippi, with the exception of the hundred miles between Vicksburg and Port Hudson, was held by the Federals, and those important fortresses were both threatened by large armies, acting in concert with a formidable fleet of gunboats. A third army, over 50,000 strong, was posted at Murfreesboro', in the heart of Tennessee, and large detached forces were operating in Louisiana and Arkansas. The inroads of the enemy in the West, greatly aided by the waterways, were in fact far more serious than in the East ; but even in Virginia, although the Army of the Potomac had spent nearly two years in advancing fifty miles, the Federals had a strong foothold. Winchester had been reoccupied. Fortress Monroe was still garrisoned. Suffolk, on the south bank of the James, seventy miles from Richmond, was held by a force of 20,000 men ; while another small army, of about the same strength, occupied New Berne, on the North Carolina coast.

Slowly but surely, before the pressure of vastly superior numbers, the frontiers of the Confederacy were contracting ; and although in no single direction had a Federal army moved more than a few miles from the river which supplied it, yet the hostile occupation of these rivers, so essential to internal traffic, was making the question of subsistence more difficult every day. Louisiana, Texas and Arkansas, the cattle-raising States, were practically cut off from the remainder ; and in a country where railways were few, distances long, and roads indifferent, it was impossible, in default of communication by water, to accumulate and distribute the produce of the farms. Moreover, the dark menace of the blockade had assumed more formidable proportions. The Federal navy, gradually increasing in numbers and activity, held the highway of the ocean in an iron grip ; and proudly though the Confederacy bore her isolation, men looked across the waters with dread foreboding, for the shadow of their doom was already rising from the pitiless sea.

If, then, his staff officers had some reason to complain
of their chief's silence and abstraction, it was by no means
unfortunate for the South, so imminent was the danger,
that the strong brain was incessantly occupied in forecasting the emergencies that might occur.

But not for a single moment did Jackson despair of
ultimate success. His faith in the justice of the Southern
cause was as profound as his trust in God's good providence. He had long since realised that the overwhelming
strength of the Federals was more apparent than real. He
recognised their difficulties; he knew that the size of an
army is limited to the number that can be subsisted,
and he relied much on the superior *moral* and the
superior leading of the Confederate troops. After long
and mature deliberation he had come to a conclusion as to
the policy to be pursued. 'We must make this campaign,'
he said, in a moment of unusual expansion, 'an exceedingly active one. Only thus can a weaker country
cope with a stronger; it must make up in activity what it
lacks in strength. A defensive campaign can only be
made successful by taking the aggressive at the proper time.
Napoleon never waited for his adversary to become fully
prepared, but struck him the first blow.'

On these principles Jackson had good reason to believe
General Lee had determined to act;[1] of their efficacy he
was convinced, and when his wife came to visit him at
the end of April, she found him in good heart and the
highest spirits. He not only anticipated a decisive result
from the forthcoming operations, but he had seen with
peculiar satisfaction that a more manly tone was pervading
the Confederate army. Taught by their leaders, by Lee,
Jackson, Stuart, and many others, of whose worth and
valour they had received convincing proof, the Southern
soldiers had begun to practise the clean and wholesome
virtue of self-control. They had discovered that purity

---

[1] 'There is no better way of defending a long line than by moving into
the enemy's country.' Lee to General Jones, March 21, 1863; O. R.,
vol. xxv., part ii., p. 680.

and temperance are by no means incompatible with
military prowess, and that a practical piety, faithful in
small things as in great, detracts in no degree from skill
and resolution in the field.   The Stonewall Brigade
set the example.   As soon as their own huts were
finished, the men, of their own volition, built a log
church, where both officers and men, without distinction of
rank, were accustomed to assemble during the winter
evenings ; and those rude walls, illuminated by pine torches
cut from the neighbouring forest, witnessed such scenes
as filled Jackson's cup of content to overflowing. A chaplain writes : ' The devout listener, dressed in simple grey,
ornamented only with three stars, which any Confederate
colonel was entitled to wear, is our great commander,
Robert Edward Lee.   That dashing-looking cavalry-man,
with " fighting jacket," plumed hat, jingling spurs, and gay
decorations, but solemn, devout aspect during the service,
is " Jeb " Stuart, the flower of cavaliers—and all through
the vast crowd wreaths and stars of rank mingle with the
bars of the subordinate officers and the rough garb of the
private soldier.   But perhaps the most supremely happy of
the gathered thousands is Stonewall Jackson.'   ' One could
not,' says another, ' sit in that pulpit and meet the concentrated gaze of those men without deep emotion.   I
remembered that they were the veterans of many a bloody
field.   The eyes which looked into mine, waiting for the
Gospel of peace, had looked steadfastly upon whatever is
terrible in war.   Their earnestness of aspect constantly
impressed me. . . . They looked as if they had come on
business, and very important business, and the preacher
could scarcely do otherwise than feel that he, too, had
business of moment there ! '

At this time, largely owing to Jackson's exertions,
chaplains were appointed to regiments and brigades, and
ministers from all parts of the country were invited to
visit the camps. The Chaplains' Association, which did a
good work in the army, was established at his suggestion,
and although he steadfastly declined to attend its meetings,

deeming them outside his functions, nothing was neglected, so far as lay within his power, that might forward the moral welfare of the troops.

But at the same time their military efficiency and material comforts received his constant attention. Discipline was made stricter, indolent and careless officers were summarily dismissed, and the divisions were drilled at every favourable opportunity. Headquarters had been transferred to a tent near to Hamilton's Crossing, the general remarking, ' It is rather a relief to get where there will be less comfort than in a room, as I hope thereby persons will be prevented from encroaching so much upon my time.' On his wife's arrival he moved to Mr. Yerby's plantation, near Hamilton's Crossing, but ' he did not permit,' she writes, ' the presence of his family to interfere in any way with his military duties. The greater part of each day he spent at his headquarters, but returned as early as he could get off from his labours, and devoted all his leisure time to his visitors—little Julia having his chief attention and his care. His devotion to his child was remarked upon by all who beheld the happy pair together, for she soon learned to delight in his caresses as much as he loved to play with her. An officer's wife, who saw him often during this time, wrote to a friend in Richmond that " the general spent all his leisure time in playing with the baby." '

But these quiet and happy days were soon ended. On April 29 the roar of cannon was heard once more at Guiney's Station, salvo after salvo following in quick succession, until the house shook and the windows rattled with the reverberations. The crash of musketry succeeded, rapid and continuous, and before the sun was high wounded men were brought in to the shelter of Mr. Yerby's outhouses. Very early in the morning a message from the pickets had come in, and after making arrangements for his wife and child to leave at once for Richmond, the general, without waiting for breakfast, had hastened to the front. The Federals were crossing the

Rappahannock, and Stonewall Jackson had gone to his last field.[1]

[1] The Army of the Potomac was now constituted as follows:—

Engineer Brigade.

First Corps.	Reynolds.
Second Corps.	Couch.
Third Corps.	Sickles.
Divisions.	Birney. Berry. Whipple.
Fifth Corps.	Meade.
Sixth Corps.	Sedgwick.
Eleventh Corps.	Howard.
Divisions.	McLean. Von Steinwehr. Schurz.
Twelfth Corps.	Slocum.
Divisions.	Williams. Geary
Cavalry Corps.	Stoneman.
Divisions.	Pleasonton. Averell. Gregg.

NOTE

Headquarters, Second Corps, Army of N. Va. :
April 13, 1863.
General Orders, No. 26.

I. . . . .

II. Each division will move precisely at the time indicated in the order of march, and if a division or brigade is not ready to move at that time, the next will proceed and take its place, even if a division should be separated thereby.

III. On the march the troops are to have a rest of ten minutes each hour. The rate of march is not to exceed one mile in twenty-five minutes, unless otherwise specially ordered. The time of each division commander will be taken from that of the corps commander. When the troops are halted for the purpose of resting, arms will be stacked, ranks broken, and in no case during the march will the troops be allowed to break ranks without previously stacking arms.

IV. When any part of a battery or train is disabled on a march, the officer in charge must have it removed immediately from the road, so that no part of the command be impeded upon its march.

Batteries or trains must not stop in the line of march to water; when any part of a battery or train, from any cause, loses its place in the column, it must not pass any part of the column in regaining its place.

Company commanders will march at the rear of their respective companies; officers must be habitually occupied in seeing that orders are strictly enforced; a day's march should be with them a day of labour; as much vigilance is required on the march as in camp.

Each division commander will, as soon as he arrive at his camping-ground, have the company rolls called, and guard details marched to the front of the regiment before breaking ranks; and immediately afterwards establish his chain of sentinels, and post his pickets so as to secure the safety of his command, and will soon thereafter report to their headquarters the disposition made for the security of his camp.

Division commanders will see that all orders respecting their divisions are carried out strictly; each division commander before leaving an encampment will have all damages occasioned by his command settled for by payment or covered by proper certificates.

V. All ambulances in the same brigade will be receipted for by the brigade quartermaster, they will be parked together, and habitually kept together, not being separated unless the exigencies of the service require, and on marches follow in rear of their respective brigades.

Ample details will be made for taking care of the wounded;

those selected will wear the prescribed badge; and no other person belonging to the army will be permitted to take part in this important trust.

Any one leaving his appropriate duty, under pretext of taking care of the wounded, will be promptly arrested, and as soon as charges can be made out, they will be forwarded.

By command of Lieutenant-General Jackson,

A. S. PENDLETON,
Assistant Adjutant-General.

CHAPTER XXIII

CHANCELLORSVILLE

It has already been said that while the Army of Northern Virginia lay in winter quarters the omens did not point to decisive success in the forthcoming campaign. During the same period that Lincoln and Stanton, taught by successive disasters, had ceased to interfere with their generals, Jefferson Davis and Mr. Seddon, his new Secretary of War, had taken into their own hands the complete control of military operations. The results appeared in the usual form : on the Northern side, unity of purpose and concentration; on the Southern, uncertainty of aim and dispersion. In the West the Confederate generals were fatally hampered by the orders of the President. In the East the Army of Northern Virginia, confronted by a mass of more than 130,000 foes, was deprived of three of Longstreet's divisions ; and when, at the end of April, it was reported that Hooker was advancing, it was absolutely impossible that this important detachment could rejoin in time to assist in the defence of the Rappahannock.

A full discussion of the Chancellorsville campaign does not fall within the scope of this biography, but in justice to the Southern generals—to Lee who resolved to stand his ground, and to Jackson who approved the resolution—it must be explained that they were in no way responsible for the absence of 20,000 veterans. Undoubtedly the situation on the Atlantic littoral was sufficiently embarrassing to the Confederate authorities. The presence of a Federal force at New Berne, in North Carolina, threatened the main line of railway by which Wilmington and Charleston communicated with Richmond, and these two ports were of the utmost

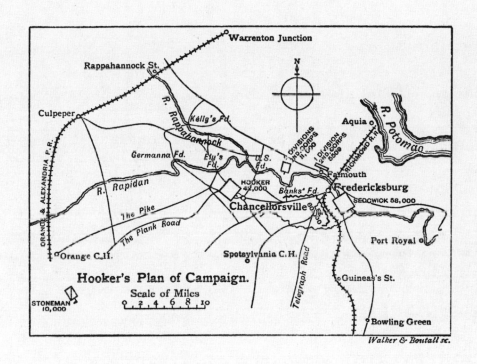

Hooker's Plan of Campaign.

Scale of Miles

Walker & Boutall sc.

importance to the Confederacy. So enormous were the
profits arising from the exchange of munitions of war and
medicines [1] for cotton and tobacco that English shipowners
embarked eagerly on a lucrative if precarious traffic.
Blockade-running became a recognised business. Companies were organised which possessed large fleets of swift
steamers. The Bahamas and Bermuda became vast entre-
pôts of trade. English seamen were not to be deterred
from a perilous enterprise by fear of Northern broadsides
or Northern prisons, and despite the number and activity
of the blockading squadrons the cordon of cruisers and
gunboats was constantly broken. Many vessels were sunk,
many captured, many wrecked on a treacherous coast, and
yet enormous quantities of supplies found their way to the
arsenals and magazines of Richmond and Atlanta. The railways, then, leading from Wilmington and Charleston, the
ports most accessible to the blockade-runners, were almost
essential to the existence of the Confederacy. Soon after
the battle of Fredericksburg, General D. H. Hill was
placed in command of the forces which protected them,
and, at the beginning of the New Year, Ransom's division [2]
was drawn from the Rappahannock to reinforce the local
levies. A few weeks later [3] General Lee was induced by
Mr. Seddon to send Longstreet, with the divisions of Hood
and Pickett,[4] to cover Richmond, which was menaced both
from Fortress Monroe and Suffolk.[5]

The Commander-in-Chief, however, while submitting
to this detachment as a necessary evil, had warned General
Longstreet so to dispose his troops that they could return
to the Rappahannock at the first alarm. 'The enemy's
position,' he wrote, 'on the sea-coast had been probably
occupied merely for purposes of defence, it was likely that
they were strongly intrenched, and nothing would be gained
by attacking them.'

[1] Quinine sold in the South for one hundred dollars (Confederate) the
ounce. O. R., vol. xxv., part ii., p. 79.
[2] 3,594 officers and men. Report of December 1. O. R., vol. xxi., p. 1082.
[3] Middle of February.
[4] Pickett, 7,165 ; Hood, 7,956—15,121 officers and men.
[5] Lee thought Pickett was sufficient. O. R., vol. xxi., p. 623.

The warning, however, was disregarded; and that Mr. Seddon should have yielded, in the first instance, to the influence of the sea-power, exciting apprehensions of sudden attack along the whole seaboard of the Confederacy, may be forgiven him. Important lines of communication were certainly exposed. But when, in defiance of Lee's advice that the divisions should be retained within easy reach of Fredericksburg, he suggested to Longstreet the feasibility of an attack on Suffolk, one hundred and twenty miles distant from the Rappahannock, he committed an unpardonable blunder.

Had Jackson been in Longstreet's place, the Secretary's proposal, however promising of personal renown, would unquestionably have been rejected. The leader who had kept the main object so steadfastly in view throughout the Valley campaign would never have overlooked the expressed wishes of the Commander-in-Chief. Longstreet, however, brilliant fighting soldier as he was, appears to have misconceived the duties of a detached force. He was already prejudiced in favour of a movement against Suffolk. Before he left for his new command, he had suggested to Lee that one army corps only should remain on the Rappahannock, while the other operated south of Richmond; and soon after his arrival he urged upon his superior that, in case Hooker moved, the Army of Northern Virginia should retire to the North Anna. In short, to his mind the operations of the main body should be made subservient to those of the detached force; Lee, with 30,000 men, holding Hooker's 130,000 in check until Longstreet had won his victory and could march north to join him. Such strategy was not likely to find favour at headquarters. It was abundantly evident, in the first place, that the Army of Northern Virginia must be the principal objective of the Federals; and, in the second place, that the defeat of the force of Suffolk, if it were practicable, would have no effect whatever upon Hooker's action, except insomuch that his knowledge of Longstreet's absence might quicken his resolution to advance. Had Suffolk been a point vital to the North the question would have assumed a different shape. As it was, the town merely covered a tract of conquered territory, the Norfolk dockyard, and the mouth of the James River. The Confederates would gain little by its capture; the Federals would hardly feel its loss. It was most improbable that a single man of Hooker's army would be detached to defend a point of such comparative insignificance, and it was quite possible that Longstreet would be unable to get back in time to meet him, even on the North Anna. General Lee, however, anxious as ever to defer to the opinions of the man on the spot, as well as to meet the wishes of the Government, yielded to Longstreet's insistence that a fine opportunity for an effective blow presented itself, and in the first week of April the latter marched against Suffolk.

His movement was swift and sudden. But, as Lee had anticipated, the Federal position was strongly fortified, with the flanks secure, and Longstreet had no mind to bring April 17. matters to a speedy conclusion. 'He could reduce the place,' he wrote on April 17, 'in two or three days, but the expenditure of ammunition would be very large; or he could take it by assault, but at a cost of 3,000 men.'

The Secretary of War agreed with him that the sacrifice would be too great, and so, at a time when Hooker was becoming active on the Rappahannock, Lee's lieutenant was quietly investing Suffolk, one hundred and twenty miles away.

From that moment the Commander-in-Chief abandoned all hope that his missing divisions would be with him when Hooker moved. Bitterly indeed was he to suffer for his selection of a commander for his detached force. The loss of 3,000 men at Suffolk, had the works been stormed, and Hood and Pickett marched instantly to the Rappahannock, would have been more than repaid. The addition of 12,000 fine soldiers, flushed with success, and led by two of the most brilliant fighting generals in the Confederate armies, would have made the victory of Chancellorsville a decisive triumph. Better still had Longstreet adhered to his original orders. But both he and Mr. Seddon forgot, as

Jackson never did, the value of time, and the grand principle of concentration at the decisive point.

Happily for the South, Hooker, although less flagrantly, was also oblivious of the first axiom of war. As soon as the weather improved he determined to move against Richmond. His task, however, was no simple one. On the opposite bank of the Rappahannock, from Banks' Ford to Port Royal, a distance of twenty miles, frowned line upon line of fortifications, protected by abattis, manned by a numerous artillery, against which it was difficult to find position for the Federal guns, and occupied by the victors of Fredericksburg. A frontal attack gave even less promise of success than in Burnside's disastrous battle. But behind Lee's earthworks were his lines of supply; the Richmond Railway, running due south, with the road to Bowling Green alongside; and second, the plank road, which, running at first due west, led past Chancellorsville, a large brick mansion, standing in a dense forest, to Orange Court House and the depôts on the Virginia Central Railroad.

At these roads and railways Hooker determined to strike, expecting that Lee would at once fall back, and give the Army of the Potomac the opportunity of delivering a heavy blow.[1] To effect his object he divided his 130,000 men into three distinct bodies. The cavalry, which, with the exception of one small brigade, had moved under General Stoneman to Warrenton Junction, was to march by way of Rappahannock Station, and either capturing or passing Culpeper and Gordonsville, to cut the Confederate communications, and should Lee retreat, to hold him fast.[2] General Sedgwick, with two army corps, the First and Sixth, forming the left wing of the army, was to cross the river below Fredericksburg, make a brisk demonstration of attack, and if the enemy fell back follow him rapidly down the Bowling Green and Telegraph roads. Then, while Lee's attention was thus attracted, the right wing,

---

[1] Hooker to Lincoln, April 12, O. R., vol. xxv., part ii., p. 199.
[2] The cavalry was to take supplies for six days, food and forage, depending on the country and on captures for any further quantity that might be required.

composed of the Fifth, Eleventh, and Twelfth Corps, with Pleasonton's brigade of cavalry, under Hooker's own command, would move up the Rappahannock to Kelly's Ford, push forward to the Rapidan, cross at Ely's and Germanna fords, and march upon Chancellorsville. The Third Corps was to remain concentrated on the Stafford Heights, ready to reinforce either wing as circumstances might require. The Second Corps was to leave one division on outpost at Falmouth, and to post two divisions on the north bank of the Rappahannock opposite Banks' Ford.

It will be observed that this design would place a wide interval between the two wings of the Federal army, thus giving the Confederates, although much inferior in numbers, the advantage of the interior lines.[1] Hooker, however, who knew the Confederate strength to a man, was confident that Lee, directly he found his position turned, and Stoneman in his rear, would at once retreat on Richmond. Yet he was not blind to the possibility that his great adversary, always daring, might assume the offensive, and attempt to crush the Federal wings in detail. Still the danger appeared small. Either wing was practically equal to the whole Confederate force. Sedgwick had 40,000, with the Third Corps, 19,000, and a division of the Second, 5,500, close at hand; Hooker 42,000, with two divisions of the Second Corps, 11,000, at Banks' Ford; the Third Corps could reinforce him in less than four-and-twenty hours; and Stoneman's 10,000 sabres, riding at will amongst Lee's supply depôts, would surely prevent him from attacking. Still precaution was taken in case the attempt were made. Sedgwick, if the enemy detached any considerable part of his force towards Chancellorsville, was 'to carry the works at all hazards, and establish his force on the Telegraph road.'[2] The right wing, 'if not strongly resisted, was to advance at all hazards, and secure a position uncovering

[1] From Franklin's Crossing below Fredericksburg, where Sedgwick's bridges were thrown, to Kelly's Ford is 27 miles; to Ely's Ford 19 miles, and to Chancellorsville 11 miles.
[2] O. R., vol. xxv., p. 268.

Banks' Ford.' [1] Were the Confederates found in force near
Chancellorsville, it was to select a strong position and await
attack on its own ground, while Sedgwick, coming up
from Fredericksburg, would assail the enemy in flank and
rear.

Such was the plan which, if resolutely carried out, bade
fair to crush Lee's army between the upper and the nether
millstones, and it seems that the size and condition of his
forces led Hooker to anticipate an easy victory. If the
Army of the Potomac was not 'the finest on the planet,' as
in an order of the day he boastfully proclaimed it, it
possessed many elements of strength. Hooker was a strict
disciplinarian with a talent for organisation. He had not
only done much to improve the efficiency of his troops, but
his vigorous measures had gone far to restore their confidence. When he succeeded Burnside a large proportion
of the soldiers had lost heart and hope. The generals who
had hitherto commanded them, when compared with Lee
and Jackson, were mere pigmies, and the consciousness
that this was the case had affected the entire army. The
Official Records contain much justification of Jackson's
anxiety that Burnside should be fought on the North Anna,
where, if defeated, he might have been pursued. Although
there had been no pursuit after the battle of Fredericksburg,
no harassing marches, no continued retreat, with lack of
supplies, abandoning of wounded, and constant alarms, the
Federal regiments had suffered terribly in *moral*.

'The winter rains set in,' said Hooker, 'and all operations were for a while suspended, the army literally finding itself buried in mud, from which there was no hope of
extrication before spring.

'With this prospect before it, taken in connection with
the gloom and despondency which followed the disaster of
Fredericksburg, the army was in a forlorn, deplorable
condition. Reference to the letters from the army at
this time, public and private, affords abundant evidence
of its demoralisation ; and these, in their turn, had their
effect upon the friends and relatives of the soldiers at

[1] O.R., vol. xxv., p. 274.

home. At the time the army was turned over to me desertions were at the rate of about two hundred a day. So anxious were parents, wives, brothers and sisters, to relieve their kindred, that they filled the express trains with packages of citizens' clothing to assist them in escaping from service. At that time, perhaps, a majority of the officers, especially those high in rank, were hostile to the policy of the Government in the conduct of the war. The emancipation proclamation had been published a short time before, and a large element of the army had taken sides antagonistic to it, declaring that they would never have embarked in the war had they anticipated the action of the Government. When rest came to the army, the disaffected, from whatever cause, began to show themselves, and make their influence felt in and out of the camps. I may also state that at the moment I was placed in command I caused a return to be made of the absentees of the army, and found the number to be 2,922 commissioned officers and 81,964 non-commissioned officers and privates. They were scattered all over the country, and the majority were absent from causes unknown.' [1]

In the face of this remarkable report it is curious to read, in the pages of a brilliant military historian, that ' armies composed of the citizens of a free country, who have taken up arms from patriotic motives . . . have constantly exhibited an astonishing endurance, and possessing a bond of cohesion superior to discipline, have shown their power to withstand shocks that would dislocate the structure of other military organisations.' [2] A force which had lost twenty-five per cent. of its strength by desertion, although it had never been pursued after defeat, would not generally be suspected of peculiar solidity. Nevertheless, the Northern soldiers must receive their due. Want of discipline made fearful ravages in the ranks, but, notwithstanding the defection of so many of their comrades, those that remained faithful displayed the best characteristics of their

[1] *Report of Committee on the Conduct of the War.*
[2] *Campaigns of the Army of the Potomac.* By William Swinton, p. 267.

race. The heart of the army was still sound, and only
the influence of a strong and energetic commander was
required to restore its vitality. This influence was supplied
by Hooker. The cumbrous organisation of Grand Divisions
was abolished. Disloyal and unsuccessful generals were
removed.   Salutary changes were introduced into the
various departments of the staff.   The cavalry, hitherto
formed in independent brigades, was consolidated into a
corps of three divisions and a brigade of regulars, and under
a system of careful and uniform inspection made rapid improvement. Strong measures were taken to reduce the
number of deserters. The ranks were filled by the return
of absentees.   New regiments were added to the army
corps. The troops were constantly practised in field-
exercises, and generals of well-deserved reputation were
selected for the different commands. ' All were actuated,'
wrote Hooker, ' by feelings of confidence and devotion to
the cause, and I felt that it was a living army, and one
well worthy of the Republic.'

On April 27, after several demonstrations, undertaken
with a view of confusing the enemy, had been made at
various points, the grand movement began.

The Confederate army still held the lines it had
occupied for the past four months.   Jackson's army corps
extended from Hamilton's Crossing to Port Royal.
McLaws' and Anderson's divisions occupied Lee's Hill
and the ridge northward, and a brigade watched Banks'
Ford.   Stuart was with his main body, some 2,400 strong,
at Culpeper, observing the great mass of Federal horsemen
at Warrenton Junction, and the line of the Rappahannock
was held by cavalry pickets.

The strength of the Army of Northern Virginia, so far
as can be ascertained, did not exceed 62,000 officers and
men.

Second Corps.

A. P. Hill's Division .	11,500
Rodes' Division	9,500
Colston's (Jackson's own) Division .	6,600
Early's Division	7,500
Artillery .	2,100

First Corps.

Anderson's Division 8,100
McLaws' Division 8,600
Artillery 1,000

Cavalry.

Fitzhugh Lee's Brigade 1,500
W. H. F. Lee's Brigade (two regiments) . . . 900
Reserve Artillery 700
Add for reinforcements received since March 1, date
    of last return 4,000
                                                            ————
                                        Total . . 62,000
                                        and 170 guns.

Thus the road to Richmond, threatened by a host of 130,000 men and 428 guns, was to be defended by a force of less than half the size. Ninety-nine generals out of a hundred would have considered the situation hopeless. The Confederate lines at Fredericksburg were certainly very strong, but it was clearly impossible to prevent the Federals outflanking them. The disparity in strength was far greater than at Sharpsburg, and it seemed that by sheer weight of numbers the Southern army must inevitably be driven back. Nor did it appear, so overwhelming were the Federal numbers, that counter-attack was feasible. The usual resource of the defender, if his adversary marches round his flank, is to strike boldly at his communications. Here, however, Hooker's communications with Aquia Creek were securely covered by the Rappahannock, and so great was his preponderance of strength, that he could easily detach a sufficient force to check the Confederates should they move against them.

Yet now, as on the Antietam, Lee and Jackson declined to take numbers into consideration. They knew that Hooker was a brave and experienced soldier, but they had no reason to anticipate that he would handle his vast masses with more skill than McClellan. That the Northern soldiers had suffered in *moral* they were well aware, and while they divined that the position they themselves had fortified might readily be made untenable, the fact that such was the case gave them small concern. They were agreed that the best measures of defence, if an opening offered, lay in a resolute offensive, and with Hooker in command it was not likely that the opportunity would be long delayed.

No thought of a strategic retreat, from one position to another, was entertained. Manœuvre was to be met by manœuvre, blow by counterblow.[1] If Hooker had not moved Lee would have forestalled him. On April 16 he had written to Mr. Davis : ' My only anxiety arises from the condition of our horses, and the scarcity of forage and provisions. I think it is all important that we should assume the aggressive by the 1st of May. . . . If we could be placed in a condition to make a vigorous advance at that time, I think the Valley could be swept of Milroy (commanding the Federal forces at Winchester), and the army opposite [Hooker's] be thrown north of the Potomac.'[2] Jackson, too, even after Hooker's plan was developed, indignantly repudiated the suggestion that the forthcoming campaign must be purely defensive. When some officer on his staff expressed his fear that the army would be compelled to retreat, he asked sharply, ' Who said that ? No, sir, we shall not fall back, we shall attack them.'

At the end of the month, however, Longstreet with his three divisions was still absent ; sufficient supplies for a forward movement had not yet been accumulated ;[3] two brigades of cavalry, Hampton's and Jenkins', which had been sent respectively to South Carolina and the Valley, had not rejoined,[4] and Hooker had already seized the initiative.

The first news which came to hand was that a strong force of all arms was moving up the Rappahannock in the

---

[1] ' The idea of securing the provisions, waggons, guns, of the enemy is truly tempting, and the idea has haunted me since December.' Lee to Trimble, March 8, 1862. O. R., vol. xxv., part ii., p. 658.

[2] O. R., vol. xxv., p. 725.

[3] ' From the condition of our horses and the amount of our supplies I am unable even to act on the defensive as vigorously as circumstances might require.' Lee to Davis, April 27, O. R., vol. xxv., p. 752.

[4] On April 20 Lee had asked that the cavalry regiments not needed in other districts might be sent to the Army of Northern Virginia. His request was not complied with until too late. O. R., vol. xxv., pp. 740, 741.

direction of Kelly's Ford. This was forwarded by Stuart on
the evening of April 28. The next the Federal
movements, which might have been morning
no more than a demonstration, became pronounced. Under
cover of a thick fog, pontoon bridges were laid
at Deep Run below Fredericksburg; Sedgwick's
troops began to cross, and were soon engaged with Jackson's
outposts; while, at the same time, the report came in that a
force of unknown strength had made the passage at Kelly's
Ford.

April 28.

April 29.

Lee displayed no perturbation. Jackson, on receiving
information of Sedgwick's movement from his outposts, had
sent an aide-de-camp to acquaint the Commander-in-Chief.
The latter was still in his tent, and in reply to the message
said : ' Well, I heard firing, and I was beginning to think
that it was time some of your lazy young fellows were
coming to tell me what it was about. Tell your good
general he knows what to do with the enemy just as well
as I do.' [1]

The divisions of the Second Army Corps were at once
called up to their old battle-ground, and while they were
on the march Jackson occupied himself with watching
Sedgwick's movements. The Federals were busily intrenching on the river bank, and on the heights behind
frowned the long line of artillery that had proved at
Fredericksburg so formidable an obstacle to the Confederate attack. The enemy's position was very strong,
and the time for counterstroke had not yet come. During
the day the cavalry was actively engaged between the
Rappahannock and the Rapidan, testing the strength of
the enemy's columns. The country was wooded, the
Federals active, and as usual in war, accurate information
was difficult to obtain and more difficult to communicate.
It was not till 6.30 P.M. that Lee received notice that
troops had crossed at Ely's and Germanna Fords at 2

---

[1] On March 12, before Hooker had even framed his plan of operations,
Lee had received information that the Federals, as soon as the state of the
roads permitted, would cross at United States, Falmouth, and some point
below; the attempt at Falmouth to be a feint. O. R., vol. xxv., part ii.,
p. 664.

P.M.   Anderson's division was at once despatched to Chancellorsville.

The next message, which does not appear to have been received until the morning of the 30th, threw more light on the situation. Stuart had made prisoners from the Fifth, the Eleventh, and the Twelfth Corps, and had ascertained that the corps commanders, Meade, Howard, and Slocum, were present with the troops. Anderson, moreover, who had been instructed to select and intrench a strong position, was falling back from Chancellorsville before the enemy's advance, and two things became clear :—

1. That it was Hooker's intention to turn the Confederate left.

2. That he had divided his forces.

The question now to be decided was which wing should be attacked first. There was much to be said in favour of crushing Sedgwick. His numbers were estimated at 35,000 men, and the Confederates had over 60,000. Moreover, time is a most important consideration in the use of interior lines. The army was already concentrated in front of Sedgwick, whereas it would require a day's march to seek Hooker in the forest round Chancellorsville. Sedgwick's, too, was the smaller of the Federal wings, and his overthrow would certainly ruin Hooker's combinations. ' Jackson at first,' said Lee, ' preferred to attack Sedgwick's force in the plain of Fredericksburg, but I told him I feared it was as impracticable as it was at the first battle of Fredericksburg. It was hard to get at the enemy, and harder to get away if we drove him into the river, but if he thought it could be done, I would give orders for it.' Jackson asked to be allowed to examine the ground, but soon came to the conclusion that the project was too hazardous and that Lee was right. Orders were then issued for a concentration against Hooker, 10,000 men, under General Early, remaining to confront Sedgwick on the heights of Fredericksburg.

We may now turn to the movements of the Federals.

Hooker's right wing had marched at a speed which had

been hitherto unknown in the Army of the Potomac. At nightfall, on April 30, the three army corps, although they had been delayed by the Confederate cavalry, were assembled at Chancellorsville. In three days they had marched forty-six miles over bad roads, had forded breast-high two difficult rivers, established several bridges, and captured over a hundred prisoners.[1] Heavy reinforcements were in rear. The two divisions of the Second Corps had marched from Banks' Ford to United States Ford, six miles from Chancellorsville; while the Third Corps, ordered up from the Stafford Heights, was rapidly approaching the same point of passage. Thus, 70,000 men, in the highest spirits at the success of their manœuvres, were massed in rear of Lee's lines, and Hooker saw victory within his grasp.

'It is with heartfelt satisfaction,' ran his general order, 'that the commanding general announces to his army that the operations of the last three days have determined that our enemy must either ingloriously fly or come out from behind his defences, and give us battle on our own ground, where certain destruction awaits him. The operations of the Fifth, Eleventh, and Twelfth Corps have been a succession of splendid achievements.'

Hooker was ' skinning the lion while the beast yet lived,' but he had certainly much reason for congratulation. His manœuvres had been skilfully planned and energetically executed. The two rivers which protected the Confederate position had been crossed without loss; the Second and Third Corps had been brought into close touch with the right wing; Lee's earthworks were completely turned, and Stoneman's cavalry divisions, driving the enemy's patrols

---

[1] The troops carried eight days' supplies : three days' cooked rations with bread and groceries in the haversacks; five days' bread and groceries in the knapsacks; five days' ' beef on the hoof.' The total weight carried by each man, including sixty rounds of ammunition, was 45 lbs. The reserve ammunition was carried principally by pack mules, and only a small number of waggons crossed the Rappahannock. Four pontoon bridges were laid by the engineers. One bridge took three-quarters of an hour to lay; the other three, one and a half hour to lay, and an hour to take up. Each bridge was from 100 to 140 yards long. O. R., vol. xxv., pp. 215, 216.

before them, were already within reach of Orange Court House, and not more than twenty miles from Gordonsville. Best of all, the interval between the two wings—twenty-six miles on the night of the 28th—was now reduced to eleven miles by the plank road.

Two things only were unsatisfactory :—

1. The absence of information.

2. The fact that the whole movement had been observed by the Confederate cavalry.

Pleasonton's brigade of horse had proved too weak for the duty assigned to it.   It had been able to protect the front, but it was too small to cover the flanks ; and at the flanks Stuart had persistently struck.   Hooker appears to have believed that Stoneman's advance against the Central Railroad would draw off the whole of the Confederate horse.   Stuart, however, was not to be beguiled from his proper functions.   Never were his squadrons more skilfully handled than in this campaign.   With fine tactical insight, as soon as the great movement on Chancellorsville became pronounced, he had attacked the right flank of the Federal columns with Fitzhugh Lee's brigade, leaving only the two regiments under W. H. F. Lee to watch Stoneman's 10,000 sabres.   Then, having obtained the information he required, he moved across the Federal front, and routing one of Pleasonton's regiments in a night affair near Spotsylvania Court House, he had regained touch with his own army.   The results of his manœuvres were of the utmost importance.   Lee was fully informed as to his adversary's strength ; the Confederate cavalry was in superior strength at the critical point, that is, along the front of the two armies ; and Hooker had no knowledge whatever of what was going on in the space between Sedgwick and himself.   He was only aware, on the night of April 30, that the Confederate position before Fredericksburg was still strongly occupied.

The want, however, of accurate information gave him no uneasiness.   The most careful arrangements had been made to note and report every movement of the enemy the next day.

No less than three captive balloons, in charge of skilled

observers, looked down upon the Confederate earthworks.[1] Signal stations and observatories had been established on each commanding height; a line of field telegraph had been laid from Falmouth to United States Ford, and the chief of the staff, General Butterfield, remained at the former village in communication with General Sedgwick. If the weather were clear, and the telegraph did not fail, it seemed impossible that either wing of the Federal army could fail to be fully and instantly informed of the situation of the other, or that a single Confederate battalion could change position without both Hooker and Sedgwick being at once advised.

Moreover, the Federal Commander-in-Chief was so certain that Lee would retreat that his deficiency in cavalry troubled him not at all. He had determined to carry out his original design. The next morning—May 1—the

May 1. right wing was to move by the plank road and uncover Banks' Ford, thus still further shortening the line of communication between the two wings; and as the chief of the staff impressed on Sedgwick, it was 'expected to be on the heights west of Fredericksburg at noon or shortly after, or, if opposed strongly, at night.' Sedgwick, meanwhile, was ' to observe the enemy's movements with the utmost vigilance; should he expose a weak point, to attack him in full force and destroy him; should he show any symptom of falling back, to pursue him with the utmost vigour.' [2]

But Hooker was to find that mere mechanical precautions are not an infallible remedy for a dangerous situation. The Confederates had not only learned long since the importance of concealment, and the advantage of night marches, but in the early morning of May 1 the river mists rendered both balloons and observatories useless. Long before the sun broke through the fog, both McLaws and Jackson had joined Anderson at Tabernacle

[1] Balloons, which had been first used in the Peninsular campaign, were not much dreaded by the Confederates. ' The experience of twenty months' warfare has taught them how little formidable such engines of war are.' Special Correspondent of the *Times* at Fredericksburg, January 1, 1863.

[2] O. R., vol. xxv., p. 306.

Church, and a strong line of battle had been established at the junction of the two roads, the pike and the plank, which led east from Chancellorsville. The position was favourable, running along a low ridge, partially covered with timber, and with open fields in front. Beyond those fields, a few hundred paces distant, rose the outskirts of a great forest, stretching far away over a gently undulating country. This forest, twenty miles in length from east to west, and fifteen in breadth from north to south, has given to the region it covers the name of the Wilderness of Spotsylvania, and in its midst the Federal army was now involved. Never was ground more unfavourable for the manœuvres of a large army. The timber was unusually dense. The groves of pines were immersed in a sea of scrub-oak and luxuriant undergrowth. The soil was poor. Farms were rare, and the few clearings were seldom more than a rifle shot in width. The woodland tracks were seldom travelled; streams with marshy banks and tortuous courses were met at frequent intervals, and the only *débouchés* towards Fredericksburg, the pike, the plank road, an unfinished line of railway a mile south of their junction, and the river road, about two miles north, were commanded from the Confederate position.

When Jackson arrived upon the scene, Anderson, with the help of Lee's engineers, had strongly intrenched the whole front. A large force of artillery had already taken post. The flanks of the line were covered; the right, which extended to near Duerson's Mill, by Mott's Run and the Rappahannock; the left, which rested on the unfinished railroad not far from Tabernacle Church, by the Massaponax Creek. For the defence of this position, three miles in length, there were present 45,000 infantry, over 100 guns, and Fitzhugh Lee's brigade of cavalry, a force ample for the purpose, and giving about nine men to the yard. On the rolling ground eastward there was excellent cover for the reserves, and from the breastworks to the front the defiles, for such, owing to the density of the wood, were the four roads by which the enemy must approach, might be so effectively swept

8 A.M.

as to prevent him from deploying either artillery or infantry.

But Jackson was not disposed to await attack. Only 10,000 men remained in the Fredericksburg lines to confront Sedgwick, and if that officer acted vigorously, his guns would soon be heard in rear of the lines at Tabernacle Church. Work on the intrenchments was at once broken off, and the whole force was ordered to prepare for an immediate advance on Chancellorsville.

10.45 A.M. Before eleven o'clock the rear brigades had closed up; and marching by the pike and the plank road, with a regiment of cavalry in advance, and Fitzhugh Lee upon the left, the Confederate army plunged resolutely into the gloomy depths of the great forest. Anderson's division led the way, one brigade on the pike, and two on the plank road; a strong line of skirmishers covered his whole front, and his five batteries brought up the rear. Next in order came McLaws, together with the two remaining brigades of Anderson, moving by the pike, while Jackson's three divisions were on the plank road. The artillery followed the infantry.

About a mile towards Chancellorsville the Federal cavalry was found in some force, and as the patrols gave way, a heavy force of infantry was discovered in movement along the pike. General McLaws, who had been placed in charge of the Confederate right, immediately deployed his four leading brigades, and after the Federal artillery, unlimbering in an open field, had fired a few rounds, their infantry advanced to the attack. The fight was spirited but short. The Northern regulars of Sykes' division drove in the Confederate skirmishers, but were unable to make ground against the line of battle. Jackson, meanwhile, who had been at once informed of the encounter, had ordered the troops on the plank road to push briskly forward, and the Federals, finding their right in danger of being enveloped, retired on Chancellorsville. Another hostile column was shortly afterwards met on the plank road, also marching eastward. Again there was a skirmish, and again Jackson, ordering a brigade to march

rapidly along the unfinished railroad, had recourse to a
turning movement; but before the manœuvre was completed, the Federals began to yield, and all opposition
gradually melted away.   The following order was then sent
to McLaws :—

'Headquarters, Second Corps, Army of Northern Virginia,
2.30 P.M.   'May 1, 1863, 2.30 P.M. (received 4 P.M.).

'General,—The Lieutenant-General commanding directs
me to say that he is pressing up the plank road; also,
that you will press on up the turnpike towards Chancellorsville, as the enemy is falling back.

' Keep your skirmishers and flanking parties well out, to
guard against ambuscade.

' Very respectfully, your obedient servant,

' J. G. MORRISON,
' Acting Assistant Adjutant-General.' [1]

There was something mysterious in so easy a victory.
The enemy was evidently in great strength, for, on both
roads, heavy columns had been observed behind the lines
of skirmishers.   Several batteries had been in action;
cavalry was present; and the Confederate scouts reported
that a third column, of all arms, had marched by the river
road toward Banks' Ford, and had then, like the others, un-
accountably withdrawn.   The pursuit, therefore, was slow
and circumspect.   Wilcox' brigade, on the extreme right,
moved up the Mine road, in the direction of Duerson's
Mill; Wright's brigade, on the extreme left, followed Fitzhugh Lee's cavalry on the unfinished railroad; while the
main body, well closed up, still kept to the main highways.

At length, late in the afternoon, Hooker's tactics became
clear.   As Jackson's advanced-guards approached Chancel-
5 P.M.   lorsville, the resistance of the Federal skirmishers,
covering the retreat, became more stubborn.   From
the low ridge, fringed by heavy timber, on which the
mansion stands, the fire of artillery, raking every avenue of
approach, grew more intense, and it was evident that the
foe was standing fast on the defensive.

[1] O. R., vol. xxv., p. 764.

The Confederate infantry, pushing forward through the undergrowth, made but tardy progress; the cavalry patrols found that every road and bridle-path was strongly held, and it was difficult in the extreme to discover Hooker's exact position. Jackson himself, riding to the front to reconnoitre, nearly fell a victim to the recklessness he almost invariably displayed when in quest of information. The cavalry had been checked at Catherine Furnace, and were waiting the approach of the infantry. Wright's brigade was close at hand, and swinging round northwards, drove back the enemy's skirmishers, until, in its turn, it was brought up by the fire of artillery. Just at this moment Jackson galloped up, and begged Stuart to ride forward with him in order to find a point from which the enemy's guns might be enfiladed. A bridle-path, branching off from the main road to the right, led to a hillock about half a mile distant, and the two generals, accompanied by their staffs, and followed by a battery of horse-artillery, made for this point of vantage. 'On reaching the spot,' says Stuart's adjutant-general, ' so dense was the undergrowth, it was found impossible to find enough clear space to bring more than one gun at a time into position; the others closed up immediately behind, and the whole body of us completely blocked up the narrow road. Scarcely had the smoke of our first shot cleared away, when a couple of masked batteries suddenly opened on us at short range, and enveloped us in a storm of shell and canister, which, concentrated on so narrow a space, did fearful execution among our party, men and horses falling right and left, the animals kicking and plunging wildly, and everybody eager to disentangle himself from the confusion, and get out of harm's way. Jackson, as soon as he found out his mistake, ordered the guns to retire; but the confined space so protracted the operation of turning, that the enemy's cannon had full time to continue their havoc, covering the road with dead and wounded. That Jackson and Stuart with their staff officers escaped was nothing short of miraculous.'[1]

[1] *Memoirs of the Confederate War* Heros von Borcke.

Other attempts at reconnaissance were more successful. Before nightfall it was ascertained that Hooker was in strong force on the Chancellorsville ridge, along the plank road, and on a bare plateau to the southward called Hazel Grove. ' Here,' in the words of General Lee, ' he had assumed a position of great natural strength, surrounded on all sides by a dense forest, filled with a tangled undergrowth, in the midst of which breastworks of logs had been constructed, with trees felled in front, so as to form an almost impenetrable abattis. His artillery swept the few narrow roads, by which the position could be approached from the front, and commanded the adjacent woods. The left of his line extended from Chancellorsville towards the Rappahannock, covering the Bark Mill (United States) Ford, which communicated with the north bank of the river by a pontoon bridge. His right stretched westward along the Germanna Ford road (the pike) more than two miles. . . . As the nature of the country rendered it hazardous to attack by night, our troops were halted and formed in line of battle in front of Chancellorsville at right angles to the plank road, extending on the right to the Mine road, and to the left in the direction of the Catherine Furnace.'

As darkness falls upon the Wilderness, and the fire of the outposts, provoked by every movement of the patrols, gradually dies away, we may seek the explanation of the Federal movements. On finding that his enemy, instead of ' ingloriously flying,' was advancing to meet him, and advancing with confident and aggressive vigour, Hooker's resolution had failed him. Waiting till his force was concentrated, until the Second and Third Corps had crossed at United States Ford, and were close to Chancellorsville, it was not till eleven o'clock on the morning of May 1 that he had marched in three great columns towards Fredericksburg. His intention was to pass rapidly through the Wilderness, secure the open ground about Tabernacle Church, and there, with ample space for deployment, to form for battle, and move against the rear of Marye's Hill.[1]

[1] O. R., vol. xxv., p. 324.

But before his advanced-guards got clear of the forest defiles they found the Confederates across their path, displaying an unmistakable purpose of pressing the attack. Hooker at once concluded that Lee was marching against him with nearly his whole force, and of the strength of that force, owing to the weakness of his cavalry, he was not aware. The news from the Stafford Heights was disquieting. As soon as the fog had lifted, about nine o'clock in the morning, the signal officers and balloonists had descried long columns of troops and trains marching rapidly towards Chancellorsville.[1] This was duly reported by the telegraph,[2] and it was correctly inferred to signify that Lee was concentrating against the Federal right. But at the same time various movements were observed about Hamilton's Crossing; columns appeared marching from the direction of Guiney's Station; there was much traffic on the railway, and several deserters from Lee's army declared, on being examined, that Hood's and Pickett's divisions had arrived from Richmond.[3] The statements of these men who we may suspect were not such traitors as they appeared—were confirmed by the fact that Sedgwick, who was without cavalry, had noticed no diminution in the force which held the ridge before him.

It is easy, then, to understand Hooker's decision to stand on the defensive. With a prudent foresight which does him much credit, before he marched in the morning he had ordered the position about Chancellorsville, covering his lines of retreat to United States and Ely's Fords, to be reconnoitred and intrenched, and his front, as Lee said, was undoubtedly very strong. He would assuredly have done better had he attacked vigorously when he found the Confederates advancing. His sudden retrograde movement, especially as following the swift and successful manœuvres which had turned Lee's position, could not fail to have a discouraging effect upon the troops; and

[1] O. R., vol. xxv., pp. 323, 336.
[2] *Ibid.* p. 326. The telegraph, however, appears to have worked badly, and dispatches took several hours to pass from Falmouth to Chancellorsville.
[3] *Ibid.* p. 327.

if Sedgwick had been ordered to storm the Fredericksburg lines, the whole Federal force could have been employed, and the Confederates, assailed in front and rear simultaneously, must, to say the least, have been embarrassed. But in abandoning his design of crushing Lee between his two wings, and in retiring to the stronghold he had prepared, Hooker did what most ordinary generals would have done, especially one who had served on the losing side at Fredericksburg. He had there learned the value of intrenchments. He had seen division after division shatter itself in vain against a stone wall and a few gun-pits, and it is little wonder that he had imbibed a profound respect for defensive tactics. He omitted, however, to take into consideration two simple facts. First, that few districts contain two such positions as those of the Confederates at Fredericksburg ; and, secondly, that the strength of a position is measured not by the impregnability of the front, but by the security of the flanks. The Fredericksburg lines, resting on the Rappahannock and the Massaponax, had apparently safe flanks, and yet he himself had completely turned them, rendering the whole series of works useless without firing a shot. Were Lee and Jackson the men to knock their heads, like Burnside, against stout breastworks strongly manned? Would they not rather make a wide sweep, exactly as he himself had done, and force him to come out of his works? Hooker, however, may have said that if they marched across his front, he would attack them *en route*, as did Napoleon at Austerlitz and Wellington at Salamanca, and cut their army in two. But here he came face to face with the fatal defect of the lines he had selected, and also of the disposition he had made of his cavalry. The country near Chancellorsville was very unlike the rolling plains of Austerlitz or the bare downs of Salamanca. From no part of the Federal position did the view extend for more than a few hundred yards. Wherever the eye turned rose the dark and impenetrable screen of close-growing trees, interlaced with wild vines and matted undergrowth, and seamed with rough roads, perfectly passable for troops, with which his enemies were far better acquainted than himself. Had Stoneman's cavalry been present, the squadrons, posted far out upon the flanks, and watching every track, might have given ample warning of any turning movement, exactly as Stuart's cavalry had given Lee warning of Hooker's own movement upon Chancellorsville. As it was, Pleasonton's brigade was too weak to make head against Stuart's regiments; and Hooker could expect no early information of his enemy's movements.

He thus found himself in the dilemma which a general on the defensive, if he be weak in cavalry, has almost invariably to face, especially in a close country. He was ignorant, and must necessarily remain ignorant, of where the main attack would be made. Lee, on the other hand, by means of his superior cavalry, could reconnoitre the position at his leisure, and if he discovered a weak point could suddenly throw the greater portion of his force against it. Hooker could only hope that no weak point existed. Remembering that the Confederates were on the pike and the plank road, there certainly appeared no cause for apprehension. The Fifth Corps, with its flank on the Rappahannock, held the left, covering the river and the old Mine roads. Next in succession came the Second Corps, blocking the pike. In the centre the Twelfth Corps, under General Slocum, covered Chancellorsville. The Third Corps, under Sickles, held Hazel Grove, with Berry's division as general reserve; and on the extreme right, his breastworks running along the plank road as far as Talley's Clearing, was Howard with the Eleventh Corps, composed principally of German regiments. Strong outposts of infantry had been thrown out into the woods; the men were still working in the intrenchments; batteries were disposed so as to sweep every approach from the south, the south-east, or the south-west, and there were at least five men to every yard of parapet. The line, however, six miles from flank to flank, was somewhat extensive, and to make certain, so far as possible, that sufficient numbers should be forthcoming to defend the position, at 1.55 on the morning of May 2, Sedgwick was instructed to send the First Army Corps to Chancellorsville. Before midnight, moreover, thirty-four guns, principally horse-artillery, together with a brigade of infantry, were sent from Falmouth to Banks' Ford.

Sedgwick, meantime, below Fredericksburg, had contented himself with engaging the outposts on the opposite ridge. An order to make a brisk demonstration, which Hooker had dispatched at 11.30 A.M., did not arrive, the telegraph having broken down, until 5.45 P.M., six hours later; and it was then too late to effect any diversion in favour of the main army.

Yet it can hardly be said that Sedgwick had risen to the height of his responsibilities. He knew that a portion at least of the Confederates had marched against Hooker, and the balloonists had early reported that a battle was in progress near Tabernacle Church. But instead of obeying Napoleon's maxim and marching to the sound of the cannon, he had made no effort to send support to his commander. Both he and General Reynolds[1] considered ' that to have attacked before Hooker had accomplished some success, in view of the strong position and numbers in their front, might have failed to dislodge the enemy, and have rendered them unserviceable at the proper time.'[2] That is, they were not inclined to risk their own commands in order to assist Hooker, of whose movements they were uncertain. Yet even if they had been defeated, Hooker would still have had more men than Lee.

[1] The following letter (O. R., vol. xxv., p. 337) is interesting as showing the state of mind into which the commanders of detached forces are liable to be thrown by the absence of information :—

' Headquarters, First Corps, May 1, 1863.

' Major-General Sedgwick,—I think the proper view to take of affairs is this : If they have not detached more than A. P. Hill's division from our front, they have been keeping up appearances, showing weakness, with a view of delaying Hooker, and tempting us to make an attack on their fortified position, and hoping to destroy us and strike for our depôt over our bridges. We ought therefore, in my judgment, *to know something of what has transpired on our right.*

' JOHN F. REYNOLDS, *Major-General.*'

[2] Dispatch of Chief of the Staff to Hooker, dated 4 P.M., May 1. O. R., vol. xxv., p. 326.

CHAPTER XXIV

CHANCELLORSVILLE (*continued*)

AT a council of war held during the night at Chancellorsville House, the Federal generals were by no means
unanimous as to the operations of the morrow. Some of
the generals advised an early assault. Others favoured a
strictly defensive attitude. Hooker himself wished to con-
tract his lines so as to strengthen them ; but as the officers
commanding on the right were confident of the strength
of their intrenchments, it was at length determined that
the army should await attack in its present position.

Three miles down the plank road, under a grove of oak
and pine, Lee and Jackson, while their wearied soldiers
slept around them, planned for the fourth and the last time
the overthrow of the great army with which Lincoln still
hoped to capture Richmond. At this council there was no
difference of opinion. If Hooker had not retreated before
the morning—and Jackson thought it possible he was
already demoralised—he was to be attacked. The situation
admitted of no other course. It was undoubtedly a
hazardous operation for an inferior force to assault an
intrenched position ; but the Federal army was divided,
the right wing involved in a difficult and unexplored country,
with which the Confederate generals and staff were more
or less familiar, and an opportunity so favourable might
never recur. 'Fortune,' says Napoleon, 'is a woman, who
must be wooed while she is in the mood. If her favours
are rejected, she does not offer them again.' The only
question was where the attack should be delivered. Lee
himself had reconnoitred the enemy's left. It was very
strong, resting on the Rappahannock, and covered by a

stream called Mineral Spring Run. Two of Jackson's staff officers had reconnoitred the front, and had pronounced it impregnable, except at a fearful sacrifice of life. But while the generals were debating, Stuart rode in with the reports of his cavalry officers, and the weak point of the position was at once revealed. General Fitzhugh Lee, to whose skill and activity the victory of Chancellorsville was in great part due, had discovered that the Federal right, on the plank road, was completely in the air; that is, it was protected by no natural obstacle, and the breast-works faced south, and south only. It was evident that attack from the west or north-west was not anticipated, and Lee at once seized upon the chance of effecting a surprise.

Yet the difficulties of the proposed operation were very great. To transfer a turning column to a point from which the Federal right might be effectively outflanked necessitated a long march by the narrow and intricate roadways of the Wilderness, and a division of the Confederate army into two parts, between which communication would be most precarious. To take advantage of the opportunity the first rule of war must be violated. But as it has already been said, the rules of war only point out the dangers which are incurred by breaking them; and, in this case, before an enemy on the defensive from whom the separation might be concealed until it is too late for him to intervene, the risks of dispersion were much reduced. The chief danger lay in this, that the two wings, each left to its own resources, might fail to act in combination, just as within the past twenty-four hours Hooker and Sedgwick had failed. But Lee knew that in Jackson he possessed a lieutenant whose resolution was invincible, and that the turning column, if entrusted to his charge, would be pushed forward without stop or stay until it had either joined hands with the main body, or had been annihilated.

Moreover, the battle of Fredericksburg had taught both armies that the elaborate constructions of the engineer are not the only or the most useful resources of fortification. Hooker had ordered his position to be intrenched in the hope that Lee and Jackson, following Burnside's example, would dash their divisions into fragments against them and thus become an easy prey. Lee, with a broader appreciation of the true tactical bearing of ditch and parapet, determined to employ them as a shelter for his own force until Jackson's movement was completed, and the time had come for a general advance. Orders were at once sent to General McLaws to cover his front, extending across the pike and the plank roads, with a line of breastworks; and long before daylight the soldiers of his division, with the scanty means at their disposal, were busy as beavers amongst the timber.

It only remained, then, to determine the route and the strength of the outflanking force; and here it may be observed that the headquarters staff appears to have neglected certain precautions for which there had been ample leisure. So long ago as March 19 a council of war had decided that if Hooker attacked he would do so by the upper fords, and yet the Wilderness, lying immediately south of the points of passage, had not been adequately examined. Had Jackson been on the left wing above Fredericksburg, instead of on the right, near Hamilton's Crossing, we may be certain that accurate surveys would have been forthcoming. As it was, the charts furnished to the Commander-in-Chief were untrustworthy, and information had to be sought from the country-people.

'About daylight on May 2,' says Major Hotchkiss, 'General Jackson awakened me, and requested that I May 2. would at once go down to Catherine Furnace, 2.30 A.M. which is quite near, and where a Colonel Welford lived, and ascertain if there was any road by which we could secretly pass round Chancellorsville to the vicinity of Old Wilderness Tavern. I had a map, which our engineers had prepared from actual surveys, of the surrounding country, showing all the public roads, but with few details of the intermediate topography. Reaching Mr. Welford's, I aroused him from his bed, and soon learned that he himself had recently opened a road through the woods in that direction for the purpose of hauling cord-wood and iron ore to his furnace. This I located on the map, and having

asked Mr. Welford if he would act as a guide if it became
necessary to march over that road, I returned to head-

3.30 A.M.   quarters.   When I reached those I found Generals
Lee and Jackson in conference, each seated on a
cracker box, from a pile which had been left there by the
Federals the day before.   In response to General Jackson's
request for my report, I put another cracker box between
the two generals, on which I spread the map, showed them
the road I had ascertained, and indicated, so far as I knew
it, the position of the Federal army.   General Lee then
said, "General Jackson, what do you propose to do?"
He replied, "Go around here," moving his finger over the
road which I had located upon the map.   General Lee
said, "What do you propose to make this movement
with?"   "With my whole corps," was the answer.
General Lee then asked, "What will you leave me?"
"The divisions of Anderson and McLaws," said Jackson.
General Lee, after a moment's reflection, remarked, "Well,
go on," and then, pencil in hand, gave his last instructions.   Jackson, with an eager smile upon his face,
from time to time nodded assent, and when the Commander-in-Chief ended with the words, "General Stuart
will cover your movement with his cavalry," he rose and
saluted, saying, "My troops will move at once, sir."[1]
The necessary orders were forthwith dispatched.   The
trains, parked in open fields to the rear, were to move to
Todd's Tavern, and thence westward by interior roads;
the Second Army Corps was to march in one column,
Rodes' division in front, and A. P. Hill's in rear; the First
Virginia Cavalry, with whom was Fitzhugh Lee, covered
the front; squadrons of the 2nd, the 3rd, and the 5th were
on the right; Hotchkiss, accompanied by a squad of
couriers, was to send back constant reports to General Lee;
the commanding officers were impressed with the importance of celerity and secrecy; the ranks were to be kept
well closed up, and all stragglers were to be bayoneted.

----

[1] Letter to the author.   A letter of General Lee to Mrs. Jackson, which
contains a reference to this council of war, appears as a Note at the end of
the chapter.

The day had broken without a cloud, and as the troops began their march in the fresh May morning, the green vistas of the Wilderness, grass under foot, and thick foliage overhead, were dappled with sunshine. The men, comprehending intuitively that a daring and decisive movement was in progress, pressed rapidly forward, and General Lee, standing by the roadside to watch them pass, saw in their confident bearing the presage of success. Soon after the first regiments had gone by Jackson himself appeared at the head of his staff. Opposite to the Commander-in-Chief he drew rein, and the two conversed for a few moments. Then Jackson rode on, pointing in the direction in which his troops were moving. ' His face,' says an eye-witness, ' was a little flushed, as it was turned to General Lee, who nodded approval of what he said.' Such was the last interview between Lee and Jackson.

4.5 A.M.

Then, during four long hours, for the column covered at least ten miles, the flood of bright rifles and tattered uniforms swept with steady flow down the forest track. The artillery followed, the guns drawn by lean and wiry horses, and the ammunition waggons and ambulances brought up the rear. In front was a regiment of cavalry, the 5th Virginia, accompanied by General Fitzhugh Lee ; on the flanks were some ten squadrons, moving by the tracks nearest the enemy's outposts ; a regiment of infantry, the 23rd Georgia, was posted at the cross-roads near Catherine Furnace ; and the plank road was well guarded until Anderson's troops came up to relieve the rear brigades of the Second Army Corps.

Meanwhile, acting under the immediate orders of General Lee, and most skilfully handled by McLaws and Anderson, the 10,000 Confederates who had been left in position opposite the Federal masses kept up a brisk demonstration. Artillery was brought up to every point along the front which offered space for action ; skirmishers, covered by the timber, engaged the enemy's pickets, and maintained a constant fire, and both on the pike and the river road the lines of battle, disposed so as to give an impression of great strength, threatened instant assault. Despite all precautions, however, Jackson's movement did not escape the notice of the Federals. A mile north of Catherine Furnace the eminence called Hazel Grove, clear of timber, looked down the valley of the Lewis Creek, and

8 A.M.   as early as 8 A.M. General Birney, commanding the Federal division at this point, reported the passage of a long column across his front.

The indications, however, were deceptive. At first, it is probable, the movement seemed merely a prolongation of the Confederate front; but it soon received a different interpretation. The road at the point where Jackson's column was observed turned due south; it was noticed that the troops were followed by their waggons, and that they were turning their backs on the Federal lines. Hooker, when he received Birney's report, jumped to the conclusion that Lee, finding the direct road to Richmond, through Bowling Green,

11 A.M.   threatened by Sedgwick, was retreating on Gordonsville. About 11 A.M. a battery was ordered into action on the Hazel Grove heights. The fire caused some confusion in the Confederate ranks; the trains were forced on to another road; and shortly after noon, General Sickles, commanding the Third Army Corps, was permitted by

12.15 P.M.   Hooker to advance upon Catherine Furnace and to develop the situation. Birney's division moved forward, and Whipple's soon followed. This attack, which threatened to cut the Confederate army in two, was so vigorously opposed by Anderson's division astride the plank road and by the 23rd Georgia at the Furnace, that General Sickles was constrained to call for reinforcements. Barlow's brigade, which had hitherto formed the reserve of the Eleventh Corps, holding the extreme right of the Federal line, the flank at which Jackson was aiming, was sent to his assistance. Pleasonton's cavalry brigade followed. Sickles' movement, even before the fresh troops arrived, had met with some success. The 23rd Georgia, driven back to the unfinished railroad and surrounded, lost 300 officers and men. But word had been sent to Jackson's column, and Colonel Brown's artillery battalion, together with the brigades of Archer and Thomas, rapidly retracing their steps, checked the advance in front, while Anderson, manœuvring his troops with vigour, struck heavily against the flank. Jackson's train, thus effectively protected, passed the dangerous point in safety, and then Archer and Thomas, leaving Anderson to deal with Sickles, drew off and pursued their march.

These operations, conducted for the most part in blind thickets, consumed much time, and Jackson was already far in advance. Moving in a south-westerly direction, he had struck the Brock road, a narrow track which runs nearly due north, and crosses both the plank road and the pike at a point about two miles west of the Federal right flank. The Brock road, which, had Stoneman's three divisions of cavalry been present with the Federal army, would have been strongly held, was absolutely free and unobstructed. Since the previous evening Fitzhugh Lee's patrols had remained in close touch with the enemy's outposts, and no attempt had been made to drive them in. So with no further obstacle than the heat the Second Army Corps pressed on. Away to the right, echoing faintly through the Wilderness, came the sound of cannon and the roll of musketry; couriers from the rear, galloping at top speed, reported that the trains had been attacked, that the rear brigades had turned back to save them, and that the enemy, in heavy strength, had already filled the gap which divided the Confederate wings. But, though the army was cut in two, Jackson cast no look behind him. The battle at the Furnace made no more impression on him than if it was being waged on the Mississippi. He had his orders to execute; and above all, he was moving at his best speed towards the enemy's weak point. He knew—and none better—that Hooker would not long retain the initiative; that every man detached from the Federal centre made his own chances of success the more certain; and trusting implicitly in Lee's ability to stave off defeat, he rode northwards with redoubled assurance of decisive victory. Forward was the cry, and though the heat was stifling, and the dust, rising from the deep ruts on the unmetalled road, rose in dense clouds beneath the trees, and men dropped fainting in the ranks, the great column pushed on without a check.[1]

About 2 P.M., as the rear brigades, Archer and Thomas, after checking Sickles, were just leaving Welford's House, some six miles distant, Jackson himself had reached 2 P.M. the plank road, the point where he intended to turn eastward against the Federal flank. Here he was met by Fitzhugh Lee, conveying most important and surprising information.

The cavalry regiment had halted when it arrived on the plank road ; all was reported quiet at the front ; the patrols were moving northward, and, attended by a staff officer, the young brigadier had ridden towards the turn-pike. The path they followed led to a wide clearing at the summit of a hill, from which there was a view eastward as far as Dowdall's Tavern. Below, and but a few hundred yards distant, ran the Federal breastworks, with abattis in front and long lines of stacked arms in rear; but untenanted by a single company. Two cannon were seen upon the high-road, the horses grazing quietly near at hand. The soldiers were scattered in small groups, laughing, cooking, smoking, sleeping, and playing cards, while others were butchering cattle and drawing rations. What followed is best told in General Fitzhugh Lee's own words.

'I rode back and met Jackson. "General," said I, "if you will ride with me, halting your columns here, out of sight, I will show you the great advantage of attacking down the old turnpike instead of the plank road, the enemy's lines being taken in reverse. Bring only one courier, as you will be in view from the top of the hill." Jackson assented. When we reached the eminence the picture below was still unchanged, and I watched him closely as he gazed on Howard's troops. His expression was one of intense interest. His eyes burnt with a brilliant glow, and his face was slightly flushed, radiant at the success of his flank movement. To the remarks made to him while the unconscious line of blue was pointed out

---

[1] There were three halts during the march of fourteen miles. Letter from Major Hotchkiss.

he made no reply, and yet during the five minutes he was on the hill his lips were moving. "Tell General Rodes," he said, suddenly turning his horse towards the courier, "to move across the plank road, and halt when he gets to the old turnpike. I will join him there." One more look at the Federal lines, and he rode rapidly down the hill.'

The cavalry, supported by the Stonewall Brigade, was immediately placed a short distance down the plank road, in order to mask the march of the column. At 4 P.M. Rodes was on the turnpike. Passing down it for about a mile, in the direction of the enemy's position, the troops were ordered to halt and form for battle. Not a shot had been fired. A few hostile patrols had been observed, but along the line of breastworks, watched closely by the cavalry, the Federal troops, still in the most careless security, were preparing their evening meal. Jackson, meanwhile, seated on a stump near the Brock road, had penned his last dispatch to General Lee.

'Near 3 P.M. May 2, 1863.

'General,—The enemy has made a stand at Chancellor's,[1] which is about two miles from Chancellorsville. I hope as soon as practicable to attack. I trust that an ever-kind Providence will bless us with great success.

'Respectfully,
'T. J. JACKSON, *Lieutenant-General.*

'The leading division is up, and the next two appear to be well closed.

'T. J. J.

'General R. E. Lee.'

25,000 men were now deploying in the forest within a mile of the Federal works, overlapping them both to north and south, and not a single general in the Northern army appears to have suspected their presence. The day had passed quietly at Chancellorsville. At a very early hour in

---

[1] Melzi Chancellor's house ; otherwise Dowdall's Tavern.

the morning Hooker, anticipating a vigorous attack, had ordered the First Army Corps, which had hitherto been acting with Sedgwick below Fredericksburg, to recross the Rappahannock and march to Chancellorsville. Averell's division of cavalry, also, which had been engaged near Orange Court House with W. H. F. Lee's two regiments, was instructed about the same time to rejoin the army as soon as possible, and was now marching by the left bank of the Rapidan to Ely's Ford. Anticipating, therefore, that he would soon be strongly reinforced, Hooker betrayed no uneasiness. Shortly after dawn he had ridden round his lines. Expecting at that time to be attacked in front only, he had no fault to find with their location or construction. 'As he looked over the barricades,' says General Howard, 'while receiving the cheers and salutes of the men, he said to me, "How strong! how strong!"' When the news came that a Confederate column was marching westward past Catherine Furnace, his attention, for the moment, was attracted to his right. At 10 A.M. he was still uncertain as to the meaning of Jackson's movement. As the hours went by, however, and Jackson's column disappeared in the forest, he again grew confident; the generals were informed that Lee was in full retreat towards Gordonsville, and a little later Sedgwick received the following :

'Chancellorsville, May 2, 1863, 4.10 P.M.

'General Butterfield,—The Major-General Commanding directs that General Sedgwick cross the river (*sic*) as soon as indications will permit,[1] capture Fredericksburg with everything in it, and vigorously pursue the enemy. We know that the enemy is fleeing, trying to save his trains. Two of Sickles' divisions are among them.

'J. H. VAN ALEN,
'*Brigadier-General and Aide-de-Camp.*'

'(Copy from Butterfield, at Falmouth, to Sedgwick, 5.50 P.M.).'

[1] Sedgwick had crossed the river on April 29 and 30.

At 4 o'clock, therefore, the moment Jackson's vanguard reached the old turnpike near Luckett's Farm, Hooker believed that all danger of a flank attack had passed away. His left wing was under orders to advance, as soon as a swamp to the front could be 'corduroyed,' and strike Lee in flank; while to reinforce Sickles, 'among the enemy's trains,' Williams' division of the Twelfth Corps was sent forward from the centre, Howard's reserve brigade (Barlow's) from the right, and Pleasonton's cavalry brigade from Hazel Grove.

The officers in charge of the Federal right appear to have been as unsuspicious as their commander. During the morning some slight preparations were made to defend the turnpike from the westward; a shallow line of rifle-pits, with a few epaulements for artillery, had been constructed on a low ridge, commanding open fields, which runs north from Dowdall's Tavern, and the wood beyond had been partially entangled. But this was all, and even when the only reserve of the Eleventh Army Corps, Barlow's brigade, was sent to Sickles, it was not considered necessary to make any change in the disposition of the troops. The belief that Lee and Jackson were retreating had taken firm hold of every mind. The pickets on the flank had indeed reported, from time to time, that infantry was massing in the thickets; and the Confederate cavalry, keeping just outside effective range, occupied every road and every clearing. Yet no attempt was made, by a strong reconnaissance in force, to ascertain what was actually going on within the forest; and the reports of the scouts were held to be exaggerated.

The neglect was the more marked in that the position of the Eleventh Army Corps was very weak. Howard had with him twenty regiments of infantry and six batteries; but his force was completely isolated. His extreme right, consisting of four German regiments, was posted in the forest, with two guns facing westward on the pike, and a line of intrenchments facing south. On the low hill eastward, where Talley's Farm, a small wooden cottage, stood in the midst of a wide clearing, were two more German regiments and two American. Then, near the junction of the roads, intervened a patch of forest, which was occupied by four regiments, with a brigade upon their left; and beyond, nearly a mile wide from north to south, and five or six hundred yards in breadth, were the open fields round the little Wilderness Church, dipping at first to a shallow brook, and then rising gradually to a house called Dowdall's Tavern. In these fields, south of the turnpike, were the breastworks held by the second division of the Eleventh Army Corps; and here were six regiments, with several batteries in close support. The 60th New York and 26th Wisconsin, near the Hawkins House at the north end of the fields, faced to the west; the remainder all faced south. Beyond Dowdall's Tavern rose the forest, dark and impenetrable to the view; but to the south-east, nearly two miles from Talley's, the clearings of Hazel Grove were plainly visible. This part of the line, originally entrusted to General Sickles, was now unguarded, for two divisions of the Third Corps were moving on the Furnace; and the nearest force which could render support to Howard's was Berry's division, retained in reserve north-east of Chancellorsville, three miles distant from Talley's Farm and nearly two from Howard's left.

The Confederates, meanwhile, were rapidly forming for attack. Notwithstanding their fatigue, for many of the brigades had marched over fifteen miles, the men were in the highest spirits. A young staff-officer, who passed along the column, relates that he was everywhere recognised with the usual greetings. 'Say, here's one of old Jack's little boys; let him by, boys!' 'Have a good breakfast this morning, sonny?' 'Better hurry up, or you'll catch it for gettin' behind.' 'Tell old Jack we're all a-comin'. Don't let him begin the fuss till we get there!' But on reaching the turnpike orders were given that all noise should cease, and the troops, deploying for a mile or more on either side of the road, took up their formation for attack. In front were the skirmishers of Rodes' division, under Major Blackford; four hundred yards in rear came the lines of battle, Rodes forming the first line ;[1] Colston, at two hundred yards distance, the second line ; A. P. Hill, part in line and part in column, the third. In little more than an hour-and-a-half, notwithstanding the dense woods, the formation was completed, and the lines dressed at the proper angle to the road.

5.45 P.M. Notwithstanding that the enemy might at any moment awake to their danger, not a single precaution was neglected. Jackson was determined that the troops should move forward in good order, and that every officer and man should know what was expected from him. Staff-officers had been stationed at various points to maintain communication between the divisions, and the divisional and brigade commanders had received their instructions. The whole force was to push resolutely forward through the forest. The open hill, about a thousand yards eastward, on which stood Talley's Farm, was to be carried at all hazard, for, so far as could be ascertained, it commanded, over an intervening patch of forest, the ridge which ran north from Dowdall's Tavern. After the capture of the heights at Talley's, if the Federals showed a determined front on their second line, Rodes was to halt under cover until the artillery could come up and dislodge them. Under no other circumstances was there to be any pause in the advance. A brigade of the first line was detailed to guard the right flank, a regiment the left ; and the second and third lines were ordered to support the first, whenever it might be necessary, without waiting for further instructions. The field hospital was established at the Old Wilderness Tavern.

The men were in position, eagerly awaiting the signal ; their quick intelligence had already realised the situation, and all was life and animation. Across the narrow clearing stretched the long grey lines, penetrating far into the forest on either flank ; in the centre, on the road, were four

[1] Rodes' brigades were formed in the following order :

```
  ...................................................    .........
: |    ____     ____     ____     ____
: |  Iverson  O'Neal    Doles   Colquitt
                                         _____   :
                                         Ramseur  :
```

Napoleon guns, the horses fretting with excitement; far
to the rear, their rifles glistening under the long shafts of
the setting sun, the heavy columns of A. P. Hill's division
were rapidly advancing, and the rumble of the artillery,
closing to the front, grew louder and louder. Jackson,
watch in hand, sat silent on 'Little Sorrel,' his slouched
hat drawn low over his eyes, and his lips tightly compressed. On his right was General Rodes, tall, lithe, and
soldierly, and on Rodes' right was Major Blackford.

'Are you ready, General Rodes?' said Jackson.

'Yes, sir,' said Rodes, impatient as his men.

'You can go forward, sir,' said Jackson.

A nod from Rodes was a sufficient order to Blackford,
and the woods rang with the notes of a single bugle.
6 P.M.   Back came the responses from bugles to right and
left, and the skirmishers, dashing through the
wild undergrowth, sprang eagerly to their work, followed
by the quick rush of the lines of battle. For a moment
the troops seemed buried in the thickets; then, as the
enemy's sentries, completely taken by surprise, fired a few
scattered shots, and the guns on the turnpike came quickly
into action, the echoes waked; through the still air of the
summer evening rang the rebel yell, filling the forest far
to north and south, and the hearts of the astonished
Federals, lying idly behind their breastworks, stood still
within them.

So rapid was the advance, so utterly unexpected the
attack, that the pickets were at once over-run; and,
crashing through the timber, driving before it the wild
creatures of the forest, deer, and hares, and foxes,
the broad front of the mighty torrent bore down upon
Howard's flank. For a few moments the four regiments
which formed his right, supported by two guns, held
staunchly together, and even checked for a brief space the
advance of O'Neal's brigade. But from the right and from
the left the grey infantry swarmed round them; the second
line came surging forward to O'Neal's assistance; the
gunners were shot down and their pieces captured; and in
ten minutes the right brigade of the Federal army, sub-

merged by numbers, was flying in panic across the clearing. Here, near Talley's Farm, on the fields south of the turnpike and in the forest to the north, another brigade, hastily changing front, essayed to stay the rout. But Jackson's horse-artillery, moving forward at a gallop, poured in canister at short range; and three brigades, O'Neal's, Iverson's, and Doles', attacked the Northerners fiercely in front and flank. No troops, however brave, could have long withstood that overwhelming rush. The slaughter was very great; every mounted officer was shot down, and in ten or fifteen minutes the fragments of these hapless regiments were retreating rapidly and tumultuously towards the Wilderness Church.

The first position had been captured, but there was no pause in the attack. As Jackson, following the artillery, rode past Talley's Farm, and gazed across the clearing to the east, he saw a sight which raised high his hopes of a decisive victory. Already, in the green cornfields, the spoils of battle lay thick around him. Squads of prisoners were being hurried to the rear. Abandoned guns, and waggons overturned, the wounded horses still struggling in the traces, were surrounded by the dead and dying of Howard's brigades. Knapsacks, piled in regular order, arms, blankets, accoutrements, lay in profusion near the breastworks; and beyond, under a rolling cloud of smoke and dust, the bare fields, sloping down to the brook, were covered with fugitives. Still further eastward, along the plank road, speeding in wild confusion towards Chancellorsville, was a dense mass of men and waggons; cattle, maddened with fright, were rushing to and fro, and on the ridge beyond the little church, pushing their way through the terror-stricken throng like ships through a heavy sea, or breaking into fragments before the pressure, the irregular lines of a few small regiments were moving hastily to the front. At more than one point on the edge of the distant woods guns were coming into action; the hill near Talley's Farm was covered with projectiles; men were falling, and the Confederate first line was already in some confusion.

Galloping up the turnpike, and urging the artillery forward with voice and gesture, Jackson passed through the ranks of his eager infantry; and then Rodes's division, rushing down the wooded slopes, burst from the covert, and, driving their flying foes before them, advanced against the trenches on the opposite ridge.   Here and there the rush of the first line was checked by the bold resistance of the German regiments.   On the right, especially, progress was slow, for Colquitt's brigade, drawn off by the pressure of Federal outposts in the woods to the south, had lost touch with the remainder of the division; Ramseur's brigade in rear had been compelled to follow suit, and on this flank the Federals were most effectively supported by their artillery.   But Iverson, O'Neal, and Doles, hardly halting to reform as they left the woods, and followed closely by the second line, swept rapidly across the fields, dashed back the regiments which sought to check them, and under a hot fire of grape and canister pressed resolutely forward.

The rifle-pits on the ridge were occupied by the last brigade of Howard's Army Corps.   A battery was in rear, three more were on the left, near Dowdall's Tavern, and many of the fugitives from Talley's Farm had rallied behind the breastwork.   But a few guns and four or five thousand rifles, although the ground to the front was clear and open, were powerless to arrest the rush of Jackson's veterans. The long lines of colours, tossing redly above the swiftly moving ranks, never for a moment faltered; the men, running alternately to the front, delivered their fire, stopped for a moment to load, and then again ran on.   Nearer and nearer they came, until the defenders of the trenches, already half demoralised, could mark through the smoke-drift the tanned faces, the fierce eyes, and the gleaming bayonets of their terrible foes.   The guns were already flying, and the position was outflanked; yet along the whole length of the ridge the parapets still blazed with fire; and while men fell headlong in the Confederate ranks, for a moment there was a check.   But it was the check of a mighty wave, mounting slowly to full volume, ere it falls in thunder on the shrinking sands.   Running to the front with uplifted swords, the officers gave the signal for the charge.

The men answered with a yell of triumph; the second line, closing rapidly on the first, could no longer be restrained; and as the grey masses, crowding together in their excitement, breasted the last slope, the Federal infantry, in every quarter of the field, gave way before them; the ridge was abandoned, and through the dark pines beyond rolled the rout of the Eleventh Army Corps.

It was seven o'clock. Twilight was falling on the woods; and Rodes' and Colston's divisions had become so inextricably mingled that officers could not find their men nor men their officers. But Jackson, galloping into the disordered ranks, directed them to press the pursuit. His face was aglow with the blaze of battle. His swift gestures and curt orders, admitting of no question, betrayed the fierce intensity of his resolution. Although the great tract of forest, covering Chancellorsville on the west, had swallowed up the fugitives, he had no need of vision to reveal to him the extent of his success. 10,000 men had been utterly defeated. The enemy's right wing was scattered to the winds. The Southerners were within a mile-and-a-half of the Federals' centre and completely in rear of their intrenchments; and the White House or Bullock road, only half-a-mile to the front, led directly to Hooker's line of retreat by the United States Ford. Until that road was in his possession Jackson was determined to call no halt. The dense woods, the gathering darkness, the fatigue and disorder of his troops, he regarded no more than he did the enemy's overwhelming numbers. In spirit he was standing at Hooker's side, and he saw, as clearly as though the intervening woods had been swept away, the condition to which his adversary had been reduced.

To the Federal headquarters confusion and dismay had come, indeed, with appalling suddenness. Late in the afternoon Hooker was sitting with two aides-de-camp in the verandah of the Chancellor House. There were few troops in sight. The Third Corps and Pleasonton's cavalry had long since disappeared in the forest. The Twelfth Army Corps, with the exception of two brigades, was already advancing against Anderson; and only the trains and some artillery remained

within the intrenchments at Hazel Grove. All was going
well. A desultory firing broke out at intervals to the eastward, but it was not sustained ; and three miles to the south,
where, as Hooker believed, in pursuit of Jackson, Sickles
and Pleasonton were, the reports of their cannon, growing
fainter and fainter as they pushed further south, betokened
no more than a lively skirmish. The quiet of the Wilderness, save for those distant sounds, was undisturbed, and
men and animals, free from every care, were enjoying the
calm of the summer evening. It was about half-past
six. Suddenly the cannonade swelled to a heavier roar,
and the sound came from a new direction. All were
listening intently, speculating on what this might mean,
when a staff-officer, who had stepped out to the front
of the house and was looking down the plank road with
his glass, exclaimed : ' My God, here they come ! '
Hooker sprang upon his horse ; and riding rapidly down
the road, met the stragglers of the Eleventh Corps—men,
waggons, and ambulances, an ever-increasing crowd—
rushing in blind terror from the forest, flying they knew
not whither. The whole of the right wing, they said,
overwhelmed by superior numbers, was falling back on
Chancellorsville, and Stonewall Jackson was in hot pursuit.

The situation had changed in the twinkling of an eye.
Just now congratulating himself on the complete success
of his manœuvres, on the retreat of his enemies, on the
flight of Jackson and the helplessness of Lee, Hooker
saw his strong intrenchments taken in reverse, his army
scattered, his reserves far distant, and the most dreaded of
his opponents, followed by his victorious veterans, within a
few hundred yards of his headquarters. His weak point had
been found, and there were no troops at hand wherewith
to restore the fight. The centre was held only by the two
brigades of the Twelfth Corps at the Fairview Cemetery.
The works at Hazel Grove were untenanted, save by a few
batteries and a handful of infantry. The Second and Fifth
Corps on the left were fully occupied by McLaws, for Lee,
at the first sound of Jackson's guns, had ordered a vigorous
attack up the pike and the plank road. Sickles, with

20,000 men, was far away, isolated and perhaps surrounded, and the line of retreat, the road to United States Ford, was absolutely unprotected.

Messengers were despatched in hot haste to recall Sickles and Pleasonton to Hazel Grove. Berry's division, forming the reserve north-east of the Chancellor House, was summoned to Fairview, and Hays' brigade of the Second Corps ordered to support it. But what could three small brigades, hurried into position and unprotected by intrenchments, avail against 25,000 Southerners, led by Stonewall Jackson, and animated by their easy victory? If Berry and Hays could stand fast against the rush of fugitives, it was all that could be expected; and as the uproar in the dark woods swelled to a deeper volume, and the yells of the Confederates, mingled with the crash of the musketry, were borne to his ears, Hooker must have felt that all was lost. To make matters worse, as Pleasonton, hurrying back with his cavalry, arrived at Hazel Grove, the trains of the Third Army Corps, fired on by the Confederate skirmishers, dashed wildly across the clearing, swept through the parked artillery, and, breaking through the forest, increased the fearful tumult which reigned round Chancellorsville.

The gunners, however, with a courage beyond all praise, stood staunchly to their pieces; and soon a long line of artillery, for which two regiments of the Third Army Corps, coming up rapidly from the south, formed a sufficient escort, was established on this commanding hill. Other batteries, hitherto held in reserve, took post on the high ground at Fairview, a mile to the north-east, and, although Berry's infantry were not yet in position, and the stream of broken troops was still pouring past, a strong front of fifty guns opposed the Confederate advance.

But it was not the artillery that saved Hooker from irretrievable disaster.[1] As they followed the remnants of the Eleventh Army Corps, the progress of Rodes and Colston had been far less rapid than when they stormed forward

---

[1] Lieutenant-Colonel Hamlin, the latest historian of Chancellorsville, has completely disposed of the legend that these fifty guns repulsed a desperate attack on Hazel Grove.

past the Wilderness Church. A regiment of Federal cavalry, riding to Howard's aid by a track from Hazel Grove to the plank road, was quickly swept aside ; but the deep darkness of the forest, the efforts of the officers to re-form the ranks, the barriers opposed by the tangled undergrowth, the difficulty of keeping the direction, brought a large portion of the troops to a standstill. At the junction of the White House road the order to halt was given, and although a number of men, pushing impetuously forward, seized a line of log breastworks which ran north-west through the timber below the Fairview heights, the pursuit was stayed in the midst of the dense thickets.

At this moment, shortly after eight o'clock, Jackson was at Dowdall's Tavern. The reports from the front informed him that his first and second lines had halted ; General Rodes, who had galloped up the plank road to reconnoitre, sent in word that there were no Federal troops to be seen between his line and the Fairview heights ; and Colonel Cobb, of the 44th Virginia, brought the news that the strong intrenchments, less than a mile from Chancellorsville, had been occupied without resistance.

8.15 P.M.

There was a lull in the battle ; the firing had died away, and the excited troops, with a clamour that was heard in the Federal lines, sought their companies and regiments by the dim light of the rising moon. But deeming that nothing was done while aught remained to do, Jackson was already planning a further movement. Sending instructions to A. P. Hill to relieve Rodes and Colston, and to prepare for a night attack, he rode forward, almost unattended, amongst his rallying troops, and lent his aid to the efforts of the regimental officers. Intent on bringing up the two divisions in close support of Hill, he passed from one regiment to another. Turning to Colonel Cobb, he said to him : ' Find General Rodes, and tell him to occupy the barricade [1] at once,' and then added : ' I need your help for a time ; this disorder must be corrected. As you go along the right, tell the troops from me to get into line and preserve their order.'

[1] In the woods west of the Fairview Heights.

It was long, however, before the men could be assembled, and the delay was increased by an unfortunate incident. Jackson's chief of artillery, pressing forward up the plank road to within a thousand yards of Chancellorsville, opened fire with three guns upon the enemy's position. This audacious proceeding evoked a quick reply. Such Federal guns as could be brought to bear were at once turned upon the road, and although the damage done was small, A. P. Hill's brigades, just coming up into line, were for the moment checked; under the hail of shell and canister the artillery horses became unmanageable, the drivers lost their nerve, and as they rushed to the rear some of the infantry joined them, and a stampede was only prevented by the personal efforts of Jackson, Colston, and their staff-officers. Colonel Crutchfield was then ordered to cease firing; the Federals did the same; and A. P. Hill's brigades, that of General Lane leading, advanced to the deserted breastworks, while two brigades, one from Rodes' division and one from Colston's, were ordered to guard the roads from Hazel Grove.

These arrangements made, Jackson proceeded to join his advanced line. At the point where the track to the White House and United States ford strikes 8.45 P.M. the plank road he met General Lane, seeking his instructions for the attack. They were sufficiently brief: 'Push right ahead, Lane; right ahead!' As Lane galloped off to his command, General Hill and some of his staff came up, and Jackson gave Hill his orders. 'Press them; cut them off from the United States Ford, Hill; press them.' General Hill replied that he was entirely unacquainted with the topography of the country, and asked for an officer to act as guide. Jackson directed Captain Boswell, his chief engineer, to accompany General Hill, and then, turning to the front, rode up the plank road, passing quickly through the ranks of the 18th North Carolina of Lane's brigade. Two or three hundred yards eastward the general halted, for the ringing of axes and the words of command were distinctly audible in the enemy's lines.

While the Confederates were re-forming, Hooker's

reserves had reached the front, and Berry's regiments, on the Fairview heights, using their bayonets and tin-plates for intrenching tools, piling up the earth with their hands, and hacking down the brushwood with their knives, were endeavouring in desperate haste to provide some shelter, however slight, against the rush that they knew was about to come.

After a few minutes, becoming impatient for the advance of Hill's division, Jackson turned and retraced his steps towards his own lines. 'General,' said an officer who was with him, 'you should not expose yourself so much.' 'There is no danger, sir, the enemy is routed. Go back and tell General Hill to press on.'

Once more, when he was only sixty or eighty yards from where the 18th North Carolina were standing in the trees, he drew rein and listened—the whole party, generals, staff-officers, and couriers, hidden in the deep shadows of the silent woods. At this moment a single rifle-shot rang out with startling suddenness.

A detachment of Federal infantry, groping their way through the thickets, had approached the Southern lines.

The skirmishers on both sides were now engaged, and the lines of battle in rear became keenly on the alert. Some mounted officers galloped hastily back to their commands. The sound startled the Confederate soldiers, and an officer of the 18th North Carolina, seeing a group of strange horsemen riding towards him through the darkness —for Jackson, hearing the firing, had turned back to his own lines—gave the order to fire.

The volley was fearfully effective. Men and horses fell dead and dying on the narrow track. Jackson himself received three bullets, one in the right hand, and two in the left arm, cutting the main artery, and crushing the bone below the shoulder, and as the reins dropped upon his neck, 'Little Sorrel,' frantic with terror, plunged into the wood and rushed towards the Federal lines. An overhanging bough struck his rider violently in the face, tore off his cap, and nearly unhorsed him; but recovering his seat, he managed to seize the bridle with his bleeding hand, and turned into the road. Here Captain Wilbourn, one of his staff-officers, succeeded in catching the reins ; and, as the horse stopped, Jackson leaned forward and fell into his arms. Captain Hotchkiss, who had just returned from a reconnaissance, rode off to find Dr. McGuire, while Captain Wilbourn, with a small penknife, ripped up the sleeve of the wounded arm. As he was doing so, General Hill, who had himself been exposed to the fire of the North Carolinians, reached the scene, and, throwing himself from his horse, pulled off Jackson's gauntlets, which were full of blood, and bandaged the shattered arm with a handkerchief. 'General,' he said, 'are you much hurt?' 'I think I am,' was the reply, 'and all my wounds are from my own men. I believe my right arm is broken.'

To all questions put to him he answered in a perfectly calm and self-possessed tone, and, although he spoke no word of complaint, he was manifestly growing weaker. It seemed impossible to move him, and yet it was absolutely necessary that he should be carried to the rear. He was still in front of his own lines, and, even as Hill was speaking, two of the enemy's skirmishers, emerging from the thicket, halted within a few paces of the little group. Hill, turning quietly to his escort, said, 'Take charge of those men,' and two orderlies, springing forward, seized the rifles of the astonished Federals. Lieutenant Morrison, Jackson's aide-de-camp, who had gone down the road to reconnoitre, now reported that he had seen a section of artillery unlimbering close at hand. Hill gave orders that the general should be at once removed, and that no one should tell the men that he was wounded. Jackson, lying on Hill's breast, opened his eyes, and said, 'Tell them simply that you have a wounded Confederate officer.' Lieutenants Smith and Morrison, and Captain Leigh of Hill's staff, now lifted him to his feet, and with their aid he walked a few steps through the trees. But hardly had they gained the road when the Federal batteries, along their whole front, opened a terrible fire of grape and canister. The storm of bullets, tearing through the foliage, was fortunately directed too high, and the three young officers, laying the general down by the roadside, endeavoured to shield him by lying between him and the deadly hail. The earth round them was torn up by the shot, covering them with dust; boughs fell from the trees, and fire flashed from the flints and gravel of the roadway. Once Jackson attempted to rise; but Smith threw his arm over him, holding him down, and saying, 'General, you must be still—it will cost you your life to rise.'

After a few minutes, however, the enemy's gunners, changing from canister to shell, mercifully increased their range; and again, as the Confederate infantry came hurrying to the front, their wounded leader, supported by strong arms, was lifted to his feet. Anxious that the men should not recognise him, Jackson turned aside into the wood, and slowly and painfully dragged himself through the undergrowth. As he passed along, General Pender, whose brigade was then pushing forward, asked Smith who it was that was wounded. 'A Confederate officer' was the reply; but as they came nearer Pender, despite the darkness, saw that it was Jackson. Springing from his horse, he hurriedly expressed his regret, and added that his lines were so much disorganised by the enemy's artillery that he feared it would be necessary to fall back. 'At this moment,' says an eye-witness, 'the scene was a fearful one. The air seemed to be alive with the shriek of shells and the whistling of bullets; horses riderless and mad with fright dashed in every direction; hundreds left the ranks and hurried to the rear, and the groans of the wounded and dying mingled with the wild shouts of others to be led again to the assault. Almost fainting as he was from loss of blood, desperately wounded, and in the midst of this awful uproar, Jackson's heart was unshaken. The words of Pender seemed to rouse him to life. Pushing aside those who supported him, he raised himself to his full height, and answered feebly, but distinctly enough to be heard above the din, "You must hold your ground, General Pender; you must hold out to the last, sir."'

His strength was now completely gone, and he asked to be allowed to lie down. His staff-officers, however, refused assent. The shells were still crashing through the forest, and a litter having been brought up by Captain Leigh, he was carried slowly towards Dowdall's Tavern. But before they were free of the tangled wood, one of the stretcher-bearers, struck by a shot in the arm, let go the handle. Jackson fell violently to the ground on his wounded side. His agony must have been intense, and for the first time he was heard to groan.

Smith sprang to his side, and as he raised his head a bright beam of moonlight made its way through the thick foliage, and rested upon his white and lacerated face. The aide-de-camp was startled by its great pallor and still-ness, and cried out, 'General, are you seriously hurt?' 'No, Mr. Smith, don't trouble yourself about me,' he replied quietly, and added some words about winning the battle first, and attending to the wounded afterwards. He was again placed upon the litter, and carried a few hundred yards, still followed by the Federal shells, to where his medical director was waiting with an ambulance.

Dr. McGuire knelt down beside him and said, 'I hope you are not badly hurt, General?' He replied very calmly but feebly, 'I am badly injured, doctor, I fear I am dying.' After a pause he went on, 'I am glad you have come. I think the wound in my shoulder is still bleeding.' The bandages were readjusted and he was lifted into the ambulance, where Colonel Crutchfield, who had also been seriously wounded, was already lying. Whisky and morphia were administered, and by the light of pine torches, carried by a few soldiers, he was slowly driven through the fields where Hooker's right had so lately fled before his impetuous onset. All was done that could ease his sufferings, but some jolting of the ambulance over the rough road was unavoidable; 'and yet,' writes Dr. McGuire, 'his uniform politeness did not forsake him even in these most trying circumstances. His complete control, too, over his mind, enfeebled as it was by loss of blood and pain, was wonderful. His suffering was intense; his hands were cold, his skin clammy. But not a groan escaped him—not a sign of suffering, except the slight corrugation of the brow, the fixed, rigid face, the thin lips, so tightly compressed that the impression of the teeth could be seen through them. Except these, he controlled by his iron will all evidence of emotion, and, more difficult than this even, he controlled that disposition to restlessness which many of us have observed upon the battle-field as attending great loss of blood. Nor was he forgetful of others. He expressed very feelingly his sympathy for Crutchfield, and once, when the latter groaned aloud, he directed the ambulance to stop, and requested me to see if something could not be done for his relief.

'After reaching the hospital, he was carried to a tent, and placed in bed, covered with blankets, and another drink of whisky and water given him. Two hours and a half elapsed before sufficient reaction took place to warrant an examination, and at two o'clock on Sunday morning I informed him that chloroform would be given him; I told him also that amputation would probably be required, and asked, if it was found necessary, whether it should be done at once. He replied promptly, " Yes, certainly, Dr. McGuire, do for me whatever you think best."

'Chloroform was then administered, and the left arm amputated about two inches below the shoulder. Throughout the whole of the operation, and until all the dressings were applied, he continued insensible. About half-past three, Colonel (then Major) Pendleton arrived at the hospital. He stated that General Hill had been wounded, and that the troops were in great disorder. General Stuart was in command, and had sent him to see the general. At first I declined to permit an interview, but Pendleton urged that the safety of the army and success of the cause depended upon his seeing him. When he entered the tent the general said, " Well, Major, I am glad to see you; I thought you were killed." Pendleton briefly explained the position of affairs, gave Stuart's message, and asked what should be done. Jackson was at once interested, and asked in his quick way several questions. When they were answered, he remained silent, evidently trying to think; he contracted his brow, set his mouth, and for some moments lay obviously endeavouring to concentrate his thoughts. For a moment we believed he had succeeded, for his nostrils dilated, and his eye flashed with its old fire, but it was only for a moment: his face relaxed again, and presently he answered, very feebly and sadly: "I don't know—I can't tell; say to General Stuart he must do what he thinks best." Soon after this he slept.'

So, leaving behind him, struggling vainly against the oppression of his mortal hurt, the one man who could have completed the Confederate victory, Pendleton rode wearily through the night. Jackson's fall, at so critical a moment, just as the final blow was to be delivered, had proved a terrible disaster. Hill, who alone knew his intention of moving to the White House, had been wounded by a fragment of shell as he rode back to lead his troops. Boswell, who had been ordered to point out the road, had been killed by the same volley which struck down his chief, and the subordinate generals, without instructions and without guides, with their men in disorder, and the enemy's artillery playing fiercely on the forest, had hesitated to advance. Hill, remaining in a litter near the line of battle, had sent for Stuart. The cavalry commander, however, was at some distance from the field. Late in the evening, finding it impossible to employ his command at the front, he had been detached by Jackson, a regiment of infantry supporting him, to take and hold Ely's Ford. He had already arrived within view of a Federal camp established at that point, and was preparing to charge the enemy, under cover of the night, when Hill's messenger recalled him.

When Stuart reached the front he found the troops still halted, Rodes and Colston reforming on the open fields near Dowdall's Tavern, the Light Division deployed within the forest, and the generals anxious for their own security.

So far the attack had been completely successful, but Lee's lack of strength prevented the full accomplishment of his design. Had Longstreet been present, with Pickett and Hood to lead his splendid infantry, the

Third Corps and the Twelfth would have been so hardly pressed that Chancellorsville, Hazel Grove, and the White House would have fallen an easy prize to Jackson's bayonets. Anderson, with four small brigades, was powerless to hold the force confronting him, and marching rapidly northwards, Sickles had reached Hazel Grove before Jackson fell. Here Pleasonton, with his batteries, was still in position, and Hooker had not yet lost his head. As soon as Birney's and Whipple's divisions had come up, forming in columns of brigades behind the guns, Sickles was ordered to assail the enemy's right flank and check his advance. Just before midnight the attack was made, in two lines of battle, supported by strong columns. The night was very clear and still; the moon, nearly full, threw enough light into the woods to facilitate the advance, and the tracks leading north-west served as lines of direction.

The attack, however, although gallantly made, gained no material advantage. The preliminary movements were plainly audible to the Confederates, and Lane's brigade, most of which was now south of the plank road, had made every preparation to receive it. Against troops lying down in the woods the Federal artillery, although fifty or sixty guns were in action, made but small impression; and the dangers of a night attack, made upon troops who are expecting it, and whose *moral* is unaffected, were forcibly illustrated. The confusion in the forest was very great; a portion of the assailing force, losing direction, fell foul of Berry's division at the foot of the Fairview heights, which had not been informed of the movement, and at least two regiments, fired into from front and rear, broke up in panic. Some part of the log breastworks which Jackson's advanced line had occupied were recaptured; but not a single one of the assailants, except as prisoners, reached the plank road. And yet the attack was an exceedingly well-timed stroke, and as such, although the losses were heavy, had a very considerable effect on the issue of the day's fighting. It showed, or seemed to show, that the Federals were still in good heart, that they were rapidly concentrating, and that the Confederates might be met by

STUART   457

vigorous counter-strokes. 'The fact,' said Stuart in his
official dispatch, 'that the attack was made, and at night,
made me apprehensive of a repetition of it.'

So, while Jackson slept through the hours of darkness
that should have seen the consummation of his enterprise,
his soldiers lay beside their arms; and the Federals, digging,
felling, and building, constructed a new line of parapet, protected by abattis, and strengthened by a long array of guns,
on the slopes of Fairview and Hazel Grove. The respite
which the fall of the Confederate leader had brought them
was not neglected; the fast-spreading panic was stayed;
the First Army Corps, rapidly crossing the Rappahannock, secured the road to the White House, and Averell's
division of cavalry reached Ely's Ford. On the left,
between Chancellorsville and the river, where a young
Federal colonel, named Miles,[1] handled his troops with conspicuous skill, Lee's continuous attacks had been successfully repulsed, and at dawn on the morning of May 3 the

May 3.   situation of the Union army was far from unpromising. A gap of nearly two miles intervened
between the Confederate wings, and within this gap, on the
commanding heights of Hazel Grove and Fairview, the
Federals were strongly intrenched. An opportunity for
dealing a crushing counterblow—for holding one portion of
Lee's army in check while the other was overwhelmed—appeared to present itself. The only question was whether the
moral of the general and the men could be depended upon.

In Stuart, however, Hooker had to deal with a soldier
who was no unworthy successor of Stonewall Jackson.
Reluctantly abandoning the idea of a night attack, the
cavalry general, fully alive to the exigencies of the situation, had determined to reduce the interval between himself and Lee; and during the night the artillery was
brought up to the front, and the batteries deployed
wherever they could find room. Just before the darkness
began to lift, orders were received from Lee that the assault
was to be made as early as possible; and the right wing,
swinging round in order to come abreast of the centre,

---

[1] Commander-in-Chief, U.S. Army, 1898.

became hotly engaged. Away to the south-east, across the hills held by the Federals, came the responding thunder of Lee's guns; and 40,000 infantry, advancing through the woods against front and flank, enveloped in a circle of fire a stronghold which was held by over 60,000 muskets.

It is unnecessary to describe minutely the events of the morning. The Federal troops, such as were brought into action, fought well; but Jackson's tremendous attack had already defeated Hooker. Before Sickles made his night attack from Hazel Grove he had sent orders for Sedgwick to move at once, occupy Fredericksburg, seize the heights, and march westward by the plank road; and, at the same time, he had instructed his engineers to select and fortify a position about a mile in rear of Chancellorsville. So, when Stuart pressed forward, not only had this new position been occupied by the First and Fifth Army Corps, but the troops hitherto in possession of Hazel Grove were already evacuating their intrenchments.

These dispositions sufficiently attest the demoralisation of the Federal commander. As the historian of the Army of the Potomac puts it: 'The movement to be executed by Sedgwick was precisely one of those movements which, according as they are wrought out, may be either the height of wisdom or the height of folly. Its successful accomplishment certainly promised very brilliant results. It is easy to see how seriously Lee's safety would be compromised if, while engaged with Hooker in front, he should suddenly find a powerful force assailing his rear, and grasping already his direct line of communication with Richmond. But if, on the other hand, Lee should be able by any slackness on the part of his opponent to engage him in front with a part of his force, while he should turn swiftly round to assail the isolated moving column, it is obvious that he would be able to repulse or destroy that column, and then by a vigorous return, meet or attack his antagonist's main body. In the successful execution of this plan not only was Sedgwick bound to the most energetic action, but Hooker also was engaged by every consideration of honour and duty to so act as to make the dangerous task he had assigned to Sedgwick possible.'[1]

But so far from aiding his subordinate by a heavy counter-attack on Lee's front, Hooker deliberately abandoned the Hazel Grove salient, which, keeping asunder the Confederate wings, strongly facilitated such a manœuvre; and more than this, he divided his own army into two portions, of which the rear, occupying the new position, was actually forbidden to reinforce the front.

It is possible that Hooker contemplated an early retreat of his whole force to the second position. If so, Lee and Stuart were too quick for him. The cavalry commander, as soon as it became light, and the hills and undulations of the Wilderness emerged from the shadows, immediately recognised the importance of Hazel Grove. The hill was quickly seized; thirty pieces of artillery, established on the crest, enfiladed the Federal batteries, facing west, on the heights of Fairview; and the brigade on Stuart's extreme right was soon in touch with the troops directed by General Lee. Then against the three sides of the Federal position the battle raged. From the south and south-east came Anderson and McLaws, the batteries unlimbering on every eminence, and the infantry, hitherto held back, attacking with the vigour which their gallant commanders knew so well how to inspire. And from the west, formed in three lines, Hill's division to the front, came the Second Army Corps. The men knew by this time that the leader whom they trusted beyond all others had been struck down, that he was lying wounded, helpless, far away in rear. Yet his spirit was still with them. Stuart, galloping along the ranks, recalled him with ringing words to their memories, and as the bugles sounded the onset, it was with a cry of 'Remember Jackson!' that his soldiers rushed fiercely upon the Federal breastworks.

The advanced line, within the forest, was taken at the first rush; the second, at the foot of the Fairview heights, protected by a swampy stream, a broad belt of abattis, and

[1] *Campaigns of the Army of the Potomac*, pp. 241-2.

with thirty guns on the hill behind, proved far more formidable, and Hill's division was forced back. But Rodes and Colston were in close support. The fight was speedily renewed ; and then came charge and counter-charge ; the storm of the parapets ; the rally of the defenders ; the rush with the bayonet ; and, mowing down men like grass, the fearful sweep of case and canister. Twice the Confederates were repulsed. Twice they reformed, brigade mingled with brigade, regiment with regiment, and charged again in the teeth of the thirty guns.

On both sides ammunition began to fail ; the brushwood took fire, the ground became hot beneath the foot, and many wounded perished miserably in the flames. Yet still, with the tangled abattis dividing the opposing lines, the fight went on ; both sides struggling fiercely, the Federals with the advantage of position, the Confederates of numbers, for Hooker refused to reinforce his gallant troops. At length the guns which Stuart had established on Hazel Grove, crossing their fire with those of McLaws and Anderson, gained the upper hand over the Union batteries. The storm of shell, sweeping the Fairview plateau, took the breastworks in reverse ; the Northern infantry, after five hours of such hot battle as few fields have witnessed, began sullenly to yield, and as Stuart, leading the last charge, leapt his horse over the parapet, the works were evacuated, and the tattered colours of the Confederates waved in triumph on the hill.

' The scene,' says a staff-officer, ' can never be effaced from the minds of those that witnessed it. The troops were pressing forward with all the ardour and enthusiasm of combat. The white smoke of musketry fringed the front of battle, while the artillery on the hills in rear shook the earth with its thunder and filled the air with the wild shrieking of the shells that plunged into the masses of the retreating foe. To add greater horror and sublimity to the scene, the Chancellorsville House and the woods surrounding it were wrapped in flames. It was then that General Lee rode to the front of his advancing battalions. His presence was the signal for one of those uncontrollable outbursts of enthusiasm which none can appreciate who have not witnessed them.

'The fierce soldiers, with their faces blackened with the smoke of battle, the wounded, crawling with feeble limbs from the fury of the devouring flames, all seemed possessed of a common impulse. One long, unbroken cheer, in which the feeble cry of those who lay helpless on the earth blended with the strong voices of those who still fought, hailed the presence of the victorious chief.

'His first care was for the wounded of both armies, and he was among the foremost at the burning mansion, where some of them lay. But at that moment, when the transports of his troops were drowning the roar of battle with acclamations, a note was brought to him from General Jackson. It was handed to him as he sat on his horse near the Chancellorsville House, and unable to open it with his gauntleted hands, he passed it to me with directions to read it to him. I shall never forget the look of pain and anguish that passed over his face as he listened. In a voice broken with emotion he bade me say to General Jackson that the victory was his. I do not know how others may regard this incident, but for myself, as I gave expression to the thoughts of his exalted mind, I forgot the genius that won the day in my reverence for the generosity that refused its glory.'

Lee's reply ran :—

'General,—I have just received your note, informing me that you were wounded. I cannot express my regret at the occurrence. Could I have directed events, I should have chosen for the good of the country to be disabled in your stead.

'I congratulate you upon the victory, which is due to your skill and energy.

'Very respectfully, your obedient servant,
'R. E. Lee, *General*.'

Such was the tribute, not the less valued that it was couched in no exaggerated terms, which was brought to the bedside in the quiet hospital. Jackson was almost alone. As the sound of cannon and musketry, borne across the forest, grew gradually louder, he had ordered all those who had remained with him, except Mr. Smith, to return to the battle-field and attend to their different duties.

His side, injured by his fall from the litter, gave him much pain, but his thoughts were still clear, and his speech coherent. 'General Lee,' he said, when his aide-de-camp read to him the Commander-in-Chief's brief words, 'is very kind, but he should give the praise to God.'

During the day the pain gradually ceased; the general grew brighter, and from those who visited the hospital he inquired minutely about the battle and the troops engaged. When conspicuous instances of courage were related his face lit up with enthusiasm, and he uttered his usual 'Good, good,' with unwonted energy when the gallant behaviour of his old command was alluded to. 'Some day,' he said, 'the men of that brigade will be proud to say to their children, "I was one of the Stonewall Brigade."' He disclaimed all right of his own to the name Stonewall: ' It belongs to the brigade and not to me.' That night he slept well, and was free from pain.

Meanwhile the Confederate army, resting on the heights of Chancellorsville, preparatory to an attack upon Hooker's second stronghold, had received untoward news. Sedgwick, at eleven o'clock in the morning, had carried Marye's Hill, and, driving Early before him, was moving up the plank road. Wilcox' brigade of Anderson's division, then at Banks' Ford, was ordered to retard the advance of the hostile column. McLaws was detached to Salem Church. The Second Army Corps and the rest of Anderson's division remained to hold Hooker in check, and for the moment operations at Chancellorsville were suspended.

McLaws, deploying his troops in the forest, two hundred and fifty yards from a wide expanse of cleared ground, pushed his skirmishers forward to the edge, and awaited the attack of a superior force. Reserving his fire to close quarters, its effect was fearful. But the Federals pushed forward; a school-house occupied as an advanced post was captured, and at this point Sedgwick was within an ace of breaking through. His second line, however, had not yet deployed, and a vigorous counterstroke, delivered by two brigades, drove back the whole of his leading division in great disorder. As night fell the Confederates, careful not to expose themselves to the Union reserves, retired to the forest, and Sedgwick, like Hooker, abandoned all further idea of offensive action.

The next morning Lee himself, with the three remaining brigades of Anderson, arrived upon the scene. Sedgwick, who had lost 5,000 men the preceding day, had fortified a position covering Banks' Ford, and occupied it with over 20,000 muskets. Lee, with the divisions of McLaws, Anderson, and Early, was slightly stronger. The attack was delayed, for the Federals held strong ground, difficult to reconnoitre; but once begun the issue was soon decided. Assailed in front and flanks, with no help coming from Hooker, and only a single bridge at Banks' Ford in rear, the Federals rapidly gave ground.

May 4.

Darkness, however, intensified by a thick fog, made pursuit difficult, and Sedgwick re-crossed the river with many casualties but in good order. During these operations, that is, from four o'clock on Sunday afternoon until after midnight on Monday, Hooker had not moved a single man to his subordinate's assistance.[1] So extraordinary a situation has seldom been seen in war: an army of 60,000 men, strongly fortified, was held in check for six-and-thirty hours by 20,000; while not seven miles away raged a battle on which the whole fate of the campaign depended.

Lee and Jackson had made no false estimate of Hooker's incapacity. Sedgwick's army corps had suffered so severely in men and in *moral* that it was not available for immediate service, even had it been transferred to Chancellorsville; and Lee was now free to concentrate his whole force against the main body of the Federal army. His men, notwithstanding their extraordinary exertions, were confident of victory. 'As I sheltered myself,' says an

---

[1] It is but fair, however, to state that Hooker, during the cannonade which preceded the final assault at Chancellorsville, had been severely bruised by a fall of masonry.

eye-witness, 'in a little farmhouse on the plank road

May 5.   the brigades of Anderson's division came splashing through the mud, in wild tumultuous spirits,
singing, shouting, jesting, heedless of soaking rags, drenched
to the skin, and burning again to mingle in the mad
revelry of battle.' [1]   But it was impossible to push forward,
for a violent rain-storm burst upon the Wilderness, and the
spongy soil, saturated with the deluge, absolutely precluded
all movement across country.   Hooker, who had already
made preparations for retreat, took advantage of the

May 6.   weather, and as soon as darkness set in put his
army in motion for the bridges.   By eight o'clock
on the morning of the 6th the whole force had crossed;
and when the Confederate patrols pushed forward, Lee
found that his victim had escaped.

The Army of the Potomac returned to its old camp on
the hills above Fredericksburg, and Lee reoccupied his
position on the opposite ridge.   Stoneman, who had scoured
the whole country to within a few miles of Richmond,
returned to Kelly's Ford on May 8.   The raid had effected
nothing.   The damage done to the railroads and canals was
repaired by the time the raiders had regained the Rappahannock.   Lee's operations at Chancellorsville had not
been affected in the very slightest degree by their presence
in his rear, while Stoneman's absence had proved the ruin
of the Federal army.   Jackson, who had been removed by
the Commander-in-Chief's order to Mr. Chandler's house,
near Guiney's Station, on the morning of May 5, was asked
what he thought of Hooker's plan of campaign.   His reply
was: 'It was in the main a good conception, an excellent
plan.   But he should not have sent away his cavalry; that
was his great blunder.   It was that which enabled me to
turn him without his being aware of it, and to take him in
the rear.   Had he kept his cavalry with him, his plan
would have been a very good one.'   This was not his only
comment on the great battle.   Among other things, he said
that he intended to cut the Federals off from the United
States Ford, and, taking a position between them and the

[1] Hon. Francis Lawley, the *Times*, June 16, 1863.

river, oblige them to attack him, adding, with a smile, 'My men sometimes fail to drive the enemy from a position, but they always fail to drive us away.' He spoke of General Rodes, and alluded in high terms to his splendid behaviour in the attack on Howard. He hoped he would be promoted, and he said that promotion should be made at once, upon the field, so as to act as an incentive to gallantry in others. He spoke of Colonel Willis, who had commanded the skirmishers, and praised him very highly, and referred most feelingly to the death of Paxton, the commander of the Stonewall Brigade, and of Captain Boswell, his chief engineer. In speaking of his own share in the victory he said: 'Our movement was a great success; I think the most successful military movement of my life. But I expect to receive far more credit for it than I deserve. Most men will think I planned it all from the first; but it was not so. I simply took advantage of circumstances as they were presented to me in the providence of God. I feel that His hand led me—let us give Him the glory.'

It must always be an interesting matter of speculation what the result would have been had Jackson accomplished his design, on the night he fell, of moving a large part of his command up the White House road, and barring the only line of retreat left open to the Federals.

Hooker, it is argued, had two corps in position which had been hardly engaged, the Second and the Fifth; and another, the First, under Reynolds, was coming up. Of these, 25,000 men might possibly, could they have been manœuvred in the forest, have been sent to drive Jackson back. And, undoubtedly, to those who think more of numbers than of human nature, of the momentum of the mass rather than the mental equilibrium of the general, the fact that a superior force of comparatively fresh troops was at Hooker's disposal will be sufficient to put the success of the Confederates out of court. Yet the question will always suggest itself, would not the report that a victorious enemy, of unknown strength, was pressing forward, in the darkness of the night, towards the only line of retreat,

have so demoralised the Federal commander and the
Federal soldiers, already shaken by the overthrow of
the Eleventh Army Corps, that they would have thought
only of securing their own safety ?   Would Hooker, whose
tactics the next day, after he had had the night given him
in which to recover his senses, were so inadequate, have
done better if he had received no respite ?   Would the soldiers of the three army corps not yet engaged, who had
been witnesses of the rout of Howard's divisions, have
fared better, when they heard the triumphant yells of
the advancing Confederates, than the hapless Germans ?
'The wounding of Jackson,' says a most careful historian
of the battle, himself a participator in the Union disaster,
'was a most fortunate circumstance for the Army of
the Potomac.   At nine o'clock the capture or destruction
of a large part of the army seemed inevitable.   There was,
at the time, great uncertainty and a feeling akin to panic
prevailing among the Union forces round Chancellorsville; and when we consider the position of the troops
at this moment, and how many important battles
have been won by trivial flank attacks—how Richepanse
(attacking through the forest) with a single brigade ruined
the Austrians at Hohenlinden—we must admit that the
Northern army was in great peril when Jackson arrived
within one thousand yards of its vital point (the White
House) with 20,000 men and 50 cannon.' [1]   He must be a
great leader indeed who, when his flank is suddenly rolled
up and his line of retreat threatened, preserves sufficient
coolness to devise a general counterstroke.   Jackson had
proved himself equal to such a situation at Cedar Run, but
it is seldom in these circumstances that Providence sides
with the 'big battalions.'

The Federal losses in the six days' battles were heavy:
over 12,000 at Chancellorsville, and 4,700 at Fredericksburg, Salem Church, and Banks' Ford ; a total of 17,287.
The army lost 13 guns, and nearly 6,000 officers and men
were reported either captured or missing.

The casualties were distributed as follows :—

[1] *Chancellorsville*, Lt.-Colonel A. C. Hamlin.

First Army Corps 135
Second   „   1,925
Third   „   4,119
Fifth   „   700
Sixth   „   4,590
Eleventh   „   2,412
Twelfth   „   2,822
Pleasonton's Cavalry Brigade 141
                                         ‾‾‾‾‾‾
                                         16,844

The Confederate losses were hardly less severe.   The
killed and wounded were as under :—

SECOND ARMY CORPS.

A. P. Hill's Division 2,583
Rodes'   „   2,178
Colston's   „   1,868
Early's   „   851
Anderson's „   1,180
McLaws'   „   1,379
Artillery   227
Cavalry   11
Prisoners (estimated) 2,000
                                         ‾‾‾‾‾‾
                                         12,277

But a mere statement of the casualties by no means re-
presents the comparative loss of the opposing forces. Victory
does not consist in merely killing and maiming a few thousand men.   This is the visible result ; it is the invisible that
tells.   The Army of the Potomac, when it retreated across
the Rappahannock, was far stronger in mere numbers than
the Army of Northern Virginia ; but in reality it was far
weaker, for the *moral* of the survivors, and of the general
who led them, was terribly affected.   That of the Confederates, on the other hand, had been sensibly elevated, and
it is *moral*, not numbers, which is the strength of armies.
What, after all, was the loss of 12,200 soldiers to the Confederacy ?   In that first week of May there were probably
20,000 conscripts in different camps of instruction, more
than enough to recruit the depleted regiments to full strength.
Nor did the slaughter of Chancellorsville diminish to any
appreciable degree the vast hosts of the Union.

And yet the Army of the Potomac had lost more than all the efforts of the Government could replace. The Army of Virginia, on the other hand, had acquired a superiority of spirit which was ample compensation for the sacrifice which had been made. It is hardly too much to say that Lee's force had gained from the victory an increase of strength equivalent to a whole army corps of 30,000 men, while that of his opponent had been proportionately diminished. Why, then, was there no pursuit?

It has been asserted that Lee was so crippled by his losses at Chancellorsville that he was unable to resume operations against Hooker for a whole month. This explanation of his inactivity can hardly be accepted.

On June 16 and 18, 1815, at Quatre-Bras and Waterloo, the Anglo-Dutch army, little larger than that of Northern Virginia, lost 17,000 men; and yet on the 19th Wellington was marching in pursuit of the French; nor did he halt until he arrived within sight of Paris. And on August 28, 29, and 30, 1862, at Groveton and the Second Manassas, Stonewall Jackson lost 4,000 officers and men, one-fifth of his force, but he was not left in rear when Lee invaded Maryland. Moreover, after he had defeated Sedgwick, on the same night that Hooker was recrossing the Rappahannock, Lee was planning a final attack on the Federal intrenchments, and his disappointment was bitter when he learned that his enemy had escaped. If his men were capable of further efforts on the night of May 5, they were capable of them the next day; and it was neither the ravages of battle nor the disorganisation of the army that held the Confederates fast, but the deficiency of supplies, the damage done to the railways by Stoneman's horsemen, the weakness of the cavalry, and, principally, the hesitation of the Government. After the victory of Chancellorsville, strong hopes of peace were entertained in the South. Before Hooker advanced, a large section of the Northern Democrats, despairing of ultimate success, had once more raised the cry that immediate separation was better than a hopeless contest, involving such awful sacrifices, and it needed all Lincoln's strength to stem the tide of disaffection.

The existence of this despondent feeling was well known to the Southern statesmen; and to such an extent did they count upon its growth and increase that they had over-looked altogether the importance of improving a victory, should the army be successful; so now, when the chance had come, they were neither ready to forward such an enterprise, nor could they make up their minds to depart from their passive attitude. But to postpone all idea of counterstroke until some indefinite period is as fatal in strategy as in tactics. By no means an uncommon policy, it has been responsible for the loss of a thousand oppor-tunities.

Had not politics intervened, a vigorous pursuit—not necessarily involving an immediate attack, but drawing Hooker, as Pope had been drawn in the preceding August, into an unfavourable situation, before his army had had time to recover—would have probably been initiated. It may be questioned, however, whether General Lee, even when Longstreet and his divisions joined him, would have been so strong as he had been at the end of April. None felt more deeply than the Commander-in-Chief that the absence of Jackson was an irreparable misfortune. 'Give him my affectionate regards,' he said to an aide-de-camp who was riding to the hospital; 'tell him to make haste and get well, and come back to me as soon as he can. He has lost his left arm, but I have lost my right.' 'Any victory,' he wrote privately, 'would be dear at such a price. I know not how to replace him.'

His words were prophetic. Exactly two months after Chancellorsville the armies met once more in the clash of battle. During the first two days, on the rolling plain round Gettysburg, a village of Pennsylvania, four Federal army corps were beaten in succession, but ere the sun set on the third Lee had to admit defeat.

It is needless to linger over the closing scene at Guiney's Station. For some days there was hope that the patient would recover; pneumonia, attributed to his fall from the May 7. litter as he was borne from the field, supervened, and he gradually began to sink. On the Thursday his wife and child arrived from Richmond; but he was then almost too weak for conversation, and on Sunday morning it was evident that the end was near.

May 10. As yet he had scarcely realised his condition. If, he said, it was God's will, he was ready to go, but he believed that there was still work for him to do, and that his life would be preserved to do it. At eleven o'clock Mrs. Jackson knelt by his side, and told him that he could not live beyond the evening. 'You are frightened, my child,' he replied, 'death is not so near; I may yet get well.' She fell upon the bed, weeping bitterly, and told him again that there was no hope. After a moment's pause, he asked her to call Dr. McGuire. 'Doctor,' he said, 'Anna tells me I am to die to-day; is it so?' When he was answered, he remained silent for a moment or two, as if in intense thought, and then quietly replied, 'Very good, very good; it is all right.'

About noon, when Major Pendleton came into the room, he asked, 'Who is preaching at headquarters to-day?' He was told that Mr. Lacy was, and that the whole army was praying for him. 'Thank God,' he said; 'they are very kind to me.' Already his strength was fast ebbing, and although his face brightened when his baby was brought to him, his mind had begun to wander. Now he was on the battle-field, giving orders to his men; now at home in Lexington; now at prayers in the camp. Occasionally his senses came back to him, and about half-past one he was told that he had but two hours to live. Again he answered, feebly but firmly, 'Very good; it is all right.' These were almost his last coherent words. For some time he lay unconscious, and then suddenly he cried out: 'Order A. P. Hill to prepare for action! Pass the infantry to the front! Tell Major Hawks——' then stopped, leaving the sentence unfinished. Once more he was silent; but a little while after he said very quietly and clearly, 'Let us cross over the river, and rest under the shade of the trees,' and the soul of the great captain passed into the peace of God.